Being and Ambiguity

Being and Ambiguity

Philosophical Experiments with Tiantai Buddhism

BROOK ZIPORYN

OPEN COURT
Chicago and La Salle, Illinois

To order books from Open Court, call toll-free 1-800-815-2280, or visit www.opencourtbooks.com.

Open Court Publishing Company is a division of Carus Publishing Company.

Copyright © 2004 by Carus Publishing Company

First printing 2004

All rights reserved. No part of this publication may be reproduced, stored in a retrieval system, or transmitted, in any form or by any means, electronic, mechanical, photocopying, recording, or otherwise, without the prior written permission of the publisher, Open Court Publishing Company, 315 Fifth Street, P.O. Box 300, Peru, Illinois 61354-0300.

Printed and bound in the United States of America.

Library of Congress Cataloging-in-Publication Data

Ziporyn, Brook, 1964-
    Being and ambiguity : philosophical experiments with Tiantai Buddhism / Brook Ziporyn.
       p. cm.
    Includes bibliographical references and index.
    ISBN 0-8126-9542-9 (trade pbk. : alk. paper)
  1. Tiantai Buddhism--Doctrines. 2. Philosophy, Buddhist. I. Title.
    BQ9118.3. Z56 2004
    294.3'42042--dc22
                                                2004010772

For my brother

It is clear that the world is purely parodic, in other words, that each thing seen is the parody of another, or is the same thing in a deceptive form.

Ever since sentences started to *circulate* in brains devoted to reflection, an effort at total identification has been made, because with the aid of a *copula* each sentence ties one thing to another; all things would be visibly connected if one could discover at a single glance and in its totality the tracings of an Ariadne's thread leading thought into its own labyrinth.

But the *copula* of terms is no less irritating than the *copulation* of bodies. And when I scream I AM THE SUN an integral erection results, because the verb *to be* is the vehicle of amorous frenzy.

Everyone is aware that life is parodic, and that it lacks an interpretation.

Thus lead is the parody of gold.
Air is the parody of water.
The brain is the parody of the equator.
Coitus is the parody of crime.

Gold, water, the equator, or crime can each be put forward as the principle of things.

And if the origin of things is not like the ground of the planet that seems to be the base, but like the circular movement that the planet describes around a mobile center, then a car, a clock, or a sewing machine could equally be accepted as the generative principle.

— GEORGES BATAILLE, "The Solar Anus"[1]

---

[1] Georges Bataille, *Visions of Excess: Selected Writings, 1927–1939*. Edited and with an introduction by Allan Stoekl, translated by Allan Stoekl, with Carl R. Lovittt and Donald M. Leslie Jr., *Theory and History of Literature*, vol. 14 (Minneapolis: University of Minnesota Press, 1985), 5.

Contents

ACKNOWLEDGMENTS   xi
PREFACE   xiii

INTRODUCTION: WHAT IS TIANTAI?   1

PART ONE
NEO-TIANTAI BASICS: ENFRAMEMENT,
COHERENCE, AND AGENCY—THE THUSNESS AND
OTHERWISENESS OF ALL COHERENCES   35
    What Else Is There?   35
    Meaning à la Mode   37
    More to Come   40
    Quiddity Qua Quaddity: Oneness, Coherence and Agency   41
    Perception, Conceptualization, Imagination   45
    Properties Are Theft   49
    Centrality: Local Coherence as Global Incoherence
    (Intersubsumption)   55
    Four Ways of Being Thus and Otherwise: Impermanence,
    Illusion, Tertium Quid, Asness   62
    Transpositions of the Four Ways   73
    Omnicentrism   82

The Process of Transformative Recontextualization: Setup and Punch Line as the Basic Categories of All Possible Experience	91
Enchantment, Disenchantment, Reenchantment	100
Asness as All-pervasion	101
The Transcendental Unity of Apperception and the Principle of Charity	103
Content and Category in Kant and Tiantai: A Priori Categories and Inherent Entailment	109
"Natural Law" as Global Incoherence	124
Sense, Reference, and Private Language	130
Composition, Temporal Succession, and Contrast	139
On the Fire Not Burning Itself	146
The External World(s)	149
Categories of Asness and Their Attributes: Summary of Part One	151

PART TWO

Desire and the Self: Toward an Ethics and Psychology of Constitutive Impossibility — 155

Presence as Hyper-absence; Absence as Hyper-presence	155
Correspondence and Coherence: Epistemological Implications	163
Control and Its Lack: Practical Implications	164
Unavoidable, Unobtainable	166
The Cunning of Cunning	167
What It Is Like: Being as Cunning, Cunning as Metaphoricity	168
Non-X Is Just Like X, Only More So	176

Can't Get No-Satisfaction	179
Rival Centers and Reversibility: Desire and Aversion	181
Desire to Be	187
Aversion	188
A Note on Crawling through the Desert	191
The Self: Subject and Object, Punch Line and Setup	193
Identity as Constitutive Impossibility (as All-pervasion)	202
The Good as the Intersection of Two Impossibilities	215
Krug's Pen Revisited	220
Pleasure and the Self	222
Freedom	234
More about the Will	251
Full Exertion: Repetition, Intensification, Meaninglessness, All-pervasion	253
Language, Mindfulness, and the Obvious	256
Adequation, Openness, "Moretoitivity," Energy	260
The Desire of Desire: The Intersubsumption of Self, Affect, and Object	271
Bad Faith versus the Innocence of Becoming: The Moral Benefits of Inherent Evil	278
Ethical "Layering"	286
Personality as Symptom and as Pregnancy	288
Buddha *Sive* Time *Sive* the Inscrutability of the Other . . . Or: The *Samadhi* of Not Knowing What You're Doing	289
Sive . . .	300
Boredom, Anxiety, Narrative, Addiction, and Love: Human Time	302
Death and Embarrassment	308

PART THREE
HERMENEUTICS AND AUTOEROTICS: TRUTHS AND OTHER HIDDEN PARTS, AND HOW THEY WELCOME THEIR DEMISE — 313

- Why There's Anything: Habituation and Solidarity, with Some Reckless Reasoning about Entropy and the End of the Universe — 313
- Atomicity, Otherness, and Violence (Co-starring Whitehead, Levinas, and God) — 322
- Eroticism and Continuity, with Bataille — 350
- The Rival and the Double: Oneself as One's Own Indigestible Kernel — 360
- Beauty, Harmony, and the Mystical — 369
- Humor — 381
- Sex and Drugs — 393
- Catharsis and/or Addiction: Asness, Art, and the "Repression Hypothesis" — 398
- The Limits of Sublimation — 405
- Hegel and/or Zen — 405
- The Revolutionary Impulse and Revolutionary Charisma, with Gotama, Jesus, Nichiren, Lennon, Dylan, et al. — 410
- Boredom or Truth: A "Critique" of Critique — 417
- Onany, Interpretation, and Love: Truth and the Libidinal Community — 420
- Proof that All Previous Errors Have Spoken This Truth, and Vice Versa; Or: How to Believe Everything You Read — 428
- Invitation to a Recantation — 439

INDEX — 441

Acknowledgments

I would like to express my gratitude to three astute readers of early versions of this manuscript. David Levin, my colleague in the Department of Philosophy at Northwestern University, took the time to read and comment upon a still rather rough-and-ready version of the text, and his encouraging words and subtle appreciation of some of the finer points involved in the discussion not only greatly improved the finished manuscript, but gave me the courage to continue with this somewhat risky—not to say insane—project, as did his own example of combining broad-mindedness, extensive scholarship, and intrepidity as a thinker. Another of the rare living American philosophers whose work harmonizes rigorous thinking and adventurous experiment, Andrew Cutrofello, also provided me with invaluable encouragement and suggestions for improvement, with the inimitable synthesis of unassuming clarity and true profundity of thought that is distinctive to him. Finally, my least-convinced and longest-standing reader, fan, and heckler, Alan Cole, refused as always to let me get away with anything, providing stubborn resistance to the most basic premises of the argument, forcing me to torture them into the of course incontrovertibly apodictic and all-victorious form in which they now appear here. On the other hand, the pleasure he took in some of the more idiosyncratic and perhaps clownish sideroads I took in playing out the hand was as gratifying to me as the few points I was able to get him to swallow without reservations. All three of these readers made this an incomparably better book than it would have been without their interventions, and, knowing what a burden it can be to devote the time and energy to force-feed oneself a colleague's torturously irrelevant alternate universe, I can only thank them again for their patience, good-will, and encouragement.

Preface

Suppose a book published at the beginning of the twenty-first century proclaimed in its first sentence: "This work contains the answers to all philosophical problems which have hitherto existed and which ever shall exist. All other books are included in and superseded by this book, which finally reveals the absolute truth about the universe and its application to all possible facets of human experience. The crucial paradigm shift has been discovered which reduces to irrelevance all the bitter struggles of past and present philosophers and theorists in all fields; this discovery has been made by me and explicated in the work you are now holding. Whatever conversations you have hitherto been having with yourself and your alter-selves are picked up here, tweaked into a slightly better vocabulary, integrated with all other conversations so that it is revealed that all were about each other, and resolved into a far richer set of possibilities and vistas of new experience than you had dared hope for. All possible phenomena are given the optimal explanation as to their meaning, origin, function, end, and value by this work." There is much to be grateful for in the fact that such claims are nowadays immediately taken as irrefutable signs of crankdom, found only in fanatical and naïve street-corner tracts or deliberately obscurantist New Age self-help manuals. The consensus of modern intellectual conscience seems to be that such self-advertisements, whether explicit or implicit, are to be consigned to the ranks of sinister ideological posturing, which ignore both the epistemological revolutions of the past two hundred years, and the relativizing thrust of self-historicization that came in their wake. For ethical as well as intellectual reasons, this kind of self-mythologization, still possible, say, for Spinoza and Leibniz, and also, more complicatedly but nonetheless unmistakably, for Hegel or Schopenhauer, has been thoroughly discredited, and appears ludicrous to us now. All things considered, most concerned parties have no trouble agreeing that this is an enormous boon which is to be applauded, and for which we latter-born cynics have much to be grateful.

But now suppose that you had in your hands an ostensibly philosophical work, concerned with all the big questions of being, presence, experience, nothingness, time, value, and so on, which began by stating: "The following work is completely devoid of objective validity of any kind. It is just a bunch of crap assembled in a totally contingent manner, according to my whims and sensations of a particular time as conditioned by the weather, my diet, my chemical mood swings, my love life, what was on TV that day, and moreover by a person, myself, who is through and through a contingent jumble of influences, who can see and think only as his organs of perception and thought, created chaotically by particular historical and natural forces beyond anyone's or anything's control, allow him to. This is just how things happened to *seem* to me at a particular time, and this was determined not by my insight into eternal or universal truths of some kind, but merely by the accidental tangle of conditions that constitute me. There is nothing universal or objective in what follows: it is a bunch of impressions which have no binding force of any kind, and no predictable applicability to any other things in the world besides the appearances from which it sprang." We might consider the book in question as a work of art, of fiction, or poetry, in that case. It might lay claim to a form of "truth," perhaps even a higher form of truth, as an aesthetically incisive or accurate portrayal of someone's personal experience at a particular time. It may even be that this would be what is left of philosophy in some quarters, a new conception of the vocation of the writer who wishes for some unknown reason to seriously consider the big useless eternal questions, but who wants to do so without entangling himself in the self-deception and questionable ethical position of claims to objectivity, and the authoritative power claims that go with it. This would seem to be the obvious alternative to the braggadocio know-it-all-ism of the classical "truth" approach caricatured above, and one that successfully avoids its most troubling embarrassments.

On the other hand, it seems there is still, to most readers, something rather unsatisfying about this position as well. Why, they might ask, should I read this and take it seriously any more than I should spend my time studying transcripts of your daily calorie intake, or x-rays of your intestinal functions? What does it have to do with me, or anyone else, what you saw or felt at some particular time? Given the contingency and particularity of your subjective experience, and the impossibility of ascertaining its relation to any objectivity and hence to any link to my own subjectivity, why, in a word, should I care or consider what you think?

Perhaps one might answer that the value of such a work could lie in precisely its thorough actualization of that contingent particularity, as an artist might claim a particularly refined sensibility which allows her to render the concrete contingencies of her life in a way which reveals something profoundly important about her—something which might be called her truth or her universality, but which need not be so called—something which is open to the reader as a spur for reapplication to other specifics, although it does not restrict the range of what these applications will turn out to be. But this intuition arguably still contradicts the radicality of the initial claim to pure contingency and meaninglessness; it posits something in the place of truth, or something better than truth, which it is delivering, but the exact nature of this relation between the contingent, contextualized impressions and this looser form of their "applicability," and what kind of guarantee it has, remain unsettled. Most readers, I suspect, will probably find this sort of proclamation just as unsatisfactory as the claim to have discovered universal truth once and for all.

It would seem then that in our millennium-beginning moment we have a beautiful epistemological double bind on our hands: neither the claim to universal truth nor its denial its making any sense to us. It is not just that both alternatives are unjustifiable; more seriously perhaps, they have both become morally repugnant. It would seem that the only way to endure walking into the Babel of a bookstore or library, or even glancing through a record shop, a magazine rack, faces on a bus or pictures in a newspaper without being driven to despair is to somehow block out the overabundance of superfluous viewpoints. Most obviously in the case of books, some poor schmuck has poured his heart and soul into each and every one of these things, is convinced that he knows what's what, at least what's important and possible if not what's true and false, and is screaming the world he sees from the rooftops. The traditional way to avoid this almost surreal but nonetheless ordinary fact—the simultaneous superimposition of so many contrary subjectivities, and hence so many contrary worlds—has been the first attitude adduced above: the belief in a single objective truth, one perspective which is correct as opposed to all others that are wrong. Aside from the one truth, all the other views are mere "falsehood" and hence ultimately negligible. I describe this as morally repugnant with tongue only partly in cheek; we are so used to this commonsense view of conflicting opinions that we no longer feel what an affront and an outrage it is to regard another subjectivity and its world in this way, and the cost of doing so. It has begun to be noticed that the notion of objectivity per se is a mode of imposing the "hegemony" of one perspective over others, and that this is, at least among other things, a form of violence; we have grown too morally sensitive to tolerate these outrages called objectivity and truth. In the end, this marks a decisive advance in our respect for subjectivity, let us say for experience, for life, for being in any sense, per se. And, to make it clear once more, this is something I can only heartily applaud.

On the other hand, in the shadow of the old notion of truth, and in its absence, all eggs having been put in the basket that has now been swiped away, we are left with a chaos of conflicts where any possible structuring or arrangement, indeed any mutual regard or embrace of conflicting viewpoints, is viewed suspiciously as another surreptitious establishment of a power relation; we do not have any idea of how two different and contradictory viewpoints can be related to each other unless one is right and one is wrong, or both are wrong, or perhaps, at best, that each is "partially" right, whatever that might mean. The consequence of the moral fanaticism that will protect us from the tyranny of truth then becomes a fragmental chaos of solipsistic universes, forbidden any contact with one another; the atomistic assumption that in fact underlay the mutually exclusive picture of truth and falsehood here rears its head in another form. It is not only the impossibility but also the desirability of each of these two alternatives that has now come into question; would it really be such a good thing to have all the answers? We think not. But would it be such a good thing *not* to have all the answers? No again. What we want perhaps is both to reinstate the mysteriousness of all quiddities and to be at home in them in their mysteriousness, and, more importantly, in the mysteriousness of our knowing anything about them, of their coherence. It would seem to me that only a simultaneous preservation of ineluctable coherence and ineluctable mysteriousness would do justice both to our experience and to our aspirations. But how can this be achieved?

But whenever we encounter this kind of irresolvable dichotomy, where either half seems to be unsatisfactory, where the answer bounces back and forth endlessly without any apparent chance at settling one way or the other, we can be confident that we have here a bad pair of categories—that is, a false dichotomy—which needs to be transcended. Many have intuited as much for some of the great battles waged through the history of philosophy—that the reason the questions of freedom versus determinism, for example, or materialism versus idealism, are irresolvable is that there is something wrong with the categories by means of which the question is posed in the first place. One of the main concerns of this work will be to apply a rigorous justification for this intuition, and indeed extend its application to all contrary positions. The case at hand at the moment is the epistemological one. The presupposition that any claim must be *either* universally or objectively true *or* just a bunch of contingent, context-dependent subjective appearances is the source of the problem. In the fashionable phrase, we need a new epistemological paradigm here, one which does not make this presupposition, one which can allow the full and audacious claim to be making a statement of eternal and universal validity while at the same time acknowledging that one is just spouting groundless claptrap in reaction to the obscure needs of the current situation. We may think here of Kierkegaard's famous remark about Hegel's *Logic*: If this had been prefaced by the words, "The following is all only a thought experiment," it would have been the greatest work of all time; as it is, it is merely laughable. Nowadays we are most comfortable saying of any philosophical work that it is first and foremost a thought experiment, a working through of a line of thought to see where it leads and, in the best empirical spirit, to allow it to either function or fail to function as a catalyst for further experiments. That is what I want to say here too, not only because it is prudent, but also because it so nicely describes the intuitive sense we have of what we are doing when we philosophize; not necessarily plumbing the depths once and for all, but playing around with some ingredients to see what will happen. We are rightfully wary of hanging too much on what we come up with, of making everything that comes up in the mix into an earnest assertion of a conviction that must be defended to the death.

In the work that follows, however, I want to explore a paradigm that has as one of its greatest advantages the ability to combine these two apparently irreconcilable positions. That is, what we have here is a thought experiment one of whose conclusions is to knock out the supports from under the distinction between thought experiment and earnest assertion. For, as I hope will be clear soon enough, what we come up with here resembles a "thought experiment" in that it comes with a willingness to adopt alternate approaches instead, indeed insists on them, and that it is guided in its concrete choices first and foremost by a "mere" pragmatic interest in where it will lead. On the other hand, the picture that emerges resembles the "earnest assertion" in that it brings with it a risk that puts the contours of our entire lived world at stake and, more crucially, entails seeing this picture as ineradicable from the real world outside of our speculations, and in this sense as binding and inescapable. How these two opposed epistemological positions will prove to be not only compatible but also in fact identical will be, it seems to me, one of the more interesting aspects of this particular experiment/assertion. This identity, as one might expect, has far-reaching consequences, not the least of which is the anticipation that, when the day inevitably comes when I may say of this work, "Oh yeah, that was all claptrap, I don't know what I was thinking of when I wrote that" (and this day will come, whether on my senile deathbed or just on the verge of sleep, if not more dramatically as a conversion to some other ideology), this will in no way refute what is said here, but will rather exemplify it, such that if and when this particular way of thinking does appear in my experience again, or anyone else's, it will see these refutations *as* versions of itself. But what this might mean will become clearer, it is hoped, as we proceed.

And the following should be said about this work itself as well: This work contains the answers to all philosophical problems which have hitherto existed and which ever shall exist. Moreover, this work is completely devoid of objective validity of any kind. I hope in the following pages to make clear how I can make both these claims at the same time and, moreover, why I hold them to be ultimately, not two contradictory positions, nor even two harmonious aspects of the situation which compensate for one another, but two different ways of stating one and the same thing. To be objective truth is to be subjective claptrap, and vice versa. The "omnicentric" presuppositions of this claim, as well its epistemological, ontological, phenomenological, and axiological consequences, will be elucidated in the pages that follow. It is hoped that the specialness of the epistemological situation that follows from this will be appreciated in good time; I will be, like everyone else, twisting the world to fit my paradigm and projecting my own obsessive concerns into universal principles, but it should be kept in mind that this is all I am claiming to do, and moreover all I am claiming can be done—but what is much more, also that this is the means by which universal truths are delivered, "universal" in a peculiar sense to be defined below. So when I give an analysis of, say, desire, I will enter from an angle that has to do with where and when and how I am; but we will try to pursue these projections to the point of their *breakdown* into universality.

Before getting to the meat of the matter, some words should be said about the sources of the ideas to be developed here. More strictly, although this may seem nitpicky and precious at this stage, we should perhaps describe these rather as the precedents of whom one might presently choose to see this work as an intellectual descendant, since the conceptual category of a single finite set of identifiable causal sources for a set of ideas, and indeed for any datum of experience, will be among the things the work itself will have occasion to call into question below. Be that as it may, it is certainly worth pointing out that most of the main strains of thought in these pages have made their appearance and been developed in the course of "my professional duties as a Sinologist," as A. C. Graham once wryly/pathetically put it when trying to compose a philosophical work of general, non-Sinological import. In my case, the most central by far of the influences relevant to this study is the classical Tiantai tradition, by which I mean the thought of Zhiyi, Zhanran, Zhili, et al., of course, as interpreted by me. I have devoted a previous work to elucidating some features of the way I understand their thought, mainly within the confines of a standard intellectual historical framework, focused especially on the question of "value paradox and omnicentrism" in Tiantai thought, with, however, a few more general considerations interspersed here and there, and addressed head on at the end. The present work may in a certain sense be considered a continuation and expansion of the latter aspect of that work, and indeed is consistent with it to such an extent that I would not hesitate to call this a work of "Neo-Tiantai" philosophy—the only one in existence, so far as I know. Indeed, I may have occasion to use the locution "in the Neo-Tiantai view . . ." in the following pages, which is to be understood as an evasive way of saying "in my view," or "in the view developed in this book." This work, however, is not a technical Sinological, Buddhological, or intellectual historical study; it is an attempt to isolate, restate, and develop the kernels of a handful of the most distinctive ideas and insights from the Tiantai tradition, using methods and applied to problems which were of no interest to the classical Tiantai theorists. The methods will be, with some misgivings, the old-fashioned ones of deduction and induction, phenomenological description, logical proof, and occasional rhetorical hand-waving—in short, all the stock-in-trade of the Western philosophical tradition. My misgivings in using these methods derive not from their irrelevance to the classical Tiantai project—for what has that to do with us?—nor any Tiantai scruple about one-sided theorizing at the expense of "practice," another concern which we will allow ourselves freely to embrace or diverge from as we deem appropriate, but because it could be convincingly argued that all these techniques are functions of the first of the two epistemological positions caricatured above, that is, the claim that I am in possession of unique philosophical proofs to which I will now compel my readers to assent. To attempt to prove something is, in an important sense, an attempted act of violence on alternate perspectives in the name of a particular notion of objective truth—as exclusive of its opposite, as demonstrable, as commanding obedience. The last point is particularly important; objectivity as a standard which must be obeyed, which must be accorded with, on pain of being simply in the wrong, is one of the central notions to be called into question in the epistemology to be expounded in the pages to follow. The moral implications of this notion of truth—you must adopt this position whether you want to or not, because the facts prove that it alone is the right one, and that truth is supposed to provide some secure refuge from the shifting unpredictability of appearance and opinions—are parasitic on notions of the relation between obedience and rightness, and of truth and appearance, which are, in my view, far from obvious and worth far less than they cost.

Nonetheless, invoking the second view caricatured above, I too am a child of my time, and the fact is that this "traditional" kind of argument is more convincing, clearer, more easily deployable and applicable in new contexts, than mere dogmatic assertions and finely-wrought epigrammatic insights. Systematic exegesis has the advantage of spelling out a pattern of connections, which the reader can internalize by tracing its contours in operation after operation, thereby actually learning a new skill, the skill of applying the same operations on new material. This, rather than the use of an arsenal of arguments meant to compel submission, is the intended effect of the almost anachronistic or atavistic creation of what looks like a "system" in this book, in spite of the fact that this particular system is centered on an attempted demonstration of the felicitous impossibility of any complete or unilaterally coherent system.

A similar consideration is relevant to the application of these ideas to topics well outside the concerns of classical Tiantai thinkers. It is not that I am trying to reconstruct what, say, Zhili would say if, *per impossibile*, he decided to write an essay on sex, or the nature of pleasure or humor or time, or academic customs of the early twenty-first century; I apply these patterns of thought here because these are issues I am concerned about, and because immersion in Tiantai ways of thinking has sometimes suggested ideas about these subjects which I believe to be potentially useful to contemporaries with similar concerns, and which have not been otherwise developed. Indeed, I make no claim to be faithful to the Tiantai tradition, because obviously in some respects I am and in some respects I am not, however one may choose to define that orthodoxy. Biographically, it so happens that most of these ideas took shape in the process of trying to puzzle out what the Tiantai writers were trying to say, and I would be delighted to give them credit for whatever insights may have emerged thereby, which I certainly would never have come by otherwise. Nonetheless, there are obviously many other important influences to be owned up to here. In the first place, the central epistemological insight on which this work is based can really be credited to Zhuangzi, as I interpret him (controversially, however, among my Sinological colleagues), which very likely had something to do with the fuller development of this position in the classical Tiantai works themselves.[2] The Laozian "invisible center" too is a crucial category for us, in the form given it, again, in its expanded Tiantai version. Closer to home, the ultimate philosophical concerns that inform this discussion have been formed largely by traditional Western philosophical categories and interests, and the lens provided thereby—forged by extended entanglements with the pre-Socratics, Plato, Aristotle, Leibniz, Spinoza, Kant, Schopenhauer, Sartre, Polanyi, Freud, Merleau-Ponty, Lacan, and, above all, the unlikely duo Nietzsche and Hegel—has much to do with what aspects of Tiantai thought have seemed especially important to me, and have suggested a way to think out their implications which in many ways is deeply foreign to that of the Tiantai thinkers themselves. I say all this, at the risk of appalling self-indulgence, out of a perhaps misguided sense of obligation and desire

---

[2] See my article, "How Many Are the Ten Thousand Things and I? Relativism, Mysticism, and the Privileging of Oneness in the 'Inner Chapter'," in *Hiding the World in the World: Uneven Discourses on the Zhuangzi*, ed. Scott Cook (Albany, N.Y.: SUNY, 2003).

for frankness, although the question of influence is not one that particularly interests me personally. Nor would I be displeased if specialists in Western philosophy, committed Buddhists and/or Buddhologists and Sinologists all found this work initially an unwieldy addition to their own discipline, being neither fish nor fowl—it's not Buddhism, it's not philosophy, it's not scholarship—but which will be at least enjoyable or interesting enough to provoke a long enough engagement to allow other aspects of its strangeness, its seeming insouciance, its effrontery and so on to dawn. I hope this book will, to use the language developed within, become its own punch line, and that its indigestibility in each of its parent disciplines will prove the setup of a joke that ends with it playing the role of a useful contribution to each.

This book is divided into four main sections. The first is the Introduction, which gives a somewhat technical overview of the Buddhological background and doctrinal development of the classical Chinese Tiantai school, singling out those aspects of both which are relevant for our purposes here. Readers with a special interest in Buddhism will find this section useful at least in making plain where the connections lie and how we got from there to here, interpreting which old tropes in what way, although its approach may strike them as idiosyncratic and selective, to say the least. It is not, and does not purport to be, a history of Buddhist thought as such, or even of classical Tiantai thought, but does help to ground the following discussion in its sources, and might also satisfy the curiosity of those who wonder what this odd recurring word "Tiantai" refers to and where it came from. Readers uninterested in these background issues can, I think, skip this Introduction without thereby missing any of the main premises of what follows.

"Part One: Neo-Tiantai Basics" presents the fundamental philosophical claim of the book, building it, as it were, from scratch and from the ground up. Here an attempt is made to construct a fairly rigorous ontological and epistemological argument that will be presupposed as the basis of the rest of the discussion. No familiarity with or acceptance of any other thinker or tradition is assumed, but the ideas of a few thinkers are invoked here and there for clarification, to make the nuances of the Neo-Tiantai position stand out in contrast, rather than to discuss these thinkers themselves, as later parts of the book do. The topic under discussion here, broadly speaking, is the most general question imaginable: what is the relation of determinacy to indeterminacy, or coherence to incoherence, and what does this imply for how we are to understand what it means for something to exist? In other words, what is it to be something, or for something to be there, and to be what it is? This part of the book may be experienced by some readers as somewhat difficult, focusing as it does more or less exclusively on abstract philosophical issues.

"Part Two: Desire and the Self: Toward an Ethics and Psychology of Constitutive Impossibility" attempts to draw the psychological and ethical implications from the ontological and epistemological conclusions of Part One. A theory of the self, the will, desire, the Good, the body, the personality, identity, possession, experience, and so on, are what are at stake here. Hegel, Schopenhauer, and Nietzsche make important cameo appearances.

"Part Three: Hermeneutics and Autoerotics: Truths and Other Hidden Parts, and How They Welcome Their Demise" is the "spiciest" section of the book, where the previous conclusions are pushed a bit further in order to comment on cultural and social issues of various kinds, from sex to God to humor to mysticism to aesthetics to standards of truth in our current cultural situation, taking a final crack at the metaphysical and epistemological issues along the way, and initiating a Neo-Tiantai response to such figures as Freud, Bataille, Whitehead, Hegel, Heidegger, and Levinas, among others, and also to deconstruction, the Zen tradition, and certain forms of historicism. Probably this section is the one that is the most fun to read, and for certain readers it might not be a bad idea to lower oneself gradually into these waters by starting with this section, to see where the rest is really heading and whether the conclusions are attractive enough to merit expending the time and attention required by the dialectics of Part One, which, I hope, will "prove" that this fun is actually there to be had—albeit only by means of rather radical redefinitions of what is meant by "proving," "fun," "having," and "actually there."

Introduction

WHAT IS TIANTAI?
THE CLASSICAL TIANTAI SCHOOL AND ITS PLACE IN/PLACEMENT OF TRADITIONAL BUDDHIST THOUGHT

I should briefly explain the intellectual history of Buddhism, where the Tiantai school fits into it, and how it reads that history, before going on. What is the Tiantai school?[1] And what is Buddhism in the eyes of the Tiantai school? It is no small hint about the nature of this school of thought to realize that in this case these two questions ask for the same answer. Tiantai, as I mean it here, is a school of Chinese Buddhism, expressed definitively in the works of three figures, Zhiyi, Zhanran, and Zhili, who lived in China between the sixth and eleventh centuries of the common era. It is a school that provided a distinctive hermeneutic approach to the massive Buddhist canon that had come into China. This approach, known as "the classification of teachings," was based on a reading of a very peculiar Mahāyāna Buddhist text known as the *Lotus Sūtra* (*Saddharma Puṇḍarīka Sūtra*). Without getting bogged down in the technical details of the case, this text was read as providing a way both to harmonize the contradictions noticed in the vast array of differing doctrines taught in the canon, and to distinguish itself from them, precisely by virtue of this harmonization. But to see the importance of this, we must take a quick tour through the history of Buddhist thought, in terms of the themes that will become prominent in the Tiantai reading of that tradition, which rereads these doctrines as more or less obscure expressions of its own.

An account of early Buddhism from this perspective highlights certain aspects rather than others, and suggests a reading of its structural problematic that differs in some ways from more straightforward interpretations. The most important precedents for Tiantai thought discoverable within earlier Buddhism are the doctrines of the Four Noble Truths, Dependent Co-arising,

---

[1] A more detailed and technical account of philosophical aspects of Tiantai Buddhist can be found in my previous work, *Evil and/or/as the Good: Omnicentrism, Intersubjectivity and Value Paradox in Tiantai Buddhist Thought* (Cambridge: Harvard University Press, 2000).

Momentariness, Emptiness, Two Truths, Nonself, and the Middle Way. The Four Noble Truths proclaimed by the Buddha in the Pali canon can be read as an uncomplicated diagnosis and prescription: there is suffering, its cause is the presence of desire for what is not the case, and hence this suffering can be eliminated by eliminating the desire through a program of discipline, concentrated awareness, and wisdom. But the description of what constitutes this suffering and its range (it applies to *all* conditioned events, including experiences of pleasure and happiness) and the analysis of the desire that is its cause suggest a more intricate picture.

The desire in question is described as three types of craving: (1) the craving for certain experiences, for pleasure; (2) the craving for being, that is, to have a particular identity, to be one determinate entity rather than another; (3) the craving for nonbeing, that is, *not* to be some particular thing, or, as it is sometimes interpreted, to get rid of certain experiences, to have them cease to be. The first of these, the desire for pleasure, appears quite straightforward, a familiar condemnation of hedonism as leading to long-term frustration and sorrow; but close attention to its deployment suggests, as some interpreters have pointed out, that what is at stake here is not really the occurrence of the psychological event "desire for pleasure" but the second-order attitude toward this event: in fact, the solution to the problem is described as lying in the "letting go" of desire (i.e., a clinging to some particular object or experience) but rather the *clinging to this desire itself*. "Clinging to desire" introduces a more complex motif that in fact feeds into the questions of temporality and selfhood, the centerpieces of early Buddhist thinking. This is implicit even if we speak simply about the desire for any specific experience, for example, for pleasure. If pleasure is *desired*, not just enjoyed and renounced, *repeatability and availability* of some past state are demanded. One would otherwise not have any particular *object* or desire, even the recognizable object "pleasure." Implicit in the desire for the repetition of this precise event in the future is a desire that oneself, the prospective enjoyer of it, will also persist to that time, and even that the desire that wants it will still be there. If the desired experience is obtained but the desire for it is gone, or the subject who was supposed to enjoy it is gone, the desired object is no longer desirable. Hence, desire for pleasure is also always an implicit desire for persistent selfhood, attachment to these desires as possessions of this self, which are supposed to benefit this self some way. The desire for repeatability is a process whereby objects are reified as targets of grasping and, correlatively, the self as the power to be a possessor, a master, a determiner, who owns the previous pleasure (as his "experience") and thus must be in a position to make it available to himself again. More crucially, it is not really the pleasure that is desired in this scenario, but rather precisely the power to make it available to oneself again, the power to create an exact repetition, which means the power to transcend time, to be unconditioned. One does not want a pleasure that is forced upon one, or that one is unable to escape from at will. Desire for pleasure is disguised desire for power, for unconditional selfhood. It should be stressed that the *first* experience of any given pleasure is not what is meant here. *Desire presupposes memory*, that is, the intent to repeat a pleasure, *repetition*. All desire is desire for repetition, and this is precisely will to selfhood, to the possession of the *power* to recreate some specific experience, to have control over it.

What is really wanted in the first type of desire for pleasure, then, is self-being, that is, power, autonomy, self-mastery, ownership, control, unconditioned continuity. But this is precisely the second type of desire, the "desire to be," to be something or other definitively, or to be a self, an owner and possessor of experience, an independent and free subject and agent. The third type of desire, for "nonbeing," also reduces to a desire to be, whether interpreted as desire "not to be" something in particular (a reverse form of desire to be something in particular) or desire to get rid of some experiences (a reverse form of the desire for pleasure). Desire to have, desire to be, desire not to be: all these are ultimately desire to be a self, a particular being with an unconditional identity, and the power to determine its own nature, attributes, and experiences.

But the doctrine of dependent co-arising, the main pillar of early Buddhist theory, shows that this is precisely what is impossible. For this doctrine is perhaps most easily summed up by an interpretive boiling down of the treatment given in the early scholastic formulation from the *Visuddimagga:* it is not merely an assertion that all things are causally conditioned, but rather more specifically that no *single* cause gives rise to a *single* effect, nor does a single cause give rise to multiple effects, nor do multiple causes give rise to a single effect, but that *in every occurrence, multiple causes give rise to multiple effects.* This is enough to establish the "nonself" teaching which is the central soteriological and, later, ontological principle of all Buddhism, along with the other "marks of existence": Impermanence and Suffering. For a "self" would be either a singular cause or a singular effect, a "one" which is in sole control of its effects, or which could emerge an unambiguous singular result of a set of causes. It would be, in a word, a master and owner of its experience. Desire is the endeavor to create a single effect through a single cause: my self, acting alone, wants to produce precisely this experience and no other. But this is doomed both because no single self acting alone can create any single effect; it always needs other conditions, by definition outside its control, and it always produces something more that the single effect it wanted.

Desire is present as a dissatisfaction with the total phenomenal reality of the present moment, with a given set of what "there is." But this desire is itself a part of aspect of this moment, this "there is." A dividedness of the moment appears here, constituting the subject-object split, a tension tied to the aspiration to be the absolute sole master of this moment. Desire is a demand for reality to be otherwise, but it exempts itself from this desire for change. It wants *part* of reality to change, but another part of reality—itself—to stay the same: it demands its own survival into a future moment, to be the enjoyer of the object it has desired when it finally arrives. This is also viewed as impossible, given the Buddhist idea of universal impermanence, applying equally to the subject and to the object, neither of which can possibly persist identically from one moment to the next. Here we have a fundamental division or split in experience, the subject-object split, which is seen as a ceaseless matrix of suffering.

Early Buddhist tradition suggests three possible ways to eliminate this tension: indulgence of desire, suppression of desire, and "the Middle Way." The first two of these are, on this account, doomed to failure. The first strategy, that of ordinary hedonistic life, is to fulfill the desire, to indulge it, to get rid of it by providing what it asks for, by obtaining the demanded pleasure. But this necessarily fails because, first of all, the particular object is not really lastingly fulfilling; it is conditioned, impermanent, a series of events rather than a single thing that persists through time. Hence, the image desired cannot really match up to the real which is later attained, since both are unique temporal occurrences. The experience is never the same; at the very least it is a repetition, modified by the previous memory, plus many other new conditions. But *inattentiveness*, ignorance, crudity of attention, allows the willed repetition to appear successful in normal worldly experience. The external conditions are close enough to the original set to allow a result that crude ignorance can construe as the *same* as the original desired result. This *ignores* the *difference* between the desired and the attained, and also the *fortuitous similarity* of conditions that allow them to appear identical. I ignore all the conditions that enable me to have this experience, attributing it only to my own agency, and also the ultimate conditionality and hence passivity of this apparently active agency itself—my desire, which I am laboring to satisfy, is conditioned by the previous experience of pleasure. Moreover, I ignore the difference between what I finally obtained and the previous experience that defined my desire for it. This inattentiveness is what allows the illusion of genuine unconditionedness, freedom, mastery, selfhood to arise. Thus does "action" (karma, apparently successful action) plus ignorance (inattentiveness) reinforce "the view of self." This sense of selfhood in turn motivates further action, for having defined myself as this determinate and yet unconditioned self, I am predisposed to find pleasure in those things which serve this sense of control and displeasure in those which contradict it, and act to confirm, consolidate, or enhance this sense of my own power to own these things. And so the cycle perpetuates itself.

Second, what is really wanted in desire for specific pleasures is, as we have seen, selfhood, mastery, power, autonomy, ownership, control, eternity, which is likewise impossible. The fulfillment of the desire reinforces the splitting of the moment as a habitual structure; it reestablishes the subject-object split in a new form for the next moment. The sense-of-self in turn conditions desire—either, if construed as an absolute self, to verify and exercise this putative master, or if construed as a conditional self, to meet its particular determinate needs for sustenance, of goals, commitments, projects. It establishes a set of sensitive organs for contact, predisposed to find some things congenial and others not, leading to new feelings of pleasure and new volitions, hence more sense of separate self.

Note that here what seems to be an expression of freedom is seen as really only a further bondage. To satisfy this desire is not to satisfy your "self"—the absolute independent agent of freedom—but to satisfy your "master," an other. The apparently "purely active" agent is in reality also conditioned, hence passive, "suffering" in its root sense. Moreover, this desire hides itself, reinforces the tendency for inattentiveness. It is painful, and we have a vested interest in not seeing our own pain, since it contradicts our pretension to absolute selfhood. Pain is humiliating to our sense of autonomy. Moreover, this desire hides itself, reinforces the tendency for inattentiveness. It is painful, and we have a vested interest in not seeing our own pain, since it contradicts our pretension to absolute selfhood. Pain is humiliating to our sense of autonomy. Moreover, this desire transforms itself into the subject-object relation, that is, a neutral, free, wise self seeing an objectively valuable object, which it wants, it thinks, because of that objective value, not because of its own desire as a conditioned aspect of itself. All desire is thus the desire to be unconditioned, to be master, owner, and enjoyer who can freely conjure up the desired thing into existence; *but this desire itself is conditioned, is not owned by me or anyone else, cannot be freely conjured up or eliminated.* As Schopenhauer says, interpreting Spinoza, people believe they are free because they can do what they wish, but ignore the fact that they cannot wish whatever they wish. It is conditioned by the experience of pleasure, by its disposition in relation to objects, by the structure and relation of particular sense organs and objects, by its retention of remembered images of objects and so on. Every particular act of volition is conditioned by the organs that instantiate it and its pleasure/pain relations that pertain thereto. Not only do I not own this desire to be master, not only does any other person or agent or being not own it, but *it does not even "own" itself*. Even if it succeeds, it fails; for to succeed in the project of being an unconditioned master is only further undermined the more it is accomplished, if the desire to do so itself is just one more conditioned thing, one more imposition from outside, one more form of servitude, with no single cause and no owner. No single cause, neither I nor anyone else, including "itself," is in a position to make it what it is.

Given these difficulties, the second way of dealing with this tension of desire is the ascetic attempt to eliminate or suppress it entirely. But the early Buddhist tradition insists that this is equally hopeless and impossible. For the desire to get rid of desire is simply one more desire, setting up a vicious circle of desiring to not desire and so on. Moreover, the original desire is a conditional entity, and will continue to arise as long as its conditions are present. Adding one more condition—the desire to destroy it—will not eliminate it; the only thing that can eliminate it is to remove the conditions of its arising. And again, if eliminated, the desire remains unseen, unexamined, hence its conditions become even more hidden, and thus further entrenched. On top of all that, since the real desire is not for this particular object, but for selfhood, power, mastery, the suppression of any particular desire will be useless—it will simply change forms to find another way to prop up the notion of a self.

Since neither the fulfillment nor the elimination of desire is of any use, or even possible, according to the early Buddhist tradition, the "Middle Way" between them is proclaimed. What is this Middle Way? It is neither indulging nor destroying the desire. Rather it resides in being "mindful" of the desire, closely attentive to it. This means: (1) Seeing the desire; (2) Knowing "there is desire" as a present explicit fact—that is, no longer as tacit, hidden, flooded into the apparent "desirableness" over in the object or the future, but as a positive present state pertain to one's own body-mind; (3) Seeing it as arising, dwelling, vanishing—as temporal; (4) Seeing it as involving displeasure, as leading to and resulting in displeasures of various kinds; (5) Seeing it therefore as conditional, as nonself, as not entirely subject to my will as a sole agent; (6) Releasing, relinquishing the desire, no longer clinging to it, considering it mine or me, controlled by me, coming from self, benefiting self, establishing self, reinforcing self or in any other way affecting my putative self, as a unitary and unconditioned agent and owner of experience. Since ignorance about this was one condition of the arising of the desire, this attentiveness removes one of the necessary conditions of its arising. Deprived of it, the desire fades and ceases. We have let the desire be what it is, be itself—i.e., conditioned, impermanent—and this *allows* its fading, rather than indulging it or destroying it. What then, on this reading, is the early Buddhist solution to desire, inasmuch as it all reduces to desire for selfhood and thus inevitable frustration? Neither the elimination of desire, nor the indulgence in desire, but the Middle Way. This means the awareness of desire, and the letting go of desire—not its annihilation, which is impossible, but simply letting it be an entity in its own right, letting it be itself, which is to say, an impermanent, unsatisfactory, nonself, conditioned and *co*-arising thing, which arises and fades in accord with conditions which are not in the control of any single agent. This endeavor to be mindful of the process of desire's arising and perishing is of course still a desire of sorts, situated, as it were, between the active and passive modes. But this particular desire, the practice of Buddhism itself, is regarded in early Buddhism as a "raft," temporarily exempted from the critiques of clinging and desire because of its putative ability to overcome all other desires and finally also itself, in that in the end it too is to be let go of, when no longer necessary.

This is, in nutshell form, the early Buddhist notion of liberation. This plays out, especially in later Abidhammic literature, into the theory of momentariness, holding that the ultimate constituents of reality are extremely short-lived mental and physical events which are nonself and impermanent. In the earliest version, these events have a definite, but very short, duration. Later the circle is closed and in the Mahāyāna it is asserted that they arise and perish simultaneously—they are literally instantaneous. This amounts to a very radical temporalization of reality which is also designed with a mainly soteriological intent, with an eye again to the problem of clinging: for these instantaneous events cannot be objects of desire because they could not possibly be possessed, they are literally gone as soon as one becomes aware enough of them to desire them. Desire to possess (i.e., to be a possessor, a self) is a category mistake, for there are no things (possessables), only events. It is to be noted in this connection that there is no term in this literature that strictly corresponds to the concept of "things," or for that matter even of "phenomena," with its basic meaning of a showing or shining forth. Instead, the basic elements of experience are designated as "dhammas." The same word is used to denote the behavior proper to a particular caste or role, and in its prescriptive sense the same word is used for the Buddhist teaching as a whole. As such, this term can perhaps be translated as "regularities," here descriptively as indicating what is objectively found in the world of experience. This implication will be of some use to us in our discussion of "coherence" in the pages that follow.

The same problem can also be approached by means of the Five Aggregates doctrine: what we normally call our self is made up of impersonal momentary processes which can be generally categorized as belonging to five groups: Form, Sensation, Memory/Perception, Volition, Sense of Self (consciousness in the sense of a subject aware of an object). What we have here is a Sensation/Desire/Reification/Self-Identity feedback loop.

A certain disposition of a conditioned entity, that is, the sensitive material, tissue, or chains of events that we call our experience of existence in the world—physical organs contacting objects, giving rise to pleasant or unpleasant feeling—is conditioned by, among other things, ignorance. Ignorance here means above all nonmindfulnesss, not knowing this *as* a conditional, composite aggregate process, which would imply also knowing it as suffering, impermanent, momentary, nonself. Nonmindfulness of this fact conditions memory, classification, judgments of repeatability, sameness and difference, reiterability, perception, identification as object, reification, detemporalization (in the terms we are to develop below: de-as-ification). With this, we have a condition for volition, as if something could be done about or to this object (which is an error: no such object persists to be acted upon, and it is not repeatable). This is an indispensable condition for what we normally call consciousness, that is, a sense of self existing over against these objects which it *has* before it to manipulate, acquire, eliminate, avoid, and so on. This in turn further disposes the sensitive tissue in some particular way rather than another, so that it is once again susceptible to pain or pleasure, and to the category mistake which separates itself from this experience creating two separate entities, subject and object. The weak link here is ignorance, which can be overcome by means of mindfulness and attention to just these facts, of impermanence and nonself. Mindfulness of the body as body, of feelings as feelings, of mind as mind (sense of self as sense of self), of objects as objects (the classical "Four Foundations of Mindfulness") is thought to be enough to show them to be nonself, impermanent, suffering; this can be further extended to the simple awareness, with nothing added, of sounds as sounds, of sights as sights, of cognitions as cognitions, of volitions as volitions, and so on. In each case, the process itself is to become the focal point of awareness, rather than the means for focusing elsewhere, on a putative object. We will discuss this technique in its Tiantai context extensively below. But the objective even in the earliest texts can be described as simply letting these things be themselves, that is, in this case, impermanent and nonself, nonreified natural processes which arise and perish in accordance with necessarily multiple conditions.

The implications of mindfulness are well expressed in the following passage from the early Buddhist *Udāna*, a kind of tell-me-all-the-Dharma-while-standing-on-one-foot summary of the Buddha's teachings:

> [Y]ou should train yourself thus: "In the seen there will be merely what is seen; in the heard there will be merely what is heard; in the sensed there will be merely what is sensed; in the cognized there will be merely what is cognized.". . . Then . . . you will not be "with that." When you are not "with that," then . . . you will

not be "in that." When you are not "in that," then . . . you will be neither here, nor beyond, nor in between the two. Just this is the end of suffering.[2]

To unpack the implications of this passage, let us first ask what is implied about ordinary, "naïve" experience, suffering-laden experience, in this description? Naïve experience would seem to be that in which there is more to the seen than merely what is seen, more to the heard and cognized and sensed than merely what is heard and cognized and sensed, and this "more" makes it the case that one is "with something," which makes it the case that one is "in" something, and that this being positioned in a particular locus is the source of suffering. What is this "more" that is in the seen? The first clue toward answering this comes from a consideration of the fact that each of the realms described is a totality of *unrepeated* data. Each token in "what is seen" appears only once in that field. It is not repeated by another "seen." However, it does seem to be repeated by a token in the field of, say, what is cognized. That is, each of these fields of perception is, to use an odd phrase of Spinoza's, "infinite in its own kind": each describes an unbounded field with items that can only be limited by other items in the same field, which inscribes all of reality in its own register, with nothing left out, in terms of its own particular mode of apprehension. It is noteworthy that it would be unnecessary to say, "In what is seen on the floor there will be merely what is seen on the floor . . . in what is sensed by the right foot there will be merely what is sensed by the right foot," and so on. For the various "parts" of the field of the seen do not overlap or superimpose on one another, there is no "reiterability" implied. The problem, then, seems to come from the superimposition of these various totalities onto a single putative system of coordinates. Because of this superimposition of my "cognizing of X" and my "seeing of X," I am given to assume that there is a *real* called X, which is reiterable. This is the "more" that normally pertains to seeing, hearing, sensing, and cognizing—each is the "more" to the others—and it is this that posits us as "in" something which is "with" something else—the subject/object mode of experience. For the real X is posited as completely abstracted from any mode of experience, indeed as unexperienceable. The "more-to-it-ivity" of each phenomenal aspect as such is converted into an impossible real that is however, in itself, putatively "non-more-to-it-ive." It is the collation of the various fields of experience, their mapping onto one another by means of the assumptions of persistence of objects, limitable causality, and repeatability, which posits the object which is out there beyond my experience of the object, self-identical but acting as

---

[2] John Ireland, trans., *The Udāna and The Itivuttaka* (Kandy: Buddhist Publication Society, 1997), 21.

the single cause of these multiple effects. Each effect is abstracted from the total process which differentiates them; for my seeing of object X is conditioned not only by the putative object, but also by my eyes, etc., while my feeling of object X is conditioned also by my tactile nerves, and so on. The seen X and the felt X do not by any means have a single cause. This again confirms that there is no single cause which by itself could produce multiple effects. It is thus that the world of objects is set up over and against—what? Here the self is posited; "being-with-that" conditions "being-in-this." The inaccessibility of the putative self-identical object requires the positing of the self that is equally outside of experience, and correlatively acting as a single cause of multiple effects. With this, we have a finite self confronting a world of finite objects, reinforcing the desire for reiterable objects and experiencing and necessitating suffering.

Pushing this a step further, however, there is perhaps a sense in which "what is seen on the floor" has also "what is seen on the ceiling" "in" it. That is, the mutual determination of the elements within any given field entails a kind of mutual reference between them. When seeing what is on the floor, one is comparing, connecting, or otherwise referencing whatever else could be seen—the background making up the rest of the field of the seen. Now it could be said that this mutual referencing is precisely the work of the field of "cognizing." That is, the mutual references between things in any given field of perception, which fixes their determinate identities within a coherent system of coordinates, is added on to "pure sensation" by the agency of the thinking mind and its categories, implicitly or explicitly. This indeed seems to be the psychological model operative in much of early Buddhism. In this case, "not seeing the ceiling" while "merely seeing the floor" would be a special case of superimposing "what is cognized" over "what is seen." Mutual referencing is the essence of cognition, on this model. It is noteworthy that the mindfulness position does not, even on this reading, call for the elimination of that mutual referencing, the activity of cognition. Rather, the point is to see cognition as cognition, and seeing as seeing, again so that the two not be superimposed. So even the attribution of the "single cause" which is the real object causing the various manifestations is a legitimate function; the referential datum of cognition (which "refers" to other objects and sensations, and thus fixing its unique identity) and the nonreferential datum of pure sensation are to coexist, but not overlap. The idea here again would concern repeatability: the cause of suffering is the false belief that what is found in cognition could ever also be found in perception, or vice versa. Within the field of cognition itself, of course, the implication would be, more critically, that each act of identifying the "same" universal object by cognition is to be seen as a separate, nonrepeatable process of identification, beyond which there is no such object to be found in experience. This takes us close to certain familiar philosophical themes, both Kantian and phenomenological. It may be wondered, above all, whether the nonreferential "Suchness" of pure sensation is not even more a cognitive fiction than the ordinary object; on some accounts, it would be argued that all perception is already referential in this sense, that the raw nonreferential sensation is an intellectualist fiction that betrays the very conditions of real possible experience. Early Buddhist phenomenology, it seems, might contest this point, appealing to the exceptional states of mind of accomplished meditators. But what is most intriguing about this way of setting up the issue is the way in which this plea for ultimate nonreferentiality in early Buddhism develops, not back to ordinary referentiality of experience, but to what might be called ineluctable and constitutive omni-referentiality. This is the Tiantai move, toward which we now turn.

The above themes of early Buddhism come to play an important role in classical Tiantai, but especially as filtered through several Mahāyāna refinements, which will alter and expand the implications of what it means to "let things be what they are" to something beyond mere impermanence and nonself. These further implications emerge through the mediation of the general Mahāyāna idea that impermanence is really of zero-duration, that arising and perishing are simultaneous, that nonself is universally applicable, even to the momentary events, which are not only not oneself, but are not even "themselves," which is understood according to the development of the concept of Emptiness in the Mādhyamika school of Nāgārjuna and in the *Prajñā-pāramitā Sūtras*; and the idea of the Bodhisattva and Buddha as developed in the *Sūtras*; and the idea of the Bodhisattva and Buddha as developed in the *Lotus*, especially the notion of skillful means, as what is entailed in letting something be itself.

Perhaps the most comprehensive way of grasping the famous doctrine of emptiness, in its classical form, is its argument concerning the thing and its mark. The argument goes as follows: To exist is putatively to be a thing which is just itself and nothing else; to do this it must have (at least) one "mark" or characteristic that distinguishes it, which is unshared by anything else. Is the distinguishing mark the same or different from the thing it is the mark of? If the same, then no marked thing is distinguished—just a mark has arisen, not a marked thing, and hence no existence. If the mark is different from the marked thing, it is not this thing's own mark, but another *thing*; we have two existent entities, a marked thing and a mark, each of which demands the mark/marked structure in order to count as "existent entity," and again no marked thing is established. Does this mark itself "exist"? If not, how can the thing be marked by a nonexistent mark? If so, the mark must itself *possess* a mark, the same mark/marked structure must apply to it as any other existent thing, and we have the same problem. Hence it is concluded that the mark/marked structure makes no sense, and with it any meaningful claim that "some particular things, disposed in some way or other, with some characteristic or other, exist" cannot be established. In this sense, it is said that the existence of things is purely illusory, a category mistake. They are not "real existences" in the sense of being entities with properties, characteristic marks.

The argument is also posed in terms of causality: the reality of every thing or definitive entity is rejected in the sense that things are not self-caused, self-supporting, guarantors of their own being thus—hence they too are not eternal, free, masters of themselves, owners of themselves, just as was shown in the early teaching to be the case for personal sentient beings. They are not self-identical. They are entirely reducible to something qualitatively other, fail to be exclusive of what they are not, and are not conceivable in terms of categories like same, different, coming, going, born, dying, and so on.

Nāgārjuna critiques causality in the literal sense by means of a typical *reductio ad adsurdum*: either a thing is caused by itself, by another, by both, or by neither. If it is caused to arise by itself, then first of all, no arising has taken place, but merely a repetition of the cause—"itself" gave rise to "itself," hence there was no "effect," and if there was no effect there was indeed no "cause." If it is caused to arise by another, why does not any "other" at all give rise to it? Otherness pertains to every other entity, so it cannot be otherness per se that makes this X arise, but some other quality or mark in these causes and conditions which are somehow related to the X which arises. Now, are these related conditions the same or different from X? If different, we have the same question all over again. If the same, we have the problem raised in the first case. Hence a thing does not arise from another or others. How about a combination of both self and others? But this involves the difficulties of *both* of the previous cases, rather than eliminating them by combination. Then do things arise without causes? But this would contradict the observed connections between things, and allow corn to grow from wheat seeds, and so on. Indeed, if their arising were truly unconditional, they would have to arise in all times and places, in fact, be always already present, and hence in reality no arising of them would ever take place. Hence it is concluded: "things" do not arise at all. The sense here is the same as in the previous paragraph—"real" things, defined as guarantors of their own being thus and so, equivalent to themselves, possessing a mark which distinguishes them from all other things, exclusive of what is not themselves—have never arisen and can never exist. With this comes a critique of the reality of the "dharmas"—the ultimate momentary constituents of experience—which likewise fall victim to the mark/marked critique, and of dependent co-arising thought of as a straightforward real causal process where one thing arises from another.

Put more strictly: For any entity X, to exist means to be determinate, for its nonexistence must differ in some real way from its existence. There must then be some range, whether conceptually (i.e., among conceivable entities), or of literal time and space, where X does not apply, some place, time, or conceivable entities in which X is lacking. Hence X cannot be omnipresent and eternal. Otherwise it would be indeterminate, and hence nonexistent. Thus it appears only under certain conditions, at a certain time and a certain place. Now the conditions of the existence of X must have some kind of relationship with X in order to accomplish the work of "conditioning" it, of causing it to exist. Conditioning, in other words, is some kind of relationship between two entities, the conditioning and the conditioned. This applies whether we are speaking of material causality or any other kind of conditioning (e.g., conceptual contrast). But for two entities to have any kind of relationship, they must both exist. These two terms must both exist for there to be any kind of relationship between them, and "conditioning the existence of" is a kind of relationship. This however can never be the case if we are speaking of the conditioning not of the state of X, but of the very emergence of X into existence. If we imagine a ground of X's existence, which coexists with X and sustains it in being, we must ask why X arose at some particular time after the ground was already in existence. The cause of X cannot be simply the preexisting ground itself, for otherwise X would have to have arisen as soon as the ground was present. If X and the ground came into existence in the same instant, then we can call the entire system "X and its ground" one entity and must ask about the causes of the emergence of this entity. X can coexist with the conditions that sustain it, but it cannot possibly coexist with the conditions of its own arising, the causes that begin its existence. For if it did, X would already exist prior to this relationship, and thus would require no conditions to allow it to exist. Moreover, even in the case of conditioning the state of a pre-existent thing, we must if this "state" exists or not. If not, it cannot modify the thing it is the state of, but if this state in any way "exists," the same impossibility also applies to the conditioning of its existence. Therefore, X cannot possibly arise, cannot possibly be X as a real "simply located" entity so conceived. X as such is "empty."

This is easy to understand if we consider the state of the entire totality of being at moment M and at moment $M + 1$. The state of things at M is thought to have the power to cause the arising of the state of things at $M + 1$. But if M is gone when $M + 1$ arrives, it cannot "reach" $M + 1$ to do anything to it; it is already gone, nonexistent, and thus can do nothing. If the state of things at M continues to exist when $M + 1$ arrives, however, time has failed to move ahead, or we must admit the coexistence of two alternate total states of being at the same time. If the appearance of $M + 1$ does not necessitate the disappearance of M (which by definition possesses the power to bring about M + 1), M would then continue to generate precisely M + 1 repeatedly forever. In either case, time would not be possible, and no real entities could arise. Hence the Mahāyāna claims that *without* Emptiness, if there were any being that were not empty, nothing could come to exist. The same argument applies equally to causality of one state by another in space, or of one part of the totality causing or conditioning another. We have a parallel argument about coexistence or superimposition in space, about the impossibility of contact between two diverse entities in a single unit of space.

However, Nāgārjuna allows for the use of the concepts of older Buddhism by means of his notion of "Two Truths." The old categories of Buddhist practice—such as momentary dharmas, causal conditioning, Five Aggregates, Nirvana, karma—as well as the common usages of terms like "I," "You," "Cause," "Effect," "Thing," "World," and so on, as well as his own concepts such as "Emptiness," are all "conventional truths," that is, propositions and practices with a pragmatic usefulness in terms of the goal of realizing "ultimate truth," which is beyond all conceptualization or verbalization. On the status of other sorts of claims, however, Nāgārjuna is a bit ambiguous. For he sometimes says that the Buddha has taught all sorts of contradictory doctrines—self and nonself, eternity and annihilation, and so on—as conventional truths, and hence that every claim is potentially true and every claim potentially false; but on the other hand he is very concerned to refute any claims for real metaphysical or ontological consistency of non-Buddhist philosophical theories. In practice, we seem to have three epistemological categories here: conventional truth (Buddhism and ordinary speech); ultimate truth (unspeakable); and plain falsehood (non-Buddhist metaphysical, religious, and philosophical theories which claim to give a thoroughgoing, ontologically consistent, universally applicable account of the world in discursive terms, or of cause and effect, of creation, of God or gods, of karma, of the soul, and so on; claims that these are "ultimately real" are just plain false.)

These two approaches to truth are not incompatible, and the Tiantai tradition begins, in a way, with seeing their compatibility, by means of its engagement with the *Lotus Sūtra*. This is a strange Mahāyāna text, very short on doctrinal content as Mahāyāna sūtras go, at first reading seemingly philosophically unsophisticated, fanciful, mythological, superstitious, self-serving and self-righteous, ill-tempered and polemical in a way which is very exceptional for a Buddhist scripture. It appears to be the product of some obsessive sectarian in-fighting, between the "Hinayana" disciples and the new Mahāyāna movement, aggressively selling its idea that, contrary to the Hinayana claim, the goal of Buddhist practice is not the extinction of individual existence and suffering in Nirvana, but rather to practice the Bodhisattva path, to become a Buddha, which means to be endlessly engaged in the project of knowing, interacting with, relating to, guiding, educating, and liberating all sorts of sentient beings, coming up with lots of different ways of edifying them in accordance with their particular dispositions and desires. But the polemic takes an odd turn in that the claim is not that the Hinayana practitioners—called *śrāvakas* or "hearers of [the Buddha's] voice" in this text—are just plain wrong, but rather that they themselves, *precisely in denying Bodhisattvahood*, are in fact practicing the Bodhisattva path, are on their way to becoming Buddhas, are in fact already educating, transforming, setting an example for sentient beings and at the same time working their way step by step toward Buddhahood, without knowing it. This disjunction between "what you are really accomplishing" and "the goal you have in mind in order to make that accomplishment possible" is the distinctive contribution of the *Lotus Sūtra*. It proceeds to claim, in effect, that all beings are Bodhisattvas, that being and Bodhisattvahood are in a way convertible terms, and further that there is really no difference between a Buddha—the end of the process of the Bodhisattva path—and a Bodhisattva—the means; the Buddha himself is eternally a Bodhisattva, being born, taking on various forms, educating beings, striving to find the truth, becoming enlightened and dying over and over again. This is significant because of the collapsing of the ends-means relation implied, made possible by the content of Bodhisattvahood/Buddhahood: it means (1) to assume an infinity of forms, in accordance with the needs of *other* sentient beings, in order to (2) liberate and enlighten them so that they may do the same and thereby (3) educating oneself and moving toward Buddhahood. If both are going on at the same time, it means that both participants in any relation are simultaneously the deluded sentient being and the enlightening Bodhisattva, taking on this deluded form *without knowing it*, as the *Lotus* says is possible, to enlighten in all directions, both self and others. The possibilities opened up here for reconceiving the relation between affirmation and negation, and oneness and manyness, are to be noted. The *śrāvakas* affirm, embody, practice Bodhisattvahood, not in spite of denying it, but *by* denying it, neglecting it, knowing nothing about it or even actively rejecting it. That *is* their Bodhisattva practice. They are Bodhisattvas in the form of the antithesis or rejection of Bodhisattvas. They are Bodhisattvas *as* non-Bodhisattvas. This is precisely how they are going about doing the three things listed above which constitute the work of a Bodhisattva: taking on various forms (in this case, as a *śrāvakas*), enlightening other beings, and working toward Buddhahood.

Tiantai takes the clue from this sutra, filters it through the category of Emptiness developed by Nāgārjuna, and arrives at what it calls the Three Truths: Emptiness, Provisional Positing, and Centrality. We will have much to say about the implications of these terms and their precise content below; but put simply, we have here a formulaic crystallization of the affirmation/negation relation described above in the *Lotus*, where they are identical to one another, and their reversible "asness"—here called Centrality. Philosophically, we will call these three truths "Global Incoherence, Local Coherence, and Reversible Asness," respectively. Nāgārjuna had Two Truths, with a clear hierarchy between them, based on a one-way means-end relation—conventional truth is subordinate to ultimate truth, deriving its value solely therefrom, by being a means thereto, which is to be dispensed with once the end is attained—which allowed for the existence of a third category (plain heretical untruth). Tiantai, in contrast, claims the Two Truths are exactly equivalent in value and ultimacy, and that this fact itself constitutes the third truth about them and everything they had severally pertained to; in fact, the Two Truths are not two separate realms or claims at all, but two alternate restatements of the same fact, namely, dependent co-arising itself. This means the differentiations between things, their conventional designations, *as well as any cockamamie philosophical or religious theory or personal illusion about them*, are just as ultimately true and untrue as their Emptiness or their beyond-conceptualization Suchness, and also that both of these aspects are just as ultimate as the fact that these two aspects are simply aspects of one another. This is the interfusion of the Three Truths, which means even Centrality is not more ultimate than the other two. To indicate any of the three is to indicate all three; they are three ways of saying the same thing. Hence Tiantai wants to go beyond what it calls the "Exclusive Center," which sees the Center as a sort of tertium quid beyond the two extremes of Emptiness and Provisional Positing, which grounds them both and expresses itself as both, to the point of the "Nonexclusive Center," which makes it possible to say that any of the three, taken alone, already says all there is to say about the other two, and entails all the functions of the other two. The Center is the convertibility of the truths of Emptiness and Provisional Positing, their mutual reducibility, which also maintains their distinction, as we shall see below.

This end-means loop, and the peculiar epistemology involved, where "provisional" and "ultimate" truth end up being identical, so that the provisional is never simply dispensed with, but instead is "made ultimate," is handled in a distinctive way in Tiantai exegesis. The technique is called "opening the provisional to reveal the ultimate" (*kaiquan xianshi*), and consists of a *recontextualization* of the provisional propositions to reveal their further implications, which allow them to *always already have been* disclosing the ultimate truth, without having to be changed in the least. The *Lotus Sūtra* tells us precisely this kind of story again and again. We have children who think they are running toward promised toys, but when more of the situation is revealed, these very steps thought to be headed toward the toys turn out to have been steps out of the danger of a fire and toward a much more magnificent reward. The steps themselves, however, are unchanged. We have a worker whose toil for minimum wage turns out to be, when the full context is revealed, actually a process of preparing himself to accept his status as son and heir to the household, who was from the beginning actually already in possession of the treasury from which his meager salary was doled out. We have travelers whose steps toward an illusory city are revealed to have been steps toward a treasure beyond it. We have of course the *śrāvakas* whose practice of Hinayana Buddhism is revealed to be part of a larger Mahāyāna Bodhisattva practice. All activities are to be regarded as recontextualizable to reveal that they have always been Bodhisattva practices both expressing and leading to Buddhahood; hence a Bodhisattva says to the *śrāvakas* who scoff at his prediction that they will become Buddhas, "I do not disparage you, since you are [thereby, even in reviling me] practicing the Bodhisattva path, and will all become Buddhas." That is, their very practices, even the rejection of Bodhisattva, can be recontextualized *by this very claim* to be revealed to be Bodhisattvahood. In Tiantai exegesis, we find a method that corresponds to this feature of the sutra, which is first to make intricate divisions and contrasts, establishing various qualities and characteristics of things by means of their differentiations, and then "opening them up" to reveal their identity in and by means of this very division. We will have more to say about the exact implications and content of this move, philosophically, below. Here some of its doctrinal implications can just be baldly stated.

First there is the claim that all entities are Empty–Provisionally Posited–Central, and that the same relation of identity qua contrast that pertains to these Three Truths also pertains to the threefold structure of all entities, in various mutually recontextualizing registers. Hence all things are karma-delusion-suffering, and also, recontextualized, all things are volitional activity-cognition-reality, and also, recontexualized, all things are Buddha-activities-Buddha-knowledge-Buddha-world/body, and also all things are liberation-wisdom-ultimate reality. These are all just alternate names for the same thing, which is all things, all activities, all thoughts, all conceptions, all views, all dispositions, all experiences. In each triad, the first two elements are opposites, and the third is the identity between these opposites, which makes all *three* ultimately synonymous and mutually inclusive. All three aspects are everywhere, and mutually entailing, indeed mutually identical, reducible to one another.

Since this is all everything is, this also implies that each entity enfolds or entails all others, and not only all "entities," but all views of all entities, all possible existential engagements of all entities. This attitude of egalitarianism between every possible fleeting illusion and ultimate truth is another very distinctive aspect of the classical Tiantai teaching. The "inherent entailment of all entities in each entity" is traditionally described in terms of the doctrine of "the Three Thousand Coherences entailed in each moment of experience," which plays also on the old notion of momentariness, the "one moment" of experience. The locus classicus for this doctrine is a text of Zhiyi's that runs as follows:

> If there is the slightest experience of any kind, it inherently includes all Three Thousand Coherences. This does not mean this moment of experience is prior [i.e., the cause] and the Three Thousand Coherences are posterior [i.e., the effect], not that the Three Thousand Coherences are prior and the one moment is posterior. It is just like the eight marks that constitute the flux of any object [arising, persistence, decay and extinction[3]]; if the object is prior to the marks, it would not be in flux, and if the marks were prior to the object, it would still not be in flux. Neither prior nor posterior is permissible; it is just the thing we mean when we refer to its flux, and just the flux we mean when we refer to the thing. A moment of experience is also thus. If the mind created all dharmas, this would be a 'vertical' way of looking at it [i.e., with a hierarchy of cause and effect, where the mind is ontically prior or 'higher']; if the mind simultaneously encompassed all dharmas, this would be a 'horizontal' way of looking at it [i.e., a definitive side-by-side equality of distinct objects, or a synchronic includer/included relationship, where these two roles are viewed as ontically distinct]. But neither the vertical nor the horizontal view is permissible; rather, it is just the mind that is all dharmas, and just all dharmas which are the mind. . . .[4]

All Three Thousand Coherences are inherent in the mind in the same manner as the characteristics of a thing are inherent in that thing, or as the process of a thing's arising and decay is identical to the thing itself. The included and the includer are not to be thought of as two separate entities, one of which is enclosed in the other. Rather, whatever vantage point is chosen as a point of reference is provisionally called the "includer" ("entailer") in that case, and all the others are called the "included" ("entailed"). If the vantage point and referencing are changed to another focus, that dharma will equally be the includer.[5] In terms of the formulation developed above, all coherences in the

---

[3] Technically, there is said to be a primary arisal and secondary arisal, primary persistence and secondary persistence, hence yielding "eight" marks rather than four.

[4] *Taishō shinshū daizokyo*, ed. Takakusu Junjirō and Watanabe Kaigyoku (Tokyo: Taishō issaikyō kankō-kai, 1914–1932), 46.54a. Henceforth cited as T.

[5] At least in the Shanjia version of the tradition; this is one of the great points of controversy in the Shanjia/Shanwai debates. The former say that any reference point is equally the includer of all coherences, the latter say this is only true directly of the Mind, and indirectly, through the medium of the Mind, of all other dharmas.

universe are appearing here *as* my mind—not as mind per se, be it noted, but as this particular moment of subjective experience, this particular moment of anger, greed, confusion, and so on, with all its specific lineaments. This moment of experience is composed of all coherences. In the terms we will develop below, it is what all things are appearing *as* at this moment. It is a center, than which there is nothing other, identical to the whole it unifies. It is the end toward which all things are working together as means, in such a way that the means are absorbed into the end, no longer immediately discernible as themselves, appearing rather as the end. The relation can be reversed: this moment of experience can in turn appear *as* all things in the universe, the objective world, or any one particular element thereof, likewise construed. The Three Thousand appear as this mind; this mind appears as the Three Thousand. It is one and the same in either case, but never definitively reducible to one side at the expense of the other.

This entails another distinctive feature of classical Tiantai doctrine, the universal application of the category of mutuality, reciprocal grounding or what we will call reversibility or mutual reducibility. Against atomism of any kind, reducibility to asserted, but asserted universally, so that nothing can be reduced to only one side, in only one direction. And indeed, ultimately, Centrality is taken to imply that every entity is reducible to and reducible from all other entities; it is the foundation and the telos of every other possible being. The classic formulation of the principle involved in this "omnicentric" turn, marking a sea-change in all Buddhist metaphysics, comes in Zhiyi's *Sinianchu*, in a critique of the unicentrism of the "consciousness-only" school, and by the same token, of any unilateral foundational metaphysic:

> In Vasubandhu's theory of consciousness-only, there is only the one consciousness, but it is divided into the discerning and the undiscerning forms of consciousness. The discerning consciousness is what we usually call consciousness, while the undiscerning consciousness [i.e., what is discerned about, rather than what is doing the discerning] is "consciousness appearing to be an object." All the physical objects in the universe, vases, clothing, carts and carriages, are all this undiscerning form of consciousness. . . . But since they are all one nature, we can equally say that there are two forms of matter, the discerning and the undiscerning. . . . It is in this sense that mind and matter are nondual. Since he [Vasubandhu] is able to say there are these two different forms of consciousness, we can equally say they are two different forms of matter. . . . In the Integrated Teaching, we can also say that all things are matter only, or sound only, or scent only, or flavor only, or tactile sensation only, or consciousness only. In sum, every dharma inherently includes all the dharmas throughout the dharma-realm. . . .[6]

---
[6] T46.578b–c.

"Discerning"—the process of making distinctions—is, initially, the characteristic feature of consciousness, which distinguishes it from matter, which is that concerning which consciousness makes its distinctions, while making no discriminations about other things itself; matter is discerned but "undiscerning." However, as soon as we say that all is consciousness, we have to allow that what appeared to be matter, because it performed no discerning, was in fact just a deceptively undiscerning "form" of consciousness. The meaning of the term "consciousness" has thereby been expanded. But if the meaning of this term can be thus expanded to include what was precisely its opposite, in distinction to which it was defined, why can any other term not also be so expanded? That is, if we can say that matter is really just a deceptive form of mind, we can equally say that mind is just a deceptive form of matter. As soon as we admit the principle of "one thing being expressed in many forms," or even the possibility of explaining any one thing in terms of another, interpretability as such, whatever X we happen to posit as this center will be emptied of its specific meaning by the very fact that it is, by this very hypothesis, also something that appears as its opposite. "Consciousness" turns out to mean "everything that appears, either as consciousness or as matter." But then, says Zhiyi, matter can also have two forms of appearing, qua consciousness or qua matter. It can also mean "everything that appears, either as consciousness or as matter." Hence matter and consciousness are nondual. But the real import of this theory is just that anything can be used to explain anything else, that all things interconnect and transform into each other such that any particular coherence may be read as pervading everywhere. When any "all is X" theory is taken seriously, it implies, "X really means everything we formerly called X as well as everything we called non-X," and thus, "non-X also means just this same X, which really means X plus non-X," and therefore ends up meaning equally that "all is *any* X," and moreover that "X is therefore identical to anti-X."[7] This is what I will be calling "omnicentrism."

This is the typical Tiantai expository technique. First a distinction is made: mind is different from matter, X is different from non-X, on the basis of its

---

[7] The extent to which any form of explanation of one thing in terms of another, any interpretation of phenomena at any level whatsoever, inevitably brings with it some kind of "all is X" claim, at least for the limited field of its metaphrand, is well worth considering. It may well be that the only way to avoid this omnicentric conclusion is to eschew all explanation whatsoever, returning to the old Abidharmic notion of momentariness, where each appearance is just itself, totally unconnected to anything else. And yet the historical connection of these two extreme possibilities is itself an intriguing clue to what may be a necessary relationship between them.

naïvely apprehended distinguishing features. Only on the basis of this distinction is the coherence of Xness established at all—for example, mind *as* discerning, matter *as* nondiscerning. But once this is done, by the holistic principle of Centrality, each is seen to be a provisional expression of the other; mind is a deceptive form of matter (discernment is a deceptive form of nondiscernment), matter is a deceptive form of mind. Thereby "mind" becomes absolute (literally transcending its defining contrast, so that it pervades everywhere, even in its opposite) and "matter" also becomes absolute, each in its very determination of contrast to the other. Without the contrast, *neither* could pervade anywhere, since no such coherences could be established at all. The arbitrary starting point is the necessary supplier of determinacy per se, and the "absoluteness" does not destroy the particular coherences, revealing a pure transcendence to which none of these particular designations pertain, but on the contrary, fully and thoroughly establishes them, as pertaining everywhere.

The above two citations come from Zhiyi, the de facto founder of the school. His great successor Zhanran brings out the implications, as applicable to meditational practice, in a famous passage:

> All possible objects of experience can be considered in terms of either the totality of which they form a part or as the differentiated parts of this whole. The totalizing whole is always some single moment of experience, while the differentiated parts can be divided into the two categories of mind and matter. . . . Once we know how mind and matter are differentiated, we can see how these differentiated parts are integrated into the totalizing whole: all things without exception are the mind and [hence] simultaneously all are the Nature.[8] Thus there is only one Nature. But one Nature is no Nature. Thereby the three thousand particular existences are all just as they always were [only more so].[9] Thus it should be known that since mind-and-matter [qua the Nature] are here as the mind,[10] just the mind is what is meant by its transformations. These transformations are what

---

[8] Zhili's reading of this controversial line. It is alternately read as, "All things without exception are of the nature of mind." But Zhili argues that this reading, typical of the heterodox Shanwai writers, loses precisely what is distinctive to Tiantai theory, assimilating the text to the doctrinal position of Huayan and most other mainstream Mahāyāna thought.

[9] The meaning here is clarified by the restatement a few lines later: "First comprehend that all external mind and matter are this one moment of experience, which is itself not this one moment of experience, not definitively a moment of experience at all; they are all this thought, which is thus no longer this thought. Just this Three Thousand of the inner substance is the mutual identity of Emptiness, Provisional Positing, and Centrality, and hence all the external things are entirely the Nature, all are the mind. . . ."

[10] Literally, with respect to the mind-and-matter of mind, i.e., the mind-and-matter which are this moment of mind.

is meant by the creation [by the mind of individual things, which are distinct from and opposed to mind]. Creation [in this sense] is what is meant by [the entire] substance [being expressed as] the function. Thus there is neither mind nor matter, there is both mind and matter, there is only mind, there is only matter. . . .[11]

According to Zhili's extensive commentary on this passage, "mind" here refers to any single moment of attention in its capacity of (1) predicating sameness or difference concerning things, making distinctions among them, (2) standing apart from them and against them with a (false) sense of autonomy, and (3) actively taking an attitude toward them.[12] This is the process by which the experienced identities of these things are constituted. As Zhanran says, on their own the things never declare themselves "the same as" or "different from" one another;[13] the very carving out of how much or how little of the perceptual or conceptual field is to count as this or that thing, or even to count as an object as such, set up over against the subject, is a function of a particular subjective mental process of selective attention. Both objective and subjective quiddities are constituted by this meaning-giving function of some particular moment of subjective attention, which is what is described here as "creation" by mind. It is the process of "seeing-as," or rather "coming to see as some X." The claim is that all coherent objects of cognition and experience exist only in this way, appear only as instances of seeing-as. All experiences of specific coherences come into being, they begin and end at a particular point in time, they have a before and after to them, and this brings with it a *process* of coming into focus as this particular identity, and an active *deed* of coming to see as X.

Moreover, if one lacks this ability to see a set of elements "as" some par-

---

[11] Zhanran, *Shibuermen* (originally excerpted from his *Fahuaxuanyi shiqian*), T46.703a.
[12] Zhili, *Jinguangmingjing wenjuji*, in *Xujangjing* (Taipei: Xinwenfeng, 1988), 31, 70a–b.
[13] Zhanran, *Zhiguan yili*, T46.452a.
[14] As Zhanran says, "Because sentient beings inherently entail the Three Thousand [as their Nature], they are able to serve as stimuli [i.e., make themselves felt by the others among the Three Thousand Coherences]; because the Buddhas fully realize this same Three Thousand as their nature, they can respond [to the others among these Three Thousand]. Otherwise, how could [the Buddhas appear in the consciousness of sentient beings effortlessly] like a shape appearing in a mirror? *The mirror must inherently possess the principle [Nature] of manifesting these forms; the forms must inherently possess the Nature [principle] of generating images*. . .The principle of each thing inherently and originally entails both the provisional and the real, but manifests as one or the other according to beginningless habitual influences. Its being one or the other depends on these habitual influences, but in their inherent principle [Nature] they are perfectly equal; it is just that in encountering various situations and times they form habituations, in dependence on their practices and intentions. *But if within them there were no original cause [to manifest as just this form], these influences would be exerted to no effect.*" (*Shibuermen*, T46.704a–b [emphases added].)

ticular coherence, there is no way to experience this coherence.[14] For example, we may see three line-segments, touching each other at their tips to enclose a space, and yet fail to see this mysterious entity "triangle" that everyone keeps talking about: yes, we might say, I see the lines, but where is this triangle? Similarly, we might say, I see the contiguous series of points, but where are these "lines" you keep talking about? And so on. For anything at all to appear, some subjective ability for seeing-as, and for seeing-as-just-this-coherence, is necessary. It is this process which is meant here by "mind." The contemplation of mind here means to experience each object of consciousness as an aspect of the power of one's own mind to see-as this particular coherence, and hence as an aspect of one's own mind at this moment.

This is not idealism, not even a limited subjective idealism of the Kantian stamp. Zhili stresses that this focus on "creation by mind" is merely a meditational convenience, a kind of start-where-you-are tool or exercise by which a more general point is made palpable to the beginning student. Indeed, this process of creation is for Zhili in an important sense an illusion, the primal illusion: for myself, I am the center of the world, all things exist only to the extent that they exist "for me," and have reality only as whatever they appear to be "to me." The being of these objects created by mind, then, is to be understood only as what would be lacking if I were not present to regard them at all, that is, the present experience of them as this or as that. Consciousness is for Zhili far from a mysterious revelation of pure spirit or the immediate presence of the unconditioned transcendental reality. Rather, he describes it as a natural process, "constituted by the habituating influences of views and attachments" (*jianai xunxi suocheng*),[15] a kind of sedimentation formed by accumulated habituation and deluded karma—deliberate deeds and, left to itself, tending to perpetuate the momentum of these delusions. For that very reason it must be utilized as the starting point for meditation practice, which reveals this illusion to be false if taken literally, but true in another, unexpected sense. In fact, he says, it is equally true to say that all things, including our minds, are "created by" and "reducible to" matter, or any particular object, in just the same way. Moreover, all sentient beings are simultaneously doing this kind of "creation by mind" in various ways, each with his or her own equally real "creating", i.e., differentiating mind. Further, the available determinations that are so "created" in each case in fact pre-exist each particular act of creation, as we shall see below. As Zhili puts it, "There is just one and the same Three Thousand, which is in itself neither internal [mental, subjective] nor external [material, objective], but can be viewed as entirely resolvable into either the

---

[15] Zhili, *Jinguangmingjing wenjuji, Xujangjing*, 31, 70a–b.
[16] Zhili, *Simingshiyishu* T46.836c.

inner or the outer according to the method of contemplation adopted."[16]

The terms "mind" and "the Nature" are to be understood according to Zhanran's statement elsewhere: "Although presencing in some particular, conditioned way, it is unconditioned and unchanging, and hence it is the Nature. Although unconditioned and unchanging, it is this particular, conditioned presencing, and hence it is this moment of mind."[17] That is, both "mind," this moment of seeing-as (or according to Zhili, any other particular conditioned entity), and "the Nature" are terms that include two opposed but mutually encompassing poles, with a difference in emphasis. Each name implies both meanings, and ultimately refers to the same double-faceted fact, as when we use "equilateral triangle" and "equiangular triangle" to refer to the same triangle, each term necessarily implying the other, but with the emphasis temporarily on one side or the other. The two opposed but ultimately mutually entailing poles in this case are the conditioned particular (in this case, a moment of coming-to-see-as) and the unconditioned universal. The unconditioned, the Nature, means what is findable everywhere, which is presencing under any and every condition. The term "nature" is used here in the sense in which we speak of the nature of something as what is unchangeable about it, as we might say that the nature of water is to have a chemical composition of H_2O. Whether it is a river, an ocean, steam, ice, droplets of dew, snow, whatever else might change about it, as long as it is water it has this unchanging nature of a chemical composition H_2O. This chemical structure is findable everywhere in the water at the bottom of the lake, in the steam above it, in the cup, in the kettle, in the ice-swan's neck or wings or beak. So by "the nature of this thing" we mean what is present or findable everywhere and at all times in this thing. In other words, it is the unconditioned aspect of this thing, what is present under all conditions in which it might be found and excluded by none. It is what water "really is," its essence, whether it looks like a swan or like a cloud or like a lake. It is also what every other aspect of the water is in some sense reducible to, or resolvable into.

Now Zhanran claims that each experienced quiddity is, on the one hand, a "creation of" a particular moment of subjective attention or seeing-as, and, on the other hand, this same quiddity is precisely the unchangeable Nature of this moment of subjective attention, its essence, what it really is. This transition from product of mind to essence of mind is due to certain considerations about relation in general, which can be stated as a question about what it means for any coherence to be "in" another coherence: a predicate in a subject, a characteristic in a substance, a part in a whole. Indeed, we are dealing here with the problem of what it means for any two distinguishable quiddi-

---

[17] Zhanran, *Zhiguan dayi*, T46.460b.

ties to be linked by any kind of "in," "of," or "as." The point here, derived from the application of Mahāyāna ideas about Emptiness to mind-contemplation, is that nothing can get "in" to anything else unless it is already in it. However, if X is able to be in Y *without thereby simply replacing X in that place*, X and Y cannot be mutually exclusive entities, and hence cannot have the simple identities as Y and X that depended on a contrast of genuinely distinguishable qualia. This problem of the coexistence of differences is at the heart of the Tiantai application of Nāgārjunian ideas to meditation. As Zhili says, it is the observed fact that all these diverse qualia coexist in a single moment of seeing-as, *or* in a single object so seen, that reveals the one Nature, not because this one moment of mind or one object as such *is* the Nature that subsumes differences in the manner of universal mind or universal matter, but because the coexistence of distinct qualia, overlapping and yet not overlapping, is the direct manifestation of "the Nature" in the Tiantai sense, that is, the Three Truths.[18]

The crux of the problem is that some kind of coexistence (at least at their interface) is necessary for the phenomenal existence of distinct coherences as contrast, as succession, as predicates belonging to a single subject or moment in time, as parts belonging to or composing a whole but is at the same time impossible if the coherences are mutually exclusive, i.e., genuinely distinct. Note that this coexistence is still a problem even when we are talking about the succession of experienced qualia. Although we may seem to be experiencing only one coherence at a time—now red, now blue, now cup, now table, now a memory, now a desire—in fact some coexistence is necessary for the contrast between these moments which establishes their distinct identities; they must overlap somewhere, with each other or with some shared third medium "in" which they both exist, for us to be able to tell the difference between them, but if they truly overlap they are no longer distinguishable. Hence, Zhili speaks of all coherences or qualia "co-present in" or

---

[18] Zhili, *Shibuermen zhiyaochao*, T46.710a: "Although the Nature is one, there is no one fixed Nature. Because the Three Thousand quiddities share this same single Nature, when presencing as the various quiddities any one among them chosen at random subsumes and totalizes all the others. When we show that a single moment of attention subsumes and totalizes all quiddities, this is to make it manifest that they share this same Nature. [Zhanran in] the *Shiqian* says, In terms of Conventional Truth [provisional positing, local coherence] they are the hundred realms and the thousand suchnesses; in terms of the Real Truth [Emptiness, global incoherence], they are co-present in a single moment of attention. What must be understood here is that it is only because they share the same Nature that they are able to be co-present in a single moment of attention. It is not designating this moment of attention itself as the Real Truth. For the fact that all dharmas are co-present in a single speck of dust equally reveals the Real Truth."
[19] Zhili, *Shibuermen zhiyaochao*, T46.708c.

"converging toward" any single moment of seeing-as,[19] not because one is explicitly aware of all things simultaneously, but because whenever one becomes aware of any other object, turning from awareness of X to awareness of Y, it turns out to be impossible for Y to have been entirely absent from X, or vice versa, or indeed for X to have been present in Y, if they are genuinely distinct. Here we have the problematic of the Three Truths in a nutshell, which we will be explicating at length below. Entities can neither overlap nor fail to overlap. This problem applies to the thoughts and perceptions "in" my mind, the objects of awareness "in" this moment of awareness, the effect of the past "in" the present and so on.

The commonsensical concept of "inside" is perhaps derived from a concrete model of, for instance, a coin in a pocket; but the coin is really "external" to the pocket, both molecule for molecule and conceptually (in that coin does not equal pocket). If something truly other and external to some X (that is, mutually exclusive to X) came "into" this X, it would simply *replace* X at that locus, not be "in" it. But neither X nor Y can be distinguished as such, or meaningfully be said to be established as existent, without some form of overlapping, some "in" relation, some coexistence between at least two mutually exclusive quiddities. For example, contact or overlap is necessary for causal efficacy (X must touch Y, or both must touch some third medium "in" which they both exist, for any "effectivity," whatever that might be, to pass between them); subsumption and composition is necessary for the whole/part relation (parts which are "in" and "compose" the whole, and yet are qualitatively distinct from it); contrast between X and Y is necessary for any discernibility (X can be seen and known to be not-Y, which means somehow the two are held in mind at the same time to be compared). All of these are "in" relations, and none can intelligibly exist for truly mutually exclusive and distinct entities. For Y to be truly in X, then, X must have "the Nature" of Y to begin with. In Tiantai terms, however, this "having the Nature of Y" means that Y is neither really present in X nor that it is really absent from X. The "Nature" is the Three Truths, in other words, that Y is a local coherence that is globally incoherent, and that these two are synonymous. Neither simple presence in X nor simple absence from X could ever explain the appearance of Y in X. Rather, Y's presence as the Three Truths, and absence as the Three Truths, is the Nature of X.

This ultimately means that Y is another name for X in its entirety. When I see Y, I am seeing an intrinsic, pre-existent power to manifest Y that belongs intrinsically to my mind. But a pre-existing, unchanging power "of" my mind *is* my mind itself, and for the same reason. Otherwise, this "power" would have to be something "in" something else, namely, my mind, or the entirety of my nature, identity, or self. The same can be said of the relation between "potential" and "actual" functioning of this supposed power, between having this power and "manifesting" it, or between this moment of experience and the effect of past mental experiences or the nature of mind as such "in" it. The subject, nature, or identity of something is, as we said, what is unchangeable, always findable about it, while whatever is only sometimes present is an attribute possessed by this subject. An unchangeable power, findable everywhere in this subject, is this subject itself. A genuinely unchangeable aspect of me is myself.[20]

The claim then is that any distinct object of attention of which I become aware at any moment is none other than my own eternal unconditioned self. To see X is to have it revealed that X is what I have always been and must always be. To see X means that it turns out that X is my own secret identity. The revelation of the secret identity which something turns out to be is not as peculiar as it sounds; any time we experience an object and separate appearances from realities, or come to understand that some perception belongs to an attribute of some substance, to which it is reducible, we have a partial application of the same principle. When I see the rim of a glass foreshortened according to the laws of perspective so as to appear to me as an oval, and instantaneously make the interpretive mental adjustment which simultaneously understands it as "really" a circle, I understand that this apparent oval, just as it is, is really a circle, and has been all along, no matter how many different ways it may appear to me at various times. It turns out to have always been a circle, which means that I can be confident that it will behave as a circle in other contexts, for example, if I touch it with my hand and feel its circularity. In the present case, when I see a chair, I learn that "chair" is what I have always been. And

---

[20] One might ask in opposition to this conclusion, Could there not be multiple unchangeable aspects? For example, we might imagine a constant mass *and* a constant volume of a piece of wax that changes its shape and color. But we must recall here that unchangeable here also means unconditioned, which is to say, *omnipresent*, inescapable, applicable in every time and place, under all conditions. It is unchangeable in both time and space, there to be found *wherever and whenever* one cares to look. So for this mass to "have" this volume, or to be "in" it, or vice versa, these two must be intrinsic "powers" of each other in the same way, and hence alternate names of one another. The question here is what it is to be mass, and what it is to be volume. If "being volume" were *either* the same as *or* different from "being mass," their relation or coexistence would be impossible. For coexistence already implies both "in" and "out"—there must be the coexistence of these two "in" some third thing, and "outside" of each other. But the concept of "outside" becomes unintelligible as soon as the concept of "inside" becomes unintelligible. If non-X is in X, it replaces it, but if non-X is not in X, or if both are not in some third medium in which they can be brought together, no contact, and hence no contrast between them, is possible. This interchangeability of diverse but equally omnipresent quiddities is what Zhili calls "creation in terms of principle" (*lizao*), pertaining to the Three Thousand as each omnipresent and unconditioned. Each "creates" the others in the sense that it is equally readable as any of the others, inherently entails the others.

here, too, this means that I can be confident that chairness will be forever findable in all the various ways I express myself in the future and in the past, that all the various appearances I go through are reducible to chairness and can be deduced from knowing all the properties of chairness.

It should be noted that self-knowledge is treated here as exactly the same as any other knowledge; equally possible, equally impossible. This is to be contrasted to the position developed in much Mahāyāna thought, most notably in some versions of Chan or Zen, that concrete knowledge of the self is uniquely impossible, systematically elusive as "an eye that cannot see itself," such that any concretely recognized quiddity cannot be the self. In the Tiantai view, on the contrary, all dharmas, self and other, mind and matter—are on the same footing; they are locally coherent, globally incoherent, and intersubsumptive. In terms of the self, this means that I am (for example) a chair, and that knowing myself as such constitutes genuine self-knowledge, telling me what I can expect of my powers and tendencies in the future, and providing me with the master key for understanding my own behavior and responses in the past. The trope used in Tiantai, to be contrasted to the assertion about the invisible eye in Chan, is that "the sword cannot cut itself." Here, however, the meaning of this claim is that what appears to be an external impingement, for example, a painful stab from outside, is in fact merely a further revelation of one's own power; one is oneself's pain, and thus cannot be harmed by pain. Similarly, the highest value, Buddhahood, is not covered over or obstructed by delusions and evils, but further manifested by them, and vice versa. Neither destroys the other, as a sword does not cut itself. These claims sound very bizarre, of course; but much of what follows will be devoted to showing their plausibility and importance.

The same argument applies to the relation of my mind or my self, "in" which this moment of mind is supposed to exist, to anything else. It is not just my self that turns out to be eternally chair; all things are likewise eternally chair. For this moment of seeing-as is generally thought to be a member "in" some larger aggregate of existents: for example, a "series" (of other moments of mental experience), the world, or some thinking substance called "the mind." But an in-relation between two genuinely distinguishable entities cannot exist here either. If my present act of seeing were genuinely different from the larger whole of which it is putatively a part, in which it occurs—the world, or time, or my self—it would simply replace them when it arose; in that particular position there would be just this event itself, not those other entities "world" or "time" or "self." But it must be genuinely different from, mutually exclusive with, this larger whole for its occurrence to take place at all; for if it is the same as the world, or time, or my self, no such event ever occurs, for there is no difference to mark the beginning of an event. So again it is not "in" the world, time, or my self as a distinct event. It cannot enter the world unless it is already the world's "nature" in the sense delineated above: unconditioned, unchangeable, present everywhere in the Three Truths sense of presence-absence. Thus, this deed of seeing-as is the world's nature, which is the entirety of the world itself, the world's own self. Hence, whatever is the nature, in the above sense, of any given entity, must be the nature, in the same sense, of all possible entities; it must be unconditioned, findable everywhere, not only "in" this one particular entity, but "in" all entities.

The result is a transition from the contrast between subject and object, to the encounter or coexistence between them, to object as product of subject, to object as unconditioned essence of subject, to object as identity of subject, to each subject and each object as the unconditioned essence of all things without exception. Each perceived coherence is a function of the mind, hence an intrinsic unchangeable aspect of mind, hence the sole essence of mind, what mind really is and always has been, and thus equally what all other entities really are and have always been. But in that case, Zhanran continues, all these natures, since they are all findable everywhere, are one and the same nature. We might think here of Spinoza's argument for the impossibility of multiple substances. Otherwise there would be change from one to another; none of them would be truly unchangeable and findable everywhere if something were truly "other" to it, if the appearance of something could displace it. There cannot be multiple unconditioned existences, because in that case each would be limited by the "condition" of the presence of the other.

However, this means that there is no particular coherence one could point to that is unchangeable, that must be appearing *simpliciter* everywhere, or even anywhere. For the very same reason that they are all one nature, there is no specifiable nature at all. For although a given X may be the nature, unchangeable and present everywhere, since X is equally Y, X need not be present anywhere at all as X itself, it might be present *only* as Y. There is no X one could point to that is unconditioned and present everywhere, that can be found under all conditions, except in the form of other coherences. No specific nature can be the one unconditioned nature, and at the same time any particular coherence that appears in experience must be the entirety of this one nature. Hence, Zhanran concludes that each function is the entirety of the Nature, is in fact all Three Thousand quiddities appearing *as* this particular thing. Thus one can say that there is mind and matter, or that there is neither mind nor matter, or that there is only mind, or that there is only matter.

Now we may give a freer rendering of the above quotation from Zhanran, spelling out its real implications more clearly:

Each subjective and objective coherence experienced, each entity or event taken to be existing either in my own mind (thoughts, intentions, feelings, memories, my character) or in the world (objects, facts, states of affairs), is a "creation" of a particular, conditioned moment of subjective seeing-as, seeing them as such and such. Each is thus also an inalienable aspect of this act of seeing-as, is what is unchangeable in this conditioned particular moment of experience, its nature or essence, for nothing can "enter" this mental experience from outside unless it was always already a part of its nature. By the same token, all are unconditioned characteristics of all things, present not only in this moment of mind but also in all times and places. All these unchanging coherences are in reality one unchanging omnipresent nature, for otherwise there is change from one to another; a true plurality of unchangeable, omnipresent, unconditioned coherences is impossible. In that case, however, there is no particular coherence that is unchangeable and omnipresent. But then each of the Three Thousand objective and subjective coherences remains there as it always was, but now understood to be, just as it is, the entirety of the unconditioned, absolute nature, findable everywhere and in all conditions. Hence, all these unconditioned subjectivities and objectivities, belonging intrinsically to this moment of experience as its ownmost identity, are such that just this moment of subjectivity is what is meant by the process of its transformation into various forms. These transformations of itself into various forms are what is meant by the creation by subjectivity of individual things which are distinct from and opposed to it. Creation in this sense is thus precisely the entire unchanging and unconditioned Three-Thousand-as-the-nature present *as* each particular function. Thus we can say equally, "There exists neither subjectivity nor objectivity," or "Subjectivity and objectivity both exist," or "Only subjectivity exists," or "Only objectivity exists."

It is important to note how "oneness," derived from "a single moment of experience," or a "single experience," reduces immediately to "noneness" here, the self-emptying of the coherence in question that comes as soon as it is seen to be universally applicable, to be all-pervasive. Here the coherence in question is "mind," or "mindlikeness," or better, "relevance to me, being a part of my world in this particular moment of experience." After delineating the contrast between mind and matter, the parts that make up this whole experience, earlier in the passage, so that this concept of "me" as opposed to "nonme" is established and given a content, Zhanran "opens the provisional to reveal the real." This quality of "mindlikeness" or "me-relevance" is found to be everywhere in any given experience; even in the act of being distinguished from its opposite, matter or nonme, the content and clarity of this content was being further revealed. The more sharply distinguished and isolated from its negation, the more vividly and clearly this particular content is revealed. But if its negative is revealing it, it is present in its negative as well. For this "presence" is just this revealing of a particular coherence. The negation of mind, therefore, reveals both mind and nonmind. Here, in terms of the practice of meditation, we are instructed to consider how the quality "mind-likeness" or "me-relevance" is findable everywhere, even and especially in its very negation and exclusion. But if it is everywhere, it has lost all meaning, it is no longer contrasted to anything, it has emptied itself of any determinate content. Note that here again a contrast is first made to establish the content of the categories—mind *versus* matter, self *versus* nonself—establishing the importance of "provisional" truth, and then it is "opened up" to reveal that *each* half in fact pervades the entire field, that precisely in being related they are each findable throughout the relation, and hence empty themselves of meaning. Hence we are told that, once we see that everything is (this moment of) mind, we immediately also see that everything is *neither* mind nor matter (Emptiness), manifesting as both mind and matter (Provisional Positing), and nothing but mind, but simultaneously nothing but matter (Centrality—what we will call Reversible Asness or Intersubsumption).

Tiantai proceeds simultaneously in the purely theoretical dimension, with the doctrine of the Three Truths applicable to any dependently co-arisen entity whatsoever, and in the practical dimension, which focuses on the dimension of mind versus matter or self versus nonself, as in the passages here. In understanding the latter, we may think here of Kant's "transcendental unity of apperception," the possibility of the "I think" or "I experience" which necessarily accompanies all representations. Without this one universal quality, which can apply to every act of awareness, nothing can appear at all. But this really just boils down to an a priori "possibility of being linked to something other than itself." This possible connection with other representations is what allows all representations to be anything at all, to appear in experience at all. For this transcendental unity of apperception consists of and necessarily contains a synthesis of multiple, diverse representations; otherwise it would not be a "unity" or "synthesis," since it would have nothing to synthesize. Empirical consciousness is diverse, unrelated to the identity of the subject—there is relation to identity only insofar as I conjoin one representation to another. Only by uniting a "many" (others, differences) into one consciousness can I represent to myself the identity of consciousness; but correlatively and equally importantly, each of the contrasted terms appears as itself only on the condition of the possibility of being contrasted to some otherness, which is only possible if both are embraced in some overarching dimension, and thereby connected. Some term must be applicable to the entire field for there to be a field of differences per se at all. Zhanran's point here is that if there is anything at all, there must be a field of at least two differences, and if there are differences, there must be a term applicable to the entire field; but any term applicable to the entire field, since the content of a term is established only by being contrasted to some other term in the same field which is outside itself, is both everywhere and nowhere, for it turns out not to have any content or meaning at all, and also to mean, in this way, everything else: hence, "the one nature is no nature." What must be stressed here is that this self-emptying is the result of the process of universalization itself, of this term's *success* in finding itself everywhere in the field: indeed, the all-pervasiveness *is* the emptiness here. In classical terms, to be ungraspable is to be unevadable. Unattainability is unrenounceability. And this allows "the Three Thousand to appear clearly just as they are"—meaning qua external, qua themselves, qua obstacles, qua resistances to and denials of their subsumption into this "oneness." They become *more* manifest as this one subsuming universal term becomes more manifest, because its full manifestation, as applying everywhere in the field, is exactly its *crash* and self-emptying, its revelation that it has no content whatsoever. This simultaneously increasing manifestation of the affirmation and the negation, and of their identity, is another very distinctive feature of classical Tiantai thought. It leads to the proposition that the *more* divided and differentiated things are, the *more* they are joined and unified, that the more isolated they are the more they are united and vice versa. This can be seen also in the role played by the unity of "one moment of experience," separated and isolated, in establishing that all entities are aspects of this one, that there is nothing outside it. Hence we have Zhanran's remarkably concise chain of equation: Mind as mind/matter, which means mind is its transformations, which means these transformations are precisely the creation of objects distinct from mind, which means the entire substance (in this case mind, the creator) is the function (the objects distinct from mind).

This last step deserves special attention. "Creation" implies here the separation between the formative term designated as the first point of reference, in this case mind, and something qualitatively other and independent. But it is precisely this separation between them, the fact that the transformation is the creation, that the continuity is the discontinuity, that ensures that the entire substance has bled into the function. The substance has crashed; one nature is no nature. It has entirely emptied itself into its function. But this includes the function of "substantiality" as such as well. That is, once the "entire substance" is seen to be the qualitatively other "function" here, we can immediately reverse the terms. Now "matter" can be the substance, and mind the function, as the next line in the citation asserts. More strictly, in accordance with Zhili's interpretation, we should say not "mind" and "matter" here as general terms, but "this particular qualitatively distinct moment of experience" and "all other possible coherences, e.g., that speck of dust, that fragrance, that tone, etc." This moment of experience is the totality of this quality and the other possibles that form its world. Hence it is not altered substantially in its transformations into these others, hence when it leaves itself behind to "create" some otherness, the entire substance—this particular qualitatively distinct moment of experience as unifier"—has emptied itself into the function—"the other." The other is now the unifier, which incorporates the initial experience. Here we have arrived at the reversibility and "intersubsumption" which are of the essence of the Tiantai view of the world.

Zhanran had specified two forms of "creation": the creation in terms of *li*, principle, designating the Three Truths as implying the necessary, categorical omnipresence and intersubsumption of all coherences, and creation in terms of *shi*, or finite, contingent (but causally intersubsumptive) spatiotemporal events. The former designates all determinate beings as unconditioned and hence uncreated; and yet a kind of "creation" is attributed to them. Zhanran explains, "Creation in terms of *li* means simply inherent entailment." Inherent entailment is the unconditionality of each coherence itself. This pronouncement formed a pillar of Zhili's doctrine of the "Twofold Three Thousand," which will be discussed at length in the treatment of the Kantian categories in Part One. But for now it is useful to note what this startling claim might mean. Zhanran's assertion is that X, say, regarded as "principle," "creates" Y in the sense that X inherently entails Y. That is, X is constitutively, ontologically ambiguous, and can also be read as Y; indeed, precisely by being determinate as X, it cannot help demanding to be read in alternate ways, including Y. This spilling over of each coherence into every other is here viewed as another way of reading the spatio-temporal causal "creation," the arising and perishing of contingent events, which constitutes the phenomenal world. The upshot of this is *an equation between ambiguity and temporality*, a Tiantai move which will bear much fruit in our further discussion. From here we can understand the Tiantai insistence on the importance of the claim found in the *Vimalakīrti Sūtra*, that "All coherences are established from the root of nondwelling" (*cong wuzhuben li yiqie fa*). Zhili interprets this last term, "nondwelling," to mean "undecidable" or "ambiguous." Simple ambiguity as such is also readable as every other coherence, both categorically and spatio-temporally. What all coherences are being at all times is this nondwelling, this ambiguity, but understood as played out into the intersubsumption of the Three Truths: to be a coherence is to be ambiguous, and to be ambiguous is to be a specific coherence—indeed, being determinate and being ambiguous are undecidable, are themselves ambiguous.

This has profound ethical and pragmatic implications, in that it comes to be stated that *fully realizing* any entity—including suffering, desire, and so on—is precisely *liberation from* that entity; in classical terms, as Zhili puts it, "the more one dwells in it, the more one is liberated from it." This is a result of the same line of thought: the more manifest it becomes, the more it is seen as a single distinct experience, isolated from all others, and hence totalizing the field and allowing contrasts within it, the more it self-undermines, and makes room for the more manifest appearance of all othernesses appearing here *as* it. We will be expanding on the implications of this doctrine at length below.

Later in this passage, Zhanran says, "How can the one moment of experience be divided into active agent and passive patient? And yet it allows the active and the passive to appear just as they are." This is a restatement of the same point, the simultaneous and proportional manifestation of the affirmation and the negation, and their identity. It again concerns the pragmatic or meditational aspect of the classical teaching—all the aspects of the world present in a single, isolated experience are undividably here *as* it, without any separation of self and others, of doer and done-to. However, since this "one experience" empties itself, turns out to mean nothing, is precisely "not this experience," it equally manifests precisely the qualities of "selfness" and "otherness," "active" and "passive," and so on. This is the basis of the further doctrine of the identity-qua-difference of self and other, and of organism and environment, what we might call the inescapability of situatedness and intersubjectivity. This has a particular religious and ritual function within classical Tiantai, but we will be elaborating its philosophical implications in detail in the pages to follow.

The above should give the reader some idea of what is going on in classical Tiantai, and those distinctive features of its teaching which we are taking as the springboard of our thinking here. Let us now proceed to a more strictly philosophical consideration and elaboration of these points.

PART ONE

Neo-Tiantai Basics

ENFRAMEMENT, COHERENCE, AND AGENCY—
THE THUSNESS AND OTHERWISENESS
OF ALL COHERENCES

What Else Is There?

It is customary to begin a work such as this one by announcing to the readers what it will be "about," what topics are going to be addressed and discussed in the pages that follow. As literary customs go, it must be admitted, this is certainly a most understandable and reasonable one. Its utility is obvious; it allows the readers to decide whether this is the kind of thing they care about, something which has some peripheral connection to something else in which they have at least a passing interest, and thus whether to bother with it, to devote precious time and attention to working through it. But this convention calls forth a peculiar difficulty in the present case. The question for us is not what we will be talking about. The question is, rather, *as* what we will *begin* talking about it.

The reason for this is simply that the approach we will take here results in an apprehension of the *necessary impossibility* of definitively limiting the "what" of any assertion, or even of any perception. This has been noticed many times before, and perhaps even felt in its full force here and there; but in almost every case, some reason is found to ignore this consideration and go on talking about some restricted range of particular things anyway, apparently necessarily, since otherwise, it is thought, it would be impossible to say anything. But in this work we will be trying to find a way to hold uncompromisingly to this insight, and yet to push it far enough through its own bottom, as it were, for it to become not an obstacle to any possibility of practical application or rigorous discourse, but rather the very underpinning and condition of all such endeavors. Hence we will not shy away from taking this apparently debilitating consideration as our centerpiece right from the beginning, and declaring it up front. For somewhat complicated reasons that are to exercise us considerably below, we shall hold unequivocally that to be talking about anything is always, in the strictest possible sense, to be talking about "everything," a flaccid term that we would normally feel more than a little embarrassed to be adducing so loosely at such an early point in the game. But there is no way to avoid it: this book is, we must admit without any ambiguity, "about" everything—and it must be added immediately, to even greater peril, that the same can be said of *anything else* as well. This means that I will be holding in all seriousness, and attempting rigorously to demonstrate, that all events of any kind—conversations, encounters of percepts, daydreams, volitions, sensations—are not only necessarily describable in terms of referentiality (all facts per se are "about" something—i.e., other facts), but also that what they are about is necessarily "everything." All experiences, we shall try to show, are in a situation somewhat like what is described in the old Second City routine: the professor begins his lecture saying, "The topic of today's lecture is the universe." "Why the universe?" asks the straight-man student. "What else is there?" says the professor.

This claim itself, of course, belongs at the end, is exactly what we will be trying to demonstrate, and yet we must make it a bare methodological dogma here at the beginning in order to even begin. But the multiplicity of topics—and the seriousness of the question of what to talk about, what to spend our time and energy on, since they are all everything anyway—is by no means to be glossed over by appeal to this point. There is always the question, as I suggested in passing above, not of what is going to be the matter at hand—it is indeed always everything—but *as* what it is going to be approached to begin with. Indeed, this notion of "asness" itself will be the central thread of the following discussion. In that sense, I can state simply what this book is "about": this is a book about asness. But to get to that discussion itself, to explore what exactly we mean by "asness," we need a starting "as"—which local approach is going to get us to that "asness" question most expeditiously? *As* what shall asness be introduced? The problem that will guide us, and that we will try to ride to a very broad range of practical and philosophical implications, very generally stated, is: What exactly is going on when we say, for example, that "X is present *as* Y, X appears *as* (in the form of) Y"? But the central dilemma involved here appears in a number of forms, *as* a great mass of pairs of opposed terms, each of which defines an axis or dimension in which the problem might be detected, which could well have served as our starting point. So here I will say (in no particular order): we will begin by raising this question of asness not exactly as the question of content and form, not as certainty and uncertainty, not as dependence and independence, not as mediation and immediacy, not as suffering and liberation, not as will and ideation, not as time and space, not as creator and created, not as love and aggression, not as flux and reification, not as totalization and dissemination, not as freedom and oppression, not as reason and sensibility, not as a priori and a posteriori, not as being and beings, not as mind and body, not as eternity and time, not as intersubjectivity and withdrawal, not as development and stagnation, not as finite and infinite. Rather, we will be starting with the question *as* the question of *coherence and incoherence*. Once our foot is in that particular door, we will try to make our way through all the other rooms of asness just listed and passed over.

Meaning à la Mode

Let us start by going back as far as we can go in this particular dimension, to a proposition that plays the role of the *cogito*, as it were, in relation to the question of coherence: Some things, we think, "make sense." By this we perhaps mean, very generally stated, that these things *cohere* with other things in a particular way, that is, fit in consistently with the rest of our percepts or beliefs in some way that is meaningful to us. Two important aspects of this situation are to be noted here. First,"coherence" here means both the cohering, or sticking together in a particular way, of the elements that compose the thing, and its cohering, sticking together in a particular way, with what surrounds it, with its environment, with everything else. This means both that it coheres with everything else that "makes sense" within a given system, and also that, precisely by contrast, it sticks together in a particular way with that class of things deemed not to make sense. Making sense is contrasted with not-making-sense.

If we have some experience of what it means for something to make sense, to be coherent, we necessarily also have the contrasted experience of what it means for something not to make sense, to be incoherent. It is this contrast that provides both terms with their content. It is here that we can see how this consideration delivers a strictly and literally incontrovertible starting point for our further reflections here. For a truly incontrovertible proposition can only be accomplished through this peculiar form: it must be a proposition whose denial will only serve to further confirm it. An absolute and inarguable statement is thus easy to provide. Following Zhuangzi, one could state it like this: " Sometimes there are disagreements." This statement can qualify as an "absolute truth" in the peculiar sense that both agreeing to and disagreeing with this claim confirm it, and the latter actually proves it. It includes within itself, as it were, the form of unclosability and disagreement with itself, its own self-denial, which alone makes it impossible to deny. Similarly, the terms "coherence" and "incoherence" are only "coherent" because of the peculiar way in which they "cohere" with one another, namely, their necessary contrast. The claim "some things are coherent" brings with it the claim "some things are incoherent," and the latter is of this same form of incontrovertibility and inescapability, but in the register not of cognitive claims about what is true or false, but, even more fundamentally, of what is or is not an intelligible proposition about which one could ask whether it is true or false. If one fails to understand what is meant by the claim that "some things are incoherent," one is only exemplifying it. Moreover, in feeling this incoherence, one is at the same time positing the contrasting experience of coherence, which one is judging to be lacking, and which one must hence have some familiarity with. It is in this sense impossible to fail to recognize coherence and incoherence, and their inherent coupling.

This brings us to the second point: it would seem that, even under the aegis of this commonsense dichotomy, there is a peculiar time lapse that allows a thing to have what might be called a deceptive appearance of incoherence, which means that it might *turn out* in the end to be coherent after all. We have cases where something does not make sense at first, but upon close consideration, recontextualization, experimentation of various kinds, coherence dawns in this mass of incoherence. It turns out to belong to the other category, the category of things that make sense. In certain modes, we call this process "thinking," and often this procedure is precisely what is supposed to distinguish for us which of all the possible things or ideas in the world ultimately do make sense and which do not.

We will return to the first point, the significance of the dual meaning of coherence, between its internal parts on the one hand and with its environment on the other, at length below. Here I want to focus on the second point. For this little time lapse, this introduction of the categories of apparent and real incoherence (as well as the correlative categories of apparent and real coherence), and the various directions in which coherence seems to dawn for various coherence-seekers, complicates the picture considerably. We may approach this complication through a particular form of coherence: the way in which new or tricky propositions are judged to be "true" or the contrary in terms of some previously accepted notions of the criteria and content of truth—for example, the hermeneutic ingenuity with which religious thinkers are able to incorporate initially incoherent doctrines or scriptures into their discourses. Rationalistic moderns are constantly bemused and disgusted by the ease with which our superstitious forebears, those comically fanatical true believers of one stripe or another, were able to make any proposition, no matter how preposterous, believable to themselves, if only they had adequate motivation to do so. The history of religions is fraught with this phenomenon, indeed almost composed of it. When the literal sense of some hallowed text or dogma—that is, the plain intent of the original authors—is proved to be incontravertibly false—for instance, when Christ failed to appear within the allotted time, or when the Chinese alchemists' potions and techniques killed enough people—the "mystics" always appear to provide the allegorical sense: Christ returned in our souls, the real alchemy is the inner alchemy of spirit and energy, and so on. Of course this is not merely a complaint about the ancients; the reasonable, however self-defined in a given milieu, never tire of complaining about the astonishing capacity for self-interested self-deception exhibited by their less rational brethren. Nor, indeed, is it merely a modern complaint; it is precisely what Plato has Socrates railing against in the *Phaedrus*, the hermeneutic ingenuity of the poets and myth-mongers. Socrates says that he has no time for such nonsense, preferring to pursue self-knowledge.

The "Neo-Tiantai" position that we will be developing here, however, is that these two apparently opposed and incompatible endeavors are one and the same thing. To know how to squeeze new meanings out of old premises is to know oneself, for one has no self but this constant, somewhat desperate, and vaguely disreputable rereading and recontextualizing of old claptrap. This book will be arguing, in fact, that "identity" per se—the fact that some particular thing is just this thing and no other, its being what it is—is synonymous with its own constitutive impossibility. We will try to show that identity does indeed exist in an important sense, but only as its own failure to be free of the need for rereadings, the impossibility of *definitive* identity *simpliciter*, and that this in turn is another name for a distinctive type of all-pervasiveness, qua absence, of the identity in question. Indeed, as we shall see, this endeavor of seeing new secret meanings revealed in old tokens without changing them, so ridiculous, so transparent a rationalization, so obviously a pathetic case of grabbing at straws to protect an outworn creed to which one is attached for no longer particularly rational reasons, this gerrymandering of the parameters of interpretation to fit one's present purposes itself, ironically enough does turn out to be the profound inner content of all religions, or all philosophical systems, indeed of all propositions or even experiences of any kind. It is this that is the real message, and the real truth that is delivered by all these mad histories of exegetical ingenuity. The interpreters who claimed to be getting at the real meaning in this way were thus right in spite of themselves, in a deeper way than they knew, precisely by being so wrong. They were getting at the true kernel of the matter by straying so unjustifiably from the "original meaning," although the true kernel was not what they believed they saw revealed there in the old lies but rather the very process of "finding true kernels in old lies." As Wittgenstein came close to saying once, an error of a great enough magnitude turns out to be a revelation of a new dimension of truth.

For what exactly is revealed by the fact that any proposition, no matter how plainly false, can be read to reveal the highest truths (however defined by the interpreter)? That, in effect, even if one tried with all one's might to come up with a statement that was necessarily false, one could not do so, for there would also be some context or interpretative principle, which some nimrod or other would be crazy enough to employ, by which it could be read as true. The Kabbalistic readings of the Torah, and the Tiantai readings of the *Lotus*, give fine examples of this style of exegesis. Nothing can be false, no matter how hard it tries—*as long as one has decided in advance to read it as true*. What does this tell us about the world in or as which we live?

The consideration I'm working up to here works equally in the other direction: any apparently true statement's truth is conditioned by someone's wanting to read it as true, and applying the appropriate parameters to its interpretation. The same can be said, of course, of the present inquiry; like all others, on its own it will be partial and inconclusive. All philosophers and theorists, indeed anyone trying to make any kind of point or argue any thesis, inevitably comes to a point where they must say, "The constraints of time and space of the present format make it impossible to develop all the implications and details of this view here, and work out all the implicit questions; this will be done elsewhere; this will be a topic for future research." As Slavoj Žižek has pointed out, however, this is not a chance feature, which just happens to appear, explicitly or implicitly, in every assertion of any point; what is crucial to realize is that this is a *structural necessity* of positing any assertion, any theory, any view of what is so. It is this structural necessity, and its implications, with which I want to start this discussion. This will appear initially to be, broadly, an epistemological or hermeneutical issue, and this will indeed be as it were the "home ground" of our inquiry, but one which will be shown to lead us directly to phenomenological, ontological, and ethical consequences, and indeed in such a way that ultimately the unique status of the epistemological issue as grounding source is directly effaced.

More to Come

This is by now, in our age of giddy postmodern self-reference, I think, an uncontroversial, perhaps even boringly passé, suggestion: no text, no matter how vast, would be able to effect a complete, self-disambiguated disclosure of any position. We know all too well the postmodern mode of carrying on about this reflection, as well as its overflow toward the mathematical "incompleteness theorem" of Gödel, which perhaps assists in giving the same idea the glamour of rigorousness. In either case, and for us too, this necessary incompleteness is not due to an overly vast and multifarious array of details and implications of the intended claim. On the contrary, it is because *the appearance of coherence in experience is dependent on the limitation of the exposition to a certain restricted realm.* There is always, constitutively, "more to come."

This is not hard to comprehend; besides the usual modern panic about textuality and historicity, we will be considering several structural features of awareness itself which, for us as presently constituted at least, ensure this self-limitation as a structural necessity. But the upshot of this notion that we want to pursue here, which is going to be doing the fun work later on, is that any proposition, "fully developed," will at the same time universalize and destroy itself, in such a way that these two are one and the same thing. Much of the following inquiry will be concerned with delineating what is meant by "fully developed" here. In the course of it, we will inevitably be reinventing many a wheel, explicitly or otherwise, but the course of these spinners will be tweaked enough by the crucial Tiantai momenta, it is hoped, that the slight variations in their derivations and premises, determined by the direction from which we are beginning, will yield wildly divergent results, ones that will pull us further into the redoubtable richness of the experienced world, expanding the range of what it may be read as—not only in terms of what it is but, more importantly, what it is possible to do with it, in it, as it.

Quiddity Qua Quaddity: Oneness, Coherence, and Agency

Let us proceed, then, to consider the question of *coherence*. What I wish to mean by this term is the appearance in experience—visual, aural, hermeneutic, conceptual, mathematical—of a particular whatness, a "quiddity" of any kind. The term "coherence" is meant here in the most general and nontechnical sense, which will allow the term to apply also to many items that would be quickly excluded from a more narrowly construed concept of coherence. Anything of which anything can be said or felt, any something, any determinacy, anything that appears as excluding anything else, is a coherence. This is meant to include anything whatsoever which might be a part of any experience. We include here the classical examples of redness, greenness, hardness, softness, darkness, warmth, coldness, and so on, but also more complex qualities, like tiredness, vagueness, objectiveness, troublingness, gracefulness, telephoneness, waiting-ness, having-to-go-up-the-stairs-ness, looking-out-the-window-ness, existing in time-and-space-ness, avoiding-a-topic-ness, trying-to-decide-which-shirt-to-wear-ness, shirt-ness, deciding-ness, trying-ness, sleeve-ness, fabric-texture-ness and so on. "Indeterminacy" is a coherence; "vagueness" is a coherence; "determinacy per se" is a coherence; "nothingness" is a coherence. "The whole universe" is a coherence, even if the universe turns out to form no sort of whole; "two-thirds of the whole universe" is also a coherence. Anything that is apprehendable or positable or readable or intelligible in any sense at all, any putative regularity or quiddity or somethingness, is a coherence.

Indeed, even "nine-eighths of the whole universe" is a coherence, as are "furiously humming equality" and "square circle." These latter cases, where we are dealing with incoherent or meaningless notions, should be especially noted in grasping what we mean by coherences here. Any determinate effectivity that is for any length of time even apparently distinguishable from any other, according to any fanciful notion presently engaging any cognitive apparatus of whatever kind, whether as a proposition, an image, an instance of perception, a fact, a sensation, a meaning, or a concept, is in the same boat as far as our present inquiry is concerned. Our claim will be that all of these are alike in being coherences which remain coherent in the sense of being readable as such, like a picture fuzzily or clearly received on a television screen or a vague rabbitiness in a cloud shape, within certain contexts and not within others. If I can adduce the words "square circle," if I can raise it in conversation or in any half-asleep reverie as an example of something—even as an example of a phrase which is incoherent, something to be avoided, something impossible—as opposed to anything else—for example, something coherent, desirable, possible—then it counts as a coherence. If I can experience the inherent impossibility of square-circle-ness as opposed to the possibility of right-triangle-ness such that some feature of the latter thereby is disclosed, it counts as a coherence. Whatever torque of self-aborted momentum, whatever image of dead-ended tail-swallowing it brings, whatever Möbius sensation of wall-colliding self-cancellation it evokes, it constitutes a process of attempted establishment and the discovery of the failure of this attempt, and that much experienced content is more than enough to qualify it as a coherence in good standing in our present sense. In the context of a discussion about meaninglessness or a priori impossibility, for example, the phrase "square circle" has a distinct function, and if it has a function it has a meaning, appears as a distinct something contrasted to other somethings, and is a coherence. Outside of the context of this discussion, the phrase will be meaningless and incoherent, will fail to denote. But the same could be said of any phrase, if the range of possible "contexts" is large enough. The coherence of the sentence, "Dick sees Jane" is, as we shall see in more detail below, equally effaced when placed, for example, in any situation which lacks a cognitive apparatus capable of understanding English, but also in any context where whatever has locally been designated as "Dick" is simultaneously and explicitly shown not doing what is locally designated as "seeing" to what is locally designated as "Jane." Here we usually say that the statement is coherent, but false. However, under the present definition of coherence, we will find that a strict division between truth and coherence is no longer supportable.

The point here, of course, is that incoherence is no more "immediate" than coherence, or anything else. As Merleau-Ponty puts it, we are *condemned to meaning*.[1] This is true of both senses of the term "immediate"; it takes some time for the incoherence of something to dawn, and it is dependent on the cooperation of mediating conditions, as will be explored at greater length below. "Square circle" is a notion that breaks down very quickly, when the context that had initially been applied to it, and which accounted for its ability to appear at all, expands ever so slightly. Another way of putting this is to say that there is a very small number of uses to which this coherence can be put, very few types of effects it can elicit. In contrast, a sentence such as "Dick sees Jane" breaks down somewhat less quickly, and only upon encountering a larger contextual field of ulterior considerations, and has a much larger field of applications. Perhaps "the law of contradiction" as a logical principle is readable, make-out-able, consistency-maintaining, applicable within an even broader field of parameters. But in each of these instances we have something that is readable or applicable or appearing to a given line of conscious regard while certain things are excluded from consideration and becomes blurry or incoherent when the field of relevances expands beyond a certain point, as we shall make clear below. Whatever can be *entertained*, even for the briefest span of time, by any consciousness, even an "insane" one, and even if only to be immediately rejected as absurd and ridiculous and incoherent, is a coherence. Whatever can be raised for consideration, or evaluated as to its coherence, is a coherence; it is not only what is possible, but anything which one can raise the question of possibility about, whatever *might* be possible. Indeed, we may say a coherence is to be strictly defined not as a possible but merely as a *possible possible*. It should be obvious that the category coherence as we are using it here is much broader than categories like "things," "entities," "clear and distinct ideas," "possibles," "essences," or "beings." It just means any possible whatness (I deliberately avoid the phenomenologically overloaded term "essence") that can appear in experience,

---

[1] Maurice Merleau-Ponty, *Phenomenology of Perception*, trans. Colin Smith (London and New York: Routledge, 1989), xix. Henceforth, this work will be referred to as PhP.

for any possible observer, for any length of time, from any side, whether as part of any other or as includer of others, or otherwise.

Now, the claim we want to make here is that any such coherence, to be experienced at all, must be experienced *as* some *one*, that is, as some particular coherent homogenous something. This is not affected by the fact that in another experience, this same "one" can in turn be analyzed as constituted by a great number of other coherences. Indeed, this will be true for all the coherences, no matter how apparently simple or complex. To appear is to appear *as* some one. One here simply means "something," some determinate being, roughly in the way Hegel defines the category of *Dasein* in the *Logic*. If it is not a one in this sense, it has not appeared. But the term "determinate" here should not mislead us. We are in the process of radically redefining what determinacy *is*. This one can be a set of heterogenous elements which do not cohere exclusively into any one figure, but in this case we have the appearance of a chaotic array or set of elements, which is to say "chaoticness" or "set-of-incongruent-elements-ness" is the "one" which is appearing. It is in this sense that we may understand the arresting Whiteheadian assertion that "oneness" (along with "manyness") is among the indefinable starting categories that cannot be understood analytically, but only intuitively:[2] this is because to appear, to have any identity or meaning at all, is already to appear in the mode of oneness, as some particular one. In one form or another, this inescapable equation of "oneness" and "being" has served as a foundation of every traditional Western metaphysical system. It is given perhaps its most definitive statement already by Aristotle (*Metaphysics* X.2.1054a13ff.). Coherences should not be understood as what are present only in clear and distinct, or thematized, self-reflective, or thetic experience; the claim here is that they are constitutive of experience per se, in the broadest possible sense (one that perhaps extends beyond the scope of what is usually regarded as sentience). This does not mean that everything in experience is a coherence, except in a very special sense. That is: are there any experiences or beings other than coherences? Yes: aspects of other coherences, and more of these aspects are necessarily always discoverable, as we shall see. Whatever is implicit or confused in experience, then, functions as an aspect or part of some other focal concern; some coherence, some focus, is always operative, *against which*, in the most inchoate case, indistinctness and indefinability are felt. As we shall soon see, to be a "one" in this sense is precisely what is impossible, but nec-

---

[2] A. N. Whitehead, *Process and Reality: An Essay in Cosmology* (New York: Harper and Row, 1957), 31. Henceforth cited as PR. We will return to this assumption of Whitehead's more critically later in this work, in the section entitled "Atomicity and Otherness (co-starring Whitehead, Levinas, and God)."

essary, in all experience. Some coherence is always at least *discoverable* in any experience, and where there is one coherence, there are always more coherences. The peculiar relationship between explication, verbal and otherwise, and the experience of coherences will be explored in greater detail below.

Perception, Conceptualization, Imagination

It should be noted immediately that an implicit conception of attention and perception is operative here, and moreover, as a first approach, that it is the mode of perception, as opposed to conceptualization or imagination, which we are taking as primary here, and which we will show to be the underlying mode of experience even of the apparently opposed latter two modes of consciousness. We have here a kind of modified Merleau-Pontian "primacy of perception." However, since I will go on to reinstate the other two modes of consciousness as equally primary, but only at the end of an inquiry which proceeds first from the direction of perception, this primacy must be considered only provisional. That any set of contrary elements or modes can equally serve as the foundation or source of the others is indeed the primary feature of what we will be calling omnicentrism, which is a serviceable general term to describe the type of theory we are developing here. Before continuing, then, a few words are in order about these alternate modes of consciousness of objects and how I wish them to be understood.

Sartre made the commonsense distinction between (1) perception of an object, which is the encountering of something which can be explored, which can surprise one or teach one something, and (2) conceptualization, which he claims presents the whole object all at once, in its entirety, without leaving anything further to be explored or revealed, and also (3) imagination, which presents the image in the immediacy of perception but in the unexplorability and uninstructiveness of the concept, a hybrid form which presents the object precisely *as absent*.[3] We shall have occasion to return to this point a bit later, where I will try to show that indeed all three of these modes are in fact occurring in each, with one or the other brought provisionally to the fore, which is precisely an instantiation of what I will be calling omnicentrism. That is, (1) the "explorability and ability to surprise" of the encountered object also implies (2) the "fullness" of the concept and (3) the "presenced nothingness" of the image; in the same way, the concept also functions as an encountered explorable percept and a present-absent image, and so, *mutatis*

---

[3] Jean-Paul Sartre, *The Psychology of the Imagination*, trans. Bernard Frechtman (New York: Washington Square, 1966), 8–17.

mutandis, for the image. Indeed, we will see that the three modes of engaging an object correspond importantly to the classical Tiantai "Three Truths." The best way to arrive at this conclusion, however, is to start with the model of perception, the appearing in experience of some encountered "one," some coherence. I will present the process of perception here on the basis of slightly modified Gestalt theory, as prefigured to some extent in Polanyi's work on tacit knowledge and Merleau-Ponty's development of the Heideggerian notion of the openness pertaining to the horizon-structure of experience.

We begin with the Gestaltist premise that when some "one" appears as an explicit coherence in the above sense, it appears as a figure against a background. The figure is the explicit coherence we are experiencing—this cup, some embarrassment at remembering an idiotic remark made two days ago, irritation at the bus being so late, the fact that there is a city called Phoenix in Arizona. But the coherence of this experience is also tacitly an apprehension of the nonthematized background, which is constitutive of the coherence in question, and without which it does not appear as such—the table on which the cup sits, the clay from which it is made, the potter's studio where it was done, along with the structure of my eye and nervous system, the chair I am sitting on, the amount of sleep I had last night and how much food I ate today; or, the people present when I made my stupid remark, the clothes I was wearing at the time, the other things preoccupying me at that time; or, the traffic, where I have to go, my not having brought a book with me, my bad mood because of losing an important slip of paper earlier; or, the history of the settling of the American West and European mythology, and so on. The point I will be making here is that when the cup appears, it is all these other things appearing *as* cup, and so for the other examples, or for any "one" that is appearing. We have here, as it were, the mediation and immediacy of the coherence in question, which, as Hegel says, are always *both* present for any determinacy.

Polanyi develops a useful paradigm for considering the means/ends relationship as a function of the part/whole relation. Polanyi describes awareness as coming with a structure whereby we are always aware *from* some set of conditions *to* some object of awareness. The set of conditions, which includes our bodies and sense organs, the instruments by which we come to know something (a probe by which we feel our way in the dark, a signal preceding an electric shock, the individual features in a facial expression, a semantic signifier), and the "background" portion of a Gestalt, may be equated with the *means* of knowing. The object which appears nontacitly to awareness (the texture we discover at the end of the probe, the electric shock, the facial expression itself, the meaning of the signifier) is precisely the object of our *interest*, the *meaning* of the other terms, which absorbs them into itself as aspects or "moments," quite often completely effacing their presence to us as discernible contents. Here we have the integration of several models of relation: figure/background, end/means, whole/part, signified/signifier, explicit/tacit, distal/proximal (we will soon add others, most crucially: object/subject, and punch line/setup). What is emerging here is a convertibility and mutual implication of these relations that verges on identity.[4] Figure is end is whole is signified is explicit is distal is object is punch line; ground is means is part is signifier is tacit is proximal is subject is setup. The "is" in these equations must be understood: they are not juxtaposed, not parallel, not mutually exclusive, but also not indistinguishable, not reduced to blankness; rather, they exist only *as* one another, as we shall elucidate below. But this is getting ahead of ourselves. For the moment, let us simply note that this object of awareness and interest is also the locus of ultimate value in the whole in question, and may be equated with the "center" in the sense to be described more fully below. The "whole" in this sense will be mostly tacit, that is, not explicitly present to consciousness. But this is tantamount to saying that all the parts appear merely *as* the object, which subsumes them, makes them aspects expressive of itself, while their own particular qualities vanish from experience. As Polanyi's examples demonstrate, we may behave in such a way that proves that we are in some sense aware of changes in these tacit contents without being able to specify what they are. This is the guarantee of their genuine experienced presence, in spite of the fact that we are not explicitly aware of them as such; we are indeed aware *of them*, but only *as* the explicit focal object. Any object of awareness will be implicitly unifying a vast totality of means—indeed, in the Tiantai recension, *all* things, indeed, all *possible* things, indeed all coherences—which will include even what is not possible but could possibly be possible, including the direct opposite of the object—are included in the whole (which, as we shall see, may also be equated with the unperceived but perceivable body-subject which is "that which" is perceiving the object). This means that this vast collection of means is appearing *as* the end in any given case; what appears in experience is just the end—the facial expression per se as a visceral coherence of anger or joy, say, or the anticipation of shock—while the means whereby this is accomplished, though also necessarily "tacitly" known and experienced, are known and experienced only *as* this end, rather than as coherences in their own right. When one sees an object on a table, many means are involved—the function of cones and rods in the eye, the nervous system, nutrition, oxygen, light, molecular vibrations, the nuclear explosions of the sun, and so on—but normally none of these comes explicitly to consciousness; they are, however, experienced, but only

---

[4] Cf. Merleau-Ponty, PhP, 183.

as the object in question. The movements and processes in the eye, for example, are "read" *as* the appearance of the object, rather than as eye-processes per se. Again, that they are nonetheless a part of the experience—that they are being experienced—is clear in that, as Polanyi points out, it can be experimentally verified that alterations in the tacit triggers of the object of attention and concern can be responded to without one's being explicitly aware that one is doing so. When the subject came upon the syllables with which he was conditioned to associate an electric shock, he "instinctively" avoided uttering them and triggering the pain, although he could not specify that this was what he was doing, or why he was avoiding these particular sounds.[5]

This implies that it is no longer adequate to consider the figure and the ground as two discrete elements that are in some manner combined to bring out the features of the coherence serving as figure. Instead, we must conclude that the figure is the ground, or more strictly, that what we experience as the figure is in fact the figure/ground appearing *as* the figure, while what we apprehend (or ignore) as the ground is the figure/ground *as* the ground. The relationship is not additive, but mutually constitutive, or better, is a question of the "asness" deployed in the case in question. Which of the coherences this totality will appear *as* is determined by the interest, that is, the value-orientation, presently prevailing. A portion of the whole is singled out, and the rest of the whole is then seen *in terms of* that portion, indeed, is completely subsumed in the appearance of that object, is transformed into its tacit ground.

To appear, then, is not only to appear as a one, as an identity, as a something, a coherence; more importantly, to appear is to be appearing *as* something or other. That is, there is no direct atomistic appearance of anything *simpliciter*; we have instead always the appearance of some multifarious set of elements under the organization imposed by some perspectival interest, which organizes these elements *as* something. This applies in both directions: the background elements are appearing *as* the focal coherence, but the focal coherence itself is only appearing *as* the combination and organization of these elements, as a manner of focusing and orienting this whole set of what can equally well be viewed as alien coherences, that is, coherences which are nonidentical to this focal coherence, which negate it and, as ones, exclude it. The appearing of a coherence necessarily carries with it the ability to be seen *as* something other, and can only appear by being mediated by these others. This particular contortion of lips and eyes is seen *as* a smile; to be a smile

---

[5] For a full explication of Polanyi's notion of "tacit knowledge," from which these examples are drawn, see Michael Polanyi and Harry Prosch, *Meaning* (Chicago: University of Chicago Press, 1975), 22–45, and Michael Polanyi, *The Tacit Dimension* (Garden City: Doubleday & Company, 1966), 3–25.

means never to be a smile *simpliciter*—there is no "smileness" which is not also "contortion of lips and eyes," or "graphite marks on flattened wood pulp," or some other non-smile set of coherences—and therefore always to be susceptible to being seen also as some set of non-smile coherences. To be a coherence is to be a one which excludes all other coherences; but every coherence appears only *as* these other coherences. My point here can be summarized pithily though clumsily as follows: Quiddity is, if I may coin a phrase, quaddity. To appear is to appear qua something or other. Isness is asness. Or perhaps more accurately: we shall here be considering isness *as* asness.

Properties Are Theft

We start then with the premise that no coherence can ever appear just as itself, *simpliciter*. Let us explore this claim a little more carefully. To be a coherence is to display a certain readability, a certain homogenous somethingness, and this can never be said of a simple, and yet could only be said of what is taken as a simple. The arguments for this are fairly straightforward and old-fashioned. For a coherence to appear *simpliciter*, it would have to a be a true simple, something with no parts, not an expression of something else, not a link in a chain, not a collection of elements arranged in a particular way. But what has no parts can have no determinacy. If we imagine a flashing of a certain coherence into momentary presence, without duration, we cannot possibly find any characteristics that would pertain to it. This is true not only because of its lack of internal or external relations, which alone could determine its qualitativeness, as we shall see in more detail below, but also because such a flash of an impression would not qualify yet as a thing, or as a given particular. What has no duration or relations will have no content at all. So unavoidable is coherence of some kind that it cannot fail to be subsumed as the content of some other particular, to be an attribute of something else, *as* which that something else is now manifesting itself. This flash of simple coherence will be read as a sudden spasm of the eye, or a revelation from God, or a meteorological peculiarity, which is understood in terms of some other set of identifiable coherences, that is, given content by virtue of its role as an interruption of some already existing coherence. We have neither a pure indeterminacy nor a hard-and-fast in-itself determinacy, but rather one ambiguous, tentative determinacy replacing another.[6]

However, once we have admitted this coherence to be a part of the complex concatenation of elements that make up a thing or a determinacy in general, we then have the question of how these parts are to be related. Are all

---

[6] Cf. Merleau-Ponty, PhP, 5.

these coherences that are tied together as the thing to be viewed as aspects and expressions of the otherwise unexpressed "thingness" of the thing? Or is one an indirect expression of the quality that is more directly expressed by the other? What other kind of relation can bind together these two disparate qualities as "belonging" to the same "thing"? Take an electric current, which manifests here as light perceived by the eye and there as an electric shock perceived by the hand. We say they are both "expressions" of the same thing, "electricity." But as everyone knows, this electricity, upon analysis turns out to be no more than a name linking all its expressions, an empty X for the thing which appears now as light and now as a shock, perhaps at most indicating the convertibility and conservation of the quantity involved in one case or the other, but even there only very inexactly and only under the control of carefully specified test conditions. Electricity never appears, even conceptually, *simpliciter*; it always appears *as* one thing or another—if not *as* a shock or a light, than *as* a quantity linking the two, the latter being an even more complex equation involving a larger set of constitutive terms, and hence all the farther from an appearance of electricity *simpliciter*. If we try to privilege one of its expressions as its *simpliciter* appearance—say, claiming that it is light which appears as an electric shock, so that light is the direct expression and the shock and all other electrical manifestations indirect expressions, we soon have another problem: the initial *simpliciter* coherence which serves as the explainer in terms of which all the other appearing coherences are understood, once it is put to this use, empties itself of its determinate meaning to the exact degree that it succeeds in being read into these disparate expressions, a crucial point we shall explicate in detail momentarily.

If on the other hand we try to dissociate all these expressions, granting full "thinghood" to each, such that they have no inner connection and are simply momentary flashes of experience with nothing underlying them, besides reducing the phenomenal world to a chaos of unintelligibility where all predictability becomes inexplicable, we find we have simply pushed the problem back a step. Now the coherence "light" must be investigated: does it have parts? It can certainly be analyzed, both as indicated above into its components and by delineating its limits and what distinguishes it from its other. That is, this experience of light is a joining of certain reflexes of the eye, certain conditions of the lamp, and so on; how are these parts to be related? They all come into consciousness as an immediate coherence, called light; but how is this immediate coherence to be related to the parts that can easily be discerned therein? Shall these constitutive parts be seen simply as additional discrete coherences flashing into experience? That would mean that light is one thing, while the reactions of the eye and motions of photons that can be viewed as component parts of this experience of light are simply other things, experienced at separate moments. But again, besides the counterintuitive and indeed strictly unimaginable unintelligibility of the world that results, we have the further problem that this shaving down of the definition of how much thing is a thing has no nonarbitrary stopping point; we can only go until we have pure simples with no determinate content whatsoever.

The same problem occurs, however, in the opposite direction, that is, when we allow that some coherence is an expression of at least one other coherence, as we have seen we must. This means that coherence X appears and can only appear *as* some non-X coherences. But as soon as we admit this principle of *as*ness, it is impossible to establish a nonarbitrary stopping point to it. That is, if light and shock are expressions of electricity, and were found to have content only to the extent that they were read as expressions of something, as manifestations of something else, or as shorthand ways of designating complex relations between other coherences, will not the same thing apply to the coherence "electricity" itself, however we are conceiving it? It too will have to derive its content solely from its asness, from being the expression of something else, or by appearing as something else. All this is of course just a clumsy rehashing of the old Hegelian critique of immediacy, of which I thoroughly approve but which, as we shall see, I hope to take a few steps further, or at least in other directions, leading to conclusions that Hegel himself would, we may safely say, repudiate with considerable ill temper.

This leads us to the following consideration. Determinacy of any kind, the appearance in experience of any coherence, requires duality, distinction, that is, the presence of some *twoness*. Any given coherence appears only in relation to some other, and indeed is always readable *as* some other coherence. At the very least, there must be the subject/object distinction, the sense organ and the sense object, which is also an exfoliation of the principle of figure/ground, or text/context, as we shall explore in Part Two of this work. Without this twoness, nothing appears. For any one "something" to appear, there must be "two." To be a coherence, a one, is to be a coherence, which is to be not only the appearance of some determinate something but also a *cohering*, a bringing together of a manyness.

But this means that, in an important sense, no "one" *can* appear at all: appearing always requires at least "two"; no effect can be produced by any "one" *simpliciter*. There is always a necessary, but necessarily excluded, complement, the background, which is appearing *as* this one, and in such a way that indeed this one is nothing but its background appearing as such, with all the othernesses appearing *as* it, such that the asness is reversible. But where there is duality, there is *in*determinacy, that is, ambiguity. For disambiguity, definitive determinacy, requires that some *one* is in possession of the thing to be determined, that is, *controls* it, a single and unified power to determine and sustain determination in some particular way, or at will; someone or something has to be able to force it to be read *as* one coherence rather than all the others that are also appearing as this coherence. In short, true determinacy would require that some *one* has *mastery*. But given the fact that all determinacy requires duality, this is impossible. Neither side of the duality can ever attain this, since each is eternally in a position of requiring the other in order to accomplish the determinacy; neither one can do so self-sufficiently. Conditions can never be reduced to any unified *one*, however complex; the circle of conditions must always be expandable, must always point beyond whatever is already determined. Whatever set of coherences is designated as the "one" in question, whatever attempt is made to redefine it so as to include all its conditions, some further coherence is needed to make this new "one" be what it is. And here we can see the importance of Merleau-Ponty's late account of perception as a paradigm here, that is, in the notion of the invisibility of the visible; to see is always to see more than one sees. If you say, in the perhaps deliberately naïve manner of early Buddhism, "Eye plus visible object are, together, the one which creates visual consciousness, the one self-contained whole that has mastery over it, that can always successfully determine it in accordance with its own finite set of laws," this will fail; these two need another condition, for example, whatever brings them together in this particular way, to produce this vision, and so on ad infinitum. Any one (and by the way, as we shall be getting to, this applies all the more urgently in the case of any *felt* unity, any sense of "oneself") is always in a position to have to negotiate with some silent partner, someone more. We could say, no finite cause can accomplish anything, but we must add also that even an infinite cause, if considered as some kind of one, as a determinate coherence with any kind of meaning whatsoever, can also do nothing. Where there is this necessary "twoness," there is not any particular and definitive "one coherence" for sure—everything requires the cooperation of something more, nothing is ever quite settled. As dominance, however conceived, shifts between the "two," the determination itself changes (while not changing at all, as we shall see; all its component coherences, everything that can be specified about it, may remain the same, while the coherence *as* which they are appearing changes). Is it subject or object that makes some experience "so"? Who is responsible for anything? Who is the master determining what is experienced? No one can own anything, including himself, because ownership means that something "belongs" to one as a "property" belongs to a substance, that one is in a position to determine everything about it at will, that is, in accordance with one's own self or laws or whim; but what does this can never be any finite or even infinite one. It must be stressed again that this denial extends even to abstract coherences like laws or Nature; no law owns its instantiations, Nature does not own its elements. Not matter, not God, not Nature, not the laws of physics, not freedom, not time, not anything—that is, no one, no determinable coherence, is in the position to make anything the case, to make anything so. That is, the agent that makes any coherence so is not I, not you, not it, not something else. Perhaps in a certain sense the doer of what is done can be called "we," but only if this is understood in its full open-ended sense, that is, myself as understood as the moment in partnership with some tentatively engaged and mysterious silent partner, a fragile agreement negotiated between two unpredictable and nonfinite parties, where I can do nothing without the consent of my other, but have no reliable information about that other, and where no matter how much the circle of the known "me" may be expanded, the otherness and unpredictability of this silent partner can never be exhausted. No finite cause produces any effect. The putative attribution of any coherence, then, is the surreptitious attribution of the mastery or ownership of that property to the degree that would enable some one to determine it definitively.

This is a confirmation of the anxieties of worried old theists that without God, some true owner, as creator or judge or omniscient observer or all of the above, there could be no order of any kind, indeed, nothing could be anything at all. Things cannot have any true nature to them, any fact of the matter pertaining to them, without some sort of owner of this kind, even if it is a virtual "law of nature" which itself can come to be known by finite minds after the fact. No one is in the position to judge what anything is, no one can ensure that it is one way or another, or be sure he is seeing all that is relevant of it, or control it, or make it so or otherwise completely on his own power. And, indeed, as the theists feared, this means that there is no fact of the matter concerning what anything is—not even what we have said in this sentence. Its epistemological status is not to be a report on the fact of the matter, but the making explicit of a particular kind of seeming, a working-it-through so that all its implications may become manifest, and a demonstration of some of the possibly useful-to-us consequences to which this working-through may lead—not the least of which is the overcoming of the need for something to be a report about the fact of the matter in order to be an important and indeed "universally valid" proposition. This is possible because this elimination of *the* fact of the matter means for us that there is no limit to the facts of the matter, not that there are no facts of the matter. These redefined facts of the matter will be just as nongainsayable as the old kind in their way, but will arrange themselves a bit differently, as we shall see. Indeed, while confirming the theistic fear about the godless chaos, we are reversing the value judgment; for us this is the best possible news, and suddenly allows us to untie once and for all the knots that have bound our thought. It is no less than a liberation. No one really owns or determines these coherences. To claim otherwise is the primal usurpation. Properties are theft.

All coherences have an "unseen back" to them, either as context or as implicit explorability, horizon. But what is crucial is to apply this also to all experiences, to thoughts; they are no more "transparent" than anything else, they too come with unseen roots, and turn out to be otherwise than they appear to be at first. The point is that the unseen back of anything is not *another* appearance, another positive something which we happen not to be seeing at the moment (a flat surface of representations out there), but an essential part *of* this surface that I can see, the "more" to it, that belongs to it *exactly as much* as the part seen, for the reason just indicated. Since nothing can belong to anyone, nothing belongs any more to this one than to any other one. I myself belong as much to anyone else as to me. I must not think, "at least I am seeing and knowing all there is to see and know about this one surface, or this one sense impression." These sense impressions are not separate facts; they are the other side *of one another*. And, given what we have established above, if there is more to the thing, even the part we can see turns out to be otherwise than it appears, is otherwise ramified, is recontextualized. The power of a new datum to transform all others through recontextualization, it should be noted, is not directly related to any measurable quantity, or predictable rule; no accumulation of hard facts, no matter how internally consistent, bound together by no matter how perfect a theory, is proof against some feather that will change them all. The believability of a thousand-page book, carefully and intricately wrought such that there are no loose ends, where everything fits together with staggering consistency and indubitable vividness, is completely recast by the single word "fiction" printed on the spine. Whatever we are experiencing is concealing its back, has more of itself to reveal, and thus is not what it appears to be. But this must happen *no matter how much we can see at any time*. It is structurally necessary. Everything is more than it is, everything is not what it is. Indeed, this is perhaps the one thing we can confidently say about any X that presents itself: it is "not just X." For us this means that it is marked by an unlimitable susceptibility to recontextualization and reinterpretation, which however is nothing added to it, but is the very fact of its appearing, is inherent to its being any Xness at all, as we shall see presently. As Merleau-Ponty nails it, "What enables us to centre our existence is also what prevents us from centring it completely."[7] But this formulation, in terms of "that which centers (gives coherence)" and "that which prevents complete centering," asserting that the agent of both is one and the same, and hence that the two (centering and failure to completely center, emergence as

---

[7] PhP, 85.

X and failure to be completely X) are two aspects of one and the same thing, does not go far enough from a Tiantai perspective; it falls into what we will characterize as the third of four ways of understanding the relation between any coherence's being X and its not being X. The fourth way is to understand that "centering" and "failing to completely center" are strictly synonymous. To get to this distinction, however, we must make a few more intermediate steps.

"Centrality": Local Coherence as Global Incoherence (Intersubsumption)

The above conclusion, in classical Tiantai terms and in the parlance of much of Mahāyāna Buddhism, is what is referred to as the "Emptiness" which pertains to all coherences. But in Tiantai this is only the beginning of the matter. The truth is not just Emptiness, but "Emptiness, Provisional Positing and Centrality." These are the so-called Three Truths, or better, the Threefold Truth. All coherences (possible possibles) are describable equally as Empty, as Provisionally Posited, and as Central. These terms make sense in Chinese, but they are awkward and obstructive in English philosophical discourse, obscuring more than they reveal. Hence here I will translate them in accordance with their actual implications.

Provisional Positing means "Local Coherence": whatever is is coherent from some local perspective or other, in some context or other, can be made sense of and read consistently within some limited range of connections. These connections are determined by factors such as desire, interest, sensory, cultural, linguistic, and neurological dispositions, which exclude certain contexts and allow others. Only thereby is anything identifiably a coherence at all.

Emptiness means "Global Incoherence," or ambiguity, or what David Bohm has called "asynordinacy"—the inability to be coherent in every context at once.[8] It means the failure of any local coherence to remain identifiable as such in every possible frame of reference, when all possible connections are allowed to manifest their relevance. It means that nothing is irreducibly what it is, nothing is an object with a particular mark that distinguishes it unambiguously in all contexts and from all perspectives.

Centrality signifies that Local Coherence *is* Global Incoherence. These are not separate facts at all; they are two ways of stating the same thing. A coherence is locally coherent if and only if it is globally incoherent, and indeed

---

[8] See David Bohm, *Wholeness and the Implicate Order* (New York and London: Routledge, 1996).

its local coherence is its global incoherence, and this is what it means to be a coherence at all. Local Coherence is reducible to Global Incoherence, and vice versa; to think through what one has stated when either has been adduced is already to adduce the other one. Centrality, then, is the mutual reducibility of Global Incoherence and Local Coherence, what we will call their "Reversible Asness," or their "Intersubsumption." This means, further, that Global Incoherence cannot be simply a blank blob or blur; rather, it means infinite mutual reducibility, or the reversible asness of this particular local coherence with every other possible local coherence. That is, Reversible Asness (Intersubsumption) signifies that this coherence is reducible to and from any other coherence, that all are reducible to it (qua locally-coherent-globally-incoherent) and that it is reducible to all of them (in the same way). Hence, to define its final implications, Centrality signifies that every coherence is the foundation, the substance, the ultimate telos, the Being, the explainer, the center, of all other coherences, and vice versa. Its synonyms then are: Reversible Asness, Intersubsumption, Subsumer, Subsumed, Foundation, Substance, Being, Telos, Explainer, Center, Principle, Arche, Universal, Particular, Set, Member of Set, Reciprocal Readability (i.e., Readability of X as Any Other, Readability of Any Other as X), Mutual Reducibility, Reducibility to and from Any Other, Infinite Coherences, Infinite Readability, Infinite Mutual Reducibility. Every coherence has the character of being all of these.

These may be called three aspects that are necessarily discoverable for every coherence, or three alternate ways of describing and apprehending its mode of being, in terms of both its essence and its existence. Moreover, there is no precedence among these three, no question of greater or lesser ultimacy. Each is equally valid, each is equally the ultimate and foundational (and indeed, *singular*) truth about each coherence, beyond which nothing more can be said, and to which all other attributes and conditions are reducible. The crucial point, however, is that each turns out to be just an *alternate way of stating the other two*, with various emphases. To be Empty is to be Provisionally Posited and to be Central. To be Provisionally Posited is to be Empty and to be Central. To be Central is to be Empty and Provisionally Posited. To be Globally Incoherent is to be Locally Coherent is to be Infinitely Coherent qua Reversible Asness. To be Locally Coherent is to be Globally Incoherent is to be Infinitely Coherent qua Reversible Asness. To be Infinitely Coherent qua Reversible Asness is to be Locally Coherent is to be Globally Incoherent. But more needs to be said about these other two aspects that result from the thinking through of the ambiguity or Global Incoherence which constitutes Emptiness.

Local Coherence ("Provisional Positing") means, in the simplest case, what we have called the appearing or presencing of coherences, the disclosure of seemingly mutually exclusive coherent "ones." The panorama of mutually exclusive and differentiated entities, particulars, qualities or even mere aspects which are distinguishable from one another, whatever anything is appearing to be or seeming to be—all this falls under the category of Local Coherence. Strictly speaking, it is a way of indicating that if and when the local context is fixed in such and such a way, this coherence appears as X rather than Y.[9]

But like the classical Tiantai writers, we can stop at neither Emptiness nor at Provisional Positing: we must press on instead to what is known there as Centrality, what we are calling Intersubsumption. Centrality, in traditional terms, is at its simplest level the identity between Emptiness and Provisional Positing (which, as we shall see, is effected precisely by their ineradicable contrast). Intersubsumption (All-pervasion as All-pervadedness) *is* the fact that that Global Incoherence and Local Coherence are just alternate ways of describing the same situation, the absolute contradiction as absolute identity between them which is their truth, i.e., that to which they are reducible without remainder. But in traditional Tiantai, Centrality can be further thought-through to reveal that it is not merely a Center *exclusive* of the two extremes—something which is neither one nor the other, but is capable of appearing as either, as a substance with two types of expression, a presumed tertium quid deriving from the undecidability between them, which is known as the *Exclusive Center*. This would be reversibility which is itself not reversible with "non-reversibility," which for us would limit "infinite meanings" and make for at least one unidirectional reduction.

Intersubsumption (All-pervasion as All-pervadedness) is not elevated above Local Coherence and Global Incoherence, as that which is "really" expressing itself in these two contrasted forms, which finally tells the final truth that explains them, to which they are reducible. (That is, the Center is not transcendent to Emptiness and Provisional Positing.) It must also be apprehended as the *Nonexclusive Center*. Intersubsumption can be reduced to the simple notion of Global Incoherence, or of Local Coherence, or of any given local coherence, just as successfully as they can be reduced to it. This signifies that each of the extremes, considered strictly in itself, entails and includes

---

[9] Note that no claim is yet made here about whether or how the context is fixed; we have indicated above the path we will pursue in considering this question below, which follows once again the import of the classical Tiantai doctrine; there, a provisional posit is ultimately conceived on the model of a Buddha's putting forth of provisional teaching, an *upāya*, in accordance with the desires, dispositions, beliefs, and needs of some sentient being or moment of sentience; here, we understand this to mean that the context is determined by desire, interest, need, previous local coherences (beliefs), volitions, and so on, on the part of some receptive and engaged sentient apparatus.

both its opposite and Intersubsumption, which is to say, either extreme as such equally functions as the "substance" which can express itself *as* the other two, which are then seen as aspects *of* it. This means that, just as Global Incoherence and Local Coherence are reducible to Intersubsumption without remainder, so that just by adducing Intersubsumption one has automatically also said all there is to say about Global Incoherence and Local Coherence (this is all that is meant by "substantiality" and "truth" here), the adducing of Global Incoherence says all there is to say about Intersubsumption and about Local Coherence, and the adducing of Local Coherence already says all there is to say about Intersubsumption, and about Global Incoherence, if any of these is "thought-through to the bottom." In other words, it must be stressed that "Intersubsumption" too can never appear *simpliciter*; it must always appear *as* Local Coherence/Global Incoherence, as the extremes. The relation of the apparently more abstract term (in this case, Intersubsumption) to the apparently more concretely subsumed terms (in this case, Local Coherence and Global Coherence) can no longer be one-way, given the principle of Intersubsumption itself. Transcendence is always bilateral, as is immanence, and the most "abstract" possible term, Intersubsumption, appears only *as* its "instantiations."

The same holds for any lower relation of apparent subsumption. That is, for example, Local Coherence never appears *simpliciter*, but always *as* some particular locally reified coherence. From this point we can go on to see that merely to adduce *any* provisionally posited or locally coherent coherence as such in its positedness and coherence—this blue cup, the redness of that folder, the vague sense of having forgotten something, and so forth—is already to have said all there is to say about Local Coherence as such, and Global Incoherence, and Intersubsumption. To apprehend any "this" as a "this" is, it turns out, to apprehend the Three Truths. But to think "this" as the nonduality of "this" and "not-this" is already to have thought every other possible coherence, to have apprehended the openness to every other coherence, which is, as will become clear presently, the pervasion of this coherence by every other coherence. This applies to any quiddity, any provisional posit, any local coherence, which will come to imply, as we shall see, that any coherence pervades all times and places, entails and includes all other coherences, and is also entailed and included in them, which is what we will be calling the principle of omnicentrism. All things are "something," some one, some coherence. Therefore all things are impossible, unable to appear *simpliciter*, constitutively ambiguous. These two claims are restatements of the same situation, as we have seen, and yet they are not indistinguishable; each is merely the thinking-through of the other, the other one considered more fully—the other one, as we shall see, only *more so*. They feed into one another like the two sides of a Möbius strip, which are in reality only one side, but at the same time contrasted back to back, revealing their oneness only when one travels along one all the way to its endless end. Therefore all things are Intersubsumptive, and indeed are Intersubsumption (All-pervasion as All-pervadedness, readable as any other coherence and readable into any other coherence). Therefore all things are all-pervading and all-pervaded. The center is everywhere: omnicentrism. The rest of Part One of this book will be devoted to arguing out the details and making manifest this point.

The Center, significantly, is traditionally the "substance" of any thing,[10] as opposed to, and uniting, the opposed moments of determinate "external" appearance or attributes of the thing[11] and the purely transcendent "internal" character or nature of the thing.[12] That is, besides the specifiable appearance of something and the purely unlocatable but apprehended meaning of that appearance, there is the thing itself, the identity of the thing, considered here to be precisely the meaning expressing itself *as* the appearance (hence the unity of the two in their contrast, as the divergence between them). The asness is the thing itself, the substance, and this asness, as we are beginning to see, necessarily entails the reversibility that makes it equally permissible to say that the appearance expresses itself *as* the meaning.

In classical Tiantai, Intersubsumption is also "that which one realizes through practice," in other words, the object of cognition which is disclosed through various activities and praxes. This cognition, however, is considered an expression of Global Incoherence, and the praxis that underlies and embodies that cognition an expression of Local Coherence. To translate this rather naïvely into philosophical terms, this means that the truth that the mind apprehends is nothing besides a certain relationship between its own function of apprehension and the practico-inert preconditions of this function in the body and the world. The relationship is precisely that described above between Global Incoherence and Local Coherence, that is, one of undecidability, reversibility, opposition, and mutual subsumption. We will develop some of the implications of this conception of the function of mind in its relations to its objects and its preconditions in the section on the Mind-Body relation below. But for the moment, to enhance our grasp of the category of Intersubsumption itself, the following point is to be stressed. Centrality, Intersubsumption (All-pervasion as All-pervadedness), as we have said, corresponds

---

[10] In traditional terms, the "suchlike substance" (*rushi ti*), corresponding to Centrality. It should soon become apparent in what way this is to be distinguished from the traditional Aristotelian notion of "substance," although there are points of contact between them.

[11] In traditional terms, the "suchlike appearance" (*rushi xiang*), corresponding to Provisional Positing.

[12] In traditional terms, the "suchlike nature" (*rushi xing*), corresponding to Emptiness.

to what in occidental thought would be the *substance* which possesses attributes rather than an attribute possessed by any substance. Intersubsumptivity is the very being and life of any coherence, is what that coherence *is* itself. Its Local Coherence is its own constitutive contradiction, its Global Incoherence, its own impossibility of ever appearing *simpliciter* or unambiguously. But in this case, due to the special characteristics of the relations between the Three Truths, rather than reducing these attributes to itself, Intersubsumption-as-substance has the peculiarity of restoring its own power of substantiality, i.e., the power to be that which binds together and is expressed *as* these contradictory others, to all those things *as* which it appears. In the end, to be the substance which has attributes is to be the attribute possessed by all other coherences as substance, and this alone constitutes the substance in question. That is, it is substance that establishes a kind of *reversibility* between substance and attribute—the relation of asness described above—so that once it is fully grasped the substance becomes as much the attribute of the attribute as vice versa.

The result is that any given coherence may be strictly described as the *sole* substance of the universe, that which is always being expressed as all others, and vice versa. Once Intersubsumption appears (i.e., becomes locally coherent), Global Incoherence is also Intersubsumption, Local Coherence is also Intersubsumption, and indeed any particular locally coherent coherence is also Intersubsumption; and this signifies also that Intersubsumption is also Global Incoherence, Local Coherence is also Global Incoherence, and so on.

This coherence before me is "green cupness"—green cupness is Locally Coherent. This coherence before me is "not just" green cupness, hence is not green cupness—green cupness is Globally Incoherent. "Green cupness" is not "green cupness"—that, as a first approach, is the simplest implication of the claim that "green cupness" is Intersubsumption. Green cupness—this coherence per se—is the substance of which all other coherences are attributes, is what is revealed by all other coherences, is what binds all coherences together, is the source and end which is expressed as all other quiddities—that is a further implication of the claim that green cupness is Intersubsumption, as will be explored in detail in a moment. It is this that entails the reversibility whereby we can equally validly describe the situation by saying that green cupness is an attribute which belongs to any other coherence considered as substance, and equally that all coherences are attributes of the substance we are calling green cupness.

In the language we have been employing here, Intersubsumption is the consideration that, given the necessary establishment of the claim[13] that any

---

[13] Or, more strictly, the exposition of a view in which the coherence of this claim is seen to appear in all possible cases, for you epistemological quibblers out there.

datum that presents itself insistently as a nonnegotiable qualitative fact depends on some unseen putative data fixed obsessively as its relevant frame, at the expense of other, neglected data, it follows also that these framing determinacies, which have been carelessly assumed to be definitive factual qualities or simple unambiguous coherences of some kind, in reality in just the same manner are appearing to be a certain determinate X only with respect to another arbitrarily narrowed frame, are themselves incapable of appearing *simpliciter* but exist rather in a chronic state of reversible asness. The context, too, is just a text, and is equally ambiguous, and for the same reason. That which is fixing the meaning of the ambiguous token itself has no fixed meaning, in just the same way; and indeed, the ambiguous token itself is part of the context which will fix the meaning of the meaning-fixer. Intersubsumption (All-pervasion as All-pervadedness), we may say, is a term used to designate the fact that the "context" *is* the contextualized; the figure *is* the ground; hence the "recontextualization" is internal to the figure, not imposed on or added to it from outside.

We may take up again the example of perceived object and organ sensation. What I call "appearance of cup on table" may equally well be called "function of rods and cones and nerves and light and molecular structures and atomic processes," without having altered any of the contents of the experience; the latter appears *as* the former, and vice versa. But more is involved in the means by which and as which this cup appears. If the cupness appears explicitly, it will have to do so *by means of* its exclusion of, hence positing of, the concept or apprehension of noncupness per se (the third type of Provisional Positing, or Local Coherence, in classical Tiantai thought), that is, the exclusion-of-cupness as a coherence in its own right. Indeed, this noncupness is "on the side of" the eyes and brain, something not explicitly thematized as focal awareness but functioning tacitly *as* the cup. Absence-of-cupness is one of the proximal terms by means of which the distal term, cupness, is appearing, closer to me than the cupness. We may even say, in that case, that I am embodying noncupness when I experience cupness, and vice versa, my "body" being all those coherences *through* which I experience other coherences, which appear to me *as* those other coherences, as the function of my eyes and brain appear to me *as* the image I am perceiving. Noncupness is in just the same position as eyes and brain in the experience of cupness. We shall take up a more detailed analysis of this structure of "having" and "being" below.[14]

---

[14] For the moment, though, we may drop a quick hint of the extensive existential implications such a vision will entail. When I perceive pain, pleasure is the proximal term and pain is the distal term. When I perceive pleasure, pain is the proximal term and pleasure

One way of summing up the implications of this line of thought is to say: to be present as X is also to be present as not-X. One simple sense of this principle is that of ideality: X is always the perception of X, not the X-in-itself, hence not X. It is contextualized by its requirement of a second, the subject, in order to appear. To put it another way, we may note that the whole set of words and notions given above under the heading "emptiness," the thoughts in my head that all things are more than they appear, is itself a thought which is appearing; hence there must be more to "there is more to any X than is known at any time" than is known at any time. There is an unseen back to the idea "there is an unseen back to everything." There is a constitutively unseen context or ground to "there is always a constitutively unseen context or ground to any figure which ambiguates it" which ambiguates it. Necessary ambiguity is ambiguous, necessarily. But this ambiguity simultaneously confirms and disconfirms the fundamental ambiguity: it is one more instance of it, hence confirms it; but in this case it also means that the ambiguity of ambiguity implies determinacy, is identical to determinacy. Ambiguity in this sense will mean that it is also just as possible to say that everything is just as it appears. Everything is thus exactly as it appears, and can never be what it appears. Everything is exactly thus and exactly otherwise. But we have many ways of playing out the implications of this notion, depending on how thoroughgoingly and uncompromisingly we think it through. The above claim, as we shall see in the following section, is not enough; following out the vision we have developed so far, we must further specify: *to be thus is to be otherwise, and to be neither*. But this formula—which defines Centrality, Intersubsumption (All-pervasion as All-pervadedness), the "absolute," the only thing that qualifies as the actual "identity" of any coherence—can be played out in a number of alternate ways.

Four Ways of Being Thus and Otherwise: Impermanence, Illusion, Tertium Quid, Asness

We have established so far that to appear as an element of experience is to appear qualitatively, that is, as some definite homogenous "one." This means, we said, that any given datum, to appear in experience, must appear as a definitive, nonnegotiable, unavoidable fact or coherence, a "something" which *excludes its other*, that is, every other "something," everything which is qualitatively other. Commonsensical experience (which here incorporates negli-

---

the distal. I perceive the distal term *by means of* the proximal. Both are always present, one is always tacit and one manifest. What is more, the tacit one is an element in what is usually referred to as subjectivity per se, while the manifest is the object.

gence of both phenomenological attentiveness and speculative thinking, both of which lead away from this characterization of experience) appears as a series or array of such coherences, in a sequence or side-by-side spread, as a mutually external "many."[15] On some level of abstraction or other, some group of final terms tends to be posited as a set of in-itself "ones." This goes for ordinary affect-laden perception, for atomic or even sub-atomic theory, even for Merleau-Ponty's "rays of the world" or "intentions," if naïvely (mis)construed. My claim here is that if there is *literally no term* which can be reduced to this in-itself manner of being, by virtue of the very structure of what it means to be, *even* to be a "one" (as I have tried to show), the result will be the radical ambiguity and interpervasion of coherences described here, with the implications to be explicated below.

However, we went on, there can be no appearance of any "one" without a context of "others"—as causes, conditions, background, conceptual or perceptual contrasts, and so on. Therefore, no "one" which appears is what it seems; no true "one" is ever present. The appearing of a coherence always requires *at least two* coherences. This "two," however, also cannot be construed as a "one," that is, a finite set which fully accounts for the appearance. No effect can be produced by any "one," and that also means, by any finite or determinate set of causes. There must always be a figure and a ground, a necessary but necessarily excluded "otherness" going into each appearance; as soon as this nonappearing set of conditions is included in the known, it becomes instead the conditioned, the figure, the "one," and another set of supports is implied, and so on *ad infinitum*. There is always this unknown unseen "other half" of every experience, what Merleau-Ponty calls the invisibility *of* every visible. We added also that even this coherence, of "always having more to it than meets the eye," is apprehended as a "one," and thus must have more to *it* than meets the eye.

We could restate this by saying that the coherence or whatness of any experience is determined by the *horizons of relevance* (to borrow Peter Hershock's term) which are allowed to serve as its effective context. Relevance is determined by an active *neglect* of certain facts or other coherences, all of which, by virtue of the fact that no finite set can be the determiner of any coherence, are potentially relevant. Again, this same problem applies equally to all other possible coherences that might serve as determining contexts;

---

[15] Merleau-Ponty and others contest just this for perception. Nonetheless, "common sense and science" continue to construe experience in this way, making it a fair characterization of experience as it manifests prior to any phenomenological explication of what it "always already was." The transformation that occurs without changing anything, which is typical of the effect of phenomenology on naïve experience, is one of the mysteries we will be in a position to explicate a bit in the pages to follow.

they are all equally determinate and indeterminate, context-dependent ("Empty"). This means that the way they can fix the indeterminacy of the first coherence is itself indeterminate. Indeed, what makes them determinate as "determiners of X" (i.e., read in this particular way among all possible other ways) is the ambiguous appearing of X itself as something to be determined. Thus the determinacy of each coherence is identical to its indeterminacy: to be present as X is also to be present as non-X. ("Identical" here, of course, must be understood to imply also difference from, and both, and neither.) Therefore, the defining relativity or contrast between its presence and its absence has been seen to be no contrast at all.

Every coherence is, to use the picturesque traditional expression, like space, whose presence is the same as its absence, which therefore necessarily pervades all times and place. It has no inside or outside, nothing that is itself and nothing that is other than itself, and has both, each being an expression of the other. It is "not thus and not otherwise." This aspect of all things is known as Intersubsumption (All-pervasion as All-pervadedness). It signifies that the context *is* the contextualized thing itself, the figure is the ground, and hence that "transformative recontextualization" is not something external "done to" the token or figure, but is something it is itself doing, just as much as it is "other," and each is always both. The figure is the figure/ground *as* the figure; the ground is the figure/ground *as* the ground. Thus there is no determinable difference between "the context is done to me" and "I create the context myself"—hence any one of these formulations has always been saying (being) all three: X, non-X, and both (neither). But since this applies in all cases, it also means that X is expressing itself as all other coherences, and all other coherences are expressing themselves as X.

Note that this does not mean that the *écart* between figure and ground is done away with when we assert that "the figure is the ground"; rather, the split between them subsists in and as this very identity, is what makes it possible. The "contextualizing relation" itself is what makes the context and the contextualized identical in their opposition. We will begin to see the practical consequence of this somewhat subtle refinement shortly; it will mean, for example, that we do not say it is all the same whether something is present or absent, so much as to say its absence is its hyper-presence, and its presence is its hyper-absence, not just that X and non-X are the same, but that non-X is *more Xish* than X. Most of the more interesting implications of our reflections here derive from this crucial point, as we shall see.

From here we can begin to push toward further Tiantai consequences of this situation. Intersubsumption describes the relation between the determinacy and the indeterminacy of each coherence, its appearance as such and its being transcended or negated as such. One of the most brilliant strokes of classical Tiantai was the exposition of the various meanings and implications of this same insight at various stages of practice, or in the context of various teachings. We will follow the broad outline of this "classification of teachings," and also its structural peculiarity, namely, the manner in which it asserts both the identity and the difference between the different teachings, in the setup/punch-line manner to be described presently. This progressive but in the end self-equalizing division of modes of experience, stripped of its wealth of specifically Buddhist details, gives us four general modes in which the relation between the appearing and the transcending of any coherence can be understood:

1. Whatever appears in experience will be transcended, i.e., will disappear, will be recontextualized, will assume a meaning other than the one it has appeared *as*. (Analytic Global Incoherence, Impermanence)

2. Whatever appears *is* transcended already. Appearance is apprehended here *as* (mere) appearance. Appearing and being transcended are always copresent; wherever there is appearance of any coherence there is also necessarily already transcendence of that appearance; the two are necessarily inseparable. (Global Incoherence, Mirage, Illusion)

That is as far as we have gotten in the above exposition. But a further thinking through of just the same situation reveals it "to turn out to" entail further implications:

3. Whatever appears is *thereby* transcended.

Here the necessary causal relationship is further articulated and seen in its necessity. Two closely related versions of this are possible:

A. That by which it appears is that by which it is transcended; there is a single cause of both of these two contrary aspects. The reason it appears is the reason it is transcended. (The Exclusive Center)

B. It appears *because* it is transcended; it is transcended *because* it appears. Here we have two looped and mutually entailing aspects, each of which serves as the ground of the other.

Here we have a sort of tertium quid (either the neutral reason which grounds both, as in case A, or the mutually grounding relation itself, as in case B), which is neither the appearance of X nor the transcendence of X, neither thus nor otherwise, which however is what is expressing itself either as thus or as otherwise. This third thing may be the single reason that accounts for both its being thus and its being otherwise, or may be, in the second case, the whole looped structure, the causal relation itself; it is thus because it is otherwise, it is otherwise because it is thus, and this "becauseness" that links them here serves as the tertium quid. Phenomenologically, this can be described as the *undecidability* between them *per se*, rested in or apprehended as a particular coherence in its own right. At this stage we still have the lingering notion that there must be some true fact of the matter. Given the fact that we have a situation where the thusness and otherwiseness of X are not only necessarily linked, always simultaneously copresent, and completely balanced (i.e., neither side can claim any kind of ultimacy over the other), we have a true undecidability pertaining to the two; since the analysis has found itself incapable of settling on either thus or otherwise as the truth of the matter, a third thing is posited, defined simply as something which is neither thus nor otherwise, which transcends both in some unthinkable matter but expresses itself equally well and freely as one or the other (X and non-X in case A, X-grounded-in-non-X and non-X-grounded-in-X in case B), being given a content in only this way. Whether thus or otherwise, what is really being presenced is this neither-thus-nor-otherwiseness that can disclose itself in either way.

4. Appearing per se is being transcended per se. To be thus is to be otherwise. They are not separate aspects at all. To appear is itself to appear as transcended; to be transcended is itself to be transcended as something which appears. This is asness, or Nonexclusive Centrality. This means also that to appear is itself also (1) to be transcended, and (2) to presence the identity (*and contrast*, n.b.) between appearance and transcendence. To be transcended is also (1) to appear and (2) to presence the identity between appearance and transcendence. To presence the identity between appearance and transcendence is also (1) to appear and (2) to be transcended. Each of the three entails the other two. To be transcended *always* means to appear. That is, the only form of "disappearance" possible is not a retreat into utter annihilation but only into a modified *form of showing oneself*, that is, showing one side, behind which the rest is hidden. It follows from the universal applicability of this premise that all things are "forms" of one another. Similarly, to appear *always* means to be transcended. Thus are the pseudo-concepts "being" and "nothing," "eternity" and "annihilation," "sameness" and "difference," "birth" and "death" overcome. To be thus is to be thus as otherwise; to be otherwise is to be otherwise as thus.

This is the same as the previous position (tertium quid), with the last vestige of the notion that undecidability must somehow land us somewhere, perhaps in "undecidability" per se, finally transcended. The consequence of this slight switch is however great, and easily testable. For here, unlike in the previous case, the *degree* to which it is thus is exactly the *degree* to which it is otherwise—and indeed, the degree to which it is the neither-nor tertium quid. The more thus, the more otherwise, the more neither. It is no longer the case that the tertium quid discloses itself at any given time and place *either* as thus *or* otherwise, without changing; in that case we can say that the more it is either thus or otherwise, the more it is neither-thus-nor-otherwise, but we cannot yet say the more thus, the more otherwise, the more neither-thus-nor-otherwise. It is only at this last stage, where full asness is grasped, that such a complete mutual identity between being thus and being otherwise can be asserted.

So: to be thus *is* to be otherwise (which also means, to be "neither thus nor otherwise" in the naïve, mutually exclusive sense of "being thus" and "being otherwise"). But this cannot be construed to mean merely "whatever is thus is also necessarily otherwise," or "it is thus for the same reason it is otherwise" (which might imply merely two aspects, to effects of a single cause, hence an Exclusive Center). We have to say instead that *to be* thus *is to be* otherwise, its being thus is its being otherwise. To appear as X *is* to appear as non-X. E.g.: to appear as the front side of this tree is to appear as more than just the front side, i.e., to appear as "tree." But then also to appear (conceptually) as "tree" *is* to appear as "more than tree, hence not (just) tree, hence not (what was originally meant by) "tree." To perceive explicitly the thought "the whole tree, including the parts I can't see or know," is already tacitly to perceive more than that.

We may think of this as a kind of curved logical space (to borrow a phrase from Steven Laycock): straight lines, that is, coherence as some one particular coherence which excludes all others, exist only in an abstract sense, for a very limited scope; but any straight line *extended far enough* becomes curved, that is, becomes something else, loses that original coherence, begins to fall apart. By recontextualizing itself into all possible contexts, its original meaning and significance will be effaced.

What is it then for something to have an "appearance"? You see it, but you do not see all of it. This object shows me one side of itself; no matter which side I view it from, I am never seeing all of it at the same time. What I am not seeing is part *of* the thing itself. This too must be seen as a structural necessity; the attempt to escape it by positing a kind of phenomenological transparency of immediate experience is nothing but a dodge. That is, we cannot say even that I am at least seeing all there is to see of this thought, this emotion, this impression, this appearance, as when it is suggested that to think one is in pain is to in fact to be in pain. The point is to retrieve the reality of pain by seeing that when we perceive pain, we are not perceiving all of what it is to be this pain. And this being the case, precisely by giving it back its objective reality, we free it of its objectivity: for the part of what it is to be pain that we are not seeing when we see pain is its constitutive *pleasure*, as we shall see below.

There is *always* a "way things look" (*jia*, or Local Coherence, in classical Tiantai terms) *and* "some doubt about it" or ambiguity to it (*kong*, Global Incoherence) because of the moretoitivity that necessarily pertains to it, and these two are one and the same, to appear is to appear as something in doubt (which is saying more than merely saying that everything that appears is *also* something which is in doubt), but they are the same precisely by virtue of their contrast, as the identity between seriousness and humorousness accomplished by the dawning of the punch line of a joke, as we shall explain in more detail below. This last point is what is referred to in classical Tiantai as *zhong*, or Intersubsumption.

In a sense our final position, as we shall see in Part Two, can be seen as a *reestablishment* or final justification of the view of naïve consciousness: the assumed "realness" of each experience comes back as as "inherence," that is, as all-pervasiveness qua self-destruction, unevadability qua unattainability; each is indeed a revelation of the true nonnegotiable nature of reality.

The final Tiantai position on the mode of being of all coherences could also be described this way: all coherences are constitutively *at a distance*. They are *necessarily* "before me," or "over there." They are not at a distance *from* anything, but "distanced" per se. Even the feeling of air in my lungs, or of my throat at the back of my mouth, or my eye, or the *back* of my head, is "over there," "before me," "at a distance." Once we see this not as a contingent distance from some other thing—myself—which is *not* at a distance, but as a necessary distance which pertains to the coherences themselves, which is the mode of their being there at all, we are seeing the Three Truths. That is, "at a distance" *means* simply being capable of being moved around, of changing in perspective, of being recontextualized, of being seen otherwise while remaining the same thing. If this is seen as something extraneous to what the thing is, then we have relativity with respect to a genuinely unchanging thing. But if this is part of what the thing is, we have grasped that being thus is being otherwise. Nothing is "right here." Anything that was would be imperceptible, would be crammed too close up to the lens to appear, if you like. But only something that was "right here" in this sense would qualify as being in-itself, a coherence *simpliciter*, which is simply what it is, full stop.

Hence for a thing to be experienced *is* for it to be multiply experienceable, to admit of many perspectives or sides, to be more than itself (as Merleau-Ponty puts it, to "outrun itself"), to be "open." To be thus is to be otherwise (which does not mean it is not thus, as some of our postmodern contemporaries seem to think, but rather precisely that it *is* thus.)

The next question that would come with this consideration would be to reconceive the order of coherences at *various* distances, in a system of degrees of distance and blocked or mediated by other things. "At a distance" also means uncertain, not finalized, bearing further inspection. What we have here is a system of *degrees* of uncertainty, at any given moment. They are themselves "at-a-distance" in various ways, but this creates the illusion of a particular, empty self that lies at the center of the system of distances, the zero-point which is right here, is itself, is just as it is, which in turn is projected onto these perceived coherences, as the truth which must pertain to them ultimately in spite of all appearances to the contrary.[16] It is this also that equals the "situatedness" that pertains to any configuration of coherences. This "at-a-distance" quality, however, gives us the Three Truths in a single intuition: Each coherence is not here, less than absolute, a little out of my grasp, contextualized, admitting of further discoveries and other perspectives, and hence constitutively "moretoitive." But this is the condition of its appearing at all: if it were *right here* I could not see it, as the eye cannot see itself. It has to be "before me"—to be over there—to be present—to be here—at all. Being here is being there, being thus is being otherwise, and this is Intersubsumption.

This sheds important light on what it means to be an "object" at all, and on the question of explicitness, to be explored further below. To be at-a-distance means to be susceptible to at least one more viewpoint. In this context, we may think of the relative distances of objects from my putative self as in reality denoting simply increasing levels of explicitness in the sense of implying a greater number of intervening views of the object. To be "farther" means "to have more points of perspective between this one and it." (It is not necessary to insist that this corresponds exactly to measurements of physical distance; we mean rather degrees of explicit objecthood and realness, rather than spatial distance, here, although the two are related.) But of course to be seen from more viewpoints is to reveal more aspects, to be seen *as* part of more projects, as pervaded by more diverse quiddities, indeed to be manifesting *as* a greater number of more diverse coherences at once. For whatever sees X

---

[16] We can perceive here the contours of the controversy between Sartre and Merleau-Ponty. For the latter's critique of the former, with which the present analysis accords closely, see Maurice Merleau-Ponty, *The Visible and the Invisible*, trans. Alphonso Lingis (Evanston: Northwestern University Press, 1968), 50–104. Henceforth cited as VI.

pervades X, is expressed by X. The object—for example, the back of my head, which seems so close—is cramped by its original "short" distance, which simply means it was remaining in a relatively stable and unthreatened sense of its identity, unsusceptible to exposure to the infection of other perspectives. To "pull back" from it, to continue this spatial metaphor, would mean nothing other than "there are more and more positions between me and it," where "position" means point of view, perspective. These possible other perspectives are present *on* the object, as it were, *as* its degree of distance. This is one way in which we may approach a definition of objectivity per se, and its essential relativity, and with it the subject-object relation as a whole. "More objective" means in effect "seeable by more subjects," registering from a greater number of perspectives (i.e., as susceptible to an intersubjective agreement of which one is confident), which in turn means, "expressing more coherences, present *as* more coherences, even without in any way changing what it is here and now, fitting into a greater number of meaning-contexts, hence given a greater number of meanings."

This is one way in which we can understand the central Tiantai proposition that the more X becomes X, the more explicitly and manifestly it becomes X, the more it realizes its Xness—the more non-X it becomes, the more it expresses all other coherences. The more thus it is, the more otherwise, the more itself, the more something else. Its being-thus and its being-other become manifest or implicit in precisely proportionate degrees, for in fact they are one and the same fact. Its being-thus is its being-other. Close by, or when its at-a-distance-ness is conceived of as merely contingent, as simply being a certain distance from some one particular point but being at zero distance from some other point (e.g., itself), both its thusness (Local Coherence) and its otherness (Global Incoherence) are indistinct, as is the fact that at-a-distance-ness is a necessary condition, and these two are thus one and the same fact (Intersubsumption). When its inherent and necessary at-a-distance-ness becomes manifest, it becomes manifest too, and as it becomes manifest as X, it simultaneously becomes manifest as non-X, and every non-X.

Another way to state this would be to say that all coherences are fundamentally *pivots*. The Three Truths means, in effect, that "pivotality" is the most basic and essential of categories which constitutes the condition of possibility of all presencing. Much more will be said about this in the following section, and indeed throughout the rest of this book, but a few words should be said about it here.

The cupness of this cup before me, qua inherently distanced, is the fact that it can be seen from elsewhere. But to be seen "from somewhere else" for us just means "to be seen as an aspect of something else." This cup is an aspect of my situatedness, of my sitting-here-writing-with-a-sense-of-urgency coherence. But that this coherence can also be seen as the cup means that this cup is also open to other views, to other coherences that equally pervade it, that equally are expressing themselves as it. Its being is not only a matter of "disclosure" (which still sounds too objective, as if it is a piece of information that is being given), but rather "exposure," in the sense of being exposed to an infection or a disease. To be is to be exposed in all directions to gazes that not only perceive, but infect, that make this coherence an element of themselves, of these other coherences, so that they become saturated with it, and share its coherence. This cup is exposed to the joyful drinker, the angry fighter, the indifferent table. For us this means this cup expresses joy (it is saturated with the joy as it enters the hand of the drinker), expresses anger (the fighter spies it as something to throw), expresses indifference (the table bears it up). It *is* joy, it *is* anger, it *is* indifference. Its being is this vulnerability, this *duḥkha*-problematicalness, this exposure to other pervading coherences of which it is a part and an expression, which absorb it into themselves.

A more obvious example would be this piano sitting before me. This piano is inherently, in its being-a-piano, exposed to a plethora of styles. It is exposed to Thelonius Monkness, to Bill Evansness, and so on. When played by Monk, this piano becomes part of his body, of the coherence of Monkness, saturated by that quality, such that seeing and hearing this piano is then seeing and hearing Monk. But as a discernible coherence, it is also the pivot of intersaturation with Bill Evansness, and all other styles, including the style of the chainsaw that would saw it in half. To see the piano as such would be to see this intersection, this pivotality, this density of intersaturation which inherently presences all styles. One may ask, is this presumptive presence of, say, Monkness discernible in the dormant piano sitting there equal to that which is there when Monk is "actually" playing it? One may feel that it is more directly or genuinely present in the latter case. But even then, Monkness is not present *simpliciter*, as we have established above. It is the proximal term *through which* all other things are presenting themselves, which saturates them, but which can be there only *as* these others. But just the same is true when the piano sits there unplayed, and some cognitive apparatus happens to think of Monkness at the same time. We have noted the mutual inclusion of part and whole that goes with the infinite divisibility of coherences.

Insomnia, for example, is a coherence that *includes* other "smaller" parts of which it is constituted. These parts, backgrounds, and setups of insomnia might include "not-finding-a-comfortable-position," "being in this uncomfortable position," "texture of sheets," "low hum of heater in the corner," "breathing," "tension and constriction of chest," "mental image of things to do tomorrow," "fear of not getting enough sleep," and so on. All these are pervaded by the coherences "insomnia" which is their collective name at this moment, they express it, they are "insomniacal," indeed they are insomnia itself, for in adducing the latter I can only adduce them, and indeed to induce any one of them, as it presents itself now, is already to adduce insomnia itself. But another of insomnia's "parts" would be apparently "larger" coherences like "being in the space-time continuum," "the existence of the world," and so on. These are equally pervaded by insomnia at that moment. All these coherences are pivots for all other pervasions. This pivotality is what is meant by Intersubsumption, or Centrality.

We begin here to see both the importance of the Sartrean triadic division and its limitation. First of all, it should be noted that the Sartrean triad is implicitly based on what David Levin calls certain "ocularcentric" presuppositions;[17] he is talking about seeing a visual object, conceptualizing a geometrical figure, or visualizing an image. For in the case of perceiving a sound, or imagining a tone, we no longer have the obvious disjunction of having an unseen "back" in the case of perception as opposed to full disclosure in the case of conceptualization. The sound has an unheard back to it only in the sense describe above: as the components going into its appearance which are absorbed and synthesized so that they appear completely *as* that sound—the vibrations of the air, the structure of the human ear and nervous system, and so on. This in no way differs from imagining a tune in one's head, or conceptualizing the ratios of a musical scale, for example. But what Sartre's analysis, if recast into our current form of thought, does bring out is that these three aspects are in fact all relevant to whatever seems to be either a perception, a conception, or an imaginary object: in all cases, there is a "turning out to be more" than what first appeared, and also an immediate fullness, and also a presencing of an absence. A perception is explorable because it is always in a process of recontextualization that reveals the other components that were appearing *as* it, and which it can also appear *as*; but the same is true for a concept or an imaginary object. An imaginary object is presenting an absence because it is a coherence which is composed solely of what is excluded from that coherence, and indeed, in such a way that the excluded concepts are in an important sense *more present* than the explicit contents, for they form the subject side of the relation, closer to the experience than the explicit concept, as an eye which cannot see itself. But the same is true also for concepts and percepts; in all cases, the nonthematized "absent" contents are what is most present, what one is implicitly identifying with while encountering this object as "other." A concept is whole and nongainsayable, has said all it can say as soon as it says anything, because it has no separable parts, and nothing which

---

[17] See David Michael Levin, *The Listening Self: Personal Growth, Social Change and the Closure of Metaphysics* (London and New York: Routledge, 1989).

is outside it; its appearance depends on the inclusion of all relevant factors, beyond which there can be nothing more to be added or explored. It is a manifestation of all possible coherences in a particular form, *as* this particular concept. Whatever else comes to be revealed will do so not as additions of other things, but simply as what was always already present; this process of "noticing" other things about it, then, which Sartre denies for the concept, does happen, but in another way: there is a "noticing" but not of "other things or aspects"; whatever is noticed is just more of this same thing. But the same is true for percepts and images.

We have here the mutual interpenetration of the Three Truths spoken of in classical Tiantai. If the perceptual mode pertains to Local Coherence, the imaginary to Global Incoherence, and the conceptual to Intersubsumption, when one is adduced, all are adduced, but without reducing to an undifferentiated whole. All the characteristics initially thought to pertain to them in contradistinction to each other turn out to pertain to every one of them; but these characteristics themselves only became manifest by means of the initial (erroneous, as it turns out) distinction. This is Tiantai thinking in a nutshell.

Comprehension of Intersubsumption in this last sense thus implies also seeing that all appearances and all transcendences were themselves also Intersubsumption. That is, whatever appeared to be merely an appearance (or a negation, or both) was always actually all three; this is revealed not by adding anything to it, but by attending to it more closely. This is what we shall refer to in a moment as *Kaiquan xianshi*, or Transformative Recontextualization, where this power attributed to this understanding of Intersubsumption will be spelled out a little more closely. Before doing so, we must clarify another important feature of the notion of Intersubsumption, with which this aspect will converge momentarily.

Transpositions of the Four Ways

We have described four ways in which the relation of a coherence to its own negation may be conceived, ways in which its appearance as coherence X can be related to its overcoming as X, or its disclosure as non-X. But to see the full implications of this, we would do well to transpose the same structural point into a number of related keys, as it were. For the same point may be made, perhaps more pertinently, in several alternate ways, with respect to several related dimensions of experience. The first of these, which has played a privileged role in Buddhist thought since its enthronement in the Abidharmic system, relates to what is known as the doctrine of *momentariness*, the notion that the ultimate constituents of existence are as it were momentary flashes of being, which in Abidharmic thought have a definite but extremely short duration (some hundred-thousandth of a second, and so on), while in Mahāyāna texts the claim is made that there is in fact no duration between the time a dharma appears and the time it vanishes, that the two are simultaneous. We may Tiantaify the implications of this move into the following four levels:

1. Whatever appears will vanish. Here again we have a simple commonsense impermanence doctrine, that entities come into being, exist for a while, and then cease to exist.

2. Whatever appears has already vanished. This is the Mahāyāna doctrine of the simultaneous appearance and disappearance of dharmas.

3. Whatever appears has *thereby* vanished. Appearing and vanishing are two inseparable but distinct aspects of a tertium quid, for example, a Whiteheadian actual event or occasion. As in the third level in the preceding section, two possible versions are possible here, i.e., that coherences appear because they vanish and vanish because they appear, or that both are what are indissolubly involved in the single act of "existing": to exist is to appear/vanish. To sense the "already goneness" of whatever is appearing determinately, such that it cannot be acted upon any longer and cannot be any different, is already the definition of what it is to be a present determinate fact *and* the definition of what it is to be already over with, gone. Before this is true, it has not happened yet; as soon as it is true, it is already gone. But here this same definition grounds two inseparable but distinct facts about every entity.

4. To appear is to vanish. Appearing is vanishing. Again, they are not two separate aspects at all, as in the fourth level in the preceding section. We may think here of fuel and its burning, a flashing forth which is at the same time the consumption of the coherence in question; its combustion means both its appearing and its expenditure, its vanishing. It is an error to think of appearing as one side of what is occurring and vanishing as another. Appearing is vanishing. The more thoroughly it has appeared, the more thoroughly it is gone, and vice versa. This Möbius strip structure is, we may say, the mark of the Tiantai position; it says not only that X and not-X are related, or are inseparable, or are correlative, or mutually grounding, or are aspects of the same thing, but that they are identical in the sense that the two sides of a Möbius strip are in fact one side, such that the more one travels on one side, the more one travels on the other, and such that their oneness is maintained precisely *as* their opposition and distinctness. When one goes all the way

on one side, one finds one has gone all the way on the other. The more X, the more non-X. Whatever appears is, we may say, already gone, and gone not only because, but also precisely to the extent that it has appeared, a point which will in fact have considerable practical implications when we come to discuss the self, desire, the Good, and time in the pages to follow.

We may play out the same riff in a few other keys, perhaps without having to belabor the reasoning in each case, since they follow from the same premises:

1. Whatever is disclosed will also be concealed, or whatever is disclosed in one way is concealed in another.
2. Whatever is disclosed is also concealed.
3. Whatever is disclosed is *thereby* concealed. Disclosure and concealment are two aspects of what it is to be at all, or each is the cause of the other.
4. To be disclosed is to be concealed. Disclosure is concealment. A thing is disclosed to the exact extent that it is concealed, and vice versa.

1. Wherever there is separation, there can and will be connection.
2. Wherever there is separation, there is already connection; whatever is separated is also connected.
3. Wherever there is separation, there is *therefore* also connection; these are two aspects of what it means to be at all, or causes of each other.
4. Separation is connection. To be separated is to be connected. A thing is separate from all else to the exact extent that it is connected to all else, and vice versa.

1. Wherever there is continuity there can and will be discontinuity, and vice versa.
2. Wherever there is continuity there is also discontinuity; whatever is continuous is also discontinuous.
3. Wherever there is continuity there is also *therefore* discontinuity, as two aspects of what it means to be, or as causes of each other.
4. To be continuous is to be discontinuous. Continuity is discontinuity. A thing is continuous with its environment to the exact extent that it is discontinuous, and vice versa.

1. Whatever is determinate can and will also be ambiguated.
2. Whatever is determinate is already also ambiguated.

3. Whatever is determinate is *thereby* ambiguated; these are two aspects of what it means to be at all, or causes of each other.
4. Determination is ambiguation. To be determinate is to be ambiguated. A thing is determinate to the exact extent that it is ambiguated, and vice versa.

1. Whatever appears as irreducible to anything else can and will also appear to be reducible.
2. Whatever appears as irreducible is already also reducible.
3. Whatever is irreducible is *thereby* reducible, they are reducible because irreducible and irreducible because reducible, or two aspects of what it means to be at all.
4. To be irreducible is to be reducible. Irreducibility is reducibility. A thing is irreducible to the exact extent that it is reducible, and vice versa.

This can be extended, unmodified, into much more controversial but, I claim, equally legitimate cases:

1. Whatever is red can and will also be blue; whatever is part of me can and will be part of you; whatever is good can and will be evil.
2. Whatever is red is already blue; whatever is me is already you; whatever is good is already evil.
3. Whatever is red is *thereby* blue; whatever is me is *thereby* you; whatever is good is *thereby* evil.
4. To be blue is to be red; to be me is to be you; to be good is to be evil. Blueness is redness; me-ness is you-ness. Goodness is evilness. A thing is blue to the precise extent that it is red, is me to the exact extent that it is you, is good to the exact extent it is evil, and vice versa.

This last set of permutations will perhaps cause some alarm, and it will be up to me to show in the subsequent pages why this is not at all a nihilistic conclusion, but one that alone is able to open up the way for a satisfactory epistemology and ethics. But before going there, we may note that although the Neo-Tiantai system is in one sense the extremest possible form of holism, it is also a very distinct form thereof, the form we will call omnicentrism. This is a holism whose motto from beginning to end must be "isolate, isolate, isolate," for it is the isolation and atomicity of things that alone is the privileged means by which their interconnection and indeed reversibility is disclosed; what connects and integrates them is precisely their momentariness, as seen in the classical Tiantai formula, "One moment of experience, three thousand coherences." Indeed, the *worst* way to integrate and interpenetrate is to try to unify or amalgamate or relate terms into a whole or a system of the panoramic kind, as all previous holisms have tried to do. The Neo-Tiantai method on the contrary takes the "momentary" approach from beginning to end: it is only as a "snapshot," completely isolated from all other moments and beings, discontinuous, irreducible, unconnected, fully determined, that the *how and whereby* of any coherence's connection to and indeed identity with all other coherences is disclosed. There is no panoramic array of interconnected coherences that make up the whole. Rather, all other coherences are copresent with this coherence only *as* this coherence, as its components; the present coherence, and each coherence, is quite literally *all there is*, and in each case the rest of any putative totality is present only in the form of the particularity itself, completely subsumed into it. Figuratively speaking, we may say that there is *no room* within a moment or a single "one" coherence for any "other," which is what makes all its relations and determinations internal, which makes the figure reversible with the ground, so that every coherence permeates the entire field of its constituent coherences, and vice versa. To hate X or love X, indeed to have any relation to X at all, is accordingly to *be* X, as we shall see. The division of hater and hated is done in a subsequent moment, or through comparison with another moment, or through taking this moment as only end or only means, or of regarding its determination and its ambiguation, its distinctness and its connection, as two separate aspects of the event.

We may think here of Merleau-Ponty's description of what he calls the "anonymity of perception." In describing the relation of "subject" and "object" in sense experience, and the implications close observation of this relation will have for understanding the relations between the *a priori* and the *a posteriori*, on the one hand, and *natura naturata* and *natura naturans*, on the other (all these relationships collapse together into intertwining chiasms), he writes:

> The sensor and the sensible do not stand in relation to each other as two mutually external terms, and sensation is not an invasion of the sensor by the sensible. It is my gaze which subtends colour, and the movement of my hand which subtends the object's form, or rather my gaze pairs off with colour, and my hand with hardness and softness, and in this transaction between the subject of sensation and the sensible it cannot he held that one acts while the other suffers the action, or that one confers significance on the other . . . a sensible datum which is on the point of being felt sets a kind of muddled problem for my body to solve. I must find the attitude which *will* provide it with the means of becoming determinate, of showing up as [e.g.] blue; I must find the reply to a question which is obscurely expressed. . . . I do not possess it in thought, or spread out towards it

some idea of blue such as might reveal the secret of it, I abandon myself to it and plunge into this mystery, it 'thinks itself within me,' I am the sky itself as it is drawn together and unified, and as it begins to exist for itself; my consciousness is saturated with this limitless blue.... of the sky, as it is perceived or sensed, subtended by my gaze which ranges over and resides in it, and providing as it does the theatre of a certain living pulsation adopted by my body, it can be said that it exists for itself (i.e., as aware of itself), in the sense that it is not made up of mutually exclusive parts, that each part of the whole is 'sensitive' to what happens in all the others and 'knows them dynamically'.... Every perception takes place in an atmosphere of generality and is presented to us anonymously. I cannot say that *I* see the blue of the sky in the sense in which I say that I understand a book or again in which I decide to devote my life to mathematics.... So, if I wanted to render precisely the perceptual experience, I ought to say that *one* perceives in me, and not that I perceive. Every sensation carries within it the germ of a dream or depersonalization such as we experience in that quasi-stupor to which we are reduced when we really try to live at the level of sensation.... I am no more aware of being the true subject of my sensation than of my birth or my death. Neither my birth nor my death can appear to me as experiences of my own, since, if I thought of them thus, I should be assuming myself to be pre-existent to, or outliving, myself, in order to be able to experience them, and I should therefore not be genuinely thinking of my birth or my death. I can, then, apprehend myself only as 'already born' and 'still alive'—I can apprehend my birth and my death only as prepersonal horizons: I know that people are born and die, but I cannot know my own birth and death. Each sensation, being strictly speaking, the first last and only one of its kind, is a birth and a death. The subject who experiences it begins and ends with it, and as he can neither precede nor survive himself, sensation necessarily appears to itself in a setting of generality, its origin is anterior to myself, it arises from sensibility which has preceded it and which will outlive it, just as my birth and death belong to a natality and a mortality which are anonymous. By means of sensation I am able to grasp, on the fringe of my own personal life and acts, a life of given consciousness from which these latter emerge, the life of my eyes, hands and ears, which are so many natural selves. Each time I experience a sensation, I feel that it concerns not my own being, the one for which I am responsible and for which I make decisions, but another self which has already sided with the world, which is already open to certain of its aspects and synchronized with them....[18]

Here we are coming closer to the Neo-Tiantai implications of perception and moretoitivity than we did in Sartre's account. The comparison of each act of perception to a birth and death is a commonplace of Buddhist momentariness theory, and Merleau-Ponty's development of the implications moves

---

[18] PhP, 214–16.

in a direction closely parallel to what we find in the Tiantai works. This other self who is me perceiving, this non-me who is more intimately me than me, brings us close to the Tiantai "single moment of experience," where also there is no way to disentangle the agent from the patient, the seer from the seen, the doer from the done to; hence we saw above that for Zhanran, where all Three Thousand coherences, of matter and mind, pertaining to every possible subjectivity and objectivity, are identical to the moment of experience, we were already able to reverse the creator and the created, the subject and the object: mind creates matter, matter creates mind, I am performing the world, the world is performing me, I am thinking myself in the sky, the sky is thinking itself in me; the Intersubsumption of self and other allows us to see how we can claim that any single coherence in this simultaneous Three Thousand can be singled out as the center, as the unifier, as what is expressing itself as all the others.

But we must also see here how the "primacy of perception," if perception is understood in this way, undermines the clear-cut irreversibility of subject/object relations even in the other two realms adduced by Sartre, namely, conceptualization and imagination. Merleau-Ponty clearly recognizes the "self-awareness" that applies to, say, the sky when "I" see it: "it sees itself in me." But here he contrasts this I of perception to the I of knowing and understanding on the one hand ("I who understand a book") and the I of willing and action ("I who decide to devote my life to mathematics"), the one who understands ideas and concepts, or even the "things" in the world as identifiable entities, and the one who "commits himself" and wills his own projects. Here, the implication would seem to be, as opposed to what takes place in the realm of pure sensation, I am indeed the real agent of my actions, the one who makes myself. But the fundamental tangling of subject and object in any act of disclosure rooted in perception, as all acts of disclosure can be seen to be, their reversibility and Intersubsumption, pushes us beyond this clear-cut distinction, even in the realm of volition.

Merleau-Ponty himself moves in the same direction. First he notes the correlativity of this incompletion of the self with the necessary incompletion of any coherence that is appearing to me: "Sensation can be anonymous only because it is incomplete. The person who sees and the one who touches is not exactly myself, because the visible and the tangible worlds are not the world in its entirety . . .,"[19] i.e., because any coherence we perceive is always inherently moretoitive. Because the object is not quite itself, I am never quite myself. But he goes on to connect perception with a kind of impersonal *action*:

---

[19] Ibid., 216.

> My first perception and my first hold upon the world must appear to me as action in accordance with an earlier agreement reached between x and the world in general, my history must be the continuation of a prehistory and must utilize the latter's acquired results. My personal existence must be the resumption of a prepersonal tradition. There is, therefore, another subject beneath me, for whom a world exists before I am here, and who marks out my place in it. This captive or natural spirit is my body, not that momentary body which is the instrument of my personal choices and which fastens upon this or that world, but the system of anonymous 'functions' which draw every particular focus into a general project.[20]

Here we have an acute phenomenological description of the temporal presituatedness of all our *actions*, which makes each of them more than it conceives of itself to be and more than any single act of intention can determine, which corresponds closely to the Tiantai reading of the revelation of everyone's prehistory in the *Lotus*. It is not just that the I who perceives is more me than me, and the world as perceived is more than it is; the I who knows and acts and undertakes projects is also not just me, and its objects, its world and goals, are also constitutively moretoitive. And the full fruits of this advance come to light in the discussion of time in the same work, where the active/passive dichotomy is fully broken through: "We are not in some incomprehensible way an activity joined to a passivity, an automatism surmounted by a will, a perception surmounted by a judgement, but wholly active and wholly passive, because we are the upsurge of time."[21] The reader of this work will by now be familiar with these "both completely X and completely non-X" types of claims, which Merleau-Ponty has arrived at through his own descriptions. We hope that the present work will make this fact not only apparent, but thinkable, and indeed known in its inevitability, and with its full implications. Of the latter, we find some also in Merleau-Ponty, who prefigures what we are to say below in some detail very pithily when he says of time itself, "We shall be obliged to say of [time] what we have said of other objects; that it has meaning for us only because 'we are it.' . . . It discloses subject and object as two abstract 'moments' of a unique structure which is *presence*."[22] This is so because, among other things, "The world is inseparable from the subject, but from a subject which is nothing but a project of the world, and the subject is inseparable from the world, but from a world which the subject itself projects."[23]

---

[20] Ibid., 254.
[21] Ibid., 428.
[22] Ibid., 430. Cf. 325: "In order to perceive things, we need to live them."
[23] Ibid.

Here we are more than halfway to the omnicentric Intersubsumption characteristic of the view we are developing here. But one crucial adjustment must be made. From our current point of view, it is not quite adequate to say simply, "there is *another* subject, an anonymous subject, a pre-subject, underneath my subjectivity, which already belongs to the world." The problem with this formulation is the *singularity* of the "other" subject that I am. This transposes the putative "oneness" which has just been displaced from my surface subjectivity, as if it resided elsewhere. But our point is that this "other subject" is precisely "the world" itself, and "the world" can never be a single synordinate world. The anonymous subject which acts, feels, perceives, wills, and thinks in my every single moment of experience is not any single unequivocal being with a particular unambiguous project of its own, for instance, some determinate orientation to the world. It is the "Three Thousand," all possible conflicting coherences and expressions of quiddities, *each* of which can equally be read as the doer of my deeds, the seer of my sights, the willer of my will. Merleau-Ponty, with his focus on the inseparability of ambiguity and being, is in a position to appreciate this, but his quasi-existentialist notion of a single "project" or consistent orientation to the world which coordinates all our relations into a single unambiguous narrative identity, or one way of "being-in-the-world" which corresponds to a particular unambiguous pre-understanding of the world, or mode of being-there.

A similar confusion can be found in vulgarized Freudianism, where *the* unconscious serves as a stand-in for the consistency displaced from the control of the conscious self, and we get monolithic, unilateral explanations of what a person's actions *really* mean and what they *really* want, i.e., what *the* unconscious wants. But strictly speaking, even for Freud, there cannot be any meaning to speaking of *the* unconscious; the realm of the unconscious is precisely untotalizable, overdetermined, incapable of understanding either time or negation, and hence of any semblance of unequivocality.

For us, too, this preunderstanding is no more impervious to ambiguity than the explicit understanding, and our basic orientations, actions, and projects which lie below our explicit consciousness are just as much necessarily ambiguous, readable as parts of three thousand alternate and conflicting projects, as the conscious self undermined by this anonymous perceiver which we also are. Nor do we want to in any way attribute a greater degree of "reality" to this underself than to the conscious explicit I; that illusory puppet, too, is the center of all experience, is found to be the doer of all other acts, the implicit agent of all that happens, here or elsewhere. Given the premises we have established above, we cannot be biased any longer: each and every one of these interpretations, including the mass of rationalizations and misrecognitions which is the conscious ego, covers the entire field, so that it is isolated from all the others, indeed, is *all* there is anywhere, as we shall see in more detail below. (Indeed, in the case of the ego, this is its own explicit sense of itself, as revealed for example in the *cogito*. But this insane overestimation of its own certaintly can now be "opened up" Tiantai fashion to reveal its truth.)

We have spoken of isolation as the mode in which interpenetration alone can take place. Indeed, "that to which all others can be reduced, which is itself irreducible" is one of the traditional definitions of "Intersubsumption (All-pervasion as All-pervadedness)" as such, which is accordingly also "unrelated to any other," completely isolated, alone in the universe, the one thing that exists, irreducibly itself; all is passivity, all is activity, all is *a priori*, all is *a posteriori*, all is *natura naturata*, all is *natura naturans*. Moreover, every momentary flash of experience, of whatever kind, is all there is, and has no connection to anything else. This is the very mode of its "being identical to everything else." But before taking on the implications of this, let us say some more about omnicentrism.

Omnicentrism

According to what we have said so far, any coherence that appears in experience can be equally well described in any of these three simultaneous and mutually entailing, indeed mutually identical, ways: (1) as (all three appearing initially as) appearing to be some exclusive coherence, (2) as (all three appearing initially as) the ambiguity of this coherence due to its moreness, the negation of itself which haunts it and is inherent to it, the fact that its very appearing demands a context which is necessarily excluded from itself, presupposes a demand for a more thorough investigation of itself which however would entail its destruction and fading into incoherence, and (3) as (all three appearing intitially as) the fact that to appear and to appear ambiguously and self-destructively are one and the same, such that appearing as X is appearing as non-X, and appearing as non-X is what it is for X to appear, that contextualized coherence is self-recontextualizing.

This last "aspect" of each coherence is what we call Intersubsumption. But given this characterization, it may also be described, as the original Chinese terms suggests, as a sort of *center*, that is, *the point in reference to which all other points attain their significance, consistency, identity, and value.* It takes on, in a new way, the role we just described as impossible, that of being the controller that determines the identity or meaning of other things, precisely by embodying that impossibility, by being the absence of any determinate one coherence that it takes as its self, by being in principle applicable in every possible case. The center is the one independent variable, the one constant in terms of which all other variables are defined, the determiner of all coherences—but what it determines them all as, is equally the determiner of all coherences and of it. If "centrality" or "mean-ness," once it appears as a coherence, makes all other coherences appear *as* itself, as centrality, it has thereby emptied itself, for thereby each coherence is just as much the center, the definer, the controller of all other coherences as it, the abstract determination "center" had been. This is the quintessential Tiantai move, the role of the *Lotus* or ultimate teaching which functions only to reveal that all other teachings were each the ultimate teaching. This is the way out of the epistemological impasse that would otherwise result from our reflections so far.

It should be noted also that the center is the locus of *ultimate value* within the whole. Since holistic doctrines, of which ours is one rather peculiar variant, by definition locate ultimate legitimacy, that is, the power to determine the "true" identity, meaning, and value of any of the parts, in the whole per se, in the relatedness of the parts to one another, we may also think of the center as the point within the whole that accurately represents the whole qua whole, the point within the whole that has direct and undistorted access to all the parts, as the center of a circle is the point of convergence of all its radii, which form direct contacts to every point in the circumference, and moreover is the point in reference to which the position of all points on the periphery is determined. The center is the "bottom line," the standard by which things are judged, and in relation to which anything that happens in the whole is viewed to matter or not to matter. Take a large set of processes, let us say, the international activities of a large corporation. A holistic analysis will insist that the meaning and identity of each of these individual activities is to be understood in the context of the whole, that is, all the activities of the corporation. What they are to be understood *as* must take into account all the other activities; what appears as philanthropy may thus appear also as publicity, what appears as charity may also appear as public relations. So far all its activities exist in a sense of constitutive ambiguity. If we understand this holism as "centered," however, we may identify one overriding concern to which all these activities may be interpreted as ultimately reducible, for example, making money. All the effects of these wide-range processes will only matter inasmuch as they effect making money; they are good if they contribute to this goal, and bad if they do not. They are *motivated* by and also *judged according to* their relation to this one central concern. The fact that a teenager in Tahiti wears a Pepsi T-shirt is good for Pepsi if it makes them money; it does not matter that he does not know or care what it says, or that he is unconvinced by Pepsi-centric rhetoric, and would show no veneration for the CEO of Pepsi if they met. If the center lies in being loved, or being obeyed, these will be the standard, and the same set of parts, the Pepsi corporation, may be seen as a different whole, and one that is judged differently, in the way it coheres around these different centers. The center is the crossroads of all the connections, all the relationships between the parts, what ties them together and gives them a specific coherence or meaning.

This has many implications. Epistemologically, it is only from a "center" of this type that the whole appears as coherent at all. On the premise of holism, this means that only for a center can a whole be considered a true whole, and only therefrom are any of the parts themselves coherent. Ethically, this means that only a center can know what the legitimate activity of any part, or of the whole, would be, assuming that this is connected with a coherent vision of what it is. Since only a center can know what anything truly is, or how it is connected with the vectors of lack (for what it lacks are other parts of the whole, which only a center can see comprehensively), only a center can know what anything should do; the center is a locus of *value arbitration*. Moreover, this is almost always connected with being a locus of value itself; to be a center is in some sense to be good, as defined by that whole. Value, as we shall see in more detail below, is connected with power to obtain some goal defined in terms of a perceived lack, the ability to be also the contrary of one's present state, thus defining a dyadic good/bad whole to the sentient being in question.

An example may make all this more clear.[24] In any system of terms, there will be one master term by reference to which all the other terms have their content fixed. For example, if I am a feminist, I may also support Marxist and ecological movements, because I see them as aspects of the general problem of patriarchy and as contributing to that struggle for equal rights for women. In that case, I would believe that, once the real problem, patriarchy, has been solved, the ecological crisis and capitalist exploitation will automatically also be solved, for the feminist problem is the real root of the others. "Feminism" in this case is the ultimate value, the "center" of my system. However, if I am a radical Green ecologist, I will feel on the contrary that only a solution to the ecological crisis can solve the problems of patriarchical and capitalist exploitation; man's warped relation to nature is the real root problem, the "center," the ultimate value. A Marxist, of course, will feel that feminism and ecologism are just epiphenomena of the root problem of capitalist exploitation and class

---

[24] I have borrowed this example from Žižek's brilliant exposition of the Lacanian concept of the "quilting point." See *The Sublime Object of Ideology* (New York: Verso, 1989), 87–89, *For They Know Not What They Do* (New York: Verso, 1991), 16–20, and *The Indivisible Remainder* (New York: Verso, 1996), 214–16. Much of the following exposition is quoted from my book, *Evil and/or as the Good: Omnicentrism, Intersubjectivity, and Value Paradox in Tiantai Buddhist Thought* (Cambridge: Harvard University Press, 2000).

struggle. Similarly, if my ultimate value resides in egotism, I may support feminism, Marxism, or ecologism if I think they will benefit me personally; my personal interests, in that case, form the center of the whole of value signifiers I employ. Feminism is good *to the extent* that it furthers my interests as a woman; Marxism is good because I am a proletariat, and so on.

This means that the "noncentral" terms are always *fundamentally ambiguous* until tied to some center in a particular context. Their identity and content are not otherwise fixed. As Žižek points out,

> Ecologism['s] ... connection with other ideological elements is not determined in advance; one can be a state-oriented ecologist (if one believes that only the intervention of a strong state can save us from catastrophe), a socialist ecologist (if one locates the source of merciless exploitation of nature in the capitalist system), a conservative ecologist (if one preaches that man must again become deeply rooted in his nature soil), and so on; *feminism can be socialist, apolitical . . . ; even* racism could be elitist or populist. . . .²⁵

It is the connection to a center which fixes or stabilizes these terms in any particular case, bestowing on them a definite content or identity.

Legitimate autonomy or freedom of action can only emanate from a center, for any other part of a whole is dependent on others extrinsic to itself for its meaning, purpose, and role. From the vantage point of the center, one can survey the whole, and know that the whole is indeed a whole, in spite of the fact that one is located *within* the whole itself. It is a point within the whole from which one can know the whole as whole, and see each part as reflective of the whole. It is also representative of the whole, and may be said to include the whole, in some virtual form, within itself. This may also imply that from the center one can control the whole, can have a direct influence on any and all points of the whole. The center is the focal point around which all the other parts revolve.

On this basis, we may broadly distinguish two types of holism. *Unicentric holism*, briefly, holds that the true meaning of the collection lies only in the whole as such; the source of all error lies in mistaking a mere part for the whole. Epistemologically, the comprehension or vision of this whole may or may not be possible from within the system, from the viewpoint of a particular privileged part. (Such a point may also be asserted, in a given case, to lie outside the system as a whole.) This point sees the whole, is directly connected to all parts, and can in some sense control the whole. It is a part that is also in some sense the whole, or may legitimately and adequately represent the whole, as all the radii of a circle are extensions of the center.

---

²⁵ Žižek, *Sublime Object*, 87.

If the feminist in our previous example has a unicentric underlying conceptual system, she will have to claim that feminism truly occupies a special and privileged place among signifiers, that is, that it is the real and true root of all the other problems, the uniquely adequate way of regarding the problem as a whole; ecologism and Marxism are merely parts. The same will go, *mutatis mutandis*, for the other two examples. If we are outside observers, we will, if we are unicentrists ourselves, have to believe that one and only one of these three contesting views is correct. One of these three terms truly represents the whole; the other two are just partial representations, and have mistakenly elevated their own status to the central position.

Omnicentric holism, on the contrary, holds that we may in fact take the part for the whole, since any part, simply considered in itself, in its own characteristics, already implies the whole of which it is a part. The part, in other words, is the whole, and any part can thus adequately stand for the whole. An omnicentrist, observing the above disagreement, would not have to insist that one of these three combatants was correct and the other two were mistaken. He would say, instead, that the whole field of phenomena and questions to which they are all referring can be described equally in these three ways, or anywhere else, that the master signifier can in fact be located anywhere at all in the whole. The entire complex functions meaningfully in all these ways at once. Feminism can indeed be seen as the unifying thread running through capitalist and ecological exploitation; on the other hand, class struggle can also be viewed as the unifying thread, or ecological exploitation, or my personal interests, or anything else. The holistic mutual dependence of the parts is so thorough that the system of causality can not be conceived of simply as one-way, with one unique root which causes all the other parts of the whole.

The concept of root or cause is here only provisional, as we shall see in more detail below. And yet it is not illegitimate; the claim here is not that we must forget about having any master signifier or center at all, that nothing is the root of anything else and all are simultaneously present, but rather, a both/and position; the categories of cause and effect, of root and branch, of appearance and reality, are unavoidable if there is to be any meaning at all, but it always works in both directions at once. It is not that there is no real center (and center is therefore a mere ideological invention); rather, "centrality" is an indispensable category, such that all points are center, all points are periphery.[26] What is ideological distortion, if anything, is just the claim

---

[26] We may think here of the Kantian categorical imperative, which demands that all other persons be treated *not only* as means (periphery) but *also* as ends in themselves. This gives us a picture of all persons as ends in themselves, but also as means—an intriguing ethical form of omnicentrism.

that some one of these centers is the sole point of which centrality can be asserted. In short, omnicentrism holds that the identity and significance of any entity is so thoroughly and completely a function of its relations to others—so completely "holistic"—that every identity is a sliding identity whose significance is always susceptible to grounding in something else, always ambiguous, changeable, and instrumental. However, *since this is also true of all the other entities in which it is so grounded*, every entity equally can and must itself serve as a ground, as a master signifier from which everything else attains its significance and identity, as a center.

We can perhaps understand this better by recalling the comment above about the *ambiguity* of the identities of all noncentral terms prior to their connection with a determining center. At first glance, this seems to suggest that the center is the one entity which is definite, fixed, "full," unambiguous, that is, which has a fixed meaning or identity which need not depend on the connection to something else. This is true, but for omnicentrism it is only part of the truth. In omnicentrism, the holistic premise is pressed to the point of rendering this center at the same time completely *empty* of its own meaning or identity as well. For example, to use the ideological example of meanings cited above (in which context it is perhaps easiest to grasp this point), if "class struggle" is the center of my meaning system, it will seem as if all other particular issues get their meaning just from class struggle, they all end up to be nothing but particular expressions of class struggle; the meaning of class struggle seems to remain constant and prior, while the meaning of terms like "feminism" is transformed by the connection to this center. But if this mode of interpretation succeeds to the ultimate extent, it will come to explain everything as forms of class struggle; when this happens, "class struggle" will turn out to be, not the most meaningful term in the system, but the one term that is completely devoid of meaning, since it means literally *everything*. It will have come to be so modified by its use as the metaphier for all these disparate phenomena that it will end up being no more than a null point in the system with no specifiable content.

At this point, it is the dependent peripheral terms that actually provide the content and meaning for what had been the center. As long as there was something outside it, to which it could not be applied, this central term retained a determinate content in contrast to that outside; now, however, its content is supplied only by the contrast between ground and grounded, between center and periphery, or between the basic thing and the forms *as* which it expresses itself. But since, as we have seen, it never appears *simpliciter*, but only *as* these others, this contrast between the thing itself and its expressions ends up being only provisional. It is nothing but what it appears *as*, and thus this relation supplies the center with no definite or privileged content.

What remains is merely the formal structure or relation of central coherence X expressing itself as non-X, unfixed to any particular X and hence functioning in all directions, from all centers, at once. Thus, when any one of these centerings (interpretative systems) succeeds to the utmost point, the center in question comes to mean both nothing and everything. At this point, any given term in the system can function equally well as the center—all the terms explain each other, and the starting point can be anywhere, as long its function is pushed to its ultimate. When "class struggle" completely succeeds as a center, it ends up revealing, in all things, not just the character of class struggle, but since at the end this term has become meaningless, just the fact of interconnection itself, the fact that one thing can be used to explain another, that, when its work is complete, any term can be used to explain all others; it reveals omnicentrism. In this sense, it ends up revealing not only that "class struggle" is present everywhere, but also that "patriarchal oppression" is present everywhere, that "sin" is present everywhere, that "exploitation of nature" is present everywhere, that "sexual repression" is present everywhere, that "glorious enlightenment" is present everywhere, and so on. Any term at all ends up being just as meaningful as the unifier of all phenomena as the one initially chosen, and pushed to its limit. Similarly, when "feminism" completely succeeds as a center, it shows that gender issues are everywhere, which similarly empties the term "feminism" of meaning and ends up revealing most centrally just interconnection itself. When they succeed fully, these two opposite centers end up revealing the same thing, their meaning ends up being one and the same—the fact of interpretability from all perspectives, omnicentrism.

To put the same point in a "classical" rather than "postmodern" idiom, let us suppose that I say, with Thales, that "all is water." That is, "water" is the center, that all other things—fire, air, and earth—are to be understood in terms of water, that they are "really" water, that they are all identical to water. Initially, this term "water" means the wet element as opposed to the fiery, earthy, or aery elements. But if this theory is really taken seriously, then the metaphier changes along with the metaphrand; that is, by my own theory, "water" refers not only to the wet element, but also to all things that appear to be fiery, earthy, or aery. "Water" no longer means that which appears as wetness, but rather that which appears sometimes as wetness, sometimes as fieriness, sometimes as earthiness and sometimes as aeriness. In effect, the term "water" now really means "water-fire-air-earth," with an emphasis on the central term of water. So in saying "Water, fire, air, and earth are all water," I am just saying, "Water, fire, air, and earth are water, fire, air, and earth." But actually I am asserting a little more; I am saying that when I name any one of these four, I am really referring to something that includes all four. By the same token, if I now say "fire," since fire is just water and water is just water-fire-air-earth, I can equally say, "All things are fire." Any term can be the center, since each of the four really refers to all four at once. This also means that I can say, "fire is identical to water." In all this, I have really just asserted that all the four terms transform into one another, that they are inseparable, and that any starting point can serve as a point of reference by which to explain the others. This is omnicentrism, which can thus be viewed as simply a fuller thinking-through of the basic premises of holism per se.

Omnicentrism is here viewed not as one specific teaching among many, but as the real significance of what it means for there to be any teaching at all, what is really at stake when anyone suggests any center, any way whatsoever of interpreting experience.[27] What is revealed as omnicentrism is simply that whatever is is always revealed *as something else*, that manifestation is always manifestation in the form of some other, that all experience is interpretable, and always reducible to something other than itself. If this "always" is taken seriously, this will also imply, "to *anything* other than itself."

To review: the identity of any token of experience is fundamentally ambiguous and dependent on a particular restricted context for its establishment. This ambiguity is what is meant here by Global Incoherence. The provisional, dependent identity acquired in this fashion is equivalent to Local Coherence. However, since this same ambiguity applies also to whatever term might be chosen as the grounding center, and since, once successfully extended to explain all other parts as expressions of itself the initial grounding center loses its determinate character, obtaining all its contents and identity solely from the "expressions" of which it was posited as the ground, all points end up equally being the grounding center, and any point can be chosen as the starting point for a system of interpretive connections and groundings. This further reversal is equivalent to Intersubsumption (All-pervasion as

---

[27] For the sake of completeness, and to avoid any misunderstandings, I should spell out the connection between these considerations and the Tiantai teaching of inherent inclusion and the Three Truths. I have just shown that any center will end up being both the most meaningful and the most meaningless term in the system. Its totalizing meaning corresponds to Centrality, its meaninglessness to Emptiness, and its character as some specific starting point (e.g., "Marxism" as opposed to "feminism") corresponds to Provisional Positing. The doctrine of inherent inclusion seeks to preserve the specific starting points with all their differences, in spite of the fact that at their ultimate point they all end up meaning all-and-none. This is possible essentially due to the doctrines of intersubjectivity and compassion in Tiantai, which mean that both sides of the process must always be in operation; even after this interpenetration is accomplished, it is *always* possible to speak of everything in terms of specifically Marxism, or feminism, or fascism, or democracy, rather than forcing us into a final situation where all we can say is "everything means everything."

All-pervadedness). The fact that any entity thus ends up being both center and periphery, the ground and the grounded, the explainer and the explained, the root and the branch, is the Nonexclusive Center. The final effect of setting up some X as the center, the grounding term by reference to which all others are explained, is not just to show that all are expressions of this particular X, but more importantly to show that *any* X can serve to explain everything else, that all things are expressions of any chosen X, that every X pervades all times and places, because the interconnections of things are precisely what comprise each thing's identity.

But it may be asked, is expression or instantiation the only form of contextualization? That is, when something "derives its identity from its relation to an other," that is, its context, does this necessarily take the form we have been mainly discussing in the above examples, namely, the form of instantiation, as "feminism" may be seen, if contextualized in a certain way, as merely an expression or facet or instantiation of "Marxism" or "ecologism," or "water" may be seen to be an indirect "expression" of fire? The implicit model of the situation in the slightly jargony postmodern idiom we have been using, speaking of "contexts," or of Gestaltist figure/ground relations, would suggest not. For in neither of these pictures do the "contexts" or "backgrounds" seem necessarily to involve the "self-emptying" of the determinate content; it does not seem to be the case, at least *prima facie*, that the identity of a background is changed when it serves as a background for a figure, for instance, black remains black when it is used to contextualize a white figure. It is possible to argue that the context or background is itself contextualized or grounded in some larger context or ground, thus again making its identity nondeterminate; this may well be so, but it raises certain difficulties of infinite regress and the identity of the whole, as well as old onto-theological specters of first cause arguments, which we may not want to involve ourselves in. It is also possible to assert that in fact the identity of the context *is* in fact modified by the mere act of serving as context; it has, at least, one additional characteristic—that of serving as the context for something—which it did not have before, which would perhaps, on some holistic or internal-relations-only accounts, be considered a change of identity. On this view, more or less plausibly, the content and identity of a metaphor, or any other explanatory sign, is always modified by the content of that to which it comes to be applied.

However, I would rather suggest at this juncture that this is just the place where our metaphors of context and background break down, and must be replaced by a more nuanced one, which will really account for the omnicentric properties of Tiantai speculations, and allow us to pursue their implications. That is, it has become necessary to specify exactly *what kind* of contextualization we have in mind here. Contextualization of semiotic tokens in differential networks is here only the general notion, which explicates the Tiantai omnicentrism only to a limited extent. To get us over the remaining hump, a more precise specification of the relevant subset of semiotic contextualization is especially necessary here. The new metaphor I am suggesting is based on the uniquely Tiantai doctrine of transformative recontextualization, literally, "opening the provisional to reveal the mean" (*kaiquan xianshi*). This notion is best understood by the metaphor, not of figure and ground, nor of semiotic marker and context (although both of these are involved and as it were presupposed by the modified metaphor), but by the model of *a joke*, in particular a joke with a setup and a punch line, as we shall explicate presently. To understand the applicability of this concept, however, let us first take a look at the Tiantai doctrine from which it derives.

The Process of Transformative Recontextualization: Setup and Punch Line as the Basic Categories of All Possible Experience

In these reflections I have simply adumbrated what is writ large and in another idiom in the Tiantai system of omnicentrism. The central pillar of this system, however, by consideration of which I hope to explicate the manner in which the real meaning and content of any center ends up being just the principle of "centrality" (mutual explication) itself, is to be located in the Tiantai view of the purported *Lotus Sûtra* teaching of "opening the provisional to reveal the real" as the ultimate truth revealed by *all* teachings. To explicate this I will have to delve into a few technical Buddhological details. In spite of considerable trepidation at complicating the picture and raising difficulties for nonspecialists, this will necessarily involve us in a brief excursus into the Tiantai understanding of some specialized Buddhist religious and mythological concepts, such as "Enlightenment," "Nirvāna," "Bodhisattvahood," "Provisional and Ultimate Truth," "Skillful Means," "Becoming a Buddha," "Universal Buddhahood" and so on.

The *Lotus*, a text with minimal doctrinal content, except for a meta-level consideration of the relationship between different teachings, is, in the Tiantai view, the ultimate truth. It is not some specific teaching about *what* the real is, but just the act of opening and revealing, of bringing teachings together so they are revealed to be versions of one another, one may say of *teaching per se*, that is the ultimate teaching. Omnicentrism is here viewed not as one specific teaching among many, but as the real significance of what it means for there to be any teaching at all, what is really at stake when anyone suggests any center, any way of interpreting experience.[28] This hinges on the work done by Intersubsumption (All-pervasion as All-pervadedness). "Intersubsumption," we must repeat, is itself just another concept, is itself a sensation and a determinacy, whose specific quality is "seeing that all things are reducible to any thing." All things are reducible to *this* thing, "Intersubsumption," as well. But its specific character is to make it possible for everything to also be reducible to anything else. It is established as the absolute truth above all other truths; but once this is done, it simultaneously establishes every other possible thing, sensation, or concept as the absolute truth. This is how Intersubsumption transformatively recontextualizes all other coherences, how it "opens up the provisional to reveal the real." Let us explore this in more detail.

The Tiantai tradition's unique position rests on its claim concerning the relation that obtains between Local Coherence and Global Incoherence. It will come as no surprise for those familiar with Buddhist rhetoric that they turn out to be "neither the same nor different," denoted here as the "Nonexclusive Center." But as the above reflections have already begun to suggest, rather than relegating this claim to a facile unthinkable identity of contraries or blank "everything is everything" story, the Tiantai tradition has something very specific in mind here: the neither-sameness-nor-difference of the provisional and Global Incoherence in Intersubsumption is to be understood on the model of the relation between provisional and ultimate doctrines preached by the Buddha, the process of preaching false but necessary provisional doctrines, on the basis of one's realization of ultimate truth, in order to lead other beings to that ultimate truth, especially as described in the *Lotus*. The ontological problems of the relation of appearance and reality, and of oneness to multiplicity, are to be understood here according to the blueprint provided by this basic paradigm. That is, Local Coherence is to Global Incoherence as provisional truth is to ultimate truth. And what precisely is this relation?

---

[28] For the sake of completeness, and to avoid any misunderstandings, I should spell out the connection between these considerations and the Tiantai teaching of inherent inclusion and the Three Truths. I have just shown that any center will end up being both the most meaningful and the most meaningless term in the system. It totalizing meaning corresponds to the Mean, its meaninglessness to Emptiness, and its character as some specific starting point (e.g., "Marxism" as opposed to "feminism") corresponds to Provisional Positing. The doctrine of inherent inclusion seeks to preserve the specific starting points with all their differences, in spite of the fact that at their ultimate points they all end up meaning all-and-none. This is possible essential due to the doctrines of intersubjectivity and compassion in Tiantai, which mean that both sides of the process must always be in operation; it is always possible to speak of everything in terms of specifically Marxism, or feminism, or fascism, or democracy, rather than forcing us into a final situation where all we can say is "everything means everything."

According to the *Lotus*, the provisional doctrines, valid in some local context, are posited (1) *on the basis of* the ultimate truth and (2) *in order to reveal* ultimate truth. That is, to put it in the technical terms of traditional Buddhist mythology, a Buddha creates these doctrines on the basis of his own wisdom and compassion, his own embodiment of ultimate truth, and designs them for the sole purpose of leading other sentient beings to the same state. The doctrines, understood in the sense specified by their original local context, do not literally describe this state of realization, or match its contents, but do both derive from and lead to it. However, this is not yet the whole story, for according to the Tiantai understanding of this relation, in terms of "opening the provisional to reveal the real," this content is itself purely context dependent; that is, just the same content, when "opened up" and revealed in this context of deriving from and leading to ultimate truth, suddenly *reads differently* without having changed in the least. It is not that the provisional is refuted and replaced by ultimate truth, but that it is revealed in this manner to have always been, token for token, ultimate truth itself.

On this picture, it is possible to be practicing both ultimate and provisional truths at the same time, in that one may believe himself to be practicing a particular practice, which, when recontextualized, turns out to have always had quite a different meaning and efficacy. Hence, in the *Lotus*, the *srāvakas* ("Hinayana" disciples) are told that they have actually been practicing the Bodhisattva path all along,[29] as are the tormentors of the Bodhisattva Never-Disparage.[30] As Zhiyi points out,[31] these tormentors are not instructed to change their behavior in any way; rather, they are told that, in doing what they are doing (tormenting Never-Disparage) they *are now actually practicing* the Bodhisattva path, which proceeds from and leads to enlightenment,

---

[29] In Mahāyāna Buddhism, the Hinayana disciples are viewed as practicing an inferior path, aiming only at personal liberation and predicated on an inferior understanding of emptiness, as opposed to the Bodhisattvas, who strive eternally for the liberation of all beings on the basis of a more profound understanding of emptiness.

[30] The story is of a monk who says to everyone he meets, "I dare not disrespect you, for you are practicing the Bodhisattva path, and will definitely become a Buddha." (The straight present-tense rendering is based on Zhiyi's reading of the Kumārajiva's Chinese translation.) Everyone is understandably annoyed by this, so they ridicule him by giving him the epithet Never-Disparage and eventually even take to beating him, in response to which he says just the same thing. In the end, these tormentors do indeed become Buddhas—after a detour in purgatory and continued encounters with this teaching—and Never-Disparage is revealed to be a previous existence of Śākyamuni Buddha.

[31] "This is the opening of the provisional to reveal the real, so that in all dharmas one sees the Middle Way. Hence the text says, 'What you are practicing is the Bodhisattva path.' They did not need to change their road or move into different tracks to seek the truth, but rather could reveal the glorious within the coarse." (T33.740.b.21-23)

and hence will all become Buddhas. This claim is made possible by the presumption that "the Bodhisattva path" is a particular state of being which is understood as having at least the following two attributes: (1) It can assume any form because it is (2) always involved in responding to and bringing enlightenment to other sentient beings. Hence any particular form may turn out to be an instantiation of the Bodhisattva path, and have the effect of bringing enlightenment to both oneself and others. The previous teachings are shown to have been provisional (merely *forms* of Bodhisattvahood), and their real intention and source is revealed (they are forms *of Bodhisattvahood*). They were not literally "true" as understood in the original context, but when placed in the context of the original intention and result (both of which are the Bodhisattva path), a beginning before the previous supposed beginning and an end after the previous supposed end, it is revealed that these very teachings, token for token, were revelations of the ultimate truth as well—that is, they were forms assumed by enlightenment and which reveal enlightenment.

When a previous teaching is "opened up" in this way, it is not exactly refuted. Instead, the hermeneutic context in which it reveals itself to have always have been speaking the ultimate truth is revealed. The teaching itself is not changed, but now it is seen that all along it was teaching the ultimate truth, the content and implications of which are very different from those assumed to pertain when this provisional teaching was heard in isolation, or taken in its literal sense. As Zhiyi says, "When we open up the *upāya*s to reveal the real ultimate truth in them, we see that precisely the former bodies [of Buddhas preaching inferior doctrines] are the perfect eternal body, and that the former doctrines are all the perfect Integrated Teaching, that the former practices and former principles are all precisely the ultimately real."[32]

This entails also that once the ultimate is revealed, it reveals itself both in contrast to the previous *upāya*s and as a new contextual nexus in the light of which the former teachings are themselves revealed as identical to this ultimate teaching, thereby in the same gesture overcoming this very contrast. This is made most explicit in the Tiantai doctrine of the "two marvels," the relative and the absolute, which is traditionally explained with respect to the relative status of various sutras—but this is the model for the Tiantai vision of reality. Let us draw out the implications. Both the distinction between value and antivalue and the subsequent abolition of that distinction are necessary here. By means of the distinction, the concept of value is gained; without first having the contrast, there would be no notion of what was meant by value. Moreover, this alone assures that value will be able to perform its work of transforming antivalue into itself. Once this concept is in hand and granted

---

[32] T33.691b.

its place hierarchically above antivalue, with which it is given meaning by contrast, it is revealed that this value subsumes antivalue within it, that by virtue of itself, antivalue is no longer antivalue, but rather is, paradoxically, value itself. This can serve as a template not only for the relation between the *Lotus* and other sutras, but also for the development of the Mahayana claims of identity between *nirvāna* and *samsāra*. We begin with suffering, deluded beings, which have always existed. The Buddha comes along and says, "Notice that you are suffering and deluded, that all reality is nothing but delusion and suffering." By grasping those concepts, they simultaneously grasp the contrasting opposite concepts: enlightenment and bliss, defined so far only as far-off ideals contrasting in every detail with reality: Nirvāna. Nirvāna is so far quite simply the pure opposite of reality, its unmitigated negation. Reality is impermanent, painful, selfless (unfree) and defiled: *therefore* Nirvāna means the opposite state, the state that is permanent, blissful, free, and pure. Nirvāna defined in this way is the relative marvel. Then comes the punch line, the twist: this further revelation is made that existing reality is Nirvāna. Nirvāna is *samsāra*., in other words, the ordinary cycle of birth-and-death itself. It is reality that possesses these qualities of permanence, bliss, and so on, *precisely by virtue of the impermanence and pain that led to their positing*. Value consists in revealing that the antivalue with which it was contrasted in order to become defined is itself the source and locus of this value, is itself identical to value. To say from the beginning, "This is all value," would have no meaning at all, would not *reveal* anything to sentient beings, because they simply would not know what value (marvel) means.[33] As Zhiyi says, "How could the coarse thinkable be different from the marvelous unthinkable? Without leaving words and letters we can thus speak the meaning of liberation. The crux is just to realize how the thinkable is identical to the unthinkable."[34]

As noted, this notion of opening and revealing does not only apply to doctrines and teachings, much less merely to the groupings of the Buddha's teaching, although this is its initial and formative point of reference. It is deployed

---

[33] In passing, let me note that we have here an answer to Schopenhauer's complaint about pantheism: he said he agreed with it, except that it really said nothing. If you took away the emotional associations with the term "God," to say everything is God just means that everything is everything. Thus, what pantheism really means is that the awe and love that were formerly accorded to God should instead be accorded to the world. This Schopenhauer rejected. (See Schopenhauer, *The World as Will and Representation*, vol. 2, trans. E.F.J. Payne (New York: Dover Publications, 1966), 640–46.) But the Tiantai position is that these are two steps in one process, the only way to sanctify the world. First the world must be contrasted with God, so to speak, so that the awe and love can be established. Then this contrast is broken down: God is the world. Now we have these notions of value in hand, and can apply them to the world.
[34] T33.700b.

as general metaphysical notion. This entails not only an emphasis on the preservation of individual deluded forms and even names in their glorified form, but also the way in which the actual qualities, appearances, characteristics of the "nine realms" (that is, all forms of existence other than Buddhahood), are treated as a kind of *upāya*, or skillful means of teaching, which are opened up and revealed to be the Buddha realm. By this very act, they are all again both provisional and real at the same time.[35] The relation between provisional and ultimate *teachings* is here used as a model for the relation between the ontic realms themselves. Ordinary reality is to the realm of enlightenment as a provisional teaching is to the ultimate teaching that it leads to.[36]

---

[35] Zhiyi says a little later on, "Each dharma realm possesses ten thusnesses, so the ten have a total of a hundred. But since each inherently includes the other nine, each has a hundred dharma realms with a total of a thousand thusnesses. Now these can be arranged into five levels: (1) The evil [hells, hungry ghosts, animals, asuras], (2) the good [humans and gods], (3) The Two Vehicles, (4) the Bodhisattvas, (5) the Buddhas. If we divide these in two, we can say that the first four are provisional (*quan*) and the last one is the real (*shi*). But a more detailed exposition reveals that each one possesses both the provisional and the real." (T33.693)

[36] The final form this ontological application of the notion of opening the provisional to reveal the real takes is in the famous Tiantai doctrine of the "mutual inclusion of the ten realms," or, even more pithily, "the three thousand coherences inherent in each moment of experience." The implication of stating the standard Chinese Buddhist notion of mutual inclusion in this very particularist manner must not be overlooked here. That is, by referring explicitly to the "ten realms," or the "three thousand," rather than simply stating, in the Huayan manner, an ambiguous "everything is each, each is everything," the Tiantai version of this doctrine explicitly ensures the inclusion also of subjective states of delusion and suffering, since these ten realms include the specifically enumerated realms of purgatory, animals, asuras, hungry ghosts, and so on as pervading and being pervaded by the realm of Buddhahood. Since, in pan-Buddhist mythology, all such realms are constitutively subjective as much as objective (that is, creations of karma), this means not just that a set of morally neutral entities, the things making up the world, are all mutually pervasive, but specifically that delusion and enlightenment, which in Tiantai terms means provisional and ultimate truth, are mutually pervading, each one being an adequate description of the whole process of delusion-enlightenment. We may say then that the ultimate truth cannot be separated from provisional truth, and would not be itself without the lesser teachings that precede it. The provisional truth can never be eliminated or left behind, because then the ultimate truth would fail to be the ultimate truth; it is only ultimate by virtue of its mutual inherence with the provisional truth, which is also, therefore, ultimate. Here the real nature of all phenomena is asserted to be none other than the principle of *upāya* itself, of a provisional positing which is perpetually exposed as false and superseded. The truth, in other words, is the process of falsehood (partial truth) leading to truth. The world is thus to be experienced as a teaching device, something that is in itself false if taken literally but true in that it is manifested by and in fact inherent in the truth itself, as a means devised skillfully to lead one to the truth, which will turn out to be this principle of truth and half-truth itself, fleshed out. But this is only half the story, since it is as true to say, "the Buddha realm

This structure adumbrates the procedure Zhiyi uses in every section of the *Fahuaxuanyi*, and his other main works. First he makes a distinction, allowing the contrast to define the two poles, usually a hierarchical contrast or a straight value contrast, and then at the end he "opens the provisional to reveal the real," showing that actually all lower or negatively valued parts are identical to the higher or positive part, and have been all along. All falsehoods *will turn out always to have been* the truth. This is not to say they already are the truth, or that they will become the truth; there is both a necessary forward motion ("will turn out") and a realization, constituted thereby, that this opposite value has been copresent all along ("always to have been"). But how in the world are we to understand this, and gain an intuitive sense of its plausibility?

It is here that I must beg readers to indulge me in suggesting what I have found to be a highly useful comparison; for the entire Tiantai concept of the relation between provisional and ultimate truth can, as I have already hinted, be illuminated by means of a very commonplace example: I refer to the structure of a joke. Provisional is to ultimate as setup is to punch line. Enlightenment is here equal to humorousness, delusion to seriousness. The whole setup of the joke is experienced as serious until the punch appears; once the punch line is understood, however, the entire setup is seen to also have been "funny." One does not say, after all, "The punch line is funny, but the joke as a whole is not." One simply says that the whole joke is funny, including the seriousness of the setup. Every atom of the setup is thereby understood to have also been funny. But this does not mean that one was laughing while hearing the setup. On the contrary, *the punch line will only work, will only be experienced as funny, if the setup has been temporarily, "provisionally," taken seriously.* It is precisely the contrast between the solemnity of the setup and the absurdity of the punch line that constitutes the humor of the latter, and thereby, of the entire joke, including the serious setup. In this way we can see how the setup can be simultaneously "serious" and "funny," and how these two are identical to one another, and yet exist in a *necessary* conflict and contrast. As I understand it, this provides a remarkably close approximation of the relation between provisional and ultimate in Tiantai, and thereby, of the relation of value and antivalue; this model provides us with one model by which to understand how "antivalue" (purgatory, karma, afflictions, sentient beings, provisional teachings) can be both identical to and opposite to "value" (Bud-

---

too is merely a provisional *upāya*," as it is to say, "the nine realms are really the ultimately real Buddha realm." In fact, all have to be both at once, and thus we could say that all our evils are teaching devices of the Buddha *or* that even the Buddha is just another delusion resulting from ignorant clinging. Both of these must be equally valid for all experience.

dhahood), without changing in the least, and without renouncing the experienced conflict between the two. Their conflict itself is experienced as harmony, as the contrast between the seriousness of the setup and the humor of the punch line is also experienced as their harmony, in the retrospective understanding of the humor of the joke as a whole. Thus Tiantai writers can say, "All things, including evil, are Buddha, Nirvāna, enlightenment, ultimate truth, etc.," without thereby destroying the meaning of these terms through the paradox of asserting any predicate of "all things," without denying the contrast between evil and good, and without absorbing all the particulars and distinctions among individual things into one indeterminate universal Suchness or "night in which all cows are black." On the contrary, the goodness of all things is dependent on the eternal uncompromising contrast between evil and good. The *Lotus Sūtra* is the punch line of the universe, which reveals all Local Coherences, without altering in the least their immediate coarseness, illusion and evil, simultaneously to be marvelous like the marvelous *Lotus* itself. Once the punch line appears, everything is always both funny and serious.

It is the last point that needs stressing, for it is here that our new model comes to our aid. For we can now understand not only how the recontextualized token (here, the setup) comes to be both *entirely* characterized by two opposite qualities (here, humurousness and seriousness, each of which will apply to the *entire* setup once the punch line appears), but also how the same can be true, in an assymmetrical manner, of the punch line itself. For the quality of "humorousness," once it is revealed that it can also "turn out always to have been present" even in the most serious and even tragic of qualities (the setup), no longer has a determinate and identifiable significance in contrast to the serious; nothing can be imagined or pointed, however serious, of which it could be said with assurance, "This is not funny." "Funny" no longer means anything in particular, no longer has a specifiably limited range of meaning; it no longer means, for example, that when you are in the presence of something "funny" you will burst out laughing, or experience pleasure, or even not be in misery and terror; all and any experience can turn out to always have been funny. Hence funny no longer denotes any determinate meaning. This being the case, the predicate "funny" empties itself of determinate concept, in the manner required for a truly omnicentric picture.[37]

---

[37] This modification of our model has many important consequences. One, which I will not go into in depth here, is to provide a possible response to Whiteheadian critiques of Chinese Buddhism (usually based on a picture derived from the Huayan tradition, where this notion of opening the provisional to reveal the real is no longer of any real importance) concerning the symmetrical relation of mutual inclusion between past and future (in preference to which

We are now in a position to understand what is meant by the term transformative recontextualization. It should be stressed that nothing is changed in this process, so this is "transformation" only in the restricted sense. Moreover, there is no actual recontextualization, for there are *always already* an infinite number of relevant contexts out there. It is just that by a *sui generis* act of active neglect some are (and must be) excluded from consideration habitually in every case, thereby yielding our usual world of determinate coherences. Recontextualization therefore means more an *undoing* of this chronic previous habitual focus or mental grip, or seeing its groundlessness, arbitrariness, in other words, that another set of equally obvious facts, if attended to, change the significance, meaning, *identity* of the token in question. Think suddenly of the skeletons in everyone's bodies, or their intestines, or the Big Bang, or the Roman Empire, or the ocean floor; does that not change the way the present moment is experienced?[38]

In other words, any datum that presents itself insistently as a nonnegotiable qualitative fact depends on some unseen putative data fixed obsessively as its relevant frame, at the expense of other, neglected data. These framing determinacies are assumed to be factual qualities, but in reality they are also only a certain X with respect to another certain arbitrarily narrowed frame, and so on. In terms of our holistic paradigm, we can put the case this way: it is never possible for all parts of any whole to "appear" at once—that is, as distinct coherences, none of which are concealed. By the holistic premise, any data about the whole of which something is a part is relevant to determining the identity of that thing. Therefore, some relevant data concerning the identity of anything that appears is always missing from experience. Hence it is never possible to determine the identity of anything. However, everything appears as some identity, some coherence. This appearing, in toto, is all the data we have. So all we know about the whole which we cannot see in its entirety is its capacity to appear *as* this form, which means to appear as a

---

process philosophers suggest an assymetrical situation where future prehends or includes past but past does not include future). In the Tiantai picture, past includes future and future includes past, indeed, but this is itself an asymmetrical situation, as suggested by the setup/punch-line structure: the sense in which "inclusion" (copresence of two contrary identities) occurs in the two cases is quite distinct. Although it is true to say that the serious part of the joke is both serious and funny, and the funny part of the joke is both serious and funny, this is so for different reasons in the two cases, as explained above.

[38] In terms of praxis, this is why mere consciousness of the relevant contexts is curative: as long as they are not figures of awareness they implicitly function as brute facts in the frame, determining the fixity of the figure. But once they become figures themselves, this whole configuration calls out for contextualization; the fixed determining contexts turn out also not to be experienced brute facts, but to depend on an arbitrary narrowing of relevant contexts.

coherence while equally presenting to experience the nonultimacy of this form, the provisionality, the explorability, the more-to-come-ness of it. We only know that whatever does appear in the future will be a further expression of what we are now calling "X," by the general holistic premise—something which will be, by being revealed, transforming the identity of this X but also will necessarily be transformed by this appearance *as* X of one of its determining contexts.

Enchantment, Disenchantment, Reenchantment

Take for example: we have some sneaky clique of professionals—probably shamans or priests—who manage by means of a kind of pompous mystification to impress on the rest of the population that they are different from everyone else, that what they do is not like ordinary work, that their very existence is sacred in contrast to the profane lives of everyone else. We might think of the caste system in India for a particularly apt example, but it is no different when later on, after many crashes, some other group assumes this mantel of sacredness or specialness—artists, for example, or philosophers. At some point someone wises up and says, But what you do is no better than what anyone else does, it's just one more form of labor; you take a bunch of materials and you put them together and transform them into a product, that's just what all the rest of us are always doing. But this universalization of the coherence that has been identified already as sacred can have three possible consequences: either the profanization of the previously sacred, or the sacralization of the previously profane, or the abolition of these categories altogether, as meaningless. That is, having established the two categories "sacred" and "profane" by means of their contrast, the discovery that there is really nothing in the one which is not also in the other allows us to say either, positivistically, (1) the contrast no longer holds, let's abolish it (the Exclusive Center), or else, humanistically, (2) see, everything is profane, the concept sacred was a hoax, or else, pantheistically, (3) see, everything is sacred. The Neo-Tiantai view is that all three of these are applicable; we abolish the two concepts only in a very special sense, namely that their contrast is no longer what we initially thought it to be, that is, a relation of mutual exclusion; sacred means sacred/profane, profane means profane/sacred. However, we will not rest even with this "Exclusive Center": we will say also, if we wish, Everything is profane, including the sacred; the coherence "profanity" extends everywhere without exception. However, it is also unattainable as something that excludes its opposite, sacredness. Hence, we have the reversibility as well: Everything is sacred, including the profane. These coherences, sacred and profane, once established by the erroneous contrast, are forever with us, and indeed forever applicable everywhere. The setup is both serious and humorous, and the punch line too is both serious and humorous; they are equal but only by virtue of this very contrast and inequality. This is how the nature of things gets any determination whatsoever, and indeed is just what justifies and, if you will, redeems, all the errors of which our lives are composed. Whatever appears, for whatever reason, appears *as*, and whatever appears *as* pervades all times, places, and coherences.

Asness as All-pervasion

It is worthwhile to pause to explicate this notion of something appearing "as" something more thoroughly, recalling the discussion earlier in this book, for this may be the shortest route to an understanding of the true implications of the Tiantai notion of Intersubsumption (All-pervasion as All-pervadedness). In the Marxism-Feminism-Ecologism example, we may say that, for instance, Marxism appears *as* Feminism when an instance of gender prejudice is seen *as* a subset of the broader category "class struggle." Two things should be noted about this situation. First, Marxism always has to appear *as* something besides "class struggle" *simpliciter*. Even if I happen to come across a guy dressed like the capitalist from Monopoly hitting a striking worker on the head with his gold cane, an active interpretive choice is needed to name this as a "direct" appearing of class struggle—rather than, say, a biological phenomenon, an exemplification of the laws of physics, or a personal vendetta. More generally, everything that appears must always appear *as* something else. Some other examples, from other realms, will make this clearer. Take love, or hate. Love appears only as some nonlove coherences—particular gestures, acts, facial expressions, states of consciousness, pleasurable sensations and attributions of those pleasures, experiences of loops of desire, perhaps physiological states, perhaps the emptying of certain chemicals into the bloodstream at particular times, and so on. As much as we search, we can never find "love" *simpliciter*, that is, not appearing or presenting itself in the form of some other, strictly nonlove coherences. The same may be said of each and every one of the components of love so designated; a facial expression appears *as* the tensing or broadening of certain facial muscles, together with a particular social context which allows a certain interpretation of these muscular changes, and the physiological processes of the perceiver and namer of this set of actions as "this particular facial expression." The same goes for the physiological processes themselves, and so on, on this view, *ad infinitum*. Opposite qualities, such as hate, are susceptible to the same analysis; hatred too cannot be found anywhere *simpliciter*. It is *always* "read in" to other, "nonhate" coherences. Or take an even less abstract example: the triangularity of a triangle, something with clear objective characteristics, can only appear *as* some nontriangle elements—lines of ink on a piece of paper, a mathematical formula, three matchsticks on a floor, and so on. Even more concretely, a good old primary quality like a patch of blue, something which seems to be immediately perceived as itself plain and simple, is always also some nonblue things appearing *as* blue, which can thus also appear *as* these nonblue things: processes in the eye and nervous system, frequencies of molecular vibration, ink, paper, matter. This fact, that everything must always be appearing *as* something else, something not unequivocally itself, is equivalent to the Truth of Global Incoherence. The fact that there is always some coherence that is doing the appearing *as* these nonself things is the Truth of Local Coherence.

But the second thing to be noted, for all these examples, is the implication that, if this "necessarily always appearing as something else" really applies universally, to all elements, to all possible coherences and configurations, then *anything* can be a form in which this thing appears, it can appear *as* anything at all. Class struggle can be seen operating in feminism, in Christian charity, in ecologism, in fascism, even in apparently contradictory expressions like liberal egalitarianism or philanthropy; there is in principle nothing that cannot be interpreted as an expression of class struggle. Love can be expressed as kindness, as sternness, as indifference, as murder; hate too can be expressed as kindness, as sternness, as indifference, as murder. These two examples, dealing with complex abstract concepts like "class struggle" and "love" are relatively easy to comprehend. It is more difficult to see the same thing operating in the case of, say, triangularity or blueness. The manner in which this works will hopefully be clear after the discussion of the distinctive Tiantai notion of transformative recontextualization (*kaiquan xianshi*) above, but even on abstract or general grounds, it can be understood. Anything can reveal itself to be an expression of "triangularity," no matter how "non-triangular" it may appear to be at first. A trivial-sounding but I think ultimately quite important example would be demonstrated by drawing three nonunilinear circles on a blank sheet of paper; circularity being a strong case of "nontriangularity," which, by virtue of the whole to which it turns out to belong, reveals itself to be actually an expression of triangularity. I suspect that even more "nontriangular" things, such as "hope" or "the Roman Empire," could also be shown to reveal triangularity with just a little ingenuity. Blueness is perhaps an even tougher example; how can, say, redness turn out to be an "expression" of blueness, how can blue appear "as" red? Again, a little ingenuity can devise a solution in this particular case; we all know that colors perceived as homogenous to the naked eye at the macro level may turn out to be composed of a composition of many disparate colors at a micro level; imagine a spot of red, then pull the camera back to reveal a vast field of dots of the same size, which as a whole read to the eye as blue. This is just another example of recontextualization on holistic premises. We can even imagine, say, "whiteness" being expressed by "blackness": imagine a black arrow pointing to a black square, inside of which is whiteness. Here we have a different sort of relation, that of referentiality (i.e., the arrow, which necessarily points "to" something), rather than of composition, but the holistic point is the same. The point to be grasped here is simply that since X can never appear except as something else, X can appear as *anything* else. If it could only appear as a certain finite set of "something else's," this principle would no longer be universal; this complete set of expressions would simply be X itself appearing as it is, rather than X appearing as something else. This seeing of X in every other appearance is Intersubsumption (All-pervasion as All-pervadedness).

Here we have, in a nutshell, the Three Truths in their identity and their difference: That *some given X* always appears (as something else) is Local Coherence. That (some given X) *always* appears *as something else* is Global Incoherence. That (some given) *X always appears* (as something else) is Intersubsumption (All-pervasion as All-pervadedness).

The Transcendental Unity of Apperception and the Principle of Charity

In discussing Zhanran's account of classical Tiantai meditation in the Introduction, we offered an analysis which made use of Kant's notion of the transcendental unity (or synthesis) of apperception. We are now perhaps in a position to expand a bit on this connection, and bring out some of its implications. I mentioned Kant's adduction of the possibility of an "I think" or "I experience" which necessarily accompanies all representations. Without this one universal quality, which can apply to every act of awareness, nothing can appear at all; this possible connection with other representations is what allows all representations to be anything at all, to appear in experience at all. It must be presented as contrastable with, and in a stronger sense, already contrasted with, other representations; but these are on the surface level outside the present representation; Kant calls the agent which allows this contradictory interconnection of the necessarily absolutely distinct the "I." For us, of course, the substantiality of this relation is to be reversed: the I is merely an expedient which on analysis turns out to mean nothing but the "sense of contrastedness, already connectedness to, what is necessarily excluded, hence moretoitiveity, Intersubsumption, asness, and so on." Nonetheless, this relation is for that very reason reversible—I can be an aspect of moretoitivity just as well as moretoitivity can be an aspect of Iness. Hence the error of attributing Iness need not be repudiated, any more than, in Tiantai thought, any other error need be repudiated. On the contrary, it is another locally coherent Provisional Posit which can, if recontextualized, serve as a skillful means to reveal its own self-overcoming, and its being as Intersubsumption itself. Indeed, in traditional Tiantai, as in Kant, this delusory I is given a privileged place in practice—for it is indeed the fundamental error, the best one, the one from which all others grow and which can be attacked like the trunk of a tree to chop down all the rest simultaneously.

So every particularized object of experience, to the extent that it is appearing in experience, consists of and necessarily contains a synthesis of representations. Empirical consciousness is diverse, unrelated to the identity of the subject—there is relation to identity only insofar as I conjoin one representation to another. Only by uniting a "many" (others, differences) into one consciousness can I represent to myself the identity of consciousness; but correlatively and equally importantly, each of the contrasted terms appears as itself only on the condition of the possibility of being contrasted to some otherness, which is only possible if both are embraced in some overarching dimension, and thereby connected. Some term must be applicable to the entire field for there to be a field of differences per se at all.

For Zhanran this is not so much a transcendental I as a qualitatively distinct singular moment of experience, a "momentary" somethingness which has a definitive quality only to the extent that it is isolated from and contrasted with others, that it excludes them, that it is a "one" in the sense delineated above. The point here is that if there is anything, there must be a field of at least two differences, and if there are differences, there must be a term applicable to the entire field; but any term applicable to the entire field, since the content of a term is established only by being contrasted to some other term in the same field which is outside itself, is both everywhere and nowhere, for it turns out not to have any content or meaning at all, and also to mean, in this way, everything else: any "one" nature is *for that very reason* no nature. What must be stressed here is that this self-emptying is the result of the process of universalization itself, of this term's *success* in finding itself everywhere in the field: indeed, the all-pervasiveness *is* the emptiness here. In classical terms, to be ungraspable is to be unevadable. Unattainability is unrenouncability. And this allows "the three thousand to appear clearly just as they are"—meaning qua external, qua themselves, qua obstacles, qua denials of their subsumption into this "oneness." They become *more* manifest as this one subsuming universal term becomes more manifest, because its full manifestation, as applying everywhere in the field, is exactly its *crash* and self-emptying, its revelation that it has no content whatsoever.

This simultaneously increasing manifestation of the affirmation and the negation, and of their identity, is another very distinctive feature of classical Tiantai thought. It leads to the proposition that the *more* divided and differentiated things are, the *more* they are joined and unified, that the more isolated they are they more they are united. This can be seen also in the role played by the unity of "one experience," separated and isolated, in establishing that all entities are aspects of this one, that there is nothing outside it. This has profound ethical and pragmatic implications, in that it comes to be stated that *fully realizing* any entity—including suffering, desire and so on—is precisely *liberation from* that entity; in classical terms, as Zhili puts it, "the more one dwells in it, the more one is liberated from it." This is a result of the same thought: the more manifest it becomes, the more it is seen as a single distinct experience, isolated from all others, and hence totalizing the field and allowing contrasts within it, the more it self-undermines, and makes room for the more manifest appearance of all othernesses appearing here *as* it.

This consideration provides us with an unexpected link to a theme that has assumed considerable importance in recent analytic philosophy, namely, Donald Davidson's "principle of charity," which is often regarded as the very bedrock without which any intelligibility is unthinkable. As Davidson says, rejecting radical incommensurability, "Different points of view make sense, but only if there is a common co-ordinate system on which to plot them; yet the existence of a common system belies the claim of dramatic incomparability."[39] One of the upshots of this consideration is that "if we cannot find a way to interpret the utterances and other behaviours of a creature as revealing a set of beliefs largely consistent and true by our own standards, we have no reason to count that creature as rational, as having beliefs, or as saying anything."[40] In other words, we must presuppose a huge area of agreement to even raise the question of the agreement or disagreement of individual elements in the position of the other, for without this background of massive agreement, there is no coherence at all, nothing has been said, there is nothing to be judged as either agreeing or disagreeing with what we believe. "[D]isagreement and agreement alike are intelligible only a gainst a mackground of massive agreement."[41]

> the aim is not the absurd one of making disagreement and error disappear. The point is rather that widespread agreement is the only possible background against which disputes and mistakes can be interpreted. Making sense of the utterances

---

[39] Davidson, *Inquiries into Interpretation and Truth* (Oxford: Clarendon Press, 1984) 184.
[40] Ibid., 137.
[41] Ibid.

and behaviour of others, even their most aberrant behaviour, requires us to find a great deal of reason and truth in them. To see too much unreason on the part of others is simply to undermine our ability to understand what it is they are so unreasonable about.[42]

And again,

> The method is not designed to eliminate disagreement, nor can it; its purpose is to make meaningful disagreement possible, and this depends entirely on a foundation—*some* foundation—in agreement.... Since charity is not an option, but a condition of having a workable theory, it is meaningless to suggest that we might fall into massive error by endorsing it. Until we have successfully established a systematic correlation of sentences held true with sentences held true, there are no mistakes to make. Charity is forced on us; whether we like it or not, if we want to understand others, we must count them right in most matters.[43]

Davidson goes on to assert that this makes "massive error about the world ... simply unintelligible."[44]

We can, I think, easily detect the structural parallel between the principle of charity, applied in the area of language theory, commensurability, and translation, and Kant's transcendental unity of apperception on the one hand and Zhanran's "one nature is no nature" account of Tiantai meditation on the other. In each case we have the startling realization that contrast, differentiation, difference, disagreement—and therefore assertability, appearance, experience as such—is only possible against a background of unity, a field of correspondence and agreed-upon reference, against which the comparisons can be made. Without the "I" unifying experiences, for Kant, at least potentially, there can be no experiences to be compared. Without the background of massive agreement, for Davidson, there can be no assertability, reference, agreement, or disagreement, no meaning whatsoever. Without "this one moment of experience," or "mind," for Zhanran, there cannot be the differentiated array of mental and physical objects to be unified thereby and appear therein, or thereas. But the further Tiantai move is not made by either Kant or Davidson, and in both cases it restricts the implications of this insight in a way which we would like to correct here.

Tiantai's next move, translated into the terms of the principle of charity, would be to say, "First we have seen that both agreement and disagreement make sense only against a background of massive agreement; indeed, we can

---

[42] Ibid., 153.
[43] Ibid., 197.
[44] Ibid., 201.

say that both agreement and disagreement are aspects of this massive agreement, that his agreement expresses itself both as what we normally call agreement and what we normally call disagreement. But what has happened thereby is that we have changed the meaning of the term 'agreement.' Agreement is not only what appears as what we call agreement; it appears equally as disagreement. Unity expresses itself equally well as contrast and disunity. But in that case, why do we continue to call that background level 'agreement' only? Agreement and disagreement alike are terms derived from the foreground, in accordance with their supposed contrast and mutual exclusivity; but that contrast and mutual exclusivity has just collapsed, and cannot be applied to that which grounds both, to the background. It is what allows both agreement and disagreement to appear, indeed what appears *as* both agreement and disagreement. The claim so far has been somehow that agreement expresses it more directly, as in our 'all is water,' example above. But there as here, the explaining, all-extensive term changes its meaning in succeeding to pervade the entire field. 'Agreement' now means 'what can express itself as either so-called agreement or as so-called disagreement.' If an instance of first-order agreement turns out to be, in reality, this 'both agreement and disagreement,' the same will be true for an instance of first-order disagreement. 'Disagreement' thus equally means ' what can appear as both'; if we are going to use any first-order term at all, we are equally authorized to use 'disagreement' to characterize the background. In other words, both agreement and disagreement rest on their subsumption against a background of massive 'disagreement.'"

Hence Zhanran says, in effect, "since all is mind, all is neither mind nor matter, all is expressed as both mind and matter, all is nothing but mind and nothing but matter," and "since all is mind, mind is not mind, and all not-mind things appear all the more brilliantly as what they are." The equivalent here would be, "since all is expressive of agreement, all is expressive of neither agreement nor disagreement, all is expressed as a system necessarily including both agreements and disagreements, and all is nothing but agreement, and all is nothing but disagreement," and again, "since all agreements and disagreements are expressive of a massive agreement, agreement is not agreement, and all disagreements appear all the more brilliantly as what they are, that is, as real disagreements"— as disagreements which directly express the disagreement which is the massive background of all intelligibility. This is, of course, nowhere that Davidson or any other analytic philosopher wishes to go, but I do wish to suggest that it does the job he wants done, and then some. We have seen Davidson's concern to make sure his principle of charity is not construed as outlawing all disagreement, but rather as making it possible. We have done the same here. But we have also rooted out the one-sidedness that appears to continue to haunt Davidson about this discovery. We want to say not only that agreement and disagreement are always correlative, or two sides of a tertium quid (the now neutral background) but rather that to agree is to disagree and to disagree is to agree, and that all assertions and communications are always not only instances of both, but entirely reducible to *either*, in accordance with the above considerations. Agreement and disagreement lose their definite meanings, their one-sided mutual exclusivity; they become intersubsumptive, which does not mean they become meaningless or useless, or cease to function, but that they function more so as what they have always been. We have very different aims in mind, a very different image of life, if you like, than the one assumed by analytic philosophy as desirable. We are, if anything, inveterate enemies of the "common sense" to which they always explicitly or implicitly appeal when setting up standards of the "good life." And indeed, some of the implications of this bleed into the consideration of the typical analytic questions of intelligibility, reference, and commensurability; for us, commensurability just is incommensurability, and vice versa, and this is a good characterization of what it means to be a speaking being. For we know well enough what the principle of charity is really designed to do within its own original "local context"—as quoted above, to make radical error impossible, which is to say, to make most of what *we* think basically right, and to make it impossible for alternate viewpoints to differ in any radical, incommensurate way. This horrific (or to some, comforting) reactionary consequence, so dear to analytic philosophers who are concerned to make science and common sense reliable, and to exclude crazy alternate versions of the world, is for us nothing but a constraining bit of short-sightedness, with terrible human implication, and one which we feel we can now easily circumvent.

So we accept the consequence—"It is impossible to say anything intelligible which is not largely true"—for this means for us only that to be is to be Locally Coherent. But we need not share Davidson's other worries, since for us this *means* also that whatever can be said is largely false—Globally Incoherent. This frees us from the conclusion Davidson and others desire here, in other words, the certainty of our own common sense and scientific knowledge, but also from nihilistic skepticism. The complacent dogmatism of common sense falls by the very same blow that cuts down nihilistic irrealism. There just cannot be meanings at all if they are not very much true and also very much false. What they *are*, in other words, is the Intersubsumption of these two—and that alone, as we shall see in more detail in the next section, is precisely what is "referred to" by the word itself.

This has both epistemological and ethical implications. We will return to this question when we discuss the distinctive (Neo-)Tiantai notion of compassion, which underlies the possibility of all human activity in much the same way that Davidson's "charity" underlies the possibility of all intelligibility and meaning. But there as here, the implications of the typical Tiantai conversion free this from the one-sidedness of its initial formulation, and provide the possibility for a genuine ethics. There as here, we can equally name this all-embracing "compassion" universal conflict, à la Heraclitus, and we now have a way to understand how these two propositions are convertible.

Content and Category in Kant and Tiantai: A Priori Categories and Inherent Entailment

We can clarify the Neo-Tiantai position by a further comparison to Kant. To "be," we have tried to demonstrate above, always means to be definitively, to be determinate, to be finite, to have, to borrow a felicitous bit of Whiteheadese, simple location—which is to say, to have borders or boundaries. To appear in experience at all, X must be "non-all," must be contrasted to some non-X, must have an "outside." To be present is to be determinately, which is to "be-with" an outside. But to *necessarily* have an outside means the outside is not really outside. The relation between the internal and the external is itself internal. For if we really assume simple location as the mode of all existence, we can always ask of any border, Is it part of the inside or the outside? Does the outside come to an end before making contact with the outside or not? If there is a gap, what is the relationship between them? Does this "relationship" exist or not? If it exists, it must itself be "simply located," a determinate something with borders of its own, separating it from what is other than it. This means there must be another border between "the relationship" and the things of which it is the relationship. But then we have the same problem over again, an infinite regress, and the necessary relationship is lacking. If there is no gap between the boundary and the bounded, what makes this the boundary rather than the bounded? Does one end before the other begins? Is there another border between the boundary and the bounded? There is no coherent way to answer these questions, if "to exist" is assumed to mean "to be simply located."[45] Hence, the interface always proves unintelligible, and the

---

[45] This is of course a very abbreviated summary of Zhiyi's favorite method of meditative inquiry. This method, described in greatest detail in the *Mohezhiguan*, T46.63b–66c, considers a single moment of experience as putatively arising from itself, or from something other than itself. Each of these possibilities is refuted. If it arises from itself, no arising has actually occurred: it was already there before the event. It is arises from something other than itself—the organ of perception, the previous moment of experience, the contrasting absence of it against which it is experienced, the conjunction of a set of causes—we are asked why *this*

outside proves both ineradicable and paradoxically impossible, since it always proves to really be equally internal, and hence not an outside at all. Therefore, the inside, the X, is equally ineradicable and impossible (*bukede, bukeshe*).

But if this is so, a very startling conclusion ensues. For it turns out not only that being = determinacy-finitude = ambiguity = indeterminacy, but also that determination or "finitude" as such, in other words, the quality of being-bounded, of having borders, equals "being this shade of red" as such, but also equally "being the French Revolution" as such, and so on for any possible determinacy, for any coherence. That is, not only is the shade of red one example among many of being-bordered, so that it both has borders as such and also, in addition or more specifically, the particular borders that made it red rather than blue; but also, that to have borders, any borders, *is* to have just these borders. To be "locally coherent," in Tiantai terms, is, since it is identical to Emptiness and Centrality, also "to be provisionally posited as this shade of red, as this woman's toe, as the French Revolution, and as their mutual inclusion, as all Three Thousand Coherences." This is because the argument just advanced applies equally to the *particularity* of the borders or determiners themselves, as putative existences (which they must be to have any efficacy at all; that is, to experience these boundaries as particular is to experience their particularity, and this particularity is itself then a particular entity which must arise in tandem with othernesses, and there must be a border between "particularity" and "nonparticularity"). That is, take the borders that divide the inside of being-red from its outside, which define it as red. Do these exist or not? If not, they do not define red. If so, what are their defining borders? In other words, what separates "defining-as-red" from "defining as not-red" or "failing to define as red"? What is the borderline between "the determining as red" and "the failure to determine as red"? These borders too prove to be incoherent, and the borders defining any other thing, in contrast to which they were defined as just these borders, as just this act of determination and no other, turn out to be outside-as-inside this mode of determination in the same way. All the borders are equally ineluctable and impossible. Hence, if there is any defining border at all (and there must be, since being = presence =

"other," among all the things that are "not" the arisen event in question, is able to generate it. If we say that this particular "other" alone possessed the pre-existing "potential" for this event, we must again ask if this "potential" itself is the "same as" or "different from" the generated actual event, and so on ad infinitum, with the same result. Again, we are asked if it co-exists or not with the generated event. If so, neither precedes the other and no generator/generated relation can pertain to them. If not, it cannot be there to cause the event. What all this amounts to is a critique of the adequacy of the concepts "same," "different," "existence," and "nonexistence" to account for real events in the world, in this case a moment of experience—in other words, a critique of simple location.

determination = finitude), it must be none other than *this* border, this particular operation of limiting, this particular mode of determination. If there is any determinacy at all, it must be being-red, and being-red must be being-the-French Revolution, and so on. In other words, nothing is just "determinate-as-such." Being-determined must be further determined as being-determined-as-red, and so forth, at which level the same argument applies.

Concretely, this applies to each coherence, each moment of experience. Each has some qualitative coherence, which unifies its diverse parts. If it is a moment of anger, all the nonanger elements which arise together with it—the particular bodily feelings which are interpreted as "anger," the mental pictures of undesirable situations about which one is angry, the object of anger, the organ of anger, the narrative as part of which the anger appears, the context of values and facts which make this anger meaningful—are also to be noticed as necessary complements, othernesses which arise together with it. The interfaces between this anger and this nonanger are examined closely with the Three Truths, until we see them to be ungraspable and incapable of producing the determinate, unambiguous quality they had implicitly promised. The inside is the outside, the anger is globally incoherent, hence locally coherent, hence intersubsumptive, hence "anger" pervades, is discoverable in, all the nonanger coherences that appeared in tandem with it. This inference is made on the grounds that to be contrastable is to be relatable, and to be relatable requires the sharing of at least one characteristic: belonging to the same relation, or field of relations. Every experience is a "oneness" in this sense, i.e., in that the experienced is a single field of relations and contrasts, including precisely whatever it seems to define itself by excluding; for even this "excluding" is an internal relation intrinsic to this experience. The mind, in this specific sense, has to itself no outside as such; its outside, manifestly and not only logically, is immediately recognizable as also its inside. To know a limit is already to know beyond that limit. Otherwise the limit is not known as a limit. When this particular moment is known, and it is seen that all its elements dwell together as this particular moment without losing their difference (when it is seen as the unifying totalizer of these differences), the inference is made that these various elements must share the same nature. They could not all appear as aspects of anger unless they all had the same nature, or unchanging identifying characteristic: *namely, the nature of being able to appear as either anger or nonanger without changing in the least*. Their nature, in a word, is "nondwelling," i.e., ambiguity, multiple readability, determinateness-as-undecidability. This Nature is thus the Three Truths: the fact that being, being finite, being anger, being the determinateness of anger, being the ambiguity of anger, being the synonymousness of the determinateness and the ambiguity of anger, being the all-pervasion and eternity and necessity and universality of anger, and being the necessity and universality of all other determinacies, are all synonyms.

We must thus be careful to correctly understand what a writer like Zhili thus means when he says that all things dwell together as a single moment "because" they have the "same nature." This is not to be understood as "the Exclusive Center" (*danzhong zhi li*), a tertium quid that is neither "this" nor "not-this" but is the underlying reason manifesting as both, which is arguably what Fazang and the Huayan tradition mean by "principle" and what Whitehead means by "Eros" or "Creativity as such," which he sometimes identifies with the Spinoza's One Substance.[46] This is because, for Zhili, this "same nature" is "nondwelling," i.e., because the "dharma-nature" is precisely "ignorance," and hence this fundamental principle or nature cannot be construed as a positive determining power prior to what it determines. It functions not so much as a determining cause (which is impossible on the pan-Buddhist premise of dependent co-arising, which stipulates that no single cause can account for any existence), but as a condition of possibility, in the strict Kantian sense.

This is why Zhili makes a point of warning us, "We cannot one-sidedly cling to the maxim that 'each phenomenal function is possible only because it is inherently entailed as a principle' to claim that the true (enlightened) mind is the (sole) creator of dharmas. We must understand that the deluded conditional mind is itself precisely principle—it is principle as (phenomenal) functioning."[47] Principle, the Buddha-nature, Truth, Ultimate Reality, Original Enlightenment, the Nondwelling root are not to be construed as some

---

[46] Whitehead, *Science and the Modern World* (New York: Macmillan, 1925), 177: "Each individual activity is nothing but the mode in which the general activity is individualized by the imposed conditions. The envisagement which enters into the synthesis is also a character which conditions the synthesising activity. The general activity is not an entity in the sense in which occasions or eternal objects are entities. It is a general metaphysical character which underlies all occasions, in a particular mode for each occasion. There is nothing with which to compare it: it is Spinoza's one infinite substance. Its attributes are its character of individualization into a mutliplicity of modes, and the realm of eternal objects which are variously synthesized in these modes. Thus eternal possibility and modal differentiation into individual mutliplicity are the attributes of the one substance." Very clearly here, the general activity is "not an entity" like actual occasions and eternal objects; there is nothing with which to compare it. This is similar to the Huayan conception of Principle, which is not a dharma. In Tiantai, however, the symmetry goes all the way: even the Three Truths, Principle, are another dharma, which themselves interpenetrate just as all other dharmas interpenetrate. "Emptiness" is Empty, Provisional, and Central. Likewise "Provisional Positing," likewise "Centrality." Each is a "dharma" treated like any other. Principle itself has a non-dwelling root, and is not exempt from the categories applicable in all other cases. This is a very crucial point for understanding the distinctiveness of the Tiantai position.

[47] *Siming shiyishu*, T46.835b.

pre-existing (in)determinate ground which single-handedly creates or emanates to form all phenomenal existences, the literal "source of all things." Indeed, it would be more accurate to say that for Zhili *each* dharma-as-principle, not "principle as such," is a condition of all experience in the precise sense of a Kantian a priori category. Zhili says the "one nature" is not a "fixed single nature," which is equivalent to saying also that this "same nature" is not a "fixedly same nature." It is not definitively "the same." Rather, it is the nature in the sense of unchanging, but unchanging only in the sense of nondwelling, which is the only sense in which it can serve as a ground or "root." In fact, we can say it is a multitude of alternate "Ones" or different "Samenesses." That is, when one thing is determined as X, all other things are also Xish, no matter what X is. The universe is an infinity of *alternate* Onenesses. The Nondwelling "One" nature is that by virtue of which all things are readable as "of the same nature as" *whatever* X might be adduced. This is the "one same nature"—*not some particular characteristic that is "the same" in all cases, but the characteristic of "sameness" as such*. For all Three Thousand are in one sense "the same" in all cases, applying everywhere as categories, as we will discuss in more detail momentarily.

"Sameness" is one of the characteristics that is "the same" for all things, shared in all cases. "Difference," however, is another one. But Zhili here points to the shared characteristic of *"allowing all difference to be unified or read as the same one, no matter what that one is"* as "Principle" (i.e., the Three Truths, Local Coherence as Global Incoherence as Intersubsumption), because it is what allows us to come to see the undecidability, and hence the interpervasion, of all the other shared characteristics. In contemplation of the mind, we see that the phenomenal, determinate, simply located moment of mental experience unifies all other dharmas, that all dharmas converge here as this moment of experience and share its nature, in the border between this quality and the others which are internal-external to it can never be established. All dharmas have the nature of this moment of experience, which means they all have the characteristic of "being able to assimilate to and form a part of this determinate experience without ceasing to be what they are."

Matter is experienceable as mental, mind as material—in either case what is important is their undecidability. That is, they are experienced here *as* this moment but also as something distinct from this moment ("converging as this moment" and "not losing their own essences"). This is the "phenomenal totalizer," sameness on the level of phenomenal occasions. The deluded mind transforms into and creates all things: this means that as soon as my mind becomes X, it makes all things appear as aspects of X, converge as X, as X's inside-outside. This reveals something about both this experience and about all other things, as phenomenal occurrences. *It reveals that X is X in spite of being nothing but non-X. It also reveals that all non-Xs can be Xish without changing in the least, without ceasing to be non-Xish.* This reveals that *all* of them are Principle, i.e., the Three Truths, which is to say, determinate only as undecidable, which is to say, categories, determinacies which are nowhere and everywhere, as we shall see below. We may indeed say that all things are creations or aspects of some one particular—of mind, or of delusion, or of the Buddha-nature—but only to the extent that we are seeing this X as precisely also non-X, as subsuming all its internal-external conditions, i.e., seeing it as principle. Mind creates all dharmas because mind is not only mind, but rather mind-matter, mind/non-mind. Thus it can fulfill the "multiple conditions" stipulation of the doctrine of dependent co-arising. All things are produced by X because X can never be just X.

This is important because it clarifies for us that "inherent mutual entailment" or "eternity and omnipresence" is not "dwelling," but rather just the opposite. To say "X is inherently entailed in the nature (of any *other* dharma)" then just means, "Given that X has appeared in experience, it is impossible to conceive it as having come from any other determinacy, or from itself as a fixed determinacy. Its 'being X' transcends all determinable categories, it is neither eternal nor noneternal. It is an ineluctable *category* of existence which never appears *simpliciter,* but must appear integrated *somehow* into every possible appearance." The status of a dharma-as-principle is thus just like that of a Platonic Idea as understood by Whitehead, i.e., an eternal object. It is never a simply located datum, but is always and everywhere operative as variously ingressed. What should this "one-not-one" nondwelling nature than be named? Any name applies as well as any other: it can be called "creativity as such" or "Eros" or "the One Substance," but equally "this table," "the French Revolution," "determinacy as such," "Emptiness as such," "neither determinacy nor Emptiness as such," "both," "my shoe," and so on.

We may restate this by thinking a little about Kant's Transcendental Aesthetic and Transcendental Deduction, and the distinction between "categories" and "contents" in general. For each thing as principle is precisely each thing as universal and necessary, which is to say, as a Kantian category. Kant says, for example, that space, time, and causality are a priori categories applying to all sensory experience. This means they are conditions for sensory experience, that every particular sensory experience instantiates them in some way, but that space, time, and causality themselves, as such, are never present in sensory experience. One never experiences "causality" as such, as a simply located datum. On the other hand, "causality" is necessarily and universally discoverable in every sensory experience. Nothing could be experienced unless there existed this possibility of association with causality, time, space, and so on. They cannot be learned from experience, nor can they ever begin or end within experience, because they are conditions of experience. This is exactly what it means for a dharma to be Principle in Tiantai: it is nowhere and everywhere, and these are the same fact about it. The Mahāyāna scriptures often state that all dharmas are "like space." In the *Jingangpi*, Zhanran makes very clear how this metaphor is to be understood in the Tiantai sense: space has no inside or outside, is discoverable everywhere and nowhere, can neither be obtained nor relinquished, *is equally present as empty space and as the filled-in space which initially appears to be opposed to it, defining it by contrast.*[48] We may think here of the Cartesian notion of "extension," as reconceived by Kant as an a priori intuition conditioning all empirical experience. All things are like space in just this sense: they are a priori intuitions. So when we say, for example, that my shoe is Principle (Local Coherence as Global Incoherence as Intersubsumption), we mean that my shoe is an a priori Kantian intuition—or indeed *category*, for Kant's distinction between intuition and category, like Sartre's between percept and concept, no longer applies here. It is never discoverable as such or simpliciter: this is the denial of simple location, for what seems to be a phenomenal shoe is in fact the application of the category shoe to a bunch of nonshoe things, just as causality is "found," and necessarily always findable, in any phenomena which I choose to interpret "causally." Shoeness is found in the leather and laces, which I choose to interpret "shoe-ishly." It can also be found in other coherences, if I choose to interpret them shoe-ishly, as the inside-outside of the determination "shoeness." The Three Thousand as Principle, then, are all coherences seen as Three Thousand categories, which all coherences must instantiate in some way or another when we choose to analyze in terms of them, but which never appear *simpliciter*. All these categories are universal and necessary, applicable at all times and places, and discoverable equally in their putative opposites. They are conditions of experience.

They are also mutually subsumptive and reducible, so that in adducing any of them, one is adducing all of them. The thought here is similar to the Hegelian ambition to derive all the Kantian categories, and more, from one another, showing that each is implicit in each. Kant had adduced twelve categories, in

---

[48] T46.781b–782a.

[49] These are, of course: Quantity: Unity, Plurality, Totality; Quality: Reality, Negation, Limitation; Relation: Inherence/Subsistence, Causality/Dependence, Community; Modality: Possibility—Impossibility, Existence—Nonexistence, Necessity—Contingency. The last triad, of modality, presents special issues, in that here an either-or is operative; every experience is *either* possible or impossible, existent or nonexistent, necessary or contingent. This would seem to militate against the "all-pervasion" typical of the Tiantai case, but in fact, by the argument of the Three Truths outlined above, this exclusion is precisely the means by which they are seen to be all-pervasive.

four groups of three, all of which are a priori conditions applicable to all experience.[49] Hegel criticizes the merely empirical listing of these categories, and Kant's failure to produce an account of their deduction and mutual relation, although something of this kind is attempted in the Transcendental Deduction, elucidating the necessary relation between the twelve categories, time, space, and the synthetic unity of apperception, which is the "highest point" making possible all other transcendental categories. Hegel comes up with a much more extensive list of categories, all of which are to be conceived as necessary and universal, i.e., as discoverable in any and every experience, applicable in all cases.[50] But in Tiantai, every particular thing is such a category. On the level of principle, each thing-as-category is the unifying totality of all the other things as differentiated particular categories. That is, by simply saying "causality-as-universal-and-necessary" I am ultimately also saying "time, space, being, determinate being, identity, distinction, etc." as universal and necessary. To think "space," in other words, is to think "time, causality, etc." *as* space. When I experience space as a concrete content (to be discussed in a moment), I find it comprised of time and causality, as its inside-outside, that "time" and "causality" have this power to dwell together as the concept "space" without losing their own essences. In Tiantai terms, when I say "my shoe as universal and necessary, applying to all experiences but never present *simpliciter*" I am also implying all other universal and necessary categories, because of their "nondwelling root," because the Three Truths mean that the inside is the outside of each determinate category. In the Tiantai case, however, "all other universal and necessary categories" means all other possible coherences.

A synthetic a priori deduction is possible between these categories in the Kantian and Hegelian case, rooted in the transcendental unity of apperception. But in the Tiantai case, no such attempt is made; rather, the interpervasion of the categories is derived from their relation to each particular moment of experience. The difference from the German idealist position is most evident here, in that, in addition to being a condition for all experience, each category is also actually experienced as a simply located datum. That is, in the final analysis it is not true to say, à la Hume and Kant, that "causality" as such is never experienced. It is experienced when we think about the concept "causality." This is because, for Tiantai as for Buddhism generally, mental engagements of conceptual objects are another type of experience, not qual-

---

[50] For example, Being, Becoming, Nothing, Determinate Being, Being-for-itself, Quantity, Quantum, Degree, Measure, Essence, Identity, Distinction, Ground, Existence, Thing, Appearance, Content, Form, Relationship, Actuality, Possibility, Contingency, Necessity, Substantiality, Causality, Reciprocity, Concept, Judgment, Syllogism, Object, Mechanism, Chemism, Teleology, Idea, Life, Cognition, Willing, Absolute Idea.

itatively or ontologically different from sensual experience. The criterion of experience is simply that something becomes present, which is to say, is determinate, is finite, has borders, has a necessary outside. What makes some of these occurrences count as "categories" is that they come with a necessary sense of universal applicability and pre-existence, and are discoverable in their putative opposite, the contrast to which defined them. When the content "causality" was first discovered, when someone first directed his attention to this abstract concept, it included a necessary sense that it had pre-existed this discovery, that "causality" had been functioning also in all prior occasions, even those hitherto imagined to be noncausal.

The case is the same for space and time, and indeed all the Hegelian categories. It is impossible to think these concepts without simultaneously allowing that they have always been discoverable or operative in all prior experiences. It is impossible to imagine a beginning or end for them, because all beginnings and ends presuppose them. The same goes for Whitehead's eternal objects, as we shall see in Part Three. This is what makes them categories. It is generally held that the case is different for noncategorical occurrences, i.e., actual occurrences, "contents."

For example, Kant is careful to distinguish between the principle of the possibility of the categories, as derived through the Transcendental Deduction, and the mere "occasioning causes" (*Gelegenheitsursachen*) of these categories, in other words, the empirical experiences leading to the first application of them in their generality.[51] They are, he allows, not only the forms of all experienced contents, but, at specific times and places, also themselves contents. By allowing this complication, however, Kant admits a doubleness to the status of the categories, which is what opens up the possibility of the alternate interpretation offered here, as developed in the Tiantai tradition. Lightning strikes a tree, and then the tree catches on fire; I may interpret this sequence of events as involving a causal relation, as an instantiation of a universal and necessary category. Causality as such here is a category, which necessarily pre-exists and applies everywhere, but this particular following of one thing by another, or indeed the lightning and the fire themselves, are seen as the contents, the terms to which causality applies in this case, a specific instance of causality. This content is seen as having a definite beginning and end, not pre- and postexisting, not something that is instantiated in some way or another in all instances of anything, which conditions the appearing of experiences as such.

Tiantai, by virtue of the Three Truths argument, denies this difference between content and category. Each content turns out to be a category, each

---

[51] Immanuel Kant, *Critique of Pure Reason*, trans. J. M. D. Meiklejohn (London: Dent Everyman's Library, 1969), 86–87.

category a content. So causality, time, space, being, becoming, identity, difference, and so on are experienced whenever we use these words and think these thoughts. Similarly, my shoe is experienced—when I call it a shoe. In either case, the content is determined by a particular act of mental narrowing and abstraction. This is what is meant by "the creation and transformation of all Three Thousand by the deluded mind" (*wangxin bianzao sanqian*). The shoe is neither shoe nor nonshoe; it is made definitively shoe by my regarding it as such. Otherwise, it would not be experienced at all. The same is true of space, time and causality. When I turn my attention to them, abstracting accordingly, I am experiencing causality, and in no other way (i.e., nonabstractly) is *anything* experienceable at all. For if each determinacy is all determinacies, it is this abstract and arbitrary habitual limitation of implications which is responsible for determining this shoe as shoe, rather than as all contents at once.

All Three Thousand are simultaneously categories which are conditions for all experience, necessary and universal, discoverable in every experience but never appearing as such, *and*, particular, simply located, finite determinacies which are experienced whenever the partial, deluded mind turns its attention to them. There are not two realms, one of categories and one of contents. The categories are the contents, the contents are the categories. All the differentiated categories are unified as each category. All the differentiated contents are unified as each content. When a content unifies all other contents, *all* these contents are seen to also be categories. These two unifications are thus seen to be one and the same. This is realized, Zhili tells us, when we examine closely any given content appearing in experience. This content is the unifier of all other things both as contents and as categories. This moment of experience totalizes the Three Thousand as-principle and the Three Thousand as-phenomena, and these are thus seen to be one and the same. Every experience reveals a content to us. Close examination of this content reveals all other contents to be implicated in it. They are not findable separate from this content; they are inside-outside it. But for another content to be inside-outside this content is for that content to be a category applying to this content, i.e., discoverable in it, but appearing as the other content, just as the content "causality" appears as the content "X following Y," not as "causality" *simpliciter*. Once all contents are seen to be present here *as* this content, all contents are seen to be categories. Their presence in each other overcomes their simple location, but their determinacy as such is a function of their simple location, of their finitude. So to be a content is to be a category, and vice versa. This means each experience of any content is a revelation of:

1. this content;
2. this category;
3. all other contents;
4. all other categories;
5. the fact that this content is all other contents;
6. the fact that this content is all other categories;
7. that this category is all other contents;
8. that this category is all other categories; and
9. that to be a content is to be a category, and vice versa.

The unifying whole in the Tiantai perspective is just this moment of experience. It is simultaneously unifying the all coherences in three distinct senses. First it unifies them qua their conditionality and finitude, as historical facts, as shadowy future prospects, as unselected alternate paths, as contexts and components and antecedents—as contents. Second, it unifies these same coherences as each pervading all times and places, as eternal and omnipresent, as unevadable-unobtainable, as universal and necessary, as principle, as the nondwelling root which manifests itself in all forms and places without changing—as categories. Third, it unifies these two distinct senses of unity.

Here again a comparison to the Kantian position is useful. For Kant, all the categories are ultimately forms of unity derived from the transcendental unity of apperception, the mind's a priori unity. This above all is what makes all experience possible; the unity of the mind cannot be discovered in experience because it conditions all experience. Every experience must be connectable to the "I think." In fact, this means that all experiences must be distinguished from something else, which means they must be related to something else, which means this something else must be part of a single field allowing for the relationship. This single field of relations is the unity of apperception. From this Kant derives the transcendental ego as distinguished from the finite empirical ego—the ego as category as opposed to the ego as a particular content, occurring in a particular time and place, with particular characteristics. In Tiantai, again, this distinction is abolished, and with it the Kantian subjectivism. The unity is discovered in the contemplation of "consciousness-only," which Zhili emphasizes is the contemplation of mind as phenomenon, as content, not directly as principle or category (of categories), but as *revealing* that both mind and matter, and all other contents, are necessarily *also* categories. It means revealing that mind is indeed a category, but only one category among many, which however are all intersubsumptive and hence in a more complex sense all "the same" category. This means to see that whatever I am experiencing right now has no outside that is not also its inside, revealing that all of these initially outside contents are intrinsically both determinate and ambiguous, and that these are the same facts about it. This is easiest to see in the case of a mental experience, or of mind as such, since to know a border as a border is already to know beyond the border. But the Three Truths argument applies to any content as such, precisely to being-content as such, and the contemplation of phenomena could also be done concerning any particular bit of matter with the same result.

Let us take a random example. The waiter spills coffee on me, and I am angry. That is an actual occasion, simply located in time and space. There is my left shoe, also an actual occasion. This shoe dwells in my moment of anger, as this anger, in two distinct senses, which are finally seen to be one and the same without losing their distinction. This shoe as a particular fact, finite in time and space, located simply at the bottom of my leg, is integrated into this anger as an element of its arisal as a phenomenon. My anger relates to, and therefore, by the Three Truths, integrates, the feeling of foot in shoe, the fact that I can get up and walk out on it, the possibility of kicking the waiter with it, the anxiety that some coffee may spill on it and stain it—all these are elements of my anger, bearing internal relations to it, without which it could not be what it is, and the interface between these factors and the anger as such is Empty, indeterminable, upon examination. The same goes for my previous experience of not-being-angry, and the indifferent nonanger of my insentient shoe, and of all the bystanders, all of which are defining horizons of otherness which make my anger experienceable as such.

Because all dharmas share the same nature—the Three Truths—this phenomenal anger has the power to integrate and the shoe has the power to be integrated, such that they reveal their ultimate categoricality. That is, because both "anger" and "shoe" are categories, they are both determinate and ambiguous, and this is the same fact about them. They are present everywhere, instantiated as all others, like space, time, or causality. The shoe is the eternal and omnipresent ultimate truth that expresses itself everywhere in differing forms without losing its shoeness. This anger is "shoeness as anger," a "transformation body" of the shoe, which is eternal, has no inside or outside, expresses its determinacy in an infinite number of indeterminate ways, and vice versa. This anger is also "nonanger in general" *as* anger.

There is no need to appeal to a transcendental ego here, because the unity is expressed precisely in the phenomenality of the phenomena. Moreover, the conclusion is not Kant's conclusion, that since these are a priori categories they should not be taken as applying to the things-in-themselves, but only to our experience of them; rather, it is that each moment of experience is an instance of "the entire dharma-realm facing the entire dharma-realm, and the entire dharma-realm thereby arising"—that is, the totality of all existences in their mutual pervasion. It is true, as Kant holds, that I could not experience instances of causality unless my mind was constructed so as to already always be applying the category of causality. Tiantai adds also that it would be impossible to experience "shoeness" unless this category similarly pre-existed. The deluded mind "reads shoeness into" a bunch of nonshoe data, and it could not derive shoeness as such from experience; shoeness is inherent in the mind. The point, however, is not that therefore the "real" thing out there definitively *lacks* shoeness, or are unreachable by my consciousness. Rather, the point is that shoeness as category pre-exists both in/as my mind and in/as the object I regard as shoe, and in every other possible locus. All other categories and contents also pre-exist in each locus. Hence the subject and object are unified, in that both contain all the same contents and all the same categories. Thus is the absoluteness of the perception attained. It is no longer dependent on an other. It is thus not only impermanent, painful, non-self. It is also permanent, blissful, free, self—absolute value itself, because it is a content, and to be a content is to be a category, which means to be immortal, invulnerable, incapable of disappearing or of ever appearing *simpliciter*. As we shall see, it is pure omni-directional desire. Put another way, it is Value itself.

In sum, *that which unifies* is the momentary, conditioned, organ-object ignorant moment of consciousness, the deluded mind in a particular state, determining all its objects accordingly.

That by virtue of which it unifies is the Principle, its unchanging "Nature": The Three Truths, i.e., the Global Incoherence and Intersubsumption—of the particular Local Coherence we have been calling this moment of consciousness, in particular, the deluded, creating, conditioned mind, the unchanging which follows conditions, the condition-following which remains unchanged.

That which is unified is:

1. All coherences as contents, i.e., as created in practice, as conditioned by a particular sentient-being project—as transformations and creations, as simply located, contingent, and finite.

2. All coherences as categories, i.e., unconditioned, as inherently entailed, as pervading all times and places, as omnipresent and eternal because they never appear in experience as such.

3. These two levels of "all coherences," these two aspects; to be conditioned is to be unconditioned, to be here and now as part of this project, is to be everywhere, as part of all possible projects, and vice versa. A moment of experience "unifies" all three of these diversities, while maintaining the particular essence of all of them. That is to say, *"nec-*

essary universality as such" and "contingent finitude as such" also converge as this moment of experience. To be a content is to be a category, and vice versa. It is this last unification that is really the point of the first two.

For Tiantai, then, "principle" means inherence, categoricality. This means the inescapability, all-pervasion, unchangeableness of the thing, *and* its unattainability, undecidability, ambiguity, *and* the identity between these two (The Three Truths). This means both what unifies things (they are all everywhere, and have the same nature) *and* what differentiates things (this nature is inherently differentiated into the Three Thousand, none of which can be blurred out of existence, all of which are always present everywhere), and ensures that the unification and the differentiation are one and the same act.

This is opposed to contents, phenomena, which means transformations, creations, conditioned co-arisings. This refers to things qua or in their becoming, their conditionality, their contingency, as decentered and impermanent, as substanceless, as done by some partial agent, as created, as intended, as owned, as local-context determined, as simply located—not as differentiation or particularity as such, but as partiality; it means what appears as something which could also not be, and hence is bound up with attachment, delusion, desire, and suffering.

Principle is inherence, i.e., these same things qua their unchangingness, their readability as all others and vice versa, their ambiguity, their ineradicability, their inescapability/unattainability, hence their necessity, and their universality in the literal sense. This literal universal reverses into ineradicable division. This is all things seen under the category of categoricality, not unity or coherence per se. The identity of principle and event means here not only that the whole is the parts, and each part is the whole, i.e., each one is all others as it, but also that *their conditionality/becoming per se is their necessity per se.*

If we look at a particular coherence as a content, that is, as a phenomenal, simply located event, all things are unified as this event because they are what is being excluded from it, its necessary accompanying outside—they are part of its pragmatic concern, *umwelt*, background. That means also, they are present-with-it as its opponents, as what threatens it, as what it is avoiding, as what it is seeking, as negative prehensions, as vague horizons, as explicitly excluded. It is interested, attached, partial, and hence "takes a stance" on *all other entities.*

If we look at this same occasion as omnipresent and eternal, having thought through the implications of the necessary outside in terms of the Three Truths, this very event is thus readable as all other events and vice versa.

The identity of the two "totalities" thus means that taking an exclusionary or opposed stance on all the other X's, or being full of anxiety about their loss, attached to them, taking a stance toward them, *is the very mode* of their being readable as X and X being readable as them. To experience or confront X as an other is to be opposed to or attached to X, and *to be opposed to X or attached to X is to be readable as X*. And this means simply to *be* X—for even "X" is X merely to the extent that it is "readable as X."

This means the all-pervasiveness of their unity/order/value/ruliness, and also of their differentiation/disorder/particularity/valuelessness/unruliness, and of the second-order identity between these two. It always includes both this unity and this differentiation at any level one cares to focus on. It is what "makes" them unified, but it is not their unity, or even that in/as which they are unified. But it is also what "makes" them differentiated, but is not their difference. But precisely because it is "not" their unity or their difference, it is the identicalness of their unity and their difference. And this identity of unity and difference is really the "identity" of any coherence as such, its being in the sense of "who" it is.

In a sense, this is an overcoming of strict immanence on any level—principle never appears alone or as such. But this also means true immanence, in other words, no internal dualism, where it is one part against another, where principle and phenomenon are two parts of a greater whole, or even two determinately different aspects. It is not just "never alone" in that it is composed of phenomena as its members or parts, but rather in that the principle that unifies and differentiates always appears as some one simply located phenomenon which unifies all others, that is, some one determinate, contingent, ignorant, local-context-dependent coherence. We have a clear example of this "phenomenal unifier": the mind as ordinary cognition, which provides an example of unifying and differentiating all Three Thousand precisely in its contingent, changing, owned, partial ordinary function. My greed unifies the world around greed, as expressions of it, rivals to it, obstacles to it, challenges to it, contrasts to it; the impure mind as such pervades. But in so doing, it demonstrates that this can only be done because all these things revealed thereby to be functions of it have the same nature, what Zhili calls "the Three Thousand nature," i.e., of all possible coherences qua unfindable and yet ineradicable categories, hence it also unifies these coherences qua necessary, readable as its own nature, ineradicable, all-pervasive, and so on. The latter is these things as permanent, blissful, free, beautiful.

The point here is thus that contingency as such is necessity as such, not merely that the contingent is always also necessary. We may say, that it is the contingency, finiteness, partiality, greed-hatred-delusion that *accomplishes* the unification of all, the all-pervasiveness. This all-pervasiveness is necessity, value, and so forth. So the efficacy of unifying things goes to the phenomenality (content), finiteness, as such. But once this efficacy is seen in finiteness, this finiteness is seen *as* categoricality. So in this sense this efficacy is attributable to categoricality. The crucial point here is the Möbius strip function of this contemplation of categoricality and phenomenality. Contemplating phenomena *qua phenomena* ends up being the contemplation of categoricality. To contemplation of categoricality as categoricality ends up being the contemplation of phenomena. To dwell in is to be free from it, and vice versa, as Zhili says elsewhere. So at every level they do break apart again, and the accomplishment of interpervasion goes to the "principle" side, or equals this going to the principle side. For Principle is categoricality is Intersubsumption, which simply means "the fact that this Möbius strip structure necessarily always applies."

"Natural Law" as Global Incoherence

The position we are developing here is obviously not meant to deny the observed coherences in the world, i.e., the regularities and continuities described either as contents or as categories, as "things" or as "principles" or for that matter as "laws of physics." (For indeed, as we have just endeavored to show, the distinction between "thing" and "law" is only one of scope, not an ontological divide: as our mention of the Buddhist usage of the term "dharma" in the Introduction suggested, both "things" and "laws" are coherences applying to a certain span of space and time, insistent realities which are to be discovered in our experience.) We claim rather that all the particular coherences we see and hear and feel around us, and all the predictable patterns that can be found in them, have an absolute realness and ineradicability described in classical Tiantai as "inherent entailment." This applies not only to patterns and laws but also to the identifiable properties of things, which can be regularly found in them and cannot be thought away—the redness of the tomato, the hardness of the rock, the "selfliness" of myself, the sadness of my mourning, and so on. But entailed in this claim is the further assertion, not merely that this lawfulness or regularity "emerges" from ambiguity or chaos or incoherence, but rather that it always remains completely identical with ambiguity, with Global Incoherence, through and through, and that indeed its determinacy and regularity is nothing other than this Global Incoherence itself. That is, the particular properties, characters, patterns, and laws are not some kind of constraint of or positive addition to Global Incoherence or ambiguity—they are simply Global Incoherence as such, whole and entire, in every single case, in spite of the fact that they are particular, identifiable, reliable, differentiated, and determinate.

To clarify this perhaps still puzzling position, I would like to borrow and expand upon an example put forth by Erwin Schrödinger in his discussion of the statistical nature of physical law. Schrödinger adduces the commonplace and seemingly unexciting phenomenon of ordinary diffusion, often used by physicists to illustrate the basic principle of entropy, to make his point. If we place a colored fluid nonuniformly within a vessel filled with water—say, bunched up initially all at the left side of the vessel—we know what to expect: the colored fluid diffuses toward the right side, until finally it is evenly distributed throughout the water. This is a regularity or a property of these molecules which might seem to be a positive law or principle restricting their behavior; it is certainly repeatable, quantifiable, predictable, and independently confirmable. What is the law that "governs" this predictable activity? A very naïve observer might suggest that it was in the nature of colored fluids to move from left to right, that there was a law of nature that determined them to do so. Fortunately, further experiments would show that this was too narrow a conception of the operative law, the real driving force that determined this phenomenon; for when the colored fluid starts on the right side, it presses reliably leftward; when it starts on top, it presses downward; when it is beneath, it presses up. We have here already an example of what is meant by a "nondwelling root," as discussed in the previous section—as a "principle" used to explain some subsumed instances, an ambiguity is located; it turns out that "the tendency to drift leftward" and the opposite "tendency to drift rightward" were here expressions of one and the same law, which "dwelt" neither in leftwardness nor in rightwardness, but served as the "root" of both.

But we perhaps feel we have finally arrived at the operative "dwelling point" at this point: after much experiment, we conclude that the fluid *always* moves from the more densely toward the less densely populated regions. That is, it is the law of such fluids to move away from the places where its molecules are more densely packed toward the "elbowroom" of the more sparsely packed areas. This would seem to apply in all cases. We might imagine that the molecules of this substance are thus under the sway of a force which drives them away from each other, or toward open spaces, a pressure or exploratory nature that pushes them in the direction of the sparser areas. However, as Schrödinger points out, if we examine the individual molecules of the substance, we find that this is not at all the case. In fact, each molecule's motion is entirely *random*. It has just as much chance of moving toward the denser as toward the sparser regions. It might be thought that this simply means that "the whole is greater than the sum of the parts," and that being a part of a group changes their nature. But in fact each behaves exactly as it would have if it were alone in the water. A single molecule in the extreme reaches of the most sparsely populated region will zoom toward the denser region with the same likelihood as the crowded molecules push toward expansion. The molecules scarcely affect each other.

> Every one of them behaves quite independently of all the others, which it very seldom meets. Every one of them, whether in a crowded region or in an empty one, suffers the same fate of being continually knocked about by the impacts of the water molecules and thereby gradually moving on in an unpredictable direction—sometimes toward the higher, sometimes toward the lower, concentrations, sometimes obliquely. The kind of motion it performs has often been compared with that of a blindfolded person on a large surface imbued with a certain desire for 'walking', but without any preference for any particular direction, and so changing his line continuously.[52]

What then accounts for the determinacy of the law governing the motion of these molecules on the "macro" level? Why, if they remain random, do they move always in so regular, predictable, even quantifiable a way? Their determinacy, lawfulness and direction is not something other than their randomness; *it is their randomness itself.* Schrödinger explains the very simple mechanism involved:

> If... thin slices are made [vertically through the vessel] of approximately constant concentration, the ... molecules [of the colored fluid] which in a given moment are contained in a particular slice will, by their random walk, it is true, be carried with equal probability to the right or to the left. But precisely in consequence of this, a plane separating two neighbouring slices will be crossed by more molecules coming from the left than in the opposite direction, simply because to the left there are more molecules engaged in random walk than there are to the right. And as long as that is so the balance will show up as a regular flow from left to right, until a uniform distribution is reached.[53]

This example is, I think, clear, simple, and quotidian enough for all readers to grasp both intellectually and intuitively. But the actual implications are quite astonishing. Whether the fluid is flowing from left to right, or right to left, or upward, or downward, or even standing still in a uniform distribution, *it is doing exactly the same thing.* Flowing left is flowing right is flowing upward is flowing downward is standing still, *because all of these are simply random, aimless, directionless motion.* This applies to each and every molecule in the group in all cases. The behavior of each and every molecule

---

[52] Erwin Schrödinger, *What Is Life: The Physical Aspects of the Living Cell* (Cambridge, England: Cambridge University Press, 1967), 15.
[53] Ibid.

is just the same whether we are talking about a mass flowing upward, downward, leftward, rightward or not at all. Indeed, we can say that every molecule of a leftward drifting fluid is always drifting rightward (since "drifting rightward" is actually in itself none other than moving randomly), and is always standing still, and is always drifting up and down and in all directions. Note also that the lawful, predictable, particular direction of the drift in any case is not a separate fact, constraining this randomness which always applies to every single molecule, particularizing this universal lack of direction, or positively added to or derived from it, such that this very same randomness can "manifest" as these definite, predictable, quantifiable laws and properties; rather, these properties are just this randomness itself. The same can be seen of the "law" of Natural Selection, which in perhaps an even more obvious and striking way is not any positive law but rather precisely the absence of any positive law. Nonetheless, it can function in a determinate, predictable, even quantifiable way.

There seems to be only one positive property of the molecules; they are, in Schrödinger's picturesque expression, "imbued with a certain desire for walking." But this too is not the addition of some positive quality or the possession of some determinate property or character, but precisely the lack of one. Here we have what we described in the Introduction as "the nondwelling root," "creation in terms of Principle as inherent entailment," ambiguity as temporality, a kind of restlessness and lack of any containable single determinate character, the inability to stay in one place or continue in any one direction, the susceptibility to any and every influence, to be readable in only one way—in short, the inability to be fully determinate to the exclusion of ambiguity. In Part Two we will be talking about human character in terms of the idea of "Pure Desire," that is, desire without any particular goal or object, but which is nonetheless desire, that is, a constant inability not to change. This is also what we call here Global Ambiguity. As we have argued extensively above, Global Ambiguity does not exclude local coherence, rather it is itself (every) local coherence. We have here a very striking example. Random restlessness does not exclude determinate lawfulness, it is precisely determinate lawfulness—indeed, it is precisely *every* such particular lawfulness, however opposed (upward, downward, etc.).

Again, this applies not only to regularities in the sense of "laws" "regulating" natural processes, but also "properties" inhering in "things," and "characters" and "identities" of objects—and persons. To drift leftward is to drift rightward is to stand still is to move randomly. To expand the implications of this metaphor, we need only replace the quality of "drifting in a particular direction" with "having a particular coherence, identity, quality." The molecules move in no particular direction, and in a certain very real sense can be said to move in all directions at once at any given time. Similarly, every coherence, every element of any coherence, is constantly devoid of any determinate quality and also, in a very real sense, possessed of every possible identity at once. To be Brook is to be a pool table is to be Hitler is to be a cup of coffee is to be life is to be death is to be ambiguity as such. I may think that I am alive as me because the particular constituents making up my body and brain are determined to behave in particular ways, thus functioning smoothly and producing this activity—being alive as Brook—rather than others. The constituents in my liver, I assume, behave in some way differently from non-liver things, which is why they can perform my necessary liver functions. Similarly, the constituents and processes in my brain have some properties or others which I assume distinguish them from other brains, from nonbrains, from nonliving matter and so on, which is what I believe makes them function as brain while these other constituents and processes do not. But on the view we are developing here, these differentiated functions are also one and the same random function. In fact, the dead matter is doing exactly what the living matter is doing; the brain is doing exactly what that rock is doing; just as the leftward drift was doing precisely what the rightward drift was doing. And precisely by doing so, the brain is brainlike and the rock is rocklike, just as precisely by doing so the leftward was leftward and not rightward, and the rightward was rightward and not leftward. They are all simply moving randomly, so to speak, directionlessly and goallessly desiring, the nondwelling root—they are being ambiguity. Their determinacy and mutual opposition is not something other than this indeterminacy, nor is it derived from it; the determinacy is the indeterminacy is all other determinacies.

We will develop further implications of this idea of "Pure Desire" in Part Two. Here I merely want to point out that "Global" Incoherence applies with respect to *any* change of scale, for in a way, this example could be seen as one of "Global Coherence as Local Incoherence"—the larger whole is coherent while its parts are not. My point is that for us these are the same problem. Global Incoherence simply means that it is impossible for them to be coherent in the same way in every context and on every scale. The independence of the elements in any putative "whole" is also to be noted here; as we have already suggested, omnicentrism is in one sense the most thoroughgoing possible holism, but in another, or for that very reason, a strict antiholism, the overcoming of foundational or unicentric holism. The fact that the "smallest" level here is one of pure incoherence is convenient for our example, and might suggest a synordinate cosmology largely parallel to the asynordinate view we are developing here, a foundational claim that all things are "really" pure chaos or flux or goalless Schopenhauerian "will." Nonetheless it is important that these two positions be distinguished. We do not claim that this "randomness" is the basic underlying principle or source or stuff of the world. Indeed, our whole argument here is that, just as "leftward" is in this example another word for "rightward," and both are alternate names for "randomness," we need not assert any priority between these terms. That is, we do not have to "reduce" leftwardness and rightwardness to their "true" nature, randomness—that would be the "tertium quid" of the Exclusive Center. Rather, leftwardness just *is* randomness; all molecules can be said to travel leftward, leftwardness can be used as the term to describe the basic nature of all other types of motion and stillness, to which they all reduce. Once we realize that "leftwardness" really means only "randomness," either term will do as the name for what is "really" going on when the other is appearing. Randomness appears as lefwardness, leftwardness appears as randomness. This is why it is important to stress that we do not have a relation of "derivation" here in any sense, but of strict identity or asness. Brainness, livingness, deadness, Brookness, and leftwardness are inherently entailed, and moreover inherently entail all other coherences. Each functions as the grounding ambiguity, because each is, from beginning to end, from top to bottom, nothing but this random ambiguity itself. To be sad would be just like this. To be happy would be just like this. In either case, it would be to be ambiguity itself—no other ambiguity need be sought outside "being sad" or "being happy" itself, just as no other randomness need be sought outside leftwardness or rightwardness.

This example does not constitute a proof, of course, least of all a proof that the same claim can be made of all cases of natural law; it is rather put forward here as a way to make the concrete content of the claim we are making imaginable and plausible. Indeed, Schrödinger himself raises this point as part of an elaborate argument to show that, while all the laws of physics may be statistical aspects of randomness in this sense (rejecting Max Planck's suggestion that that there are both "dynamical" and "statistical" laws in physics), he does think that the regularities displayed by organic life processes cannot be explained in the same way, but do require a principle of "order deriving from order" (like Planck's "dynamical laws"), as opposed to the "order deriving [sic] from disorder" seen in the rest of nature. This is not the place to take up this argument in the literal sense, not wanting at this point to enter into any disputes of a speculative nature about the literal "foundations" of the known world, since we believe the notion of foundations is itself only provisionally legitimate here. Certainly, there are important questions we can raise on the basis of our premises about the customary definition of "order" in physics, and with it the problem of entropy as currently understood. This I will do in a less formal way in the first section of Part Three, entitled "Why There's Anything." And indeed, we do wish to claim that randomness and incoherence is the essence of all possible coherences, on the grounds argued above. But it may seem that we are abusing the flexibility of language or surreptitiously jumping levels in an illegitimate way when we claim that, for example, leftwardness is rightwardness on the grounds that the meaning of leftwardness changes when it is seen to be constitutively random and multidirectional. This is the question I would like to address at this juncture.

Sense, Reference, and Private Language

A possible objection to our procedure here could be framed in terms of Frege's distinction between sense and reference (or "meaning"; *Sinn* and *Bedeutung*). For it could be urged by some that when we speak of "meaning change," we really mean just, as it were, "sense change," and that genuine meaning change is, precisely by virtue of the principle of charity, really unintelligible. If the reference or meaning is not understood in some consistent way between speakers, there is no way to say anything at all about "that," and thus no way to change its meaning through its use. This is related also to the "private language" argument accepted as axiomatic by many post-Wittgensteinians. In other words, the argument might go, the range of application of a term is one thing, while the criterion that determines where it is applicable is something else. To adopt Hilary Putnam's critique of Nelson Goodman, it might be said that there is in this a crucial difference between a proper noun and a common noun; the former "has an extension that can be fixed by giving a list." (In Putnam's example, the Big Dipper, the extension of which is fixed by linguistic convention, applying to a finite group of starts; "one learns which stars are in the group and how they are arranged when one learns the meaning of the term."[54] Putnam is subtle enough not to consider this relation exactly analytic, for the list can conceivably sustain change without necessarily altering this linguistic practice—John is still called John after he loses his hair—but he is right that this does not undermine his basic claim here.) The same is not true of a common noun like "star"—"no particular object is in the extension of 'star' simply by virtue of being *called* a star [as in the case of proper nouns like the Big Dipper]."[55] The difference is made clear by Putnam as follows:

> It might be crazy to doubt that Sirius is really a star, but someone who thought that Sirius is really a giant light bulb . . . wouldn't thereby show an inability to use 'star' in the way in which someone who doubted that that constellation is

---

[54] Hilary Putnam, *Renewing Philosophy* (Cambridge: Harvard University Press), 113.
[55] Ibid., 114.

really the Big Dipper would show an inability to use 'Big Dipper'. . . . The fact that the concept *star* has conventional elements doesn't meant that *we* make it the case that that concept applies to any particular thing, in the way in which we made it the case that the concept 'Big Dipper' applies to a particular group of stars.[56]

Although Putnam does not explicitly make this connection here, this is in fact a skillful application of Frege's distinction of sense and reference. In Frege's classic example (also, oddly, drawn from the realm of astronomy), "the morning star" and "the evening star" are two ways of referring to one and the same object, namely, the planet Venus. The two can be said to be equivalent because they share the same meaning, that is, refer to the same object. "Morning star" and "evening star" are what Frege means by sense, the actual object Venus by meaning or reference. Frege himself, while rejecting out of hand the possibility that *all* terms could perhaps have only a sense but no real meaning (i.e., that only an idea and not an "actual object" is meant when these terms are used, a proposition he regards as "skeptical" or "Idealist"), he had already allowed for the *possibility* of some intelligible terms with *only* a sense, terms that have a clear and comprehensible sense but do not have any agreed-upon reference (in particular, cultural products); but Carnap and others, adopting this distinction, have tended to consign such possibilities to the realm of meaninglessness, so that "to be intelligible" and "to refer to something" have tended to become synonymous, and analytic philosophy in general seems on the whole to have moved in the same direction. Now when we say, for example, that the term "water" or "mind" or "me" changes its meaning when it comes to be applied to a larger and larger field of instantiations, it could be argued that we are erroneously treating a common noun like a proper noun. Water is not a term whose significance is determined by giving a list of the objects to which it refers. We may change the "sense" by expanding the range of application, seeing the various implications and instantiations to which water is subject, but we can in no way change the reference or meaning of the term without entering into an unintelligible private language, and thereby subverting any linguistic effectiveness whatsoever. For the meaning in this case is of "whatever really turns out to accord with the definition, for instance, of being a fluidic substance with the chemical composition H_2O." The meaning is *not* "whatever we choose to use the term 'water' to designate in any given instance," although this may be the sense, i.e., a way of delineating an aspect of that object, or to say something *about* that object. Only in the case of a proper noun do reference and sense coincide.

---

[56] Ibid.

Our response to this is, of course, that this whole distinction presupposes a metaphysical commitment which we have found reason to challenge. This is the assumption of a self-same object (under any conceivable definition of sameness which is exclusive of otherness) that persists between instances of reference, which can be referred to *twice*. This is precisely why the previous reflections on the principle of charity, and by extension, the private language argument, are so important here, for both of these doctrines argue that without "selfsameness" of reference in some sense, all intelligibility and communication, indeed any appearing of any meaning whatsoever, is impossible. But we have here developed an alternate perspective that we think can adequately overturn these objections. For if *no* coherence can ever under any circumstances appear *simpliciter*, if Local Coherence just *is* Global Incoherence, then we can no longer imagine any selfsameness which excludes otherness; a coherence is self-same to exactly the extent that it is other to itself. If sense is a necessarily partial way of picking out a particular object, that object itself being the reference or meaning, we here see a collapsing of the two. Indeed, the distinction between them, considered a hard and fast absolute fact (rather than a merely Locally Coherent one, as we would deem it), rests on an unintelligible analytic/synthetic distinction which most of its adherents would reject, as well as on an absolute disjunction between the abstract and the concrete which is hard to maintain without some sort of surreptitious Platonism. But the collapsing of the two is not to be understood as an undifferentiated subsumption of the two into a blank tertium quid that is neither, but rather in the Tiantai manner we have established. For the question is not, "Are there any senses without meaning," but rather, "are there any meanings or referrings without at least one particular sense?" To this we answer a resounding no. Above and beyond "X in the sense of Y" and so on, there is no other X *simpliciter*. But this is for us no longer either a skeptical or an Idealist proposition. Frege is quite right that no intelligible account is possible without taking into our notice the "something more" than the various "senses" that is always meant when we refer to something, which goes beyond the various senses, aspects of ways of indicating the object. But this something more is for us not the object *simpliciter*, but the moretoitivity of *each* sense, of each aspect or asness itself. In a word, it is the Intersubsumption pertaining to any given aspect or sense, the Intersubsumption *of* that sense, but which we have seen *is* the very being of that sense or aspect. The Intersubsumption of the various aspects or senses is the being of each of them, and plays the role which the chimera of the object *simpliciter* to which we are referring was supposed to play; it connects the senses, it unifies them, it allows them to bleed into one another and reverse and explain and correlate with one another. But this is done not through the agency of some phantom tertium quid above and beyond all the senses, but from within any given sense itself, as the Intersubsumption of every other sense, every other aspect, which is accomplished by that very sense or aspect itself. What is referred to is always this Local Coherence (sense) qua Global Inocoherence (other senses) qua their Intersubsumption (reference, meaning).

Once the phantom object *simpliciter* is "opened up" to reveal it to be a limited view of Intersubsumption itself, we may resolve the difficulties we just raised. First, we notice that the distinction between proper nouns and common nouns is dispelled. Proper nouns, we may say, are also *universals*. Contrary to Putnam's assertion, they do not name a unique list of particulars; like any universal, they are a synthesis of an *indefinite* plurality of coherences. The correct use of any proper noun, just like a common noun, involves an indefinite number of distinct acts of adjudication, of application, of identification, or of subsumption. This must be done again and again, any time a potential category for identification is presented; is this still John or not? Does this fit the criterion or not? No finite number of such identificatory procedures, as temporal acts, can constitute the identity of this object, or even the correctness of any particular application of the term, once and for all. This is immediately obvious if we recall the rewriting of the one/many relation (and with it the same/different relation) that is entailed in our account of coherences. Oneness *simpliciter* is as unthinkable as manyness *simpliciter*, likewise sameness and otherness. The only kind of "sameness" that ever appears anywhere is the Intersubsumptive kind pertaining to a so-called universal—but on our account, not superimposed by the universal from above onto the particulars, but as the very Intersubsumption which is the very being of the particulars precisely qua particulars. This is obvious if we restore the temporality to experience, in accordance with the fundamental Buddhist move; the name "John" names an indefinite and inexhaustible set of experiences, which cannot all be known and enumerated in advance; the identity between them is much closer, in an analytic register, to a kind of primal baptism of a locally coherent kind, and a historical connection *which is equally only locally coherent*, in partial accordance with Kripke's antidescriptivist account. "John" is a link between all these separable moments of experience, of which there can never be a complete finite list. The same goes for the Big Dipper: this name is a synthesis of zillions of individual experiences, and the promise of more to come. It does not name a finite list of elements. Put another way, even leaving the temporal experiential aspect out of account, we may say that the aspects and coherences constitutive of this item named with a proper noun are never exhaustible; if it is in any sense a "real" thing, there is always more to be discovered about it. We have taken this point up in accordance with the Sartrean distinction among imagination, conceptualization, and perception above. The distinction between proper nouns and common nouns rests not only on a detemporalization, but also a de-as-ification, of experience; the coherences *as* which this named item referred to here can appear without losing its identity can never be definitively delineated. Its senses are literally limitless—indeed, if the thing itself is the Intersubsumption pertaining to any of the senses or aspects, what allows them to convert into and reduce into one another, we will have to say again that in fact every other coherence is an aspect of this coherence here, that any other way of describing anything will eventually, with enough ingenuity, be found to describe a "sense" of this one here. This will become clearer when we discuss the role we assign to metaphoricity below.

This being the case, we no longer have a problem with our meaning-change hypothesis: it is not that we have been surreptitiously treating common nouns as if they were proper nouns, whose meaning was defined by a finite sphere of reference. On the contrary, we hold that even proper nouns are actually in the same boat as common nouns, not the other way around. But our account of the referentiality of common nouns is not that of correspondence between a definition or a sphere of usage and an object found to have the appropriate properties. It is not the case that words fail to refer if their references, as opposed to their senses, keep changing. In fact, we will claim instead just the opposite: words have meaning *only by changing meaning*. Words signify only by changing their signification. Words refer only by altering their range of reference. Words apply by applying otherwise. To have meaning is to change meanings. What we mean by this is simply that every instance of signification is necessarily a joining of a pre-existing set of instances with a new instance, of a tentative range of meaning with a new exemplification of that meaning. If there is no new instantiation to be judged to belonged to the series, according to any Locally Coherent standard, nothing is referred to. If there is not some pre-existing series, tentatively but constitutively groping to mark out its range, to be applied to this new questionable instantiation, there is also no signification and no referring. The referring is what happens when some Locally Coherent perspective decides to join some such series to a new instance, to recontextualize the instance into the series and simultaneously, therefore, to recontextualize the series by means of this new instance. Meaning is always, consitutively, meaning change. But change is not for us the exclusion of continuity or sameness; quite the contrary, they have been shown to be identical.

We can easily see how the same consideration impacts on the question of private language. For there again, the objection is based on a mistaken notion of sameness and difference. The idea was that a language is inherently a conventional system that pre-exists any individual speaker, which always presuppose an other who also knows the legitimate usages of the word within a given language game, to whom one can address them or from whom one has learned what moves are lawful in this particular language game. Rightness and wrongness in a language game are internal to that game, and are not invented by any individual or subject to any individual's will. Hence I cannot just decide to change the meaning of the word in the language I speak, and make it mean what I say it means; meaning always presupposes an other who shares my meanings, who can verify the accuracy of my usage; otherwise, I have failed to say anything at all, signification has not taken place. But here again, the problem is the detemporalized and de-as-ified definition of "private," i.e., the metaphysical assumption that defines a particular as an "individual," i.e., as a true "one." For every supposedly private language, even if one day in the shower you decided that "bBlms" would henceforth mean "asparagus," would already be a language shared by many "others" who agree to some continuity of meanings—these "others" are other *moments*, other *coherences*, of "your own" prospective experience, standing in an explicitly intersubsumptive relationship with this one. These usages are promissory notes to one's future selves. Without this, the "decision," even the "utterance" of your new definition would not be possible. Wittgenstein compares the proposition "Sensations are private" to the proposition "One plays patience by oneself" (248).[57] Patience is a game of solitaire, and Wittgenstein's point here is simply that to say "by oneself" adds nothing to "one plays patience"; in the same way, "sensations are private" adds nothing to "there are sensations" (cf. 306). The point here cannot be that an inherently intersubjective two-person game, like chess, can never be played by a "single" person; for it is not at all senseless to imagine playing a game of chess with oneself, in fact it happens all the time: it depends on there being *more* going on in any move than once can see at any given time, which is there to be discovered in its manifold implications when one goes across the table to see it from the other perspective, as the opponent. This is again dependent on how we conceive the self-identity of what is "contained" in a so-called "single" move or position. On our view, it is never finitely containable, but is Locally Coherent precisely as Globally Incoherent. A more pertinent case would perhaps be *inventing a game* which one played by oneself, complete with its own set of rules known only to oneself. But this is no more intrinsically absurd than the previous case; again, it merely depends on defining the rules to oneself and being committed to adhering to them in *future* instances. Wittgenstein proposes that we imagine someone keeping a journal where he made a particular mark, E, every

---

[57] The references here are to the section numbers in Wittgenstein's discussion of pain and private language in *Philosophical Investigations*, trans. G.E.M. Anscombe (Oxford: Basil Blackwell, 1953).

time a particular sensation occurred in him. He asks how we could ever know if the term was used correctly, if the diarist had correctly identified "the same" sensation on subsequent occasions. One must remember the connection between the sign and the sensation *correctly* on future occasions, "but in the present case we have no criterion of correctness. One would like to say: whatever is going to seem right to me is right. And that only means here we can't talk about 'right'" (258). We heartily agree with this conclusion, in a sense: but we hold that no use of a linguistic convention is ever any better off. In the sense proposed here, we never have a hard-and-fast criterion of correctness, and can never talk about 'right' in the sense Wittgenstein wants to presuppose here. For in every case all the rightness we're going to get is what seems right—Local Coherence as rightness, which *is* Global Incoherence of rightness. For when I say "whatever seems right to me on future occasions of identification is what will count as right," I mean that on those occasions I will have to judge whether a continuity can be read between what I recall at the moment, "rightly" or otherwise, of what was happening to me when I made the sign the first time, and what is happening now; this judgment will be entirely a function of my present decision to search for a precedent for the present sensation. But this is always the case. Wittgenstein thinks it would be senseless for someone to say, "I do not know if what I have got is a pain or something else"—in that case, we would simply think that he does not know what the English word "pain" means, he would not have used it correctly, and hence would have said nothing in this particular language game (288). But this is not necessarily senseless. Consider the case of love, and the common pop song lyric, "I thought I'd been in love before, but. . . ." What does "love" mean here? Let us suppose I am going back over my journal in which I noted, during a previous affair, "I am feeling love." Now, looking back, I say, "Aha, that was not what love is supposed to mean; what I'm feeling now is love." Indeed, it is not at all unusual for people to query whether what they are feeling *presently* is or is not love. Now one sense here is, "Aha, this is what other people, songs, movies and so on have meant by 'love'; it accords more closely with the kind of behavior that combines coherently with my present sensation than it did with the sensation I *now* recall myself to have been experiencing on the day I wrote this journal entry." And indeed, this does not make sense without the intersubjective reference to an external standard. But the point here is the constitutive *ambiguity* (global incoherence) of this standard, which is in no way in conflict with its externality or even its nonnegotiability. No one is ever quite sure about how to use any word, which does not mean we do not know how to use them; every usage is a provisional one, locally coherent, but bringing with it inherently the possibility of gainsayability. But more than this, we can also imagine a case where I say, "I have a strange sensation, let's call it 'X', which is like what I think others mean when they say 'love', but more intense." Then on a future occasion I may say, "Well, I thought that was X, but now I know that this is the real X; what I called 'X' last time was merely common love." What is happening here? We simply have judged the present X as more X-like than the original, defining Xness. This is possible only because *no X is fully constituted*; the original X, as remembered or even as experienced, was never *perfectly* X, was always an approximation given a locally coherent form as coherent Xness, situated in some way in relation to other terms of the shared language, to be sure, but capable of being exemplified by an *other* which is more "it" than it itself. The establishment of the sign was a promise to keep looking for better examples of it. None of this contradicts the main thrust of the private language argument as developed by Wittgenstein himself. On the premises developed here, we would obviously be the last to assert that a truly "private" anything is possible; Intersubsumption is what being is, and the inner and outer are inherently inseparable in every instance. We only object to the idea that this excludes certain possibilities, or applies any differently to so-called private languages and so-called shared language games. We agree when Wittgenstein asks,

> What reason have we for calling 'E' the sign for a *sensation*? For 'sensation' is a word of our common language, not of one intelligible to me alone. So the use of this word stands in need of a justification which everybody understands.— And it would not help either to say that it need not be a *sensation*; that when he writes 'E', he has something—and that is all that can be said. 'Has' and 'something' also belong to our common language. (261)[58]

Yes: these words are part of shared language games, and stand in need of a justification that everyone understands. That is undeniable. All we add is: but none of them can *ever* actually acquire this justification that everyone understands. Their being in need of one and their being unable to get one are, in fact, one and the same fact, the Intersubsumption that is in fact the meaning of the term. Justification, Wittgenstein says, consists in "appealing to something independent," so he thinks a subjective justification of the kind suggested here is impossible; to appeal for justification from one memory to

---

[58] Cf. the more pointed version in 294: "If you admit that you haven't any notion what kind of thing it might be that he has before him—then what leads you into saying, in spite of that, that he has something before him? Isn't it as if I were to say of someone: 'He *has* something. But I don't know whether it is money, or debts, or an empty till." The point is that, like the beetle in the box in section 293, this has no place at all in the language game, not even as a something. But importantly, "it is not a *something*, but not a *nothing* either!" (304). This is where Wittgenstein potentially forges the bridge over to the position we are developing here.

another is like checking against an imaginary train time-table, which can only be of use if somewhere down the line I can test my memory for correctness against a nonimaginary one. Otherwise it is "as if someone were to buy several copies of the morning paper to assure himself that what it said is true" (265). But this is just what we are always doing. We always need to appeal to something independent as a test of correctness, but this process never ends, and never succeeds. We are in fact buying the paper over and over again, but we never find anything independent to serve as a standard. Wittgenstein thinks that there "are " criteria in a man's *behavior* for the fact that he does not understand a word, but thinks mistakenly that he does, i.e., attaches some meaning to the word but not the "right" one. "And sounds which no one else understands but which I '*appear to understand*' might be called a 'private language'" (269). Here he has overstated his case; by hypothesis it would really be senseless to say he understands these sounds correctly or incorrectly. There is also perhaps a category mistake in the deproblematization of these supposed "criteria of behavior," which are surely as fraught with interpretative difficulties as the usages of words. The real point is that, as Wittgenstein himself notes, "it is quite indifferent whether I have recognized the sensation *right* or not. Let us suppose I regularly identify it wrong, it does not matter in the least. And that alone shews that the hypothesis that I make a mistake is mere show" (270). This is precisely the point. Right and wrong in the sense intended here are quite pointless, and if I identify wrongly "regularly" it ceases to make any sense to say I identify wrongly. But there is a begging of the question in this word "regularly," which conceals that this is precisely the case not only in my use of my supposed private language, but in all use of language.

If we call this a private language, we can equally call any language a private language—they all have some presently delineated range of application, which is in principle never completable once and for all. I always use words—and indeed, I would be happy to extend this to thoughts, gestures, sense of self, and any other coherence whatsoever—in a way that inextricably references other coherences outside itself and outside any possible way I could conceive "myself" or "my language" or "the rules of this game," in such a way that it is constitutively impossible for me to be completely certain of the appropriateness or lawfulness of my use in the audacious sense searched for here. I am always on trial as a speaking being, awaiting a verdict from some "community" or others, and that verdict is never in once and for all. Every single use of every single word is in accordance with some tentatively established local set of putative rules of coherence, but the sphere and range of this coherence can never possibly be closed of or absolutely certain of itself. Each usage is necessarily idiosyncratic, binding the perceivable rules of coherence in its own way, questioningly and imploringly, making it through for the purposes at hand but always coming with a question and a need for further and further verification. For to be is just to be locally coherent, which is just to be globally incoherent, which is just to be the Intersubsumption of the two, which is to be all-pervasive as all-pervaded. Indeed, we wish to say just that, in the Tiantai spirit: the meaning of "private" and "shared" must be opened up to their Intersubsumption, which will allow us to assert unequivocally: every language, in order to signify at all, is a private language, every language is a shared language, every language is neither, every language is an array of both (idiosyncratic usages referring to public ranges of meaning), every language is only private and only shared. This connection between temporality and intersubjectivity, by the way, will come up again in more detail toward the end of this book.

Composition, Temporal Succession, and Contrast

The above explication, speaking in terms of the elements "as" which something appears, is perhaps most easily understood as an elaboration of Intersubsumption (All-pervasion as All-pervadedness) as resulting from what in classical Tiantai is known as the *first* type of Local Coherence, in other words, (1) the Local Coherence of X on the basis of the *components which comprise it*, its elements (*yincheng jia*). It may be more difficult to see how this analysis applies to the other two types of Local Coherence, namely, (2) in terms of succession in time and (3) in terms of semantic and experiential relativity. In reality, in the Tiantai view, these two types of positing, which are altogether more central in the Tiantai system, will also be revealed to be relationships exactly equivalent to the relationship of "composition from elements" presented here, but this may not be very easy to see at this juncture.

To clarify, let us return to the question of Intersubsumption. Intersubsumption is what "opens up" the provisional to reveal itself, the ultimate. Some X, let us say love, appears in experience. It never appears *simpliciter*, but always expressed *as* some non-X things which, according to our previous analysis, *comprise* it, in accordance with the first type of Local Coherence: words, gestures, actions, thoughts, sensations, physiological phenomena. It interpenetrates with *all* forms of non-X, on this level, only because this situation is universally applicable: hate is also always expressed as some nonhate things, and the same goes for each of the data as which each of these is expressed, and so on. But now we can see another sense in which, say, hate and love, or any X and non-X, are directly identified. X is to non-X as marvelous is to coarse, as the *Lotus* is to all previous teachings. The *relative* marvel means that X *contradicts*, undermines, cuts off, destroys non-X: love eliminates or replaces hate, Marxism eliminates or replaces feminism or Christianity, and so on. The seriousness of the setup is in perfect contradiction to the humorousness of the punch line. But the *absolute* marvel means that in this very process it *reveals* non-X to have been its precondition, the ground of its being, and indeed a continuing participant in its being, that indeed this non-X, *precisely qua non-X*, is itself an expression of X. The setup too is funny, and can now be seen as simply a deceptive form *as* which this humorousness was appearing; what is more, it appears *as* precisely the absence of humor itself, as seriousness *per se: what is funny about it is precisely that it is serious*. All forms of non-X are tricky forms in which X was showing itself, and *what is Xish about them is precisely their non-Xness*. The perfection of the Buddha's enlightenment is expressed by teaching imperfect doctrines, and it is their imperfection which makes them perfect. When love appears, it sees the hate as a way of revealing what love is, and finally, regarding itself as the happy ending of the story, as all moments of experience do, it sees the hatred qua contrast to love as a way love expressed itself, made itself felt. When class struggle establishes itself as a particular theory with its own coherence, it does so first by distinguishing itself from shallower or illusory other doctrines; then, to succeed as the "true" doctrine, it sees that all these other doctrines are in fact just expressions of itself, forms in which it had been appearing. Intersubsumption as a coherence per se (that is, realization of the above point in the mind of some practitioner, and its "objective correlative") is this point as universally applicable; that all non-Central things turn out to be Central expressed necessarily as non-Central, because and only because of its non-Centrality; but also, since it is the universal case applicable to all coherences without exception, it signifies that *any* coherence is in the same situation as Intersubsumption (All-pervasion as All-pervadedness) itself; each X is expressed by each non-X, because and only because of its non-Xness. Each coherence has been cunningly assuming these forms of not-itself, by means of which alone it has been able to manifest itself—somewhat as, say, the *śrāvakas* are expressing their Bodhisattvahood precisely by forgetting they are Bodhisattvas and instead appearing, even to themselves, as *śrāvakas*. To accomplish the Bodhisattva work it was necessary to be non-Bodhisattva for a while. Hegel has spoken of the "cunning of reason," that is, the way in which universal Reason utilizes the passions and all forms of irrational behavior to carry out its own ends. Here we have something similar, except that it is applicable not only to reason, as we shall see in more detail below, but to every coherence whatsoever: every coherence is "cunningly" appearing as its opposite so as to accomplish itself. This coffee cup here has sneakily been manifesting as all the other experiences of my life so that I could now apprehend it here and now as precisely this coherence; the same goes for all my other experiences. Each one is the sole agent, actively conniving to bring itself forth by means of various "skillful means" of its own. Just as a Buddha appears in every possible form, this coffee cup has had to appear as all forms of non-coffee-cup to express itself, and indeed, seen retrospectively, all these non-coffee-cup forms have been adequate expressions of it, just as all previous skillful or cunning appearances of a Buddha are actually the one Buddha-vehicle. We will explore this "cunning of cunning" in more detail below. I said before that to understand the relation between the Three Truths, we had to understand their structural affinity to the provisional/real problem. Local Coherence is to Global Incoherence as various not literally true doctrines are to the Buddha's own enlightenment. Now we see how Intersubsumption too fits into this picture. Intersubsumption is the opening of the provisional to reveal the real, that is, that the local coherence is the negation of itself, Global Incoherence, it turns out to lead to, that the former is an expression of the latter, *as* which it had been appearing. The non-Xness that comes when the Global Incoherence of the Provisional Posit X is revealed is a form of X, just as the seriousness of the setup is a form of the humorousness of the punch line.

Intersubsumption (All-pervasion as All-pervadedness) is this idea, seen as universally applicable. For in the Three Truths, unlike our example of a joke, *everything* is a punch line to everything else, that is, the setup is also punch line to the punch line, in that everything reveals itself to be a negative form of everything else, revealed precisely by this negativity. Moreover, since this is the Nonexclusive Center, it is equally true, obviously, to say that everything is a setup to everything else. All is center, all is periphery. It is here too that we discover the answer to the possibly most vexing question of naïve consciousness, i.e., What if there is no punch line? What if, in classical Tiantai terms, there is no Buddhahood, no one has achieved it? This problem will haunt us as long as we see it as more or less equivalent to the question, What if there is no God? in a theistic context, even with the help of an attempted Anselmian ontological proof. But that is not exactly the question here. Instead, we must note that *all* experience is the experience of the clash and synthesis of a setup and a punch line; wherever there is coherence, that is, wherever any coherence of any kind is appearing, it is absorbing into itself its own setups, is the punch line which is recontextualizing a disparate group of conditions, components, and contexts which it is allowing to manifest here *as* itself. We need have no fear of punch lines not occurring, for that too would be a kind of punch line, inasmuch as it is a definite condition. Hence in classical Tiantai, everything derives from the simple presence of impermanence, suffering, and egolessness as observable conditions; it is as these, in identity to these, as the posited background that makes them appear, that permanence, bliss, and free selfhood come to be guaranteed. That is, to the extent that "impermanence" is itself a coherence, it must also be impermanent. Selflessness must also be without self; impossibility to establish any constant self-guaranteeing coherence is itself a coherence that cannot be established. Hence, in the intersubjective context of Zhanran's *Jingangpi*, we find the claim that the Buddha, looking upon all the world, including the delusions of sentient beings, sees only himself, sees only Buddhahood, expressed in these various forms. But at the same time, when sentient beings see themselves as being so seen, they also see themselves as nothing but Buddhahood, but this means that "there is no other Buddha at the condition of result (punch line), there is no Buddha outside of these sentient beings (who are viewing themselves as viewed by a Buddha who sees them as himself)." That is, the sentient beings themselves posit, *as a function of their delusion*,[59] a Buddha who views them as a function of his enlightenment, and this is all that is necessary to establish the existence of Buddhahood, indeed, this is all Buddhahood is. In our language, while any coherence is appearing (even the coherence "All coherences are subject to revision, are dependent on an unseen background, are explorable and can never be present as fully revealed or explored"), as soon as its revisability is felt—its impermanence, its dependence on conditions, it togetherness with an unseen aspect which is equally itself and will change the meaning of the presently seen aspect—as soon as it is known that *some* punch line can appear which would undermine the present determinacy, the work of the punch line is *already accomplished*. That is, the undermining of the appearance of this coherence as fully disclosed X *simpliciter* is already complete once we know that it is the set up to a punch line to come. We do not need to know what the punch line is, nor even ever have it come—indeed, by our premises, it too can never arrive *simpliciter*. We are giggling in the midst of the intensely serious story we are hearing because we know that it is a joke; nothing funny has been said yet, and we have no clear idea of what particular aspect of this story will be hit upon by the punch line when it comes, what will be the axis of its transformation; we are attentive to the nuances, since any of them might turn out to be the crux of the joke; but this experience of humor does not depend on there ever actually being a punch line. To simply know this is a setup is already to experience the effect of the punch line, even if it never actually comes. The setup's experience of its own nonfinality is itself the punch line. This experience is made present by the constant seriousness of small setups and punch lines which constitute time and experience as such; but the apocalyptic punch line for the world—in old-time language, "enlightenment"—never has to arrive as such, or rather, only arrives

---

[59] Specialists please note: this is Zhili's interpretation of Zhanran, not necessarily Zhanran's own.

as its own eternal postponement in the form of the unimaginability of the whole of experience not being a setup, since all experience is necessarily a setup and also a punch line.[60] We will have more to say on this in the section "Buddha *Sive* Time *Sive* the Inscrutability of the Other," below.

Here we can see that all three forms of Local Coherence coincide: as composition of elements, as sequence in time (for the temporal aspect is crucial to the whole notion of opening the provisional to reveal the real, which, indeed, may be viewed as precisely an insight into temporality per se), and as semantic or phenomenal contrast. We can say also that the preceding moments in the sequence leading up to X, and the pure negation of X, are forms *as* which X was appearing, just as in the case of composition, with the further wrinkle that what makes them forms and expressions of X is precisely their non-Xness, their contrast to X, their negation of X. This, in essence, is the significance of the Nonexclusive Center, which is determined as the overcoming of the distinction between "inner" and "outer." It accomplishes finally a complete equivalence between Local Coherence as component (*yincheng jia*) and as context (*xiangxu jia, xiangdai jia*). The non-X components of X and the non-X contexts (temporal and semantic) of X are equally all included in what is appearing here *as* X. There is no longer any qualitative difference in the way these various types of non-X contribute to the manifestation of X. Picking up Polanyi's example again, we may say that the tacit knowledge of X always involves both its component parts, e.g., the features of a facial expression which are read only as the expression, perhaps to the neglect of any awareness of the individual features, and its context, temporally and semantically, e.g., in the sensations on the hand which are read only as the information experienced at the end of the probe, or the external clues of the background which tell us whether the object we see before us is becoming nearer or is growing in size. The contractions of the muscles of the eye (component) and the beating of the heart or the brightness of the sun (context) are equally appearing here *as* this visual impression I am experiencing. No non-X of any kind fails to be either a component or a context determining X, and so all coherences are appearing here as this coherence.

In other words, we can state that composition, succession, and semantic contrast (contextualization) are *three alternate names* for the same fact about

---

[60] Cf. Sartre, *Being and Nothingness*, 133–46. "Value in its original upsurge is not *posited* by the for-itself; it is consubstantial with it—to such a degree that there is no consciousness which is not haunted by *its* value and that human-reality in the broad sense includes both the for-itself and value" (145). But for us, of course, pace Sartre, the in-itself exists *only* as a value consubstantial with the for-itself, of the for-itself. It exists, but only as a form of value-haunting-the-for-itself.

any coherence; a coherence is composed of what contextualizes it in a series, and is contextualized in a series by what composes it. Each of these is a word for all three, with a different emphasis, but any one of them thought through reveals the other two, in the typical Tiantai sense. Given the infinite divisibility of coherences, and their attendant discreteness from one another (momentariness), "noticing more about X" is also another name for the coherence *after* X in the series, and what is contrasted to it to manifest its meaning. The same applies the other way around. Here we find ourselves in line with the most fundamental insight of Whiteheadian process thought, and can perhaps add something to its intelligibility and necessity, namely, that every actual entity is both the totality of all other entities *and* one further entity in addition to them. The components of coherence X are also other coherences, all other coherences, and vice versa, and it is the relation between this "whole" and these "parts" as contrast which manifests the meaning of both. Here we see how the relations of "internality" and "externality," or of "self" and "other," must be understood in a Tiantai context.

This should also make obvious what our response would be to the criticism that our analysis of coherences surreptitiously makes them all basically quasi-Saussurian signifiers, i.e., mutually referring markers of difference within a flat synchronic system. For us, this aspect is indeed one that is basic to all appearing, but it is one of three, i.e., the aspect of semantic contrast, which turns out to be mutually reducible, like all Tiantai categories, with the aspects of succession (with all its contingent historical implications) and composition (with its implication of materiality and opacity). The relation between coherences is not simply that between differential signifiers; rather, each is both the reference to/inclusion of all others, *and* also one additional coherence, uniting the aspects of pure symbolic differentialism and a sort of atomistic positivism of coherences. When classical Tiantai writers affirm the mutual convertibility of "meanings" and "objects," they have, I think, a similar point in mind.

We have arrived at the point where we can say that the presence of coherence X is revealed more fully in its absence than in its actual presence, and vice versa. This can indeed be viewed as a standard by which to identify Tiantai omnicentricm, but only with further qualifications. In itself, we have here something that also can be said at the farthest reaches of, say, speculative onto-theological dialectics of the Hegelian type, under a certain reading. As Žižek says, "Our experience of the 'loss', of the fissure between us (the subject) and the Absolute, is the very way the Absolute is already with us."[61]

---

[61] Slavoj Žižek, *For They Know Not What They Do* (New York: Verso, 1991), 91.

The absence of the Absolute is its very mode of presence, its identity is precisely its radical impossibility; God per se, correctly grasped, is *deus absconditis*, the hiddenness of God, and our experience of this Absolute, its presence to us, is precisely our not-knowing it. This is the understanding of the situation in many forms of Buddhism as well: non-self-nature, Global Incoherence, is precisely the nonresistance to the assumption of forms other than itself—that is, any particularity, any something, anything other than the "non-self-nature"—and thus is revealed precisely in not being revealed as such. We may understand this after the trope of the actor sometimes encountered in this connection. The Absolute is here like a great actor; a great actor is one who makes one forget his presence when he is performing. The less aware one is that this is Actor So-and-so, the more fully revealed is the character of Actor So-and-so, i.e., the character of being a great actor. His consummate skill, his "actorliness," is revealed precisely by the lack of his presence in experience, the fact that solely the character in the play is present to consciousness. The less he is there, the more he is there.

This is the case in the Tiantai view as well, with however one extra point to be stressed. For here we want to say that this actorliness, this deadpan skill which constitutes the Absoluteness of the Absoluteness—in Tiantai terms, Intersubsumption (All-pervasion as All-pervadedness), which is also the identity of all coherences—is not simply that which is revealed by its absence in all determinate coherences. When we say, "This cupness is precisely Intersubsumption," we do not mean only that this cupness is a revelation of Intersubsumption precisely to the degree that it is not a revelation of Intersubsumption, that precisely in being cupness it is being Intersubsumption. We mean also that the cupness per se is Intersubsumption (All-pervasion as All-pervadedness)—that is, that cupness is what is revealed by its absence in, say, tableness, hatness, being-late-ness, even "Intersubsumptionness." Cupness per se has the qualities that we have seen here to be revealed in Absoluteness—i.e., the ability to manifest itself by means of its absence, its deadpan or actorly presence qua absence. The absence of cupness—or better, the constitutive impossibility of the coherence of cupness *simpliciter*, an impossibility which is its very identity—is the disclosure by which cupness is revealed to be what all other coherences were expressing, by their very noncupness, by their very exclusion of cupness. The fissure between the cupness and me, or between the cupness and glowing with bliss, or with agony, is the very way in which the cupness is already with me, or already expressed in bliss or in agony, and vice versa. The constitutive absence and impossibility of any coherence is the form in which it accomplishes its omnipresence and inescapability, its absoluteness. More will be said about this in the section on "Presence as Hyper-absence; Absence as Hyper-presence" which stands at the beginning of Part Two of this book.

On the Fire Not Burning Itself

I mentioned this familiar Zen trope above in the discussion of constitutive self-distance, and it is indeed one of the most direct ways to gain an intuition of Global Incoherence as the very constitution of any coherence: fire burns but does not burn itself, water does not wash itself away, the eye does not see itself, the subject does not objectify itself. Neo-Zen thinkers like Nishitani have zeroed in on this line of thought as the innermost kernel of their teaching, and one that carries them through the koan tradition. The case of Dongshan and the fire is perhaps the central koan for this tradition: where can we go to escape the cold and heat? Let the cold freeze you to death, let the heat burn you to death, so that there is no longer any subject there to experience the cold or heat, just the heat itself or the cold itself, which feels no heat or cold. As we will have occasion to remark in more detail below, this is also our bridge no only to the logic of the *Diamond Sutra*, as Nishitani cites (X is not X, therefore it is X), but even into the implications of Plato and with them all of Western metaphysics. But here I would like to develop some of the implications of Tiantai thought that this trope helps us toward.

Nishitani's treatment nicely stresses that this "not being fire" is also the *being* of fire as such, that is, what allows it to sustain itself as fire.[62] His position is that of what in Tiantai would be called the Exclusive Center, the third form of thusness and otherwiseness outlined above. That is, fire is fire in that it combusts or destroys whatever it contacts, but fire is fire in that it does *not* destroy itself in its contact with itself. Water is water in that it washes things away, but water is water in that it sustains itself as water by not washing itself as water. Fire is fire because it is (in some region of its relations, i.e., with itself) not fire; water is water because it is not water. Similarly, the subject is subject because it objectifies whatever it contacts, but the subject is subject because it does not objectify itself. To the extent that it is not objectifying, it is not a subject; hence it is subject because it is not a subject. We may generalize this consideration for all coherences, and extend its implications in the Tiantai manner, beyond Global Incoherence and toward the Nonexclusive Center. We can start by considering the simple logical Spinozistic point that determination is negation. In this sense, to be X is to deXify whatever X relates to, to posit the rest of the world as specifically "non-X," as the contrast and background to X. However, to be X is to not deXify itself. But note that since "to be X" means "to deXify" and X does *not* deXify with respect to itself, X is not X with respect to itself. *But this means that X is deXifying itself as well.*

---

[62] Nishitani Keiji, *Religion and Nothingness*, trans. Jan Van Bragt (Berkeley: University of California Press, 1982), 115–18.

X is X if and only if X deXifies all other things; but we add first: all things, including itself, and second, the real Tiantai point, *and thereby Xifies all things, including itself*. For if X means "the process of deXifying things," then to Xify means "to establish the process of deXification," which means that wherever there is deXification, X is established; X is present wherever X is absent. All X means, since it is not *simpliciter* X even to itself, is the presence of the process of deXification, and this process—that is, X itself—is present in X's entire non-X world. Moreover, inasmuch as we have established the absence of Xness in X itself, X is Xifying (since all this means is making manifest the absence of Xness) itself as well. Let us try to get at this conclusion slowly.

To expand on this beyond the merely logical point and into more "existential" territory, we may say that there is a certain aggressivity and hostility involved in being a coherence: to be X is to take all the rest of the world as non-X in the very specific sense of possible *food or fuel* for X, potential grist for one's own mill, fodder to be distorted, chewed up and destroyed in order to be incorporated, made into aspects of X. To be X is to look for the confirmation of Xness in the *Umwelt* that contextualizes one, which is thereby set up as the contrast but also as the field of activity for "the project of attempting to be X" which is, as we have seen, all it means "to be X." To be X is to be engaged in the project of consuming and converting non-X into X, of testing Xness against non-Xness so as to manifest Xness, of confronting and defining a world in which Xness is made the central issue to be revealed, concealed, evaluated, sustained, or destroyed. It is to posit the rest of the world both as "not me" and as "relavant to me" in a single stroke, relevant in the sense of being the possible field on which (or rather *as which*) Xness can become manifest in one way or another, either directly or by contrast. But then, following the logic developed above, X is not X to itself since it is not engaged in this conversion project in that sphere; it is not making Xness itself relevant to Xness, and hence it is not X-ing with respect to X, it is not X to itself. Hence when it succeeds in being most itself, in making all non-X into X, it simultaneously ceases to be itself, since itself was just the project of conversion itself, which is no longer possible. To "be engaged in the conversion process" (to "eat," to "consume fuel," that is, to "exist") is simultaneously "to posit as food, i.e., as specifically non-*X*, to deXify while regarding the possibilities of making this non-X into X." X does neither of these to itself, hence "in itself" or "when it succeeds" it is already non-X. But then the "X" into which it it converting everything is in fact *non-X*—the place where X, the process of conversion, does not apply. But then things are already converted—they are all just as X as X is; even in their most radical non-Xness they are already revealing the dimension of relevance to Xness, which is all that Xness is. Hence: to be X is to deXify all, to deXify itself, and to Xify all, and to Xify itself.

We can restate this a little more strictly as follows: to be is to be some X. To be X is to sustain itself as X (over at least two moments, i.e., such that a relationship is involved—X "lives" by finding Xifiability in at least one *other*, non-X coherence). This requires fuel or food as conditions. To sustain itself is to *resist* the imposition of some non-X, while inviting and converting the rest into X. Now X neither resists nor converts itself. It grants a certain *exemption* to a particular realm of being, where its hostility abates. My antibodies must know not to attack my own cells. This is almost the definition of which region of being counts as (my) self. My being/positionality is thus inherently *polemical*, and never preaches to the converted (although ultimately the purely and completely converted do not exist; coherences, as interpervasive, inherently *backslide*). To this extent, in sustaining itself as X, X is not X. X is both X (the process of positing Xifiability) and not X. We move on to assert that X is X (the process of positing Xifiability) *only* by being not X (sustaining itself by suspending the process of positing Xifiability). Pushing farther toward the Tiantai position, we say also that whenever and wherever it is X it is also non-X. These are not two separate regions. Every act of X-ing (positing Xifiability) is also an act of not-X-ing (sustaining itself as X, exempting and suspending positing Xifiability so as to establish that which is positing Xifiability). They are two aspects of the same act, the tertium quid position, or mutually grounding flipsides of one another (so that the relationship between them itself is the final, most ultimate term, the tertium quid, of which they are the two contrary expressions). Finally, we arrive at the full Tiantai version, the Nonexclusive Center: These are not two aspects at all. Rather, to be X is to be non-X, to posit as Xifiable is to refrain from positing as Xifiable. In each detail and in every case without exception, each object that is posited as Xifiable is also not posited as Xifiable; since X is X by not being X, Xifiability is also non-Xifiability. The more X something is, the more non-X it is. The function of positing Xifiability is the function of refraining from positing Xifiability. The presence of X is its absence, only more so, and vice versa. Hence we can say that the "not burning" experienced as nonfire is fiercer than fire itself—it is being fire, the experience of fire itself. Nonfire is more fire than fire. This is also reversible: "nonfire" is fire and nonfire, "fire" is also fire and nonfire. We must then claim that the nonfieriness of nonfire also *burns* all things, just as the nonfieriness (self, being, self-sustaining) of fire does. We will come to understand this point better when the discussion turns to the constitutive status of metaphoricity, below. But for the moment let us face squarely the consequences for every possible coherence. For example, if I am Brook, then all that absolutely non-Brookish stuff out there "Brooks," discloses my essence, my being, is more than me, and *equally* posits Brookifiability, de-Brookifies in order to Brookify, the rest of the world—including myself.

But it should be stressed that in all these cases it is the contingent, momentary appearance of some particular coherence, like fire or Brookness, in experience (however "illusory") which discloses this dimension of fire and nonfire, Brookishness and non-Brookishness, pertaining to all things without exception. This alone bridges the gap between mere "non-X" and the true specific othernesses, A, B, C, and so on. Water is "nonfiery, hence more fiery than fire" only after fire has appeared, and thereafter wetness is always inescapably specifically "nonfiery qua fiery, fiery qua nonfiery," and more fire than fire. Thus is the "inherent entailment" of fire in all coherences revealed by any particular contingent appearance of fire. Hence in Tiantai, to see any coherence is to have an entire dimension open up, to see "principle" itself, a new way of defining all things. This is the meaning of the classical claim that "every sight and scent is the Middle Way itself," or is identical to Intersubsumption (All-pervasion as All-pervadedness). This does not mean that "all things are the absolute principle" in the sense of being composed of certain substance which is the absolute, like cookies made from cookie dough, or as instantiations of a form or idea, or as objects perceived expressing an absolute mind, or as effects directly issuing from an absolute cause, or as contents encompassed in an absolute whole. Rather, it means just what it says: each thing, alone, is *the* absolute, the final term, the principle (beginning, end, explanation, substance, telos, essence) of all other things. This is real pantheism, not panentheism or acosmism, as other purported pantheisms always defended themselves as being). It should also be noted, however, that it is *thereby* also "pan-dog-ism, pan-cup-ism, pan-fire-ism, pansolipsism," and so on.

The External World(s)

I will take up the question of the mind-body relation in the second part of this book. Here, however, I want to say a few words about the specter of idealism that may be felt to be haunting us in these pages. To offset any misunderstanding, let me state my meaning as clearly as possible here: not only do I wish to assert the real existence of an external world, I believe that, appearances to the contrary, the mode of thinking here described makes more of this principle than almost any other. In a word, there is *always, constitutively* an "external world." That is, for any coherence, there is necessarily an "outside." I could rewrite that more strikingly: every coherence "has" (i.e., is constituted by) its outside. To be a coherence is to have an "external world" relative to that coherence. To be X is to be (-with) non-X.

The importance of this point must not be overlooked. I do not mean it merely as a cheap equivocation, for I believe this adequately answers to the worry that underlies the concern about the existence of the external world in the more restricted and more usual sense, i.e., the question of whether anything really exists outside our own experiences, the old *ding an sich* question. Our experiences—in old-fashioned language: ideas, mind, conceptual content, consciousness—is what we are asking whether there is anything outside of; and the one unmistakable feature of ideas, mind, consciousness, and concepts is intentionality, or reference to something besides itself, or, in Hegelese, mediation. A concept refers to something outside itself; an idea is an idea *of* something; an experience is an experience *of* something. To ask if there is something outside consciousness is to ask, "Is there something outside of that which is mediated, necessarily and constitutively referential to something outside itself?" To this we answer no—hence the deceptive appearance of idealism in these pages. But with this answer we also converge with the opposite position; there is always an outside. The significance of this is by no means abstract. The worry about idealism is that it fails to do justice to the recalcitrance of the something which our ideas, our will, our consciousness *encounters*, which does not accord with its wishes, which imposes limits on it, which contravenes its own inner coherence, which it must struggle with or against, which blocks or obstructs it. This is meant both in an abstract sense and in the most everyday sense possible. But it is precisely this recalcitrance of the something other which we wish to affirm when we affirm that there is always an outside. For any X whatever, there is a necessary surrounding and indeed constitutive non-Xness that will undermine this Xness, more or less manifestly, but necessarily. There is always an "external world." No possible conceptual system can be proof against this wall; it will crash against it somewhere or other, it will never encompass everything, it cannot, for structurally constitutive reasons as traced above. There is always "more."

But for us this goes also for the so-called "external world" itself. The external world is undermined by what lies outside itself, what it cannot master, by what mediates it and yet contravenes it. The apparently in-itself is no better off than us in this regard; it has an outside too, and one that is just as hard to contend with: us. Objectivity is as much undermined by subjectivity as subjectivity is by objectivity, and this reversible relation will be explored in fuller detail below, where we attempt to offer a more strict definition for these terms. The "external world" can no more rest secure in being what it is, unreferencing and unmediated, than can we. It is susceptible to being smashed, eaten, transformed, but also—experienced. All of these are enough to destroy its simply "being-so," and all are always going on.

But this is not at all what is wanted when people demand that proper respect be given to the "external world"; what is wanted, in fact, is not for there to be an external world, but rather for there to be *one* external world—that is, an external world which itself has no outside, which forms a closed system, which is simply what it is, that is, an external world which is genuinely *independent* and hence able to be consistently itself. What is wanted is a single authoritative, unmediated external world which itself has no external world. This is precisely what an omnicentric system cannot countenance. What is really at stake here is the status of knowledge—of determinate knowledge—and especially of science. But this is another problem entirely, one which we shall take up in the section below entitled "Onany, Interpretation, and Love: Truth and the Libidinal Community" below. The demand for an external world, strictly speaking, we fully grant, and indeed, can only insist that the further demand, for this world to be stable and single, for there to be one fact of the matter or one set of facts of the matter, is merely a failure to take seriously one's own demand for an external world; if one really takes this rightful demand to its fullest development, the problem evaporates. Full appreciation of the outsideness of the external world, the really eradicable nature of "external reality," already overcomes the problem itself. The demand for this world to be one set of facts of the matter is merely a sign of a half-hearted failure to think through all the implications of one's own initial demand. Here we have a special case of a principle to be discussed in general terms in the following section: the presence of the external world (i.e., the sense of a single set of facts of the matter) is its hyper-absence (i.e., the most thoroughgoing denial of precisely the principle of necessary [self-]externality); the absence of the external world (any one set of facts of the matter) is its hyper-presence (full development, ultimate thinking-through). But this the more global implications of this outcome should become more evident in the sequel.

But does this bring us full circle? Do we come back to a self-mediation of the Hegelian type? Close. Indeed, we do wish to do away with any absolute distinction between an inner breakdown of a coherence and its destruction at the hands of some purely external force; for us these do indeed turn out to be one and the same in the final analysis. Nonetheless, the case is not as simple as this might suggest. The exact implications and conclusions we wish to draw from these premises, as well as some of the less predictable ramifications, will be explored in Part Two.

Categories of Asness and Their Attributes: Summary of Part One

It should be obvious by now in what we way intended the claim made at the beginning, that the vaguely disreputable reinterpretation of past selves and past lies into new truths is for us precisely that the self is, that self-redefinition, self-recontextualization, and mutual readability of alien coherences is the very nature of being a self; it is hoped also that my initial remarks about incompleteness as a necessary condition of any coherence (i.e., disclaimers that "space and time prohibit a further exploration of this topic" as structurally necessary to making any coherent claim at all) are by now easily comprehensible. We have begun to see a few of the implications of this view, and will proceed to draw out quite a few more in what follows. But before we move on, it would perhaps be useful at this point to give a more schematic summary of the types of relations that we have seen to undergird this claim, the parallel categories that we mean to indicate when we say of all beings that they are constitutively "asness," and the attributes of each of them. We might chart these dimensions of asness as shown in Table 1.

It should be noticed here in which each of our metaphorical aspects of asness enriches our total conception of what is meant by asness. These attributes or implications are of course mutually implicating and overlapping. The implications of each relation are to be understood as "what we get" for asness by thinking of it in terms of the relation in question. These need to be understood as applying to each other as well. For example, if we get the sense of "agency" from the object/subject aspect of asness, this must be cross-referenced with the sense of reversibility from the figure/ground relation, and of mutual pervasion from, say, the punch line/setup relation. This will mean that the attribute of agency is itself reversible with passivity, and that activity and passivity interpervade. This is because we have endeavored here to show that the figure/ground relation itself, thought through to the end and freed from any extraneous presuppositions, turns out to be also an end/means relation, and a signified/signifier relation, and a punch line/setup relation, and so on. Needless to say, this is always reversible; these are all merely alternate ways of describing the fundamental mode of appearing of all coherences, which we describe globally as asness. In each case one aspect or set of implications is brought into focus, in order to illustrate and make palpable what is in fact implicitly occurring when any of these relations is in play, and our contention must be that in every experience of coherences all these categories are in fact in play, for they are merely restatements of one another with varying emphases. Our comprehensive conception of asness must be of a relation which is manifested as subject/object, as punch line/setup, as figure/ground, all simultaneously, so that the peculiarities proper to each of these relations ends up pertaining to all of them. For a coherence to be present in the mode of asness is for it to be all of these things at once. Only this discloses for us the full dimensions of the asness relation. If is from this cross-referencing of all the implications of asness that the concrete philosophical conclusions of the following sections are to be derived.

TABLE 1: DIMENSIONS OF ASNESS

Constituent Relations of Asness		Implications
Figure	Ground	Inseparability, reversibility, ambiguity, undermined inside-outside dichotomy, alternate readability
Whole	Part	Ambiguity, contextualization as determination of quality, coherence, indetermination of identity of parts outside their relation to the whole
End	Means	Value orientation, Subsumption (one-way, means into end), "Centering" as value standard, primitive form of interpervasion of contrary qualities
Signified (Meaning)	Signifier (Expression)	Meaning, coherence-emergence intelligibility, coherence, centering
Explicit	Implicit	Tacit function, presence as absence
Object Subject/body	Subject/body Object [63]	Existential situating, agency, being and having, awareness (presencing to), qualitative world-pervasion, exposure as life-worlds, intersubjectivity
Punch Line	Setup	Mutual pervasion of opposite, "mutually exclusive" coherences as identical *because* contrasted

---

[63] We put subject and object on both sides here, each playing the role of both figure and ground, of both setup and punch line. The reason for this confusing doubleness is precisely the structure of subjectivity and desire, as will be explored in Part Two, on desire and the self. It is here that we have the central role of reversibility in all existence most manifestly disclosed.

PART TWO

Desire and the Self

TOWARD AN ETHICS AND PSYCHOLOGY OF CONSTITUTIVE IMPOSSIBILITY

Presence as Hyper-absence; Absence as Hyper-presence

Several interesting results follow from what has been said so far. First, we find we have here the makings of a doctrine about presence: presence is hyper-absence. And equally about absence: absence is hyper-presence. The implications of this result remain to be explored. They will lead us to a practical, perhaps even ethical, maxim: Any coherence can be gotten rid of only by making it fully present. Conversely, it can be obtained only by completely excluding it. This advice is of course founded on the insight that *neither of these is possible*. To put it otherwise, it is not only that "emptiness" or "Inter-subsumption (All-pervasion as All-pervadedness)" or "The Absolute" can neither be attained nor evaded (and *is* the fact that this unattainability is this unevadability); the same is true of any *other* coherence per se.

Let us elaborate the grounds for these cryptic remarks. When we try to make some coherence fully present to ourselves, we find that a necessary rhythm emerges, noticed by Freud in his image of the mental apparatus as the "Mystic Writing Pad," but depicted there only as a kind of adventitious medium for atomizing bits of experience before transferring them to the unconscious, allowing a new blank slate for perception. We are now in a position to specify the necessity and inner structure of this rhythmic process of perception. Perception of an encountered coherence, we may say, consists in a gradual growth in the consistency of, belief in and experienced reality of the figure or coherence in question, an accumulation of momentum of believability, of what is called presence. The figure is first a mere possibility, a suggestion; it grows in force and conviction as more and more elements from its periphery—its background of otherness—are seen to be consistent with it, to form a single unified field of compossibles. All this of course normally happens very quickly. I see a flash of green over there, which I tentatively identify as the coherence "green cup on table." This coherence expands outwards, in search of confirmation, in a split second: it turns out that it is in no conflict with anything else I am aware of, it fits the picture of other things I know—things like the law of gravity, the common presence of drinking utensils in houses, the lines of perspective currently applying, the whole universe as I know it. More importantly, as we have seen above, this entails the gradual expansion of the field of apparent other coherences which are appearing here, not only as consistent-with, but *as* the coherence in question.

But for the figure to remain, there must be *at least one* peripheral background element, one otherness *not yet* so synthesized, whose identity remains undecided. Indeed, this is precisely what constitutes the sense of self, i.e., oneself, one's perceiving "mind," as opposed to the object perceived; oneself as perceiver is, in one important sense, whatever elements are not yet synthesized in the cancerous growth of the perceived object, a point we shall return to below, although the status of the subject is slightly more complex than this factor alone would indicate. Once this last otherness is also explicitly brought into the picture, when *full consistency* is finally achieved and complete certainty attained, it necessarily *crashes*; this whole split figure/ground process can now become simply a figure in its own right, which then calls forth a new undermining/supporting context, a new questionability, what Douglas Hofstadter has called a "jumping out of the system."[1]

For example, I see a glass. First there is a collecting of relevant impressions beginning to cohere; then a figure of "what this glass is" increasingly certain as more and more surrounding impressions (coherences, past, present, and future) are checked against it and seen not to exclude its possibility. First this process would approach and incorporate all other objective conditions, things on the same plane of experience—in this case, other seen objects. But this process cannot stop on any one plane; the seen objects bring in other conditions, physical laws, temporal processes, and even one's own brain and eyes, one's beliefs and experiences of the cup. I include even modifications of my own eyes and nerves in the system that coheres with the appearance of this

---

[1] Douglas R. Hofstadter, *Gödel, Escher, Bach: An Eternal Golden Braid* (New York: Vintage Books, 1980), esp. 461–79.

glass, or my "mind" or "soul" however conceived, and then further the realm of intersubjective agreement, the activities of other brains and speaking mouths and writing pens. But coherence, fully thought through in the manner demonstrated above, is precisely asness; Local Coherence is precisely Intersubsumption (All-pervasion as All-pervadedness). If the coherence in question were fully achieved so as to include *all* other coherences (as it never quite does in real life), the coherence in question would be fully certain, immediate, transparent; nothing lies behind it left to explore, no thing-in-itself is over there and no self over here. "The glass presenced here" turns out to be a way of indicating the entire universe of conditions which are appearing here *as* the glass. Then what we have is a completely flat and unexplorable fact: there is simply this universe of brains and matter and laws and words appearing as glass on table. But this has nothing supporting it, nothing left to guarantee its truth or consistency, nothing to be checked against. One can say of it, like one's own imagining of a cup, that there is no more to it than what I see, it is just what I think it is. But this is, then, by definition, only an imagining, it has lost the quality which originally posited it as a reality rather than a mere imagining, namely, the moretoitivity which is the mark of realness, the unfinishedness which is the price of being actual, the supposition that there was something other than it, or another side *to* it, which could support and confirm it, either some further experiences or some form of consensus. For these further experiences and consensus are themselves already present here as the glass itself; it is meaningless to check it against itself, to double it into its own mirror image and then confirm it by its correspondence with itself. The question, "Is it real or just something I think is real?" emerges anew, now asked not only about the cup per se but about the whole system of background conditions which have now been brought explicitly to awareness as that which is appearing *as* this cup. It requires new confirmation, but none is available, as there is no longer any "other" by which it can be confirmed. The system crashes. Certainty, determinacy, coherence is self-undermining.

It should be noticed that this is simply a restatement of what was said earlier about Intersubsumption (All-pervasion as All-pervadedness), that is, the "emptying out" of the metaphier when it reaches its fullest success. When we succeed in seeing, for instance, class struggle, everywhere, even in its antithesis, the term "class struggle" ceases to mean what it did when we began—indeed, it ceases to have any determinate meaning at all. And so for any hermeneutic project where anything is understood in terms of anything else, and this means all experience without exception. There is no failure like success, to vice-versify an old balladeer. Indeed, what the total success of any interpretive project (i.e., any project, any sense of being at all, any attribution of coherences) brings about is its crash, which is a revelation of the initial explaining "central" coherence's *bankruptcy* when considered as exclusive of any others. The moment of success is the moment when *contingent* failure is transformed into *necessary* failure. What appeared to be blocking the consistency and universal applicability of our pet central coherence was formerly some *external* obstacle, some indigestible kernel it encountered which it just could not handle; now it must be seen that the failure of the system to work as originally planned was built in. This built-in-ness is what is revealed when it does apparently succeed. (On the other hand, it cannot help succeeding on some level; it always remains as a player, always appearing in some constrained arena of relevancies.) Moreover, with this failure comes another, unsuspected form of success; all-pervasion, not as a positive coherence, but as already canceled, impossible, a universal haunting, an emptied-out coherence that excludes nothing, which has no *simpliciter* being of its own, and is as much nowhere as it is everywhere.

But for the moment let us dwell on the necessary failure, which is arguably more interesting here; for what we are led to conclude is that in fact the attribution of an external indigestible obstacle that blocked success was, in the strict sense, a defense mechanism, a way of avoiding the full success which, it was perhaps always suspected, would lead to the crash and the necessity of the failure. Our interpretive apparatus claims not to be able to explain away something in terms of itself, draws up short against some fatal disconfirming data, as a means by which to *avoid* confronting its *inherent* bankruptcy. The (sole, definitive) objective world, to put it crudely, is a defense mechanism. Ironically, it is a defense against acknowledging the impossibility of the subject, of the subjective project, its complete beholdenness to its own self-contradiction, its own emptiness, precisely what the *realness* of the external world, in contrast, is always meant to prove, as noted in the previous section on the "External World(s)."[2] But it should be noted again immediately, lest there be any thought of a kind of idealism or solipsism here, that exactly the same thing applies to the objective world; its allowance of subjectivity is a way for it to maintain an illusion of consistency and presence *simpliciter* for itself, if I may put it that way. If "objectification" succeeds completely, it too crashes and is unfindable; it can only maintain itself by cravenly pretending, if you will, that subjectivity exists.

What is operative in both of these avoidance rituals is the split, the difference between the two, or uninterpretability per se; that is, the cowardly halting of interpretations which, whether by dint of "intellectual conscience" or just laziness, draw back from reading themselves into the immediate data

---

[2] Cf. Merleau-Ponty on the strictly correlative constitution of the contentless unsituated subject and the objective world, PhP, 218 and 298.

when the going gets too far-fetched. To draw the line somewhere, to say, There is a point beyond which I will not go in reading my pet theory into apparently conflicting data, a dodge whereby that pet theory—in a moment, we will as much as call it the self—maintains itself, its integrity. Of course I do not mean this is done only by avoiding appearing ridiculous to itself (i.e., the humiliation and embarrassment which are constitutive, I will argue below, of the fear of death, that is, the exposure of the nonmastery of the self, its inescapable reversibility with objecthood), although that may be involved as well, but more crucially, by being able to pretend that it has some content which distinguishes it from any other position. This is not to be criticized, as we shall see shortly; it is the *only* way we get coherences of any kind in the world—either of the mutually-exclusive, doomed-to-crash kind or the inescapable, unobtainable kind—and is absolutely necessary, even analytically, to any other datum at all, including the non-assumption of any datum. But more on this below.

This is the "optimal" case, as it were, where in fact no inconsistent element is found anywhere, no matter how much the system of explicit connections expands. We have already argued above, however, for a kind of Laycockian "curved logical space," in accord also with Žižek's remarks about the necessary limits of every inquiry, our touchstones at the very beginning of this book. That is, there is no quiddity, no coherence, that will remain what it is when all the relevant data is brought to bear. Each and every one can only remain what it is by limiting the "horizon of relevance," and begins to break up as more elements come into the picture. Coherence is bought at the price of excluding some contexts. When all contexts are brought in, we have irreducible ambiguity to the figure. Imagine the Wittgensteinian duck-rabbit; alone on the page it is ambiguous, but if one has been looking at several pages of duck diagrams, of which this is one more in the series, it appears as duck. If on the other hand we have been covering what lies beneath it with a piece of paper, and pull that away to reveal that underneath it a rabbit body is drawn, it appears as a rabbit head. However, if we then place this whole page as part of a huge collection of diagrams arranged in a circle, to be viewed from afar, we see this only as part of a circle; if then this circle is part of an even huger diagram, forming the picture of a ring on the finger of a portrait of Liberace, this same thing is simple appearing as ring; when looking at that spot one is looking at the ring. There can be no way of knowing when this process of context expansion can finally be stopped. The coherence *as* rabbit, duck, circle, ring depends on the limiting of the horizon of relevance; once this is exceeded, the same figure explodes into a new coherence, without changing in the least. Hence, "curved space": any line is "straight" only when viewed from a very limited set of parameters; *if we keep it going long enough*, it turns out to have been curving into another direction, no matter how straight may have seemed locally.

We have two different but related points here. The first was the best-case scenario, where everything worked out and everything turned out to be consistent with the original figure; in the latter account, it was suggested that this could never be. In either case, however, the facticity of the coherence crashes inevitably, and this is the crucial point. This necessity of the crash, this pivotality and inherent distance, as the existence of the thing, as identical with its establishment, is what we described as Intersubsumption (All-pervasion as All-pervadedness). By expanding the horizon, by further developing the consistency or the field of relevant backgrounds, the figure must crash. It is this that we refer to as "fully developing" the coherence in question. We apply it in all possible directions and contexts, we take it fully at its word that it simply is what it is, irrespective of contexts or conditions, and try plugging it into all possible contexts. We "dwell" in it, to use the classical Tiantai expression, trying to find out what it is in all aspects and as placed in all possible situations. By doing so, we are also "freed" of it, it vanishes as any *simpliciter* coherence, and also becomes "all-pervasive" it is what is appearing *as* all these other coherences into which it has transformed.

What has happened here is that what appeared to be two contrary cases—on the one hand, a system of coherency succeeding without impediment but then crashing due to a structural necessity as a consequence of its own total success, and on the other hand, a system of coherence which expands a bit and then *encounters* some indigestible external element, which is inconsistent with its original coherence, and *causes* it to crash, as it were, prematurely—have turned out to be alternate views of the same occurrence. Case 1, total success equaling crash, if examined all the way to its bottomless bottom, reveals itself to be case 2, an encountered impediment, and vice versa; this is the application of the same principle at the meta-level. The coherent quiddity "self-overcoming" when pursued to the end turns out to be instead the coherent quiddity "banging up against an external something," and vice versa. This hinges on what is meant by the "self" of the system in question, which we must trace back to the question of perception, conceptualization, and imagination, defined in terms of explorability and encounteredness, and will bear heavily on our general discussion of the self below. Simply expanding the initial coherence means inquiring into its conditions, its contexts, taking its word for its applicability in all contexts; without adding anything to it, it is itself revealed to be all the contexts which are appearing here *as* it. It turns out to be a tissue of metaphors, as we will see in more detail below, each of which comes to the fore in accordance with a set of horizons of relevance which appear in the same gesture of the coherence itself; it is self-contextualizing, and its contextualizations are also self-contextualizing, and it is therefore an inexhaustible treasury of coherences. These remain consistent with the initial coherence, that is, are seen as successes of its initial project, just as long as it remains possible to keep that coherence in view. It has two choices; either recoil at some encountered obstacle, or press on. We will have to inquire into the status of these two options, and what they imply for the meaning of the self. What we find is that they are not two options at all, but in fact, that each is, on a meta-level, an expression of the other; this means both that they are inseparable and that they also that they appear to be mutually incompatible. One and only one is appearing at any time, but whichever one is appearing is always necessarily implicity expressing the other, which it has momentarily absorbed into itself. But, as Zhili says, this also means that when either one is functioning, both are functioning; they are both always functioning *as* one another. We may recall Polanyi's example of the avoidance of unexperienced syllables as an instance of this function of both as each.

We can see here the epistemological consequences of this inevitable rhythm of experience, of realness and illusion, which will lead us also to the Tiantai notion of time, of transformative recontextualization, and of ethics. But we can see already that there is no qualitative difference between the experience of the crashing of the belief posited in the claim, say, "The world is made of pretzels," and the claim, "The world is made of atoms." There is a difference in scale, and that is not without importance. However, it should not mislead us. "The world is made of pretzels" has coherence for a split second, while the mental image of a pretzel-constructed world flashes into the mind of the listener. A few microseconds later, other considerations come into view which disconfirm this: wait a minute, what about molecules, atoms, what about wood and metal, what about everything "nonpretzelly" I have been experiencing so far? What about the fact that this is not what anybody says, and if I say it I will be regarded as insane? What about the fact that pretzels are made of nonpretzel materials, that this term which has been selected as the center or foundation for explanation can itself be read in terms of other things? That is, what about the fact that, when contemplated closely—that is, analyzed or taking full notice of the contextualizations that allow the coherence "pretzel" to emerge—this coherence loses its coherence, falls apart, no longer stands as a figure, appears completely as nonpretzel? This "pretzel-world" image crashes, as a result of its encounter with a greater sphere of contexts than were first allowed it. But this is exactly what will happen with "The world is made of atoms," or "of matter," or "of spirit." It is perhaps not too much to say that the attempt to create one account that will be consistent in all contexts has been the tragic chimera haunting human history. For it is easily disposed of; it survives only at the expense of completely devaluing the "illusory" impressions of individual experience. No one of these stories succeeded in making itself consistent with all coherences ever experienced; it can only pretend to do so by excluding certain ones—for example, the impression that the world is made of pretzels that might fleet through some loony's mind one day—as pure illusion. It might give a mechanical account of this illusion—a malfunctioning brain, and so on—but this again at the cost of excluding at least a part of the total set of coherences appearing to experience; the coherences appearing to the physiologist are included—the cyst on the brain, and so on—but not those to the loony as he thinks of his pretzel-world. We can now give equal time to both of these sets of experiences, and feel anything less as an unholy affront to the dignity of human subjectivity.

But in saying this I am backtracking; I have already shown how simply to succeed would be to crash; so that even if, *per impossibile*, the account in question accounted for every coherence without exception, this in itself would a priori guarantee the crashing of the certainty of this account. We are all in the same boat, then: whatever you say or think, it will certainly be true—coherent, an immediate figure of experience, for that is the only definition of truth that will be of any use to us here—within certain sets of contextualizing conditions, and incoherent in others. This is the case for "the world is made of pretzels," for "God exists," for "God does not exist," for "we can only know what our senses tell us," for "our senses are unreliable," for "life is not worth living," for "everything is beautiful," for "the law of gravity," for "the periodic table," for $E = mc^2$, for $F = ma$, for "an equilateral triangle is always also equiangular," and so on. The moment other considerations of environment, other contexts, interfere with or blur the coherence of the formula in question—if sudden sexual arousal causes me to *lose interest* in $F=ma$ for a moment and no longer perceive it clearly, its validity in all contexts has thereby been compromised. It does not apply in all situations, it is not an account which remains true in all contexts. Only this view of truth can restore to human experience the dignity and autonomy (if it turns out that we want these) that have been robbed of it by inveterate and oppressive notions of objectivity, and epistemologies that insist that some things must be accepted even if we do not want to at the moment. Here we begin to touch on the philosophical foundations of the phenomenon of *boredom*, perhaps the most serious of all philosophical problems, although it has almost never even been noticed as a problem, so deeply ingrained has been the notion of objectivity as something that does not concern our whims. No wonder we are bored. But we will take this topic up in more detail toward the end of this book.

Correspondence and Coherence: Epistemological Implications

This account of the inevitable crash of every coherence should be taken on the one hand as hearty recommendation of the continued usefulness of *both* the correspondence theory of truth *and* the coherence theory of truth, and also, on the other hand, as a demonstration of the inherent limitation of both theories, the impossibility of making either one fully succeed, the self-undermining contradiction that resides in both—to an extent that would in almost any other context constitute a thoroughgoing critique of these notions of truth, presumably in favor of some other. For us of course this is not the case, and it is of no small significance that these usually opposed pictures of what it means for a proposition to be true—it corresponds to something outside the proposition, a fact of the matter, *or* it forms part of a coherent system of propositions—are for us in exactly the same boat—indeed, put the proposition in just the same boat as a perception or a feeling or any other coherence. In each case, we have the question of the *coordination* of the primal twoness which we have described as the necessary condition of any coherent one, the figure and its ground, the text and its contexts, bearing all the same features already noted of this necessary relationship. In each case, when this coordination or consistency, whether as correspondence or as coherence or in any other form, becomes explicit, we have instead another term demanding again the explication of its unseen other, a twoness overflowing the explicit oneness, a new token that has to be confirmed. The correspondence between proposition and fact—corresponds to what? The consistent coherent system—is consistent with what? The newly established and explicit item requires another coordination with some other. Knowledge can never be confirmed if knowledge means correspondence with a fact outside knowledge; to confirm it brings it within knowledge, and calls for another confirmation outside this knowledge, and so ad infinitum. Knowledge can never be confirmed if knowledge means "what is consistent with other knowledge"; the system is unclosable, and considered as a whole it fails to be consistent with any other which could confirm it by this standard, for whatever it is consistent with is by definition inside it and not outside it, and thus in no position to confirm it. Both of these pictures are the same picture for us, the picture of any coherence.

But, again, for us this is no critique; we are perfectly happy with various degrees of correspondence and/or coherence, or rather, the appearance of these, or any other picture of validity. For us validity resides simply in appearing as such, and pertains inalienably to whatever appears, to every coherence, within whatever context grants it whatever fleeting shimmering degree of discernibility it may have as a possibility to be entertained. But it is in the nature of every type of coherence not to be able to retain this discernibility as a possibility in all cases, or even when the present context and discernibility is fully explored, for these turn out upon examination to be unfindable, to melt away in one's fingers. Every coherence is valid (somewhere), no coherence is valid (everywhere)—but somewhere always turns out to be everywhere (nowhere).

Control and Its Lack: Practical Implications

A precisely parallel consideration obtains if we turn our attention not to knowing, but to willing. Here again we confront a question of coordination between (at least) two elements, one of which, the "self" or "subject," is endeavoring to alter the other, "the world" or "the object." And here too we have the same *constitutive contradiction*. The self holds up a value standard with which it wants to make reality conform; a contrast is established between "fact" and "value." However, if the willing process succeeds, and these two are made one, we no longer have the contrast necessary to establish value as value. Realized value ceases to be value, by virtue of the very structure of the category "value" itself, as requiring, being defined by, its divergence from fact. Indeed, from our point of view, this divergence is the concretization or imaginary domestication of the fact that success equals failure, that each coherence can only be itself by being impossible, the slide or split which *is* each coherence.

We may restate this notion in terms of the question of Control: However much I am able to control my world, there is always something beyond it; at the very least, my controlling act itself is spontaneous and not done by me. My will is not willed by me. Moreover, and more importantly: The very notion of "control" implies something to be controlled, and therefore something initially not in one's control, something confronted which is external to one's will (even the movement of the body plays on the body's givenness and inertia). Total control is a contradiction in terms; but less than total control is really no control at all, as can be easily deduced from the considerations set forth in the first part of this book.

Needless to say, the same thing works in reverse for "loss of control," if that is made the goal: the more you succeed in attaining it, the less you have suceeded in attaining it. The more you succeed in losing control, the more you have gained control.

This indeed is the central argument of this work. What is demonstrated here for the coherence "will" is in fact applicable to all coherences. Any coherence is coherent only by virtue of its inherent impossibility (it can never appear *simpliciter*), and this very fact constitutes not only its specific identity but also its all-pervasiveness, its unevadability. Its unobtainability is its unevadability. The present case, the case of the coherences of will and control, is merely one of many such "constitutive contradictions" which we will be considering, all of which are equivalent to the *identity* of the coherence in question as well as its *deadpan omnipresence*. But this particular constitutive contradiction, of the will, is of special practical importance for us. I will not venture to judge whether it has a special significance for all communities and beings, or if its importance is peculiar to our age, for example, a manifestation of a particular individualistic focus on freedom and control. It is just as possible that this is merely one of many possible focal points that contitute the quickest and most direct access to the unraveling of problems pertaining to the realm of praxis, somewhat in the manner of Spinoza's infinite unknown attributes which happen to be irrelevant to those of us confined to knowledge of only thought and extension. It is this topic that will primarily engage us for the rest of this work. At this point, however, it is important only to make sure we are clear on the truly omnicentric way of understanding this sort of constitutive paradox.

Our claim will be that *identity* per se for any coherence *simply means nothing but* this constitutive paradox, *which simply means nothing but* the impossibility of appearing *simpliciter, which simply means nothing but* all-pervasiveness in the form of deadpan asness. In the present example, the identity of the coherence "control" is obtained *only* as the paradox just described, as the attempt and necessary failure for "control" per se to appear, which also entails the all-pervasion of this coherence "control." But what is crucial here, lest we fall into an "Exclusive Center," is to appreciate that this will apply to any coherence in the field. That is, we do not wish to say, "The truth of the opposed finite categories (control verses noncontrol) lies in the realization (and, as we shall say later, 'embodiment') of the fundamental paradox which is constitutive of both of them (necessary impossibility of control); once we have realized ('embodied') this constitutive paradox, we have solved the problem of control and noncontrol, and no longer fall into a one-sided clinging to either, since we know them to be coextensive." Rather, as we have seen in our consideration of "Intersubsumption (All-pervasion as All-pervadedness)," to see "Control" as an identity comprised of such a paradox allows us at once to embody the Center ("neither-control-nor-noncontrol, but expressing itself as control and noncontrol"), *as well as either of the extremes per se*, and to find in each case that the same kind of interpervasive asness applies. "Control" alone or "noncontrol" alone will serve just as well as the all-pervasive term, once any of them has been thought through or "embodied." In other words, the practical solution to any such dilemma comes not from, for example, locating the one unique constitutive paradox which structures it and will therefore, when embodied (i.e., as we shall see, comprehended precisely as impossible (qua *simpliciter* appearance and therefore as all-pervading asness), resolve (by seeing as unavoidable) the difficulty. Rather, we must assert that *any coherence at all chosen at random* from within the entire field making up the "situation," however construed, has only to be embodied, hence seen as ineradicable, to bring about the desired effect, and to allow the same all-pervasion simultaneously to emanate from alternate centers. But we are getting ahead of ourselves here.

Unavoidable, Unobtainable

Before going there, however, let us return to hyper-presence and hyper-absence, and the simultaneous unevadability and unobtainability of every coherence. The unevadability of a particular coherence is perhaps easier to demonstrate and appreciate in the case of an *already* experienced coherence. Once I have seen this red lamp, there is never any way to exclude its impact on all subsequent experience. Its relevance can never be excluded from any future experience. It must evermore be checked against, serve as a contextualizer for all other coherences, none of which can close themselves to its impact. This inability of any possible other to close itself off from this coherence constitutes its unevadability, and, as we shall see eventually, the mode of its omnipresence.

But what of never-yet-experienced coherences? They are indeterminacies, absences, which haunt the current coherence; they are its future as question mark. Note that it is impossible to adduce the never-yet-experienced to verify that it is indeed not yet experienced without thereby experiencing it. Never-yet-experienced-ness is itself thus just one more experienced coherence. The coherence called time, or openness, or sensitivity, what waits to be imposed upon by the not-yet-experienced coherences, the raw vulnerability to further relevances—this ability to experience them is their absence as hyper-presence: they are *more present* in this form of pure expectation than in their concrete presence. In the latter case, the synapse has already fired, as it were; the coherence's ability to intrude itself as a haunting of all other coherences, to stand as a threatening "further consideration," has been diminished. It has come and localized itself, become fully immediate as described before, and hence appears to be no longer a threat anywhere else for the moment; it has narrowed to this *weaker*, lesser state of presence. We may think here of the commonly reported feeling, after the worst has finally happened, that avoiding/fearing/expecting/protecting against it was much worse than its simple presence, which is met with a sense of relief. This is no mere neurotic symptom; it is built into the absence-presence rhythm that makes up experience.

The expected worst coherence's threat has finally been confined, by appearing, by "happening." *Fully* present, or hyper-presence, here means present all-pervasively, that is, having the *power* to transform itself and perform its particular work in other forms, *as* any other coherence. When it is absent, it is displaying its power to appear here even as its other; for as long as it is not present, it threatens to be the transforming punch line for which the present coherence will turn out to be the setup; this future punch line will thus prove to have the power to pervade nd presence itself in the present. This *threat* itself is its hyper-presence, its display of its all pervading ability to transform its other into itself and vice versa, to posit its own ground in the form of its other, its setup; for this is the classical Tiantai understanding of the old Buddhist concept of *upāya* or skillful means as well. The hyper-presence and unevadability enacted by absence, and the implication of the power of the absent coherence displayed in its appearance as something else, call to mind Sartre's amusing description of watching the performance of a female impressionist on the stage: "The absent Maurice Chevalier chose the body of a woman to make his appearance."[3]

The Cunning of Cunning

Another classical premonition of the doctrine of "asness," perhaps the most abstract and sophisticated version we have, is Hegel's notion of the cunning of reason. There we have a case of "reason" contriving to appear as nonreason, and indeed, once again, displaying its power, indeed precisely what makes it reason, its ability to see itself in its other, by this manifestation as nonreason, as which alone it is able to accomplish its "reasonable" aims, and indeed in the process disposing of the nonreasonable which thought it was acting for its own good. Indeed, if we can accept the Hegelian notion of *vernunft* as itself a disclosure of "asness" per se, in its role as the overcoming of sunderedness as such, we have a very close approximation of what we are talking about here, with certain modifications. Among the latter, the most crucial is the fact that the specification of this asness as "reason" begs the question and fatally limits its applicability. We would do better to speak of the cunning of *cunning* itself. That is, the principle of "X being able to appear as its opposite, non-X, as a form of hyper-presence by which alone it can accomplish its Xish aims"—that is, cunning per se—is what is cunningly appearing as non-cunning, as straightforwardness, as transparancy of any kind, as coherences *simpliciter*. Cunning appears as innocence, as its opposite, and thereby thoroughly accomplishes its of "being cunningness."

---

[3] Sartre, *Psychology of the Imagination*, 37.

If we stop here, however, we have landed in another "Exclusive Center"—and this seems as far as we can push Hegel, even in the revisionist Žižekian reading. But all we have to do is think through this very claim, push it so that all its implications become manifest, and we see that "the cunning of cunning" will also entail "the cunning of any X, arbitrarily chosen," and also the "Xness of every cunning," and so on. The indeterminate "cunningness per se," once seen to be all-pervading, ensures the all-pervadingness of any coherence chosen at random. That is, this-cup-ness is cunningly accomplishing itself by appearing everywhere as non-this-cup-ness. This is the means by which it pervades all other possible coherences; it has established itself as the punch line to the setup which all of these other coherences are. This experience of cupness here on this table before me, this moment of apprehending it, reveals itself as that which all else has hitherto been leading up to; they have turned out to be the deadpan self-expressions of the joke that is its own coherence—and as everyone knows, deadpan humor is the highest form of humor, indeed the funniest: absence as hyper-presence.

What It Is Like: Being as Cunning, Cunning as Metaphoricity

This notion of "cunning" is really another statement of what we described as the constitutive "at-a-distanceness" and "pivotality" of all coherences in Part One, which, it will be recalled, were simply ways of explaining what was meant by Intersubsumption (All-pervasion as All-pervadedness). Let us talk about the "cunning" of something even more specific, to make clear just how far we must be willing to take this point. Say whatever you can about whatever coherence is presently serving as the focus of attention—or better, experience it as closely as possible, as fully as possible. All you will be able to come up with is a sense of some aspect or other, some further coherence. Sitting here in this coffee shop reading may reveal itself to be composed of, let us say, a feeling of sitting, of what you see, and also other qualitative sensed coherences such as, say, "carrying a burden," or "recalling a past event and slightly regretting it," "waiting for a further development," "unexpectedly having to endure something previously desired," and so on. You will not find anything else about the present "this" besides such coherences of experience. But any and all of these are applicable to any and all other experiences as well. A potentially infinite number of distinguishable coherences can be apprehended as *constituent of* any other coherence. This is because each part is a coherence and each whole is also a coherence, and no nonarbitrary limit can be set to this dividability. That is, there is the "pageishness" of the page, and the "bookliness" of the book, and the "wordliness" of the word, and so on.

These qualitative coherences are not reducible to a single unilateral arrangement as a quantitative series or set of parts. They overlap infinitely and indefinitely, and precisely in this lies their explorability.

This being the case, *all* possible coherences are apprehendable in this experience, in this coherence: everything is just like this, only more so. This can go from the most general ("being," "murdering," "resisting," "accepting") to the most specific (e.g., "resisting the conclusion that you have a gum disease, mainly because your annoying aunt warned you about it once when you were seven"). What we must assert here is that this specific coherence is discoverable in any other specific coherence. This is because, even for proper nouns or other nonrepeatable specifics, we can always ask "What is it to be an X?"—that is, an aunt, an annoying aunt, resistance, resistance to a conclusion, gums, a gum disease, and so on. Any penetration into the experienced quality yields other coherences that are *strictly universal*. Of course, to some extent I am repeating the old Hegelian argument of how the particular dissolves into an aggregate of universals upon examination. But the Neo-Tiantai universals are *literally* universal in a rather different sense: they are actually applicable everywhere without exception, these specific coherences pervade all times and places, and this indeed applies to every possible coherence without exception.

For example, take the coherence, "Browsing with a slight sense of tedium the magazine rack at the airport because your flight has been delayed half an hour due to bad weather." Let us see how this pervades the coherence "Resisting the conclusion that you have a gum disease, mainly because your annoying aunt warned you about it once when you were seven" and vice versa. What is "browsing?" There need not be any one answer to this, precisely because we will have a complete interpervasion of each and every coherence with every other; one can define this coherence in whatever way one likes, and it will eventually get us where we want to go—and also, of course, everywhere else, including everywhere we do not want to go. All that we need is the way a particular coherence *seems* when considered by anyone at any time, in any state of mind. Let us be as arbitrary as possible. Let us say browsing is "a kind of hunting with only a vague idea of any concrete goal, undertaken in a mood of waiting to discover where the true goal is to kill time and overcome boredom in the process itself." Let us locate each of these new coherences over in every component coherence of the other coherence about the gum disease. As an example, we will just spell out the process with the very first one listed, namely, "Resisting" per se. "Hunting": manipulating the field of awareness so as to encounter a desired object. "Resisting": manipulating the field of awareness so as to avoid a feared object. But to hunt for X is to resist non-X; hunting is resisting. "Vagueness": a presence that promises to deliver itself more fully, combined with a sense of a standard of clarity which is not being met. "Resistance": a presence that threatens to deliver itself more fully, combined with a sense of pushing it away. But where something is threatened, something is promised; wherever the coherence of promise is presence, the coherence of threat is present. To push away is to set up an ideal state of unsullied noncontamination by the threatening presence, a singularity unharrassed by this undigestible otherness; but clarity is also a singularity that can be read as a one with no interfering contrariety within it. "Idea": a partial presence of an object that leaves something to be encountered in experience, a tally to be matched in experience. "Resisting": the partial presence of an object with which a portion of encountered reality is to be matched. But where there is a tally to be matched there is a holding off, a resisting of all possibilities that do not match, lest the tally be absorbed into pure immediacy. "Concreteness": a definiteness that can be used to exclude. "Resisting": a definiteness that can be used to exclude. "Object": a coherence that sets up an opposition between the whims of my conscious desires and what is actually encountered in experience. "Resisting": a coherence that sets up an opposition between my conscious desires and what is actually encountered in experience. . . . And so on.

Obviously these "definitions" are meant to be caricatures of arbitrariness, but the point should be clear: one can determine these coherences however one wants, always leaving something out, always finding each attempted specification matching any other attempted specification. In each case, one feels something has been left out: "Resisting" is not *just* this or that; but the point is that whatever else is specified—and we claim that there are literally an infinite number of such formulations—as constituting this coherence will also be discoverable anywhere else in just the same way.

Initially it would seem that we have here a kind of "kaleidoscope" effect, that is, each specific coherence turns out to be a rearrangement of the same finite set of elements. But this picture is complicated by the following considerations: (1) Each of these coherences is already made up of nothing but the other coherences. (2) An "arrangement" is itself a coherence, one more coherence added to the set. (3) The set of components is therefore not finite, in that it possesses a literally infinite divisibility; we have here not a collection of discrete parts, like chunks in a kaleidoscope that are each individually one and the same, but rather a set of provisional "components" each of which is analyzable in an infinity of different ways as to what is a part and what is a whole coherence.

We may approach this point from, as it were, the other direction. Here I am resisting the conclusion that I have a gum disease. Now what is it I am doing? One thing that is going on right now is that I am wearing shoes, and if I so desire I can feel them on my feet. Is this a part of "resisting the conclusion . . ." or not? Perhaps the commonsense answer is no: I experience my resistance to the conclusion at one moment, and then, when I switch my attention to something else that is going, my wearing of shoes, I am experiencing something else, a different coherence. They are not experienced simultaneously, so there need be no contradiction here, nor any perplexities arising from the question of which experiencer is myself, whether I have one mind or many, where my identity resides and so on. But this is, on our current account, a not very accurate description of this experience, and one that is founded on a particular and much discredited notion of consciousness and its transparency. We would prefer to say that the coherence "feeling foot in shoe" is in fact part of the constitutive background of the coherence "resisting the conclusion . . .," that this is indeed what is meant by "preconsciousness" in the Freudian sense, which is predicated of aspects or objects that can be experienced at will in this way. But this means that "feeling foot in shoe" is absorbed into "resisting the conclusion . . ." when the latter is the focus that is being named and attended to; the former is a component of the latter. When I shift my attention to "feeling foot in shoe" I have reversed this relationship: "resisting the conclusion . . ." has now become the background element which is absorbed into "feeling foot in shoe" as one of its components, which makes it what it is, which is discoverable within it upon examination or consideration. The whole of the former is within the latter, and vice versa. This being the case, which of these I have selected to make the focus, which determines the name given to the coherence I am now experiencing, is strictly *arbitrary*: that is, in our language, I can experience the current situation as "resisting the conclusion . . ." or *as* "feeling foot in shoe," and in either case I will be experiencing the whole set of coherences, indeed, as we have seen above, all possible coherences. "Resisting the conclusion . . ." is indeed *nothing but* "feeling foot in shoe," and vice versa. Any one particular specification of the situation is an arbitrary limiting of the field of the frame of reference, which in one sense is far from doing justice to the plenitude of the situation. To experience immediacy—"I feel pain" for example—is a kind of stubborn narrowing of the nature of the experience. But this is only half the story; as with all half truths, this one is by that very token the whole truth; "feeling foot in shoe . . ." it will turn out, is exactly as adequate a description of this whole as "the whole" or "all possible coherences" or "resisting the conclusion . . ." or "something indeterminate which can express itself in all these ways." When I say "exactly as adequate a description of it" I of course also mean "exactly as accurate and valid a way of experiencing it."

We are also obviously in agreement with certain modern trends that impel toward the conclusion that metaphoricity is in fact more primal than literalness, extending this also to the realm of experience, not merely to the symbolic system, and indeed to being as such, to the extent that this word means anything at all. Literalness is indeed an effect created by metaphoricity. That is to say, to exist is to be like something, in the strictest possible sense, and to exist here means to have some particular quality or other. That is, simply to be a coherence is to be all other coherences, and there is no more literalness about my foot- in-shoe's foot-in-shoe-ness than in its trying-to-figure-out-which-bus-will-take-me-to-the-movie-theater-ness. It is "like" itself in exactly the same way that it is "like" any other coherence. This is just what was meant earlier when we repeatedly insisted that no coherence can appear *simpliciter*. This is what allows the spiral of equivalences to expand without end in a way that will doubtless be profoundly annoying to anyone with the least literalist bent. When I say, "foot-in-shoe-ness is a kind of being-embraced in the lowest part of something I am identifying with and which is supporting that embodiment," and so on, and then say, "See, the same thing is true of trying-to-figure-out-which-bus-to-take-to-the-movie-theater-ness: the film which is the object of my desire is now that which I am identifying with, and through which I am perceiving the world, and searching for a particular object; to be in the midst of a network of "busliness" is a being-embraced-ness; this embrace encompasses the lowest or most fundamental part of that which I am embodying at this moment, my project of going to the movie," or some such shameless blather, and moreover mean it in all seriousness, and moreover again, assert that this very unlimited and unlimitable sophistry is exactly the true function of the self and its intellect, and moreover that giving free rein to this sort of interpretive ingenuity is the only way for that intellect to make its may out of the traps it has otherwise set for itself, this rests on the assertion that the so-called immediate experience itself, foot in shoe, is itself completely metaphorical in exactly this sophistic way from the beginning, that the idea that it has an immediacy which is not based on similarly flimsy or whimsical judgments and procedures is an illusion. It has never been anything but a network of fanciful metaphors from the beginning, so tightly woven together by a cramped habitual focus as to appear as natural and immediate, as a literal fact. The thing itself, the hardness of a hard thing, the brightness of the bright, the wetness of water, all those supposedly irreducible elements of experience, all are already elaborate metaphorical constructs—otherwise they could not be experienced at all. They are all experienced only in contrast to and *thus* in identity to the other expressions of themselves *as* other qualities, in the deadpan *umwelt* surrounding them. Most simply, in the case of the so-called subject and object, as described above, the subject encounters the hardness of this hard thing as an expression of himself, in the form of resistance to himself. When this happens, the openness of the subject is posited in contrast as something which could come up against a resistance—hence as a hardness itself. Hardness is a metaphor for the self, self is a metaphor for hardness. Moreover, each is nothing but that metaphor of the other, to the extent that each other is, for this very reason, every other other as well. The same goes for anything you like. Isness is asness is metaphoricity. It is no accident that to ask what something is is to ask what it is like.

What is it to experience a "simple quality"—to experience green, or speed, or hesitation, or anxiety, or the rippling surface of water, or sunlight on the face? It seems that nothing can be thought about them—any effort to understand the experience of greenness, any particular instance of greenness, well, it seems that all the ministrations of the intellect merely compare and combine it more or less quantitatively (externally) to other experiences—but what can I do to become truly "aware" of what I experience when I experience this greenness? What allows me to penetrate it fully, feel it "directly," vividly?—only comparison, metaphor. But even more essentially: even a bad, totally inappropriate metaphor will bring this experience into sharper focus for me, make it more vivid. Any token at all in the metaphor position will help. And in fact any word at all is such a metaphor. An envelope lies on the floor. If I stare at it trying to feel its rectangularness, its whiteness, the contours of its materials and its folds more clearly and focusedly, without words, I find I cannot improve my reading much. But if I say it looks like an aerial shot of a large flat building, in the very looseness of the metaphor, even if I have never seen any even vaguely similar building situated in such a way, as it were in the backwash of the falling away of this inappropriate metaphor from the facticity before me, I am suddenly able to see the envelope. Even if I say it looks like a sleeping dog, I see it better. However lame the metaphor, as long as there is one, I see more, in fact it could be said that only then do I finally see it at all. I can say, it looks like the elbow of Benjamin Franklin, and indeed, I suddenly am able to see the envelope there on the floor, as the image of Franklin's elbow crashes and breaks and drains away over it.

This crucial point also makes sense of many tricky metaphysical issues. To take the classical Buddhist and then the related classical Tiantai example: in some forms of meditation, one trains to see all dharmas *as*, for example, red, then blue, then as earth, as water, as light, and finally *as* impermanence, suffering and nonself, or as Global Incoherence. We may feel that seeing all things as, say, earth, is feasible, in that earth might be the substance from which all things are formed, but to see things as instantiations of, say, "impermanence," is not, since the latter is an abstract noun that is always the predicate of some prior thing, which *is* impermanent. To resolve this, we must fully realize the impact of the reversibility of subject and predicate, or substance and attribute, in the Tiantai perspective, which is really what establishes the current point about metaphoricity. Impermanence seems to be facts about things; how are we to see the thing *as* a certain fact about that very thing (i.e., impermanence), as one of the many predications that are unified in it as a thing? But this question is misguided. "Thing" is already seeing "as" thing, *as* particular, *as* relevant to my desire, and so on, i.e., in the framework of a certain motivated metaphysical orientation, a certain way of fixing the subject/predicate relation. One is in any case excluding much, abstracting, neglecting. "Thingishness is one among many properties belonging to impermanence" (or to the Three Truths, to Inherent Entailment, and so on) in exactly the same way that "impermanence (etc.) is one among many properties belonging to things." In each case one chooses one aspect (regarded as unchanging and unified) as the subject or substance, and the other (regarded as multiple, arrayed, and changing) as the predicate or property. The key point is to see how everything is already just as much a (merely) "abstract" noun as "impermanence, Emptiness, Three Truths, Inherent Entailment," and so on. "Cloud is white," we could say, or "cloud is impermanent," or "Cloud is Locally Coherent, Globally Incoherent and Intersubsumption," or "Cloud is Inherently Entailed in all other coherences," but we could also say, "white is cloudy," "impermanence is cloudy," "Local Coherence is cloudy," "Intersubsumption is cloudy," "Inherent Entailment per se is cloudy, is white, etc." Any of these may be the substance, with the coherences accordingly taking the role of the attributes or predicates. Once Intersubsumption has become clear, of course, any coherence at all can function in the role of the one substance; we can say, "shoe-tying is white," or "stringiness is cloudy," or "in-between-ness is Republican," and so on, and, of course, equally that any of these is Intersubsumption as such, that is, the Absolute as the substance, beginning, and end of all other coherences. Reversibility is once again the ultimate meaning here; we do not mean to assert simply, à la the physics of David Bohm, that "things" are actually derivative and "flux" (impermanence) is really primary, or make any such unilateral metaphysical claim. The point for us is that either can function as the primary, the subject, and the other as the derivative, the predicate. Nor does this entail any sort of critique of the subject-predicate or substance-accident forms; rather, in a Tiantai context, these are perfect examples of *upayas*, "skillful means," which are locally true, misleading if taken as globally true or literally, but which can be opened up to reveal more truths; in this case, we are grateful to the subject-predicate form for revealing even more truths to us, that is, not "there is no such thing as a subject or a predicate, a substance or an accident," but rather, "now that we have these useful categories in hand, we can see the universal applicability of both sides, in other words, that everything has the character of a subject or a substance that has been revealed by this false division, and everything has the character of an attribute or predicate as well."

This is the same reversal we get in the *Prajñā* sutras when they tell us, "Form is Empti(ness), Emptiness is Form," and so on. Emptiness is initially construed as a predicate characterizing form and everything else; without the Tiantai step of thoroughgoing universal metaphoricization of being, the reversal cannot hold. The point here is that "Form," "Sensation," and so on are from the beginning just as abstract as "Emptiness." We may relate this also to the being/having problem, to be discussed in further detail below, for the subject or substance is what one is, while the predicates or attributes are what one *has*. What we see when we see metaphoricity is that the predicate can equally be the substance of the substance, that the roles can always be reversed, that having and being can always switch places. Judged by the one/many or the changing/unchanging axes that seem to be implicit in these categories, we find the importance here also of the necessary oneness as manyness as oneness, and changingness as unchangingness as changingness, of all coherences, which we have established as the basic Neo-Tiantai position.

Here I may perhaps be allowed to consider the impact of this point on a particular Buddhalogical issue. I refer to the central Buddhist practice of "mindfulness," the careful and concerted attention to all sensations in their immediate temporal concreteness. The precision with which things present themselves, the vivid and intractably present aspect we see, in the wake of poetry, of the razor-sharp image or metaphor—how are we to compare this enhanced form of seeing the particular with that involved in the practice of mindfulness? In the latter practice, one is to note that one is breathing in a long breath, a short breath, an obstructed breath, the coolness of the air on the nostril, the expansion of the diaphragm, the emotional wavering going along with it along the skin and in the chest—or, that one is experiencing a pleasant bodily feeling, an unpleasant psychological feeling . . . or, that one's mind is tensely appropriating objects, or greedily appropriating objects . . . or, this material object appears like this, persists like this, disappears like this. How does this kind of direct, matter-of-fact, apparently nonmetaphorical apprehension of bare facts in their concrete particularity relate to the vividness with which a fact shines forth in the wake of a poetic metaphor?

Perhaps we could say that what you experience premetaphorically of any quality is precisely emptiness. That is, emptiness is what you actually experience of the whiteness as whiteness—such that it is as adequate to say that emptiness is white (which is to say, that it is adequate to assert this as to assert the opposite). And also that it is red, green, blue, round, tall, waiting, agitated, ironic, salty, to the extent that these words, as metaphorical markers within a semiotic network of differences, have not yet been applied to the experiences which, after such application, bear these names. We tend to assume that each quality, as perceived prelinguistically, is still distinguishable from other qualities—but is this true? "Distinguishable from other qualities" obviously already refers to the comparison with something other that lies at the heart of the process I here call metaphor. Mindfulness is an effort to see any given quality in isolation from all other qualities, and its success lies precisely in the inevitable and eternal failure of this effort—all that is left without these metaphors is emptiness. This emptiness is a plenum of qualities (Local Coherence), each of which is itself all qualities (Intersubsumption).

In that case, we may say that the challenge in each moment of experience is to look head on at the presented quality before one, to investigate it until it becomes transparent, evaporates, proves unfindable, *and yet remains present.* Only from the side, viewed in haste and as it were while averting the eyes, do qualities appear side by side in a quantitative array, as a sum of entities existing as the world. But this "remains present" remains only a dull registering until the full application of *all possible metaphors* to this quality has been accomplished—that is the real fulfillment of the "contemplation of Local Coherence" on the heels of the "Contemplation of Global Incoherence"—and this is what constitutes the Contemplation of Intersubsumption (All-pervasion as All-pervadedness) proper. "This envelope is the torments of hell, a Sunday afternoon at the lake, miraculous power, shitting on the president's head, infinite undying love, the angry rejection of all human values, perfect unexcelled enlightenment, a toothache, permanent purity and freedom and bliss"—this is the density of metaphor that must wash over any quality for it to be satisfactorily experienced. This interpenetration of qualities is eloquently testified to by the flood of irrelevancies that flood the mind like a porous material whenever it is even slightly relaxed; from all over in the peripheral atmosphere come the irrelevances that make up this present coherence. If we have frequent recourse to Freud in this discussion, it is especially in deference to the revelatory importance of free association and related techniques, that is, Freud's discovery, not of what is hidden, but of the nature of hiddenness per se. There in the interstices of the chosen points of attention, not hidden underneath them somewhere, are an infinity of alternate *Gestalten*. In Tiantaiese, we call it *yini-ansanqian*—the Three Thousand Coherences Present in/as Every Moment of Experience, or, if we prefer the Neo-Tiantai equivalent, asness as such.

Non-X Is Just Like X, Only More So

Hegel noticed it, Marx made much of it: changes in quantity become changes in quality. We want to take *this* notion itself to its ultimate conclusion. In its humblest and most immediate form, this is the beloved Daoist-anarchist principle of institutionalization (the Unabomber manifesto exfoliates it skillfully); whatever is good on a small scale, within a loose, small grouping of members, becomes a voracious evil when institutionalized, when applied to everyone, when made a rule for all. It is the enlargement itself, which entails its formalization as rule and institution and its universal recognition, which changes its quality, in particular its value: as Laozi puts it, when all the world knows good as good, this is evil.

Here we want to assert that this is an adequate definition of what it means to exist at all. "I am reminded of the old Jewish joke" (as old Jewish joke tellers like to say): "Jews are just like everyone else, only more so." What we have to say here is in that case the consummate Judaization of being: Everything is just like everything else, only more so. To be X is to be non-X, *only more so*. "More so" here means made inescapable, applicable in all cases, extended in all directions, manifesting in all dimensions, intensified to the highest possible degree. Indeed, *negation* per se is nothing other than this "universalization"—to choose a pre-disliked term for this phenomenon while at the same time bringing forth the important *logical* implications of this claim. This can now be deduced from what we have established above. For us this means simply the *full realization* of the initial project embodied in any coherence simply by virtue of appearing as some qualitative, experienced "one." The coherence of "being X" is always posited in a local context which is temporarily and arbitrarily fixed, but at the same time calls forth further recontextualizations in the same gesture as it establishes its constitutive initial narrowed contextualization. When thought through to the end, aware of all relevant contexts implied in this appearance, applied in all possible ways, this Xness necessarily crashes, and the very Xness reveals itself to have always been non-Xness, and non-Xness ultimately of every conceivable kind. This can be done either through deliberately expanding the field of reference, or by doing the opposite, that is, attempting to isolate this coherence, to disengage it from all otherness, to "purify" it—and of course to necessarily fail, or, to repeat it for the first of many times, succeed by seeing the *necessity* of this failure only. Intersubsumption (All-pervasion as All-pervadedness) signifies that these two opposite procedures are mutually entailing, and ultimately identical.

Let us draw out two forms of presence as absence. (1) The full Xness of X only dawns when it is seen to extend precisely to the absence of X. This depends on seeing that it had no straight *simpliciter* Xness to begin with, that its immediate Xness was a retrospective illusion posited back by subsequent absence of X, wherein X manifested itself as "gone." The good old days appear to consciousness only when they are gone, and this type of appearance is the only true manifestation of this coherence, "good old days." My lost youth, when it was present, could not be felt as such; it was too close, it was overpopulated with details and alternate coherences—getting up in the morning, having to get to work, waiting for the bus, buying new shoes, and so on; these were the coherences that appeared to consciousness, on the basis of the larger context, the life form of "those days," which itself could never appear to consciousness since it was the overall context, crammed up too close to the lens, as it were, to appear as a coherence in its own right. Only when it recedes into the context of some otherness—some other times, worse times—can it appear as a specific coherence at all. But this is precisely the extension of that initially hidden "immediate" coherence, "the good old days," into its opposite, into the realm of non-X; non-X is the greater extension, the growth, the full application, of this X. There are several forms of this hyper-presence of X that make it disappear, which we will consider in detail in the section on Desire ("Can't Get No-Satisfaction") below.

(2) Another dimension of this presence as absence can be disclosed by considering it from another angle. For what is it that is just like X only more so, that is "more X than X"? Answer: *Full awareness* of X. This will entail the making explicit of what were initially mere hints of memory, symbolization, expansion of contexts; the coherence of the thing is more genuinely present in its anticipation and memory than in its physical presence. Attention is made possible by absence, that is, reframing in new, broader contexts, and this attention never stops revealing new aspects and significances of the thing. The fuller implications of this will be explored in the section on mind/body relations, below. As we have already seen, experience of identities, significances, coherences is always already *metaphorical*. Everything is a metaphor for everything else. This is why, in classical terms, mere consciousness of the relevant contexts was regarded as curative of the initially oppressive facticity/unattainability of any coherence: as long as they are not figures of awareness they implicitly function as brute facts in the frame, determining the fixity of the figure. But once they become figures themselves, this whole configuration calls out for contextualization; the fixed determining contexts turn out also not to be experienced brute facts, but themselves to depend on an arbitrary narrowing of relevant contexts. When these contexts come into awareness, thereby bringing forth their own contextualizations, relaxing the crimp in mental focus, the coherence no longer appears as one "one" among an array of other "one"s; its initially oppressive unevadability/unattainability—that is, as a specific incident absent everywhere else—reveals itself to be the curative unevadability/unattainability—that is, the all-pervasiveness of its constitutive absence, its virtual presence as metaphorical unavoidability which, however, cannot appear *simpliciter* or literally, even in its initial appearance.

These two alternate explanations of presence as absence, as retrospective distancing and as awareness, may appear initially to be opposed. They are, however, structurally recapitulations of one another, and to perceive this, their identity to one another, is just what is meant by the perceiving Intersubsumption (All-pervasion as All-pervadedness).

Can't Get No-Satisfaction

Sartre compares the evocation of a fantasy image of a desired object to drinking sea water to quench thirst—"a way of deceiving the desires momentarily in order to aggravate them ... a way of *playing* at satisfying my desire...." To mentally picture the desired thing satisfies the desire momentarily, in the moment of being encountered, as it were; but as this image reveals that it is a presentation of an absence, that it lacks the explorability of a perceived presence, that the pillars on this imagined Pantheon cannot be counted, it only aggravates the desire further.

This description is surely correct. However, it backhandedly makes an assumption that we have to challenge: namely that, in contrast to this unsatisfying fantasy image, in encountering the real object of our desire we are capable of being satisfied, that its presence will be present in its presence. This we deny. In both cases, it is the initial appearance of the desired coherence that dulls the desire for a moment; the Gestalt's formation, the sudden appearance of the new figure, or, in our language, the sudden taking up of all the background context into a new meaning-giving coherence, a new punch line, is wherein the pleasure resides.[4] As the moments creep on, however, this fullness of presence must crash. The explorability of the object proves to be its undoing; as more and more of itself is revealed, it is revealed to be something other than what was desired, indeed, many other things. This is another example of presence as hyper-absence, or the "more-X-than-X"ness which constitutes the negation of the desired X. Indeed, the desired object as it were maintains itself only by means of a rhythm of slipping in and out of focus, of backing out of the spotlight, retreating from the attention and teasingly reappearing, just long enough to see but not long enough to get a good look at. Once it dwells clearly in attention, indeed, it cannot fail to be "universalized" in the sense described above. The more the coherence is examined, stayed with, kept in view, thought through, the more it reveals that it is a unique way of focusing all other coherences, that, indeed all those other—mostly unwanted—coherences are present in it to the exact extent that the desired coherence is there. This process of contamination of

---

[4] See the section "Pleasure and the Self" below.

the desired by the undesired occurs at the same time as the opposite process, the contamination of the undesired by the desired, for indeed both are the same process, and both are accomplished simply by staying with the coherence in question long enough, simply letting it unfold in the heat of attention.

That the hyper-presence of the desired object is its absence—that is, that it is the absence of desirability, that it is no longer desirable—is a well-attested phenomenon on all levels of culture. It is revealed, for example, in the faux-profound saying attributed by Woody Allen to his befuddled Socrates: "When a man sings a beautiful tune, it is a pleasure, but if he won't shut up, eventually it begins to give you a headache." This is also known as "too much of a good thing"—a common complaint, to take up the question of sex and drugs for the first of many times, in cases of excessive pornographic immersion, the grotesquerie of which is also invoked in certain cures for cigarette addiction, that is, being forced to smoke nonstop. Denied a place to hide, to retreat to, the desired coherence vanishes; as a plenum it becomes a blank, or worse, a repulsive force-feeding which becomes just the opposite of the desideratum. One has no time to desire it; therefore it becomes no longer desirable. Time to desire it—a hence to provide it with value—requires a place to retreat to from it, what I have above referred to rather cryptically as the position of the subject, the unseen negation of the coherence in question. Indeed, occasionally it would seem that the coherence as object of desire can be dissipated simply by fanatically filling the imagination with it: fill the field of mental vision and hearing with the face and cheerful laugh of the desired friend Pierre, or the hungered-for moan and wriggle of the passing miniskirt-clad hips, and we have suddenly a nightmare scenario. This is one way in which the undesired contaminates the desired, merely by allowing the desired to fully expand.

Several difficulties come with this consideration. First, we may ask, is this not a different kind of "universalization" from the one described above, that is, where the coherence in question is found precisely in its nonpresence, not in its superfluous overflow? But these really amount to two versions of the same thing. The problem in either case is the revelation of too much non-X that is also precisely X, and hence is inescapable as long as X is present. When Pierre, or the grinding hips, fills my field of consciousness, they begin to reveal themselves as flesh, as molecules, as meat and bones, as senseless molecular collisions, as teeth and nostril hairs and mechanical secretions and tools of competing obsessions and embodiments of competing intentions. This is the case in either manner of dwelling in the object, either manner of holding the object in conscious focus for too long, whether as non-X absorbing focus or as surrounding repetition. In either case, the explorability works to reveal the presence of the nondesired in the desired.

Someone might also complain, "What I desire when I desire X is precisely 'X in the proper measured context of non-X's'—indeed, as you've proved, that's all X can possibly mean." But obviously this only supports our point. If Xness *means* "a certain amount of X surrounded by a certain amount of non-Xness, in a certain arrangement," we have a strange loop on our hands, and indeed this strange loop is precisely what every moment of conscious awareness presents us with. We have here again identity as constitutive impossibility, as we have referred to above and will explore in more detail below. What comes into awareness as X is always so also as a combination of Xness and non-Xness, and it is this inescapable asness, this looping infinite Möbius-strip regress, which makes each of the coherences as unavoidable as they are unattainable.

Since Plato, it has been a common move for mystical philosophers who were not fanatically axiologically dualistic to try to reconcile the desirable things we know, but which do not satisfy us in the way the philosopher would wish—sensual pleasures—and the highest Good wherein resides true ultimate value. This is done typically by means of some version of the doctrine that the former is some kind of *pale reflection* of the latter, that in desiring temporal goods we are actually confusedly desiring the ultimate good, which is appearing before us in a diluted, indirect, confused way as this temporal good. Already in what we have said so far, and much more so in what is to follow, however, we have the opportunity to reverse this judgment: temporal sensual pleasure is the Good in its purest, most intense form, in its full presence—and *for that reason* it fails to satisfy, it loses the coherence of goodness. The hyper-presence of the Good means its absence. In contrast, any philosophical or religious or even social notion of "ultimate Good" is a dilute, vague, elusive presence of the coherence Goodness—and this is what allows it to remain Good, the truly satisfying absolute Good. Its goodness resides in the fact that we do not have it, that it is hidden from us. In the end, we have here Laozi versus Plato, and all that that entails.

Given this much, what shall we say about the unsatisfiability of desire? For this we must state unequivocally: satisfaction cannot be got. But on our general principles it should also of course follow that satisfaction cannot be avoided either—or it you prefer, that we can't get no-satisfaction any more than we can get satisfaction. What can this mean, and what are its implications for our aesthetic, moral and conative experience?

Rival Centers and Reversibility: Desire and Aversion

The "too much of a good thing" picture given above suffices up to a point; there are indeed certain desires which can be "satisfied" by imagination of their hyper-presence in the way described, that is, by making them fully and pervasively present *as images*. But now we must point out that this is by no means the case with the most intense and deepest desires of our beings, the obsessional, symbolic, maddening ones that give our life its meaning and (what is perhaps precisely the same thing) its constitutive torment. To understand these desires, we have to apply the above model more strictly. That is, for an object to appear as an object, as an image, even one that fills the field of consciousness, is still not really hyper-presence in the Neo-Tiantai sense. For that, to become a true center of all other coherences, expressing itself *as* all other coherences, it is necessary for the central coherence's determinacy as such and such to be effaced in its expressions, to be present *only* as its expressions, or at most in a relationship of undecidability between its direct presence and its indirect presence as expressed in other coherences. The central X is the punch line of the periphery, by means of which all the peripheral coherences are revealed to express Xness, but which at the same time loses its own exclusive Xness in this process, so that it no longer appears as simply X. X as a simple determinate exclusive coherence vanishes from the scene. In other words, a true center, i.e., one that has really succeeded in finding itself expressed in *all* other possible coherences without exception, does not appear directly as an image: a true center, as the Laozian tradition would have it, can only be an invisible center. We may also note here, to anticipate, that this is precisely equivalent to *identifying* with the X in question: what it means for some X to *be myself* is for me to embody it by making it the central-disappearing coherence of experience, the one that appears nowhere explicitly or *simpliciter* but which for that very reason appears everywhere, "in" all other coherences. "I," the transcendental ego, am present to myself only as my world of representations, none of which is "I" as such, but all of which are modifications and expressions of my "Iness." With this consideration, we begin to approach the question of "the self," which will occupy us for most of the rest of this work. It is to be noted from the outset that "the self" for us refers to a certain structural peculiarity, rather than any particular set of contents. The self is one side of a relation that is always operating, but the contents that fall on the "self" side are not fixed; whatever coherences happen to be on the "self" side of the dividing line at any given time are for us what constitute the self at that time. Here we begin to approach this relation in terms of the problem of "identification" and its relation to the various forms of desire.

Now there are some desires which not only cannot be wished or fantasized away, but which will not go away even when they are satisfied. These are the ones that really structure our lives, as I said, and it is here that I think the omnicentric theory can really aid our understanding.

First let us divide these desires into two structurally distinct types: desire to *have* and desire to *be*. These two categories, being and having, always seem to have something especially unhelpful and fuzzy about them, if not pointlessly evasive; but we cannot do without them here, and indeed we hope to be able to provide a more satisfactory theory for them which will elucidate their relation to one another. Of course, there is a reason for their fuzziness, which becomes immediately clear in light of the position we have been developing here. This division of being and having is not absolute, to say the least: being is a form of having, having is a form of being, having appears *as* being and vice versa. To desire to be something is also to desire to have something, and vice versa; if I wish to be powerful I desire to possess power, if I desire a car I desire to be a car-owner. Having and being are the backs of one another, like any other two coherences. Nonetheless, there are structurally distinctive features to these two aspects of what is classically called Local Coherence, the form in which the desire in question first comes into experience. If either one is thought through to its bottomless bottom, it reveals itself to have always been the other as well.

The claim I will be making here is that the obsessional desire to *have* some object is in fact a blocked or suppressed desire to *be* that object. The apparent desire to *be* something in particular, on the other hand, is a blocked or suppressed desire to be an *expression* of whatever it *excludes*. Let us try to understand what these conclusions mean, and how they are arrived at.

Let us say I have an obsessional desire to *possess* some fetishistic object: a particular shape of a particular body part, a particular type of sexual or emotional partner, or a certain type of car, or a certain type of friend, or a certain type of knowledge, or a certain type of enjoyment. This object is appearing to me inescapably at all sorts of inopportune times; I have begun to see everything else *in terms of* this thing, as means to attain this thing, as signs pointing toward or away from this thing, as various ways of bringing this coherence into my experience. In fact, it is becoming for me a *center* of experience in much the way I have described already. However, inasmuch as it is an *object* I desire, this is still a *visible* or explicit center, something with a fixed and undigested determinacy of its own, an image. I am fully aware that, as I walk the streets, I am alerted to the presence of women with a certain type of mouth in a heightened way, and when I see one, I am completely absorbed into that experience, the mouth becomes the center of my experience, everything else becomes merely its background. This type of mouth has succeeded to an extraordinary degree in integrating all other coherences into itself, making them all expressions of itself. Indeed, attention always involves desire. It is the concern with a particular goal that singles out certain aspects of the world around me as objects of attention. An object of perception is an object of desirous concern, and that is what we're dealing with here.

But to the extent that this center is still visible, that it is explicit, determinate, available as an image to my awareness, it is still only a *partial* center. That is, it has *snagged* somewhere, come up against some indigestible kernel that it cannot incorporate, which it has failed to bring into its system. If it *could* do this, it would *vanish* as a determinate image. Its Xness per se would crash if its project fully succeeded, as we have seen. What is it that it is failing to incorporate as a version of itself? The short answer is simply: *myself*. That is, whatever subject I'm identifying with, whatever "body" I am embodying. This, as we have seen, is just *whatever is not explicitly appearing,* whatever is serving as the proximal term *through which* all else is perceived. This means that what I desire to possess is whatever I cannot image myself *being,* whatever I cannot place myself in the position of, whatever I cannot metaphoricize myself as a version of, whatever I cannot embody as the proximate term which is to be experienced only *as* other coherences, including my present body.[5] The desideratum is an object that I can allow all experience to be absorbed into *except for whatever coherence I am implicitly identifying with as myself*. We have here the tension between two rival centers, one explicitly experienced as an image which is contextualizing the world around it (object of desire) and one which is unseen but expressing itself only as all other objects (self). The reversibility that normally would allow these each to be unseen centers, to absorb each other as alternate subjects and objects, has snagged on the fact that, for some reason, I cannot allow this "myself" to be something experienced by, expressed as, that particular object. "Cannot" here probably means usually "have been forbidden to," as we will explore below. If there is an object that would make my present self-concept break down if I were to imagine myself as it—that is, experiencing all the rest of the world through it and in terms of it—you can bet I will have an obsessional desire to possess this object which can never be satisfied. And why is this? Because to *be* X is to make it central, the unseen, proximal term, or rather that through which everything else is seen, or can be reduced to—as in the case of my own body—and where I always have available to me the option of *reversibility*. That is, I can see this cup on the table, in which case my nervous system, and so on, appears *as* this cup, but I can also always reverse this relation and experience the coherence of cupness *as* a modification of my nervous system, and so on. Where this reversibility breaks down, we have the obsessional desire. I desire those lips because I cannot imagine myself being

---

[5] As Merleau-Ponty puts it, "My body is wherever something is to be done" (PhP, 250).

those lips desirously encountering that part of their surrounding world that I now regard as the body that is myself.

Desire creates the Gestalt of the thing, carves it out as object. When something appears in experience, it wants, as it were, to be the center of the world, and normally it is. The self is absorbed into it for that moment of attention/desire, oneself and all other coherences are a function of this focus, the background that shares its coherence in the form of setup to its punch line, in the form of opposition to it. But in the case of an obsessional object, I am *implicitly* experiencing myself and all else in terms of it, but cannot *explicitly* do so; its original project of absorbing the world into itself hits an indigestible obstacle. There is a snag in the reversibility. That is, this sexy female mouth is what my whole being is appearing *as* when I am attending to it, and desiring it. This should mean that myself, my body, is now a coherence absorbed into the mouthness, and which expresses "sexy-female-mouthness" itself, because this mouth desires my body, and is thereby absorbed into my body, expressed by my body, such that the latter coherence is metaphorically available in the coherence "I-ness." But this has been, let us say, forbidden. My problem is that I can't imagine *being* the mouth that desires my body. I am not allowed to *see myself—my own body—from the perspective of sexy female mouthness*. To really identify with that mouth as an object of desire wants to be identified with, that is, as a genuine center, would mean making of my current body and self-identification a peripheral element which is merely expressive of that coherence. I will be experienced by that mouth as an object to be attracted by, kissed by, encountered by that mouth, and hence an element of its coherence, which means omnicentrically being that coherence itself. To fully identify in this way, as in the normal course of desiring, would mean to become fully *nothing but* sexy female mouthness, on general omnicentric principles as developed above. It is what I am seeing all other objects in terms of, but cannot yet see my own (unseen) self in terms of. To do so would be to *be* that object; it is a false center which could only be satisfied by becoming a true center, which is to say, of course, disappearing and in the process becoming omnipresent. If there is a particular mannerism of the opposite sex that obsesses one, one can be sure it is a mannerism one would never employ—that is, embody—oneself.

We may say that we have here a tension between two rival centers, between the posited, visible "false" (i.e., incomplete) center, and the real unseen center, and this is what is meant by desire in the current sense, where any *determinate* center is the object of desire. It follows that the only way to satisfy this sort of desire is to empathetically *become* the desired object—a principle Freud brushed against in *The Ego and the Id*, where the ego is in fact created as a substitute for the lost desired object: I will be what I desired to have. The same may be said for the general Freudian picture of the vicissitudes of desires to be and have the phallus in the course of childhood development. Philip Roth perhaps was somewhere in the same Freudian ballpark in his book *The Breast*. Given our omnicentric theory of metaphoricity and imagination above, we have an easier job of working through some of the implications and the range of applications for this principle. On our picture, the desire to have is in fact a substitute for the desire to be. But the desire to be a certain thing is not what is primarily desired; what is primarily desired is a restitution of the smooth and unsnagged reversibility of omnicentrism, instead of the tension between two rival centers. This consideration will reappear below, when we address the question of intersubjectivity and also of pleasure per se.

We might think here also of the Lacanian picture of desire, which is in many ways the most useful we have around, that is, desire defined as the difference between drive and demand, and as in its essence unsatisfiable, since it is also desire for a never-certain symbol of the Other's love/recognition, the impossible thing which would make the symbolic system consistent and thereby make its recognition of oneself certain. We, too, see the issue in desire as concerning making the self—that is, the unseen, real center—into an object perceived by the desired object. But the question for us is not so much a desire for recognition, and hence for a kind of de facto Sartrean in-itselfness which is otherwise impossible for consciousness, but reversibility, switchability itself. No *determinate* object satisfies, in our case, not because of the sliding of the symbolic chain as such, but because nothing that retains its determinacy as such is a true center. To "be" that other thing is to make yourself a visible object, hence, indeed to give yourself determinate being for a moment. But my claim is that the ability to switch around is what is really desired here. What you desire is what you cannot—or are forbidden to—imagine yourself *as*.

By speaking here of an empathetic identification with the object of desire/attention, I hope it will be clear that this in no way implies for me a means of gaining any sort of knowledge about that object, or circumventing the usual modes of information-gathering to gain some sort of direct intuitive understanding of the object, as, say, Bergsonian intuitionists (are there any?) may sometimes suggest. On the contrary, what is at stake here is obviously a question of making explicit what this object is *for me*, that is, in my own fantasy construction, as something which I simply cannot imagine myself being and which therefore provides a maddening snag to the interpenetration of perspectives which is always already the implicit tendency of my experience. What is discovered in this imaginative embodiment will be the same kind of arbitrary set of metaphorical connections elucidated above, revealed through repeatedly asking, "But what is it to be an X?" Hence, for example, if I have a powerful desire for money, the claim here is that this is an unwillingness to be money. But what is it to be money? Each desirer will doubtless give a different first set of answers to this question; let us say, to be a symbolic object, to be a medium of exchange, to be something having value, to be a stand-in for fecal matter, to be something that can be spent, something that can be saved, something universally recognized, something obtained with pleasure, the root of all evil, something that can be folded, something that is quantifiable, and so on. Whichever of these come to the fore, in the manner of a free association experiment, will probably be the ones most relevant to the case at hand, the ones the desirer is unwilling to identify with. Thus to imagine "being money" might involve for one person imagining being something passed from hand to hand in exchange for services and goods, while for another it might involve imagining being something that accumulates in a guarded place. It should be clear from this that what we have in mind here is probably more akin to a freshman acting class exercise than to a transcendent experience of at-one-ment. The necessary premise for all this is, of course, that whatever I had previously been identifying with is just as much an arbitrary metaphorical positing as this would be, as we have seen above and as we shall explore more thoroughly below.

Desire to Be

Desire to have is then disguised desire to be. But *explicitly* desiring to *be* someone or something is an entirely different case. To desire to *be* is a desire to posit a spectator (i.e., a true center) of the *opposite* kind, the kind excluded from what one wishes to be—again, to make a true center of it, so its determinacy vanishes and pervades—here again, due to a snag in reversibility. The sexy mouth defines my world, but fails to vanish, remains an image—so I explicitly want to have it, thereby actually to be it. But if there is something I cannot make explicitly central in this way, I will desire to *be* its opposite. Powerlessness, let us say, fails to pervade for me (whatever powerlessness might mean for me). I cannot make it a center into which all other coherences empty. I cannot clear the world of some coherences which I see as irreducible to powerlessness. I cannot imagine powerlessness as the sole center to which all coherences are reducible. Therefore, I want to *be* powerful, for this alone will establish the observing center "powerlessness" all-pervasively/indeterminately for me. It follows that only if I already see, for instance, goodness everywhere, in an oppressively irreversible way, such that I am unable to make badness a pervading center, can I wish to *be* good. The wish to be good is therefore always a means of allowing badness to truly pervade. Similarly, if I want to *be* a bad boy, it will mean I want to posit a good spectator, a hidden center with the coherence goodness that will thereby, by perceiving me, absorb all coherences, including myself, into the coherence goodness. In either case, we have what looks like a "if you can't beat 'em, join 'em" mentality here: we participate in an oppressively irreversible quality of the world, which is in reality a subversive attempt to force this quality to fully realize and hence undermine itself, to allow its reversal into its opposite by bringing its project to the complete success that was initially prevented by one's own nonparticipation. In all these cases, it is *reversibility* alone that functions as an ultimate value.

Let us say, for example, that I want to *be* the "wandering stranger," as in the old song. This means that for me something like "stable knownness, belongingness, community membership," fails to pervade. I am unable to imagine a world *without* wandering-strangerness, marginality. I want to see the *interchangeability* of "marginality" and "belongingness," but this is blocked by a *failure of belongingness to absorb marginality into itself*, to reveal how marginality is an expression of itself or vice versa. Only if I can be seen-as-an-other-who-is-marginal can I posit this all-pervading (marginality-absorbing) coherence of belongingness. It is a *fear* of marginality, as something my own sense of belongingness cannot "digest," which makes me want to *be* marginal. It follows that I can free myself from this desire to be only by more fully developing the centrality (pivotality, all-pervasiveness, etc.) of my concept of belongingness, by contemplation of what "belongingness" means for me, and the limits of my ability to metaphoricize it. If I could see belongingness as something that also operates *through and as* marginality (it posits its exception, etc.), I would no longer *have* to *be* marginal. (We may note in passing that this is one of the sources of the psychological power of Hegel's method, and how it manages to reach its conservative conclusions in spite of its radical methods.)

Or consider the desire to *be* famous. I have this because I cannot see famousness in (my own present) famelessness (being-admired in being-ignored). And in what way is being-admired to be revealed in being-ignored? Inasmuch as being-admired is an *object* for the coherence being-ignored as (invisible but all-pervasive) subject-body. When I feel seen by the ignored, this reversibility is restored. I want to *be* sexy because I cannot see the sexiness of sexlessness—which is revealed by being felt as desired by the undesired. Undesired unsexiness thus shows itself to include, pervade and hence appear also as, desired sexiness. Thereby reversibility is restored, which is always the ultimate desideratum.

Aversion

This is also the case for the phenomenon of obsessive aversion, although here we have yet another structure. On one level aversion can be seen as simply a form of desire: aversion to X is the desire for the absence of X. But given our reflections of absence and presence above, and on the basis of the phenomenology of aversion, we have to analyze the case a bit differently. It is, in a way, a much more straightforward and intuitively accessible case. To have an aversion to having something in one's presence is to have something that one cannot integrate into one's own present centering project of the moment. The hated object is something I cannot see *as* myself, however presently defined, that, whatever I am identifying with or using as the unseen proximal central term of all appearing coherences. Once again we have a snag in reversibility here, but where in the case of desire the problem was that I could not see myself as an aspect of the object, here I cannot see the object as an aspect of myself. That is, when I desire, it means I cannot imagine the world, and especially my own body and self-identified coherences, as perceived and encountered by, say, money or breastiness as the proximate term, as expressions of money or breastiness, as thereby being setups to the punch line money or breastiness which are absorbed into and as the coherence of moneyness or breastiness, whatever these might mean to me at a particular time. On the other hand, I cannot imagine that this cockroach, who has been lurking in my room for the past several days, is a setup to the punch line that I am, I cannot imagine it to reveal and express the coherence of me-ness (whatever I am identifying with as body, as unseen proximate term), I cannot incorporate it into my centering project. However, it has begun to form a partial center of its own, and indeed, unlike the partial centering of the desired object, it forms a center which is itself *invisible*, like me. For here is the central structural difference between desire and aversion, which are otherwise *so hard to tell apart*: the desired object wants to appear as an image, while the detested object resists coming to light as an image. As the adage has it, as Laozi and Nietzsche and Freud knew as well, we see mainly what we want to see. There is a definite resistance for consciousness to acknowledge and fix the attention on something it dislikes. It will tend to go underground, and will appear only as an encountered jarring disconfirmation, the outer limit of our absorption powers, the proof of the outer world's existence outside our fantasy, the shock to the growing consistent system which causes it to crash. We have shown already that in reality this crash is derivable *either* from the innate structure of the system of consistency-mongering *or* from some incomprehensible absolute otherness to it, which turn out to be the same thing, and that the same analysis can proceed with the same strictly undecidable outcome from the other direction (that is, a purely objective system breaks down and yields up the indigestible "self" as its other, a purely subjective system breaks down and yields up the indigestible "other" as its other), and that this means neither a real outside world nor a solipsistic world. Our word for this built-in necessary undecidability, wherein, further, either side, thought through to the bottomless bottom, yields the other, is, of course, "omnicentrism." We will have more to say about it in its relation to the mind/matter problem below. For the moment however, we simply want to note the distinctive means by which a hated object becomes a center. I prefer not to think about this cockroach that is lurking somewhere under one of these desks. But I find that as much as I push the disgusting image of cockroachness from my mind, it remains manifested in other forms: I begin to see the bottom of that counter as a possible-cockroach-hiding-place, the cookies left on the desk are now possible cockroach-attractors or cockroach-touched, this blanket must be touched carefully, for cockroachness may come scurrying out from under it, and so on. Cockroachness is becoming an invisible center for me, but one that I do not want to allow to enter into awareness. Here again we have a rival center. The smooth functioning of reversibility, which allows and dismisses any and all centers in turn, is disrupted by this alternate indigestible center. Here we have an object which my body, as invisible center, as subject, refuses to take into its embrace, refuses to take as an object, refuses to take as an element that can be worked into its system, as a form in which my me-ness could be expressing itself, could be a quality that is pervaded by me-ness. In this sense, my centering project is failing; I am excluding certain elements from my system. But they come back with a vengeance in the form of an alternate invisible center. The avoided indigestible coherence starts to spread like a cancer into the realm of objects I had already taken into my system. It is the confrontation of these two invisible centers, this snag in reversibility, that constitutes aversion.

It follows that the reinstitution of reversibility here is to be accomplished by deliberately keeping the object of aversion in consciousness, not as imaginatively *embodied* as in the case of desire, but as an object, as an aspect of myself, as something that can be viewed as posited by me as a way of accomplishing my project, as a setup to my punch line, as a form in which I temporarily appear so as to achieve the pervasion of me-ness. It must be incorporated into the invisible center of myself, seen as something as which I am appearing, rather than seeing my previous self as something as which it is appearing, as in the case of desire.

Similarly, an aversion to *being* X is, rather straightforwardly, a case of being unable to see Xness as pervading. This is obviously just the flip side of desiring to be non-X. I hate the idea of being an idiot because I am unable to see everyone as an idiot, to see all coherences without exception as expressions of idiocy. There is some irreducible coherence of "savvy" in the operation of the world that I am unable to digest into idiocy; I cannot imagine the world as functioning without some smart people in it. Here again we have a structure that is the mirrored counterpart to the case of desiring to be something, and once again the problem is basically a snag in reversibility.

It is significant that these structures are so close to one another, almost identical; the well-known affinity between desire and aversion for the same object, the basically inescapable phenomenon of ambivalence, can perhaps be illuminated somewhat by this consideration. This is what we would expect from our general principles: to hate is a version of loving, to love is a version of hating, hate appears as love, love appears as hate, without anything changing, merely by means of a very slight, indeed arbitrary and *sui generis*, focal shift.

The real gist of all this can almost be summarized formulaically. Suffering does not suffer. Pain is not in pain. Happiness is not happy. The sickness that is torturing and destroying you is having a perfectly good time. This is not only the crucial clue for solving the problem of instantiation of universals that hounded Plato, but also something many a menace to society has known instinctively: *the only way to escape the inescapable is to become it.* A horror that will not go away can only be escaped by becoming the horror oneself. But for us this is only half the story, as what is really wanted here is a restitution of unimpeded reversibility, not merely to remain being the horror without being able to be its opposite. As we shall see below, indeed, to "become" something, to make it one's "self," to bring its contingent dilemma to the position of necessary impossibility, is precisely what it means to be "free." What had encountered or possessed X as a problem, as a heteronomous piece of conditioning, becomes instead oneself, the center from which any subsequent move may follow. As an explanatory rather than an ethical principle, however, there can be no doubt: one becomes exactly what one has hitherto been unable to escape. And as a definition: pain is that alone in the universe that does not experience pain. The general consequence of this point must be stated as emphatically as possible, to wit: The identity of any coherence is nothing but a name for its constitutive impossibility, the necessity of the failure to establish this coherence unequivocally, which is nothing but a name for its omnipresence as deadpan all-pervading asness. This is the Three Truths in a nutshell. But to understand all its implications, we must take a little more time with it.

A Note on Crawling through the Desert

As indicated, the above discussion concerns mainly what I have tentatively called obsessive desire and aversion, the kind that does not seem to disappear when the object in question is presently attained or avoided, the type of inherently unsatisfiable condition that Lacan designates desire proper as opposed to drive or demand. I do not have in mind here ordinary hunger and thirst, especially when these are conditioned by extreme and obvious circumstances. Nonetheless, I do think the above principles apply equally well to those cases. Let us say I am crawling through the desert, violently desiring water to drink. It may seem fantastic to say that this really means I am unwilling to be water; after all, in the first place, why do we need an explanation of this phenomenon at all? By Occam's Razor (a principle, by the way, which we may by now have considerable reason to call into question), the biological explanation, based firmly on the old Spinozistic principle that the organism wants to remain in being, conation, or the Schopenhaurian will-to-life, or even the Nietzschean will-to-power, more than suffices in explaining why a creature who will die without water will desire water. In the second place, does the thirsty man not want precisely to become water, to be suffused with wateriness, to be inundated? But the crucial point here is that the water which serves as the object of desire for the thirsty man is water-as-something-to-be-consumed, something which will be completely absorbed into something else for the sake of that something else (i.e., himself, his life), which will lose all rights to be what it is so that it can serve some alien purpose. And it is just this, "water" in this sense, that he does not want to become; he does not want to become an element to be consumed by others, to be absorbed into some greater alien system, to lose his individuality: that is, he does not want to die. This consideration, which may appear merely fancifully clever or sinisterly sophistic, is nonetheless of some importance, not least because it allows us to do without accepting some given first principle, like the desire to exist or to live, which is exempt from the general structural principles of omnicentrism. Besides being observably an accurate description of the situation, and one that reveals something more of the deep structure involved, it integrates it with all other instances of desire and aversion, and saves us from any backdoor vitalism or substantialism. The will to exist et al. is the basis of all activity, just as these theorists say. But the same can be said of any other principle: the will to die, the will to be powerless, the will to become other—or, for that matter, if one wishes, the will to find my keys, the will to get this little chunk of rib meat out from between my teeth, or what have you. To be the "basis" of all other activity is to be a center. There is always some center, so we are not acentrist; but the centers are reversible, any coherence may serve as the basis. Hence we can avoid all the thorny ontological, metaphysical and cosmogonic problems that haunt all attempts to find *the* source of all, *the* principle that explains all else. Any principle explains all else, precisely by failing to do so. Such is omnicentrism.

The Self: Subject and Object, Punch Line and Setup

In the preceding sections, we have examined the role of desire in the structuring of experience, in particular with reference to the primal dyad of being and having. We intend these terms in the broadest possible senses; what one "is" in the sense described above is the self, what one "has" in this sense is this self's world. As noted already, it should be clear that when we speak of "self" we refer not to some particular set of coherences, but to a particular mode of relation in which any set of coherences can be situated at a given time. We have already begun to approach this idea with respect to the notion of "identification," and "being" and "having." We wish to claim in addition that "self/other" is a set of categories which is always in operation, which always appears simultaneously with the appearance of any coherence whatsoever, which can never be eradicated (any more than any *other* coherence could ever be eradicated).[6] It is simply that what is acting as self and what is acting as other are not fixed, may change places, in any given configuration—somewhat as in any Gestalt diagram there is always necessarily some figure and some background; the structural necessity that both be present is fixed, without the content of either ever being absolutely fixed. The importance of this way of regarding the matter for us should already be obvious, and will become even more apparent as we proceed.

In old-fashioned language, we may see in this necessary self/other a structure that can be profitably applied to the so-called subject/object relation. Several steps must be taken to fully grasp the Tiantaification of this relationship, before all its implications are completely explicit for us. Specifically, we will be exploring the notion of body as self in the Polanyian and Merleau-Pontian sense; that is, self is the body, and the body is the proximal term *through* which all other coherences appear, which appears *as* them but with the constant option for them to appear *as* it. This idea will develop further into the idea of the self—indeed, whether "oneself" or the "itself" of any coherence—

---

[6] This insistence on the unconquerable reality of the concept of "self" may surprise or disturb some of my Buddhological colleagues; but it is one important way to gauge the difference between the Tiantai approach and some others within the Buddhist tradition. In Tiantai the false notion "self/other" is coeval with all experience and existence, and just as ineradicable as all other illusions. See, for example, Zhili's discussion of the five aggregates in *Guanyin xuanyi yishu*, where he notes that one could as well adduce "five" or "six" components with regard to the personality—in the latter case, meaning the five skandhas plus the "soul" or "atman." His point is that in terms of illusion (i.e., Provisional Positing, i.e., Skillful Means, i.e., Ultimate Reality), the aggregates are just as illusory as the imputed "self" which they constitute.

as precisely its constitutive impossibility, its inability to appear *simpliciter*, which will also equal its all-pervasiveness qua this reversible asness, or Intersubsumption. But to get to these conclusions, we will have to start with the elaboration of these two notions self and other, or subject and object, or even, to begin with, mind and body, in terms of the setup/punch-line model we have already described as central to Tiantai thinking.

Now if the relation between provisional and ultimate, or context and figure, or setup and punch line, is as we have described it, it is also the way we are to conceive the simultaneous identity and difference of Global Incoherence and Local Coherence, which in Neo-Tiantai terms is called Intersubsumption (All-pervasion as All-pervadedness). This relation will also be the relation between mental phenomena and physical phenomena. That is, to put it in a formula, *mental phenomena are to physical phenomena as punch line is to setup, or as the humorousness of the punch line is to the seriousness of the setup*. This position will provide us with unusually fruitful and novel resources for dealing with the traditional mind-body problem. In order to clarify the relevant implications of this position, it is first necessary to review the nature of the problem, and the impasses to which it has so far led.

We may broadly characterize this problem in the following terms: given the *prima facie* assumption that there are some types of phenomena commonly identified as mental—thoughts, emotions, opinions, sensations, and so on—and some types commonly called material—chemical, electrical, physical, and biological processes—what is the relation between these two types? Are they two subsets of a larger set? Is one of them a mere epiphenomenon of the other, such that in all cases one and only one of these two types of phenomena will be the dependent variable and the other the independent, or one a more or less rough or deceptive description of what is more accurately and strictly described in terms of the other? We can crudely characterize the four most common traditional attempts to comprehend this relation as follows: (1) Mind is merely a local form of matter, reducible to matter, (2) matter is merely a local form of mind, reducible to mind, (3) mind and matter are separate and distinct realms, neither of which is dependent on or reducible to the other, or (4) some sort of parallelism between the two obtains, either because they are both aspects of some larger set or because they are correlated according to a preestablished harmony. Each of these views seems problematic, and the refusal of this issue to die in the annals of philosophy is, as usual, a strong indication that there may be something insoluble about the problem as stated. Solutions 1 and 2, which we may call "monistic solutions," seem to neglect the empirical distinction and even opposition between these two types of phenomena, or at least consign this distinction to the category of illusion; but this sense of distinction between mind and matter is quite central to our ordinary sense of the world, and hence its relegation to illusion brings with it a radical alienation between existential and theoretical realities, consigning most of our lives to a second-class status of something premised on a ridiculous illusion. Solution 3, the "dualistic" solution, is unsatisfactory for the opposite reason: it does not account for either the felt or the observable correlation and connection between these two types of phenomena, and indeed makes the question of how these two separate realms of being could possibly be connected more or less insoluble by definition. Alternative 4, on the other hand, seems to explain very little, consigning the relation between the two sets of phenomena to a realm that is necessarily inaccessible to any possible experience, thus offering merely another mystery as a solution to the first. In addition, this hypothesis gives us no insight into the peculiar nature of the oppositional and yet interlocked and inseparable nature of the relation between the two, the asymmetrical fact that mind is somehow "referential" to matter but not vice versa, and that this referentiality contains what might be called a kind of constitutive negativity which is nonetheless not exclusive of a relation of identity.

This last objection is perhaps obscure, but forms, in my view, the crux of the problem. For close phenomenological examination reveals that there is basis in experience for both the monistic and the dualistic views of the relation, which helps explain why neither alone has succeeded in winning universal acceptance. I refer here not so much to the empirical correlation between mental and bodily phenomena, combined with the difficulty of comprehending or asserting a token-by-token identity of the two, although this is of course also relevant here. Rather I have in mind the point stressed by Husserl and Sartre, that consciousness is always consciousness of something. Its structure is such that it necessarily and constitutively entails a reference to something besides itself, some positive existence. At the moment of this experience of consciousness, there is no identifiable distinction between the consciousness of, say, red, and red itself; it is impossible to point to a borderline between one's seeing of red and the red itself. Moreover, it is impossible to imagine consciousness without some object, existing as some entity which is then brought into relation to its object; instead, we find that consciousness is nothing but its object at any given moment. This is the phenomenological support for the monistic doctrines. On the other hand, when this object to which consciousness is apparently identical changes or vanishes, consciousness does not change or vanish; rather, it becomes equally identical to the next object, which means it could not have been identical to the first, or else it would have perished when that first object did. This pure negation or transcendence of the consciousness to the object, which suggests that consciousness always transcends any given or possible object, that it is separable and free, underwrites the dualistic hypotheses. This being the case, neither the monistic nor the dualistic nor the parallelistic hypothesis seems to provide any satisfactory insight into the most salient features of the relation.

It is here that I think the setup/punch-line model can help us. For in this model we have a powerful and intuitively accessible picturing of a relation that preserves both radical opposition and uncompromising identity at the same time. We have here neither a mind-body dualism, nor a reductionism of one to the other to produce a monistic idealism or materialism, nor exactly a Spinozistic parallelism or Leibnizian correlative harmony. We have a necessary contrast and relation of negation between mind and matter, and a reason, *pace* Spinoza, that they manifest as exactly two opposite categories, which nonetheless can be understood as also a relation of identity. This accounts both for the observed incongruity of the two, as in dualism, while also avoiding the sundering of the unity of the personality, and of all experience, that would be entailed by taking this incongruity as unconditional and ultimate.

The picture we arrive at looks something like the following: there are preconditions for every mental state that has ever been experienced—for example, a particular arrangement of molecules in physical objects, sense organs, and nerve tissue. That total configuration is both provisionally determinate, that is, consistently appearing *as* some coherence instead of others, when viewed within a particular local context, but to be so is to equally be profoundly ambiguous. These are not two separate facts about this configuration of putative objects. Indeed, the whole thrust of the Tiantai notion of the Nonexclusive Center is to elucidate this point, as discussed above. Rods, cones, nerve tissue, light, position of sun and earth, labor of potter, molecular activity of clay, and so on appear here *as* "cup (as) seen by me." The same coherence however is also "me seeing cup." The latter itself entails the reversal of the asness involved, that is, the *attention and thinking* which *reveal* that what is here as "cup (as) seen by me" is equally here as "me seeing cup," and as "light," as "molecular activity," and so on. "Mind" refers to this ambiguity, the unfolding of the ambiguity of asness that is involved in all determinate experiencing of coherences.

Matter as determinate would then be identical to its own indeterminacy, and the word for the latter would be Mind. The function of mind, be it noted, is here characterized not as some sort of still pure awareness, as seems to be the case in some forms of Chinese Buddhism, but as the process of recontextualization itself. Wherever recontextualization, and hence the change in the meaning and identity of tokens of experience without changing their content, occurs, it is called a mental phenomenon. The most basic form of recontextualization, that is, of mental experience, known to us is simply *time*, or subjective Bergsonian duration. That is, a particular experience is first presenced as real, as now, as present. But it is immediately recontextualized; without changing its content in the least, the same token has become past, gone, memory. The old Buddhist notion of impermanence is here recast in Tiantai terms as self-recontextualization, which is precisely the mark of the mental as opposed to the physical. Time per se is just the opening of the provisional to reveal the real, and this is the essence of the mental.

Spinoza saw the mind as the idea of the body—that is, the thought version of the particular part of extension whose mind it is. The view suggested here is that the mind is the punch line of the body. Where mind occurs, all of the physical becomes mental—as all of the setup becomes funny when the punch line appears. As indicated above, however, this does not necessitate the elimination of the physicality of the physical, that is, its resistance to and opaqueness to the mental. On the contrary, these are precisely the preconditions of the mental, as the contrast between the seriousness of the setup and humor of the punch line was the precondition for the simultaneous humor of both. It is the provisionally posited (locally constituted) determinacy of the physical, the world as self-identical, as in-itself, which calls forth the indeterminacy that makes it also equally indeterminate, without sacrificing its provisional determinacy, as we have described in the relations between Local Coherence and Global Incoherence generally. *Mental phenomena are the self-recontextualizations of physical phenomena.* These recontextualizations are self-recontextualizations because they are necessarily entailed by contextualization, that is meaning or determinacy, itself. To be something is to be something else.

The view propounded here has something in common with the Whiteheadian view that all actual occasions consist of both a physical and a mental pole, an approach which, it should be granted, does not fit neatly into any of the four general typologies (two monistic, dualistic, and parallelistic) outlined above. The view of time suggested by Whitehead's view, rooted as it is in Bergson's notion of duration, elegantly provides for the asymmetrical progression that is also of central concern to the Tiantai model. Two features should be noted which, however, distinguish the two views. The first is the

---

[7] See A. N. Whitehead, *Process and Reality* (New York: Harper & Row, 1960), 245: "Consciousness is the feeling of negation." Note however the elaboration on p. 372: "In awareness actuality, as a process in fact, is integrated with the potentialities which illustrate *either* what it is and might not be, *or* what it is not and might be. In other words, there is no consciousness without reference to definiteness, affirmation, and negation. . . . Consciousness is how we feel the affirmation-negation contrast. Conceptual feeling is the feeling of an unqualified negation; . . . Consciousness requires that the objective datum should involve . . . a qualified negative determined to some definite situation."

great stress on the necessary negation of the relation in the Neo-Tiantai view; Whitehead is well aware of this feature of the mental,[7] but arguably seems to stress the prehending and progressively inclusive nature of the mental pole in relation to the physical.

The second difference is far more crucial: the polar view of process philosophy, while making the two realms inseparable and elucidating their relation in a highly illuminating way, perhaps cannot quite make the seemingly paradoxical claim made by the Neo-Tiantai view, namely, that it is equally accurate to say not only that both matter and mind are present in every event, but also that all events are nothing but mind, and also that all events are nothing but matter. That is, on the setup/punch-line model, the entire joke, from beginning to end, can be described as funny, once the punch line has occurred, but equally, for asymmetrical reasons outlined above, as nonfunny. This omnicentric feature, so central to traditional Tiantai dogmatics, which allows the entire field to be characterized adequately in terms of any one of its instantiations, would suggest a radical modification of the Whiteheadian view: the physical pole is itself mental, the mental pole is itself physical, and each is also both and neither. In terms of the mental, all the physical is actually mental; in terms of the physical, all the mental is actually physical. Without recourse to the setup/punch-line model, it is difficult to get a grip on this claim. But I do wish to suggest that it corresponds to something not only true but also central to our lived experience of the relation of body to mind, which forms the basis not only for the parallelistic claims of correlation but the much stronger (materialist and idealist) monistic doctrines of identity. For everyone can, with very little effort, appreciate the force of the Berkeleyan claim that being is perception, that all is *Vorstellungen*, that there is no outside to mind, that everything we experience is an aspect of our own mind. The Neo-Tiantai view will grant full citizenship to this intuition.

On the other hand, it also seems intuitively obvious that this is both the whole picture and decidedly *not* the whole picture. Schopenhauer tried to preserve both these intuitions by allowing that while the world is in one sense nothing but representations, the sense that there was something more to it, that there was some insurmountable and impassable facticity to things was justified in that the world is also something else entirely, namely, Will. The Neo-Tiantai view allows both intuitions to be all-encompassing, each embracing the other at the limits of its own local intelligibility. The intuition that all is funny is true after the punch line is told, from the point of view of the punch line. The contrary intuition, that some nonfunny facticity pervades all, is also true, both because the punch line is funny *if and only if* the setup is taken fully seriously, as intractably nonfunny and contrasted to any escape hatch of humor, and in that the determinate concept of humorousness is emptied of content once any and all seriousness is seen as an adequate embodiment of it—and also perhaps in that humorousness itself may be viewed as simply one more neutral and unfunny fact, when we are talking about what neutral and unfunny facts constitute the world, i.e., in that, once reversibility of humor and seriousness is revealed by the punch line, it unavoidably rasises the same "meta-funny" possibility about itself. All is mind, in that once mind appears on the scene, it transforms everything into an aspect and precondition of itself, recontextualizing and integrating every fact in the process and thereby denuding them of their original given facticity. On the other hand, all is matter, not only in that mind must take facticity as factual and intractably other in order to function as mind, as opposed to itself, but also in that the quality of "being mental" becomes devoid of content once it is seen to apply to any and all instances of material facticity. On this view, then, it is equally true to say that the body is a mere aspect or reflection of the all-embracing mind, and that the mind is a mere reflection or epiphenomenon of the functions of the body. My claim here is that this paradoxicality is not to be considered an argument against this view, since an account has been given in the setup/punch-line of how such a thing *could* be possible, but actually as a recommendation of the Neo-Tiantai view, for only the full acknowledgment of both of these opposite claims would, I submit, be a complete and adequate correlate of our lived experience of being body and mind.[8]

Another consequence of the Neo-Tiantai setup/punch-line view is of equally great significance: namely, that the appearance/reality structure is here judged to be essential to all experience, to be ineradicable (*pace* some trends in postmodernism); there is always something being revealed to be an expression or form of something else, an immediate appearance being disconfirmed to reveal that there is more to it than had first appeared. On the other hand (*pace* foundational metaphysics of any kind), there is no content which ends up falling on one side or the other of this reality/appearance split; there is no set of coherences which is real as opposed to some other set which is merely appearance. Rather, it is the very structure of grounded and ground, of foundation and founded, which is basic and inescapable, but no particular thing, essence or determinacy which is the foundation or source itself. The

---

[8] We may note in passing here that this also gives us a strong interpretation of what is meant by the relation between consciousness and self-consciousness, or between Sartre's positional and nonpositional forms of consciousness; "consciousness" (or nonpositional consciousness) is what matter is called *after* the appearance of the punch line of self-consciousness (positional consciousness). There is in this relation something of a "missed encounter"; there is never consciousness without self-consciousness, we jump straight from matter to consciousness plus self-consciousness, which retroactively constitutes (nonpositional) consciousness as its (always) already-superseded precondition.

disconfirmation of an appearance is called mind. What becomes apparent in the wake of this clearing-away is called matter. The fact that these two are merely aspects of the same act—namely, the clearing away of appearances to reveal the real—is Intersubsumption (All-pervasion as All-pervadedness).

We may also say that it is essential and ineradicable that there be, in the ethical or axiological realm, some standard of right/wrong, and in the epistemological realm, some notion of true and false; there must be some putatively normative perspective operating at all times. For the observed coherence of the world to be accounted for this particular category will always be in play. But, again, no particular content can ever land once and for all on one side or the other, as definitively true or false, right or wrong. Here we have perhaps the blueprint for an elegant escape from the dichotomy between absolutist and relativist epistemologies and ethics, which, as another of those dilemmas in the history of philosophy that seems to be intrinsically incapable of solution, again draws suspicion on itself as a faulty question or set of categories.

Another point to be made here is that in this setup/punch-line structure we have a picture of mind/body relations that can accord with our intuitive picture of progressive scientific knowledge as well as of the transcending function of mind to matter, without sacrificing mind-body unity. We may say that an old Gestaltist paradox of change is embodied here: the setup will be revealed to be something other than it seemed, to have another identity than that which is currently appearing—but it will do so if and only if it is taken dead seriously as a facticity for the moment. The necessary condition for its self-transcendence is that it be accepted and accorded full attention as real and "serious"—that is, intractably factitious—while in operation. Indeed, all aspects of it must be attended to and taken seriously, for often the punch line will depend on the unexpected recontextualization of what appeared to be an insignificant detail, which is revealed thereby to be central. It is crucial to reiterate here that taking the setup seriously is the very means by which the humor comes into being; one must be "taken in" by the setup of the joke for the punch line to have any effect. Similarly, the facticity of matter must be taken seriously for it to be revealed to be a transcendable provisional appearance. The very means by which it can be transcended, in other words, is by taking seriously the very stubborn structures and functions by which blind matter operates—a picture which again accords very nicely with the overcoming of material conditions not by relegating them to unimportance or ontological second-class status, but by studying and taking them seriously. Here we are in accord with Spinoza's dictum that we come to know God better by better understanding particular things, Tiantaified to read: we come to know each and every thing better by better understanding *any single* particular thing. As Zhili says, when one becomes fully manifest, the Three Thousand become fully manifest simultaneously. The Neo-Tiantai system may then perhaps recommend itself as a sort of nondreamy idealism, and at the same time as a self-transcending (i.e., genuinely dialectical) materialism.

We now have made considerable headway in how to think about what is meant by a mind and by a body. It should be stated clearly here, however, lest there be a misunderstanding, that all of the above is posited within the particular context of our present mind/matter experiences. It applies to the extent that my own death and the dead matter I will become is at the moment, that is, from this particular center, just another thought I am having, another aspect of my life. This is not to deny that the symmetrical situation can also be worked from the opposite side; that is, that "matter" is the punch line and "mind" is the setup. Indeed, we have already asserted that everything is a setup for everything else, and also a punch line for everything else, and hence this conclusion is unavoidable. For it is not at all counterintuitive to imagine the "last laugh" of matter; all that thinking was just a set up for the body as something to be eaten by ants and worms, and so on; nothing could be a more hilarious deadpan setup for such a punch line, as all black humorists know. On the other hand, for us this means that this *particular* set of determinations, my body as inert object, have become the setup to be absorbed by another unseen center (i.e., subject), viz., the ants and worms, and hence to this extent we may be inclined to privilege the unseen side, the subject side, as the punch line implementer in all cases. However, this is to be understood under the provision that any particular content will necessarily belong to both categories, or rather, that the determinacy of the content, its partial success aspect, is what we refer to as the matter pole right now, given our present form of life, while the fact that this determinacy is itself its own undoing, the fact that it must necessarily fail, is the mind pole. That these may take forms other than those currently known to us as mind and matter goes without saying, as does the implication of the mutual identity of the Three Truths (the third here being the identity of the success and the failure of this coherence's project), and their complete presence in any of the three. Both terms lose and establish their particular limited meanings upon being shown to pervade the entire field of possible experiences. This follows simply from the fact that the identical procedure, being necessary and universal, also applies at the meta-level, for the coherences "mental" and "physical" (as defined here or elsewhere) themselves. For this is where these reflections must really find their clarity; for "matter" to be "matter" at all, its identity as such, is also necessarily identity as Intersubsumption (All-pervasion as All-pervadedness), as necessary failure, as constitutive impossibility, as opposed to merely contingent failure. This is what it is to "be" anything at all, and this is the real thrust of what must be said about being and having, and about mind as body. It is to this notion that we now turn.

Identity as Constitutive Impossibility (as All-pervasion)

We have said, with the traditional Tiantai dogmatics, that Intersubsumption (All-pervasion as All-pervadedness) is the true "identity" of any coherence, as opposed to its changing outer expression, its material facticity (Local Coherence), which is too fleeting and unstable to cohere into an identity, on the one hand, or its unchanging but necessarily unexpressed inner kernel, which is in principle unknowable and unspecifiable (Global Incoherence), on the other. We are now in a position to understand what this signifies. Intersubsumption, we may recall, is precisely constitutive impossibility. This is what "punch line" or "humorousness" in the above ruminations really boils down to for us: the punch line functions when the setup is seen as constitutively blocked from being itself, but where this is indeed the very condition of its positive existence, which however is now understood not as a positive something but as a deadpan all-pervasive asness which expresses itself *as* every other coherence. This is Intersubsumption. "Local Coherence" is the appearing of this coherence as this coherence, "Global Incoherence" is the "something-elseness" that was also precisely the appearing of this coherence, the impossibility of the *simpliciter* appearance of this coherence which was nonetheless the only possible mode in which it could appear; and Intersubsumption is a way of indicating the absolute coinciding of these two, of the appearance of a "one" and its impossibility; this is what this coherence actually *is*. To "be" (Intersubsumption) X is to "appear" to be X (Local Coherence) as something else (Global Incoherence) (or, what is the same here, to be something else appearing as X). What something is is its own constitutive impossibility, the impossibility of its ever appearing *simpliciter*. This, for us, must be true of the identity of each and every coherence, it must be the general definition of existence per se. Every situation, every being, every coherence, is some constitutive impossibility; constitutive impossibility (Intersubsumption) manifests in a limitless variety of locally coherent ways. The identity of any coherence is its *necessary* failure, as opposed to its *contingent* failure. The specificity of one identity as opposed to another is just the specificity of one particular necessary form of failure. All coherences are impossibility; X is the specific impossibility of X. What we mean by "impossibility" here, most generally, is the necessary failure to appear as such or *simpliciter*. Its presence is always conditioned by some ineradicable internal interference that prevents it from being "really" present in the way it is supposed to be. This has been demonstrated for a coherence in general, for the appearing of X as such; to appear as X is to appear as non-X, actual existence of pure X is impossible. The general reasons for this, it will be recalled, had to do with the fact that all actual X is composed of, conditioned by, contextualized by, framed by non-X, permeated by non-X in all dimensions, in such a way that it can never be free from being read also as non-X, from having non-X leak into its Xness, from being infiltrated by non-X. The non-X required by X to exist makes any pure Xness impossible. But now we will see this consideration extending to more specific cases; what we will want to consider here is not only the general case of the impossibility of pure appearing of X, but the specific ways in which this impossibility structures events. Each coherence is a *specific* impossibility, and its reasons for being impossible are intrinsic to the definition of the coherence in question. The necessary failure that establishes it is not only "failure to really appear" but "failure to appear as really X." That is, every X is a somehow faulty or inauthentic instantiation of Xness. In order to appear at all it must have a flaw that prevents it from counting as X plain and simple, as a genuinely exemplary X. *Every* X is a somehow second-rate, *faux*-X. The Xness of every X fails to quite live up to the standard of Xness, not contingently, but necessarily. This is what it is to be X.[4] We may indicate a few of these other such impossible identities in a thumbnail sort of way, by first delineating the "standard of Xness" in each case and then demonstrating how Xness per se makes the meeting of this standard impossible.

Subject/Object: On the simplest level, the existence of the subject/object relation, which we have approached otherwise above, can be illuminated as its own impossibility in the following way: Let us say that the standard for "subjectivity" is that it must be different from and exclusive of some other coherence called "objectivity." However sophisticated a theory we may have of subjectivity, at least this much must be true for the term to have any meaning at all. Many definitions of subjectivity might be attempted: we might say that the subject must be what apprehends something other than and independent of itself, some characteristics of which it somehow registers within itself; or that the object is the independent member of the pair of which the subject is a partial and dependent expression, or that the subject is the independent member and the object dependent. We might say that the subject

---

[9] We have here the key to the "opening up" of the Platonic theory of forms "to reveal the (Tiantai) real"; no actually existing X is the Form of X, and only the Form of X is Real X, so no X is really X. We will pursue the implications of this confluence in the final section of this book, where we attempt to "open up" a few of the most recalcitrantly and severely anti-Tiantai positions in the history of thought—Platonism, Christianity, Marxism, empiricism, and so on.

transcends the object—projecting itself beyond it, unable to be limited by or rest within the object—or that the object transcends the subject. We may speak of the subject as the privately inaccessible aspect of the experience, which only partially overlaps with the publicly accessible aspect called the objective. But all of these are made impossible by any actual subjectivity. What I find in my own experience is rather that without me, there is no world; but at the same time, without the world, there is no me. The *existence* of these two opposed poles is a function of the impossibility of there being any two separate or mutually exclusive poles, as each absorbs the other completely into itself. It is precisely this impossibility, this undecidable mutual absorption, which we refer to when we say, "There is a subject and an object." Also, in the case of an individual act of perception, as already suggested, when I perceive an object, I can locate no borderline between my perceiving and the object perceived, and anything I can indicate is the object; I find no excess called "the perception of the object," the perception and the object are identical. But when the object changes and perishes, my perception does not, as would seem to be required by an identity between the two. It is only as such that there can be subjectivity and objectivity. Subjectivity "is" its own constitutive impossibility. The same can easily be discerned for objectivity as such.

Causality: The standard for causality, we may say, is that some coherence is generated by means of some other coherence. But the effect cannot come from itself, from another or others, from both or from neither. Here we simply follow the old Nāgārjunian critique. If it comes from itself, it is merely a repetition of the cause, so no effect has been generated. Nothing has been caused, so there is no cause. The process of causality is here completely superfluous. If it comes from another, from otherness, it should appear wherever there is any "other." If one means some *specific* set of others, rather than otherness as such, we must ask if this set is the same as or different from the effect. If different, we must ask the same question again—why precisely *this* set of othernesses?—leading to an infinite regress. If the same, these others turn out to be the self-same thing, the effect itself, and we have the case of self-cause again. That is, we have only a change of form of the self-same thing: it was formerly "conditions A, B, and C," which considered together are named "Result X." If something must bring them together to produce the effect, then we have a new question—is this something which brings them together an other or not? If it is, any other will do, unless one means some specific set of others, which then must be included in the definition of the "self" of X all over again, and we have made no progress. The problem is with the categories of "self" and "other" for any coherence; we have already demonstrated that they cannot hold, which is what we indicate as Intersubsumption (All-pervasion as All-pervadedness). The claim that the effect arises from both self and other does not hold for both of the above reasons; it has the defects of both the self-cause and the other-cause arguments. Spontaneous generation (i.e., no cause) is not only empirically indefensible; it would mean any effect can spring up at any time, which itself would be a total chaos of effects and hence eliminate the meaning of causality as such. Causality functions only on the condition that it is impossible in this way. Causality "is" its own constitutive impossibility.

Love and Desire: On this I will have to be cryptic. I am certain it works in a great variety of ways in various cases. Let us start, for example, with the (Groucho) Marxian tenet, "I would never want to belong to any club that would have me for a member." This is surely an important circle in the purgatory of love; it is also a blueprint for the more general paradox of social recognition, as we shall see below. A bit more rigorously: if we define love, as some do, as a desire to unite with the beloved, the paradox is obvious. The more I succeed in uniting with the beloved, the less there is left for me to desire to unite with, the less yet-to-unite-with, and hence the less to love, and indeed the less love—for what I am united with no longer stands before me as an object of desire. I am not hungry for food I have already eaten. If love succeeds in its aim, uniting with the beloved, it vanishes. Love survives only when the fulfillment of its immanent aim is blocked. Hence love's desire to unite with the beloved is equally a desire to prevent this union, lest the desire perish and one find oneself united with an other one does not desire to be united with. This of course applies equally well to any desire, and so far we have just a special case of the paradox of will and value, which has been a central theme above and which will be further touched on momentarily. If the standard for love is instead simply some form of union with the beloved, rather than the *desire* for such union, the paradox is even more obvious, for then we have no difference between wanting the thing and simply being it. And indeed, this paradox hits the precise Tiantai truth of the matter.

In terms of the specific parameters of desire developed above: to desire to possess the beloved object or person is really to desire to *be* it or him or her. This means to have it disappear as an object of desire, and indeed disappear altogether from explicit consciousness, as this particular thing exclusive of its negation, which is how I desired it. To desire to have it always is to desire for it to vanish. To want to preserve it is to want to destroy it. The constitutive paradox here is obvious.

Other incisive definitions of desire yield the same result. Let us say that I do not know what I want, no concrete thing satisfies; on some rather convincing accounts, this is what "desire" as such means, as opposed to, say, "demand," or "need." A genuine "desire" would be a longing that transcends any particular object, for which all objects are merely symbols, which cannot be satisfied by any particular thing. But each actual desire expresses itself as desire for some specific object—even if it is merely the desire to be free from this nagging but nonspecific desire. But then do I really want it? Who wants it? Someone who is more me than me? Why should I struggle to please him? Desire is always a specific desire, but to be truly desire it can have no definite goal. Desire in this specific sense "is" its own constitutive impossibility.

But perhaps this definition of desire too stacks the deck. How about the more commonsense definition: Desire, let us say, means an unpleasant feeling of unease directed at some state of affairs, combined with some pleasurable imagination of its being otherwise, and possibly an act of will and attendant actions to make it otherwise. But this means that the situation taken as a whole is producing both pleasurable and unpleasurable sensations at the same time; if they are experienced at different times, the above definition will not be fulfilled. But if they are experienced at the same time, their mutually exclusive character, upon which the efficacy and necessity of the desire rests—that is, one need not move from an unpleasant sensation to a pleasant one, as the desire demands, if the two are coextensive—is impossible. Desire "is" its own constitutive impossibility.

If however we define love, as Spinoza does, with chilling precision, as "A feeling of pleasure combined with the idea of an external cause," with pleasure understood as "what I feel when my body/mind becomes suitable for a larger variety of modifications," or in Nietzsche's version, "the feeling of the increase in power," we have a paradox of dependence, which may get very close to the heart of the matter: when an external cause *lessens* my dependence on external causes, it is called "love." When something beyond my power increases my power, I experience love. This means that the external power either has to stop giving me this pleasure of expanding my power or to not stop; if it does not, it will make me so powerful that it has made itself unnecessary, and love will vanish. If it does so stop, however, I will by definition cease loving it. In either case, love proves impossible. If pleasure means an increased independence of external causes, the pleasure given by external causes is already a suppression of pleasure, a pleasure that is equally displeasure, a love that is equally hate.[10] Let others supply other versions of this

---

[10] We may think here of Theodor Reik's ambitious psychoanalytic redefinition of love as a reaction-formation rooted inescapably in envy, i.e., in wanting to be the other person instead of oneself, which comes close to our definition of obsessive desire as the desire to be the snagged object, i.e., precisely the one object one is normally incapable of being. See Reik, *Of Love and Lust* (New York: Bantam, 1967), 38–59.

paradox. The point is simply another example: Love "is" its own constitutive impossibility.

Normativity: Let us suppose that one wishes to accord spontaneously with some standard of value, believing that only as something truly internalized and spontaneous does it have real value, whereas as a purely formal dead imitation of a model for ulterior purposes it has none of the value it imitates. The standard of value is to "truly posses it oneself," rather than simply pretending to possess, externally imitating, the valued mode of behavior. But the model is all the content there is to the truth; your truth is not something other than that dead model. And yet repetition of it, the only way to consolidate or possess it, already falsifies it. Spontaneity "is" its own constitutive impossibility. If you say, on the contrary, only imitation matters, for value lies in the determinate content as such, and the goal is to free oneself completely from any spontaneity, to become a perfectly transparent vessel for the Law to work through, the opposite problem applies; the more one succeeds, the more one internalizes the Law, the more spontaneous it becomes, the more it becomes one's real self. The more one succeeds in "duty for its own sake," for example, as excluding any "pathological" personal desire in the Kantian sense, the more it becomes one's own personal spontaneous desire. Imitation "is" its own constitutive impossibility. Putting these together, normativity "is" its own constitutive impossibility.

Pleasure: Let us say that when a spontaneous unearned pleasure appears, I know too well that I have no control over it, that I cannot reproduce it, and this drains it of pleasure—I have to work at sucking every last morsel of fun out of it, knowing it is pure chance that it has fallen to me, that it may never come again, that I am at its mercy. It can be argued that "to experience as pleasure," to deem something to be pleasant, is already necessarily this granting of value to it, which is identical to this fear of losing it, which necessarily drains it of pleasure. In contrast I may suggest that there is no pleasure without the painful effort to achieve it. But whatever is attained with painful effort is, considered as a whole and without bias, no pleasure. Still, I must make the effort to attain pleasure. If I am not plagued by this worry, this attachment to it, this desire to repeat and control it, it is not what we mean by "pleasure" anymore, and is not experienced as such. (It is something beyond pleasure—what we have called "pure desire.") Pleasure "is" its own constitutive impossibility.

Work and Self-Worth (Obsessives Only): I am worthless unless my work is acknowledged as valuable universally; a merely private estimate of my own value is meaningless self-deception, for value itself is already a purely intersubjective category. But if what I do is universally acknowledged, I am pandering to the common taste, renouncing what distinguishes me. It is not me who has this value, it is just the value itself; the more I succeed, the more the essential moment of difference between value and myself as possessor of value is effaced.

Moreover, there is a problem concerning who is the representative of this binding standard of value. It can be neither objectively present nor a mere subjective projection. It cannot be objectively present because I am always the one deciding who is the *true* representative of the highest or mainstream or authoritative values of my society. From among all the diverse judgments flying around me, I deem some to be deviant, marginal, perverse, unrepresentative, sick, and the remainder to be "what everyone thinks." This "everyone" is clearly not statistical. If some individual to whom I have been looking for my validation turns out to be espouse some standard other than the one I regard as authoritative and representative, I will simply relegate him to the category of deviants, and my feeling that I am being judged by the orthodox standard will remain unchanged. For this reason, empirical disconfirmation will not, under normal circumstances, change one's belief about how one's society views one. One "already knows" what "everyone thinks" of one. For example, let us say I have got it in my head that to be "truly an adult" I must be ruthlessly objective and unsentimental; if I allow myself to show or experience sentimentality, I believe, I will be viewed as "childish and immature" in spite of my age. Now let us say I have learned how to be unsentimental, and am attempting to gain the approval of some exemplary unsentimental person who stands as an authoritative representative of that social judgment for me. I check myself against the reactions and behavior of this person, and feel myself to have failed if I find myself being more sentimental than him, or than he expects; I suffer from failing to live up to the standard he represents for me. But then let us say I gradually discover that he himself is even more sentimental than me, or even just that he approves of my sentimentality. I will immediately conclude that he too is not a "true adult," and divest him of his authority to serve as a representative of social judgment. The standard will not have changed simply because I discover that its embodier does not in fact hold the opinion of me that I expect him to; instead, the same standard, now temporarily disembodied or diffused into the faceless crowd, judges both of us as substandard. This will happen even if *every* adult I come to know turns out to be as sentimental as I am. So this standard cannot be objective. On the other hand, this standard cannot present itself as purely subjective. If it did, it would no longer serve as a standard at all, but would coincide exactly with one's own whims. The feeling that one is worthy means the feeling that one is esteemed by one's community, and this exists only on the condition of its impossibility. Self-worth "is" its own constitutive impossibility.

Intersubjectivity: I am safe in my self-certainly only as long as I do not speak, do not enter the communicative field; once I have entered that field, the meaning of my actions and words is no longer in my control, is subject to endless twisting and revision by others, so I have lost my former certainty. But unless I enter the communicative field, I can never be certain of myself. Self-certainty "is" its own constitutive impossibility.

Projects: Let us say I am working at some arduous achievement. I work so that I can have finished it, and it is this contemplation of the value it will have that brings me pleasure in my arduous work. I can only enjoy what I will be glad to have finished. I enjoy doing it only to the extent that I will enjoy its being-over-with, its disappearance. My project "is" its own constitutive impossibility.

Knowledge (Correspondence Theory of Truth): As touched on already, I can confirm the accuracy of my knowledge of the object only if I can know the perfect correspondence of my knowledge and what lies outside it; but as soon as I do so, this is part of my knowledge, rather than what lies outside it, hence is no correspondence, and must be further confirmed, and so ad infinitum. Truth "is" its own constitutive impossibility.

Will and Value: As already suggested, volition requires at least two items to be contrasted, viz., fact and value. But the fulfillment is the collapse of the two into one—and this one is then by definition no longer "desirable"—valuable, i.e., that which contrasts with fact. Will "is" its own constitutive impossibility. Value "is" its own constitutive impossibility.

It can easily be seen that these are all variations on a single theme, that the impossibility in each case is in one sense one and the same basic impossibility—Intersubsumption (All-pervasion as All-pervadedness)—while at the same time each impossibility is specific and determinative of a particular coherence—a Local Coherence and its Global Incoherence. The "being" of each of these quiddities as such, as what it is, is maintained only by means of the maintenance of its constitutive contradiction or impossibility. They continue to operate if and only if they fail to fully succeed in what they are "trying to do," only if they fail to be what they "claim," only if they are faulty or nongenuine versions of themselves. To exist as X is to be a fake X. In classical Tiantai terms, all posits are Local Coherences, which, in Chinese, is synonymous with "False" Posits (*jia*).

It should also be noted that each of these instances of impossibility is founded on some problem of *adequation*, of matching of two parts within a total field. Here we would do well to recall the discussion in the Introduction of the aggregate, consciousness, as *dividing/divided* awareness, and the Tiantai response to this. For each case here is an instance of the repeated collapsing of determinacy when its constitutive partiality (non-all-pervasiveness) is exploded. For to be present as a determinate object of either cognition or volition, to be present as a coherence *simpliciter*, as we have seen, it must be situated in an array of multiple coherences, at least *one* of which it excludes (in the most extreme case, just the coherence of consciousness or subjectivity as such). But where there is an array, there is necessarily a correlation, a connection, a question of fitting the pieces together. This is the *contingent* problem of every coherence: where does it fit in to the panorama of othernesses. But where there is a field of connected terms, there must be at least one all-pervasive term of some kind; otherwise there would be no field at all, these contrasted items would not be part of a single field and hence impossible to contrast. But an all-pervasive term is devoid of determinacy. What is devoid of determinacy cannot exclude any determinacy, including the determinacy of the original term to be matched. This term *within* the field turns out to be indistinguishable from the field itself. Hence, every term is all-pervasive and *stricto sensu* meaningless. This is the *necessary* impossibility of every coherence. Put another way, each term gets its meaning only by fitting together with something outside of itself in a certain way. But anything that X *must* match just to be X is no longer other than and outside of X. It is rather a part of "X" itself. But for this very reason, it can no longer do the job of identity-constituting for X. That is when we find that X's identity has failed to be constituted. But in that case, this "other coherence" really *is* outside of and other to X, and *can* do the job, since there is no longer an X for it to be a part of—that is, any and all contents are by definition "other than " X, since X has no content at all. The Tiantai view is hence that this constitutive matching with an other is impossible precisely because each X is all there is, is the whole, and hence has no other to match with. Whatever it meets with is itself "in another form." This means first that the two are a "perfect match," but also no longer satisfy the criterion of "matching or contrasting to an other" required for identity as X. *This simultaneously universalizes and eliminates the problem of adequation.* All coherences are impossible, are their own impossibility, and this is precisely their ineradicability, their all-pervasion, their definitive establishment in reality.

It should be noted here also what is underwriting this "continue to operate" and this "fail to be what they claim." For one objection that might be made at this juncture is that this transition from contingent difficulty to necessary impossibility is something executed and discovered by a process of thought or reflection, or at least close attention, and that these things maintain themselves quite well without any reference to this whole problematic if the whole rigmarole is not *mentioned* by philosophical trouble-makers. That is, in naïve experience they "maintain themselves " and "continue to operate" precisely by ignoring their own necessary impossibility (if we may anthropomorphize coherences in this way—which we may). Indeed, to naïve experience they are specific coherences that operate as such and also problematic in the sense of gainable and losable. After the transition to "necessary impossibility," they once again are both specific coherences operating as such (although now all-pervasive), and problematic (although now necessarily instead of contingently). These slight modifications are all that distinguish the two states, and in a sense the final state is thus a reinstatement of the initial condition. We shall see later in the section specially devoted to "Adequation" that the initial contemplations of impermanence and illusoriness are aimed at undermining the commonsense view that things have "more to them than meets the eye," even though this is precisely what is to be reinstated, in a more thorough and universal form, in the final contemplations. The structure here is the same: the initial naïve experience of the problematicalness is always apprehended against an assumed tacit background of unproblematicalness, of something which is *not* impossible, of some coherence somewhere which can serve as ground or standard which is not self-contradictory, which does not undermine its own survival, which does not have its own destruction built into its definition. There must be one nonproblematic something, one self-consistent something. It is against this background that the ordinary problematicalness of coherences is experienced, and it is the breakdown of this last consistent something assumed in all other acts, pointed-to in a backhanded manner by all ordinary experiences of problematicalness, which is the goal of these considerations and which effects the final breakthrough. When the necessary and universal impossibility of coherences per se is grasped, this assumed tacit ground falls too. When it is seen in this way that nothing can be consistently and universally applicable, ironically, we do in a sense get something which is "consistently and universally applicable": this failure itself. It is the strange loop so constituted that allows our exit from the perplexities of both foundational and anti-foundational philosophies. We therefore do not count the constitutive inconsistency and self-contradiction of coherences against them, making this a reason to consider them less real than some other kind of entity which is finally consistent and universally applicable, since there is nothing consistent and universally applicable outside of the failure of all coherences to be consistent and universally applicable. This is because the contrast between the two is effaced, they are alternate names for the same fact, and whatever can be said of one can be said of the other. On the other hand, we need not fall into the other extreme of regarding the definitional self-contradictions of ordinary coherences as inconsequential, which leads into serious problems of its own. For on this view, we must simply view consistent "real being" of the metaphysicians as a useless superstitious supposition with no basis, leaving only the apparent world. But as Nietzsche said, when the "real" world disappears, the "apparent" world disappears with it. That is, without the contrast between real and apparent, the apparent simply becomes the standard of reality, and once again we have established a definition of "real" being which, as a definition or standard, remains parasitic on the old notion of real being as consistency and universal applicability. "Being" now means simply "whatever appears, but cannot be thought through consistently," which itself becomes the consistently applicable definition of being. Whatever might fail to accord therewith would be a lesser being. In other words, the distinction between real and apparent cannot be abolished simply by trying to eliminate the real; it is a structurally necessary split, and simply re-establishes itself at the next level. The only way out of it is through it, as they say. This means to take the distinction between the two all the way to the bottom, make it necessary, which alone abolishes it. This distinction, like any other coherence, pervades all places precisely by necessarily failing to presence itself anywhere *simpliciter*. We will have more to say about a near-miss similar case in the section on "Krug's Pen" below.

This same thing works, by the way, in the opposite direction as well, perhaps even more pertinently. That is, it might be asked here as in the case of impermanence, are we not better off being unaware of Impermanence, of illusoriness, of necessarily failure? In ordinary experience we are very skilled at ignoring these, it might be said; is ignorance not bliss in this case? Most people, the story goes, do not worry about such things, and merely experience whatever comes to them as what it is. They do not *try* to construct any story about it at all, let alone some "philosophically consistent and universally applicable" story about what it is, so for them there is no contradiction present. What more could one ask for? The above account, in other words, applies only if one starts to discriminate, to think, to regard something as some definitive Being; but, it could be argued, this category "Being," with its implication of real consistent existence, is not at all important or operative to normal people—it is just a problem philosophers torture themselves with. As long as one does not think about it—and most people do not—there is no contradiction, constitutive or otherwise. A little thinking, in that case, as in saying, "This is X, that is Y," would bring the bad case of contingent dilemma (i.e., the sense of losability versus gainability), while thinking through this distinction would bring to necessary contradiction, which is finally no contradiction, in the sense just indicated. This talk of "a coherence fulfilling its implicit claim" to be consistently what it is means nothing if ordinary experience does not acknowledge any such implicit claim.

In response to this, though, I would say again that there is always differentiation, distinction, "thinking" in experience already, that is, that "claims" in the philosophical sense are involved in even the simplest and least self-reflective experience. I cannot argue this on the usual grounds of implicitness and explicitness, since for me all coherences, including those experienced by the insane and the stupid, have equal validity and equal being. But I can argue it again by the principle of backhanded counter-positing. That is, just as the experience of problematicalness is posited against (and thereby *by means of*) a tacit background of unproblematicalness which is functioning *as it*, and operative in it, "simple, direct experience which makes no claims about what anything *is*," always operates against a tacit background of putative certainty about at least one thing, about what at least one thing *is*. This certainty is where the claim is being made. Even if one is open-mindedly or ignorantly suspending judgment on what the truth is about anything, what anything is, what is consistent or not, this very act can, by a structural necessity of constitutive contrast and tacit instrumentality, only be accomplished by positing some thing about which one feels certain, which one deems to be X and not Y, which thereby makes the claim to be what it is, to exclude its other, to be contingently problematic, and so on. The Cartesian *cogito* is the most obvious example. There is something that is so, but which I have trouble experiencing *simpliciter* because of some external obstacle or other—"myself" or "the world" or "whatever is the case" or "chance" or "fate" or "the unknown laws of physics" or anything else that is tacitly deemed to be just what it is. It is then this something that is to be earmarked for the expansion toward necessary rather than contingent problematicalness.

Any coherence can appear only by failing to appear *simpliciter*. This allows us to understand, as it were, the "ethical" implications of our ruminations on being and having and on reversibility above. This is particularly obvious in the last named example, that of will and value, which forms a perfect parallel (in the register of "practical reason" as opposed to "pure reason," as it were) to the relation of knowledge and object in the critique of correspondence and coherence theories of truth discussed above and recapped in the preceding item in this section. But it runs equally through any of these coherences, and all coherences. The perfect equivalence of these terms must be stressed if the full implications are to become evident: to experience something as some particular coherence *is nothing but* to experience it as *a demand* for a coherence (a possible possible) which is constitutively impossible, which *is nothing but* to experience it as all-pervasive, *which is nothing but to identify with it, which is to be it, which is to (fail to) experience it as oneself.* Whatever one "is" is what has manifested fully (1) as determinate, (2) as constitutively impossible, and (3) as all-pervasive, such that these are merely three ways of restating the same thing. When one, in moments of disengagement from any other particular coherence, simply identifies with one's biological body (this appears in experience only when no other concern is pressing, in moments of "tranquil reflection"), one's body is being experienced as constitutively impossible and therefore as all-pervasive. When any part of the body is singled out for "identification" in this sense, this part is being experienced in that way. When any "external" coherence is the nodal point of world-structuring, it is being experienced in precisely this way, and thereby it *is* oneself at that time, that is, that through which, as which, all other coherences appear, such that its own appearance *simpliciter* is impossible, such that it is thereby all-pervasive in its very failure to appear anywhere in particular.

We have here in effect a real definition of what it is to *be* as such, of what it is to be an object and what it is to be a self, if we wish to continue this discussion in the register of the first case listed above, to take the next step in our investigation of what it means to be a self and what it means to be an other. That is: as long as something is experienced as only *contingently* problematic, it is an object, it is something to be "had" or possessed (or not), it is an "obstacle to" something, it is "distanced from" something, these being constitutive features of being-an-object. To experience something as distanced, as obstructive, as possessed or lacked or susceptible to possession or lack, is to be experiencing it as an object, and what this means is that its problematicalness is being apprehended as merely *contingent*, in precisely these forms. As soon as it is experienced as *necessarily*, constitutively problematic, that is, paradoxical and impossible in its very nature, as precondition to its appearance as this particular coherence at all, it is my self. For some coherence to "be my self" means that it is omnipresent by virtue precisely of its presenting its inability to appear anywhere, even here, *simpliciter* as genuinely necessary and inescapable, where reversibility is explicit. It is my "body," the proximate term *through which* all other terms appear, without itself appearing as such. It has been *fully realized* when it has become myself, when I have "identified with it" completely, and what this means is that its contingent problematicalness—obstruction, contingent distance, possession—is revealed to have been necessary problematicalness—constitutiveness otherness, inherent distance, determinacy qua ambiguity, asness, the lack of simple presence which also ensures its omnipresence. To fully realize X means to realize the constitutive impossibility of X, which means to see X as all non-X's and *only* as all non-X's. But this is just what it means when I say, "X is my body, X is my self." Just as my "me"-ness is something which (1) comes to have a meaning only by being posited in contrast to otherness and (2) turns out to be undiscoverable in abstraction from objects (must appear as some determinate nonme object, whether perceived object or substratum body) and thereby (3) ends up being the one thing which is manifest in/as *all* objects of my perception and experience (they are all constitutively "experienced-by-me" objects, even though no other "me" can be discovered to lend them this quality), which all end up being expressions of my being in the mode of its own absence—in the same way, any coherence *fully experienced* shares these three aspects. To fully experience X this means to *be* and *have* and *lack* X in precisely this way. These are of course the classical Tiantai Three Truths.

But with this we have arrived at the final meaning of desire, of selfhood, of existence. The value of this conclusion is not only theoretical; it is "ethical" as well.

The Good as the Intersection of Two Impossibilities

I have deliberately avoided including any "ethics" in the usual sense in these reflections, not only for the obvious reason that the premises here are not at all conducive to the derivation of any preference for some set of coherences over some other set which would apply in all cases (except in the sense in which, as we have seen, *anything* applies in all cases) but also because there is something pathetic and perverse about texts such as this one pretending to be legislators for anyone's behavior. Nonetheless, as my furtive parenthetical in the last sentence might suggest, the "should" itself is not to be disparaged or overlooked simply because no determinate content to it can be advocated in the form of exclusion of its opposite as binding on all occasions. On the contrary, we must say here in all seriousness that "shouldness" per se is another of those coherences whose all-pervasiveness is among the most obvious. There is no escaping the "should"; every coherence exists in the state of wanting to be other, of calling forth possibilities, of invoking questions about itself; "shouldness" per se is constitutive of being. Shouldness pervades all coherences; they all ought to be something else, and they "know" it. Nothing can rest in itself. This all-pervasiveness of shouldness is no surprise; we have said just the same thing about every coherence without exception. It remains, however, to indicate its precise manner of all-pervasion; as something which excludes others (viz., whatever the fact of the matter happens to be) and also as itself constitutively impossible, i.e., as being undermined by a "shouldness" itself.

For us, "shouldness" has no specifically "ethical" content; it is structurally just what desire is, that is, the demand that things be otherwise. The Good is the desirable, as reliable old Mencius said; ethical obligation is just one more species of desire. The reason we will speak of the "should" separately is simply as a more comprehensive delineation of what desire is. In a formula: pursuit of desire qua desire per se, rather than qua some specific desire, is ethical endeavor. To know what desire is, the structure of which we have been trying to delineate, is to know what desire per se desires, which is to know the Good per se.

Desire wants things to be otherwise. Now we have seen already that all things that are thus are also otherwise, and in a number of senses; Intersubsumption (All-pervasion as All-pervadedness) is the fact that to be thus *is* to be otherwise. But the pressure and force of desire and/or shouldness is to be sought in the specific vicissitudes of "blocked reversibility" discussed above. A kind of naïve ergonomic or hydraulic metaphor is not at all out of place here: where the flow is obstructed, pressure builds up. Ordinary consciousness confronts these coherences; it "has" or "does not have" them. But the imperative that lurks in all of them, the pressure of the hitched reversibility discussed above, demands that one actually "become" them, in precisely the sense specified there. What is wanted in wanting is to *be* something one has refused to be: namely this coherence currently appearing as an object. We should recall here again the discussion in the Introduction of "divided" as opposed to "whole" awareness and desire, the latter being "pure desire," the desire which wants *everything* otherwise, and sees everything thereby as *already* otherwise. We can now understand this a bit better. We have just seen in a number of rather general examples what it is that is the being of any coherence that is occurring: it is some form of constitutive impossibility. It is the being of this impossibility that is being refused in the ordinary consciousness that "has experiences" rather than being them. To be them is to be the contradiction that constitutes them. The case is no different with being "ourselves," however construed: to be ourselves would be to be the impossibility that constitutes us. To behave "ethically" and/or "satisfactorily" with regard to any coherence that is "encountered" (recalling what else lurks in the notion of "encountering" a coherence—imagining and conceptualizing it) is to understand that it is, in its very being, none other than its own constitutive dilemma, that it is by nature insoluble, and moreover that this impossibility which it is is inescapable, is a restatement of the primal impossibility which we have already been busy being, whatever that may have been in any particular case. We must see this coherence as an impossibility that is necessary, inescapable, all-pervading—but that means that we too cannot escape it, that there is no self in which we can safely hide from it: it means *to become this dilemma itself*. Full reversibility must be reinstated for this particular paradoxical identity by becoming it. We may perhaps say that being the contradiction or paradox itself is the only solution—rather than having the problem, being confronted by it, or "being part of the problem," as they say, we must *be the whole problem and nothing besides.*

What is meant by "being" the impossibility, "being" the paradox itself? First of all, it means that the contingent, encountered, escapable impossibility or irresolvability has been transformed into a necessary, all-pervasive, embodied irresolvability, "embodied" here implying that one can run from it no more than one can run from one's own feet. Moreover, it must be felt *as* one's "body" in the precise Polanyian sense we have delineated above—that "through which" all other things appear, which vanishes to appear "as" them but, when attention is redirected toward it, "as" which they can all be appearing. If one is confronted with a frustrating, impossible double-bind, the only solution is to see that it is "frustrating impossible double-bind" which is walking, eating, wanting, thinking, and so on. To be it is to be "that which is bothering so and so (your name here), not giving him/her any rest," to be "an utterance that makes no sense but demands attention," "that which challenges and disrupts and frustrates everyone or anything who tries to make sense of it." It is to see the whole rest of the world, including the troubled body-mind grappling with the problem, through the "eyes" of the problem itself, as aspects of itself, as forms *as* which it is appearing and expressing its particular impossible coherence.

We may state our conclusion here most succinctly: what is necessary in any situation is to identify the blockage constitutive of desire which defines the situation, and move it from contingent to necessary blockage. This is equivalent to absolute effort as the blockage, to becoming the obstacle itself, to overcoming the glitch in reversibility by putting oneself in "its" position. The primary Urvirtue here is perhaps courage, the courage to bring the situation to the point where its necessary failure becomes manifest, rather than allowing it to maintain the bad faith of the illusion that the obstacle is merely contingent. However, this "courage" must be understood in its proper "meaningless" sense; it would necessarily entail also the "courage" to "fully be" cowardice itself, or even a coward, understood to mean pressing cowardice so far that its necessary rather than contingent obstacles to self-preservation and expression become manifest, so that cowardice is present everywhere qua deadpan asness, cowardice is necessarily meaningless and precisely as such is present *as* every noncowardice coherence.

Let us adduce an example. A full explication of this ethical situation can only be accomplished by recourse to the category of intersubjectivity. We will say more about the structure of this category in the section on "Inscrutability of the Other" below, but for the moment we must note a few features of the situation that bear on the structuring of desire. Let us imagine the situation developmentally, as is our modern custom: a child confronts a world making demands on him, in the form of parents, peers, and institutions. These come to define the contours of dilemma that are his world. The false consciousness of dilemma as *contingent* would have us imagine for the sake of argument a superhumanly good-natured child who only wants to love and accept his playmates; he enters his nursery school and meets tough violent standards; he will be accepted only if he can be cruel to his peers. This is his contingent dilemma; he wants to be "nice" but external conditions demand that he be "mean," to put it pathetically-naïvely. (Obviously, we could just have easily have suggested the opposite case: he wants to be "mean" but external conditions demand that he be "nice." In our view, neither of these is more likely or more natural than the other. Indeed, we can begin with spontaneous dispositions, to which feelings of inferiority are necessarily attached, since everyone starts as the youngest, discovers himself [comes to self-consciousness, via mirror and frustration] in the situation of being the youngest, weakest, stupidest, most powerless member of the family or group. Everyone else knows more and is able to do more. So whatever one—perhaps rather arbitrarily—clings to as one's own domain is easily open to ridicule and devaluation, since it is necessarily in such an immature state of development. This becomes a definition of anti-value for oneself, and all one's overcomings are aimed in the opposite direction, to become the antithesis of the spontaneous dispositions.) We can easily imagine this particular axis continuing to operate throughout his life as the central defining point of his difficulties. It should be obvious however that this one-sided formulation, in either version, is not ultimately defensible. The demand to be mean can be found in the niceness itself; the demand to be nice can be found in the meanness itself. This follows theoretically from all we have said above, and I will not repeat the derivation here. The apparently contingent dilemma is in reality a necessary impossibility; niceness is always a form of meanness, meanness is always a form of niceness. However, the ethical or practical problem remains: how is the child to "embody" this dilemma, rather than confront it, so as to instantiate this impossibility? For this, on our view, is the only possible solution. He must find some *specific* mode of behavior that at once answers to both aspects of the dilemma, which is manifestly nice as mean and mean as nice. We may suggest in the present case an alternative to the Hegelian master-slave fight for recognition; we have rather a kind of "can't beat 'em, join 'em" approach. To overcome what he is scared of, the child becomes it, and to be sure he has become it, he has to be recognized as "it" by the other ones who he thinks are "it," but especially by those who are *not* it, who body forth for him the subjective position from which he wants to escape, as discussed above. He may, for example, become a bully to overcome his fear of bullies. More generally, we may derive the arising of subjectivity as such from the same principle: I become an observing consciousness only because observing consciousnesses have scared me; the only way to get away from them was to become one of them. Being interpreted as something in particular, being deemed to be some particular coherence, was the unbearable first cause (parents); my response is to become a consciousness that judges and interprets other things, attributes qualities to them. Then I have to get other interpreters to recognize me as such, to interpret me as an interpreter. Being object is thus, in this sense at least, logically prior to being subject. A similar structure applies in Freud's comment on guilt; the only way to overcome it is to find someone to share it with, someone else who is guilty in the same way.

But thus far we have only a partial solution. The child who has become a bully has only satisfied half of the original demand. He has capitulated to the demand made by the world, and sacrificed his own desire. He must also satisfy his original desire to be nice *in the same act*. This is possible here, for example, if he can continue to regard his own meanness as an act of consummate niceness—this is implicit in the above description: he has "sacrificed his own desire on behalf of the demands of others," and what could be "nicer" than that? If he can regard his meanness as the subversion of meanness itself in this way, even his bullydom, I am sorry to say, will be an ethical and satisfactory approach to his world. Desire for both (1) the demand and (2) its undermining, functioning at the same time and indeed as one and the same thing, alone will satisfy. If he loses sight of the pathetic niceness of his bullydom, it will fail to satisfy. In deference to more traditional moralists, I would be willing to grant that continued awareness of this doubleness of the bullydom will most likely change the nature of the bullydom itself. More detailed exposition of the intricacies involved here will have to await a future work. But in practice it would seem that this direct acquiescence will in most cases become too consuming to maintain contact with its own undermining. More generally, some third form of behavior must be found that will satisfy both of the opposing demands with a single token. The hard-boiled detective cited by Žižek comes to mind here: his rebellion (against the forces of evil) is even more radical than the rebellion (against society) practiced by the evil-doers themselves. His defense of civilization and goodness comes in the form of an *über*-cynicism which out-evils the evil, thereby satisfying both the demand to be evil and the demand to be good. I would suggest that all truly satisfying forms of activity, which answer to the obscure world-orienting desires, share this structure. I will cite another example. A child is raised in a high-culture worshipping household, and trained as a classical musician. His childhood is spent rebelling against this demand; the expected life as a professional classical musician comes to represent for him all the demands of culture and respectability, and his identity is formed, for various reasons (perhaps even because the excessive insistence and purity of the demand in this case made its immediate self-undermining abundantly evident) as a specific rejection of these demands. But neither acquiescence nor rebellion will satisfy here; value for him is defined only intersubjectively in accordance with this demand, but the demand's inherent antithesis to itself also makes such pure acquiescence equivalent to complete self-annihilation, as the paradoxes of value and normativity above make clear. If he did as he was told, there would be no self doing it. The way out of this dilemma would be to become it: he becomes, let us say, an outrageously crass heavy-metal singer, or a subway busker. This one token combines the two opposite demands just as they are inherent in the original demand: he is a professional musician, but precisely in the form most radically rejected by the original demand, as conceived, however idiosyncratically, by *him*. Needless to say, the precise axis of satisfaction operative may not be apparent to observers. He fulfills the demand by subverting it, and subverts it by fulfilling it. This embodied necessity of the impossibility of the demand alone will fulfill it, and alone will satisfy. In every case, some solution of this kind must be found to every troubling demand. This is Neo-Tiantai ethics in a nutshell.

Krug's Pen Revisited

We must be unequivocal about this. The claim here is that the terms "necessary contradiction" and "identity" are interchangeable, and that for any coherence whatsoever to "be there" is for some necessary contradiction to be there. No necessary contradiction, no coherence. This is our version of "the Real is the Rational"—and perhaps (in itself if not for itself) this is all Hegel meant by that infamous phrase, although he may have understood himself to be saying just the opposite, namely, that only where there is finally *no* contradiction is there something that qualifies as real. His practice, however, belies this understanding. Even so, the Tiantai position on this point differs from Hegel's, even if liberally construed, in two crucial, related respects. First, here we have no derivations and transitions from one constitutive contradiction to another, where one breaks down into another in a determinate order. Rather, we have here a polymorphous interpervasion of omnipresences, where anything randomly picked up or "encountered," to be seen as any identity at all, ends up being some necessary contradiction of itself, but where these are connected via breakdowns that proceed in every direction at once. Indeed, as we shall see in more detail below, to become the constitutive contradiction, to make it one's self, is to presence it precisely as freedom. To be fully X is to be non-X, that is, to be X as Global Incoherence, to manifest the inherent impossibility of X; a moment of freedom ensues wherever anything is fully realized in this manner, wherefrom its interchangeability is unimpeded, and it can be anything. Second, in the Tiantai view, nothing whatsoever that appears in experience can fail to be a necessary contradiction in its own right; everything we called a coherence, which, it will be recalled, included every possible possible as well as any part of any possible possible (any part of a "one" being another "one").

Hegel considered the existence of "contingency as such" as a necessary moment in the structure of rationality and necessity, in his peculiar sense of these terms (which we would translate, in our own terms, precisely as constitutive impossibility). But he did not grant this status to each particular contingent fact and event, considered separately. Hegel's stance on this question is made abundantly clear in his rather petulant response to Krug's challenge, in a hostile review, for Hegel to "deduce" the very pen with which Krug was writing the hostile review. Krug's assumption was that Hegel meant to show the rationality of each individual object and fact in the natural and social worlds, in the sense that each is deducible from the self-elucidation of the categories of Hegel's system. Hegel responds that something as inconsequential as Krug's pen cannot and should not be of any interest to philosophy, which deduces only the universals which subsume and actively express themselves in all these particular facts, to which all their specifiable characteristics turn out to be reducible. Philosophy can deduce pens in general, perhaps, thus demonstrating the rationality of their existence, but not this particular pen; for the details of empirical reality are, for Hegel, an unstable shimmering governed by caprice and contingency, which however must, as it were, *resolve* into the rationality of the universal categories (penhood, in this case). The existence of this "moment" of contingency itself, of course, is also a necessary category, but individual contingent occurrences are rational only in the sense that they *turn out* upon reflection to have nothing "real" in them but the categories into which they resolve. Our position, in contrast, is that there can be no Krug's pens "left outside," which have status *only* as a moment or element of some other thing which is "rational," merely aspects of some other identifiable necessary contradiction, that is, some other real identity. All those elements that *appear* to naïve experience to be reals but turn out not to be truly rational are, for Hegel, mere sides or parts or moments of something else which is truly rational; it is only these reals which must be deduced, in the belief that all the appearances that constitute them will thereby be picked up at the same time. The part/whole relation ends up being rather more rigid here than we would expect from Hegel's more acute theoretical statements; Krug's pen is a part of, say, the economy of production that manufactured it in a particular form of civil society, but the reverse is not true; Krug's pen is not the whole of which society can be revealed to be a part or, more strictly, a moment. On the Tiantai side, however, this reversibility is carried through to the end. Krug's pen is a constitutive contradiction in its own right, the contradiction which is its identity resides right in itself and reduces all other things to its moments. Krug's penness is a coherence with enough necessary impossibility to sustain it in being, without having to collapse into an aspect of some other necessary impossibility, that is, some other "rational real."

Pleasure and the Self

Let us turn now to the question of pleasure, which we have glanced on in passing above. Our understanding of pleasure derives directly from our explication of desire above. It is clear that we cannot very well accept any absolute definition of pleasure—that is, anything specific, based on the possession or lack of any given chemical compound or psychological contents. Instead, I can only view it most generally as, to borrow another helpful Chinese word, *tong* : 'penetration, unobstructedness, free reversibility, the acceleration of any flow' (*kuai*). This is nothing but another term for Intersubsumption (All-pervasion as All-pervadedness), or the function of the punch line, or constitutive impossibility, or deadpan all-pervasive asness, the overcoming of some snag in reversibility. It is precisely this that in the most naïve way is experienced as pleasure. Pleasure as we generally know it, more specifically, is the breaking through of an obstacle to reversibility such as conditions desire, the dawning of necessary failure which allows the free flow of reversibility, positionality, or intersubsumptive deadpan asness once again. It is the embodying of the dilemma such that in a single act both the demand and its undermining or obstacle are immediately present and interpenetrative. Pleasure, in this sense, is just what we have defined the Good as: the overcoming of snags to reversibility, or Intersubsumption

If this acceleration of flow or reversibility is too radical, then *in addition* to the pleasure there will also be pain—that is, the blocking off or slowing down somewhere else, as the equilibrium of the organism is damaged. Too intense a liberation (e.g., a knife wound) may indeed be painful—it brings with it not only the opening up of the flesh, but at the same time also the closing or obstruction of the senses, the blocking off of vision and feeling in other areas, the permanent loss of motility in other areas. All narrower descriptions of pleasure (e.g., the reduction or discharge of tension) must be regarded as special instances of this. The tension that was discharged, for example, had functioned as an obstruction, a wall, had narrowed the horizon somehow, had snagged the reversibility and exchange of perspectives, the free flow of identification and release of identification, the arising of foci and their unobstructed dissolution as absorbed into other foci. We may think here of Nietzsche's notes on the relation between pleasure and pain. He observes first that they are not opposites; the essence of pleasure resides in a feeling of more power—in our language, in the overcoming of obstacles. Hence "there are even cases in which a kind of pleasure is conditioned by a certain *rhyth-*

mic sequence of little unpleasurable stimuli; in this way a very rapid increase of the feeling of power, the feeling of pleasure, is achieved."[11] The opposite, however, is not the case: we do not find pain being composed of a rhythmic sequence of pleasures. Nietzsche goes on to claim, "There is no pain as such." Rather, pain is an intellectual occurrence expressing a certain judgment—namely, that "this is harmful." With an enhancement of perspective, or a revaluation, what was formerly regarded as pain might be seen as stimulus to further power, hence as one in the sequence of displeasures that *composes* pleasure. Nietzsche adds that displeasure is of two types: (a) displeasure as a means of stimulating the increase of power, and (b) displeasure following an overexpediture of power—or exhaustion. The latter is indeed an opposite of pleasure, for its essence lies in the feeling of the diminishment of power; but the former is not. Similarly, there are two kinds of pleasure, which Nietzsche describes emblematically as the pleasure of victory and the pleasure of falling asleep. The former needs and wants displeasures of the first type.[12] Here, too, we find a narrower description of what we are calling the overcoming of a snag to reversibility. In our case, however, we dispense with Nietzsche's dualism (and thereby, quite a few of his judgments and conclusions): for both the pleasure of sleep and the pleasure of victory can be seen to be instances of this overcoming, of the extension of Intersubsumption and reversibility. Victory is the breaking through of an obstacle, but so is sleep, for here the conscious individual overcomes his separation from inanimacy, from the insensate world; to the extent that all his waking activities were premised on identifying solely with being a conscious entity rather than an unconscious one, this periodic overcoming of the dichotomy, where he suddenly is on the verge of finding himself on the other side of the divide, restores the reversibility, which for us, if not for Nietzsche, is precisely what power means. The pleasure of falling asleep is another example of overcoming an obstacle, of exercising the motility of the border dividing one identification from another. Will to power is will to reversibility.

The contrast has sometimes been made between pleasure and power. Russell posits them as contraries, as do some Neo-Reichians, and there is some truth in this, but not the whole truth, as they know too. May we say that surrender is what constitutes pleasure, while control is power? But simply being raped or overpowered is not pleasant, one must voluntarily surrender, and this implies that one trusts the power, feels that it will take one in some sense

---

[11] Friedrich Nietzsche, *The Will to Power*, trans. Walter Kaufmann and R. J. Hollingdale (New York: Vintage, 1968), 371. He cites tickling and sexual pleasure as examples of displeasure serving as an ingredient of pleasure.
12 Ibid., 373–74.

where one wants to go—another form of power. Moreover, consider the phenomenon of mastery of a skill—it is control and power, but it is also pleasure of surrender in a sense, the full absorption of one's identity into the deed at hand—indeed, as Nietzsche says, all increase in power brings pleasure. In sex, compare self-surrender to the sensation with the ego-gratification and power of watching the other be melted or crazed under the influence of one's presence. But we can now say that surrender-pleasure is the feeling of releasing the repressing armor on the original disposition, the anti-value, the way you have been trying not to be—the feeling of relaxing a long-clenched muscle. This, too, is a form of power in a sense, since it reminds you of the motility and health of the muscle, and its continuing ability to function, which had been lost to you in the clench. It may also be seen as a re-establishment of contact with the spontaneous source of energy and creativity, the vegetative nervous responses, and so on, from which alienation had impoverished and depleted you; you have more powers at your disposal, or running through you, than you had suspected, you are less limited than you had thought. The ego-pleasure of control and power is the reclenching or strengthening of the clench of the same muscle. So we find that self-surrender and control turn out to be two forms of reestablishing reversibility, of reclaiming the motility of a chronically clenched muscle. This can perhaps shed some light as well on the varieties of sexual pleasure, as already suggested. For another common contrast, which has caused considerable bemusement, is that between "masculine" and "feminine" sexual pleasure. Male desire has sometimes been generalized to fit the model of the desire for control, for power; the self increases its power by invading an other, changing the other, while maintaining its own unbroken continuity. The self stays the same—only more so—but the world is changed, and changed according to the character of the unchanging self. Female desire, on this picture, would be a desire to be invaded by the world, to allow the world to maintain its continuity while altering and surrendering the self; the self changes, the world stays the same—only more so. The woman, in this view, needs a more radical faith in the world to which she surrenders herself—the proverbial desire for security—than the man needs toward the world he sets out to shake. But both of these would then be ideal types of what we have called "partial desire." Either the world or the self is supposed to stay the same. This, we have seen, is not possible. Perhaps the repetition compulsion endemic to role-defined sexuality may find its roots here. The alternative would be total desire, total alteration, of both self and world, such as we find, in the Neo-Tiantai view, to be entailed in each moment of experience.

In this context, we can attempt to answer the question concerning the initial determinate identification of a particular self. That is, we must address the question, Why was there any identification at all? Why did any group of coherences come to regard each other as extensions of one another, as versions of one another, as something that each of the others was appearing *as*, as against some other coherences to which this asness does not extend? We must enter this problem from the angle of pleasure—and I will dip in and out of it quite quickly, so as not to make it seem more important than it is; it is, after all, one of those questions which "tendeth not to edification." Nonetheless, we might as well give an account of it.

As I said before, pleasure is always a matter of nonobstruction, of *tong*, of overcoming a blockage, the formation of a figure in the breaking up of a previous one, the dawning of a punch line. If we assume that the self was originally the "pleasure ego," this then would also be the criterion according to which the division "self/nonself" was originally made. Where there was *tong*—unobstructed, reversible, intersubsumptive asness—was myself, where there was obstruction, where reversibility was blocked, was object, other. But this means I cling to that coherence *tong*, once noticed as such, once named by someone, once pointed out to me, as fixed self to be defended and protected, to be repeated—which precisely makes it into an obstruction. Once nonobstruction is apprehended as a coherence in its own right, one which excludes its opposite (obstruction) and thus has to be defended or preserved, it becomes an obstruction. Pleasure was all over the place, until we wanted to ensure that we could repeat it at any time. The threat of the loss of pleasure is what makes pleasure vanish—another primal, constitutive impossibility that ceases to be a problem as soon as one ventures to *be* it rather than merely encounter it. Our problem is that we try to possess pleasure, when in fact we *are* pleasure, and hence can never possess it. It is perhaps the primal ignorance to assume that death would not be pleasure, that it would be possible to lose anything by letting go of everything. The longing for death as a morbid symptom, then, as the Freudian revisionists insist, is just a resurgence of the resistance of that primal flux against the rigid fixed ego. But we must note here, to continue in the Freudian idiom, that this means that the death-drive proper, as Lacan saw, ceases to be morbid when it sees itself everywhere, as another name for drive *as such*, indeed, for life. This willingness to be reversed, to be the opposite of what one is, is death, is life. As we said at the beginning, and repeatedly since, the self is just the redefinition of the self. And this is equivalent to the total penetration of any given detail, the all-pervasiveness that we have seen to be another name for identity and another name for impossibility. Is this not a means of re-establishing contact with this intersubsumption, this transparency, this *tong*, this whoosh of the primal joy/agony?

There is a certain ambiguity about the subject-object relation that we are now perhaps in a position to clear up. The claim here has been that one *is* whatever one does not see or experience; whatever appears in experience is thereby defining itself for the moment as the not-self, against which whatever other coherences there can be, but in their inexplicit state, are what count as self. To be and to have are strictly correlative; whatever one has (in one's world as objects capable of being gained or lost) one is not, whatever one is one has not. On the other hand, we have just spoken of a determinate set of coherences with which one identifies, thereby constituting the self. That is, if there is an unwillingness to identify with some particular coherence, which I alluded to earlier as "that which one is unwilling to *be*," this must mean there is a prior identification with some other set of coherences that is obstructing the newly proposed identification. What is the relation between these two versions of "self"?

What we want to avoid here is any sort of true self/false self contrast between these two, however subtle. Indeed it is just this sort of dichotomy, and its vast array of accompanying problems which, in a way, all the above considerations are precisely aimed at eliminating. Instead, we must dig again into the bottomless resources of classical Tiantai; in this case, the description of the three bodies of the Buddha. A Buddha has, according to classical Mahāyāna, (at least) three types of "bodies" (*kāya*)—that is, "heaps," accumulations, conglomerations of elements, or, in our language, systems of coherence. These are the (1) *Dharmakāya*, that is the body of Dharma itself, usually identified in one way or another with the Dharma-nature, or the absolutely unconditioned; (2) *Sambhogakāya*, the "reward" or "bliss" body, the glorified body of the Buddha, or, in Tiantai dogmatics, the Buddha's inner subjective experience of liberation, and (3) the *Nirmāṇakāya* or response body, which assumes various forms in accordance with the capacities and needs of sentient beings to be educated, which in Tiantai means the visible, palpable physical body as such. In Tiantai, these are aligned with Intersubsumption, Global Incoherence, and Local Coherence, respectively. *Dharmakāya* is a word for the Three Thousand coherences *as* Intersubsumption (which always implies Global Incoherence and Local Coherence). Sambhogakāya is the Three Thousand *as* Global Incoherence (which always implies Intersubsumption and Local Coherence). *Nirmāṇakāya* is the Three Thousand *as* Local Coherences (which always implies Intersubsumption and Global Incoherence). Once again, we have the simultaneous differentiation and identity of the Three Truths, on the model of setup and punch line. Each of the three bodies *is* the Three Thousand coherences, and each is those coherences *as* all three truths, with, however, a different aspect to the fore in each case—that is, in each case all Three Truths, as aspects operative in all Three Thousand coherences, are also appearing as *one* of the three, given some particular interpretive context (determined by desire and soteriological need). In terms of the "three tracks," the first of these is the "true nature," what is simply so, the second is a state of consciousness aware of that reality, and the third, practico-inert conditions that make that consciousness possible, and which are guided by, follow from, that awareness. It is to be especially noted that what is "simply so" here, the *Dharmakāya*, turns out to be nothing but the identity/difference of the consciousness and its practico-inert conditions, Global Incoherence and Local Coherence. In other words, truth is nothing but the fact that all illusions are the-same-as-different as the conditions of the appearance of these illusions. It is the intersubsumption of the manifestation of any coherence and the unmanifest conditions of that appearance, such that each is punch line to the setup of the other.

In terms of our current question concerning the self, the last of these—the *Nirmāṇakāya*, Local Coherence, the Practico-inert conditions—is the limited set of conditions or identifications which has been assumed in any given case. The reason anything has been so identified has already been addressed above, although we will have more to say on this in a moment. The second body, however, is as it were the vague haze of indeterminacy, manifested as impermanence, as ambiguity, as explorability, as depth or thickness, as the self-outrunning, as the sense that more is revealed as it is examined or recontextualized, that there is more (or less) to it than can be specified in any one finite set of determinations. This is also the positing of the *observer* of the coherence in question as *what is left out of it*, as the negativity which always escapes it, as "something-more-ness" or "moretoitivity" as such. As we have seen, this "excluded something" is the precise precondition, indeed the meaning, of appearing in experience as such, of presencing per se; it is to have a proximal set of terms that are unseen, absorbed into a focal distal term. It is the otherness of whatever is excluded qua the self. Intersubsumption (All-pervasion as All-pervadedness), the true nature, the *Dharmakāya*, then corresponds to the universalization of this sense of the excluded "more," of there being a context, which is the sense of self conditioned by the appearance of any determinate coherences in experience, such that this coherence of "something moreness" is confronted with the same self-overturning and explorability, leading as we have seen to the unobstructed reversibility and absolute undecidability between all coherences, the fact that they are forever serving as each others' setup as well as each others' punch lines, revealing themselves in each other and each other in themselves. This is what any coherence is, once penetrated to its bottomless bottom. Whatever it is not is what is, perceiving it, what is making it manifest as such, and is immediately present in it if examined, if "thought through." It is in this sense that all other quiddities as such are the self perceiving this coherence, manifesting themselves as it.

Now it should be remembered that these three are the strictly identical and strictly opposed, for precisely the reason that the Three Truths are the identical and opposed, or that humor and seriousness pervade both the setup and punch line of a joke. The particular identification is the setup (Local Coherence) that calls forth the presence of a redefining otherness (Global Incoherence), which turns out to be another posit in the same boat, defining itself in terms of the otherness of the first posit, thereby bringing forth the effect of laughter, the mutual pervasion and reversibility expressed in the tension between the humorous and the serious (Intersubsumption). Some particular set of coherences have "banded together" as an identity, as coherence, which has desires and aversions in accordance with its particular contours, as described above. This is the self unwilling to be identified with a particular object, that is, the object of desire, as it would threaten the contours as defined. But this identified coherent affiliation, if made an object of attention in its own right, is always in a process of bleeding vaguely outward into its ambiguity and Global Incoherence, indeed, this is precisely what is expressed, backwardly as it were, as the insecurity of its unwillingness to identify with some elements. And in this process it is always already the whole set of all other possible coherences which is acting as this restricted self, which is appearing here *as* this particular constricted, self-protective identity. It is, in traditional terms, *by means of* restricting itself that the interchangeability of the unrestricted manifests. There can be no "reversibility" or "Intersubsumption" per se or *simpliciter*; reversibility, too, is a coherence and hence can never appear *simpliciter*. We must have terms that can be reversed, and, hence, we must have posits to start with. These posits only get any determinacy at all by taking seriously for a moment their restrictions, just as the joke will only work as long as the setup is temporarily taken in earnest and followed attentively. This means the bad-faith cowardly illusion of positing some specific self and being defensively unwilling to face it or think it through, lest it crash, is always happening, is the absolutely necessary condition of there being the universal intersubsumption in which it is surpassed at all. We will be exploring the structure of this necessary finite self in the section on "Freedom" below.

It is here that we have finally arrived at some insight concerning about the status of the two possible outcomes for any self-project alluded to above, that is, stopping short at some irreconcilable otherness, or continuing brazenly on until everything is absorbed into itself. The former, as we have already said, is a kind of defense mechanism guarding against the suspicion of the latter. The encountering of a contingent frustration of our desire allows us to postpone recognizing the absolute and necessary frustration of our desire. But in the three bodies theory, we have a template delineating the relation between these two outcomes. The defensively identified-with set of coherences, vaguely defined and unfaceable, the misguidedly grasped pleasure-ego, is *Nirmāṇakāya*—a response to a certain set of conditions, a limiting to a certain context, an unwillingness to reach the universal and perish there, a constriction that feigns to come up short and fail to recognize itself in certain things, or certain things in itself. It is the positing of a determinate self with a content and a context, which only sees and is so much, and which is in danger of being lost. It is one's personality, on which more in a moment. We may even say the vague unsteadiness of contour that inspires the unwillingness to face the complete freedom of interpretation that comes with the existence of any interpretation at all, the vague sense that there is more to come, that one has not thought oneself all the way through yet and there may be more that could be revealed about oneself if one did, is Global Incoherence, subjectivity-as-such, the *Sambhogakāya*. This is oneself as the awareness that is exploring one's own determinacy, encountering it and always one step outside it, always failing to grasp all of it, which is the condition for there being any awareness of it at all. But once this aspect of oneself is thought through, is made a coherence in its own right whose appearance is equally determined by the same condition, we have its universalization, its reversal, its identity with its reversal, that is, with the initial determinacy: hence we have Intersubsumption (All-pervasion as All-pervadedness), the *Dharmakāya*, all coherences as neither inside nor outside, as impossible and all-pervading, and as the identity of these two aspects. That is, we have full reversibility, whereby whatever appears is also the appearance of all the unseen coherences which are playing the subject to its object at the moment, and the fact that these coherences are in the same boat, all called into question by each other and free to convert into one another, that whatever appears is all other coherences appearing as it, and vice versa; this goes also especially for the initial coherence of the determinate self. This could not appear without the latter, indeed, it *is* just the latter, and vice versa.

In practical terms, this means that one is always toting around some self-concept to be defended, which manifests also as fear of destruction (of humiliation or embarrassment—of which more in a moment), aversion to some particular set of things, and impossible obsessional desire for certain things. But this very self-concept can equally be read as the *awareness* of this self-concept, which is just its "something-more-ness" per se, and the further expansion and reversion of that something-more-ness, which is the all-pervasion and ungraspability of that coherence and all others, that is, the full reversibility by which it is all others as it, and all others are it as all others, the inexhaustible metaphoric depth or thickness to it in which all other coherences are present already, the constitutive impossibility which is its all-pervasion, and so on. Moreover, this latter "reading" is accomplished precisely by the last aspect named, which is itself attained only by means of the former two. It should also be clear now in what sense it can be said, not only that desire is, in its nature, incapable of fulfillment, but that it is also incapable of frustration, that it is always being fulfilled.

A reference to Schopenhauer might clarify this point. Although Schopenhauer is sometimes interpreted as having posited the primacy of the "will-to-life," as opposed to, say, the Nietzschean will-to-power or the Heideggerian will-to-will, and although he does use this expression at times, he does so only after explicitly saying that he means more strictly simply "will as such," and that "it is immaterial and a mere pleonasm if, instead of simply saying 'the will,' we say 'the will to live.'"[13] Will as such is will to "life" only in the sense in which Schopenhauer specifies that by "life" he means the whole objective world of representation. In that the will is "omnipotent," being the thing-in-itself other than which there is nothing, whatever it wills is what there is. Will just means will-to-life in the sense of will-to-the-world as it is, or will-to-whatever-exists. But what Schopenhauer really means here, more strictly, although he sometimes elides this distinction, is that whatever we experience is directly the will itself, not an emanation or "accomplishment" of the will (i.e., not its goal, "what it wills," as realized), but precisely will per se, the willing itself, viewed through the lens of the principle of sufficient reason and the *principium individuationis*. In this sense it is not that the world is the *object* of what the will wills, its accomplished goal, but rather that it is the will itself, apprehended under this particular form. The knowable world, in other words, is not a depiction of the goal that the will is willing, but of the process of willing itself. For indeed, Schopenhauer states plainly that the will as such *has no particular goal*. "[The following question may be raised:] Every will is a will directed to something; it has an object, an aim of its willing; what then does it ultimately will, or what is that will which is shown to us as the being-in-itself of the world striving after? Like so many others, this question rests on the confusion of the thing-in-itself with the phenomenon. The principle of sufficient reason, of which the law of motivation is also a form, extends only to the phenomenon, not to the thing-in-itself. . . . In fact, absence of all aim, of all limits, belongs to the essential nature of the will in itself, which is an endless striving. . . . Eternal becoming, endless flux, belong to the revelation of the essential nature of the will. . . . Every individual act has a purpose or end; willing as a whole has no end in view."[14] If Schopen-

---

[13] Arthur Schopenhauer, *The World as Will and Representation*, vol. 1, trans. E.F.J. Payne (New York: Dover, 1969), 275.
[14] Ibid., 163–65.

hauer had held more strictly to this last proposition, many of the obvious flaws of his philosophy could have been averted, not the least of which those which bedevil his ethics. For what is implied here is that even the idea that "I will X rather than non-X (e.g., to eat rather than to be eaten), as *this* individual willer rather than *that* one," is merely phenomenal, is not what will really wills. The particularity of any given act of will does not belong to the reality of the will as thing-in-itself, or even as "the whole," for which there is no such thing as "my" willing of "this" end. Schopenhauer's messy and contradictory doctrine of grades of objectification, Platonic Forms, and "intelligible character" as an individual but nontemporal act of will obscures this point. For particular acts of will, with particular contents, are by his own premises necessarily only phenomenal. What we would say instead is that the phenomenal knowledge of this particular brain misperceives "will as such" to be "my particular will willing this particular end"—and that this misperception itself occurs is also the willing of the will that wills nothing in particular.

More crucially, on the ethical side, it can easily be seen that the whole distinction between "affirmation of the will" and "denial of the will" falls by the same stroke—for only on the "phenomenal" level of the principle of sufficient reason could there possibly be any distinction between "affirmation" and "denial." By this we do not mean to assert, as Schopenhauer sometimes carelessly does, that the will is therefore some kind of transcendental unity, since it is prior to plurality; more strictly, it is prior to both unity *and* plurality, again by Schopenhauer's own premises, a point he sometimes touches on with the more interesting assertion of the will's inherent self-contradiction, manifested in the conflict of "individual wills" in the phenomenal realm. But this assertion is damped down by the simultaneous assertion that all willing is also in some sense "the same" will, which is even supposed to carry ethical implications; all striving anywhere, by anyone, for anything, is supposed to be recognized via the formula "Thou art that," to be my own willing as well, and this is supposed to provide a basis for universal compassion. But if the "same will" which we all are is itself self-contradictory, it is hard to see why it should not will contradictory things for itself as well—to enjoy and to suffer, to eat and to be eaten, to survive and to perish. All of this is a result of not following through on the implications of a "nonphenomenal" will that is therefore truly neither one nor many, neither the same nor different, neither a harmony nor a conflict. It is the implications of this "neither same nor different" which concern us here.

For the real point of all this is that affirmation and denial of the will as a whole, or as thing-in-itself, amount to the same thing—as Zhili says, "to dwell in it is to be free from it," and this applies not only to "the whole" as such but to each particular thing, since being-a-part is precisely being-the-whole. That is to say, once my own particular willing of this particular end is seen to be equally readable as will as such, willing eternally with no particular end, unreferenced to motives or goals or indeed anything outside itself, it is at once also seen as omnireferential, as willing anything and everything, as wanting both the positing and the surpassing of every possible coherence. The Tiantai system takes this a point further in overcoming the distinction between the individual phenomenal act of will and goalless will as such, which are here seen to be genuinely identical. Each act of will is, precisely in being particular, at the same time willing much more than it "knows." It is at once a striving for a particular goal and a striving beyond that goal, as in the *Lotus* parables, a particular desire and pure desire—and more importantly, it is really only by being a particular desire, referencing some portion of the whole of possible coherences while definitely excluding others, that it is will at all, that it is indeed will as such, the nonreferential, omnireferential, atelic, omnitelic willing which is the same as nonwilling and also with any particular act of will, which we are here calling "pure desire."

Recalling the discussion of "the body" above, we may also here reinterpret Schopenhauer's assertion that the body is the direct objectification of the will, the intelligible character or timeless act of will which one is. For this act of will, or character, cannot be any particular act of will, willing any particular goal. It must be will as such, willing everything as such—the pure "I can," or as Nietzsche picked up on this point, the will to power. But as we have seen, there is no "I can" as such, no "power" as such or *simpliciter*. There is no *Dharmakāya* that is not some specific body, and no "aimless will" which is not some particular will aimed at a particular goal as well. To be a particular act of willing is to be the will as such, will to power, what is objectified as the unspecified omnitelic "I can" which is a body. What determines this particularity is not some specific act of will directed at a particular goal, which is, however, supposed to be "outside of time," whatever that might mean, but rather the snags that this omnitelic, atelic will encounters in its casting about for objects and aims, those particular goals which for structural reasons can never be satisfied in each particular case, those beings which this body cannot see its way to "being." The unsatisfiability of the will must be instantiated and preserved in some such goal, and it is in this way that it remains from beginning to end both wholly particular and wholly universal. We may recall here the discussion of "Natural Law as Global Incoherence" in Part One; the random motion of the particulars was itself their leftward diffusion, and so on. The pure goalless omnitelic will is the particular teleological will—the latter is not merely a "manifestation" or "emanation" or "modification" of the former. It might be called an "objectification" of the former, as Schopenhauer avers, but only in a very special and strict sense, which Schopenhauer effaces when he speaks of factual "grades of objectification." For the particular will, just as it is, both as a whole and in all its parts, is always also nothing but the universal, omnitelic, goalless will, both in "substance" and in "function." Any attempt to objectify it as a particular will with only one goal is undermined by the further recognition of further aspects, that is, the process that we call the passing of time. A given consciousness may judge it to be a specific will aimed at a specific goal, but both this "act of will" and this "judgment" itself never stop revealing that there is more to them.

This has important implications for reconfiguring Schopenhauer's insane but attractive development of the Kantian idea of "intelligible character." The idea is that each species of being and, in the case of human beings, each individual, is simply the playing out in space and time of a single, unchangeable act of will. The character of a human being is freely chosen, in this sense (i.e., there is nothing outside will to determine will, and this "act" of will occurs "outside" the realm of the principle of sufficient reason), but every particular action in time which proceeds from the effect of motivations upon this character is fully determined, given this premise. One's character can never be changed. This is the dark wisdom of the old joke about the scorpion: *A scorpion asks a frog to carry it across a river. "But if I carry you on my back, you will sting me and I will die," says the frog. "Think for a moment!" retorts the scorpion. "If you are carrying me and I kill you, certainly you will drown, but I will drown as well." Bending to the force of the scorpion's argument, the frog agrees, and halfway across the river, the scorpion stings it. "What are you doing!" says the frog as it dies. "Now you will certainly die too. Why should you sting me?" "I'm a scorpion," is the reply. "It is my nature."* That is, my character. Here we see a forerunner of the notion of a single existential project that can be discerned in an individual's various choices and actions, which we criticized in the discussion of Sartre and Merleau-Ponty. We need not repeat the reasons for that critique here. But, on the other hand, there is something useful in the idea that our own character is something that we discover, retrospectively as it were, from the pattern of our own apparently random, ad hoc choices.

Patterns of behavior can certainly be discerned in a given biography that suggest strongly an unconscious set of commitments and directives underlying apparently haphazard events. This unity of particular contents to form an intelligible category that is expressed but not created or exhausted by them is indeed one of the most significant aspects of our experience. But we have already, in our discussion of the Kantian categories, brought forth an alternate way to understand it. For as we have seen, in the Tiantai view, to be a content is to be a category. This means that, while an intelligible character is indeed *discoverable* in the multitude of our particular, unreflective actions, it is never a closed character that is insusceptible to alternate interpretations. These alternate interpretations, however, must also take the form of categories. Wherever anything intelligible is discoverable, it is also necessarily readable, discoverable, as some other intelligibility. Our whole argument rests on the demonstration that in fact these are convertible expressions. But what is useful in the "intelligible character" hypothesis is the notion that we are not at liberty to simply discard these categories, that they are indeed truly ineradicable. For omnicentrism differs from relativistic perspectivism on just this point; although every coherence is equally validly readable as another coherence, it is not the case that this makes any of these coherences negligible or alterable. It is true that it is a second, equally unthematized epistemological orientation or "focal setting" which initially read it as intelligible as just this X and nothing else—and indeed this "orientation" itself, is one more coherence which can also be so reinterpreted. But, on the other hand, one can never say, "It is not X, it is rather, as I now read it, Y." Rather, we are doomed to have to accept fully every possible reading. For our scorpion, this would mean that indeed there is no escape from the fact that it is his nature to sting frogs, even when it is tantamount to suicide. This fact of his nature can never be changed or surpassed; it can only be fully accepted. But here is where the conflation of denial and affirmation of particular willing as also *the whole* will becomes important. For although suicidal stinging can never be escaped, what it is to be suicidal stinging is never fixed once and for all. The coherence "suicidal," for example, must be fully accepted; only then can it be reinterpreted, given new meanings, self-recontextualized, which always means to completely change its meaning and significance without, however, changing itself in the least. I can never escape being a weakling, or a bastard, or an irresponsible drunk, but once I see this inescapability, I can see that to be any of these things thoroughly already implies the inescapability of recontextualizing them; hence being a weak irresponsible drunken bastard will no longer necessarily mean what it formerly did. Indeed, we would suppose that the repetition compulsion implicit in any such "character" is itself the result of some deeply embedded refusal to be or fully experience the coherence in question: you keep having to be what you cannot accept yourself to be. Our view, then, is that in the very intelligibility of our character lies the necessity of its *reinterpretability*; indeed, the very nature of being a self lies in this inescapable self-recontextualization and self-redefinition. We will now try to develop further the implications of this claim.

Freedom

Let us attempt this via a sort of object lesson, an extensive elaboration of a particularly resonant example of how the transformation from contingent to necessary failure, hence to identity qua omnipresent asness, constitutes the solution to the original problem. We will take the example of control, which is to say, the question of freedom. For now that we have a way of handling the question of *identification*, of what structural situating of coherences will count in experience as the "self," we may take up another perennial philosophical dilemma, namely, the question of freedom and determinism. Given the above discussion, what will freedom mean in the Neo-Tiantai picture? The answer can be given rather formulaically: *"Freedom" here is a word for the fact that everything is relevant.* That is, whatever assumed horizons for relevance one may be interpreting one's present experience in terms of, there is *always more* that can be relevantly brought into the picture, thereby creating a new context which will change the identity of this experience. This, in the view developed here, may be regarded as an adequate definition of human freedom, which neither separates it irreconcilably from the determinacies and regularities of material facticity nor robs it of its full experienced meaning in human existence. Indeed, it can be said both that all is free and that nothing is free, applying once again the setup/punch-line model. The question then is just *when and how* the freedom will assert itself and encompass its other, which will then reveal itself to have always been susceptible to this reinterpretation, to always have harbored this multiplicity of meanings. The distinction between determined and free, like that between matter and mind, is not a question of substantial difference or identity, but simply of asymmetrical but mutually embracing moments before and after a contrasting turning point, a question of time—or, we may say, more accurately, a question of *timing*.

Some of the more intriguing implications of this point can be elaborated by once more turning to the case of Hegel. The concept of "freedom" is introduced into Hegel's *Logic* as the fulfillment and overcoming of ("the truth of" in typically misleading Hegelese) the concept of "necessity."[15] This seems insane, and Hegel himself admitted that it was one of the most difficult transitions in the *Logic*.[16] But it is not so opaque if we examine Hegel's lecture notes on this matter, and if we may introduce the above notion of "identification" to the interpretation thereof. Hegel is reported to have said in his lectures:

> Necessity is often called hard, and rightly so, if we keep only to necessity as such, i.e. in its immediate shape. Here we have, first of all, some state of, generally speaking, fact, possessing an independent subsistence: and necessity primarily implies that there falls upon such a fact something else by which it is brought

---

[15] G.W.F. Hegel, *Hegel's Logic*, Part 1 of Encyclopedia, trans. Wallace (Oxford: Clarendon Press, 1975), 220, para. 158.
[16] Ibid., 221–22, para. 159.

low. . . . The identity of the two things, which necessity presents as bound to each other and thus bereft of their independence, is at first only inward, and therefore has no existence for those under the yoke of necessity. Freedom too from this point of view is only abstract, and is preserved only by renouncing all that we immediately are and have. But...the process of necessity is so directed that it overcomes the rigid externality which it first had and reveals its inward nature. It then appears that the members, linked to one another, are not really foreign to each other, but only elements of one whole, each of them, in its connection with the other, being, as it were, at home, and combining with itself. In this way necessity is transfigured into freedom—not the freedom that consists in abstract negation, but freedom concrete and positive. From which we may learn what a mistake it is to regard freedom and necessity as mutually exclusive.[17]

Freedom, then, is not the absolute negation of necessity (i.e., the total exclusion of causal determinedness). Necessity is when one thing pushes another thing around, as it were. Freedom is here this same occurrence, but with an added insight, namely that, since this pushing is possible and occurs, the pusher and the pushed are not in fact two separate and independent entities, despite their appearance as such. Rather, they are part of one total system. The lack of independence of the parts undermines their claims to be separate entities. The pushed *identifies* with the pusher; hence, the push comes from within himself. The pusher is the pushed; the pushed is the pusher. Hence, one is pushing oneself around; one is autonomous. There is no longer any external constraint.

It is easy to caricature the practical implications of such a doctrine, where one is advised to identify indiscriminately with all forces that affect one. Consider the following dialogue among a group of slaves, into which I will inject a few other Hegelian overtones for good measure:

> A *slave said to another slave, "How do you like it, being a slave? How is it with you and your master?"*
>
> *The slave said, "Before I was a slave, I thought there could be nothing worse than to become a slave. Just being a free citizen, I thought, was slavish and difficult enough, and the mutations of external things and con-*

---

[17] Ibid., 220, *Zusatz* to para. 158. In quoting these additions to Hegel's paragraphs, I do not want to encourage an attitude of blind acceptance of their contents. As Kaufmann has rightfully pointed out, we ought to maintain an attitude of some suspicion with respect to Hegel's students' lecture notes, stuck into the Encyclopedia years later and without any necessary connection to the paragraphs they are meant to explain (Walter Kaufmann, *Hegel, A Reinterpretation* [New York: Anchor Books, 1966], 219–24). Nonetheless, I quote this paragraph as a particularly vivid presentation of the thought I wish to discuss, in a form that highlights the problem of identification which is to be our focus here.

ditions to which I was subject already an insufferable tyrant. I felt that my fate was in the hands of others, that the pressures of nature and my fellow social beings were preventing me from attaining true freedom and autonomy. But then came the Great War, and we were all sold into slavery to serve the conquerors. And I soon discovered that, while previously I had known no one who was free, that indeed I had no clear conception of what freedom might be, now I suddenly beheld a being who was truly free: my master."

"But surely you know that this is merely relative," said the other slave. "You know that your master is nothing but an embattled free citizen just as you used to be. How can you consider him any freer than you were when you had slaves and worries of your own? This freedom you perceive is an illusory freedom."

"Is it?" said the other. "And yet from where I stand now at least I can see an other whose condition is the opposite of my own slavish condition, and this must be considered an advance. He gives me orders; I obey orders. How can you say he is unfree?"

"Very well. But it is otherwise with my master and me. I obey orders, and only then does he give them. His orders only become orders when I obey them. He needs me. He depends on me to manifest his freedom. But I need him only to manifest my unfreedom—as for my freedom, he does nothing for it, and thus my freedom is independent of him in a way that his freedom can never be of me. Indeed, I am certain it is just my superiority to him in this respect which forces him to beat me so often."

"You may say so," laughed a third slave, who had been eavesdropping. "But as for me, I've found a way to be not only the slave, but also my master as well. When he gives an order, I discover another part of myself of which I had formerly been ignorant. It is just as if one suddenly remembers something long forgotten, or dreams of things one has never thought, or when extreme emergencies call forth unsuspected ingenuity or strength in one. Parts of me formerly unmanifested are called forth by each new circumstance. If he orders me to dig a hole, I take it as a revelation that hole-digging has all along been an unsuspected part of me, latent until now, that it is included in my nature, that it is actually something inside of me to dig a hole. Every order that comes to me therefore comes from myself, since I define myself as all orders that come to me, together with my obligation to obey. Hence I am the true master."

"Yes, the truest," said a fourth slave, "but you are also the truest slave." But before he could explain what he meant he was called away to serve the masters, who were sitting around a nearby table chatting amongst themselves.

It is not difficult to agree with the fourth slave, for we can see what he is getting at: might not this unselective incorporation of whatever happens to one as a part of oneself, defined as such simply because one has thereby been proved not to be the independent entity one had formerly assumed oneself to be, be the most abject possible type of slavery? To resist this implication, we must introduce the notion of identification with which we have just been grappling. For this principle implies a *selection* of what to identify with. Rather than identifying with anything at all that happens to be able to affect us, we may choose which influences to identify as belonging to the same total system as we, the effect, belong to. The standard for what is to be included as a part of one's self need not be determined according to the question of subsistent independence or lack thereof, as Hegel claims in the above passage, which may lead us toward certain extreme conclusions of radical holism, where all things are ultimately part of a single system (since all things affect each other and none are independent), admitting of no intermediate levels of *partial* isolation, subsistence or independence—what we have been calling Local Coherence. It is doubtless true that nothing can be *absolutely* or ultimately intelligible outside of the context of the entire system of the universe, intelligible in the impudent sense of total comprehension suggested by science. Indeed, our claim is, of course, that when the context is extended to this degree, every token becomes precisely *in*coherent, the identity between this "absolute" coherence and "in"-coherence being Intersubsumption itself. But this does not prevent us from recognizing *degrees* of self-sufficiency and isolability, more or less successful tendencies in that direction, from which we can gain limited fields of coherence and intelligibility. Hegel recognizes this, but selectively locates such a limited self-subsistence in the state, rather than the individual, not both, so that the former's claim on the latter become inviolable, who must find his freedom-in-dependence in relation to the state upon which he is dependent. From this perspective, Hegel (a little further on in the passage quoted above) can recommend that a prisoner about to be punished for his deed should regard the punishment "not as a foreign constraint to which he is subjected, but [as] the manifestation of his own act: and if he recognizes this, he comports himself as a free man." It is here just the "recognition" of this that makes the difference between freedom and constraint—a claim that we may not find completely satisfying. Hegel summarizes this discussion as follows: "In short, man is most independent when he knows himself to be determined by the absolute idea throughout." Complete determinedness is recognized as freedom because the determination is ultimately in accord with "the absolute idea"—something which, in Hegel's view, we can completely identify with, since it is in fact the full "truth" of our own objective world and subjective experience. Freedom here is thus acting rationally, in identification with the absolute idea, to the extent that it is constituted in the concrete state in which one lives, which is ultimately just the more complete and fully realized version of our own selves. This means identifying with everything that affects us, to the extent that it is "rational" in Hegel's peculiar sense.

But to get a fresh perspective on this question of identification, let us approach it from the perspective of the individual. The questions then become: With *what* shall I identify? What shall I consider to be part of myself? Everything? Nothing? Both, as identical to one another? My faculty of reason? My passions? The beliefs and practices inculcated by my parents? My political party? A particular religious ideal? God? Humankind? The forces of nature? My spontaneous desires? My body? Whatever happens to come into my consciousness at any moment? Here the problem becomes quite subtle. For if we posit some independent standard to determine what we are to identify with, we have in effect posited an essential self, an independent essence which mysteriously controls my decisions—thus thrusting us back into a highly questionable conception of a soul with absolute free will, or an essential nature with a predetermined character, prior to its acts and expressions. If not, this move simply casts the question back into an infinite regress—what makes us choose to identify with this particular standard of what to identify with? And if our real identity is already constituted by this standard of what to identify with, why bother to actually go ahead and identify with anything? Our identity is already in place, in some obscure homunculus form, and cannot be affected by acting in accordance with it or not. Thus the positing of some independent standard for identification leaves the problem unsolved. Our only hope would seem to be to find some *immanent* principle of selection to determine what is to be identified with, and what excluded from my self-definition. That is to say, we would need a way for the elements already incorporated and identified with, what has already been appropriated from the environment to form the self, to choose to accept or reject new elements into their confederation. Even in this case, we seem to have here a mysterious first act of identification, which we have addressed in the section on "Pleasure and the Self" above, and will return to, in another way, in "Why There's Anything," below. But in what manner would a confederated "group" of explicitly intersubsumptive coherences, identifying with each other to form a self, determine what to choose for *further* inclusion therein? And how are we to think of this process of identification, or appropriation into the sense of self?

Let us return to Hegel for a little assistance here. One of Hegel's greatest contributions to Western thought was his emphasis on the importance and power of "negativity." What exactly is negativity? The term has an unconscionably broad spectrum of reference in Hegel's works. It can mean anything from difference, separation, differentiation, disharmony, contradiction, and disunity to alienation, evil and pain. Hegel also speaks of the power of the "absolute negativity" of *Geist*, its power to posit its own other and take that other back into itself. Indeed, the negative is the moving principle of the self, and moreover, to put it in its strongest terms: "The negative is the self."[18] What can this mean? Simply that it is characteristic of the self (i.e., qua Global Incoherence, the *Sambhogakāya*, subjectivity-as-such) to be able to abstract itself from any given determinate content to which it is related, from any particular filling it may be entertaining at any moment. The "I" can in effect "step back" from any particular content of consciousness, separate itself from it, consider that content unessential to itself—that is, the confederation can at any point *cease* to identify with one of its members, can exclude something which it formerly considered part of itself. This is an extremely important feature of consciousness. The contents of consciousness are not a bunch of objects tossed together in a drawer, which are simply there or not there. No single determinate element therein is privileged as a permanent or standing member, who can never be deposed. Rather, there is a faculty of potential abstraction that always hovers over them. The "I" per se, which as such is totally abstract (and hence totally empty of determinate content, nothing more in this case than a convenience of speech) can take any content as a part of itself or can decide to exclude any from itself, that is, can identify with or "disidentify" with anything in the field of consciousness.

This ties into another function of consciousness, besides its tendency to perpetually redefine itself: its ability to perceive and incorporate things outside itself, and in turn to interact with the outside world; it has an exchange with what is not itself, and is ever making the not-self into self, always taking into itself information from the outside world, breaking through the boundary between itself and all that is other than itself. That is, it resists isolation, it does not allow itself to be reduced to an isolable system, but is always stretching past its former boundaries and incorporating new elements into itself. *The act of perception is thus itself an instance of the tendency to relinquish former characteristics, that is, to redefine oneself.* A mind with a fixed definition of itself, of which it could be declared "the mind is thus and thus and not otherwise," would not be able to perceive, since perception implies the addition of something new to the sum of the mind's contents at any given present moment. If the mind had already been defined as something with no image of this flower in its visual consciousness, it could not perceive the flower and at the same time remain itself; it has to be willing to relinquish its

---

[18] G.W.F. Hegel, *Phenomenology of Spirit*, trans. A.V. Miller (Oxford: Oxford University Press, 1977), 21, Preface, para. 37.

self of the former moment, i.e. the sum total of its characteristics, in order to incorporate this new element, and with this new addition it is changed and becomes something other than it was. The system is not closed, but open, and this is identical to saying that its self-definition is not static, but rather in flux.

The "I" itself is thus not a content of consciousness; it is merely a word to refer to the confederacy's ability to exclude (to "abstract"—i.e., to pick some elements of the whole and leave out others, to hire and fire, as it were) or to identify, to generalize and to specify, to relate the contents that enter into it to one another. The other side of the picture is that the "I" cannot exist in isolation from these contents: consciousness must be consciousness *of* something. This "I"—this activity of hiring and firing—is dependent on the elements it identifies with or excludes from itself, the contents that it combines and separates, for its existence; it is nothing without them. Indeed, it is nothing but their combinations and separations, the faculty of identification and exclusion (rather than a fixed set of what has in fact already been identified with and included, or some mysterious independent power behind or above them) of the confederacy. But this is precisely a faculty pertaining to each coherence itself as such, to the extent that it is already not itself, is impossible, cannot appear *simpliciter*, appears only *as* the others. The ability to "see itself in" other coherences is inherent to what it is to be a coherence, and it is to this aspect of it that we are referring when we speak of this activity of hiring and firing.

Hegel speaks of this problem in terms of the "pure indeterminacy"—corresponding to the category of "pure being" or immediacy in the *Logic*, the emptiest and most abstract and most meaningless category, completely devoid of any content. This complete emptiness of determinate content makes this abstract Being identical to an equally abstract Nothing—both being simply pure immediacy, the total lack of any particular mediation, relation, internal differentiation—in short, devoid of any content. We need not quibble here about the exact nature of the "deduction" by which this "identity" is made to yield the next category, "Becoming," which subsequently yields "Determinate Being" (*Dasein*). For our present purposes it is sufficient to take Hegel's point on indeterminacy and determinacy (developed more fully in the subsequent discussion on the categories of Finitude and Infinity) in the following manner: pure indeterminacy is a kind of contradiction in terms, cannot remain fixed as indeterminacy, for this indeterminacy, as contrasted to determinacy, is obviously something in particular. To cling firmly to blank space, to forcibly kick out any and all determinations that may arrive, is obviously a kind of determination in its own right. Similarly, the will, equivalent here to the pure, empty "I," also cannot remain purely indeterminate forever; it must limit and determine itself as some particular content. By so doing, it is not contravening this original indeterminacy; on the contrary, it is fulfilling it, since abstract indeterminacy, as we saw above, turned out to be not really indeterminate. *The movement to determinacy is more truly indeterminate than pure abstract indeterminacy.* Indeed, this is simply a special case or prototype of the infamous "negation of the negation" of popularized Hegelianism. For to remain rigidly indeterminate would be simply a form of determinacy; it is not true indeterminacy. It would mean to remain fixed in only one form—that is, pure indeterminacy, unobstructed, contentless empty space—that is thus totally determinate.

This is a rather important point, which brings us closer to the solution we are seeking. For here we have an overcoming of the dichotomy between determinacy and indeterminacy. He who seeks indeterminacy (= freedom in the abstract, naïve, "bad" sense) will not find it in the total lack of determinations—as he pursues his quest, the true nature of his object will force itself on him, simply by thinking it through to the bottom. True "indeterminacy," thought through to the bottom, is not the blankness that excludes all determinations, like empty space—for this would be simply one more determination. On the other hand, this indeterminacy cannot just be a set of determinations, fixed and posited as such forever, as definitively one way and not another. True indeterminacy must be neither nothing nor some fixed something. What then? The solution is by now somewhat obvious: true indeterminacy (= freedom) includes, or rather *is, the process of positing and negating determinations*. It is not the absence of determinations; it is simply the *absence of definitive fixity to any of its determinations*. It is the fact that no X is X *simpliciter*. It is the fact that X must be X as something else. It is the fact that everything is relevant. Or better: it is the process of always making *and* overcoming determinations, and the power to do so. In the case of the self, this would mean an ability always to appropriate new elements into one's self-identification, and equally, always to exclude existing members of the confederacy. Freedom then would be neither the total exclusion of determinate content, nor the once-and-for-all embrace of some particular set of contents: it would be rather the ability to change what the contents of the self are, *the self's power to redefine itself,* thereby allowing it at any moment a broader range of possible actions with which it can identify, that is, a broader range of free actions. Freedom, in other words, is self-recontextualization, which is all that the "self" is.

We have seen how the positing of determinations is a form of indetermination, or, as we may prefer to put it, how the acceptance of limitations can be seen as itself an expression of freedom, rather than a contradiction or compromising of that freedom, just as, for example, the tolerance of a political group advocating authoritarian principles can be an expression of libertarian principles. In such a case, the strict dichotomy between authoritarianism and libertarianism will not apply. Indeed, the fact that a fascist group arises and is tolerated can be seen as an expression of its opposite, the total lack of any coercive political principles. Similarly, we would claim, it is implicit in the notion of indeterminacy, of abstract absolute freedom, to express itself precisely as its opposite—that is, as restriction, discipline, finitude. Thus restriction is an expression of freedom. But this sort of unsynthesized unity of the two extremes is by no means satisfactory; the mutual balancing, and even identity, of the fascists and the libertarians does little to overcome the dangerous one-sidedness of both. What is needed is a more fully realized overcoming of the dichotomy between them, which produces a new form preserving the value of both, while annulling their excesses. In order to arrive at this in the present case, where we are seeking the higher unity of determinacy and indeterminacy, what is most crucial is to note that restriction not only "expresses" absolute freedom, but also even serves as *a means by which it advances*, an aid to the further development of freedom. Here we have the Tiantai "three bodies" and "skillful means" again, in a nutshell. The original intention, to be totally free, is not discarded; rather, it is fulfilled, through restriction, *and only through restriction*. How? What is needed to answer this question is a concrete understanding of how limitation fulfills the original naïve desire for limitlessness, for which we will need to sketch a portrait of an ideal for human flourishing and freedom as Hegel *should* have envisioned it on the basis of these premises—that is, the Neo-Tiantai portrayal of the case. While we are at it, we will also try to show how this one fundamental desire for indeterminacy, for "freedom," can account for a very wide range of human values, for a great many more specialized desires and pursuits.

The desire for freedom can be described as a yearning not to have any absolutely fixed characteristics, not to be "gettable" as any particular thing, to stand above any possible content, since all contents are manifestly influenced and caused by something, hence dependent and unfree. But we have seen that by doing this, one undermines one's own design; one has become fixed with one characteristic (total emptiness, detachedness, continual rejection of any and all contents), definitively definable and determinable as this one particular thing.

But what does this original desire boil down to? What was it that one really wanted, and chose this erroneous, self-defeating method to achieve? We have described it already as a power of self-redefinition, an ability to hire and fire elements of the environment to be parts of what is identified with as the self, to maximize the reversible power of selective interpenetration of the organism and its environment. Would it not be fair to say that one wanted fundamentally a greater indeterminacy, a *greater* power for further self-redefinition?

Could this not be the principle by which the confederacy of contents of consciousness chooses to include or exclude members in itself? Put simply: they choose to appropriate ("identify with") elements that give them increased ability to appropriate and exclude further elements in the future, that make the ability to include and exclude more flexible, so that the contents of the self can best match new situations, can adapt more effectively, can have a broader range of future activities. The self is engaged in self-redefinition. By redefinition, I mean not only the mental act of drawing a provisional line around some set of coherences defined as "self," which for us consists in seeing Intersubsumption and reversibility among them, while remembering here that reversibility is the overcoming of a boundary with the extra omnicentric assurance of a structured two-sidedness and omnidirectionality, not the appropriation of one side by the other which remains unchanged. Also intended here is action in accord with this line drawing, and then recognition of oneself in such acts. In other words, both an active and a passive component are involved in self-definition. To define myself as a revolutionary, for example, entails both a feeling of sympathy and agreement with revolutions that occur, a kind of cheerleading sentiment, and also revolutionary acts of my own, however conceived, with which I identify and in which I recognize myself. Every new act, thought or perception, in the same way, redefines one; one can now be defined as a person who commits or has committed this sort of act, is engaging this object of perception, is thinking about this particular concept. This gives us some idea of the breadth of the concept of self-redefinition—indeed, it is almost simply another word for action and experience of any kind.

Now, the specific way or direction in which the self redefines itself is, we are suggesting, that which will *always tend to increase its power of self-redefinition*. This would not mean that one wanted to be nothing at all, nor to be something, nor even to be everything; it would rather be a desire *to be able to be anything*. One's power to make choices about what to identify with is always functioning, one is always redefining oneself, according to the principle of what makes one ever more able constantly to redefine oneself. In the self-redefinition of the self, the confederacy of coherences appropriates as its members those elements that allow it to continue to appropriate and exclude members more readily, and excludes those that obstruct it from appropriating and excluding members. The exact physical and social situation of a given person would determine just what members would be most conducive to preserving this constant ability to appropriate and exclude members, but in each case the drive would be to greater indeterminacy. The most "indeterminate" person would be simply the most powerful person, who is *able* to be this *or* that; hard *or* soft, cruel *or* kind, rich *or* poor, refined *or* vulgar, sensitive *or* callous, true *or* false, good *or* evil, beautiful *or* ugly, bright *or* dark, even, *pace* Nietzsche, weak *or* strong; the range of his possibilities is greater than someone who can only be hard or someone who can only be soft, who has identified once and for all with one or the other and can no longer redefine himself as the occasion demands; the "indeterminate" human being is able to do more, he has a greater scope of action and experience. He does not have to be either this or that, he is not forced by his own limitations to be X or non-X, he can be either, he can provisionally adopt as a part of his identity any of the alternatives, so that in the future he can respond to the environment in such a way as to be able to appropriate from it and exclude from himself what will allow him to appropriate and exclude more nimbly in the future, thereby maximizing his adaptability and interaction with the environment, *ad infinitum*. To adopt and adapt a famous simile, it is like a boat on the ocean which gathers driftwood and fish to rebuild and restructure itself (the driftwood as material, the fish as energy for this rebuilding), changing the structure of the boat as it moves so as to make this process of gathering and rebuilding more efficient, to make further changes and further intakes easier, and at the same time maintaining enough of itself as constant at any given time to remain afloat, and continue on its voyage. This need to remain afloat accounts for the necessary level of commitment to a certain fixed core of contents at any given time, and prevents pure reckless hypocrisy, nonengagement, mercurial change at all times. It is this that limits the range of changes at any given time and also insures a degree of continuity in the self. But it should be noted that, once enough other elements are in place to remain afloat, this original core, too, can be discarded, and so on *ad infinitum*. The job of keeping the vessel afloat (i.e., orienting oneself in and interacting with the environment, functioning, keeping oneself alive, and maintaining one's present level of "freedom" and recognition in the social nexus, or "matching" the standard of "Good" as intersection of impossibilities, as previously described, and fulfilling whatever social obligations are necessary to these ends), may be traded off, passed on to another structure—another belief system, another set of identifications and allegiances, another mode of orienting oneself within the world. Moreover, the environment may change—we may have to add holes and wheels to ride on land, and abandon even the guiding principle of "staying afloat." All we want to do is keep going into other places, as other selves, to increase the power for further redefinitions. There is no thus privileged eternally inviolable center to selfhood.[19]

---

[19] Another analogy for this might be to think of self-definitions as the equilibrium of a spinning top, and the power for self-redefinition as its motion, made more flexible, easy, and radical by this equilibrium. The fixity of its motion—i.e., a certain rotation—allows it to be much more changeable in its translational motion across the floor.

It goes without saying here that the continuity we intend here is that explicated above, that is, continuity constituted as setup/punch line. The continuity of selfhood constitutes itself when the present coherence finds a way of opening up whatever has preceded it as its own specific precedents, integrating them into a setup for the punch line which is itself, such that this coherence is able to read itself back into these precedents, to see itself being expressed in a deadpan manner *as* these contrasting previous coherences. It can thus be *intermittent*, reconstituting itself retrospectively over gaps, as personal identity does in the normal sleeping-waking cycle.

But this is madness, says the "plain (straw) man." Do we not strive for certain particular contents, namely in the direction of the pleasant, the healthy, things that are clearly good? Why do we strive to determine ourselves as these things, if basically all we want is indeterminacy? There are certain intrinsic values, things it is good to have and be once and for all, values besides just the power for self-redefinition! This is just crazed change for change's sake! This is the destruction of all responsible thinking and all concrete value! This is a shameless and senseless overgeneralization! But in response, I would claim that we can view the reason we strive to move in one particular direction, "upwards," toward the good, true, beautiful, rich, strong, etc. rather than their opposites, is that actually all these "positive" terms originally include the possibility for their opposites (to the extent that they are not absolutized or attached to). For example, it is assumed that it is intrinsically more desirable to be rich than to be poor. But we could reasonably argue that this is simply because the rich man has the material assets necessary to become a poor man at will, whereas the poor man cannot necessarily become a rich man: the poor man is thought to be more determinate, more thingified, more limited, less able to redefine himself. In no other sense, I would suggest, are the qualities regarded as "positive" more desirable than their negative counterparts. An increase in our strength, our power, means simply an increase in our indeterminacy (in its concrete sense, as the faculty of positing and negating determination, the power to assimilate into or exclude from intersubsumptive confederacy of any current *Nirmāṇakāya*), in the number of transformations we have immediate access to. And as it happens, for reasons easily discerned, this seems almost always to be achieved by an increase in our determinacy in some other capacity, through discipline or restraint, through restricting and limiting ourselves in some creative way.

This raises again the general question, what is the "good," according to this scheme? How can we judge whether a particular act is "correct" or not? We have every reason to be skeptical about these much abused terms, and particularly the ridiculous generality that comes with posing the question in these abstract terms; nonetheless, let us try to assign them some meaning within the context of what we have established above. As a first approach, we may say that the Good is to move from a position which has a fewer number of potentials for redefinition (of the world, of what we are) to one with a greater number of potentials for redefinition. When comparing two different acts which could issue from a single situation, we can see that one will arrive at a position which will leave open a greater number of possibilities than the other. That is what we may define as the "good" choice. In any given situation, there are a finite number of ways in which the next step can happen, in which changes can occur. But these different possibilities can be evaluated, as in the early stages of a game of chess, by the fact that a certain arrangement leaves more possibilities open for the next move than another.[20] "Good" in general is indeterminacy (the power for self-redefinition) using ever more complex and sophisticated systems of determinacy (self-definitions) in order to promote itself, ever further and new determinacies, ever new forms, shapes, and characteristics. Hence, the least good would be the most purely "Good," that is, pure indeterminacy as yet unmodified by determinacy, abstract freedom, which can only have the one characteristic, just its simple fact of indetermination—metaphorically, one shape, pure flatness or roundness. Where there is indeterminacy, there is determinacy and vice versa; neither ever appears alone and pure. Indeed, our claim is that Local Coherence is precisely Global Incoherence. But here, in "Good" things, the aspect of indeterminacy, or

---

[20] On the analogy of a chess game, we might say that the best move is always that which places one's total set of pieces in a position where they are not forced into any one particular next move, where there are always many possibilities, where one's following move can be any of a great number of things; when we are put in check, for example, we suddenly find that only two or three possibilities are open to us for this move; therefore we feel "being put in check" is a bad thing. For let it be understood exactly where the chess analogy breaks down, why it is not entirely applicable to life: in chess there is an artificially posited fixed motive to everything, an ultimate objective behind every move which is supposed to be the unified goal of all planning and motions: the checkmating of the opponent's king. But in life there is no such goal. The only goal is to have a greater and greater amount of possible moves. So we must imagine a vast game of chess with no kings and no limits to the board and no end, where we regret the loss of our rook not because it will make it more difficult for us ultimately to achieve our planned checkmate, but because having a rook affords a greater number of possible moves than not having a rook. In life, it is always "early in the game." For the objective can never be fixed; such a fixed goal as "checkmate" would be contrary to the nature of life itself, which is open-ended. Could it not be that our instinctive feeling upon losing our rook in chess is based on our fundamental sensation of life, and only secondarily or conceptually do we regret its potential use to us in checkmating the king? For after all, checkmating the king is only a way of winning the game, and winning the game is itself only a way of increasing our realm of power, of freedom, of possibilities, of what we have access to, of what we are. We have here what James Carse would call an "infinite game" as opposed to a "finite game." (See James P. Carse, *Finite and Infinite Games* [New York: Free Press, 1986].)

Global Incoherence, freedom, multiple capabilities, unfixed identity, and the relevance of all contexts, remains explicit, and in a certain (local) sense, master, utilizes determinacy for the advance of itself, of indeterminacy. No given local coherence or determinacy is taken as globally coherent, or as an end in itself—the latter forming a pretty good thumbnail definition of the Bad.

If one wished to derive a practical maxim from this then, it would be, not to avoid or look down on all self-definitions, but rather, to be careful *never to make a particular self-definition or restriction an end in itself*, that is, to always use it as a means to more power for self-redefinition, greater freedom, and always to see it thus. Let it be clearly understood then: this absolutely does not amount to an opposition to self-definition, to the possessing of particular characteristics. To oppose this would be like opposing the boundaries that circumscribe a nation, because they limit its expanse: but a nation without any boundaries would be a nation without territory. It would be no place; there would be no nation there. Rather, we should say all motions toward further indeterminacy always consist of both the establishment of new determinations and the destruction of existing determinations, such that a greater complexity or a broader plethora of possible ways of responding to the environment result. All statements about indeterminacy here are to be understood in this sense: it is the power for self-redefinion, which always presupposes a certain set of pre-existing self-definitions and the motion of annulling some of these and adopting some others.

How then shall we sum up the way in which the countermotion, toward unfreedom, restraints, limits, aids freedom, nonrestraint, limitlessness? There is one common word for a manifestation of this in daily life: self-discipline. Self-discipline can be defined as a type of unfreedom which is employed in the belief, correctly or incorrectly, that it will serve and enhance freedom, that is, power. One sets up rules and restrictions for oneself, thus limiting one's own activities. "I must do such and such each day, and I must not ever do such and such." This is, on the face of it, a direct contradiction of the "principle" of freedom, indeterminacy, unfixedness, and so on, according to which there is no definite pattern, no rigid routine, no predictable or fixed rules to be followed. But by restricting ourselves in this way, by *permitting* ourselves less, we become *able* to do more. That is, we make ourselves *stronger*. We have a skill or ability to do things we were formerly unable to do. We deliberately employ nonfreedom to develop a definite pattern of ourselves, a structure, a particular form, because by means of this new particular structure, forcibly imposed upon the old amorphousness of indeterminacy, we expand the range of our abilities.

It follows from all this that there is no single set of contents that would form the ideal personality; to search for which particular contents are the best to have, in all cases and in general, is, I am claiming, wasted effort. There can be no final result, no ultimately ideal form, either of political organization or of personality. For by our definition, fixity itself is an objection, and the fact that a result opens up into no further developments is a sign of its imperfection. Indeed, an ideal prescribing a fixed set of contents can be seen here only as a means, never as a goal—the goal must lie in some as yet unforeseeable further developments, especially the kind that make for structures which lead to further possibilities for unforeseeable developments. Thus we can only posit our ideal on a meta-level: the ideal personality is that which can add to and subtract from itself at will, as the situation demands, so as to maximize its ability to do just that—to add and subtract to itself more flexibly, to grow into something with a greater ability to grow. All the forms through which consciousness presses itself are then to be seen as attempts to become ever more all-inclusive, to build its whole history into ever new wholes, and to take on shapes that were never before possible, because they presuppose all that has gone before. At every given juncture, it redefines itself in such a way as to maximize its power for self-redefinition. I hope that the above has at least hinted at the way in which this purely formal principle (of value, of the self—i.e., as positing no other fixed goals besides the constant positing and annulling of goals) can be seen as adequate also to the development of all the varied contents in question, in accordance with the good old Hegelian principle of the mutual definition of form and content. The self-perpetuating form, far from disappearing into itself, as it were, is precisely the self-generation of the contents.

This entire discussion of freedom, of course, is only an elaboration of the fundamental problem of *control* that we gave as an example of a constitutive contradiction above. Any situation, seen in terms of its reference to the question of control seen as *contingent*, and hence as a determinate positive entity appearing *simpliciter*, presents the problem of freedom. The above solution to this problem is simply the recasting of this contingent problem of control into the necessary problematicalness of the coherence "control" itself, which is to say, its identity as Intersubsumption and as all-pervasive deadpan asness. I will repeat what I said there about control: However much I am able to control my world, there is always something beyond it; at the very least, my controlling act itself is spontaneous and not done by me. My will is not willed by me. Moreover, and more importantly: the very notion of "control" implies something to be controlled, and therefore something initially not in one's control, something confronted which is external to one's will (even the movement of the body plays on the body's givenness and inertia). Total control is a contradiction in terms; but less than total control is no control at all. To fully commit to inhabiting this contradiction, this failure of control to *ever* appear *simpliciter*, is to apprehend freedom simply as this impossibility of pure abstract freedom *simpliciter*. This means a self-limiting identification with a set of coherences which instantiate this impossibility, which is none other than the power of self-definition, of seeing itself *as* whatever coherence might be encountered, as a determinate from of all-pervasion, qua deadpan asness, of some given contents.

We have developed three ways of describing the Good, from three different angles: (1) reversibility overcoming a snag in identification, (2) embodying the dilemma so as to satisfy both the demand for X and the demand for non-X immediately and intersubsumptively in a single act, and now (3) increasing the power for self-redefinition by taking all determinations and restrictions to freedom as means to increased indeterminability. It must be made clear that again we have here three different ways of describing the same situation. The first and third descriptions are most obviously equivalent: to overcome a snag in identificatory power is to expand the range of coherences that I may be, to overcome the limitation of any finite self-identification. The second description may be regarded as the privileged means by which this is accomplished in practical life: wherever two mutually exclusive identifications confront each other, a way must be found to *be* both at the same time, thereby overcoming the snag or limitation that would come with identifying exclusively with either one or the other.

Before leaving this point, I wish to note two advantages, one theoretical and one practical, which this view can claim:

First, the theoretical advantage: as already noted in the discussion of crawling through the desert, this theory assumes nothing—exactly nothing. The only assumption is that we assume nothing, no particular determination, not even a fixed nothing, indetermination, or blankness. It shows how we can in principle derive everything simply by refusing to assume any particular starting point dogmatically, any particular essence, anything definitive. Just so long as we do not arbitrarily posit some underlying ground or determination to characterize things, all things, as a natural consequence of this lack of any particular definite characteristics, will develop all characteristics. This is not the result of positing some "drive" toward indetermination or development—on the contrary, this is not a law, but rather the absence of any law, like the "law" of natural selection, or the "laws" of chance. The precarious, metaphorical, and highly problematic nature of the concept of a *positive* natural law makes this, I think, an advantage.

Second, the practical advantage: This mode of viewing human consciousness allows us to explain all sorts of contradictory phenomena—both healthy and perverse pleasures, both constructive and destructive actions, to both Nietzsche's "sleep" pleasures and his "victory" pleasures. All are equally understandable outgrowths of this inherent self-expansion toward indetermination, toward a self that can redefine itself more and more masterfully and flexibly. On the other hand, this doesn't commit us to an indifferent leveling of all values—on the contrary, it gives an immanent foundation for valuation, and identifies how successful and unsuccessful action differ—in their resulting ability to actually expand self-indetermination or the lack thereof. At the same time, it preserves a wide margin for individuality in valuation, for differing valuations that are nonetheless compatible from a broader perspective as attempts to expand indetermination, the power of self-redefinition, in a particular circumstance.

More about the Will

More can perhaps be said to elaborate how the above discussion modifies the notion of will that characterizes the "free, finite" individual self. The Neo-Tiantai view of will and subjectivity, and the way it differs from that propounded in the Sartrean triad of perception, conceptualization, and imagination, should be clear by now. Sartre notes that the image and concept are *produced*, often having to do with an active willing, while the percept, in its essence, is *encountered*, is given from outside the self. But this particular differentiation, which summarizes quite well the commonsense view of the problem, depends on a very particular notion of will and subjectivity, which in that picture and in our usual experience are two mutually founding if not interchangeable terms. If this view is altered, the relation of perception, imagination, and conceptualization changes in the ways outlined above, and vice versa. Let us explore the picture of will that we have in place of the commonsensical one.

If we really want to play analytic hardball with this concept, in the context of our present biological world view, "Will" would perhaps be a word for the sensation of the activity and tension of the nonautonomic muscles (of course I mean this omnicentrically, not reductionistically: equally we could say, "'The tensions of the nonautonomic muscles' is a name for the Will"). These muscles are also called the "voluntary" muscles, a name which includes a circular reference to will itself. Let us call them instead "variable-response" muscles, and this too only comparatively, as a difference *of degree* from the autonomic. But what really does this difference amount to? Here as in many such cases, the answer lies in the application of *holism*. If the stimulus affects just one organ or part, and it responds itself without reference to (i.e., consistently and unmodified by things taking place in) any other organ, we call it autonomic. If it is so integrated with other parts that the response may be delayed, or transferred to another organ (for these two form parts of a single "whole") we call it voluntary. This response may include diffusion into unobservable body-surface tensions rather than overt motions, or electrical disturbances in the nervous system, which is precisely what connects the organs "holistically." This is, of course, just what we mean by the integration of mutual reversibility that constitutes any self.

Why do "acts of will" (tensing of the whole system of nonautonomic muscles, experienced as an affect of command) occur at one time rather than another, and with one content (direction) rather than another? Perhaps we may say simply that they are *waiting*, and multifarious—waiting for gaps in the sequential tensings and responses of the autonomic muscles. When the latter fall below a certain level of urgency, there is a "space" for "will" to jump in—but it may be any one of the deferred waiting responses circulating in the whole (as tonus). Perhaps there is a random access or availability contingency (proximity to the last set of external stimuli and their relative strength) that determines which among these waiting responses sets the tone and direction of the new tension, i.e., that determines what is "willed." Given the "inherent inclusion" of all coherences in/as each coherence, this means that what these *are* is as yet indeterminate, and depends on the context in which they do in fact emerge. Freedom, as we have said, simply means that everything is potentially relevant, and the same may be applied to "freedom of the will."

In this case, we may say that not will but *skill* is what is decisive in our claims to guarantee a particular outcome in the future (the modern Chinese terms for this is *hui*, meaning simultaneously "to bring together, to comprehend, to be capable of something," and also used to indicate the future indicative, "I shall"). To decisively intend something is to integrate it fully with the entire holistic system of the self, which for us means to integrate the Xness and non-Xness in a single token, and the ability to do this is a skill that is identical with what is referred to by the ordinary term "will." "I will be there at the appointed time" means "I am able to overcome the snag to reversibility between appearing as being-there then and as not-being-there now," "I am embodying the dilemma which constitutes the demand to be there, by experiencing it equally in my presently not-being-there and, interpenetratively, with my subsequent being-there." This skill which is will is what we will momentarily identify as *energy*, that is, an unfixed and freefloating proximal enabling, pure desire, capable of appearing in a variety of alternate distal forms, which will turn out to be yet another word for asness, selfhood, freedom, constitutive problematicalness, Intersubsumption, or reversibility.

Full Exertion: Repetition, Intensification, Meaninglessness, All-pervasion

This brings us to an interesting paradox that emerges most clearly in the state of total exertion and absorption in some act, volitional goal, or percept. On the one hand it seems to be an exclusion of all other things, and thus a narrowing of consciousness, a limitation of self. But it is experienced rather as an overcoming of the sense that something is left out, that one is missing something, that something is left undone. It is "satisfying," a "strong Gestalt" is formed, a vivid articulation comes into focus; subjectively, it is equivalent to a feeling of being the all, of being that than which there is no other. For total exertion in one act is really the drawing up of everything into the magnetic center of that act. It is the thing or act before one *sub species totalitas*. Or more strictly, even *qua totalitas*. The implication is that our usual mode of experiencing suffers from the opposite paradox: we are missing so much, and yet all those things we are missing are somehow present, somehow naggingly in the fringes of consciousness qua what is missing, what is negated, what is left out of the present experience, i.e., as *contingently* problematic, present as what I "have," which snags, rather than absent as what I *am*, which is constitutively problematic and hence reversible. For them to bother us they must be both present and absent. We are now in a position to understand this.

Is it not significant that both of these entail the same paradox, in reverse? Perhaps we have arrived back here, the long way around, and by a whole different set of symbols, at the real nature of repression. That is that feeling of having something there which is left out, of being present but absent, whereas what we want is to be absent but present. By devoting all the energy and attention that are affixed in the entire world of objects and pouring it into this one thing, not as an indifferent force but as the correlate of all those objects themselves, including all of them, are we not overcoming repression, and is this not what total exertion means?

Above I said that to "fully realize" any coherence was precisely to *be* it, to experience it as the self, which meant to enlarge its contingent problematicalness, as obstruction, possession, possible loss, contingently distanced, to necessary problematicalness or constitutive impossibility, as Three Truths, i.e., as identity which is impossibility which is all-pervasion. We have now come at this same point from another angle. We have here a fourth way of describing the Good, and one that again is simply a restating of the previous three (reversibility, embodying the paradox, enhancing the power of self-redefinition through self-limitation). The full realization of any coherence is just this coherence as total exertion, which fills in consciousness somewhat after the manner of the well-known repetition to meaninglessness of a word. We take a word, a supposed unit of semantic presence, and make it, rather than one in a series—something that whips by quickly enough to maintain its apparent simple consistency—the sole object of consciousness: we repeat it over and over until it drowns out all other objects, as in a mantra or a kōan punch line (*huatou*). If kept at long enough, as we know, this original plenitude of the meaning in question crashes into its utter meaninglessness. This only occurs when every other support—that is, contrasting coherence—has been pushed out of consciousness, including the sense of self and one's contingent "distance" from the coherence in question, i.e., this semantic unit. What began as a contingently problematic semantic unit—something that must be comprehended, which presents itself as a challenge and potential obstacle, which must be mastered and studied, that is embedded in contexts that may require some time and effort to uncover—becomes necessarily or constitutively problematic: its very meaningfulness was its meaninglessness. The same goes for the transformation of the determinateness of a coherence made the object of old-fashioned "one-pointedness" meditations. The point here is that this meaninglessness is both the full realization of the meaning and its crash, and that this ends up constituting its universal applicability, its all-pervasion. We have here a paradigmatic case of a single token which satisfies two opposite demands, viz., for meaning-freed-of-contextual-constraint (full presence of meaning) and for meaninglessness. Any coherence that "confronts" one, then, can also be approached in the manner of this unit of semantic presence. We normally plow over them so quickly that they appear unproblematic, or only contingently problematic—perhaps to avoid having to deal with their *inherent* problematicalness. And this treatment of coherences as problematics to be avoided, that is, that could possibly be avoided, is precisely what constitutes them as contingently problematic, as potential obstacles, objects of gain or loss, situated contingently near or far. Speed is usually crucial to this avoidance; it is rather like (the reverse of) moving the radio dial quickly through all the stations, so that each form of music blurs into indistinguishability. This allows us to maintain the illusion of a series of mutually exclusive things laid out side-by-side in an unproblematic array. If lingered over and fully developed, that is, made an object of fanatical exertion analagous to the repeated word, the appearance of this coherence—for example, the perception of this object—begins to reveal the true depth of its paradoxicality.

T. E. Hulme, in a classic polemic, defines "classicism" as an acceptance and limited celebration of finitude, the belief that human nature is a fixed and very constrained quantity that can, with a lot of work, be made fairly decent, while "romanticism" is marked by an obsession with infinity, flying off to the limitless and the affirmation of the unending perfectible potentials of man. He says this to disparage the vague flights of romanticism in favor of the down-to-earth rigor and precision, together with the light-hearted esteem for frivolity, of classicism. This is a useful distinction, but it hinges on denying even Hegel's work on the question of infinity, not to mention the Neo-Tiantai exploration of the same *problematik*. Hegel calls the usual infinity "the false infinity"—that is, everything every normal speaker of every language had thitherto meant by the "infinite" (unending succession or extension, limitlessness, etc.), what Hulme also means, is unattainable. It is even a self-undermining concept, for reasons we have outlined above. This rejection, then, would accord perfectly with Hulme's classical attitude—"infinity" is an empty fiction, not worth bothering with any longer. But then Hegel goes on to assert the existence of the "true infinite." By this he means what is self-limiting, self-determined, what is complete in itself, what absorbs its limiting other into its self.[21] This is a kind of wholeness, comparable to the state of full exertion, of total attention to any detail, of one-pointedness as the absorbtion of the organic totality of experience in each moment. Why does Hegel still keep the word "infinite"? Because this fulfills the original longing for infinity, and indeed was what that self-contradictory impulse was obscurely groping toward without realizing it—in Tiantai terms, "infinity" was the name of the *upāya* or setup which was opened up, punch-lined, to show that it led to this self-related limitation, this process of self-recontextualization of the foreground, focal, explicit coherence. Our normal experience is based on an odd fragmentation—that is, we feel otherness, multiplicity, not because we are not experiencing the all, but because, of the totality of whatever we are experiencing at any moment, we are pushing a part away, avoiding it, denying it. We make it nonself, that is, exclude it from some one part of the total experience, which we identify as ourself—this is the feeling of finitude, against which the empty longing for infinity is a rebellion. Total, vivid, thorough realization of any moment, of any detail, of any particular, total attention to what it is to have a qualitative sensation of any kind, which, in contrast to the "false infinity" would constitute the narrowest possible "finitude" (i.e., a "false finitude"), is in fact constitutive of the "true infinity," not because it includes every particle of possible experienceable coherences conceived as a set of separate things, but because it in itself has no outside, absorbs whatsoever else is in any sense present as constitutive of itself, so no sense of finitude, as a contrast between self and other, is any longer possible. In a word, all coherences are present simply *as* this coherence. But total, loving attention to finite details for their own sake—this is precisely what Hulme calls classicism.

In other words, we agree that "classicism" is preferable in this sense to this first, unselfcomprehending "romanticism"—but what is wanted is a further even more ridiculously radical romanticism, so romantic that it sees

---

[21] Compare Merleau-Ponty's note on *Offenheit* as the true infinity, which is identical to finitude (VI, 169).

in even the greatest finiteness the inevitable manifestation of infinity. This turns out to be identical to the most ridiculously radical classicism, that is, isolation and constraint to the strictest finitude. What it avoids is only division, inattention, half-way penetration, failure to go all the way into any particular detail, that is, disallow our reversibility with it—that and that alone is what constitutes our ordinary realm of "finiteness." Hulme's categories, of course, are based on this realm of finiteness, especially in the realm of concepts, i.e., the finite concepts "finite" and "infinite"—and in this he is faithful to his own program. But this finite is as false as the false infinite, and, if pressed or transformatively recontextualized, fully realized to the point of its crash, reveals itself to be identical to the true infinity.[22] Let us look more closely at how constraint to the most finite, extreme isolation and separation (as in mindfulness and full exertion practices, but also in poetry and language in general) discloses the true infinite as Intersubsumption.

Language, Mindfulness, and the Obvious

The question, put simply, is this: Why does this sort of full attention to a detail not only "fully realize" it, but also, as it were, *overcome* it? To take a naive-pathetic example, why does noticing, and especially *saying*, "I am sad" make one less sad?[23] What is it about noticing the processes of one's mind, especially the painful, negative ones, that undermines them, solves the problems they embody? To begin with we can identify the following factors:

1. By saying "I feel sadness" we objectify the sadness, separate ourselves from it, locate it as a fixed and completed object in front of which from which we are separable. We negate it by affirming it, or rather, we establish that our "selves" are pure negativity, capable of pulling away from any particular determinate content unscathed. If we can see it, it must not be us; an eye cannot see itself, a knife cannot cut itself.

---

[22] Along the same lines, we may say that early Buddhism shows already this ambiguity. The doctrines of impermanence, selflessness, etc., are surely the most striking possible affirmation of finiteness ever devised, and the methods by which they are actualized (Mindfulness, etc.) certainly among the more thoroughgoing regimes of attention to finite detail ever practiced. These are classical rigors. The vague affirmation, however, that this led to transcendence and the unborn Nirvana adds the romantic element. Later, Huayen and Chan tend toward the romantic, with their intimations of the originally pure mind from which there was a fall, while Tiantai, which asserts that there has been nothing but delusion since beginningless time, and insists on the importance of distinctions and concrete practices, strikes a more classical note. But in that all these schools start from an insight into the "true" infinity as standard, this conflict is after all only stylistic.

[23] I use this example although traditional Buddhists tend to disagree on the role of verbalization in this process.

1a. A crypto-Sartrean twist: when we are still absorbed in the feeling itself, before "noticing" it, it partakes of the existential uncertainty of anxiety—about its outcome, about its future. It is a project in which my self is being risked. But after we pull away from it, we have made it an "in-itself." There is no longer any uncertainty about it, no longer any need for anxiety: it is an eternal fact that I was feeling sad at that moment, and that is all there is to it, it is what it is. I have taken all the negativity into myself, as pure for-itself, but somehow this is no longer anxiety, at least at this level.

2. This leads to the Gestaltist angle. For we can simply say that when our attention shifts from the problem *in the world* that was causing us sadness to the sadness itself, it is only natural that the sadness dissipates—our sadness is no longer a relevant response to the object before us, since now this object is not some problem out there but simply this sadness itself, and sadness is not what we were sad about. Simply put, we have been distracted. Indeed, we might even be getting a little feeling of satisfaction for having caught this sadness in the act (the satisfaction, of course, remaining nonpositional, inexplicit at this point). We are simply occupied with a different problem when this Gestalt shift takes place, with a different set of interests, so it is no wonder our feeling tone shifts. At first our consciousness was focused on the fact that something in the world did something that contravened some of our wishes, which naturally causes sadness. Then we are focused on a completely different matter, namely, the fact that sadness exists in our body and mind, which causes a different set of emotions. And so on.

3. This point seems to me most significant, and touches on the crucial question of the (instrumental) role of language in all this. For it may be wondered why we should bother to *say* "I am sad" (or "I am breathing, this is a long breath, this is a short breath," etc.) when we notice these things, and why this seems to be more conducive to this type of effect. It should be the other way around, we think, because "as everyone knows" language distorts reality, limits our perception of the multifarious truth in front of us, focuses on some aspects at the expense of others, thereby obliterating the beatific vision of totality, which is necessarily "beyond language and discursive thought," and yada yada yada. But what is revealed by this phenomenon is precisely the distinctive value and function of language. *A word is a focus.* It does not present anything that was not already there, it is not a token representing something, it does not call something out of the nothingness of total blank unconsciousness; it merely changes the focus on the total gestalt. The word is a particular focus on the entire system of language. It was in the background, unnoticed but tacitly present in the strongest sense, when any other word was being spoken, and all other words now form its background, the context which makes it be itself, which makes it say what it says, which makes

it intelligible. It was, in our language, the proximal instrumental tacit term, that is, it was an aspect of our unseen self. That totality (call it a Saussurian *langue*) is always before us, no matter what word (*parole*) we are using, and it is always the same no matter which word is presently in focus. It is unchanging, and yet it is never without some focus or other, it is never a flat unaccented surface, we never see the totality except *in the form of* some focus and its field. It is impossible even to imagine the whole equally focused, but equally impossible for any element of the totality to be lacking in the background of any one focused item. If you must insist that reality is beyond language, it must at least be granted that we are so far gone in language that the way out of it is impossible without the use of language, lots of language, in a remedial capacity. There is no jumping out of it all at once, dropping it. This thorn must be removed with a thorn, and many thorns.

A word is a lens; it creates a focus. That means a figure/ground. When we bring anything into the language system, by assigning a word, however one-sided, to it, we bring it into a context, without which it is unintelligible as such. Sad is unintelligible without happy, or, more generally, not-sad. Like a circle drawn in the middle of a piece of paper, which can be seen either as a coin or as a rectangle missing a circular segment in the center—those two figures are the same figure, to apprehend one is to apprehend both. To apprehend sad is to apprehend happy. It is the same feeling, the same shape, the same contortion in the fabric of the total field of sentience. By focusing on one side or the other, we see that squiggle as sad or happy. In feeling sad, we are feeling its background too, happiness. The word sad brings this forth most explicitly, although it can be seen in the feeling itself too, after contemplation of this sort. Before contemplation, the feeling pretends to be self-contained, divorced from any context, a thing-in-itself, "immediacy." What the contemplation reveals is that there can never be present sadness without present happiness. There is no transience without eternity, no suffering without joy, no bondage without freedom, no defilement without purity. Without the contrast, nothing is felt, since sentience is designed to register only interfaces, and interfaces can always be read either way, reversibly, according to focus, and it is in this way that we must understand the identity of opposites in a Tiantai context. The "essence" of any one member of a contrasted pair (i.e., "what it really is") is equally the "essence" of either, and it inevitably includes both, and, since only in their contrast are they intelligible; the "whole" field is neither part, can be called neither sad nor happy. Nor can it be called simply "the whole." In a certain sense, we might even say that the essence of X is precisely non-X, and vice versa—the Nonexclusive Center. But the sort of ineffability that we encounter here is purely concrete, comes through the office of language itself, and its unspeakability is the opposite of a blank negation.

To say "sad" is to say: "sad, happy, and the happy/sad dimension or field itself, which could equally correctly be called neither or both happy and sad"—in other words, we have here again the Three Truths. Now relate this dimension to every other possible dimension, each defined by anything that occurs and the felt context that allowed it to be prehended as such, and expanded similarly into its three mutually identical aspects of plus, minus and plus/minus. Now take this dimension and make it the end point of another dimension, and play it through as another polarity with every other dimension, and so on ad infinitum. That, we may say, is the world.

We claimed in the section on "Four Ways" and its later permutations that "isolate, isolate, isolate" was the motto of this peculiar holism we are developing here, and that things are unified exactly to the extent and by virtue of the fact of their absolute separation and singularity. We have another instance of this principle here. For it is precisely the abstractness, separation, one-sidedness, and noncomprehensiveness of the word that establishes, no, *is*, the inclusiveness, interconnection, ambiguation of the word, the way it connects to and brings with it all other words. What descriptive word shall we use for any given situation of which we would like to be mindful? It seems that whatever we choose is hopelessly one-sided, abstract, incomplete, general. But this is precisely the point; we may choose whatever word is most obvious to us, whatever springs to mind first, the most clichéd and habitual way of speaking possible. For this already encodes the prevailing meaning system involved. A similar point can be made with respect to relativism in ethics; which of the many possible values, courses of actions, notions of the good should we choose to follow? Simply the one that prevails upon us as the most obvious. This is an audacious ethical claim, but one that I think can by now be understood on Neo-Tiantai premises, in that it necessarily involves its self-overcoming precisely in its fulfillment. This approach also liberates us from the sad Heideggerian dualism of authenticity and inauthenticity that still lurks in ostensibly nonnormative phenomenological discussions, the last refuge of cornered moralists. We say simply go with the stale unthinking values of *das Man* for there is no singular set of *das Man* values. How you intuit this already encodes your own "fundamental fantasy" about the world, which is precisely what you must fulfill in order to explode it. (Although we should note that we must reject the notion of a single, consistent fundamental fantasy for each person, an idea still found in psychoanalytic and existential theory; for us this is merely the last refuge of the soul theory and its attendant notion of the person. We would be inclined to say rather that every moment of experience, every coherence, has its own fundamental fantasy.)

Every moment of experience is a richly overdetermined set of coherences, overlapping information and interensted qualities (what Gendlin calls "the intricacy"), all of which are discoverable as parts of one another, a situation which *could* be validly characterized in a literal infinity of ways. But the most banal, obvious word (quality) and desire (as skimmed off, e.g., in Freudian free-association, Zhuangzian wandering in the obvious or Dōgenic biding of time) embodies the particular focal point that is currently structuring the field as an unseen center, menacing and disambiguating the intricacy in its snagging unwillingness to become explicit, to become a member of the array of exchangeable coherences. Naming it or willing it explicitly allows the "moment" to end, to crash, to realize itself as all pervading and unattainable, hence to flow and open to the next torque of time, the next curvature. The whole-hearted commitment to the obvious description and the obvious desire is our watchword for epistemology and ethics.

We might also here hearken back to our discussion of explicitness and objecthood in their relation to the inherent and necessary "at-a-distance-ness" of all coherences. There we said that a coherence is felt as "objective" to the extent that it brings with it a conviction of susceptibility to a greater or lesser number of alternate perspectives which confirm its presence, which make room for it and provide an interpretation of it. The greater contingent distance from me, the more other viewpoints can see it, the more objective and "out in the world" it feels, but at the same time, the more it reveals alternative coherences. That is, the more explicit it becomes qua X, the more explicit its identity with non-X becomes, and the more explicit the principle of the identity between X and non-X becomes. We have now come back to this point from another, more pragmatic perspective. When any one-sided obvious coherence is "made explicit" in this way, far from sealing it off against its identity with other coherences by confirming its identity, on the contrary it reveals this identity with non-Xness increasingly, and undermines itself, while re-establishing itself in this new form of asness, *as* every non-X. This is the practical aspect of the Three Truths: as X's Xness becomes more explicit (Local Coherence), so does its potential and actual non-Xness (Global Incoherence) become more explicit, and so does the identity and reversibility between these two (Intersubsumption, i.e., All-pervasion as All-pervadedness) become more explicit.

Adequation, Openness, "Moretoitivity," Energy

Let us now return to point 1 from the discussion of mindfulness above, concerning the localization of the anxiety, whether in the world or in the self. Consider again the passage from the early Buddhist *Udāna*, which we already discussed in the Introduction:

> [Y]ou should train yourself thus: "In the seen there will be merely what is seen; in the heard there will be merely what is heard; in the sensed there will be merely

what is sensed; in the cognized there will be merely what is cognized.". . . Then . . . you will not be "with that." When you are not "with that," then . . . you will not be "in that." When you are not "in that," then . . . you will be neither here, nor beyond, nor in between the two. Just this is the end of suffering.[24]

In naïve experience, whatever appears is *real*, that is, as we have seen, excludes its opposite or negation. This means it is an existent entity with some inalienable properties which are as they are purely on the power of that thing alone, which is hence nonnegotiable, unavoidable, forced on us; we have no choice but to accept it. This already implies a kind of aversion, at the very least in that this coherence is not made by my own whims, that it presents an opaque surface which butts against my will. Indeed, realness per se might be defined as that which contravenes our whims; we discover the "external world" when we come up a brick wall upon which our fantasies are suddenly smashed. Hence we may say that realness equals suffering.[25] In our terms, what is encountered as a real object in this sense, as excluding its opposite, is what is present as an obstacle (what stands in the way of some desired goal) or tool (what serves as a means toward some desired goal), as near or far, as possessed or lacked, and which is therefore problematic; it is something which can be desired and yet lacked, or hated and yet present. (When this problematicalness is seen to be not merely contingent but necessary and constitutive, on the other hand, this "objectness" is transformed into one's own *identity* per se, what one *is* substantiality as defined above, which is to say, as the Nonexclusive Center.) The same thing can be stated the opposite way for the case of desire: the *absence* of the desired thing is real, excludes its presence, is nonnegotiable, unavoidable, absolute, it cannot be attained—hence also suffering. The first step in the traditional regimen is thus the contemplation of impermanence and hence the necessity of ever lurking suffering. This means first and foremost to take the appearance seriously at face value, as presented by precisely these naïve assumptions, that is, taking each appearance in its presented absoluteness, as a presence which excludes its absence and the necessary possibility of problematicalness implied in this. This would mean to experience what appears as absolute, untranscendable: it is so, this thing is present, this experience is occurring, this sight, sound, feeling, a brute fact which is so incontrovertible and real and absolute and unmistakable a presence that no further considerations can cast any doubt on it. *It must be*

---

[24] John Ireland, trans., *The Udāna and The Itivuttaka* (Kandy: Buddhist Publication Society, 1997), 21.
[25] In classical terms, Suffering is *Dharmakāya* (the Absolute Reality), is Intersubsumption (All-pervasion as All-pervadedness), is the "real-nature" track.

stressed that full appreciation of this hard facticity is crucial to all that is to follow here. The initial contemplation of *impermanence* takes this as the primal premise, and then draws attention to the incomprehensible, paradoxical *temporality* of this absoluteness. Just as nonnegotiable as its presence *was*, its ensuing absence is *equally* absolute, brute fact, nonnegotiable. This is meant to show that apprehended realness is no guarantee of apprehended realness, that unambiguous insistent real presence is no obstacle to unapprehendability, and vice versa. The point is to see how fully real it is, and then how fully unreal it has become once it is gone.

It is noteworthy here that to experience the salvific paradox of appearance as transcended one need only take each experience *explicitly* as some "one"—and see that this never works, but also that there is no alternative. But this raises the question: how are we usually apprehending our experience, when we are not "explicitly" experiencing them as "ones"? In part, we can say, we are *wavering*. The assumption is of a *series* of "ones," each one placed in the context of many other "ones"—that is, many ones. But we do not quite come to focus on any one of these—instead we get a kind of blur where we vacillate between a bunch of putative "ones" very quickly, so as to produce the primal illusion that there exist these mutual exclusive ones *to choose from*. If instead each is explicitly taken as a "one"—one at a time—it becomes apparent that there is no such arrayed set of options: each supposed "one" is in fact more than one, which, since this point is constitutive of identity as such or of being a "one," and hence necessarily and not merely contingently applicable, ultimately means that this more-than-it-seems-ness is also applied to whatever coherences are determining the coherence in question. (We have explored the implications of this notion on the experience of "choice" in the discussion of "Will" above.) This means that its identity can only be understood as that which *all* others are appearing as, or that this present particular *simpliciter* identity is both unavoidable (present everywhere else as the appearance of any other) and ungraspable (present here only as others), where these two attributes indicate exactly the same thing. It is for this reason that we say that the Nonexclusive Mean signifies that the following three points can be made about every coherence whatsoever: it is some particular thing, but only *because* it is impossible for it to be simply this thing, and that, since this applies in all cases, this means also that it pervades all times and places, is alone in the universe, is both the source and the expression of all other coherences.

Hence, just the slowing down and making explicit of the naïve assumption overcomes it, and then reinstates it in its, as it were, glorified form. We may perhaps describe this as simply a transition from a vague sense of something to a sense of a vague something, that is, from a vague impression to an impression of vagueness. Once the vagueness or confusion or wavering itself becomes an explicit quality or coherence of experience, a "one" in its own right, its nature has changed, but at the same time, nothing has changed: it has just been more explicitly noticed, more closely and exhaustively described as what it had always already been. This sort of change but no change is what we referred to as "transformative self-recontextualization," and here we have as it were the most basic—in the sense both of most crude and of most fundamental—instantiation of this principle.

Another important feature of naïve consciousness may be noted in this connection: In considering the classical Buddhist problem of self and suffering, we soon discover that when we experience displeasure, although we are *not* tempted to identify this displeasure as our "self," it *does* intensify our self-concept in a *backhanded* way, i.e., by simultaneously positing, as a contrast in the background, a possible state of pleasure which we are missing out on at the moment and which we are thereby tacitly identifying as our real self (which is putatively in constant freedom/pleasure, but is blocked off by the adventitious interference of this accidental displeasure). Similarly, in the case of appearance and impermanence, our ordinary consciousness takes present appearances as a prelude or sign of some real, some other coherence which they will lead to or turn out to be—*and this is indeed the case*. But again, the naïve consciousness tacitly assumes that this other coherence the present appearance will turn out to be is *not* itself also a mere appearance, in other words, not something that itself will in turn turn out to be otherwise, something which presents itself only by concealing most of itself and so on. The naïve assumption is that the present appearance will at last be supplanted by a fully present and transparently self-same real. In this way, the usual (correct) apprehension that this present experience will turn out to be otherwise backhandedly posits the existence of that which it will turn out to be, as something which will do no more turning out to be otherwise. In this way, it devalues the present impermanence by tacitly assuming a permanent reality *of which* it is the appearance, or an end to which it is the means.

Let us explore in some greater detail the implications of these suggestions for our understanding of our usual way of experiencing the world of coherences around or in us (and the exact sense in which we must understand this casual bifurcation—"around or in us"—will be among the results to elucidated by this line of thought). We may recast the question *temporally*. That is, the categories of "appearance and reality," what is apparent and what it will turn out to be, the initial "one coherence" and the "twoness" that always turns out to be underlying it, can be restated as an *initial* apprehension which *subsequently* reveals itself to involve more than was explicit in that initial apprehension. The blueness over there promises to turn out to be a piece in a puzzle, a full context which will reveal itself in its entirety only upon further investigation—collation with other sensations, other premises, other coherences; it turns out to be the blueness of a cup on the table, which turns out to be the result of the reflection of light on a paint mixed in a factory, which turns out to be composed of molecules, or, in the other direction, turns out to be a reminder of the color favored by an ex-lover, a trigger to nostalgia, and so on. Again, the structural assumption is that the other coherence posited by this turning-out-to-be-otherwise will not itself turn out to be otherwise—it is assumed to be a reality of which this coherence is a mere appearance or expression. The *first* classical Tiantai remedial measure was thus rightfully a "pan-appearance" *flat depthless* world picture: that is, there are *only appearances*, no things, each appearance is just what it is, points to nothing beyond itself, as in Abidhammic doctrine of momentariness, or the *Udāna* passage quoted above. That is, an absolute sunderedness of impressions is attempted to counteract the *one-sided* emptying of the apparent into the real. Everything is just what it appears; there is no underlying reality for these appearances to empty into. This attempt, however, like any attempt, cannot ultimately stand; pushed to its extreme, fully realized, it crashes. For emptying out in this sense is the precise precondition for the appearance of coherences at all. If it is really accomplished, the appearances themselves vanish, not only is there is no place for them to empty into, but also there is no longer anything to be emptied out: they are empty, as we have seen above. Hence, the next remedial method reverses us *back* to ordinary consciousness in a sense: here, nothing is what it appears; everything is a means to some other end, everything will turn out otherwise, *including* the end, the "reality" they will turn out to be, the "otherwise." "The otherwise" is itself merely an appearance that must turn out to be otherwise. When the necessity of its realness and its unrealness, initially two discrete moments in time, are apprehended simultaneously in the form of a necessary connection and copresence, we have moved to a new and deeper appreciation of the relation between its being X and its being non-X—that is, impermanence as conditionality per se and hence as "illusion" or "appearance." This will apply even if the X in question happens to persist as it is forever. "Appearance" is thus the structural nature of all being in precisely the sense that all appearing is the appearing of one surface of a greater whole, and this "pointing to the rest" *is also an "appearance" in just this sense*. It is never fully revealed, and the present concealment too is no less revealed than what will result from it. I am riding the train: the present experience is completely devalued, emptied into the "project" of getting to the destination. It is the tacit positing of the possibility of a destination, the result or end as something that will fully reveal itself as an end in itself which destroys the ultimacy of the present. The first step is to see impermanence and momentariness: riding the train is just riding the train, arriving is just arriving. Neither is an expression of the other, or has an intrinsic relation to the other. The second step is to see that riding the train is indeed something that turns out to be otherwise, that is, to get all its meaning from the other coherence of arriving, but also from *every* other coherence, and moreover, that this is true of arriving as well, and indeed, necessarily of all experiences. It is in this sense that they are all "illusory"—all of them have to turn out to be something else. Naïve consciousness was right about the travelling, wrong about the arriving as anticipated from the position of travelling. When this whole situation, as a necessary positing of this anticipated other no matter which coherence is appearing, is apprehended as such, we have moved to a new understanding of the relation between being thus and being otherwise. In temporal terms, everything *turns out* to be otherwise; but this otherwise is also not some positive self-identical outcome; it never results in a final judgment which once and for all settles the score; hence it never turns out to be "anything" other than what it appeared to be, for all outcomes are likewise only appearances. It never turns out once and for all that something is unilaterally this or that; "turning out to have always been also something else" is constitutive of "being something," and, obviously, vice versa.

Now, every problem or difficulty encountered by a sentient being is a problem of *adequation*, as we have seen in various forms above. That is, it is always a question of matching or coordinating two or more coherences with one another, so that one of them is adequate to the other, on the assumption that it is initially an inadequate match for the other. If it is an epistemological problem—is this true or false? is this real or illusory?—it is a question of an adequation between what appears to be the case and what is in fact the case. If it is a moral question, it is a question of an adequation between what I am doing and what I should be doing. If it is a metaphysical problem—is this so or not so?—it is again a question of adequation between a manner of appearing and what the real world is like or is doing. If it is a practical problem, it is a question of an adequation between my desires and the external conditions, or the means and the end, which obstruct or could be conducive to it. Even my pleasure may be a problem for me in this way; is the pleasure I am now getting from this situation commensurate with, adequate to, the maximum amount of pleasure it could and should produce? These are all questions of coordinating the coherence *myself* (my desires, my impressions, my beliefs, my behavior) and some other objective thing that belongs to the coherence *world* (conditions, facts, realities, values, truth, etc.). What is feared in each case is that there is *something more* in self than in world, or in world than in self, generally the latter. The adequation is supposed to remedy this. We have here a disclosure of the basic existential anxiety, which means: there is something more out in the world, more than I have yet taken into account, more than I have taken care of, more than I have prepared for, beyond my grasp or control, beyond my powers of accurate depiction or adequate response, beyond my skills of adaptation. The world has some as yet unknown powers, there is something more to it than what I see, know, understand, or can handle, and this something more is incommensurate with my self, a threat to which my self is constantly exposed. There is more-to the world than there is to my picture of the world or my preparedness for the world, and this something-more will undermine, unhinge, sully, or destroy the specific coherence which I am. But if, as we claim, all coherences as such are "moretoitive," if this "more-to-come-ness" pertains to every coherence without exception, by virtue of its being a coherence at all, we have a very different situation. On the one hand, most simply, the I who is threatened is no longer any particular *simpliciter* coherence whose existence could be compromised by its intermixture with its opposite, or with any degree of otherness, since it is already other than itself through and through, and this is its very being. On the other hand, the world which we had been seeing as a group of *simpliciter* coherences than which there were more *simpliciter* coherences than we could currently handle or see, now turns out to be just a nonfinite set of coherences, each of which is itself moretoitive. One could equally say simply that we have just the self and its moretoitivity, with the latter called world, or that we have just the world and its moretoitivity, with the latter called self. On this basis, we can now assert that the originally sought adequation between self and world is both constitutively impossible and (thereby) always already accomplished. This is because whatever is singled out as the representative of self inherently includes whatever is identified as the coherence to be adequated to, and vice versa. Each is appearing *as* the other. This means also, however, that each is appearing imperfectly as itself, is incapable of appearing *simpliciter*, is never anywhere. Neither side can be absorbed into the other because each side in itself is already both; hence when one is perfectly adequated to the other, absorbed into the other, as if to form a unity, the two are still present, and the adequation still unaccomplished. But this is the already accomplished adequation itself, since what was on one side of the confrontation was always already on the other side as well (not to mention everywhere else). The split itself is present on both sides of the split, in other words, and this is the adequation between them. They are the same thing, forms of each other, all possible coherences are one both sides of the encounter, appearing *as* these two coherences, but neither of them is a unity, a *simpliciter* fact, nor is their "correspondence" such a *simpliciter* fact, nor indeed this condition of asness itself. Because there are no things, there can be no adequation, and adequation is already accomplished. Because each coherence is ambiguous, reversible with all its components and contextualizations, readable as all other coherences, every attempt at adequation is doomed to failure, constitutively impossible, and this is at once why it is hopeless and why no hope is needed.

Let us to return to the *Udāna* quote. Generally I look *through* these coherences toward an imaginary point in the distance that constitutes the "thing" (object) or the "end" (taking them as means in a project). In either case, it is "intentionality" which is positing the thinglikeness (determinate being) they appear to have, either as objects (in a realist picture) or as ideal *Vorstellungen* that, however, point to a perceiver or principle that is not ideal but real. I "squint" at them in order to constitute a particular Gestalt. This is the moretoitiveness I ascribe to them, but also posits a something more which itself has no more to it. The *Udāna* passage interdicts this: let there be no Gestalt beyond the particular data, let nothing "point to more" beyond itself, let nothing serve as sign, as means, as call, as challenge, as demand, as premonition of meaning, as promise. For the sense of my being *open to attack*, that is, *exposed* to other coherences as to a contagion, the sense that the world is demanding something of me more than I can provide and which I have an inadequate handle on, and the fear of inadequation of myself to the world and the task embodied in it, are the primal form in which the "moretoitiveness" which is the world is presencing for me. This is the impossible "self-project," the endeavor to be a determinate entity which is also unconditioned, something which is what it is by virtue of its own power, which has the inalienable property of being what it is no matter what it is, on its own power alone. The "no matter what it is," if accomplished, means there is no standard or direction for action; "it doesn't matter what I do" converts into "there's no point in doing anything." This is tedium and meaninglessness. On the other hand, if the "determinacy" side of the desire is accomplished, we are necessarily conditioned, threatened, constantly exposed to an undermining from without. We call this *anxiety*. We are now in a position to see how these two poles of human discontent, boredom and anxiety, amount to the same thing, are intersubsumptive. That is, the sense that things point to something else, and that this something else is a call to adequate reaction from me (in order to establish or justify my place as a determinate object among objects). But this same moretoitivity is what makes all my actions incapable of finally establishing anything about myself, my meaninglessness, the lack of content to the self I am striving to accomplish. What we have here then is actually a defense mechanism in bad faith, a kind of *draining off* of the primal openness which is in fact constitutive of beings; anxiety is strictly correlative to the putative objectivity of determinate beings, which reflects back as my own determinateness or as my utter indeterminacy, which is itself another form of determinacy, and amounts once again to the loss of the self I was trying to establish. We have anxiety when we think there's something I can do to further this self-project, the attempt to be both determinate and unconditioned, by fitting our actions into an external framework of identity-granting parameters, but find that we are never quite sure what it is. We have tedium and meaninglessness when we sense that nothing we can do will have any relevance to establishing such a self. These are merely alternate ways of responding to the mistaken sense that *some* coherences are simply determinately what they are, actual entities with inalienable properties established on their own power and independent of context, while others are as yet undetermined. But we see here instead that they are openness in their very selves, datum for datum—that is, ungraspable and inescapable, constitutively moretoitive and problematic, incapable of appearing *simpliciter*. When I drain this openness off into anxiety or tedium, I simultaneously *objectify* the world as world, turning the inherent or constitutive problematicalness into an all-pervasive but qualitatively contingent problematicalness.

Coherences, we might say, are originally time, mind, moretoitivity, openness in their very appearing, as whatever they are appearing as. We may also say here that are therefore *energy*, which we may define precisely as Intersubsumption, reversibility, an indeterminate enabling which can serve as a proximal term for an unknown and disparate set of distal terms, or as the impossibility of appearing *simpliciter*, or as freedom, nonobstruction, the self, necessary and constitutive problematicalness, asness. Intersubsumption is asness is reversibility is energy. That is, precisely what we normally experience as fear and anxiety are now experienced as energy; in their ordinary state, their openness as energy is conceived as openness as vulnerability of one object to another, or rather the sense of myself as a finite object confronting a larger finite (i.e., determinate) object called the world, and threatened by it. Here moretoitiveness reads out as beyond-my-graspness, as more-than-me-ness, as overpowering of one determinate thing by another, where the knowledge I have, and the action based on it, fail to be adequate to the object. All the particular data making up the world and myself, each coherence, becomes atomic, becomes determinate, completely devoid of moretoitiveness, all of which is drained over to the side of world, or of a determinate being which just happens to be, contingently, elsewhere or too large to grasp. But if this *kind* of moretoitiveness is reclaimed as the primal kind, as energy, as time, as openness of each datum in and of itself, the anxiety is *both* justified and overcome. Openness or moretoitiveness is primal, is the basic fact, and applies everywhere, to each sensation in and of itself. It is not reserved for some special province, and lacking everywhere else. The question of adequation hereby disappears, as we have seen in other contexts above. The question of squaring with another reality (the "bookkeeping" or matching activity traditionally called "karma") disappears, as is most clearly evident in the soteriological effects of the Tiantai notion that all coherences, including painful and evil ones, are inherently included in all others, and hence ineradicable, as we will take up in more detail momentarily. Also, the "objective world" disappears, in the sense that the world as a system of objects which are in themselves determinate and finite is replaced by an overlapping and mutually pervading field of sentient-being *Lebenswelten*, where all determinations are understood as openness, that is, as intended, as ambiguous, as part of projects or "vows," as in a process of constant revision, as moments in compassionate or passionate intersubjective regards, as constitutively exposed to an infinity of judgments, attitudes, projections of characteristics.

Lebenswelt-objects are open by nature. This not because the world does not overflow our intentions and grasps of it, but precisely because it always does, as noted in the "External World(s)" section in Part One. Objectivity in this sense is a true unknowable, and all attributions of objectivity in this sense are erroneous. Then shall it be a regulative goal or ideal, in a broadly Kantian sense? But then it is present as part of a sentient project, as an aspect of sentient experience. Compassion, vow, greed, anger, ignorance, and sympathetic joy are the categories to be privileged here, not matter and particles. Once again, we dismiss "meaning" for meaninglessness because we really want to dismiss "single meaning," because "meaninglessness" actually means "infinite meanings."

Hence, we may now supplement and consolidate our list of synonyms for "the Good," for freedom, for reversibility, for Intersubsumption, for asness, for self, for interpenetration. Every coherence can be described either as what it is, more than what it is, or the identity between these two—the Three Truths. When the "what it is" part is separated off and grouped on one side, as it were, we have what is called "objective world"; what is left over on the other side is the "more than what it is" *of all coherences*, which is normally called self, freedom, Good, and so on—all of these as phantoms, needless to say, which vanish when sought for. The positing of the goods as contingent is identical to the positing of the problematicalness as contingent; both are abstractions from their mutual identity, which is the necessity all-pervasion of both. The realization of the latter concerning any coherence, X, can be redescribed in the following ways:

1. To see X as necessarily and constitutively problematic, rather than contingently problematic. This will mean to see it as all-pervasive, incapable of appearing *simpliciter*, and so on.

2. To *be* X, rather than encountering X, having or lacking X.

3. To see X as reversible with its component *and* proximal/contextualizing terms (in a word, with all its *mediating* terms), to see it as subsumed into everything it is subsuming.

4. To see X as a token that satisfies (at least) two contrary and apparently mutually exclusive demands simultaneously.

5. To see X *nonreferentially* (that is, *omni-referentially*), that is, *as energy*, as appealing or pointing to no final fixed reference point from which it can derive an unambiguous identity. Rather, to be "reversibility" itself simply means to be energy, which is for us also 2 above, in other words, to be self/body, the proximal and unseen "I can" which waits unbound to be reversed into whatever it may encounter, to appear *as* some other coherence. To see all experiences (this is most easily verifiable in the case of extreme emotions like anger, lust and anxiety) as energy is to see them as *able* to be equally any of the proximal (opposite, tacit) terms, *unobstructed*, unbound to a particular form but capable of becoming any of them (hence the Tiantai dictum: "The one word 'capability' [*neng*: ability, energy] sums up our teaching."). This amounts to 1 above because it is seen that it could not *possibly* "come to rest" or resolve anywhere; it must not be imagined that some neutral coherence "energy" exists anywhere *simpliciter*, into which these instantiations could resolve. Energy, pure desire, exists only when some other coherence is seen as energy, which means that coherence is seen as a pure happening, ungrounded, and *for that very reason* inextricable from the universe, "inherently entailed" in every other coherence.

The above can be applied in two ways to human behavior. First, predictively, we may say that one will do what most successfully fulfills two contrary demands, the double-bind one feels oneself to be in, with a single token, according to one's basic focal settings (for in reality, any act or coherence *can* be seen to be doing so, if one's cognitive capacities serve one as a flexible enough focal apparatus). Second, prescriptively, we may give, if asked, the following blanket advice: *Do* that which *appears* to you to do the above (although ultimately any act can be seen as doing so), and search for what the demands are, the particular double-bind which defines the world for you, and what could be read by you convincingly, given your own prejudices, as fulfilling each of them. The former can usually be traced out by following the tracks of contingent problematics that emerge along the fault line into which the necessary problematicalness of all coherences has been drained off.[26] One

---

[26] Here again we find ourselves in close accord with a certain reading of Lacanian theory, in particular here the notion of the *objet petit a*, which stands as a plug to cover the "stain of the Real," the crack that reveals the overall inconsistency of the Big Other, the symbolic order itself, thereby conferring a sham constistency on it, on the world, constituting what we call reality. Where we differ in drawing conclusions from these similar premises in the practical sphere should, however, be quite obvious.

thing is set up as a representative or stopgap which as it were takes on itself all the problematicalness of all things, so they can be left unproblematic; if I may indulge a Christian symbol here, where you find some problem playing Christ in this way, it must be slain and glorified in a single act, crucified. Find the way in which that representative problem is both satisfied and destroyed in a single gesture, and the problem will be solved; that is, the original pristine all-pervasive, inescapable, constitutive probelmaticalness of all coherences will be restored, one will in fact have become the problem, and hence free from/as it.

The Desire of Desire: The Intersubsumption of Self, Affect, and Object

This point is quite tricky, and we must proceed slowly. We must consider the attitude toward desire and aversion themselves, considered as explicit objects, or as coherences in their own right. It is obvious, indeed trivial, according to our definition of coherences, and their necessarily infinite divisibility and mutual inclusion, that in any case where I desire X, the coherence X I am desiring also includes the coherence "desire for X" as an aspect of itself. But this means that in desiring X, I also implicitly desire desire-for-X, along with every other coherence.[27]

Moreover, the desire *for* desire is present also in the sense that desire is generally underwritten by the conviction that fulfilling it would "do some good"—for me or some other "one"—and that the desire itself is instrumental to achieving this good. This is so because, as we discussed in the Introduction, desire for an object is really desire for selfhood, for power: I want X because what I really

---

[27] But given the intersubsumptive structure of any field of experience, desire is also always desire *of* desire in the more searching sense of desiring the *other*'s desire, including the desire to "be desired." This is where the subject-object reversibility becomes especially important. When I desire to *have* X in my world, I also necessarily desire "to be seen from the point of view of X," to be seen by X. Desire always involves this desire to be seen (from the central determining perspective of, and therefore *as* an aspect of, some particular coherence). The desire-for-X is at first the proximal term through which the X is revealed, and a component thereof. It is absorbed into X-as-desired, and at first appears only *as* (an aspect of) this X, as the desirability of X. But this turns out to be reversible; the two terms are intersubsumptive, as we have seen. What we have said about "all coherences in general" must apply to both. To desire to have X in my world is to desire to be in X's world. My desire is for both of us to appear in the same world. But this desire of mine is not definitively mine, or anyone else's—it belongs as much to the object as it does to me. Hence, my desire to have X in the world is equally X's desire to have me in the world, or to have an X in the world that desires me in its world. I want to posit an X such that it is an X-desiring-me-in-its-world. Desire, again, is the desire for desire.

want is to know that I have the power to attain X. When I desire, I desire a tallying between the desire and the object; the desire must persist in the world long enough to meet its object. This means that I want both the desire and the wherewithal to obtain the object of the desire—if either is lacking, the desire remains unfulfilled. The desire is in this case itself desirable.

We can thus discern the direct desire of the self for the desire, as a part of its manner of self-definition and self-affirmation. Of all the pleasurable things experienced, the self chooses those for its desire which fulfill the larger, implicit projects by means of which the self has defined itself, whose unconditional power it wishes to prove. But this level of desire is normally not noticed. Indeed, the desire itself does not normally come to consciousness as an object in its own right; we see merely the object-as-desirable. When the desire itself becomes the explicit (distal) term of experience (i.e., when we introspect, or turn our attention toward these affects themselves, e.g., in mindfulness exercises), it becomes possible to detect the attitude of desire and aversion *for* desire and aversion among the now embodied, proximal terms, via a further redirection of attention. Something quite remarkable turns out to be hidden here. For here we have what might be called a *tacit* object of desire (i.e., the affect of desiring or hating per se, taken as an object), which occupies a very peculiar place in our general understanding of desire. For we have said that an ordinary *object* of desire is always something that insistently *appears*, due to our inability to "inhabit" it, to imagine being it, to place ourselves in its shoes, so to speak. The insistently desired object, generally, is the distal term, which is precisely what *cannot* be reversed into a proximal term *through* which other coherences are encountered, into that which is appearing only *as* these other coherences. It refuses to disappear, and can only be made to disappear by inhabiting it. But a desire, as such, is precisely an inhabited proximal term through which others are encountered, precisely what I am embodying, perhaps to an excessive degree; I identify with it. When I desire that woman's mouth, for example, I cannot embody the mouth; but the desire itself is precisely where I am in fact locating my identity at that moment. I am taking the desire for my self, in the most radical sense, through which I am seeing the world and the mouth. The desire is for the moment a part of "my body," which is invisible to itself and expressed only *as* the objects which are disclosed "through" it. We have said that a particular desire persists obsessively because of its inability to see its object as seeing it. But now we see a two-tiered structure to desire, whereby the desire desires the object, and the (rest of the) self tacitly "desires" the desire.[28] The desire is a kind of

---

[28] In a classical Tiantai context here, it is impossible not to think of Zhili's remarkable two-tiered model of contemplation, which he compares to a three-term relation between a

proxy outgrowth of the self, which at the moment is inhabited as that through which the world is seen, playing the role of the whole self. This desire itself is generally not seen, and yet is nonetheless also an object of an obscure desire, coming from "further back," from the rest of the habitual (*Nirmāṇakāyic*, "finite") self. What then does it mean to desire this invisible object (i.e., the desire itself), *along with* the visible object of desire?

Pressing our account of desire, we can see that a further and very important new wrinkle appears here. For a desire may now be thought of as a proximal term located *between* two coherences, with both of which it is resisting reversible intersubsumption at once. The first is the desired object—the woman's mouth, the glass of water, the fame, the money, the wisdom, the bliss, etc. But the second object it is unable to reverse positions with is my own body, my own customary self, my history, commitments, character, reason, or, more fundamentally, my very "sense of self" itself, my audacious intuition of myself as a master and owner of my experience, the will to self-mastery and power, the "transcendental ego," the self-contradictory volition for unconditionality, which is what I am. The desire is, to be sure, unwilling to be looked at by the object, to be seen as an aspect of "sexy mouth's" world. But the "sense of self" is equally unwilling to be looked at by the desire itself, to be seen as an aspect of *its* world. This means, of course, that we cannot really imagine *fully being* this object or this desire, with nothing left out, placing ourselves entirely in the desire itself as the subject position, without holding anything aloof from it. What we normally do is keep our sense of selfhood safely out of the "world" engaged by this desire. For that would mean making of our habitual self as a whole, or our sense of self as such, *an object* to be seen and affected *by* this desire. It would mean having our present self—whatever group of coherences is *de facto* being identified with, in a condition of explicit mutual asness and intersubsumption, or the coherence "sense of self" per se—afflicted by it, disrupted by it, which is what happens if they are so much as "seen" by it, become objects in its world. This means we cannot comprehend or imagine the affectability (the alternate readability) of our putatively affectless and definitively identified self (i.e., that which is unconditioned, impervious to conditions). We cannot accept that this "self" of ours also exists intersubsumptively in the world of any affect, as an object posited in the world of the affect for the latter to interact with and thus disrupt and

---

hammer, a chisel, and raw material worked on by the chisel. The chisel is an intermediate term through which the hammer works on the raw material. If any of the three is lacking, the work cannot be accomplished. In our case, we would call the habitual projects and commitments of the self the hammer, or better, the sense of self and overall volition, will to power as self-mastery. The chisel would be the particular mood, affect, desire, or aversion, and the raw material the object of desire or aversion or other concern.

redefine. For this is what would be revealed if my "sense of self"—that is, the coherence of feeling unconditioned and unaffectable—were to be seen—subsumed—from the perspective of a particular raging desire. What is needful here, but which keeps getting snagged (because it is precisely the one thing "I" do *not* want), is to *be* the affect not only in the outward-directed disposition, encountering the desired object, but also "backwards" toward the sense of self, so it can encounter/express-itself-as the passive body which is being afflicted and perturbed by it, my present body, or better, as my active sense of self itself, which takes itself to be an agent and unconditioned master. Desire wants the world to change, but not the self; but it can be overcome only if it learns to want *both*. Affect must "have" a body to afflict, hence must also express itself *as* this complete BZness (if I am BZ) or Iness or unconditionedness or illusion of mastery at the same time. But our understanding of affect limits its metaphorical range in such a way as to make this unimaginable.

In a normal case of unsnagged intersubsumptive reversibility, what has been first "had" (i.e., encountered as a distal, contingently problematic term in our explicit world) can then be inhabited. One can then "be" it without obstruction, it can become equally the proximal term. Here, however, we have a typical snag: I can be my affect having things in the world to afflict, manipulate, disrupt, challenge, harass, and affect (which is what happens when I do not see the affect itself, but only the object with which it is concerned), but I cannot then move on to *be* it, to be this wave of perturbations considered as directed towards, redefining and challenging all things without exception, including my own body and selfhood. I am unable to let that wave be the central unseen term expressed everywhere in the field (including in my body and selfhood), through which all others are expressed, but which appears nowhere in the field itself.

In short, I am subject to affects because I cannot imagine my own body and sense of being a "self" to be an object that is subject to affects and multiple interpretations. That is, to *be* the affect would be to perceive my present body or self as its *victim*, and the affect will be repeated until I can in fact find a way to do so, to see myself as its victim, to really make my own self not proximal but distal in the role of that-which-is-afflicted, that which is disrupted and redefined in terms of this affect, which is just what I cannot bring myself to do.[29]

---

[29] We may say with Freud that compulsive repetition is always of something that cannot be properly remembered; and indeed "sex" per se falls into this category. . . . One lacks mindfulness at the happiest moments; in ecstasy everything collapses into the single coherence, for example, "having sex," which becomes retrospectively an empty, abstract concept. If one could "snapshot" every moment of the experience, aware of all its constitutive and hence mutually

Note, however, that when we do become aware of these affects as explicit (distal) coherences, we notice that we dislike them—that desire and aversion *hurt*. They are not themselves desirable states or pleasures; they are tensions, clashes, disharmonies, demands, and, moreover, are afflicting us, are not in accordance with any list of our desiderata (only their objects belong to this list; I *want* to be respected, I *do not want* to be angry because no one respects me, i.e., I do not want to [have to] want to be respected, etc.) If pleasure is the overcoming of limitations, power, freedom from conditionality, desire, and aversion are primary forms of displeasure; they are intense experiences of dependence, of neediness, of limitation. As soon as we can see them explicitly, we come to have aversion for them. In short, when affects are proximal, it means we desire them; when they are distal, we have aversion for them. When affects are proximal, they are desired, and hence perpetuated and repeated. We implicitly desire to desire and to hate. What we want when we want X is not just X, but desire for X. Similarly, when we hate X, we desire to hate X. These are part of our project of defining and confirming some particular self to be unconditional, to be all-powerful. When they remain implicit (proximal), it means we desire them, hence repeating them, hence perpetuating them. Here we come to understand the aim of the early Buddhist deployment of mindfulness meditation, as we saw briefly in the Introduction to this work. It makes explicit the process of sensation and volition itself, and shows that it is, quite directly and simply, painful and conditioned, thus not worth wanting as a supposed source of pleasure which somehow bolsters or verifies a putatively unconditioned self. Seeing this clearly, one of the necessary conditions for the arising of this affect is removed, and the affect fades away, freed from its vicious circle of self-reinforcement. Once the desire is seen as "not-self" in this sense, its root is cut off, and it winds down toward its cessation. This is accomplished simply by making the affect an explicit distal term in its own right, rather than a proximal term through which its object is appearing.

But the classical Tiantai conception of liberation departs from the "Hinayana" notion of mere cessation of or liberation from the passions, based

---

pervading coherences, the repetition would not be compelled. Indeed, as we have seen, this "snapshot" orientation sublates in Tiantai into turning each moment into the *end* of a means/end relationship (which, simultaneously, if universalized, of course turns everything into a means as well; the final version must be, "To be an end *is* to be a means.") This signifies, in a temporal dimension, the "infinite divisibility" of coherences; where an end is seen, the means appear as mere *aspects* of the end. Seeing each coherence as an end means to see more and more coherences where formerly only one was seen. Positing a specific goal, having a desire, is an epistemological orientation that singles out a coherence-as-goal at the expense of its constituent aspects.

on an aversion for the suffering they bring. Instead, Tiantai calls for the "full realization" and universalization thereof, "dwelling" in the affect so that it pervades everywhere, and is expressing itself in an illimitable number of alternate ways, as the Bodhisattva path. We propose to do the same here. We need both the initial step of making the affect distal, thus seeing its painfulness and our aversion to it, and a further step, moving it back into the proximal position to be inhabited, until the two are completely intersubsumptive. How is this to be done?

As we have seen in any case of aversion, this aversion for the affect, once it is explicit and distal, means that we are unable to see ourselves *as* the affect, unable to conceive it as an aspect of our own agency or body. In particular, our sense of self, of our unconditionedness, of our mastery and ownership, will not tolerate the notion that it can be read, is reducible to, is expressible as, this wildly needy and conditioned emotion. This is, of course, the converse case of the implicit desire i.e., affect that occurs when it is proximal and tacit, and which leads to its repetition, where we cannot see the "self" as redefinable in terms of the affect, can be read as an aspect of this emotion. In the case of aversion for the (explicit) affect, I do not want to know that neediness can also be read as an aspect of I-ness; in the case of desire for the (implicit) affect, I do not want to know that I-ness can also be read as an aspect of neediness. But here we want to find a middle way, in accordance with the true Tiantai Center, Omnipresence qua Infinite Intersubsumptive Coherences, mutual pervasion, reversible asness, for our relation with our own affects, one which privileges neither desire for them nor aversion for them, but establishes their free intersubsumption, the manifestation of the constitutive impossibility of each, which is precisely their interpervasion.

The only possible solution is to, first, become aware of what desires and aversions you are repeating without being aware of it, because you desire them, because you cannot imagine them being a self which perceives—and therefore expresses itself as—your current body-mind and your sense of agency and selfhood. These desires and aversions have been invisible centers, quasi-selves, but now they become explicit objects, and incite aversion. One stood in their shoes, but did not look at all things from their perspective—one's "self" was excluded from their objects. So the first step is to step out of them completely, back into the "self." The next step, after you are aware of them and hence hate them, is to stand in their place *again*. That is, make them invisible again, but this time as the true, uncontested center, if only for a moment. For the former invisible centrality of the detested object would have been fine if I did not in addition hold onto that *other* invisible center which is my current self. Once again we have an oscillation or interference pattern caused by a tension between two rival centers. I was holding back, as it were, from full identification with the desire, by maintaining an auxiliary sense of self (my biography, commitments, attitudes, memories, body, or my sense of selfhood and agency as such), which I took to be something other than a mere object to be devastated and disrupted by this desire which I *am*.

Hence I had set up two invisible centers in implicit tension with one another. We recall that the first step in overcoming compulsive desire is to allow the desired object to be a "self" which incorporates also my previous self. The overcoming of aversion, on the other hand, could be accomplished by seeing the hated object as something which expresses me-ness, which is readable as the specific coherence "me" however I happen to identify it. But we may also recall, as noted in the Introduction in our discussion of early Buddhism, that in a certain sense every desire is at once a desire to *have*, to possess a particular object or pleasure, and more profoundly a disguised desire to *be*, a desire for selfhood, which is being fulfilled indirectly by this having, since it establishes me as an implicitly constant and unconditioned "possessor," a master. This latter aspect of desire is what is targeted here. The particular object of desire can perhaps be returned to general circulation by inhabiting it, seeing its intersubsumption with the self. But desire itself, inasmuch as it really wants *being*, will simply find another form of expression. The current consideration, however, targets this tacit desire. It is to be handled in the same manner, but in the opposite direction. The reversal and intersubsumption of subject/object positions must now be done on the subtler level of the relation between the customary self, or selfhood as such, and the desire or affect now serving as its avatar and proxy. The self must become an object afflicted by the desire, and the self does this only by desiring fully, by being *nothing but* the desire, by holding nothing back from it. If I could desire *fully*, if I could fully realize *desiring*, desire would be overcome (i.e., the desire for desire which makes it compulsively repeat). If I could be *wholly* this affect, this desire, this aversion, which swallows and devastates the whole world, without sparing even my own body, my own soul, my history, my sense of agency and mastery and selfhood, all of which are its victims, if I could stand joyfully in the place of the affect which ravages this pretension of mine to be someone in particular, its Reversible Asness and Intersubsumptivity would be manifested. This is what we have called *pure* desire, desire with no (specific) object, which for us means desire for *every* possible object, for *every condition* to be otherwise. Obviously this is also a thorough affirmation of exactly the way things are, the thusness and otherwiseness of all coherences. Then the mutual reducibility of desire and aversion, and the reversibility of both of these with the sense of unconditioned imperturbability, would become manifest. All three are operating in every possible case. Desire and aversion mutually pervade, as do the sense of self, the habitual self, the affective attitude toward the affects themselves, and so on. The affect is both overcome (seen through, become a distal object of aversion) and fulfilled (dwelled in truly, made a center of all, expressing itself as all objects without exception, the privileged proximal object affirmed beyond to a degree far greater than would be possible if it remained a mere distal object of another, more hidden desire, i.e., the desire for desire). "To dwell in it is to be liberated from it," as Zhili said. But he added, "As the dwelling reaches the ultimate, so does the liberation reach the ultimate," and that is the case here too; a desire is originally something we dwell in, but we must do so thoroughly, facing in all directions at once, as it were, and not sparing our own lives. A desire that wishes only to upset, consume, disrupt, challenge and berate the cosmos but not the desirer can never be satisfied, will only return again and again. Only a desire dwelt in so thoroughly as to see and devastate the desirer himself as a plank in its own fire can transform itself unobstructedly, reversibly, intersubsumptively, freely appearing as all other coherences.

Bad Faith versus the Innocence of Becoming: The Moral Benefits of Inherent Evil

There is an intriguing upshot of this which is worth dwelling on here for a moment, which returns us to our discussion of desire and the self, and unexpectedly brings into focus the Nietzschean "innocence of becoming," and pulls new meanings from it. When I "identify" with this cup here to the point of effecting my reversal of positions with it, by making "cup" equal "self" (the unseen proximal term through which all others are experienced), I make object into subject. In so doing, I simultaneously make what had formerly been the subject into an object. In other words, I objectify myself. In this simplest case, the initial "myself" in question would probably be my own body and my own mind as a set of conditions, tendencies, attitudes, dispositions, narratives—that is, whatever I may have been identifying with in my default or neutral mode prior to this reversal with the cup, assuming I am regarding it without strong or persistent desire or aversion. This is perhaps even clearer when I try to identify with something even more obviously considered an "aspect" of myself by common sense; for example, if I experience a moment of rage. Normally I am the substance of which my hatred or rage is an attribute. First, I can detach the object of rage ("that bastard") from the rage ("my hatred for that bastard"), and reverse positions: allow the object to manifest as an expression of rage itself (my hatred manifests *as* that bastard), or, alternately, allow the rage to be perceived from the point of view of the object, to be an aspect of the hated object (that bastard manifests *as* my hatred; that bastard is the substance of which my hatred is one attribute among many). The only escape from the hatred is, as I have said, to become it: I am hatred itself. This means to fully experience it, to see it as impossibility, as inescapable, as freedom, as pure omnidirectional desire, directed toward all possible objects, expressed as "its" entire world, and so on. But I cannot feel myself into "being" this moment of rage unless I make my mind-body into an object. This person, BZ, is "my"—the rage's—the victim. This mind-body organism is now a natural fact, an object or condition which "I" the object, or "I" the desire, am invading, harassing, upsetting, disrupting. It is a fact in the world that there exists this individual BZ, who is obsessed with such and such, who hates his neighbor, who's embarrassed by the shape of his head, etc., in just the same way that it is a fact in the world that the earth has only one moon. No one is responsible for it—as Nietzsche puts it, not God, not history, not fate, not society, not his parents, not his childhood experiences—not BZ himself. Now let "I-ness" belong to the rage, not this person. Here "I" am, this conflagration of rage, joyfully dancing on the head of this BZ, devastating him, upsetting him, disrupting him, smashing him, annoying him, hurting him, and so on. This is indeed freedom "from" the rage, and also freedom "as" the rage. And I would suggest that it is this reinstating of reversibility that lies at the bottom of the liberating experience Nietzsche describes as the innocence of becoming, and even, if one likes, the similar experience described by Spinoza, the regarding of oneself and all particular things by means of adequate ideas which see their built-into-ness in the nature of substance, the impossibility of their absence, the absence of free will, and so on. My point here is that the self-objectification involved in both cases is not really at bottom a kind of fatalism or evasion of moral responsibility, or a dehumanizing mechanization of human spirit. Rather, it is simply a necessary aspect of the reinstatement of full reversibility; *oneself must be fully objectifiable for anything else to stand in the subject position.*

The point here is that, when we Tiantaify this idea, it represents not determinism, but the convergence of absolute freedom and absolute determinism, and indeed shows wherein they end up being alternate names for the same thing. This is obvious if one considers the implications of the universal mutual pervasion of all possible coherences that we have established above—the doctrine that in traditional Tiantai goes by the name "inherent entailment." This means that all possible coherences are already present in/as each coherence. All is there already, there is nothing new, nothing is created when we move from moment to moment; wherever we go, we end up ultimately where we were already, there is no going beyond what one always was already—hence determinism. But since each unit *is* in fact all coherences (omnicentrism), it is a completely arbitrary choice which one will be manifest at any time or in any context, or what will follow from what—hence freedom. This is why full identification as the assumption of necessary impossibility is for us equivalent to freedom, as we have seen. Here, however, it is necessary to stress two points. First, Tiantai thought hereby frees Spinozistic or Nietzschean denials of free will from having to be taken literally. That is, we take them more seriously than they take themselves, and thereby allow them to equal their own opposites, absolute freedom. Second, there are important moral implications to this. For it frees the notion of "self-objectification" from the implication of entailing complete moral bad faith and evasion of responsibility—that is, as when one justifies some set of actions of his which have been called into question: I cannot help what I am, I did not do it, it is just my nature. For the latter would be to claim that my acts were simply in-itself facts, built into the universe, simply the way things are and therefore beyond question, rather than moretoitive coherences whose very nature is to be "called into question," being constitutively problematic and indeed impossible. But in Tiantai thought, it is *precisely for this reason* that they are in fact built into the universe, into "the absolute" or indeed into any other coherence, and therefore beyond question. Indeed, as in the fourth of our Four Ways, their being-beyond-question *is* their questionableness.

On this point, let me repeat: self-objectification is a necessary condition of other-subjectification. So stated, it is obvious that such a position has profound moral implications. Some of these I will take up in the section on intersubjectivity, below; it is important here to point out here, however, that for us true intersubjectivity entails not only I-Thou as opposed to I-It, but also, if you will, It-Thou. No true intersubjectivity in the Tiantai sense is possible if one is constantly clinging to oneself as pure subject, unwilling also to be an object. And, this is not only for obvious subjects, but also for apparent objects, even partial objects, even passing fancies—for any coherence whatsoever. I must be willing to be an "it" even for my own sensation of hunger, or lust, or anger, or curiosity, or worry, allowing these to be the "I" which is using this "it."

In every moment of experience, as we have seen, a multiplicity of components must come together. This multiplicity, we have argued, can be divided in an infinite number of ways, but can never be reduced to a single "one." We could say 3000, or 3 billion, elements come together to form this moment of experience. To simplify, we can enumerate four: (1) the "transcendental ego," i.e., the vague suffused sense of unconditionality which conditions the field of experience; (2) the empirical ego, i.e., my particular set of identifications, a group of contents which are in an explicit relation of intersubsumption with one another; (3) objects situated in a world, with which I come into contact; and (4) the response of my empirical ego to this set of conditions in the world it has contacted, in the form of affects and volitions. These are fitted together to comprise "an experience." There is some fact in the world, there is myself, and "between them" as it were, arising from their contact, there is "my" attitude (emotion and volition) toward it, which is supposed to adjust the relation between these other components, either to alter my "self" to accord with the world, or to alter the world to accord with my "self." Normally, at least one of these is to remain the same while the other(s) are to change to fit in with it, to match it, to adequate it. One of the components is to remain a *simpliciter* fact, which is not to change. Or, the transcendental ego, the non-*simpliciter* all-pervasive coherence applying everywhere and expressed only by everything else in the field, is taken as a meaningful token with some content to it which likewise is not supposed to change, while some other elements are to change so as to come to fit in with these conditions which provide a stable context. A fact emerges, and I have an attitude toward it. An object brings a painful sensation, for example, I have to climb a flight of stairs, bringing an unpleasant sensation of strain. With this comes a reaction—a desire to get rid of this sensation, to be free of it. Both of these are aspects of my world, permeated by the me-ness (transcendental ego) or me-tiredness (empirical ego), the relevance and presencing of which is findable everywhere in the field, but nowhere *simpliciter*. The sensation and reaction are thus initially just what they are, unambiguous, simply located particulars subsumed in "me" as non-simply-located universal. When we speak of "being" the elements of experience here, we mean reversing this relation, as the non-*simpliciter* reversible pervasion of the "self" or "what I am as opposed to what I have" position entails. This means allowing the object and the desire *each* to be the term that "looks upon" or subsumes, the other two. "Myself" (either as my history, commitments, social roles, memories, or as fatigued right now, etc., the empirical ego; or as my sense of being an unconditioned all-pervasive subject, the transcendental ego) and "stairs-to-be-climbed" are seen as aspects of "desire-to-be-free-of-this-sensation," which does not exist except *as* these expressions or aspects, is not discoverable anywhere outside them. Likewise, "myself" (fatigued, etc., or otherwise) and "desire-to-be-free-of-this-sensation" are aspects of "stairs-to-be-climbed," which is nothing but these aspects as which it is expressed. Each term pervades all three, and *is* nothing but a way of reading the other two. Each concept is thus just as much the other concepts as it is itself. None of them is a piece of a larger three-part puzzle. Rather, each is the three-aspected whole. This means that none is simply "what it is," playing the particular role in this three-part relation that conditioned the other two, for *each* is the whole puzzle, with nothing outside it to determinate it as this or that. Each is "free," unconditioned as a "self" is, to express itself as any otherness. This both fulfills and eliminates the original relationship, both preserves and explodes the original identities.

Normally, we easily enough intuit the object and affect as aspects of the self (the "idealist" intuition), or the affect as an aspect of object (our desire bleeds over into the object, so we see only the desirability of the object, rather than the object and our evaluative reaction to it as two separate entities), or even the object as an aspect of the affect (our desire posits the object as its desirable noematum), but rarely are able to see all three as strictly intersubsumptive and reversible. It is this three-way intersubsumption referred to in the passage from Zhiyi cited in the Introduction: the entire field encounters the entire field, and thereby gives rise to the entire field.

Here we see the importance of what was described as the inherent "hostility" or "polemicalness" of all coherences, alluded to briefly in the "Fire Not Burning Itself" section, and also why the description given above of the affect "disrupting" both its object and the self applies not only to anger and aversion, but even to desire and love, or any other affect. Not only every affect, but every coherence per se is a striving to disrupt other coherences—that is, to read itself into them, to subsume them, to establish continuity with them and overcome their exclusive identities. It is obvious too that this can be understood either as love and desire or as hatred and aggression. *To be a coherence is to want to make some other coherence otherwise*, so that it itself gets to stay as it is, maintains its coherence as applied to a broader context, while the other coherence comes to be subsumed therein in some way, on the assumption that initially X is X and Y is Y. X *is* an attempt to makes some set of Ys renounce their appearance of stubborn unambiguous exclusive Yness, either to be destroyed and replaced by more X-expressive coherences or transformed into such. Once it does this not to some set of Ys but to all non-Xs as such, it has moved from contingent to necessary willing, total willing, pervading all parts of the field (in this case, subject, object, and the mediating affect arising between them from their contact), thereby crashing into intersubsumption.

For this project embodied by every coherence, as we have stated it, is obviously impossible. Even as correlative objects, three parts in a puzzle contextualizing one another, each identity is dependent on those of the other two. Even my "unconditioned" sense of self (the transcendental ego) is such *in contrast* to the changing contents of the empirical ego (me-feeling-tired, etc.), and the other contents of consciousness. Me-tired is obviously manifested as such both against my past and the inescapable continuity of the "unconditioned" transcendental ego, but also by the presence of the stairs-to-be-climbed. My volition is most obviously determined by the presence of the feeling-of-stairs to be eliminated, and the transcendental ego (i.e., the sense that "I can exist elsewhere, *away from* this pain") and the empirical ego (the sense that "it would be better for me not to be tired, but at the moment I have to go up the stairs"). The stairs are manifested *as such* not only by their material contexts and components, but also by my empirical ego's project ("have to get up there") and cognitive capacities ("this is a flight of stairs"), and by the transcendental ego's unconditional continuity ("objects are out there in the world, as a field of connections united and contrasted by virtue of the continuous presence of a self to perceive them, pervading the field"). To change some but not all of these is therefore impossible. But this is just what is attempted, on the assumption that they are four separable actual parts of the situation. Most likely I want "pain-giving-stairs" and "volition to get rid of them" (which is otiose once the stairs are gone) to go away or change, leaving the transcendental and empirical ego intact.

Now it is easiest to see that the transcendental ego is nothing in itself, is expressed only *as* the other components. Its *simpliciter* presence is necessarily impossible, hence it is what I currently *am*. When thoroughly and explicitly realized, this makes it clear also that the same status of reversibility applies also to the other "components" of this field. We have, if you will, the transcendental volition, the transcendental pain, the transcendental stairs. The volition finds itself, not just confronting or contextualized by the other elements, but consisting of them, so that it cannot be found apart from them. Hence the coherence "will-to-get-free-of-this-stairs-related-discomfort" permeates transcendental ego, empirical ego, pain and stairs, is present only *as* them. They are collectively readable as "this will." This will hence pervades the field completely by appearing nowhere *simpliciter* within it. This will is unevadable, unobtainable, constitutively impossible, free, expressing itself in any form, uncontrasted to anything outside itself, unconditioned, absolute. I *am* then this "will-to-be-free-of stairs-related-discomfort," which is thereby the one doing the disrupting of the other elements, making them merely its own aspects, readable as itself, as this will.

So in the face of some troublesome condition—anxiety, let us say—it can first be noted that it exists only by being related to something. It must operate on, contrast to, contextualize itself in reference to something *else* in order to be present at all as what it is. For example, it requires my body and mind as the experiencer of it, or a factitious world to give it referential content. Is this "something else" the same or different from the anxiety? If the same, the necessary relation is lacking. If different, what is this "of" relation? It must refer to a tertium quid, some attempted subsumption, some stretching of a single coherence to apply and reveal itself in more than one coherence. But this other coherence, because necessary to the anxiety, ends up polluting and disrupting the "simpliciterity" of the anxiety. Is "anxiety" discoverable in "the experiencer" or "the world about which I am anxious"? If not, no anxiety. If so, intersubsumption. For "X subsumes Y" simply means Y, as Y, instantiates X, or Xness is findable in Yness.

But note also the implications here for the concept of responsibility. I am not responsible for my existence, no one is. Nor am I responsible for this desire or emotion; I did not create it. Nor did anyone else create it; no "one" of any kind can possibly be responsible for it. But this groundlessness, far from implying, "it should not be here," rather is the *only* way to finally establish that "it has (I have) a right to be here." All attempts to *justify* the existence of this coherence by means of a reference to some other—its ground, its purpose, its law—fails miserably in the collapsing of these two into another coherence which again stands in need of justification, hence an infinite regress. As a convenient brother to the point made above about freedom and necessity, we may notice here a perfect coinciding of contingency and necessity. That is, this fleeting groundless occurrence, this passing fancy, is ineradicably built into all possible coherences, all possible experience. All-pervasion *replaces* (fulfills) "logical necessity."

In terms of any one coherence's (e.g., "my") responsibility for itself, and for everything else, it must be said that here self-creation equals total nonresponsibility, and that self-creation is none other than this being built into all possible coherences. We may hereby make sense of Freud's remark that most people are not only much less moral than they think they are, but also much more moral than they think they are. That is, that cup is myself as cup; that hatred is myself as hatred; equally, I am that cup as myself, that hatred as myself. This is so whether that hatred is my hatred of you, or your hatred of me. In either case, I must embody it; it faces me and makes me into an object, a simple inextricable fact of the universe. Once I take responsibility for all these coherences, including those that are "out there" in this sense, I am in the same gesture myself made into something for which no one is responsible. So by reversal, if I "take responsibility" for everything (as we always already do, deep down; one may think here of the categorical imperative, or the Sartrean notion that everything I do is necessarily a model for all humans) we are delivered of responsibility for ourselves; all beings are responsible for what I do, and vice versa. The key here is again reversibility.

The theists like the realists and Spinoza are right in pointing to complete "other-power," but wrong in deeming it to be a "one" of any kind. If the impossibility of its oneness or manyness is perceived (hence, its interpenetrative but infinite multifariousness), other-power equals self-power.

Pushing the ethical implication a step further, a claim must be made here for the moral efficacy of this notion. This is traditionally what is called the ethical importance of the notion that evil is ineradicable, which Tiantai thinkers regard as providing the sole condition for moral improvement. Why?

The evil accomplished in the Absolute—that is, which is ineradicable, no matter what one does or where one goes, for which no one and nothing is responsible—makes it unnecessary to do evil oneself. Normally, the evil possibility ("You know, I could just kill her and get the insurance money") presents itself as something I must *do* something about—either "make good" on it (suppress it, repent it), or fulfill it (accomplish it). Some condition in the world or myself calls for some further remedial action. In either case, this means bringing it back to "Reality" in some sense, justifying it, erasing the sense that it is a contingent aberration which I, or some other one, simply decided "for no good reason" to create. An attempt is made at adequation, at matching to parts of a broader whole together, at adjusting a relation between parts, of changing some set of the totality of beings to accord with some other part which remains unchanged. The same impulse lies behind realizing my desire and making good on it (repenting it) with the Absolute—truth, or the moral law, or my notion of my own decency, etc. Inherent evil means it has already been done (along with everything else) in the Absolute, and indeed is always inescapably being done everywhere and by everyone; no need then to go on. The affair is over as soon as the impulse is registered. As long as subjective experience, moral and immoral impulses, volitions, are regarded as "groundless" (nonadequated, not fitting into a proper place in the total array of coexisting coherences, including putative standards of value) *as opposed to some other coherences which are genuinely grounded*—the ethical substance, physical reality, God, matter—they "stick out" in a way that calls for *another volition*—that is, something else which will ground them, put them into their proper place in reality. If their proper place is already given—they are an integral part of every other possible coherence, they are, as we have seen, "already adequated" in the precise sense that no adequation is possible, either for them or for any other coherence with which they could putatively be adequated—this subsequent volition is uncalled for, does not arise. There is no "what to do about it" about them; everything has already been done. My claim is that "evil" volitions, in this case, simply fizzle out without the added impetus to "make good" on them, either as actions and hence realities, or as repented perverse evil thoughts which have no good reason for being there. They have always been there and will always be there. They can be there *as* all other things, and vice versa. Their reversibility with these others is unimpeded if they are allowed this (non)place in the (non)scheme of things, on equal footing with the Grand Canyon and the Pythagorean theorem, and hence there is no longer anything objectionable about their "evil," which, in this fully realized, intersubsumptive form, is also appearing *as* all other coherences, from the most virtuous to the most debased.

In passing, these reflections allow us to specify at least three functions of the gods/symbols/metaphysical realm, of the ideals we gives ourselves:

1. As model: the holy god, the pure sage, the pure mind. Nietzsche complains: this devalues real life.

2. As company and justification: the naughty gods, the literary heroes. Plato complains: this is a poor model for humankind.

3. As compensation: this means really either of the previous, picked up from the wrong end. The naughty gods mean we do not have to bother to be naughty ourselves; we can practice good Hellenic ethical culture and moderation, in contrast to the gods. The holy god, on the other hand, means we do not have to be holy ourselves; all we need to do is have faith in this completely other Good being. We can sin as long as we have faith in the sinlessness of Jesus or Amida. The gods are wicked or virtuous *in our place*. It is already taken care of. It is already fully established in the real, in complete power. No further adequation is required.

The Tiantai Buddha, let us note, does all three of these, by means of an insight into the reversibility between 1 and 3, on the one hand, but also between 2 and 3, on the other, that is, the fact that in either case they are the same content picked up from opposite sides (a deployment of the Three Truths). This Buddha is evil—so he is good company for the evil, justifies, shares in and affirms reality, but also goads the good by making it unnecessary to do evil, making contrasting human ethics possible. This Buddha is good—so he is a good model for humankind, but he does this by not devaluing the evil, but rather by having lived it and incorporated it himself; faith in his perfection allows all practices, however evil, to be read as valid and efficient forms of spiritual practice. It is this third category that reveals the real moral power of the doctrine of inherent, all-pervasive, and ineradicable evil.

So the Tiantai thinker turns out not only to be a coincidence of Zen and Hegel, a Zenny Hegel; he must also be a coincidence of existentialism and Spinoza, an existential Spinoza, or a Kantian Nietzsche.

Ethical "Layering"

One way of restating some of the ethical implications of the Tiantai view of coherences is to speak of it in terms of a kind of "layering." That is, since coherences can and must function *as* each other, we have an infinitely broad range of what kind of coherences may be included in any form of the Good, by whatever definition might be set up at any time. Circles can be constitutive of triangles; similarly, neuroses can be constitutive of health, evil impulses of good impulses, malice of benevolence and so on. My neuroses and selfishness and malice do not have to be replaced or eliminated; they can be combined in certain ways to form new figures at other levels of attention and analysis, as combining into single tokens that form part of another higher-level figure. Once again, as we will see in our discussion of time as well, the essence of Neo-Tiantai ethics lies in recontextualization, rather than elimination or substitution (and, of course, this means also that we do not call for the "elimination" of elimination or substitution, or that recontextualization be "substituted" for them; they too can be recontextualized). My obsession or compulsion or stupidity or malice may be seen, when the camera draws back to the right distance, as it were, as a point in a curve describing bliss, generosity, health, and so on. The question lies then in how far back the camera is to be drawn. And the implication is that at any level of focus or analysis we may be resting at, it would be possible to push forward and discover that our present figure is made up of plenty of components that are horrible when judged by its standard, and vice versa; there need be no final level at which this process must stop.

Indeed, the indistinguishability of self and other, the inherent reversibility of these two structural positions which mark any experience, also reverses the ethical valence of any act, for I can always find myself to be standing on either side of the relation. What is from one side an imposition is on the other side an enjoyment, and I am not "simply located" on either side. This is perhaps most commonly seen in the pervasive power of the affect of *emulation* that seems to come into play to ambiguate all interpersonal relations. When I harm you, I impinge on you, but simultaneously also benefit you by providing you with a *model* of happiness, and even vicarious happiness. I am mortified and cheated by your selfishness, but also liberated by it, inspired by it; for that is also what I am, that also intersubsumes with what I am now, the victim, and I find myself standing over there on the other side even in the moment I perceive it. This principle has vast ethical implications, and must be understood even if its effects are to be prevented (i.e., in self-victimizing identifications with the oppressor, etc.), in the interest of some local standard of ethical desirability. But it can be counteracted only by being fully developed, for it will always be true that victims enjoy their victimization and that victimizers suffer their crimes as well, for identity, as experienced, simply cannot be restricted to any finite position within the field of experience, nor made to exclude any contents which are presented to it in whatever form. The implications are neither unilateral nor obvious. But we will have more to say about this below.

Personality as Symptom and as Pregnancy

A few remarks are in order here on the tricky question of how we view the value of the specificity of the finite self we have been describing, or the question of personality. Our reflections lead us to the following conclusions on this point. Personality is first and foremost a symptom, an aberration, a distortion to the pure flow, an obsessive protective device shaped in the shape of a given organism's particular cage, to borrow the Nabokovian image. Indeed, this image is quite exact: One becomes exactly what one could not escape, what haunted one either as object of desire or as hateful imposition. The personality one ends up with is the photographic negative of that trap one found oneself in, or a kind of defensive framework surrounding our former disaster sites.

But personality is not for this reason to be finally excluded from even these forms of the intersubsumptive flux, and in the final analysis, although personality is unmistakably a disease, as Nietzsche said of bad conscience,[30] it is so only as pregnancy is a disease: it is a first step toward a reaction formation which more than makes up for the disease. To learn how to flex and unflex this muscle is everything; building on these symptoms, a human being realizes his reversibility with whatever he is thereby constituting as the impersonal cosmos, it is his passageway in, and, to use the traditional language instead of the Lacanian *wo es war*. . ., a Buddha is simply a personality who has become all that his non-personality was. What is objectionable in the personal notion of deity is not that he has personality but that he only has one personality. The Buddhanature as substratum for billions of different Buddhas, who are identical with it and each of whom fully embodies it, reverses this judgment. To become enlightened is to become a personality, and every personality, of the world.

What is it that personality provides, once perfected? A certain direction of libidinal specificity, an angle from which to develop outwards towards the whole and fill in every quality. Sublimation: an anal personality, for example, may be a symptom of renounced infantile anal erotism. But these ugly traits too must be filled into the picture, they too are necessary for a Buddha's personality; they are objectionable only when they are compulsive or automatic, when the possessor cannot help being that way. But as part of his arsenal of character traits, to be used, for example, in the Bodhisattva practice of enlightening beings, they must be possessed and mastered. This would mean to be able to draw on all the old personalities of the past, even on their infantile roots, to be able to feel the entire process still present and tap into it at

---

[30] Friedrich Nietzsche, *On the Genealogy of Morals*, trans. Walter Kaufmann and R. J. Hollingdale (New York: Vintage, 1969), Second Essay, sec. 19, p. 88.

any part. To feel pleasure in being anyone and everyone, feeling its libidinal roots and the satisfaction of the neurotic symptom. What was originally an unconscious reaction formation becomes conscious, part of the expanding ego, and therefore also reveals its opposite as a new possibility. Thereby one grows, thereby one gains more and more symptoms, and their opposites. To possess every possible symptom, and be able to deploy them at will, is to be a Buddha. Here we may recall our discussion of the "three bodies" of the Buddha in traditional Tiantai dogmatics. Each, as we saw, is an aspect of the others; there *is* no pure world of intersubsumptive mutual pervasion (the *Dharmakāya*) except as an aspect of some finite being's personal experience (*Sambhogakāya*) and/or of that being's socially visible body (*Nirmāṇakāya*), and vice versa.

Buddha *Sive* Time *Sive* the Inscrutability of the Other *Sive* the Inscrutability of the Future . . . Or: The *Samadhi* of Not Knowing What You're Doing

I have not backed away from occasionally using the unwieldy term "Buddha" in this discussion, in spite of the plentiful obstructive side-effects that might come with doing so, most notably the confusion and even alienation of a large number of readers. It is only fair that I do some close specifying of what I mean by this sticky term. When Spinoza, Hegel, and others insist for whatever reason on using the term "God," they both intensify and alter its original scholastic meaning as creator, lawgiver, judge, savior, and so on, in an attempt to boil down and purify these meanings; but as we have seen above abundantly, to purify, to make something more itself, is already to change it without changing it. We will be doing something of the same thing for the term Buddha in the sense of "Awakener."

I have already stated that we need not worry about "there never being a punch line," that the question, "What if the truth never dawns" is moot. We do not need truth—we have delusion, which is more than enough, which does more positing of truth than even truth ever could, precisely by being delusion, by constantly falling apart, by its inevitable self-undermining. The absence of truth, "universalized," is the truth. This is, of course, a kind of transformation of the question, "What if there is no Buddha?" That is, in the old-fashioned Tiantai sense, if everything depends on the ten realms interpenetrating, what if that realm called the Buddha-realm just is not there to interpenetrate? It is to make clear the meaninglessness of this concern that we have to specify more closely what is meant by Buddha here, which will lead us directly into the questions of *time* and *intersubjectivity*.

"Boiling it down" as promised, the term "Buddha" in a Tiantai context means both

(1) "the big Other" in the God sense, that is, *not* God as creator but God as "omniscient" observor, who sees not only all relevant data but understands it all thoroughly. What that means here is of course seeing asness thoroughly, and seeing you in your delusion as Intersubsumption incarnate. The Buddha is himself a thorough embodiment of intersubsumptive asness, which means also seeing all other coherences as asness itself, that is, as himself. The term "Buddha" also means (2) your own *future*, and that of all other deluded beings, what you will become, the "punch line to come." This in-the-future-ness must be accepted as essential to the definition of Buddhahood per se, if we accept the classical Tiantai insistence that all ten realms, that is both delusion and Buddhahood, can never be eliminated. This will also apply to "in-the-past-ness" and "in the present-ness qua protentions and retentions." The presence of Buddhahood in delusion is felt not only as the clear-sighted observer gazing back at us, but also as the *anticipated retrospection* on itself, which this present delusion expects will see itself, this delusion with its anticipation right now, as an expression of itself. These two are the same gaze, backwards and toward the opposite other. The themes of temporality and intersubjectivity are forever tied together here, as we shall return to in a moment. Now, however, let it be made clear that, given this anticipated omniscient retrospection, there is no need for the retrospection to ever happen as such—indeed, it would be impossible for it to happen as such. The Buddha cannot be Buddha *simpliciter*; indeed, Buddhahood is the consciousness of the impossibility of any thing being anything *simpliciter*. It is the intuition of ineluctable Intersubsumption or reversible asness. The Buddha, as we know from traditional Tiantai dogmatics, must be the Buddha *as* something and must also be something *as* the Buddha. This is the upshot of the traditional doctrine of the indestructibility and Intersubsumption of the ten realms. Delusion is thus the *sine qua non* of Buddhahood. The mark of Buddhahood is the unhindered reversibility between these two, what Intersubsumption is appearing as and Intersubsumption appearing as this something.

This, however, means also the unhindered reversibility between the seer (the Buddha) and the seen (the deluded being), and also between the future (Buddha, punch line) and the past (you, setup). To anticipate this seeing of oneself (which is identical in its deadpan reversibility with being seen as such) is Buddhahood already. In other words, just to have the idea of Buddhahood is to have entertained the possibility of yourself looking back on yourself as a prior expression/setup for that retrospection which so sees you. This is an artful coincidence of sameness and difference which is precisely parallel to the epistemological amnesty we are granting ourselves here, and one which has great importance for the questions of temporality/intersubjectivity.[31] Just to posit "the Buddha" as a possible object—that is, as a coherence, a possible possible—is to be seen by the Buddha (since Buddhahood = awakening to, being aware of whatever ever appears, to anyone, to be there), which is to be the Buddha (since the type of seeing or awareness peculiar to Buddhahood is such that seeing is identical to being, that is, the Buddha is one who *is* whatever he sees, who can "be" whatever he "has" or encounters). This is like knowing that what one is hearing is a setup, or more precisely, like the humorousness of the very notion that anything *could* be thought of as funny. Here we have one way of grasping the *performative* nature of the very idea "Buddhahood" in Tiantai. We will find that this is structurally somewhat analogous to Anselm's ontological argument for the existence of God, or Descartes's *cogito*, in that the mere positing of the idea, the question at hand, is to serve as its own fulfillment and guarantee. For the very idea of "Buddhahood" in this sense, if so much as mentioned or entertained, already guarantees its own reality. The punch line, to go back to our earlier example, is self-positing: it is, as noted, as if one were to apprehend that the notion that "humor is possible" is itself funny. Imagine a case where to think that anything *could* be funny to someone makes me laugh; in this case, the *possibility* of humor is identical to the *actual appearing* of humor. "He might think I think his actions are funny, he might think I am secretly laughing at him, his apparently innocent and solemn actions, and my serious response to them, are so unfixed that they could conceivably be taken as humor—how hilarious!" Close observation of the acquisition of the sense of humor in small children may well confirm that this intersubjective feedback loop is really the *basic* structure of all humor.[32] The reason this applies in the present case is simply that the notion of Buddhahood is of something that appears even in its nonappearance (is

---

[31] This is borne out by the traditional Tiantai advocacy of Pure Land practices and the Japanese Tendai *hongaku* notion that Buddhahood is achieved upon attaining the "identity of name," i.e., at the moment of hearing about this idea that you are identical to the Buddha in this way, and taking it seriously as a thought. We may also think here of the predictions of Buddhahood in the *Lotus*, pointing to the presence of Buddhahood as inherently in-the-future, but present everywhere in this form. Also, the suddenness of this present of postponement is obvious in the story of the Naga girl, and the claim that, in the tenseless Chinese version of Kumārajīva, to say, "Hail Buddha" is equivalent to being enlightened.

[32] We may think also of the doctor in the Frank Oz film *What About Bob*; the patient has come to perceive his technique as so radical that any action whatsoever on the part of the doctor, including attempting to murder the patient, is perceived by the latter as a daring new form of therapy, and by this very token it functions effectively as therapy—i.e., it is in fact therapy. There are indeed quite a few Tiantai overtones in this film; it could easily be viewed as an extended meditation on the relationship between delusion and enlightenment, or Buddhahood and ordinary beings, in Tiantai thought.

intersubsumptive with its absence), guaranteed already by the *removal* (or even recontextualization) of the former baseless assumption that the identity of anything could ever be definitively fixed. If it cannot, then anything can possibly come to be seen as an exemplification of anything, and hence of a state of something that appears in its own nonappearing, which indeed is simply the principle of "anything can come to be seen as anything else" itself. To put it naïvely-pathetically, the only guarantee that "things turn out well" in this sense is simply that things are continually turning out badly, well, or otherwise, that things are always turning out to be other than they appear, that things cannot stop "turning out" to be one way or another. Every single event is always both the setup of some punch line and the punch line of some setup. An unexpectedly "bad" result guarantees this form of goodness as well as an unexpectedly "good" one. All that is needed is for the identity of all things to be continually changing in retrospect, or rather the non-appearance of any means that can successfully and decisively prevent this from happening, the continual jerking around of punch-lines that is our lived experience of time, to guarantee the presence of Buddhahood in the Tiantai sense.

In other words, to have the idea "recontexualization," even as a possibility, is already to have recontextualized all of one's experience. The word or notion "recontextualization" itself recontexualizes everything, provides a new element to the frame around the given which changes its meaning. Buddhahood can be said to be something whose possibility is the same as its actuality, somewhat like the old theological God, but it would be better to describe it as possibility as such, or even *the possibility of possibility*—which, it will be recalled, was precisely our definition of what it means to be a "coherence" per se. Is "possibility" (i.e., that there is more here than meets the eye, that the meaning of things might be changed when some unknown other thing dawns, that there is a relevant unseen back to this coherence) at least possible? Can such a notion be even fleetingly entertained? If so, you are already a Buddha. In the classic Mahāyāna formula, *samsara* is nirvana, delusion is enlightenment, impermanence is Buddha-nature.

We see this sort of thing in the favorite Tiantai *Lotus* parables (burning house, lost son, illusory city[33]), all of which indicate that one is doing *more*

---

[33] Briefly: the heedlessly playing children leave the burning house under the false assumption that they are going to get certain toys out there; the poor son is hired by his unrecognized wealthy father and made to perform years of menial tasks, being unable to accept his real status, until finally it is revealed to him that he is the natural born inheritor of the estate; the travelers are dissuaded from turning back on their long journey by the appearance of an splendid city conjured by their wise guide, where they regain their energy and spirit to pursue the treasure beyond. The false goals of toys, earned wages, and the splendid city all turn out to be illusory goads to the real, hitherto unthought-of goal beyond. At the same time, all their steps toward the false goals turn out to have been steps toward the real goals.

than one thinks, that one does not know the nature of one's own thoughts and actions, that one can be, and hence *must* be, a Bodhisattva without knowing it. This means that one's previous actions and perceptions *just as they are* are already causes and also results of Buddhahood. "One need not change one's course" in order to be practicing the Bodhisattva course, as Zhiyi says. To be a Buddha is simply to be exactly as one is right now, *only more so*. To experience as a Buddha experiences is just to experience simply as you are experiencing right now, *only more so*.

There is a looping of the two fundamental categories "ends" and "means" here. The means "vanish" (are sublated) into the end—that is, the means are the perception of the end, and ultimately, the means are the end (or, more strictly, in the setup/punch-line structure we have described, means = means/end and end = means/end, and therefore means = end). On the one hand, Buddha (enlightenment) is the end and delusion (the nine other realms) are the means. But at the same time, Buddhahood is the means and the nine realms are the end (*upāyic* transformation into all forms on the basis of Buddhahood). To reach the effect is simply to see more completely the nature of the cause. There is necessarily both a contrast and identity between them. It is this reversibility of subject and object, of the seen and unseen centers, which characterizes Buddhahood.

A moment of "enlightenment" in the Tiantai context means the following: to see all possible and real entities as expressions of, causes of, and effects of Buddhahood. Cause and effect are here equally eternal, *in that* neither ever definitely dawns *simpliciter*. All forms of activity are practices leading to Buddhahood. All forms of activity are (have always been, will always be) also the salvific activity of accomplished Buddhahood. Moreover, all are inherent in the nature of Buddhahood as principle or nature.

The crucial point not to be missed here is the implications of this concept of the observer and the future, and their parallel, indeed coincident, structure. That is, the relation between moments in time must be conceived as an *intersubjective* relation, and this relation must be understood in terms of the universal asness of the setup/punch-line relation. I have argued elsewhere for the importance of the category of intersubjectivity in classical Tiantai. Here I will forego the technical details of this argument and simply review the conclusions relevant to our present discussion. By "intersubjectivity" I mean here as there the impact on any given subjectivity created by the existence of other subjectivities. That is to say, I am assuming there is a difference between the way a conscious being feels itself related to another being with a putatively similar consciousness and the way it feels itself related when in the presence of what it regards as insentient beings. The intersubjective relation might include such things as the apprehension of being apprehended, the sense of being seen, of being challenged, confronted and judged by an independent, unpredictable other with an unseen interiority like one's own, the thought of being thought about, expressed perhaps as the desire to impress, inspire, intimidate, please. When I speak of the *primacy* of intersubjectivity, I mean the idea that in an important sense intersubjectivity is in fact prior to, and more fundamental than, subjectivity per se, i.e., the inner sense of a given individual consciousness taken in isolation, without explicit reference to any other such consciousness.[34] This implies that individual consciousnesses, in spite of their inner sense of being independent of one another, are actually codependent poles of the intersubjective relationship, and only come into existence as a by-product of a prior proto-aware intersubjective relation.

The connection between this conception and all we have said so far about Intersubsumption as deadpan reversibility should not be hard to discern. The primacy of intersubjectivity can be looked upon as another way of understanding the impossibility of reducing all to any one center, the necessary partial success as ultimate failure of all centers, as played out in the particular context of the subject/object paradigm developed above. Indeed, intersubjectivity is just one more name of Intersubsumption itself, construed through the focal settings of a particular subset thereof, a particular local context.[35]

We have already established that "properties are theft," i.e., that no coherence definitively belongs to anyone or anything—not to a particular person, not to the intersubjective network, not to the laws of nature, not to God, not to matter, not to the Idea, not to the Will, not to "the World"; none of these has the power to determine once and for all the limits of the other coherences

---

[34] Intersubjectivity is to be understood here in the sense which was introduced into Western accounts of human subjectivity by Hegel's *Phenomenology of Spirit* (1807), especially but far from exclusively in the famous Master-Slave section so important to Marx, in which was embedded the dialectical claim that a self-consciousness can only be constituted (come into being) through the mediation of (at least the belief in) another self-consciousness. For an influential semi-modern account stressing the intersubjective aspect, see Alexandre Kojevé, *Introduction to the Reading of Hegel* (New York: Basic Books, 1969), esp. 3–30.

[35] This partial success as ultimate failure must also, of course, be applied to "intersubjectivity" itself, considered as a particular coherence. That is, when I assert its primacy, I do so in order to temporarily undermine the still commonsense notion that subjectivities exist prior to their interrelation; but, strictly speaking, it would be just as grievous an error to assume the contrary, that intersubjectivity is substantially prior to subjectivity. We may prefer to say that wherever there is subjectivity, there is also discoverable intersubjectivity, and also the contrary, which is too obvious to be stated and hence is de-emphasized here. That is, subjectivity in the solipsistic sense can serve as a setup that can be revealed to have always already been intersubjectivity, its punch line, without changing in the least. Intersubjectivity can also be the setup to the punch line of solipsistic subjectivity. This is the way we understand the simultaneous mutual exclusivity, mutual identity, and complementarity that constitutes all omnicentric relations.

discoverable in any coherence, to say once and for all what it is. Whatever coherence is appearing at any particular time and context "belongs" in this sense as much to one of these as to any other, and to any other person as much as to the person who is currently experiencing it. All have equal rights to it, which is to say, no absolute rights to it at all. We have seen already that the apparent absence of this coherence may be construed precisely as its hyperpresence, in the form of susceptibility to it and its power to rewrite all other coherences which have no way of closing themselves off to its influence. This applies also to the subject-object relation, as we have seen, where the positions of being and having are strictly, omnicentrically, complementary/exclusive/identical. It also applies to the question of agency and will. What this means is that any coherence I am experiencing—let us say, a pang of regret—belongs as much to the table and chair, to the Lincoln Memorial, to Genghis Khan, to the Vienna Boys Choir and to you, as to me. The agent who is "performing" this regret can with equal justifiability be described as me, the event I am regretting itself, my unconscious complexes which fixate on it, the table and chair, the Lincoln Memorial, Genghis Kahn, the Vienna Boys Choir and you, and also equally to any combination of these elements, or to the whole set of them, or to simply the relations between the terms. Which is the most accurate description of "who is doing this regret" is strictly *undecidable*. That is to say, what is really of primary importance in this talk of intersubjectivity is precisely the eternal *inscrutability of the Other*, and what follows therefrom, as we all "know": the inscrutability of the self.

The very fact that we cannot see how we are seen by the other, that there is the possibility that we are being seen in some way that is "other" to any finite set of guesses about what the other sees, leads us directly into the arms of the self-posited Buddha-gaze seeing us as itself. For if this could be excluded, if we know for sure that that chair over there, or that cat, or that belligerent drunk on the subway, was *not* a Buddha appearing *as* such and such, we would know something definitively about what the other is experiencing. This would be possible only if that "experience" were itself a genuinely *simpliciter* coherence, incapable of being altered in its nature by further recontextualizations. But the foreclosure of that blind spot of experience is absolute; just this constitutively elusive fact of our relation with the other, that we can never know what she thinks, allows us to entertain the possibility that she is a Buddha seeing us as a Buddha, which is all that is required to have infected our actuality (the coherence which is our "real self," which, as we have long known, is only constituted by the objectification achieved by the other's look) with the possibility of alternate possibilities, *eternally and inexhaustibly* alternate possibilities. In other words, to exist is to be seen and to be judged, to be constitutively at-a-distance and exposed to the unclosable possibility of incorporation and saturation by other coherences. More: to exist is always already to be seen and judged in *all possible ways*. But to be seen or judged as X is, by our epistemological premises, all that is required for something to *be* X. That shabby sense of being is all the being there is anywhere. If it is possible to doubt what the other is seeing us as, the structure of asness has forever occupied all of experience, and this is precisely the pervasion of Buddhahood. This inscrutability of the other, as perpetual anxiety, is a pretty good definition of our worst suffering as well, and why not; here we have it once again, the strict identity as exclusivity as complementarity of suffering and bliss, delusion and enlightenment.

But as we have seen, this intersubjective relation is for us also a temporal relation; it is one moment of experience looking forward to or back to another moment and subsuming it into itself as an expression of itself, as a factor in the coherence which it is constituting as center. The point is that this same inscrutability applies here as well. Me of brushing my teeth ten minutes ago is as inscrutable to me of now stretching my back as are me and that guy sitting across from me on the train. How that past would be viewed by this present and future—these can never be beyond doubt. What will be made of this point in time, what punch line futures it will be made to serve as a setup for, is something it can never know. The assymetry we found in the enlightenment/delusion relation here accounts precisely for the directionality of time. All coherences are revisable by future coherences, future moments which will recontextualize, absorb, and thereby transform them. This sense of revisability, of not having yet closed itself off, of not yet being sure of what it means, is endemic to all present moments; we call it "having a future." The coincidence of time, consciousness and negation has been noted many times in the past two hundred years, and here, too, we must assert their identity. For time to exist is for any given X to also not be X; this X not being just X is what it is to be aware of X, awareness of X. This is precisely the Three Truths. The moment is the cresting wave of Intersubsumption, the punch line always just being cracked, the transformative recontextualization of all previously established coherences. What comes before is emptied, ambiguated, but also thereby posited; what comes after is posited as the new meaning of the whole, but in the process also negated as such.

Indeed, we can deploy the fundamental Tiantai categories to give a very precise description of the structure of time per se. The past is Local Coherence; the future is Global Incoherence. More strictly, pastness per se, as a coherence that is always applicable in all situations, is Local Coherence— that is, facticity, fixity, definiteness, determinate conditions. Futureness is Global Incoherence—that is, moretoitivity, uncertainty, openness. Intersubsumption (All-pervasion as All-pervadedness) is the Present, or presentness as such—as we have seen, Intersubsumption is the identity, the actual being of any coherence. This means here the positing/negating process itself, whereby both the humor and the seriousness come to pervade both halves of the relation, the functioning that we call time. As we can see, as the traditional writers constantly reiterate, each of the three actually functions as all three (posits, negates, and pervades), a fitting model for what they ensure all other coherences do. That is, as for all such Tiantai divisions and designations, we must immediately rewrite this partial characterization. Strictly speaking, each of the three dimensions of time is all three, is simultaneously Local Coherence, Global Incoherence and Intersubsumption, is past, present, and future. Pastness is Global Incoherence and Intersubsumption *as* Local Coherence; pastness is presence and futureness *as* the past. Futureness is Local Coherence and Intersubsumption *as* Global Incoherence; futureness is past and present *as* future. Presentness is Local Coherence and Global Incoherence *as* Intersubsumption ; presentness is past and future *as* present. This last example is in fact particularly useful in comprehending the difference and identity of the Three Truths; for past and future are present here as this moment, as aspects of this moment, having no other existence, and yet are forever clearly distinguishable dimensions opposed to presentness as such. There is no past and future outside the present, and yet the three are eternally distinct. The Tiantai view, once again avoiding the Exclusive Center, goes beyond this commonsensical paradox to add two more: there is no past and present outside the future; there is no present and future outside the past. All time is nothing but past, all time is nothing but future, all time is nothing but present, and yet the three are distinct and opposed. It is in this way that we must understand the Fourth Way of being thus and otherwise, i.e., that continuity is discontinuity. For we want to claim here both that time is absolutely discrete, breakable into quanta indefinitely, privileging momentariness and the division into separable coherences, *and* the never-ending-ness of every moment, the all-pervasiveness of each coherence as such, the permeability of moments and the inadequacy of any notion of the atomicity of moments and coherences. They pervade *because* they are absolutely separate, and even more, their mutual pervasion *is* their separation, and vice versa.

Put otherwise, for time to pass is for some setup to be transformed by some punch line, and so on. Time is self-recontextualization. This means also, however, the pre-established *intersubjectivity* of the relation of anticipated retrospection that characterizes Buddhahood; time is subjectivity/intersubjectivity, negation, the inscrutability of the other (moments). Nothing has quite happened yet; everything is still happening. A moment aware of its inability to come to a close, to conclude itself, to deliver its final punch line which cannot be overturned, is thereby overturned already by the omnipresent never-appearing punch line, the coherence "punch line" that is thus inescapable and unobtainable, and reveals the same to be the case for every other coherence.

Indeed, we may in passing perhaps suggest that the most basic malady of the human will is in effect a *confusion* of the three tenses of time, at the expense of their intersubsumption. That is, the unison that in fact pertains to them as intersubsumption is mistaken by the will for an immediate interchangeability. At the most obvious level, we may characterize the three tenses as follows: The past is what cannot be changed. The present is what is *changing*, but cannot *be* changed (by an act of will; the will is always already too late to change the present). The future is what can be changed. Indeed, anything determinate, as we have seen, anything that can be taken as a definite object of the will in one way or another, is already past, and this goes for apparently "present" conditions as well. The mantra appropriate to any fact about which one has already become aware would be, "This is already past. This already cannot be changed by an act of will." But normally we treat the present as the future, and try to act upon it by means of the will. To remedy this we have to first separate the three aspects, and then rejoin them in their true intersubsumptive form of unity. No willing is appropriate vis-à-vis the past or present, since not one jot or tittle of it can be eliminated or altered thereby. But at the same time, all of it can be altered—by *adding* some further volition, or letting an existing volition cease, by an addition that recontextualizes the unchangeable past, rather than substituting anything for any part of it. The will is mistaken when it tries to exchange any possible for any existent; what it can do is only recontextualize the whole by means of the whole—self-recontextualization. The future is recontextualization itself. But once this division is clear, the real interpenetration of the tenses comes to be revealed. For now we see that the past cannot be changed—but it can be changed, and indeed is inevitably always changed, by every molecule of future, which is always recontextualizing it. The past cannot be changed but can and must be changed. The present is changing but cannot be changed, but at the same time it can be changed, in its aspect of already-completeness, its own pastness, and also does not change. The future can be changed—but cannot be changed, for it has no being to be changed. The future is not a field where possibles can be substituted for actuals either, for it contains no actuals to be substituted for. Hence we find all three tenses equally changeable and equally unchangeable, in their own distinctive sense, each of which is revealed to be the other two senses *as* this particular sense of changeability and unchangeability. The will is fundamentally restructured when its apprehension of time follows these contours, recontextualizing rather than substituting. We may recall here the discussion of possibility and actuality in the Introduction. There is no fixed field of actuals into which some possibles can be fitted, effecting a *partial* substitution. Instead, the entire field of actuals, precisely by being fully actualized, crashes, thereby revealing itself *in toto* to be the alternate possibilities which recontextualize it. This is just what it means to say, "Time passes."

This applies not only to the will, but to the use and abuse of Reason as well. The proper function of Reason is to discern universality and necessity, not to coerce consensus or even, be it said, to guide future actions directly or independently. A certain mental labor, which we have instantiated, for example, in this text, is necessary for discerning the manner in which my already given motivations and feelings do not belong (exclusively) to me—seeing my anger, for example, as a natural or social phenomenon, its animal past, its possible futures, its haunting of every other coherence, its fulfillment of infinite unknown vows, and so on. But this anger itself arises without the intervention of any particular effort at reasoning, nor does it need to. In other words, Hegel was right in a sense when he said the Owl of Minerva flies at dusk; Reason has no legitimate guiding or prescriptive function, it deals only with the past. However, it is to be remembered that in Tiantai the past is the truth of Local Coherence, which also intersubsumes with the present and future as the other Two Truths, as seen above. This implies, we may say, that Reason can deal with the future *qua past*, i.e., seen in its aspect of being inherently entailed in the past, as, for example, in causal projections. This is a predictive function that bears explicitly with it a sense of its own fallibility in its orientation to the future, not prescription, which claims the ability to legislate for the future. But even prescriptive reason plays a role in the *upāya* of cultivation. It backfires, however, if used directly to try to influence future acts, or command compliance and consensus.

Hence, to return to the problem raised in the earlier section, continuity and coherence as such are always already forms of intersubjective compassion. This sort of solidarity between moments is prior to any and all specific conflicts, in the sense that it makes them possible; for the coherence of the combatants depends on the "principle of charity" applied in both directions. One must be assuming a coherence to find it; one must assume interpretability, a similarity to oneself, or a continuity with oneself, to even perceive the thing in question. The relations between moments of one's own experience, or any past and present, is already one of compassionate opening up and transformative self-recontextualization, a way of freeing the previous moment from its apparent *simpliciter* finitude and revealing it to be, first, an expression of the present, and second, asness itself, which is to say, to reveal the previous moment to be that which is expressing itself as the present moment, a center in its own right. In all cases we have both an immediate ignorant starting point ("Local Coherence") and a compassionate response to it to a greater or lesser degree, a revelation of its reversible intersubsumptive asness, and, further, the identity of the ignorance and the compassion, the fact that they are one and the same token, accomplished as both by one and the same act, self-recontextualizing.

It should be obvious, however, that this sort of always-prior solidarity between all perspectives may manifest itself in many disturbing ways; torture and rape, on this account, are appeals to this prior seeing-as-being-seen as the primal condition of all being, they are modes of participating with others, communicating with others, invoking a prior togetherness, which for us means also a primal reversibility. We may want to hurt and maim as an expression of this primal attraction and sympathy, the fact that we want to be felt on the other side, to be the other side, to be the receiver as well as the giver, as an expression of the primal Intersubsumption which is implicit in being. The disclosure of the latter is what qualifies such activities, this often-horrifying solidarity, for the traditional name given it in Tiantai thought: compassion, as a primal, all-pervasive condition of being. In short, all acts can be viewed as both habitual-delusional passions (passivities), closings-off into denials of reversibility, suffering, and equally as instances of solidarity, "compassion," founded in and expressing the fundamental reversibility which threatens, underwrites, subtends them, as responses, interactions, appeals, regards, displays for the infinity of gazes which necessarily pervade and modify each of them. We have demonstrated this formally in the section on the Principle of Charity in Part One. Every act is a display, an intrusion calling to another consciousness, to bridge that gap, to assert reversibility—hence, they are all compassion, as well as passion. In the one sense, as fonts of pain, all coherences are called delusions. In the other sense, precisely these same coherences are called compassion, as self-recontextualizations that disclose the primal interrelation and reversibility which is the ground, goal and resolution of this suffering: "Buddhahood."

Sive . . .

This is why we can never put a period to the end of our list of *sives*. Buddhahood not only appears as time and as the inscrutability of the other. By doing so, it is the intersubsumptive asness that is appearing as all else, and is each other particular appearing as all others, as we have seen. Once "opened," i.e., revealed to have always been causes of and expressions of the state of Intersubsumption and mutual interpretability, the setups are also revealed to be openers, capable of supplying punch lines for any other setup. Each particular appearance is thus precisely the "principle" of all things, that is, the sole explanatory foundational coherence to which all other appearances are reducible, of which all other appearances may be seen as forms of expression, the substance of which all others are accidents or modifications. "Principle" means the nonapparent background that contextualizes; "event" means the apparent foreground that is contextualized.

To be truly "Integrated" enlightenment in the Tiantai sense, however, the following must also be true: all forms of activity are expressions of, causes of and effects of, not only Buddhahood, but also of every other possible state or mode of being in the nine deluded realms. To use the traditional example of the most insignificant and lowly as all-pervasive, all things are causes leading to Dung-beetle-hood; all things are the effects of accomplished Dung-beetle-hood. All things are expressions of the inherent nature of Dung-beetle-hood.

In a nutshell, this means that it is not enough to admit the evil inherent in the Buddha-nature, while also asserting that only one function, evil or good, arises from this at a time. We must go on to see the case as one where in one sense they always "function simultaneously" and in another sense they function at different times.

They function simultaneously, both as cause and effect, and for each of the three tracks (Buddha-bodies, and so on), in the above sense. To be a dung beetle knowing that all things are causes and effects of a dung beetle is to be a dung beetle as it appears in the eyes of a Buddha, hence a Buddhified dung beetle. Its behavior, form, and structure do not change in the slightest.

It might be argued however that at least its subjectivity has changed radically, i.e., that dung beetle as dung beetle knows nothing about dung-beetle-hood pervading all times and places, while Buddha qua dung beetle knows this. In one sense this is true. In another, however, the doctrine allows for the opposite of all three Buddha-bodies to be their proper expression; that means *not knowing may be an expression of knowing as well*.[36] Everything appears in deadpan intersubsumptive form as everything else when it is seen that in the case of every coherence without exception it is possible, indeed necessary, that its absence is as much, or more, a revelation and presencing of it

---

[36] "Buddhahood" means "able to express itself as not-itself; to be unchanged whether one is X or the opposite; to be absolute." This applies for all the Three Types of Buddha-nature described in Tiantai dogmatics.

Conditioning Cause Buddha-nature can express itself by appearing as not-itself: as in the "Lifespan" chapter of the *Lotus*: the Buddha's very disappearance from the world is itself a way of appearing, i.e., a way of making his salvific presence known to all sentient beings. (Perhaps this could be the effect appearing as not-itself, in both thought and deed).

Revealing Cause Buddha-nature can express itself by appearing as not-itself: as Subhuti forgetting his Bodhisattva vow—if we take this as a fulfillment of that vow. He had to be a *śrāvaka* for a while to fulfill the Bodhisattva Vow, i.e., not know he was a Bodhisattva. The

as its (immediate or, per impossible, *simpliciter*) presence. The *sive*s or alternate names/coherences for Buddha are infinite. The alternate names for "tying your shoe" are also infinite.

Boredom, Anxiety, Narrative, Addiction, and Love: Human Time

Let us take a stab at redescribing the human condition as we have chosen to view it here: we are "beings in the world," possessed of a "dividing consciousness," willing to change some parts of the all but not all of the all, and thus, correlatively, endeavoring to be a particular, determinate entity who nonetheless possesses at least one inalienable, unconditional property, specifically, to be a particular existent entity which persists as the owner of a property called its autonomy, its unconditionality. As long as this is so, time for us is the perpetual question, "What should I do next?" This means, "What particular action can I take that will be worthwhile, so that I will not be wasting my time, so that I will be utilizing my time and energy in a way which is valuable?" But given our understanding of what underlies valuation, the paradox here should be immediately evident. Value means power. It means the ability to be free from conditions, to be what one is in spite of anything one does or any particular thing one "is." Our normal anxiety about time wants some particular condition, some specific act, that will give the self this kind of being. But this means seeking for the condition that will provide us with unconditionality. What condition will assert, demonstrate, or establish my unconditionality? Indeed, this is a good definition of human

---

whole retrospective setup/punch-line principle of transformative recontextualization speaks to this; you have been doing more than you realize, and accomplishing it only because you failed to realize it. This is true also for the lost son parable and the Phantom city parable in the *Lotus*. (The cause appearing and functioning as not itself, in both thought and deed.) We see this also in the story of the Bodhisattva Never Disparage as post-Enlightenment Buddha—no sign that he knows what he is doing. Also, in the *Lotus*, Devadatta makes Buddhas while engulfed in ignorance.

Proper Cause Buddha-nature can express itself by appearing as not-itself: as in the more standard theoretical considerations of how Emptiness does not maintain its own nature, to be empty is to have no self to lose, and thus to exclude no possible form of "selfing."

So Buddhahood does indeed in one sense "come and go," but it is a state the nature of which is to see even its "going away" as part of itself; it knows it will vanish, but sees its vanishing also as a form of its fulfillment. We may think again of the case of the doctor played by Richard Dreyfus in Frank Oz's film *What About Bob?* Given the interpretive perspective adopted by the Bill Murray character, absolutely anything the doctor does, including terminating therapy and trying to kill the patient, is a form of therapy. Therapy appears equally in the form of its absence.

desire: the paradoxical search for the one, single condition which, once attained, will make us free, valuable, existent, unconditional. The one that equals none—the one condition which makes unconditional. We have here, as it were, the quixotic nostalgia for the "oneness" which haunts and eludes our sense of self: to appear, coherences must appear as a "one," but a "one" is precisely what can never appear. Desiring time is a search for the one, the one thing that will make us finally become a one which needs no other one.

This desire tries to steer us between the two poles of human existence, as Schopenhauer called them, namely, anxiety and boredom. Anxiety means we have no answer to the question, What should I do next to ensure or establish my being? We know that it is needful; we suspect there is something out there that could do the job, but we do not know what it is. Boredom, on the other hand, is the sense that there is definitely nothing I can do right now that is in any way relevant to this self-project. This can mean either because I regard it as already accomplished, in whatever terms I have been defining it in so far, or that I can find no means to this end in my available next movements. In either case, nothing I do is relevant to allowing me to devote the next moment to the one condition that will make me unconditional, i.e., a real, determinate being, whose being there differs in some meaningful way from its not being there, but who nonetheless remains this very same being no matter what it does or what happens to it.

The similarity of boredom and anxiety should be evident from their definitions here, although they are generally experienced strictly as mutually exclusive opposites. But their similarity can be readily observed, with close attention—they are, as it were, flip sides of one another. For human desire cannot be satisfied either by a definitive answer to the question, What should I do next? or by *no* answer to that question. We require an answer we are *almost* sure of. A set of definitive demands, prescribing every action at every moment, as in a military regimen or set of detailed divine commandments, will never assuage this anxiety/boredom unless it can avoid becoming fully explicit or definite in at least some one crucial respect. We must not be able to control or determine it entirely, for we then cease to be a "real, determinate entity." There is no "outside" against which we can be compared, no standard in conformity with which we are established as being there as opposed to not being there. If we know for sure that "action X will make us definitively exist," this action and its effect together become a new fact, which cries out for some further context in terms of which it will be meaningful, i.e., become something more than just "this fact occurs," becoming instead "this fact is an action of mine which proves that I exist." This is normally made possible by the meaningless cipher placed in the grounding of the system, the unknowability of the divine nature or plan (if you do this, God will most likely be happy, but you cannot control him, and there is no telling exactly what he will do in response), the "more" to the system that is not explained in the prescriptions as such.

Whatever charm or effectiveness this approach has in combating human boredom/anxiety lies in its maintainence of this unseen part. For if the system which defines our actions for every moment becomes entirely transparent and explicit, it reasserts the anxiety of requiring something further to justify its value, to ground it. What makes it worthwhile to devote the next moment to X rather than Y? The fact that doing X makes you "a follower of these rules," provides that identity. No one wants to be valued just for what they do—this doing must somehow convert into a form of *being*. But being by definition is unconditionality; being attained through action can never be true being. The action is meant to go beyond doing into the realm of being: you are, as long as you fulfill this condition, "one who is approved of by God," or "a decent human being," or "a model officer," and so on. To "be" something means, for us, not simply to "possess some attribute" in the manner of a thing, but that there is no finite list of its attributes; it can continue to "be" that thing in other contexts, expressed in other ways. But without some moretoitivity, some hidden side, to the justifying identity-granter itself, this loses the "unconditional" impression necessary for the sense of "selfhood." The entire system becomes one more fact, one more action—"being a decent human being" may help me, but not when it becomes explicitly "being regarded as a decent human being by some determinate, identifiable agency." That is just a deed, a fact—in itself it cannot reach to the unconditionality of "being" and identity. So if our anxiety is avoided by the "bad faith" of filling in a determinate content for the prescriptions of our actions, it cannot help leading toward its full realization, which is boredom (nothing to do here to help my self-project), which is anxiety again.

On the contrary, if we take the opposite approach, the "authentic" existential (really Sartrean) pure indeterminacy and groundlessness of our being, embracing anxiety, we end up in boredom, which is anxiety again, which is boredom again, and so on. Sartre misconstrues the category of being when he allows that we are what we do, that we create our "essence" by means of our existence, i.e., through our actions. For again, *being* something is not merely a matter of having an essence, being a particular "whatness"—Sartre's being is always already implicitly objectified, which is why abstract freedom falls on the other side, the essenceless for-itself. For "to *be* X" is not to *have* the objectively determinate essence of Xness; that is still a form of "having." Rather, it is precisely the disappearance of Xness as having any simple location, of being anywhere *simpliciter*. The project of trying to "be something real" is thus not a "useless passion," as Sartre thinks, unattainable because what I am is nothing more than what I make myself, and because this something is thus always already past, beyond changing, my past deeds as in-itself but no longer genuinely for-itself, as the original demand requires. Rather, I become a truly real being, "in-itself," only when the in-itself vanishes for me as anything appearing *simpliciter* in any particular, conditioned place in the total field of experience. We want relief from the Sartrean nightmare of having to make ourselves continually through our actions, with no possibility of success, since the standard of what counts as constituting a self is also only made through our particular, groundless actions. We want some one thing, some one condition, in the presence of which our "being" is not in question, no matter what we do, and whatever we do is an attempt to get into the presence of that thing, so as not to have to do anything. That is what it means to "be" something—everything everywhere in the field is "it," no matter what they are, but it itself is nowhere in the field, simply as itself and nothing else. So we may accept Sartre's description of our basic desire: to be in-itself and yet for-itself, to be determinate, absolute, and interrelatable, able to remain itself in any activity and in any guise. But for him, the attainment of this goal is impossible. For us, it is impossible/inevitable—impossible as contingent, inevitable as this necessary impossibility itself.

Normally, as we have seen, this means desiring to be the one thing our identificatory intersubsumptions (another word for "experience") become snagged on, what we are not allowed to be, which comes to us in the form of desiring obsessively to be in the presence of that thing. Being in the presence of that thing here becomes the "one" condition that will allow us to feel fully intersubsumptive, the condition that, we think, will allow us finally to be unconditional. This drive can be seen most clearly in human narrativity, human addiction, and human love. In each case we have some single condition that allows a sensation of "being," that is, unconditional yet particular existence, and which in one way or another postpones its own crash by coming with at least one particular impenetrability or contingency, something just outside my grasp.

A narrative into which we become absorbed is one way of creating the impression of being: it is "the same story" going on in all these different events, but the story itself is nowhere except in the events. We cannot say for sure in advance which events will henceforth also be parts of this same story; it can enfold an indefinite number of possible next moves. This is made possible by the fundamental global incoherence/intersubsumption that is inherent to any local coherence; every event calls for a story around it, and indeed for many stories. A story is a temporal context that narrows the possibilities of contextualization to a manageable few. We know that this event means "more" than just itself—the story is the unwinding of some of the aspects of this "more," redefining the various meanings of the events that have already taken place. Our anxiety/boredom is alleviated by stories; they give us a sense of what it is to be a particular something which is nonetheless more than itself, which remains unexhaustible by any list of its attributes, which can freely mutate through different conditions without ceasing to be itself. The stories that interest us, the ones in which we can habitually "lose ourselves," will be those which present some subset of what we ourselves have identified with, those coherences which we have embraced and which we know to have more-to-them, the verdict on which we are awaiting from the world, or, conversely, precisely those we have most insistently excluded from our self-definition. In either case, our unconditionality is blocked here, and the one condition that we think will restore it is the all-pervasion of either the "me" or the "nonme," which obviously amount to the same thing. Anxiety/boredom cease here: we know "what to do with the next moment"—keep reading the story, find out more about this bit of the self or nonself which seems to now be doing the work we need it do, i.e., showing itself to pervade every possible experience without ceasing to be itself. If we can keep hearing the story, if we can keep the story going, we will be unconditional. Thus are anxiety/boredom abated for a while.

Another way this can happen is with an object of addiction. This applies to the more generous application which popular culture now gives to this term, but the structure is still that we see in the more clinical cases. The drink, the cigarette, the gambling room, the sex, the drug, the accomplishment, the music—in each case, the addict feels that as long as this one thing is present, "everything else" will be fine—it does not matter what else is going on, as long as I have drink, or a cigarette, or a woman. Everything else is transformed into an aspect, an expression, of "being drunk," or "being out drinking," or "gambling," or "smoking a cigarette," or "working," or "picking up a woman." The very same experiences which would be unpleasant without this one condition are now part of the bliss. The objects of addiction, while having certain physiological effects which make them especially conducive to the reduction of anxiety/boredom, also fit our description of eliminating the need for the "what to do next" by rolling all the little anxieties and boredoms into a single place, as it were: just get the drug, and you will have done what is needful. Whatever happens then will be part of this same thing, "me smoking a cigarette," for example, which I have defined as a free, happy act. So driving a car, having a conversation, reading a book, yelling at the cable company over the phone, contemplating my sorry fate, these are all just part of the fun of "smoking a cigarette." Here an action has jumped into the position of "being." With this one condition, I have become unconditional, and my anxiety/boredom have disappeared.

Another example is the state of being in love. I have already gone through several definitions of love, to show how it, like every other coherence, "is" its own constitutive contradiction. Here I will offer one of my own, which falls into the same category. Love is the feeling of being in the presence of a person who makes you feel unconditional, and whom you feel you make feel unconditional. That is, as long as she is present, I can do no wrong. Whatever happens to us will be part of the joy of "being with her." I do not have to worry about what to do next; whatever I do, and whatever she does, we are both blissful through the mere presence of the other. This requires also that some part of this "presence" is not merely an act of my will, something I arbitrarily "decide" to do and can control. There is "something special" about me in particular, which no one else has; likewise her. This provides us with the particularity, the realness of the being we desire. Sexuality plays a major role here, as that "something about me" which is in no way under my own control, which I cannot simply will; the things that determine my sexual attractiveness—my sexual vibe, not to mention the biological particulars of my appearance and endowments—are things I cannot simply decide to have or not have. Precisely this contingency provides the sense of unconditionality. The other, too, cannot simply list those things about you that make you attractive to her in this way. There is no exhaustive, finite list. Love, we may perhaps say, means that there is one person who I think will be blissfully happy on the one condition that I am present, and miserable so long as I am not, but who cannot exactly explain why, or is too proud or inarticulate to admit it. This makes me feel blissfully happy on the one condition that she is present, and miserable so long as she is not, but without being able to exactly explain why—for I am relieved of my usual form of time, of my continual question, What shall I do next in order to become unconditional and yet particular? What can I serve in order to become free? For anything I do now, as long as we are together, however that might be construed, is automatically right, just because it is precisely I who am doing it. Whatever we do or encounter—the house burns down, the police come at midnight to adjudicate our argument with the landlady, we are run out of town on a rail—is enjoyable, is part of "us being together and in love," our sweet memories of our life together. Here, as in all our examples, the point is that all one's small anxieties are rolled into one big anxiety, in the form of the "one," the being we are trying to be—the last ditch attempt to avoid the necessary impossibility which comes with the crash of any coherence. Love somehow makes us feel free while at the same time, and with the very same means, makes us feel obligated. Maximum unfreedom and maximum freedom coincide here, poised at their greatest tension before the crash. We feel obligated, hence enslaved, because we know that this person needs us, somehow, in the same way we need her, and will not provide the desired feeling of unconditionality unless we meet the condition of providing her with her feeling of unconditionality. The particular type of person who will be able to do this in each case will probably be a matter, again, of where the snags in this unconditionality have hitherto resided. It may be someone who pretends to be completely indifferent to me, but seems occasionally to reveal that she is totally dependent on me (for example, in bed). It may, on the contrary, be someone who appears to be completely dependent on me, but in some crucial way remains proudly resistant and independent of me. It may be someone who makes many demands on me, or makes no demands on me, or who declares her fidelity, or denies her fidelity, someone above me or below me, someone exuding entitlement or disenfranchisement, but in each case, we have these two poles; she is the one I cannot imagine being, the one who fulfils the two opposite demands at once, the one who rounds out the picture and allows me to feel unconditional and absolutely free, on the one condition that she loves me, which I can never control or even quite know for sure. Perhaps we should add that, in being in love, one is under the impression that one is playing the same role for the other—filling in some particular paradox of dependence and independence, one that fits the contours of her particular snags. The paradox is here presented in its most acute and explicit form, which is perhaps why this is the strongest of all the forms of time-transcendence we have listed here; it is the most effective means of avoiding the necessity of the paradox precisely because it is its closest approximation. Being in love is emblematic of that impossibility which is the being of every thing, the all-pervasiveness and inescapability which is simultaneously an unlocatability, impossibility of attainment which is simultaneously the impossibility of evasion, intersubsumption—which indeed is just a slightly more attentive description, on our view, for the anxiety/boredom which is otherwise each moment of time.

Death and Embarrassment

Our discussion of the individual finite self would not be complete without some comments on its most notable feature: its temporal finitude, manifested as its awareness and fear of it own extinction. But what does this amount to once the concept of finitude itself has been rewritten omnicentrically, where the self has no fixed contents to begin with but instead operates by constantly enhancing its flexibility in renouncing its own characteristics, in embodying its own pre-devastation, its own inherent impossibility? What is it that is then feared in the famous fear of death? Freud intuited, shockingly, that fear of death was a kind of transmuted version of castration anxiety, rather than the other way around; to fear nonexistence, loss of *being*, is in fact a form of fearing the loss of *having* something, or of being something in particular. This is an important insight, and we will go along at least with the suggestion that the fear of death is not so ultimate as it appears, that it is actually a distorted version of something else. For us, however, that something else is the fear, not of castration, but of *embarrassment*, humiliation, injured narcissism, loss of control as a disgrace, giving the lie to the ego's notion of itself as master of its ship, as some particular coherence not impinged by what it tries to exclude.[37] That is, the supposed ability of my self to be its own master, to definitively define itself, which means not only to be able to make reversals but especially to reverse whatever reversals are constantly being visited upon me, this is what is embarrassingly crushed in death.[38] This is what we have called "control" in its contingent sense, as the precise opposite of control in its necessary form, which is my ability to reverse in every possible direction, to allow every reversal upon me, as necessarily leading to a *further* reversal, since reversibility is genuinely all-pervasive. This means simply that it is not the loss of the unseen center per se that is feared in death, nor the field of awareness, the coherences as which it presences, but the fear of a particular unseen center becoming prey to other centers, that is, becoming the part of other projects without the opportunity to talk back, to put a spin on whatever spin is put on one. To fear death is, in essence, to fear being seen as dead.[39] This is what it means to be pure body; to be a setup for alien punch lines—by which I mean coherences not yet interpreted into my story, or ones which I refuse to incorporate, so as to maintain my present story. Others can then do as they like with one: worms may eat the flesh, alternate systemizers can pull one into their systems, one's history no longer has this present center as spokesperson to interpret it as it pleases, and incorporate alternate readings into its own.

It is not merely "being interpreted," that is, objectification, which is fearful here, for this is going on all the time anyway; it is, once again, fear of the lack of reversibility. I can ping-pong the alternate readings of me back into myself while alive; after I am dead, I believe, I will be at the mercy of the

---

[37] Here we are really closer to the Sartrean notion of death than either the Freudian on the one hand or the Heideggerian on the other. See *Being and Nothingness*, 689–700, esp. 692–93: "The unique characteristic of a dead life is that it is a life of which the Other makes himself the guardian."

[38] Hence perhaps the common association of fear of death with the fear of *confinement*, e.g., when one imagines with terror death as trapped enclosed within one's coffin.

[39] We may, perhaps, see a connection here with the universality of burial practices in human civilization. One must be assured, whether buried or cremated, that no one will ever *see* one's decaying corpse.

pundits, I cannot "fight back," and everything about me will be taken as brute (*simpliciter*) coherence as seen from elsewhere, read in some single, closed way. Built into this fear, then, is a certain neglect of the *multiplicity* and uncertainty of these remaining views, the openness and infinity[40] that will necessarily continue to pertain even to the supposedly finite set of coherences that had already been selected as the circle of one's identity.[41] Fear of death depends on *either* a false totalization of the "Big Other," to use the Lacanian term, into a single consistent God's-eye with a single consensus, a kind of Last Judgment on one's life; *or*, a complete inert no-eye view, unperceivedness, total lack of any "otherness" to perceive or incorporate one's story at all. It depends on belief in either one interpreter or no interpreters at all—monotheism or materialism, to put it simply. It is perhaps no accident that these two extremes—the inert materialist unperceivedness or invisibility (excluding cases of unanimous posthumous renown, which fall into the other category), or a single viewer and judge, God—are the two poles between which modern Western humanity oscillates, the *only* two conditions that could produce the fear of death as we experience it now. And indeed, for us these two amount to the same thing: for "no" view" is equally "one particular view." But if intersubsumptive reversibility is synonymous with being, as we have argued, if to see is to be seen (in Merleau-Ponty's language), if the intersubjective relation is prior to inert-single-determinateness of any kind—if to exist as such, in other words, is to be seen and incorporated into a literal infinity of views, if to be is to be something *as* which an infinity of coherences are revealing themselves, then the self is not a specific content which could be gained or lost, but rather the process of establish continuities on the basis of discontinuities. But there simply are no discontinuities that are not, by virtue of their discontinuities, also establishments of continuities; discontinuity is continuity, and time is self-recontextualization. In that case, our own meager little life will inevitably still go on to "have been" an infinity of lives and meanings.[42] Everything I have kept nicely interpreted away by means of the might of my own story is now fair game for other scriptwriters; it all comes out—my intestines, my being as meat, some particular shape of my deeds, no longer hidden in the power of my own present narrative. This is embarrassment, humiliation, pure and simple. It is not the loss of the conscious field I fear,

---

[40] I mean this in the sense suggested archly by Nietzsche in *The Gay Science*, trans. W. Kaufmann (New York: Vintage Books, 1974), Book Five, Section 374, "Our New Infinite," 336.

[41] Again we think of Nietzsche here, on the retroactive revelation of meanings that *will have* been true, e.g., of history. See Nietzsche, *The Gay Science*, 104.

[42] A consideration very central to the mythological underpinnings of the Tiantai system, i.e., the *Lotus Sūtra*.

or the ability to move my body, except in a special sense: I fear the loss of the ability to rewrite the meaning of my body, and all its perceptual aspects, and to rewrite whatever other rewritings of my body may be floating around out there.

This may be rephrased in terms of a more Heideggerian notion of death as the disclosure of a primal aloneness. To put it an almost vaudevillian formula, the really terrifying thing about death is the idea that you can't talk it over (negotiate it, interpret it, come to a consensus or to a mutually recognizing confrontation about it) with anyone afterwards—not even with "yourself."

PART THREE

Hermeneutics and Autoerotics

TRUTHS AND OTHER HIDDEN PARTS,
AND HOW THEY WELCOME THEIR DEMISE

Why There's Anything: Habituation and Solidarity, with Some Reckless Reasoning about Entropy and the End of the Universe

It is hoped that the above reflections will have already made any questions such as, "What is the source of everything? Where does it all come from? What is it all for? What is the meaning of life?" irrelevant. For the key term in each of these questions—"source," "come from," "for," "meaning"—I in each case a way of pointing to what we have called a "center," and each is a demand for a particular coherence to be specified as the unique ground or orienting point to be applied in all cases, *in terms of which* all other coherences are to be understood, either as efficient, material, or final cause. We, however, have come to regard the positing of any particular coherence as center to be a provisional but necessary function of all experience; there is always some center, but none is applicable to the exclusion of all others. We would say not that things have no source and meaning, but rather that any coherence at all, chosen at random, *is* the source and meaning of all other coherences, precisely by means of its necessary failure—concurrent with its most complete, final, ruthless triumph—to function as source and meaning for all other coherences. Its necessary failure throws the ball over to the failure of some other center, which, as in a game of "hot potato," has to get rid of it at some point as well, eventually back to the first center. We might think of this also as a game of "duck-duck-goose": whoever is running around the circle at the moment is the center at that time, looking for a way to pass that position on to someone else and to itself fade back into the realm of the options open to some other center. We have tried to specify some of the vicissitudes for what constitutes being "chosen at random" above.

There would still seem to be a kind of nonobvious assertion here, that of the *necessity* of this failure. But this is neither something that has to be proved nor something that is devoid of meaning because it cannot be disconfirmed. It does not have to be proved because, by its own hypothesis, it cannot be proved; it is claiming that nothing, not even itself, can succeed in all cases, can remain coherent in the face of all possible considerations; "necessary" here can only mean something the contrary of which cannot be imagined, and that in our case only because of the purely formal or empty nature of the claim being made. Being a claim to see all coherences in their opposites, it can also see the coherence "my success in applying universally" in the coherence "my failure in applying universally." It is enough for it to have made this claim *seem* coherent to anyone for any span of time. Hence its own breakdown at some point would not count against it. However, it could be disproved, if some other center really were capable of being shown to be applicable in all possible cases, not to fail and break down somewhere. The burden of proof rests with anyone who would want to overthrow this frankly self-contradictory premise, for the only possible refutation of this assumption would be the demonstration of some positive ontology, something which has never been done. This would include even the claim, "No system based on self-contradictory first principles can be accepted." Not only has this never been done, but for it to really "apply in all cases" in the radical sense intended here it would have to function in and as every other apparent coherence, including those which occurred before it was dreamt up. If anyone ignored it for a moment, if any moment of experience that was definitive and self-contained, in the past, present, or future, did not acknowledge it in a way that *it* could not demonstrate to be also a manifestation of itself, it would also have proved to be a failure by this standard. One of the advantages of our position is its ability, in its failure, to succeed in meeting this taxing standard.

Indeed, contrary to appearances, we may say that this claim of inherent entailment, or necessary positing and necessary failure of all coherences as centers, is intended as a statement of *the minimum possible assertion,* or the suspension of all possible definitive premises. It is meant to be the furthest reach of a thoroughgoing skepticism demolishing all possible positive claims, rather than a dogmatic and positive claim asserting the existence of a particular nonapparent metaphysical truth. The establishment of the doctrine of inherent entailment, of deadpan reversible Intersubsumption, is to be thought of not as the addition of one more unverified proposition to which we are to give our allegiance (e.g., "Contrary to appearances, X actually includes within it all other possible coherences"), but rather as the removal or overcoming of one more proposition, the final and fundamental unexamined assumption, namely, "It is either true that 'X is really X' or that 'X is really not X,' one or the other."[1] That is, the Tiantai position is that we are actually assuming *less*, not more, when we say that all coherences are mutually included and identical in this manner, even less than if we were to say, for example, "All dharmas are empty," or "Fundamentally nothing has ever existed," or "There is no subject of which anything could be predicated," or "Truth is inexpressible, nothing can be asserted, all beliefs about the nature of reality are false." This blankness, like the commonsense and substantialist/"atomistic" notions of identity already demolished by the Global Incoherence critique (and indeed, by any Skeptical system, for instance, that of Pyrrho or Sextus Empiricus) of which it is a result, actually posits one more unexamined and un-"emptied" deluded assumption than the assertion of inherent entailment and Intersubsumption in the Tiantai sense. That is, it still posits a definitive and self-identical blankness or exclusion of all coherences, which is, however, actually a coherence itself, as it has an opposite (i.e., "incoherence" is the opposite of "coherence"), and is hence not yet "absolute." The setup/punch-line identity-in-conflict structure, the opening of the provisional to reveal the real (self-recontextualization) discussed above, on the other hand, brings us to a truly absolute result which is free of all unrefuted presuppositions. We are not asserting as an unconfirmed positive hypothesis that a bunch of other unseen coherences are hidden inside this coherence; we are just asserting that this coherence is unspecifiable except in the setup/punch-line manner, that it is constantly rewriting itself as other coherences without having to change in the least, which, thought through, equals the doctrine of the inherent entailment of all the coherences in each other and their deadpan reversible Intersubsumption.

In other words, the question, Why are there any coherences at all, rather than an eternal blankness? is a nonquestion: eternal blankness is itself a coherence, and one much more difficult to establish and maintain than the situation we actually have, of ceaseless production and deadpan Intersubsumption of infinite coherences. If we did assume any one fundamental coherence, we would have a real question to ask, Why just this one? Why should it not be

---

[1] The Tiantai notions of the four meritorious properties of Nirvana—eternity, bliss, freedom and purity—as simultaneous assertions of their opposites, are established on the same basis; not as a further demand for faith in eternity, but as the removal of a previous faith, of the clinging delusion that all entities must be either eternal or not-eternal.

something else? As it is, there is no something else which things can be, since they are *already* all possible states, emphatically including their own absence. We start not at the beginning of time, but just with whatever appears to be appearing right now to whatever idiot happens to be appearing to be doing the considering. Here the reader may hear an echo of Heidegger's question of questions, Why is there anything at all, rather than nothing? On the most obvious level, we join hands here with the vilified ranks of Hegel and Nietzsche in Heidegger's account, that is, those who have "forgotten the question of Being" to such an extent that the word *Being* comes to be the most vaporous and meaningless of all terms, who see the question, as we have put it here, as a nonquestion. For Heidegger, this is symptomatic of a fundamental tragedy in the history of our relationship to Being as such, a total lostness in beings. But although we do thus confirm the meaninglessness of this question, we do also, we think, suggest a way of answering it thereby, and one that is very sympathetic to Heidegger's concern to keep this query alive. For above all we have in mind precisely the disclosure of beings, their asness, their showing of themselves as distinct from and yet identical to their being such and such a being, when we speak of Intersubsumption and Asness, and this, we think, not only does not involve an oblivion of Being into beings, but finally adequately enunciates their relationship, of identity and difference, and beyond. To be a being at all is already, for us, to be that X as non-X, or the Asness that is the showing of Xness and non-Xness. Neither the collapsing of Being into beings nor the separation of the two, which makes of Being another being, are possible from this perspective; as we saw already in the early Mahāyāna argument about a relationship between a thing and its marks, we have here a relationship for which both identity and difference are woefully inadequate predicates, which is not even a "relationship," and which calls for a fundamental rethinking of what it means to be a "being" at all, such as we have attempted here. From the old-time Buddhist soteriological perspective, the only valid point of departure for any such "why" question is always "this moment of experience," or better, "this moment of delusion and suffering." Everything is derivable from this alone. The determination of precedents as determinate particulars is a function either of (1) the present moment of delusion, that is, the particular narrowing of horizons of relevance which one is presently engaged in, or what we will call habituation, or (2) a ("compassionate") response of solidarity with this arbitrary narrowing, which is in reality just the self-recontextualization of that initial deluded coherence. One is always currently engaged in determining what the source and meaning of all things is at this very moment.

If the question is posed a little more naïvely, in a quasi-objectivist manner, we may be confronted with the query, Why any coherence? Not "Why some particular coherence?" but "Why coherence at all?" Although as I have just indicated, I consider this way of putting it a little off the point—total exclusion or lack of coherence is already, by our standards, a type of coherence—it is still perhaps worthwhile, as an *upāya* if you like, to suggest how someone intent on looking at it this way could be answered. We have said that this necessary failure, this interpervasion qua constitutive impossibility, is the elimination of all positive assumptions. But given necessary failure as the condition of all coherences, why the *appearance* of success? Why should an anti-failure, a kind of reifying motion, coherence, arise within this necessary failure? For this we have a ready answer: Necessary failure means that even the coherence "failure" must fail, that "success" must be able to appear, at least momentarily, so as to undermine the claim of "failure" to universal success. If it did not, the coherence "failure" (or "incoherence") would be appearing *simpliciter* as the one-way ultimate truth of all coherences. Hence the analytic necessity of the appearance of coherence, for discontinuity and incoherence already *are* continuity and coherence. So far no problem.

But a more serious question then arises: Why does a given "trend" of coherence or pattern, an apparent success of coherence, persist for more than an instant? Why does a given center persist in extending itself to the point where it must break down? Whence this momentum of interpretation? Why does it not just appear as a freak spark in the opposite direction that is then immediately annulled by the continuing thrust of pure flux, the pure failure of all coherence, which breaks all patterns apart? Why is this pattern, which happens to be here, "self-reinforcing and habituating," why is it able to become so forceful and universal, why does it repeat itself, why does it extend outward to see itself in a greater range of othernesses than those in which it originally appeared? Whence this continuity? This question is tantamount to asking for an explanation for the broad predictability and reliability of the empirical world. While we do not regard this continuity and coherent "lawfulness" of the world as absolute, and find any *simpliciter* assertion of its all-pervadingness subverted by every moment of subjective experience which, for whatever reason, is not directly apprehending it, we cannot deny a stronger and more enduring sense of coherence and continuity than are accounted for by the simple need to undermine the absoluteness of incoherence, the requirement that failure also be a failure, which would only require occasional islands of coherence. Are we not surreptitiously assuming a hidden definite characteristic here, namely that, if you will, "flux" is a medium which "takes" momentums, that allows patterns to repeat and extend to the point of breakdown, that it is like a loop of magnetic tape rather than like a strip of plain paper running over the recording head of the present moment?

In other words, assuming coherence to be "the perpetuation of some local pattern which is identifiable to some subjectivity," why does this pattern continue to repeat after it happens to occur once? Why does the cycle not peter out after one revolution and fly off into another random direction? Why is there momentum, or habit-formation, at all? The answer to this question is: Because of the *ambiguity* of deadpan Intersubsumption itself. For coherence is already continuity. This patternizing is not some other specific characteristic assumed in addition to this impossibility of the self-establishment of any universality of any coherence, this flux, but rather is actually inherent in the definition of this flux, i.e. the failure of all definite coherences. We may recall here again the discussion of "Natural Law as Global Incoherence" in Part One. There we saw how the randomness at the microlevel read out as determinate regularity at the macrolevel. Now it might be legitimately objected, if this point is translated into any kind of cosmological explanation, that the emergence of statistical regularity in that case is entirely due to the existence of disequilibratory—"orderly"—initial conditions. Entropy is a process whereby there is a statistical tendency to even distribution of elements that are initially distributed in an uneven way. This unevenness requires "work," and is what physicists generally mean, in the broadest sense, when they speak of "order." But it would be a mistake to take this definition of order uncritically, as the most perspicacious of modern theoretical physicists themselves also point out.[2] We need not drag in the big guns of Kant or Spinoza (naturally laughed off by any self-respecting modern physicist) to discredit the absolutizing of this concept of order, although both are useful in understanding the degree to which the application of this category is connected with subjective idiosyncracies, Kant in the well-known and obvious way, Spinoza by means of the suggestion the notion of order has everything to do with what is more or less easily imagined and remembered by us, what accords most readily with our cognitive apparatus. Rather, I would like to take up the problem of entropy and initial conditions on its own terms—and this problem is especially relevant to our discussion, since entropy is the bottom-line explanation for the observed "irreversibility of time" in modern physics, an irreversibility that is, however, admitted to be statistical, not metaphysical.

The story goes like this: We start with a high degree of order (although even this is contested by some physicists) that degenerates into disorder, even-distribution, entropy. We cannot, therefore, derive order from disorder, let alone equate the two, because the only reason determinate regular-

---

[2] Richard Feynman, for example, is careful to note, "this word order, like the word disorder, is [one of the] terms of physics which are not exactly the same as in ordinary life." See Feynman, *The Character of Physical Law* (Cambridge, Mass.: MIT Press, 2001), 113.

ities emerge from this random drift (e.g., the leftward or rightward drift of particles) is because of a high degree of unbalance—order—in the initial conditions. If we had only evenly distributed randomly drifting particles "from the beginning," no determinate marks, and no order, and no coherence, of any kind would ever appear. This would seem to be a very strong argument. But what is wrong with it is the surreptitious assumption of a fixed frame of reference in the positing of the terms. For if we really try to boil down what the "law" of entropy signifies, as some physicists have done, we come up with something like the following definition: if the microstate of a system consists of a complete description of the state of every constituent of the system, and the macrostate means the determinate character of the system as a whole, the entropy of a system in a particular macrostate is the number of possible microstates that the system might be in. Every macrostate (e.g., leftward drift) can be in a large number of different microstates without affecting its macrostate. That is, there are lots of different ways its elements can be arranged without in any way changing the properties of the macrostate. If a stagnant gas consisting of one million particles is standing still, and we number these particles, the gas as a whole will be in the same state whether particles 1 through 500,000 are moving leftward and the rest rightward, or vice versa. The number of possible arrangements can be computed exponentially, yielding an enormous number, which would be an index of the entropy of this system. If the components are few, and can move only in a small number of ways, the possibility of random reversibility increases proportionally; it is far more likely that three balls randomly thrown on the floor will arrange themselves into a line than fifty balls. The number of possible microstates is what accounts for the unlikelihood of reversibility into the initial coherence of the macrostate after it dissolves, since these elements can also be used, unchanged, to yield such a vast number of other macrostates; a line made of fifty balls has more potential for entropy than one made of three balls.

Given this definition, however, entropy can be understood only on the basis of the distinction between levels of coherence. It rests on the "holistic" principle of emergent properties of a whole that differ from those of its components. What is coherent on one level is incoherent on the other level. The "incoherence" here is judged to be so on the basis of its failure to match the standard of coherence of the other level. Reversing the terms, we would find that the macrostate fails to show the coherence of the microstates. That is, the macrostate drifts left, but the microstate moves randomly. But leftwardness fails to be randomness just as much as randomness fails to be leftwardness. We can, in fact, restate the law reversibly: the entropy of a system is the number of possible *macrostates* that a particular *microstate* can engender.

Now the question that emerges here is where we fix the frame of reference in defining "macrostate" and "microstate." When we describe the final state as "evenly distributed," we are speaking only of a particular macrostate, and moreover only over what we regard as a statistically relevant stretch of time. Given the quantum nature of particle behavior, however, this can never be true also at every microlevel, and for every possible span of time, even in the case of the imagined "end of the universe" as a homogenous spread of evenly distributed particles, total disorder. For if this stagnant macrolevel, displaying a constant steady state of stillness, is composed entirely of microlevels of random behavior, what happens if we "zero in" on a smaller subset, say a macrolevel of just two particles (as defined in a given frame of reference)? In a very short period of time, are these two particles always "evenly distributed"? Would there be no moments of disequilibrium between them? This is not even imaginable. Moreover, the definition of space as only what is "within" the whole of knowable matter and motion is a choice that obscures the situation of the "largest" macrolevel. For the "whole universe" as an evenly distributed patch of particles would then be a very dense irruption within a space which, precisely for this reason, would have to be redefined as the larger enclosing context. It would be a point within a larger space. So, to indulge a slightly science-fiction speculation, would we not expect rather that the scale of order would have to change whenever disorder is achieved? That is, another set of processes would operate at the very small microlevel of disorder, and at the very large level of disorder; there could never be any lack of initial conditions of "order," that is, the tension of unequal arrangement. The universe too, on this picture, is condemned to meaning, to order, to the extent that these terms denote anything at all—which is only to the extent that order is always also disorder to begin with.

This point can be made clear if we recall the manner in which we understand coherence itself, or what we mean when we say something is repeatably coherent to some subjectivity. This assumes all we have said about subjectivities so far, and is to be understood on the model of transformative self-recontextualizations we have developed. To put it simply, we may say that, given the figure/ground structure of all coherences, which is always accomplished by a single act which is at once an ignoring of backgrounds and a focusing on foreground, coherence as such is always present in some form or another—even if as only the coherence "confusion." Again, we are "condemned to meaning." What this boils down to is that "being X" is equivalent to "being X provisionally, only in certain contexts, exposed to the threat of alternate contexts," which is equivalent to "being an attempt to be X which requires its support outside any finite set of previously established set of X-susceptibility." By "equivalent" I mean very strictly that *whatever* can be said about any one of these can also be said about all the others. Whatever can be said to characterize, for example, "being-X" can also be said to characterize "the attempt to be X." But this is already a promissory note to disclose whatever continuities-with-self are within one's power to disclose. To be X is to be hungry for continuity and coherence, and to be doomed to extend this quest as long as one locally persists, and to fail by succeeding. This indeed is what we have called Will to Power, which as we saw was just another term for Intersubsumption. In short, "to be locally coherent as X" simply *is* "to effect as much continuity-with-X as is possible given whatever powers of other-interpretation (subsumption) are involved in being-X." And "to be locally coherent as X" *is* to have at least *some* such powers of subsumption.

However ignorant or acute the cognitive apparatus in question may be—and here we regard even a rock as a (highly obtuse) cognitive apparatus, in the sense of something that interacts with and is affected by things outside itself—it will be reacting to and registering some coherence or other, and neglecting many others. Given our analysis of the nature of coherences as such, however, these "others" are to be understood as merely appearing to it *as* the one coherence that is affecting it explicitly, and indeed, this coherence is here for it precisely *as* its effect. In this situation we already have the principle of *continuity, which is indeed nothing but the principle of asness itself*. For when the "others" become the explicit focus, they *can* in turn be seen *as* the initial coherence, or as its affect or modification of the "cognitive apparatus" in question. As this cognitive apparatus becomes more and more acute, this interchangeability of asness becomes more explicit; it can experience non-X appearing as X, and then, in turn, X appearing as non-X. This is what continuity means: reversibility. This "becoming more acute" is itself nothing more than what every self is already involved in doing. Selves read their environments as aspects of themselves, as relevant to themselves, or as contrasted challenges constitutive of themselves. The range of this interpretive self-definition is variable, but the structure is inescapable, necessary, since, as we have shown, it is equally present in its absence as in its presence. Whatever form of ignorance happens to be operative at any moment will define for itself a corresponding coherence of the world. Coherence and continuity are constituted from the perspective of each self, which contextualizes, opens up, reads all the other data in terms of its own project. This applies equally to the coherence of its own past, its own previous experience, its own previous selves. It can extend further to other selves and other coherences, and indeed, given the structure of asness, has no need to stop anywhere, given sufficient liveliness of hermeneutic valor, until it reaches the point of total coherence of the world, which, as we have shown, is identical to the confrontation of its own necessary failure, its crashing, the impossibility of total coherence.[3]

If we really wonder about the source of any starting point, the classical Tiantai answer would be not cosmological but phenomenological. First, plain old ignorance, the narrowing of horizons of relevance as it is being implemented at this moment; that is, failure to notice the full extent of relevances in the subjective consciousness to which this coherence is appearing, that is, all the contexts which would overturn it. This is just what we have called a particular habituation, which insists on reading this coherence as a univocal sign. Why this ignorance? Again, this is the minimum possible assumption; to assert any "knowing" of this fact would require the assumption of a very difficult set of conditions, that is, a sophisticated nervous system and conceptual apparatus function in complete accordance with all perception or affectibility. It is the difference between assuming a rock being hit by other things or a philosopher sitting there interpreting; the first is obviously less difficult to imagine, is a "higher entropy" state, requires a much less elaborate set of presuppositions and carefully adjusted conditions.

But given this, why does this coherence, now as center, persist forever? The answer lies in what we have called the primal solidarity which pertains to all coherences, which is merely a way of describing the *inescapable possibility of reversibility* which is inherent to them, which indeed constitutes them—and which we have seen to be, strangely enough, simply another way of describing the *irreversibility* of time in physics, that is, merely statistical irreversibility. In classical terms, this is, as we have seen, rather ironically, known as *compassion*. The peculiar meaning of this term, which diverges very radically from its ordinary meaning, and its relation to the old Tiantai notion of this reversibility as *intersubjectivity*, has been explored in an earlier section. Microstates cannot help also being macrostates, and vice versa, and precisely because they are unable to remain univocal in this arrangement, they cannot help bodying forth the alternate coherences that they always also are.

Atomicity, Otherness, and Violence (Co-starring Whitehead, Levinas, and God)

We see above, as a continuation of the discussion of the permutations of the "Four Ways of Being Thus and Otherwise," the importance of what might be

---

[3] On the basis of these considerations we can venture a definition of habituation. Habituation means: some coherence has come to function, for someone, as a sign, a symbol, which implies that it is a part of some specific whole, that it is leading to some particular completion.

called the atomicity of coherences, their isolation and "one"-ness, in this system which insists so houndingly on their interpenetration. Without atomicity of coherences, they do not interpenetrate. Unless distinct, they do not express one another. Hence the stress we have laid on explicitness, mindfulness, language, and the obvious above. In this context, we can perhaps address more explicitly the relationship between Neo-Tiantai thought and Whiteheadian process thought, with which it has quite a bit in common.

Whitehead's account of process is notable for its emphasis on atomicity and definiteness. Reality is atomic, said Whitehead;[4] every actual occurrence is a process which prehends the universe through its subjective feeling, according to the categorical obligations, in order to reach its satisfaction, which for Whitehead is identical with its definiteness. This does not mean an exclusion of relation and complexity, for Whitehead, quite the contrary, and this is the advance he makes on previous atomic theories of reality. As he notes, "atomism does not exclude complexity, and universal relativity. Each atom is a system of all things."[5] What is still atomistic about this all-inclusive atom, however, is its definiteness, its exclusion of ambiguity, its being simply what it is, period. "An actual entity has a perfectly definite bond with each item in the universe. This determinate bond is its prehension of that item."[6] Process, greatly simplified, may be described as a transition from appetite to emphasis (or exclusion, negative prehension and selection of modes of positive prehension) and finally to the satisfaction of definiteness, in which the "superject" is at last fully formed and at once perishes. This actuality, however, does not only perish; it also enjoys an "objective immortality"—that is, it may and must be prehended by further occasions, for each of which it will present a possibility of relevance. Hence its actuality is in one sense limited to the moment of its active appetition,

---

I finish my dinner, and I want a cigarette: "finishing dinner" has become a coherence which for me means "then there's a cigarette to be had." The coherence "finishing dinner" is for me *always*, nonnegotiably, part of a larger whole, "finishing dinner and then having a cigarette," which contextualizes it and gives it its identity as such. "Finishing dinner" for me *means* "a cigarette is coming." Meaning is habituation. Habituation is meaning. It signifies that some particular coherence comes with a necessary suggestion of some particular other coherences which are part of the same whole, that its identity as X is established only as a part of that whole, only on the condition that the rest of the expected whole come into place. Finishing dinner just is not really finishing dinner unless I have a cigarette afterwards. To be the coherence "finishing dinner" simple *means* "to be a prelude to a cigarette." This is to be remembered below when we consider the question of beauty.

[4] "Thus the ultimate metaphysical truth is atomism. . . ." (Whitehead, *Process and Reality* [henceforth PR], [New York: Harper, 1929], 53.)
[5] Ibid.
[6] Ibid., 66.

selection, and satisfaction; henceforth, this particular entity can be actual only through its being prehended by further, novel occurrences.

Several things are to be stressed about this account of interpervasion of all entities, before we contrast it to the Tiantai doctrine of inherent entailment and Intersubsumption parallel to it. The first is this notion of definiteness as satisfaction. This means that an event achieves real satisfaction of aesthetic harmony in its subjective form when its original appetition is definitely made actual; the appetition is construed here as having a single, definitive aim, which, when matched, spells the satisfaction and perishing of that atomic occurrence. The second point is the passivity that seems to pertain to the objective and to the past. As Whitehead says explicitly, "Agency belongs exclusively to actual occasions."[7] This means that the present actual entity is the real agent who prehends, and the past objectively immortal entities and eternal objects are definitively only prehended. There is no possibility of ambiguity about which is the prehended and which the prehender here. The third is what may, with certain qualifications, be called the givenness of the eternal objects. Whitehead, to be sure, is careful to stress that "the total multiplicity of Platonic forms is not 'given.' But in respect of each actual entity, there is givenness of such forms. The determinate definiteness of each actuality is an expression of a selection from these forms. It grades them in a diversity of relevance."[8] It would not be fair to say that Whitehead is merely equivocating here; the distinction he makes is quite crucial. It is not quite true to say that the eternal objects are not "made," that they are exceptions to the general law of creativity and the exclusive actuality of occurrences; nonetheless, it would seem that they are "made" just once, and are never henceforth truly novel. From a Tiantai perspective, at least, the eternal objects thereby certainly enjoy a considerable degree of relative givenness, a nonnegotiability vis-à-vis any non-God actual entity that relates directly to their putative definiteness. They pertain to what Whitehead calls the primordial nature of God, which is to be sure an actual occurrence in its own right, but certainly one that has a unique position among all occurrences. It is these three features I want to use as comparison points to the notion of inherent entailment, leading on to a comparison between the notion of Buddhahood implied there (and in the *Lotus*), and Whitehead's notion of God.[9]

---

[7] Ibid., 46.

[8] Ibid., 69.

[9] It should be noted that post-Whitehead process thought has often taken Whitehead to task for the latter two of these three points (i.e., the passivity of the past and the reality of the Eternal Objects), which are often modified in more recent process philosophy and theology. The first point, on the other hand, concerning definiteness as satisfaction, seems to be accepted by all process thinkers.

Whitehead is able to assert both the mutual pervasion of actual entities, and also to give an account of the apparent differences between them in spite of this omnipresence of each, their nondisclosure in some times and places, via his notion of "negative prehensions" in the process of appetition and emphasis described above.[10] The Neo-Tiantai position offers a different account of the simultaneous nondisclosure of some entities in the universe and their complete mutual interfusion, which I would like to compare to Whitehead's account, based on the idea of negative prehensions, as premised by the above three points. This is the doctrine of "inherent entailment," as expressed through the notion of "opening the provisional to reveal the real," derived from the *Lotus*. The *Lotus* tells us that there is only one Buddha-vehicle, that the lesser vehicles are in reality the Buddha-vehicle. All teachings, indeed, are the Bodhisattva path, and all practices, even those of the *śrāvakas* that explicitly reject or "negatively prehend" the Bodhisattva path, are in fact instances of the practice of the Bodhisattva path (as can be seen, for example, in the tale of Sakyamuni's previous incarnation as the Bodhisattva "Never Disparage"[11]). This means, on the Tiantai reading, to begin with, that all actions and cognitions are Buddha-actions and cognitions, and that all partial cognitions and beliefs can be "opened and revealed" to be—indeed, to have *always already* been—the cognition of the whole truth.[12] That is, one may believe that one is merely pursuing a certain local goal, in accordance with a particular sort of appetition (the sons running out of the house toward their promised carts,[13] the lost son digging the dirt to make minimum wage,[14] the travelers taking step after step to move closer to the illusory city[15]), but one is always doing more than one knows in doing these things: the sons are saving their lives and moving toward the great ox cart with each deluded step; the lost son is readying himself to learn of his inheritance with each day's labor; the travelers are moving closer to the treasure trove beyond the illusory city with each deluded step they take toward the latter. One's satisfaction is here in decided contrast to one's initially conceived aim or appetition. Each deluded step is at once completely deluded and completely enlightened; that is, one was genuinely

---

[10] See Steven Odin, *Process Metaphysics and Hua-yen Buddhism* (Albany: SUNY Press, 1982), 105–11.
[11] See ch. 20 of Kumarajiva's version, T9.50b–51c.
[12] As Zhiyi says in the *Fahuaxuanyi*, "Once the gate of the provisional *upāya* has been opened up to reveal the true real-mark, precisely the former body is seen to be the perfect eternal body, precisely the former teachings are the perfect teaching, and precisely the former practices and the former principles and ideas all turn out to to be the true and real ones." (T33.691.b.9–11)
[13] T9.10b ff.
[14] T9.16b ff.
[15] T9.22a ff.

misguided, but *precisely by being misguided and, in these cases, only thereby*, one was well guided, and practicing the correct path. To be a Buddha means to be able to withhold information and thereby to more effectively disclose it: to use *upāya*, skillful means, and then "open and reveal" them at the appropriate time.

The principle of nondisclosure here is thus radically rewritten: if all experiences are to be understood as these *upāya* (as in the Tiantai reading), then what is not explicitly included in any event is not simply dismissed as irrelevant, but is, as Whitehead's idea of negative prehension would suggest, an integral part of that entity's being what it is. However, the *Lotus* doctrine takes a further step: each entity is not only made what it is by excluding certain things, and thus to be thought of as including them via this exclusion: it is also *actually revealing them by excluding them*. The Buddha can only fully reveal the Bodhisattva path—in all its vastness and multifariousness—by concealing it for a time; the travelers can only reach the treasure by not seeing it for awhile, the sons must go through a period of misconceiving the aims of their actions in order to achieve the true end of those actions. Otherwise the true nature of those actions can never be revealed at all. So precisely what is excluded from any entity is revealed in or even *as* it precisely by means of this exclusion, or even precisely *as* this exclusion.

This involves a difference between the Whiteheadian notion of atomic events, one-way time and one-way prehension, and the *Lotus*/Tiantai idea of "neither sameness nor difference" as pertaining to the relation between provisional and ultimate truth. Here we must conceive time itself, or process itself, not on the model of appetition-emphasis/selection-satisfaction/definiteness, but on the model of "opening the provisional to reveal the real." Every actual event, we may say, is an opening of the provisional to reveal the real." In the first instance, this means only, in the special case of the Buddha's teachings, to reveal that all other ways were really the Buddha-way. But in the fully omnicentric Tiantai reading, this same structure applies to every moment of experience: each is an opening up of all other moments as provisional *upāya* which both expressed and concealed itself, and these two—expressing and concealing—as identical, as in the case of the Buddha's *upāyas*. This is the essence of the Tiantai Three Truths: Global Incoherence is Local Coherence is Intersubsumption (All-pervasion as All-pervadedness). Hence the relation between any one entity and all other entities must be understood here on the model of the relation between provisional and ultimate truth as laid out in the *Lotus*. What is this relation? I have earlier used the example of the relation between the setup and punch line of a joke to illustrate this peculiar type of identity-as-difference, where contrast and exclusion are not only means to, but in themselves already are identity and inclusion themselves. These two opposite qualities of funniness and seriousness are entailed in it, in full definiteness, at the same time, each pervading the whole thing. This is how the Tiantai doctrine of "inherent entailment" must be understood; every entity is *in its entirety* every other entity, permeated by every other quality, readable as an instantiation of every other coherence. Every X is also, in its entirety, every non-X. And, as in the case of the setup and punch line, this is not so *in spite of* the fact that X is contrasted to and excludes non-X, but precisely because it is contrasted to and exclusive of non-X; non-X is present in X as the very exclusion of non-X. Here perfect ambiguity and perfect definiteness are, we may say, combined, even identical to one another. To be determined as X is to be every non-X, and not as two separate aspects, but such that X's Xness is precisely its non-Xness. An entity is non-X (expressive of non-Xness, of alternate coherences and qualities) precisely to the extent that it is X, and vice versa. Similarly, for the *Lotus*, all previous teachings are both contrasted with the *Lotus*'s teaching of the One Vehicle, and at the same time, by this very exclusion, instantiations of it. They are simultaneously the antithesis of ultimate truth and, precisely *because* they are its antithesis, ultimate truth itself.

Applying the same line of thought to any given entity, as the Tiantai school does, we may say that this pen contrasts with all that is not-pen in the world, and this not-pen, as the internal/external condition of this pen, turns out thereby to be revealed to be this pen itself, in the form of non-pen, or precisely by virtue of its exclusion of and contrast with pen-ness. Non-pen is pen in the form of non-pen-ness, just as the *śrāvakahood* is Bodhisattvahood in the form of *śrāvakahood* (and it is an expression of Bodhisattvahood here, a part of the Bodhisattva path, only because it has forgotten its Bodhisattvahood, because it excludes it), or the setup is humor in the form of seriousness. Non-pen is pen appearing as non-pen. Here we can see the manner in which the Tiantai Three Truths provides the decisive alternative to the Whiteheadian view of unambiguous atomic determinacy as the standard of actuality. Determinacy corresponds to the Truth of Local Coherence only; but here every Local Coherence is also Globally Incoherent (always already ambiguated, readable as every other coherence precisely by excluding them), and these two are, precisely in their contrast, one and the same thing (Intersubsumption), two alternate ways of stating the same fact. There is no way to privilege the actuality of the aspect of fixed determinacy, or this thing precisely as it appears at the moment of its arising within a given context, over the further ramifications and expressions that its essential prehendability (ambiguity, objective immortality, Global Incoherence) entails, nor vice versa. And indeed, even Intersubsumption (All-pervasion as All-pervadedness), the union of determinacy and indeterminacy, or of this entity as it appears now and all the things that can henceforth be made of it, is not to be privileged over either extreme. It is on this basis that the Tiantai doctrine of "inherent entailment" is established, which holds that all coherences without exception are inherently entailed in any given coherence. This does not mean merely that every actual entity prehends all other entities, but more, that the identity of the prehender and prehended in this relation can never be definitively determined; this very coherence X here can equally validly be read as every other coherence, as expressions of all conceivable forms of non-Xness. It is this entity right here which *is* all the other entities, and it is these other prehended entities which are this entity doing the prehending. This is the essence of the interfused Three Truths as understood in the Tiantai tradition, which makes the unidirectional Whiteheadian notion of prehension, as premised on the privileging of determinacy alone as actuality, untenable.

On this model, we have a possibility for a less onesided understanding of the prehender-prehended relation than we find in Whitehead. For here the *agent* responsible for "opening" the rest of the world is no longer simply the ultimate teaching itself, but all the inferior teachings themselves. That is, once the *Lotus* has opened all the other teachings, these other teachings become the ultimate teaching itself. But to be the ultimate teaching means to have, like the *Lotus*, the ability to open up all other teachings. This point is made explicitly in the writings of the school of the Tiantai master Siming Zhili.[16] So it is not only that this actual entity currently in the process of reaching its satisfaction prehends all other entities in their objective immortality, such that they are merely passive raw materials for its work; on the contrary, it is impossible even to specify any exclusive agent of this operation. We can say with equal validity that the prehended entities participate in prehending themselves, or in opening themselves up (indeed, in strict Tiantai terms, any participant in the process can be adequately described as the *sole* agent of the process; any aspect can be the sole prehender, while all the others are the prehended, and vice versa).[17] It is for this reason that we have referred to this process sometimes as *self*-recontextualization.

This point is well illustrated by the Tiantai reading of the climactic scene in the *Lotus* where the Treasure Tower emerges from the earth. This stupa, a

---

[16] T46.880a.

[17] Compare, for example, Zhili's assertion that when a Bodhisattva responds to the stimulus of sentient beings, it is equally adequate to say that both stimulus and response come from the self, or that both come from the other, or that the two work together as both stimulus and response, or none of the above (T34.892b, 920b). In other words, the agency of the event can be located at any point within it, or in the whole, or nowhere; none of these is exclusively true, but all of these are provisionally true and equally adequate descriptions for certain sentient beings.

monument to a *part* of a past deceased Buddha, can be read as the past in its objective immortality, coming to form a part of the present. Its active emergence from the earth to bear witness to Śākyamuni's preaching of the *Lotus* already suggests the active element of this prehended element, but the parable goes farther, for the dead (objectively immortal) Buddha inside turns out not to be dead at all, and where we expected to find merely a part (as in standard Buddhist stupa worship) of this Buddha, we have instead the whole living Buddha. He speaks, he invites the Buddha of the present to open up this past, and indeed to join him in it. The live Buddha inside the stupa is a powerful image of the active participation of the past in its own prehension, and his wholeness testifies to the fact that no simple unilateral part/whole relation pertains to the relation between the prehending present and the prehended past. The objectively immortal past is here not just one element or part taken into a unicentric whole that is orchestrated by the present entity. Note that the Buddha of the present, Śākyamuni, after being instructed by the Buddha of the past, is able to open the stupa and enter it only by gathering together all the aspects of his present activity, all his transformation bodies. We may read this as suggesting that, when the present moment unifies the extent of its multifariousness, the multitude of prehended entities of various and contrasted forms as which it currently expresses itself, this has the simultaneous effect of revealing the activeness of all the seemingly dead, past, merely prehended or objectively immortal entities, and overcoming the illusion that they are merely parts within a larger whole: the stupa is revealed to have a live complete Buddha within it, Śākyamuni opens it up and, importantly, joins him inside. This suggests that not only is the past an active member of the prehending relation, but that the present has recognized itself as acting in the past as well. The deeds of the long dead Buddhas are now seen to be equally validly describable as the activities of this Buddha living now, or, in Tiantai terms, of this pen here, in such a way that no definitive judgment can be made about which is the agent and which the patient, nor what is a part and what is the whole; each is the whole of which the others are the parts, and each is the active prehender for which all the others are the passive prehended, reciprocally. It is this insight that paves the way for the true doctrinal climax of the scripture, the Buddha's revelation of his prior enlightenment and lifespan.

If the "trace-gate" of the sutra may be read as asserting that all practices of sentient beings are in reality readable as Bodhisattva practices, the revelation of the "root-gate" may perhaps be understood as taking the next step, namely that the activities of a Bodhisattva may be equally validly read as the activities of a Buddha. In the "Emergence of Bodhisattvas from the Earth" chapter, Śākyamuni says, "Since the time when I reached supreme enlightenment at the town of Gaya, at the foot of the tree, and put in motion the all-surpassing wheel of the law, I have brought to maturity all of them [the Bodhisattvas of the Earth] for superior enlightenment."[18] In this verse, any notion of a dichotomy between the "recent enlightenment" and the "original enlightenment" of the Buddha is completely effaced; Sakyamuni asserts in the same sentence both that he was enlightened at the foot of a tree in the town of Gaya forty-odd years previously, *and* that his activities as a Buddha extend to the ancient past, to the maturation of these myriads of advanced Bodhisattvas. It is in this way that we must understand his "infinite lifespan." For the implication here is that, once he became a Buddha at Gaya, he realized also that he had already been a Buddha, or rather that the activities of all Buddhas of the past were in fact equally readable as his own activities. These activities were necessarily done in the form of not knowing he was a Buddha, just as the Bodhisattvas must at times forget that they are Bodhisattvas, and believe they are *śrāvakas, in order to* fulfill their Bodhisattva vow. The parable of the doctor in the "Lifespan" chapter illustrates this point well: the Buddha's deeds are sometimes better accomplished by his absence, his death, than by his presence. That is, he is all the more present in his own absence, all the more active and efficacious. Hence, upon enlightenment he is able to see that all his previous (and perhaps future) moments of "nonenlightenment," the absence of his own awareness of Buddhahood, were precisely Buddhahood, the functioning of enlightenment, which has been enlightening beings for countless ages. Nonenlightenment is enlightenment in the form of nonenlightenment. Delusion is Buddhahood in the form of delusion, as delusion, included in it precisely by being excluded from it. Here not only does the prehended share in the work of prehending, but the prehender sees the prehended—the past deeds when he was not yet thus and so— as aspects of his present prehending, or the activity of this very actual entity which he is at this moment, and vice versa. Those past moments of otherness are not merely passively prehended: they are also this very moment of prehending itself, all the more active, all the more efficiently prehending all into the actuality of the Buddha-vehicle, by being apparently passive and absent. The dichotomy between activity and passivity is here overcome.

Intriguingly, Whitehead describes his modification of the antithetical terms "universal" and "particular" in favor of "eternal objects" and "actual entities" as an attempt to overcome precisely this sort of one-sided relationship.

---

[18] Kern's translation from the Sanskrit (op. cit., 293). A literal translation of the corresponding verse in Kumārajīva's translation would read: "I attained supreme enlightenment beneath the bodhi tree near the city of Gaya, and turned the supreme wheel of the Dharma; thus did I teach and transform them, and bring about their initial arisal of the aspiration for enlightenment. . . . Now I tell you truly, I have been teaching and transforming them for long ages" (T9.41b).

The notion of a universal is of that which can enter into the description of many particulars; whereas the notion of a particular is that it is described by universals, and does not itself enter into the description of any other particular. . . . [However,] an actual entity cannot be described, even inadequately, by universals; because other actual entities do enter into the description of any one actual entity. Thus every so-called 'universal' is particular in the sense of being just what it is, diverse from everything else; and every so-called 'particular' is universal in the sense of entering into the constitutions of other actual entities.[19]

This would suggest, however, that the eternal objects and objectively immortal past entities need not be conceived merely as the prehended, and the present actual entity merely as the prehender; in line with the position outlined above, we can perhaps see a way clear here toward reconfiguring the relation so that the prehended is also in a sense the prehender, and vice versa; that all actual entities are constantly prehending each other, serving as both universal and particular to one another, agents whose activity can never be closed off once and for all, who can recenter all reality around themselves under certain conditions—as, in the sutra, the treasure tower takes in the present Buddha Sakyamuni once all his transformation bodies have gathered together in one place.

This brings us back to the question of the givenness and nonnegotiability of the eternal objects, and the question of God. Whitehead is intensely concerned to correct what he regards as some of the errors of traditional theistic theology's conception of God. Primary among these is the one-sided transcendence of God, the "vicious separation of the flux from the permanence" which leads to the concept "of an entirely static God, with eminent reality, in relation to an entirely fluent world."[20] Bound up with these are God conceived in the image of an imperial ruler, as a personification of moral energy, and in the image of an ultimate philosophical principle.[21] All of these are pernicious errors, Whitehead thinks, which separate God from the world unduly and moreover misconstrue him. In fact, he is not an exception to general metaphysical principles but their primary exemplification. He is not eminently real, but rather, in his primordial form, deficiently actual. This primordial character of God, Whitehead says, is "the acquirement by creativity of a primordial character."[22] But this not only exemplifies, but also establishes the categorical obligations. We are told that he is the principle of concretion itself—that "whereby there is initiated a definite outcome from a situation

---

[19] PR, 76.
[20] PR, 526.
[21] PR, 520.
[22] PR, 522.

otherwise riddled with ambiguity."²³ This primordial nature of God is unconscious; he is conscious only in his consequent nature, which is the realization of the actual world in the unity of his nature, and through the transformation of his wisdom. The primordial nature is limited by no actuality that it presupposes, is infinite, devoid of negative prehensions, free, complete, eternal, actually deficient, and unconscious. The consequent nature of God is determined, incomplete, consequent, fully actual, and conscious.²⁴ It is on the basis of this dipolar notion of God that Whitehead can make his famous theses of reversibility: it is as true to say that God is permanent, one, actual eminently, immanent in the world, transcending the world, and creating the world, while the world is fluent, many, deficiently actual, pervaded by God, transcended by God, created by God, as to say just the opposite.²⁵

Now the question I want to raise here is whether Whitehead really makes good on this claim to thoroughgoing reversibility. For there is one traditional theistic attribute of God that he retains here, which goes hand in hand with the theses of atomism and definiteness and givenness referred to above. We are told that in God there is no loss, that as consequent he salvages and prehends transformatively all things in the world, all persons, with a "tender care" which in effect saves the world. Indeed, "each actuality in the temporal world has its reception into God's nature." However,

> the corresponding element in God's nature is not temporal actuality, but is the transmutation of that temporal actuality into a living, ever-present fact. An enduring personality in the temporal world is a route of occasions in which the successors with some peculiar completeness sum up their predecessors. The correlate fact in God's nature is an even more complete unity of life in a chain of elements for which succession does not mean loss of immediate unison. . . . Thus in the sense in which the present occasion is the person *now*, and yet with his own past, so the counterpart in God is that person in God.²⁶

Whitehead is quite ingeniously avoiding the conclusion that this "counterpart of the person in God" is not exactly that person himself; just as the present person is a completer summation of the route of occasions leading up to it, its own past, which it both is and is not, the person in God is a still more complete summation of that same course of events. But we must ask, do we really overcome the traditional separation of God from the individual person with this move? The worry is that God remains God, and the person

---

²³ PR, 523.
²⁴ PR, 524.
²⁵ PR, 528.
²⁶ PR, 531–32.

the person, even if the latter is transmuted into an element of the former. The reason for this is that once again we seem to have a one-sided prehender-prehended relation here, and the unambiguously fixed whole/part relation that goes with it. God as primordial is prehended by the course of events that is this temporal person, while this temporal course itself is prehended by the consequent nature of God. This is, indeed, the means by which God becomes himself in actuality, prehends his own primordial nature, through the medium, as it were, of its prehension by the intervening actual events. God is the whole, the prehender, while these events and persons are the parts, the prehended. But in that case we must ask, why can the list of reversible predicates not be extended to the other attributes Whitehead attributes to God, particularly in his consequent nature? That is, God is "a fellow sufferer who understands," who "saves the world" with his "infinite tender care" and so on. Can these also be said of the individual person, or even of the individual person "in God"? Or just of God *simpliciter*, as the encompassing prehender but not as the parts prehended per se?

Whatever the answer may be in the case of Whitehead, it is clear that this is just what is asserted in the *Lotus Sūtra*; each sentient being is practicing the Bodhisattva path (which, by the Tiantai reading, means also that he or she is always already a Buddha; we may say that the trace gate establishes that all activities are Bodhisattva activities, while the root gate establishes that all Bodhisattva activities are Buddha-activities; ergo. . . .), is the savior of the world, the fellow-sufferer who understands, extending his infinite tender care to enlighten all beings. Now one could say that here too these beings are only "revealed" to be practicing this path by the *Lotus* itself, and that it is really thus "the same person in the *Lotus*" who is the savior of the world. But this is still different from what we have in Whitehead, for several reasons. First, it is still the individual element so sublated or prehended into this new context who is attributed with the whole salvific function, not the prehending whole itself; each being will be a *whole* Buddha, not "part of" *the* Buddha. Second, the relation between the being prior to "opening the provisional to reveal the real"—for example, before the *śrāvakas* know that they are actually Bodhisattvas—and after this revelation, differs from the relation between the individual person and that person in God. For in this case, it is unmistakably the "same person," indeed, even the same practices, which are now reread as being instances of the Buddha vehicle, as the Buddha's own activity, precisely because they are exclusions of it, as discussed earlier. Their very partiality and one-sidedness is what does the accomplishing of the Bodhisattva work here; they are Buddhas precisely and only in that they are not Buddhas, or they are God not as the encompassing prehender but as the individual benighted parts which stand to be prehended. No other model will allow us to overcome the one-sided notion of sameness or difference pertaining to these two conditions. In the *Lotus*, the *śrāvakas* are truly saving the world while being *śrāvakas*, and precisely by being *śrāvakas*; the same goes for anyone who utters Namo Buddha with a distracted mind, slightly lowers his head, and so on. It is the condition of these beings, or of the definiteness of these beings and these specific practices, to be not *merely* definite. By being so, they are also ambiguous, or in Tiantai terms, definiteness itself is necessarily also indefiniteness, precisely by being definiteness (Local Coherence is Global Incoherence is Intersubsumption); it demands to be opened up and revealed to mean more than it seemed to, not as an extra action upon it added from outside, but as a part of what it is to be definite (a Local Coherence) in the first place. This is because just by being what they are and *not* being sublated, they are sublated; by excluding their own future Buddhahood (practicing the *śrāvakas* path, etc.) they are embodying, performing, exemplifying their Buddhahood.

With this understanding of the Tiantai doctrine of inherent entailment, explicating a kind of presence precisely as absence itself, we can make a few further observations. First of all, we may compare inherent entailment to the givenness of the eternal objects mentioned above. Tiantai famously proclaims that "all Three Thousand Coherences are inherently entailed in every moment of experience," as we have seen; on the surface level this would seem to imply an even more inexorable and perhaps dogmatic givenness than any Whitehead could have dreamed of for his Eternal Objects, since it implies in effect that *every* object is an eternal object, none can ever be extricated from existence, and all are as it were "built-in" to the nature of all things. But now we can perhaps see that, although the three thousand specific forms of existence are indeed in a certain sense more "given" than the eternal objects, this is to be understood in a sense which allows them also to be radically contingent, since their presence can equally be instantiated by their very absence. This makes them less given than the putative givenness of eternal objects, since givenness itself is rethought here, eliminating its dogmatic character. Givenness here is, if you will, brought to the extreme, on the venerable Chinese principle of "things brought to the extreme reverse into their opposite." Their given presence is instantiated equally by their absence.

This brings us to the question of Emptiness, or Global Incoherence, as elaborated into the Tiantai Three Truths, and whether Whitehead's critique of substance ontology adequately covers the same ground. For what is revealed by the Three Truths is that there is more to Global Incoherence than an emphasis on flux or critique of substance ontology. The doctrine that actual occasions are "always becoming, but never are" cannot do the job of Global Incoherence, because the latter calls into question not only the "substance" of entities, in the Aristotelian sense of "what can exist apart," but the *definite identity* of what is in flux. It means not only that "this X here" is what it is only through its prehension of other entities, and perishes as soon as it establishes itself, and cannot "exist apart" from them, cannot be in any one location to the exclusion of others, and so on. The Buddhist position criticizes not only the substantiality, independence, and simple location of any given X, but also the notion that "X as determinate means that X excludes non-X, and cannot be equally legitimately read as non-X." On the Tiantai reading, the determinateness and indeterminateness of X, X as X and as non-X, are one and the same, are alternate names for the same fact. This brings us back to what may be called, from a Tiantai perspective, the basic problem of process thought: the ultimacy given to the categories "one," "many," and "creativity," without disclosing their reversibility. Whitehead calls these the "category of the ultimate" and implies that they cannot be further derived or reduced.[27] The Tiantai position, on the other hand, is that they can indeed be reduced—to each other. They are three ways of stating the same thing. Oneness is manyness is creativity, and to say any one of them is to say the other two. For Whitehead, it would seem, oneness and manyness are distinct but inseparable *aspects* of any actual occasion, always copresent and indeed merely abstractions from the occasion, to be sure, but nonetheless two *different things* that may be legitimately said about the occasion, whose interrelation or mutual grounding is not disclosed. This is why the active/passive and the whole/part relations within actual occasions remain unilateral. In Tiantai, on the other hand, they are identical—it is not just the case that every one is also a many, or that every entity is at once one and many, but rather that oneness itself is manyness itself. Each turns out to be the other, in accordance with the Möbius strip structure of the Three Truths and the way in which it allows us to view the presence of the absent, and the relation of being-X to not-being-X. The inherent self-negation of any actual entity is, we may say, its necessary inner structure; it is not merely that whatever appears also disappears, or even that it disappears as soon as it appears, but rather that its appearing is its perishing, its determination as some X is also its indetermination, its ambiguation, which overcomes Whitehead's duality of one and many as inseparable but absolutely different aspects of each occasion, which is what passivizes the prehended past and allows God to slip in as the encompassing prehender whose role differs from that of the prehended parts. And indeed, if we may say so, this is perhaps why Whitehead sometimes feels so flat and uninspiring in spite of his profundity—the "selfness" of actual occasions remains ultimately unexploded, since each is just itself. Along the same lines, we may

---

[27] PR, 31–32.

say that the true "tragedy" of what Whitehead poignantly calls the tragic beauty of existence is not adequately expressed by his notion "perpetual perishing"; for the true tragic beauty of the Three Truths lies in the fact that every coherence wants what it does not want, is what it is not, and is eternally in conflict with itself, and its "harmony" subsists only in the form of this genuine conflict, not merely an aesthetic contrast of mutual noninhibition of genuinely distinct entities. Each entity is contrasted *to itself*, which is where the true tragedy and the true beauty lie. Whitehead's system turns this into merely *someone or something else*, another subsequent actual occasion, contradicting this coherence. Continuity and discontinuity are here separated; we end up with both too much "self"—each thing is just itself, period—and too little "self"—not enough for anything to bite its own tail and devastate *itself*.

This brings us back to the question of Whitehead's doctrine of "eternal objects," which he defines perhaps most clearly in chapter 10 of *Science and the Modern World*. The realm of eternal objects, according to this exposition, is that by reference to which an actual occasion of experience is "diversified." The eternal objects

> transcend that immediate occasion in that they have analogous or different connections with other occasions of experience. For example a definite shade of red may, in the immediate occasion, be implicated with the shape of sphericity in some definite way. But that shade of red and that spherical shape, exhibit themselves as transcending that occasion in that either of them has other relationships to other occasions.[28]

The particular shade of red and the spherical shape are here basic examples of eternal objects. A particular experience of a sphere of this color is "prehending" these two eternal objects, among other things (i.e., other actual occasions in the history of events leading to the actual production of this experience). In addition to these "positive prehensions" of eternal objects, there are also "negative prehensions" of other eternal objects, which are excluded from this experience:

> Also, apart from the actual occurrence of the same things in other occasions, every actual occasion is set within a realm of alternative interconnected entities. This realm is disclosed by all the untrue propositions which can be predicated significantly of that occasion. It is the realm of alternative suggestions, whose foothold in actuality transcends each actual occasion.[29]

---

[28] Alfred North Whitehead, *Science and the Modern World* (New York: Macmillan, 1967), 160.
[29] Ibid.

These negatively prehended eternal objects express the "great refusal" which is the primary characteristic of an occasion's aesthetic achievement. "An event is decisive in proportion to the importance (for it) of its untrue propositions: their relevance to the event cannot be dissociated from what the event is in itself by way of achievement."[30] In the case of the experience of the red sphere, a particular shade of blue and cubicity would be examples of such negatively prehended eternal objects.

It is notable that in the case of both the positively and the negatively prehended eternal objects, it is *precisely the same object* which is apprehended in various events. This is what Whitehead refers to as their "transcendence." These eternal objects, he tells us, are what previous philosophy has referred to as "universals," and in Western thought from Plato to Kant and beyond, the primary model underlying the idea of a genuinely reiterable object which remains the same in spite of its various instantiations derives from mathematics. It is, that is to say, inferred and extended from a consideration of the nature of mathematical truths, such as the Pythagorean theorem. This is something that is "so" of any right triangle whatsoever, and whether or not any "actual" triangle happens to exist. It is a property which is the same in the case of each right triangle, in addition to the different properties that may pertain to actually existing right triangles; this one is made of chalk, that one of toothpicks, this one is red, that one is blue, but all of them are such that the Pythagorean theorem can be truly stated of them. Indeed, if we take Whitehead at his word that eternal objects transcend their relationship to *any* actual occasion to mean that they transcend their relationship to any determinable finite set of such relationships, then in *all* cases, no matter how many actual occasions we may know this eternal object to be related to, it presents itself as possessing necessarily *other* relations with *other* occasions. This means that no finite set of relations or instantiations can exhaust them, nor can they be derived in their entirety from any such a temporally finite set of instantiations. This is what qualifies them as "eternal"—and indeed, as we shall see, this also makes them more than merely empirical. "Eternal objects are thus, in their nature, abstract. By 'abstract' I meant that what an eternal object is in itself—that is to say, its essence—is comprehensible without reference to some one particular occasion of experience. To be abstract is to transcend particular concrete occasions of actual happening." The Pythagorean theorem, on this view, is comprehensible without reference to any particular existing right triangle. It is so, and remains the same, whether there are none, one, or a million such triangles in experience. Whitehead is quick to balance this claim, stating, "to transcend an actual occasion does not mean being

---

[30] Ibid., 160–61.

disconnected from it. On the contrary, I hold that each eternal object has its own proper connection with each such occasion, which I term its mode of ingression into that occasion."[31] *Each* eternal object ingresses into *each* actual occasion: prehended either positively (with some particular degree of emphasis) or negatively.

Whitehead's exposition continues with the following assertion: "Thus an eternal object is to be comprehended by acquaintance with (i) its particular individuality, (ii) its general relationships to other eternal objects as apt for realization in actual occasions, and (iii) the general principle which expresses its ingression in particular actual occasions."[32] What is crucial to note here is that, while this specification is consistent with Whitehead's claim that eternal objects are transcendent to each actual occasion (i.e., can be comprehended without reference to any of them), *they are not transcendent to one another, nor to actual occasions as a whole and as such (i.e., the total set of all actual occasions)*. That is, they can be understood only in relation to each other (as a particular mathematical theorem can only be grasped by seeing how it is interrelated with other mathematical theorems), and also in relation to its manner of ingression into (any and every) actual occasion. In short:

> An eternal object, considered as an abstract entity, cannot be divorced from its reference to other eternal objects, and from its reference to actuality generally; though it is disconnected from its actual modes of ingression into definite actual occasions. This principle is expressed by the statement that each eternal object has a 'relational essence.' This relational essence determines how it is possible for the object to have ingression into actual occasions.[33]

This is Whitehead's way of salvaging the "unchanging essence" of universals, the fact that each "is what it is" as he says, in spite of the number of its actual ingressions, while maintaining its "relational essence" as entailed by the general premises of process philosophy. Whitehead tells us that each eternal object adds its own unique contribution to each occasion, and that this contribution is *identical* in each case. However, the "mode of ingression" in each case is what is *different* in each case.[34]

This relation between identity and difference is further specified by saying that the essence of an eternal object has a *determinate* relationship to every other eternal object, but an *indeterminate* relationship to particular actual occasions. This is because each eternal object ingresses into each actual

---

[31] Ibid., 161.
[32] Ibid.
[33] Ibid., 161–62.
[34] Ibid., 161.

occasion in a graded scale of actualization—it may stand as a possibility realized or rejected in that actualization, or realized to a particular degree in relation to other (eternal objects =) possibilities. This means, however, that although the relation of the eternal object to the occasion is indeterminate (it may ingress in a variety of different ways), the reverse relation of the occasion to the eternal object is *determinate* (it is prehended in some particular way in this occasion). "Accordingly the relationship between [an eternal object] A and [an actual occasion] a is external as regards A, and is internal as regards a."[35] This asymmetry is crucial for Whitehead's establishment of the *identity* of the eternal objects in every *differing* occasion. An actual occasion is "a limitation" or better, "a gradation," by which Whitehead means

> an indeterminateness stands in the essence of any eternal object (A, say). The actual occasion *a* synthesizes in itself every eternal object; and, in so doing, it includes the *complete* determinate relatedness of A to every other eternal object, or set of eternal objects. This synthesis is a limitation of realization but *not* of content. Each relationship preserves its inherent self-identity. But grades of entry into this synthesis are inherent in each actual occasion, such as *a*. These grades can be expressed only as relevance of value.[36]

In this connection, Whitehead tells us of the *double aspect* pertaining to the prehension of eternal objects into actual occasions: (1) each eternal object has a *determinate* relatedness to *each* particular occasion (i.e., with regard to a, the relationship to A is internal); and (2) each eternal object has an *indeterminate* relatedness to occasions generally, or as a whole.[37] But recall also that Whitehead has claimed that the relationship of A to a is *indeterminate* (A can be understood without reference to any particular a), while on the other hand the relationship of A to *all* of actuality is *determinate* (A cannot be understood apart from the general principle of its ingression into actual occasions as such; its relation to actuality *as such* is internal).

Thus on the one hand it is the relation to the particular occasions that is determinate and to the totality of occasions that is indeterminate, while on the other hand it is also just the reverse. The crucial distinction seems to be whether the relationship between A and a is seen, as it were, from the side of A or from the side of a. But is this one relationship or two? It is really possible for the same bond to be both definite and indefinite? It is Whitehead's doctrine of the transcendence of eternal objects that is supposed to make an affirmative answer to this question possible. If so, must we not redefine what

---

[35] Ibid., 160.
[36] Ibid., 162.
[37] Ibid., 163.

it means to be definite and indefinite? This is a crucial question for Whitehead, given the central role definiteness plays in his philosophy, and his need to keep it absolutely distinct from indefiniteness especially for his value theory to make sense. For definiteness is of the essence of the process of actualization, the emergence of actual occurrences which is the creative advance of the universe. An actual occasion is constituted by its exclusion of ambiguity, its being simply what it is, period. The eternal objects are supposed to have an existence beyond the definiteness of their particular bonds with particular actual occasions, while "objectively immortal" past events exist only in the definite prehensions of subsequent occasions.

The question we wish to raise here is whether this difference is really coherent. For we may ask, is a past occasion, in its objective immortality, really in a different ontological position from the eternal objects? Does it not remain the same in just the sense that an eternal object does, and transcend particular occasions in the same way? How we answer this question depends on how we answer the previous one about the relation of determinateness to indeterminateness. If these two can really be kept separate, as Whitehead wishes in spite of his doubling of the bond between eternal objects and actual occasions, a genuine difference can exist between these two modes of immortality, since a special transcendence will pertain to the eternal objects which cannot be found for the objectively immortal past occasions. If not, is there any difference between "eternal objects" and "past events"?

It is clear that Whitehead wishes to move his doctrine of universals in a "Nominalist" rather than a "Realist" direction, while also respecting the special status of the eternal objects as derived from considerations of the peculiar qualities of pure mathematics. This is evident from his assertion that universals cannot describe particulars *even inadequately*, and the reasons given: that other actual occasions also must enter into the description in all cases whatsoever. Traditional "universals" are by definition also "particular" in that they have a necessarily limited range of application. That is, "red" does not apply to all things, but only to red things; they are, as Whitehead says, "just what they are, distinct from everything else." But Whitehead's eternal objects apply to literally everything. They are involved in every actual occasion, either positively or negatively prehended. This means they are genuinely "universal" in a sense that traditional universals are not. Can they really remain simply "distinct from everything else, just what they are" if they are instantiated in some form or other in every possible occasion? Indeed, this literally universal application makes them less like traditional universals and more like an a priori *category* in the Kantian sense, although this is doubtless a result that Whitehead would not welcome. Given the alternative between negative and positive prehensions, they are specifically similar to categories of modality, that is, for which an either/or applies (Kant's examples are existent/nonexistent, possible/impossible, and necessary/contingent). Whitehead's notion of *degrees* of ingression is profoundly un-Kantian, but perhaps not incompatible with universality as category. What this means is that no actual occasion can be an object, can be experienced, can be an occasion as such, unless each and every eternal object is involved, just as, say, for Kant no object can be experienced unless it is spatial and temporal, or causal, and so on.

This brings us back to the question of the determinacy/ambiguity dichotomy in Whitehead. For the eternal objects are what "diversifies" actual occasions, an essential part of what makes them determinate. And yet they are diverse, identical in all instances, and categorical, that is, *all* of them are operative in *every* actual occasion. There is a tension here that Whitehead wants to solve with his doctrine of differing degrees and modes of ingression, the aesthetic harmony achieved between them in each actual occasion's determinateness. But if we rethink the relation between determinateness and ambiguity, there is perhaps another way of combining genuine categorical universality, anti-transcendentalism, real diversity, and thoroughgoing reversibility—one which has very intriguing consequences especially for value theory.

Do we still need the eternal objects in a Neo-Tiantai universe? The answer is yes. For the Three Thousand as eternal and omnipresent are more than just the Three Thousand as "objectively immortal." The difference is that, like a mathematical law or a particular shade of red, every particular discovery of an object comes with a sense that it is not new, that it has always been there, that it would have always been there whether or not it came about in this particular contingent situation. It could only appear if it transcended all appearance, and yet appeared in all appearance, like a Kantian category. This is because the act of determination of any possible X would always be the act of determination of this particular object as its necessarily included/excluded outside, and hence this determination is accomplished no matter what determination is made. It transcends any particular determination. It could only be here as a finite temporal appearance if it had always been here, was eternal and omnipresent, beyond this finite appearance, as long as there is any finite appearance (and there is always some finite appearance). This is the cash value of the claim that "only because X is inherently eternal and omnipresent can it be conditional and finite." But is there in the Neo-Tiantai view a separate set of eternal objects, apart from the objective immortality of occasions? No. Actual occasions are just extremely complex eternal objects. This also means that the eternal objects are not exempted from process; they too must "differ" with each instantiation as much as the objective immortality of actual occasions does. Difference and sameness applies to both the level of principle (equivalent to eternal objecthood) and the level of actual phenomena (equivalent to actual occasions), and these two are seen to be ultimately identical (and thus different!). Each of the two levels of the Three Thousand pervades all times and places, but in two distinct ways. As principle, they pervade transcendentally, with (1) an indeterminate relation to any particular occasion, but with (2) determinate relations to each other and (3) to occasions in general. As actual occasions, they pervade contingently, adopted variously into various other occasions, with an indeterminate relation to future occasions and a determinate relation to past relations. From this we can clearly see the Tiantai conclusion: all things are eternal objects and all things are actual occasions. With this goes the more radical claim that the "indeterminate" bond, the partial particular way that each content integrates all contents, thereby revealing them to be categories, is itself the only type of "determinate" bond which exists among the categories as such, and between each category and the totality of possible contents.

Whitehead sees these two types of interpervasion, but assigns them to differing sets of objects. The Huayan tradition of Chinese Buddhism sees only the latter type of interpervasion, of the contingent events among one another, the "nonobstruction of phenomenon with phenomenon," which is grounded on a Principle *of* Interpervasion (Emptiness), which however does not itself truly *inter*pervade. The phenomena are the phenomena, the principle is the principle, and their "interpervasion" (Huayan's "Third Dharmadhatu") is not thoroughgoing enough to allow the two to change places. The specific determinate qualities do not share *all* the characteristics of the principle—grounding all existence, being the foundation of all appearances; especially, they do not share the character of being "that by virtue of which all things interpervade," as in the Tiantai case. Principle remains that on which interpervasion depends, while phenomena are what, depending on their putative identity to this principle, interpervade. But *these* two do not interpervade in the Tiantai sense, where they converge as a single moment of experience. An asymmetry remains in the Huayan relation between principle and phenomena, so that "eternal objects" never enter the picture. There is just the eternal objectlessness that manifests and grounds and allows the interpervasion of all objects (Emptiness, Principle), and the contingent "objective immortality" of mutually interpervading occasions. In the Tiantai view, we have both senses of interpervasion, but both simultaneously apply to all objects. These two senses are seen to be intersubsumptive. The contingent interpervasion *is* the necessary interpervasion.

We may also note that the Tiantai doctrine rewrites the notion of the "givenness" of eternal objects, much as it rewrites the Kantian assertion that the categories are never experienced. It will be recalled that for Tiantai the categories are in fact experienced, in just the same way anything else is experienced—

abstractly, deludedly, one-sidedly, in contrast to an outside which turns out ultimately not to be an outside but rather to be another instance of the same category. Since we have the word "space," space must have been experienced, for example, in empty space as opposed to filled space, or further as space as opposed to time or another category. But upon examination it was seen that this contrast could not hold, and the contrasting category—for example, filled space—was just another form of spatiality. Similarly, it is not true to say that the eternal objects are somehow not actual occasions. They pertain to what Whitehead calls the primordial nature of God, which is, as we noted, an actual occurrence in its own right, but certainly one that has a unique position among all occurrences. In the Tiantai version, this special status is repealed. When someone first experienced the abstract mathematical quality of "triangularity," it was an occurrence. This occurrence turned out to have a content which by its nature could never have begun or ended. The same, however, is true of every occurrence, for to be a content is to be a category. All eternal objects are actual occurrences, and all actual occurrences are eternal objects.

It is for this reason that we said above that the Tiantai doctrine of "inherent entailment" and the pre-existence of all possible coherences, which appears to be a perfect example of the "narrow stuffy" doctrine of unfoldment of pre-existing contents, criticized by Whitehead, and an obstacle to any understanding of true creativity, is in fact just the opposite, that is, the most radical possible doctrine of truly creative novelty. For what the Tiantai doctrine means is that the "creative advance of the universe" is not only a succession of constantly new occasions which are perpetually coming forth, as opposed to certain primary categories, eternal objects, or God, which remain the same (as is the case for Kant, Whitehead, and Huayan in various ways), but is simultaneously the constant emergence of *new categories*. This means that every experience is a disclosure of a new universe, with a new set of rules, new categoreal obligations, and even new a priori categories of experience and understanding, new ways of unifying all previous unifying conditions of experience. The Principle of Emptiness is not "a single, same principle," as in Huayan, nor is there a fixed set of categories of understanding as in Kant, or of Reason as in Hegel, nor even the "primordial nature of God" which possesses a certain set of eternal objects and no others, as the basic overall activity of creativity, the general activity which is not an occasion but rather analogous to Spinoza's substance, assuming a primal determinateness, as in Whitehead. Rather, in a very real sense, as in the *Lotus Sūtra* doctrine of universal Buddhahood, there is in Tiantai *a new God*, a new foundation and new telos of all possible activity, with each moment of experience.

These differences have important practical consequences for ethics and value theory in all three cases. Whitehead defines determinacy, disambiguity, as a value, in a certain sense as Value itself. The adjustment of occasions to a harmony of aims is of the essence of process, and each occasion reaches "satisfaction" when it has become fully determinate, establishing a self-justifying value of beauty and harmony in unifying the totality of all existences in just this graded harmony. Then it perishes into objective immortality. In Huayan, the contemplation of interpervasion itself is seen as somehow salvific; whatever experience arises is to be seen as bringing with it all other occasions. Value resides in seeing that both determinacy and indetermination are aspects of the arising of occasions—both their formation into particulars and the openness of these particulars. But these two are seen in Huayan as two conceptually separable aspects; occasions are determinate because they are indeterminate, and indeterminate because they are determinate, but these remain two separate aspects both of which point to the tertium quid of pure, undefiled principle, which manifests as these two interlinked aspects.

In Tiantai, the interpenetration of determination and indetermination is more radical. For all our reflections about universally applicable categories are directed, in the Tiantai case, not toward the solution of logical, epistemological, or mathematical problems, but as a solution to the basic existential problem of Buddhism—the problem of suffering. It is an inquiry into value above all. To be a universally instantiated category is here to be an absolute value. This is surely surprising, for universality as such would seem to be axiologically neutral; after all, "redness" does not seem to imply any necessarily positive value, much less general concepts like "evil" or "decay" or "disharmony"—quite the contrary. The reason categorical universality is identical to value in Tiantai, however, derives from the primitive Buddhist problematic of impermanence and suffering. Very much simplified, for Buddhism, the determinate is the conditional, and the conditional is necessarily suffering. This is true whether we are speaking of the positive presence of a state that could be otherwise, or its absence, and it applies to all possible objects of knowledge and experience. Ipso facto, it applies to all possible objects of desire. Whatever can be desired is a determinate object, which therefore is conditional. But in the Tiantai understanding, whatever is conditional is also therefore not only determinate, but also, as such, ambiguous, indeterminate. As such, it will always fail to satisfy any single desire for a determinate result, which every desire must, by definition, be. The determination of things is their indetermination, their indetermination is their determination. To be truly valuable, an object of desire would have to be able to sustain itself in being, to be free, to be its own master, to be able to sustain an unambiguous determinacy. But this is impossible for any finite, phenomenal, simply located thing in time, and thus, it would seem, for any *content* whatsoever. For to arise and perish at a particular point in time ipso facto shows that an object is conditioned, has its being only under the specific condition of this time and place.

But in Tiantai, as we have seen, the finite simple location of things is precisely their all-pervasion and vice versa. Their necessary/impossible omnipresence is their contingent appearing and vice versa. Value here is conceived of as the "freedom, eternity, bliss, and beauty" of this all-pervasion qua contingency, that is, the freedom of any coherence to manifest as all other coherences, which is precisely its inescapable compulsion to depend on them, and their inescapable presence in it, whatever they are. But this means also that value is not just the transparent determinate realization of a transparent goal, as in some of Whitehead's pronouncements, where value is the achieved determinacy of a subjective aim, accomplished through the harmonization of graded prehensions of all these other coherences. Value in Tiantai contains a certain ineluctable element of opacity. This accords closely with the *Lotus Sūtra* idea that one always accomplishes more than the aim one consciously embraced, something qualitatively other. The *śrāvakas* in the sutra say that they attained Bodhisattvahood "without seeking it." (*buqiu zide* in Kūmarajīva's Chinese version). This does not mean they were not seeking anything at all; on the contrary, they were seeking something else (*śrāvaka-nirvrāna*), and indeed something that specifically excluded the aim of Bodhisattvahood. Further, it was precisely by this exclusion of Bodhisattvahood from the conscious aim that the aim was in fact achieved.

This agrees with Whitehead's more developed theory of value, for example, in the notion of "Peace" developed in the last chapter of *Adventures of Ideas*. "The experience of Peace," Whitehead says there,

> is largely beyond the control of purpose. It comes as a gift. The deliberate aim at Peace very easily passes into its bastard substitute, Anaesthesia. . . . [True Peace] results in a wider sweep of conscious interest. It enlarges the field of attention. Thus Peace is self-control at its widest,—at the width where the 'self' has been lost, and interest has been transferred to coordinations wider than personality. Here the real motive interests of the spirit are meant, and not the superficial play of discursive ideas. . . . Peace is the understanding of tragedy, and at the same time its preservation.[38]

I submit that, even with the qualification that the "motive interest of the spirit" and "not the superficial play of discursive ideas" is meant here, this wider notion of value which goes beyond purpose and self, is in severe tension with Whitehead's generally teleological notion of process, conceived in terms of

---

[38] A. N. Whitehead, *Adventures of Ideas* (New York: Free Press, 1956), 285–86.

the achievement of determinacy which is ultimate difference absolutely distinguishable from indeterminacy. It is this same irreversible distinction that also undergirds Whitehead's separation of the realm of eternal objects from the realm of actual occasions. We can suggest that the Tiantai picture of actual occasions as eternal objects, of determinacy as indeterminacy, allows for an expanded notion of "purpose as purposelessness," and hence "each purpose as all other purposes," which provides a firmer metaphysical ground for this notion of Peace.

Whitehead's final words in this citation are especially apt in the Tiantai case. Buddhahood in Tiantai entails precisely the "understanding and preservation of tragedy"—this is what is referred to by the distinctive Tiantai doctrine of the evil inherent in the Buddha nature, which can never be destroyed. As Zhiyi says, the Buddha comprehends the evil nature (the understanding of tragedy) but does not eradicate it (the preservation of tragedy). But given the doctrines just outlined, this assumes a very definite and clear meaning that is perhaps harder to grasp in its practical implications in Whitehead's own exposition. That is, to "understand" evil and tragedy—disharmony, partiality, anger, greed, delusions of simple location, and misplaced concreteness—means to see it as both principle and phenomenon, as an eternal object which pervades and expresses itself in and as all other objects, including the good, precisely by "dwelling in its own position"—being fully itself, fully finite, fully impermanent, fully evil. But it is only thus that the overcoming of evil is truly accomplished. Evil is both a content and a category, a condition of all experience, instantiated as all experience and as all other categories. As a content, it is conditioned, transient, painful, and disharmonious, but precisely by being a content it is also a category, and as such, it is free, eternal, blissful, and harmonious. Process itself, in its transient concrete contingency, is value.

*   *   *   *   *

This leads us to a conclusion that is perhaps surprising in its very unsurprisingness, for it simply restates what all teachers tell their students the first day when indicating the difference between Buddhism, even in its most wildly devotional Mahāyāna forms, and any kind of theism. The issue is not one of anthropomorphism; for the ultimate nature of the universe, the source, ground, and end of all entities, is in Tiantai certainly as anthropomorphic as it is nonanthropomorphic; humanity is the end of all, the source of all, and the same can be said even of this particular person, or this particular aspect of this person—but it can equally be said that it is, say, just as "pen-o-morphic" as it is "non-pen-o-morphic"; this pen is the source, ground, and end of all entities.

Anthropomorphism, then, is not the issue. Rather, the decisive line that divides Sinitic Buddhism from any kind of theism lies in the doctrine of universal Buddhahood. As the cliché has it, in Buddhism any one may (must) become a Buddha, while in theism the created being can never become God himself. This cliché, it would seem, holds true even in the relation between the most expanded, Buddhistically inclined forms of theism and the most theistic-looking form of Buddhism. We may say that the notion of universal Buddhahood here continues to separate Buddhist thinking decisively from any approximation in theistic-influenced philosophy, whatever other similarities there may be.

This question of the relation between sameness and otherness is really the heart of the matter, and allows us to make a few remarks about one other modern resuscitation of the notion of God, the neo-theism that stresses radical otherness, as it comes to us from figures like Buber and Rosenzweig, to perhaps its most forceful representative, Levinas, whose influence on Derrida and the latter's treatment of the concept of exteriority is not at all negligible, which gives extra resonance to the following remarks.[39] In *Totality and Infinity*, Levinas gives a strong phenomenological account of alterity which rests firmly on the observation that the Other is not a mere negation of me, therefore correlative to me and hence reducible to me, nor another member of the tertium quid, the panoramic whole which neutrally embraces both. Rather, the "face to face" other is genuinely other, absolutely strange, a world (or in our language, a center) unto himself, manifested not in any panorama of adequate ideas (or negations, or differences) but as "the idea of the infinite," which is for Levinas a very unique entity: "the idea of infinity is the mode of being, the 'infinition,' of infinity. Infinity does not first exist, and *then* reveal itself. Its infinition is produced as revelation, as a positing of its idea in me."[40] Again he says,

> The idea of infinity is exceptional in that its *ideatum* surpasses its idea whereas for the things the total coincidence of their 'objective' and 'formal' realities is not precluded. . . . The distance that separates *ideatum* and idea here constitutes the content of the *ideatum* itself. . . . The infinite is the absolutely other . . . the sole *ideatum* of which there can be only an idea in us. . . .[41]

---

[39] See Jacques Derrida, "Violence and Metaphysics: An Essay on the Thought of Emmanual Levinas," in *Writing and Difference*, trans. Alan Bass (Chicago: University of Chicago Press, 1978), 79–153.
[40] Emmanual Levinas, *Totality and Infinity*, trans. Alphonso Lingis (Pittsburgh: Duquesne University Press, 1969), 26.
[41] Ibid., 49.

It is not to be thought of as an object, for the distance between a thought and its object does not exclude but for Levinas implies the *possession* of the object, that is, the suspension of its being, it reducibility to the world of the subject.[42] Levinas further characterizes this idea of infinity in the finite as Pure Desire, the "Desire for the infinite which the desirable arouses rather than satisfies. A Desire perfectly disinterested—Goodness."[43] The latter point has important resonances with the Neo-Tiantai characterization of pure desire and the Good developed above. But one of the most central implications of Levinas's argument here is that otherness does not equal simple negation, which, if accepted, would strike right at the heart of our entire derivation of interpervasion above, depending as it does on the centrality of the self/non-self or X/non-X relation as such. Here then we would like to reaffirm the centrality of direct "correlative" negation, why it does not amount to the taming reduction Levinas has in mind, and why it is crucial to the structure of Desire and value, leading us once again back to the fundamental theism/atheism split. We will claim that the idea of infinity, as an idea whose *ideatum* by definition exceeds any idea, does not produce the notion of otherness in Levinas's sense of a "face to face," but rather otherness in the sense of infinite alternate meanings, what we have called Global Incoherence, the dawning of all possible specifications of the *ideatum*, each of which is equally adequate and inadequate to it. More importantly, we must return to the importance of the idea of the Double, and its place in value theory.

For getting back to Whitehead, we may concur that value is essentially aesthetic contrast; but as we have established above, for us this is not a contrast between two different things or even two aspects of a thing, but between a coherence and itself. A coherence's perfect value, as the Absolute, as the principle and telos of all other things, as Intersubsumption itself, is established precisely when its constituent otherness to itself is manifested, when its identity is manifested qua concealed, that is, seen to be constitutive impossibility. It is here that we must locate the importance of the apparently "correlative" relation between non-X and X. For the Neo-Tiantai redescription of the substance/accident relation (which does not abolish it, but rather makes it reversible) is our answer to Levinas's very legitimate critique of the consequences of the "reducibility" of the other to the self that constitutes the violence of all apparently "neutral" theory. We accept reducibility as correlativity, and the defining of the other as an "aspect" of the self, but with the proviso that this is reversible, that the self *thereby* becomes equally reducible to the other *precisely qua otherness to self*, qua non-Xness as such. This is still a

---

[42] Ibid.
[43] Ibid., 50.

sort of violence, admittedly, but one that constitutively works both ways at once. Rather than the dualism between violence and nonviolence entailed in Levinas's privileging of ethics, we have a *constitutive mutual violence* which, as such, is precisely the "compassion" spoken of earlier—indeed, we would claim, it is the very "face to face" immediacy that Levinas correctly identifies as standing at the origin of all apparently neutral Logos, grounding it, which now turns out to coincide with the ontological extension of Davidson's "principle of charity" which lies at the heart of all coherence as such, the neutral overarching panoramic view that Levinas rejects.

We can put this point more strictly as follows. For something to appear as a coherence, it must be accompanied by some desire, some valuation, some vector of interest. But we have established that value is, with Whitehead, aesthetic contrast, and further, the contrast of any coherence with itself. Hence the value/interest of a coherence which allows it to appear in experience is precisely its tension with itself, its constitutive impossibility, the correlativity of its own Xness with *its own* non-Xness, which comprises the *mutual* reducibility and *mutual* violence constituent of its being itself. For us, the necessity of this violence pushes it to an intimacy that allows us to characterize it as love, compassion, solidarity. This is not merely a semantic distinction; it has crucial ethical implications. For what answers Levinas's concern for infinity in this self-violence of all coherences is the fact that just by being themselves, coherences are seen as eternally resistant to any totalization. This is the essence of *mutual* reducibility, which opens up an unclosable space that is always overflowed—the "moretoitivity" which is the essence of all coherences, as discussed above. There is always "an external world," and it is this "exteriority" per se which *is the coherences themselves*.

This is where the ethical implications come in, for this means that what we have described as *constitutive* violence is always already outside itself qua violence, that compassion and concern are always already *discoverable* in it; it is incapable of closing up as violence *simpliciter*. It is always susceptible to the "ethical layering" discussed above. It is true that we therefore continue to exempt ourselves from the prioritizing of ethics as "first philosophy" enjoined by Levinas; but we think we have something here which answers better to the concern which impelled him to do so. For the ethical dimension remains, if anything, even more strictly *inescapable* in Neo-Tiantai thought; as we have cited Freud saying above, human beings are always *both* more moral and less moral than they think. Levinas is right to hold that merely speaking, indeed merely seeing, is already an ethical act, which is addressed to another face that answers back.

But there is no need to assume any longer that the only way to avoid the violence of totalized theory is to consign transcendence to a purity that artificially isolates it from immanence. It is quite true that previous attempts (e.g., the Hegelian attempt) to unite the transcendence and immanence of the self-other relation always ended up reducing the other to the self, disguised as the objectivity of the Same; but we have reason to believe that the revision of the categories of being we are suggesting here may be sufficient to overcome this difficulty. For we do not merely assert that transcendence and immanence are correlative, or even aspects of a single tertium quid; we say rather that to transcend is to inhere and vice versa, which is a very different proposition. They are identical in a way that may also be described as mutual exclusivity; transcendence appears as inherence, inherence as transcendence—there is no further transcendence outside of inherence, nor inherence outside of transcendence, so their correlativity as side-by-side coexistence is unimaginable. In other words, it is exteriority as such, the violence of the other who faces us as love, which is the self who is faced, the inherence (not just what inheres, but the immanence itself). Oneself—or better, one's selfness—is the violence which is other to oneself, never enclosable, never predictable, never totalizable. Without this self-contrast, one could never appear as a coherence, as an identity, at all.

Eroticism and Continuity, with Bataille

This question of the relations with the Other and where that fits into the self's own internal disruption can bring us, perhaps unexpectedly, closer to a Neo-Tiantai understanding of the more profoundly disruptive aspects of sexuality and eroticism. To get there, let us consider several propositions from Georges Bataille, eroticism's most suggestive modern theorist.

Bataille begins his main theoretical work on this issue with the following claim: "Eroticism, it may be said, is assenting to life up to the point of death." This is asserted on the basis of Bataille's assumption that "reproduction implies the existence of *discontinuous* beings. Beings that reproduce themselves are distinct from one another, and those reproduced are likewise distinct from each other, just as they are distinct from their parents. Each being is distinct from all others.... Between one being and another, there is a gulf, a discontinuity." However, distinct though we are, you and I, we can "experience the dizziness of this gulf between us" *together*, this gulf that is *death*, the ending of our discontinuity, for Bataille tells us,

> It is my intention to suggest that for us, discontinuous beings that we are, death means continuity of being. Reproduction leads to the discontinuity of beings, but brings into play their continuity, that is to say, it is intimately linked with death. I shall endeavour to show, by discussing reproduction and death, that death is to

be identified with continuity, and both of these concepts are equally fascinating. This fascination is the dominant element in eroticism.[44]

From here, we move to the question of violence and violation. Bataille speaks of

> the elemental violence which kindles every manifestation of eroticism. In essence the domain of eroticism is the domain of violence, of violation. . . . there is most violence in the abrupt wrench out of discontinuity. The most violent thing of all for us is death which jerks us out of a tenacious obsession with the lastingness of our discontinuous being. . . . We cannot imagine the transition from one state to another one basically unlike it without picturing the violence done to the being called into existence through discontinuity. . . . What does physical eroticism signify if not a violation of the very being of its practitioners?—a violation bordering on death, bordering on murder? . . . The transition from the normal state to that of erotic desire presupposes a partial dissolution of the person as he exists in the realm of discontinuity. . . . The whole business of eroticism is to destroy the self-contained character of the participators as they are in their normal lives.[45]

Bataille later expands on this contrast between "normal life" and eroticism as a distinctly human form of sexuality. What is distinctly human is above all *work*, and Bataille endeavors to connect this intimately with two other uniquely human features: awareness of death and eroticism/sexual continence. Work is the everyday world of reason and the constructive assembly of discontinuous beings. It is interrupted by death and sex, which have therefore to be deferred to special times and places, lest work be interfered with. These special times and places are the province of religion and eroticism, where a vicarious festival of murder and the breaking through of discontinuity is celebrated. Above all, religion is for Bataille a matter of sacrifice, where a victim is ritually murdered, its continuity with nature—with non-X, we may say—exposed. Of the essence here is "the ancient comparison of sacrifice and erotic intercourse."

> If transgression is not fundamental then sacrifice and the act of love have nothing in common. If it is an intentional transgression sacrifice is a deliberate act whose purpose is a sudden change in the victim. The creature is put to death. Before that it was enclosed in its individual separateness and its existence was discontinuous. . . . The act of violence that deprives the creature of its limited

---

[44] Georges Bataille, *Erotism: Death and Sensuality*, trans. Mary Dalwood (San Francisco: City Lights, 1986), 11–13.
[45] Ibid., 16–17.

particularity and bestows on it the limitless, infinite nature of sacred things is with its profound logic an intentional one. It is intentional like the act of the man who lays bare, desires and wants to penetrate his victim. The lover strips the beloved of her identity no less than the blood-stained priest his human or animal victim. The woman in the hands of her assailant is despoiled of her being. With her modesty she loses the firm barrier that once separated her from others and made her impenetrable. She is brusquely laid open to the violence of the sexual urges set loose in the organs of reproduction; she is laid open to the impersonal violence that overwhelms her from without.[46]

—and, of course, also from within. Bataille compares the sacrificial feast, where the victim was taken apart and eaten collectively, laying bare the organs and flesh which can now melt into the being of others, with "the fullness of the blood-swollen organs, the impersonal fullness of life itself."[47] Both the act of love and the sacrifice

> reveal the flesh. Sacrifice replaces the ordered life of the animal with a blind convulsion of its organs. So also with the erotic convulsion; it gives free rein to extravagant organs whose blind activity goes on beyond the considered will of the lovers. Their considered will is followed by the animal activity of these swollen organs .... Underlying eroticism is the feeling of something bursting, of the violence accompanying an explosion.[48]

The main thing about eroticism is thus

> the way that an ordered, parsimonious and shuttered reality is shaken by a plethoric disorder. . . . It upsets an ordered system on which our efficiency and reputation depend. In fact the individual splits up and his unity is shattered from the first instant of the sexual crisis. Just then the plethoric life of the body comes up against the mind's resistance. . . . Only the actual experience of states of normal sexual activity and the clash between them and socially approved conduct allows us to recognize that this activity has its inhuman side. The organs' plethora induces reactions alien to the normal run of human behaviour. A rush of blood upsets the balance on which life is based. A madness suddenly takes possession of a person. This madness is well known to us but we can easily picture the surprise of anyone who did not know about it and who by some device witnessed unseen the passionate lovemaking of some woman who had struck him as particularly distinguished. He would think she was sick, just as mad dogs are sick. Just as if some mad bitch had usurped the personality of the dignified hostess of a little while

---

[46] Ibid., 90.
[47] Ibid., 91.
[48] Ibid., 92–93.

back. Sickness is not putting it strongly enough, though; for the time being the personality is dead. For the time being its death gives the bitch full scope, and she takes advantage of the silence, of the absence of the dead woman. The bitch wallows—wallows noisily—in that silence and that absence. The return of the personality would freeze her and put an end to the sensual delight she has abandoned herself to.[49]

It is precisely this clash, this contrast between the ordinary realm of ordered, efficient work, reason, and personality, the realm of discontinuous beings, and the plethoric madness of sex and sacrificial violence which constitutes eroticism, and this also accounts for the importance of the affect of transgression and the complicity of the taboo with its own transgression. Truly, to put it in a nutshell, the pillar supporting all eroticism is the uncanny, fascinating, ghastly mystery of a palpitating genital that also knows how to say "I." This is why "degradation, which turns eroticism into something foul and horrible, is better than the neutrality of reasonable and non-destructive sexual behaviour." This is because at the real heart of value for Bataille there lies this notion of beauty, understood in a very important sense:

> The further removed from the animal is their appearance, the more beautiful they are reckoned. . . . But the opposite . . . also holds. The image of the desirable woman as first imagined would be insipid and unprovocative if it did not at the same time also promise or reveal a mysterious animal aspect, more momentously suggestive. The beauty of the desirable woman suggests her private parts, the hairy ones, to be precise, the animal ones. . . . If beauty so far removed from the animal is passionately desired, it is because to possess is to sully, to reduce to the animal level. Beauty is desired in order that it may be befouled; not for its own sake, but for the joy brought by the certainty of profaning it. In sacrifice, the victim is chosen so that its perfection shall give point to the full brutality of death. Human beauty, in the union of bodies, shows the contrast between the purest aspect of mankind and the hideous animal quality of the sexual organs. . . . For a man, there is nothing more depressing than an ugly woman, for then the ugliness of the organs and the sexual act cannot show up in contrast. Beauty has a cardinal importance, for ugliness cannot be spoiled, and to despoil is the essence of eroticism.[50]

It is easy to see that Bataille's categories of continuity and discontinuity are a profound oversimplification, shockingly and naïvely one-sidedly and abstract in themselves, but at the same time it is hard to deny the force and acuity of his analysis of the essence of eroticism, and indeed of value as such,

---

[49] Ibid., 104–6.
[50] Ibid., 140–45.

from our present perspective. Indeed, in his characterization of beauty he has begun to overcome the one-sidedness of his initial conceptual framework. We are perhaps justified in objecting that life/work/reason/personality/selfhood/coherence, the ordered world of efficiency and cooperation, cannot be so simply equated with "discontinuity," nor death/sex/violence/swollen organs/chaos with "continuity." Even without the Hegelian turns Bataille himself sometimes attempts with these concepts, we may be inclined to posit a more nuanced notion of structure than Bataille will allow, inasmuch as we cannot even imagine continuity without discontinuity or vice versa. We may wish to say, for example, in a commonsense sort of way, that life/work/self represents a way in which discontinuity subsumes continuity into its own form, while death/sex/sacrifice represent a way in which continuity subsumes discontinuity. The former, work and personality, would be a heightened, articulated continuity, integrated and concentrated as one's own body, history and self as an ordered system where each part wears its continuity, as it were, on its sleeve, in the semiotic continuity that we call meaning. We have described this as the explicit Intersubsumption and reversibility that apply to the confederacy of coherences that make up any finite "self." The latter, death and sex, would be a less articulated, less localized, more diffuse form of *both* continuity and discontinuity, a confused rescrambling or a transitional phase to other bindings and integrations of the two. In any case, in the Neo-Tiantai context, we would want to assert not only the inseparability of the two, but indeed their strict equivalence: to be continuous, as we have already said many times above, is to be discontinuous, and vice versa, and indeed, the more continuous something is, the more discontinuous it is.

But this allows us to restate and perhaps broaden the thrust of Bataille's main point about beauty and eroticism. Bataille realizes that his two main conceptual categories have been brought together into a fundamental ambiguity here: "Together with an effort to reach continuity by breaking with individual discontinuity, the search after beauty entails an effort to escape from continuity. The twofold effort is never at an end: its ambiguity crystallizes and carries onward the workings of eroticism."[51] In our terms, then: discontinuity is what we call the array of X and non-X's, X being X and non-X being non-X. Continuity is X being non-X and non-X being X.

The essence of erotic beauty for Bataille is the Xiness of a thing that can be sliced into to reveal its underlying non-Xiness; the face, the social composure, the self, giving way to the spasm of sexual crisis and the ugly mania of engorged organs. The value of the experience depends on the intensity of this contrast, and we are obviously trying to connect this to the staid White-

---

[51] Ibid., 144.

headian notion of value as aesthetic contrast cited above. In both cases, we make a Neo-Tiantai emendation: The contrast between any coherence's Xness and its non-Xness is precisely its identity as necessary impossibility; not something added to it from outside, but its innermost essence. It is not only that every X turns out also to be non-X, but that to be X is to be non-X, that Xiness *is* non-Xiness. We have tried to show how a sliding scale of identifications and self-definitions will constitute special objects of desire wherever snags in the reversibility of this relation occur, and our ruminations on freedom above can perhaps confirm Bataille's intuition about beauty as something that exists, like a prohibition, precisely in order to be befouled and transgressed. And this leads us directly into the crucial Neo-Tiantai transformation from the Exclusive Center to the Nonexclusive Center: it is not enough to say simply that value/beauty always lies in a contrast between the sublimely self-possessed and its befoulment, nor to say that these two even function as ends and means of one another, so that the sublime is established only to be befouled and vice versa. Rather, we must go on to see that each of these three terms—pristine sublimity of self-possession and control, befoulment thereof, and the erotic pleasure that emerges from this juxtaposition—implies the other two already, that in fact whenever one mentions any of them he has already said all three, and each possesses all the characteristics of the others. In other words, pristine civilized sublimity and self-possession is itself already erotic, in that it is always already befouled. Befoulment is always already pristine civilized sublimity and self-possession, and pleasurably erotic. And erotic pleasure is itself always already befouled and sublimely self-controlled. We would even go on to functionalize this: pristine sublimity *befouls*, and *comes*, if you will; befoulment *ennobles*, and enjoys; enjoyment befouls and ennobles.

And this point is really crucial if we are to understand the strange double negatives that seem to be endemic to the erotic realm. We have seen that certain objects come to be singled out as objects of obsessive desire because of a snag in reversibility; I cannot imagine being X, cannot imagine X relating to the me I am now from X's perspective; X is for me an impossible self, but a merely contingent impossible self, which has not accepted the constitutive impossibility that we mean when we use the word "self." Now this is just the alter ego we want to sacrifice, to tear limb from limb, in order to enjoy our own death vicariously, that is, to experience our own crash that has been blocked by the snag in reversibility. I want to see these lips, which talk so well, moaning uncontrollably. I have chosen these lips to be my particular sacrificial victim in just the way a priest chooses a taboo animal to be sacrificed and consumed in ritual feast. The taboo animal, as the old-fashioned anthropological story goes, is the totem of my tribe, the one who represents us, who is our true ancestral self, which protects and sustains us normally, and which we must never kill in any circumstance except on the one designated feast day. In the same way, perhaps we can say that the desired sexual object is an objectification of the impossibility which we experience at the heart of ourselves, our own enjoyment, which is our very life, but which is impossible for us, constitutively unable to appear as itself. It is more me than me, because it embodies the impossibility which is my selfhood in a contingent, visible form, *in my experience at all as such*. I want to overcome this contingency and re-establish reversibility. I have defined myself implicitly as some particular Xness, which confronts now the one coherence it cannot bear to read itself as an aspect or expression of; oftentimes, to indulge a very vulgar Freudian pun, we could say that we are attracted to someone who has holes where we cannot imagine having them, or lacks holes where we cannot imagine lacking them. How could she not mind that? How could she not notice or care about that? How could she do that or have that or be that way?

The negations fall wherever we cannot imagine them for ourselves, where our Xness makes a taboo of having them. We can perhaps consider this a gloss on Kenneth Tynan's famous quip about desire: We are looking for claws that fit our wounds. Now this Xness knows implicitly that it is also non-X, that it can fulfill itself only by crashing, by spilling over and making manifest the non-Xness it always embodied. But this is the one thing it is forbidden to do—in Bataille's version, it must maintain the discontinuity of the world of work and social identity. It endures, convincing itself that it is X to the exclusion of non-X, by establishing its own "totem" which is worshipped, tabooed, and also, on special occasions, to be made its sacrificial victim, and consumed.

This particular non-X will be precisely the invisible central hole around which its identity is structured. X can maintain its Xness on the condition of not seeing that this specific non-X is also readable as Xish—feeling my own body from the side of those lips, such that my body is an aspect of that particular "lipiness," for example. But X wants it both ways—to maintain itself as X by not seeing Xness as a version of non-Xness, *and* to see non-X embrace Xness in itself, since "how I— X—look to that particular non-X" is unimaginable for it. This is what is accomplished by the sacrificial/sacred nature of the totem/sexual object. I want to see the continuity of non-me with non-non-me (the double negative referred to above), but not just any non-me will do. It must be precisely the one which is constitutively non-me, but in a visible, explicit form, the snagged object, the particular totem/object of desire in which I recognize the dimension of the prohibition constituting my selfhood (the taboo), the occasional destruction of which is the only way I can vicariously overcome my selfhood while maintaining it. We said above that what is meant in Tiantai when we say such things as "Every coherence is the center which intersumes with all its peripheral coherences," or, "Each coherence is the principle of Intersubsumption itself" is that every object is the standard or measure which establishes a dimension in terms of which all other coherences are to be understood, against which they are measured. In saying they are all "expressions" of it we mean they are all unavoidably susceptible to this dimension, *both positively and negatively*, in their being it *and* their not being it, in their matching *and* failing to match the standard or dimension of being established by this coherence qua absolute principle and telos of all other things.

The importance of this notion comes to us full force here. The desired totemic victim is the one that defines the dimension, the set of coordinates against which our identity is measured, positively and negatively at once. If I am of the wolf tribe, the specific "non-me which is more me than me" is the wolf. To see the non-me melt back into the me, this form of non-me-ness alone will do, for I have prohibited only this one form. The other forms of non-me—my regular nonsacred prey—are already clearly known to be expressible as me and vice versa, there is no snag in our reversibility; I kill and eat them every day without difficulty. Only the taboo animal that is totemic to me, that represents my very life, can allow me to vicariously experience my own death, my own re-establishment of manifest continuity between Xness and non-Xness. Similarly, my interaction with ordinary objects of use shows no snag in reversibility; I make them me and me them in every act of consumption, perception, or manipulation. But some special object is excluded from this ordinary prey, which I cannot allow myself to be. That is the one that must be vicariously sacrificed for me to see my own non-me-ness. That is the object of my desire.

Given these structural concerns, it is perhaps not surprising how fraught with difficulties the erotic endeavor must inevitably be. It requires an object that can simultaneously die and reinstate itself over and over, which can remain an object while refusing to be an object, which can possess itself while letting go of itself, which can represent me while excluding me. The many peculiar permutations which accrue here are well worth closer study; the uncanny horror of persons who seem to "own" their own sexuality, and the converse sexual power of the disavowal of sexuality even in the wake of its most explicit expressions, and so on, all fall into this category. Nietzsche spoke of the increasing subtlety of men who need further and further proofs that they "truly possess" a beloved woman, which also belongs here. The object which knows how to best embody, in visible form, the impossibility of that victory, in closest tandem with its inevitability, is perhaps the most desirable. The woman who surrenders in just the right, most obscene way, and yet can never be brought quite to own up to it—well, in some cases that is enough to ensure a good decade of "enjoyment"—i.e., torture—for the right kind of man.

The same may be said, from our point of view, about any self-definition, any definiteness and determinacy, about discontinuity as such. This would be for us almost an ontological principle, at least a retrospective one, along the lines described in the section entitled "Why There's Anything." We make ourselves such and so in order to break ourselves, in order to stimulate the erotic pleasure of contrasting our intrinsic non-Xness with this Xness we have made of ourselves. We add to this the category mistake of moving this act of contrasting, i.e., enjoying pleasure, into the realm of having, possessing it, making it an object of control and ownership, which is what snags the reversibility proper to it in the realm of being it. We are pleasure, we are this contrast; for this reason we can never possess it.

But more is at stake here. For in spite of Bataille's oversimplified "active/passive" dichotomy, where the active/male is the sacrificer, the agent of the violence, while the passive/female is the sacrificial victim, the patient of the violence, we find once again that his actual descriptions surpass his own conceptual limitations, and bring us a powerful pointer toward the Neo-Tiantai reading of the situation. For what is essential to the agent/patient relationship in Bataille's conception of sex as sacrificial murder is that its main motivation lies in *vicarious enjoyment* of being destroyed on the part of the destroyer. This is what undermines the active/passive dichotomy, and brings with it also, from our point of view at least, the crucial Tiantai vice versa—the victim allows herself to be torn apart, to have her "continuity" with non-Xness exposed, as a form of vicarious enjoyment of the role of the agent who tears into her. Each is always on both sides of the relation, as we hold to be the case for every relationship, to be the very glue that makes a relationship a relationship. In this case, the vicarious structure of self-destruction in the rite of sacrifice, and in eroticism, is, as it were, a way for the perpetrator to die while still alive, to maintain his being while working through his own destruction. As Bataille puts it, "We can make do with an illusion. If we possess its object we shall seem to achieve our desire without dying. Not only do we renounce death, but also we let our desire, really the desire to die, lay hold of its object and we keep it while we live on."[52] The victim is already my double, my alter-ego; the same is true for the "victim" in the erotic situation, who surrenders to her "destruction," the spilling over of her "ugly" throbbing non-Xness and allows it to befoul her hard-earned Xness; both are allowed both to die and to witness their own deaths. In one case the

---

[52] Ibid., 142.

deceased is vicarious, in the other the witness, even if we accept Bataille's highly idealized depiction of the situation.

The Double, then, is always, constitutively involved in eroticism—and here we may perhaps be reminded of Freud's remark, in an early letter to Fliess, that every sexual act involves at least four people—or was it six? The parents of each partner are of course what is meant here, but we can easily see that quite a few additional participants are also lurking in every bed. For here it is not only, "Me qua me, me qua her, her qua her and her qua me," to put it in asness language, and all the exponential permutations thereof, but also, recalling the way asness in general opens up toward every other asness and is unable to restrict itself to any determinate realm, quite a few others.

Let us recall what we have said earlier about *objects* in general, which for us means already objects of interest and desire. "Object" always means "seen by me and at least one other." An object is a coherence, it appears in experience, hence is *at-a-distance*, hence is always seeable from other perspectives. Its objectivity, its realness, is guaranteed for me by the specter of another who could also be viewing it, in whose world it is also a part. The desired object, we may say, always posits *at least one more desirer* in order for it to be posited as "genuinely there to be desired," and the intersubjective implications of this are easily discoverable in sexuality. We desire through the intermediation of at least one "other," to slightly adapt a point Lacan has stressed to powerful effect, *who is present there for us as her desirability as such*. One knows what it means for a woman to be "desirable"—her value as object depends on the positing of one or many rivals who also want her. One's own pleasure is inseparable from the prospective pleasure of these envious others—indeed, we would say, is it, their displeasure is here as your pleasure—and your pleasure is over there, in them, in the form of envy and suffering. To feel the desirability of the woman is to feel the presence of the prospective rivals, the others who also find her desirable—strangely, although peculiar fetishes and preferences are endemic to the erotic realm, it is perhaps impossible for any of them to function without the mediation of some phantom other who shares the desire, from whom one is snatching this prize. Nothing is more difficult than pure idiosyncrasy of sexual taste. Our desires are decisively conditioned by what we think we feel looking over our shoulder.

But with this move, we have changed the stakes and parameters of the situation decisively; not only eroticizing all existence, but also moving the intrinsic problematicalness of it front and center, in a way which, we hope, will shed further light on our relations with both ourselves and with others. Let us pursue this theme a step further.

The Rival and the Double: Oneself as One's Own Indigestible Kernel

Let me hazard a case study as an example, from the realm of the erotic, where, as I have said, we get some of the most exemplary read-outs of omnicentric theory, and which can reveal some of the most distinctive features of Neo-Tiantai ethics. Let us say that you are a megalomaniac who wants to be perceived as a god, or as God, and let us say you have managed somehow to stumble into a situation that allows you to see yourself that way, which is to say, to see yourself as being seen that way. In terms of the discussion in the previous section, one has managed to constitute a discontinuous, self-possessed identity for oneself, with the power to control itself and its world. This unique, discontinuous being which alone is yourself, it seems to you, has come to master and integrate the sex-violence of discontinuity, of otherness, owning and integrating its own vicarious death in some totemized form. This might be because you have been persistently and publicly honored in some way for something that you think is unique about you, or have had some extraordinary set of things happen to you upon which you have been able to build this sense of identity. You are the one true genius, or the unique sex god, or the most wonderful being in the universe in some other way. Let us make it a love affair. With apologies, I will use a heterosexual male as an example. You met a woman under highly unlikely circumstances; she turned out to be perfect in every way, plus the most fantastically erotic creature on earth, plus she had never bloomed in this way before—no one else could get to her. Indeed she is the one true woman in the world, and she immediately recognized you as the one true man. You believe the woman of your dreams has been swept off her feet head over heels by yourself in particular. Indeed, you believe you have found the kernel of her vivacity and life, and indeed of all life, in her sexuality as it rises to meet you—she lives, let us say, for erotic love, and to her you are erotic love itself, as she seems not to respond to anyone else.

But then the woman falls similarly for some other clown—a caricature of you, so you think, an insult, a repulsive imposter; how can it be that she cannot tell the difference? Your precious identity-consolidating experience has been retrospectively stolen from you. You experience what we called aversion above, and here it is a hatred both for the woman and for her new lover. As with the cockroach cited above, the reason for this is that you cannot read these persons as versions of yourself. That is, yourself as "Self" in the audacious sense that this love affair had established for you—as a Sartrean in-and-for-itself, as a God, as a master, owner, doer, self-determiner who was miraculously also an object of desire as such, hence, a perfect free being. The sexual example is useful here because it already involves the self-beyond-self, that is, the spontaneity of you that is "more you than you" is uniquely responded to by the spontaneity of her, the perfect woman, which is "more her than her." But now it turns out that this was not the case—you could have been anyone. You just happened to have been in the right place at the right time. This sense of "being me" and the sense of being an object in the sense of being nonabsolute, susceptible to humiliation and failure, part of an array of other beings, replaceable, passive, were not seen by you as reversible, as intersubsumptive, as readable as each other, and hence you feel aversion, and your world and self are shaken. "Being the one true god" per se is not readable by you as "being that repulsive clown she's with now" or for that matter "being this humiliated cuckold." The absoluteness of your sense of self, which was your "me being me" in this relationship, was not yet readable as "me being humiliated, deceived, replaced, and abused," an object in someone else's world, and vice versa. Your identity is "threatened" by this development, by the presence of a rival who, under the conditions of scarcity of goods, takes your place, threatens the uniqueness of your place in the world, as the one sole center of all being, who defines and founds everything. That is, your identity is *contingently* problematic. How is this to be overcome?

We have established above that nonselfness readable as your selfness overcomes attachment, and your selfness readable as nonselfness overcomes aversion. If you can imagine being the loved woman, seeing the world, including your own body, through her eyes, so that the coherence "youness" is related to by, and hence an expression of, the coherence "herness," you will be free of attachment to her. If you can imagine your own coherence readable as the hated woman or the hated clown, so that the coherence "clown" is an expression of the coherence "one true sex god," as two sides of a Möbius strip, such that the more godlike something is the more clownlike it is, you will be free of your aversion. This particular situation is especially unbearable because it intertwines two impasses at once, and calls for two mutually reinforcing liberations. One is attached to the woman and one hates the man—*and vice versa*. For as we shall see, the man is oneself to the extent that he is delighted in by the woman, and to the extent that one mistakes one's own being for a possession. He is the objectification of oneself, to put it simply, which is the source of the problem, but this is only made possible by being the object of affection of the woman who has been deputized to establish one's own being. Hence it is necessary both to imagine oneself *being* the woman and seeing oneself through her eyes, seeing oneself as an attribute of the substance which is her, which alone will deauthorize her, and also to see the manner in which the objective form of the hated man is something as which one could oneself be read, an aspect of one's own world which is as legitimately permeated by the coherence one takes oneself to be as any other, as an attribute of the substance which is you. The challenge here is to see the sensation of "being godlike" *exactly as it is experienced* as also meaning "being clownlike." Moreover, you see what he has seen, the private places that no others have reveled in. They remain permeated by the repulsive coherence of "himness," serve now as pivots between youness and himness, which in effect makes you him and vice versa in certain moments. Your two worlds, and hence your two identities, overlap around this pivot that centers both of them. The crisis is resolved by seeing your identity as inherently, necessarily problematic, as its own negation, as porous, as incapable of ever having appeared *simpliciter*. You recall her loving glance and her ecstatic embrace, and the sense of identity that emerged for you under that gaze—these were read *as* "she worships me as a sex god, the center of her world, irreplaceable, sacred; hence in the eyes of the one true woman on earth I am the one true man on earth, etc."

But what was this coherence "sex god" you were being? It was that one true god. It was a bunch of "other" coherences, and a coherence is something the nature of which is to always be susceptible to "turning out" to be otherwise, hence always already to have been otherwise. Re-examine that feeling of being the one true god—it was already full of holes, contextualized by, embraced by, composed by non-one-true-god coherences. The palpable coherence one-true-godness was an emergent quality read as the meaning through a lot of other quiddities. But precisely in being that way, it was otherwise. What made it coherent made it incapable of final coherence. Indeed, its coherence was incoherent. This can be recalled existentially or reconstructed analytically, but in either case this identity of yours was certainly "Globally Incoherent," pre-transcended, already gone by virtue of its appearance. You will recall perhaps the "always having to be confirmed" sense that went with it, or "still being in the process" sense, or "so far"-ness that attended it. To be a coherence is, after all, really to be an *attempt* to be that coherence, indeed to be the tentativeness, incompleteness, provisionality, hesitancy, experimentation, mere suggestiveness, uncertainty of that coherence per se; to be X and to be the attempt to be X are synonymous. X is an attempt to be X, a halting, stopgap, ramshackle last minute process asking eternally for further confirmation or completion. More centrally, we may recall here the discussion of fire not burning itself in Part One: being the coherence "one true god" was precisely "not-one-true-god" *to itself*, and indeed this alone constituted its true being, its self-sustaining existence. Only by refraining from manifesting itself as god, not treating something (itself) as an object over which to lord, could it be god. Its being god was its being not-god, and the more god it was, the more not god it was. As "being," it was invisible to itself, manifested only *as* all the things it related to as excluding the coherence it was being, the Xifiable rest of its world. X is not X to itself; to itself X is only the Xifiability of the rest of the world. Hence, precisely in your being a god to her, you were not that god.

In this sense we share the common Buddhist, psychoanalytical, existential and Marxist approach: the self must be predevastated, its pretension to full ontological consistency exploded. In this case, this means seeing that when the woman loved you, she already loved another—the other who was yourself. You suddenly realize, "All I was to her was just a guy who happened to be there—anyone else would have done just as well; all that worship and all that ecstasy, which I was reading as establishing my identity as the one true god, really only meant You are here and I can tolerate you more or less"— all those tokens of meaning turn out to be readable otherwise. That precious identity that had been established by this relationship had never been present; the enjoyer and worshipped man was already another who was there *as* you, being read as you qua "one true god," as "Self." You were never you to begin with. That one whom she delighted in, and who took delight in her, was already also some other. The self who was the object of her delight and the subject of your own delight was also an other. This is not only because, for example, the past is other to the present, and the past self was "someone else" to you; nor only because whatever instantiates the coherence "you-ness," however construed, in one sense also instantiates various other coherences in other senses; nor only because you-ness is grounded on non-you-ness, and vice versa, and both are mere aspects of a tertium quid that in itself is neither you nor not-you. But it is also because whatever is you is also not you, in the sense that you-ness appears in experience on the condition that one is distanced from it, that it is a pivot exposed to and pervaded by other coherences and other centers, that its appearing coincides completely with its cancellation as purely and definitively you. In the very sensation of you-ness per se, however construed, non-you-ness was always equally operative. Non-you-ness and you-ness appear as each other. When she looked at you with worshipful delight, she was looking also at someone else—and the necessary possibility of many others; "you-ness" per se was always just a promise for and guarantor for itself to turn out to be otherwise. That being who was the "one true god" was other to the "one true god" whose pride is now hurt by being dethroned. This is the standard "Global Incoherence" point.

Moreover, the other she already loved was this particular pathetic clownish other, whom you must now accept as a version, a "transformation body," of yourself, whom you have always already been being, without having known it. What she saw when she saw you was apparently just some guy, or this clown, whom you now have no choice but to accept as a revelation of who you *also* are. This is the first Tiantai move. If he is in your world, but you are unable to face being him, your reversibility is snagged. The only way to overcome this is to boldly accept the humiliating consequence of being a cockroach, a slobbering idiot, a creep, and whatever else might scuttle into your awareness however fleetingly.

But the second crucial Tiantai move here is to realize that this failure of the "one true god" sense of self to ever appear anywhere on the scene *in no way obstructs its appearance on the scene*; it has been there all along *only as impossible*. This is what allows it to now be seen equally possible *everywhere*, haunting every actual, equally readable into any situation. If "one true god" could read out as "humiliated cuckold" and/or "clownish pathetic imposter," it can read out as anything. So the vainglory of being the one true god need not be given up, need not be thrown away as an unworthy megalomaniacal conceit; on the contrary, by means of its destitution and crisis it comes to be more fully realized, to pervade everywhere. By being made explicit, it is shown to be impossible, but by being shown to be impossible, it is restored in its more extensive form, as inescapable, built into all coherences, all-pervasive. It is handed back and glorified by being destroyed.

Let us say more about the way this "you not having been you to begin with" is to be understood here. The thing that disrupts or traumatizes any coherence, in this case you qua god, is the Other, the real, indigestible, repulsive Other who is my intrinsic enemy because we exist side by side in a world of goods which are limited, and we cannot both occupy the same place at the same time. This undeniable aspect of what it is to be a determinate coherence prohibits any easy positing of non-X as correlative to, hence included in as excluded from X, as we mentioned in our discussion of Levinas. But the Neo-Tiantai point not to be missed here is that in reality this Other, this absolutely traumatic imposition, is oneself, or is any coherence "itself." This is perhaps easiest to see if we think of the asness relation of coherences in the sense of momentariness. All other coherences are here only *as* this coherence, not outside it in an array or panorama; in this moment or this oneness of a particularity there is no room for any extrinsic trauma. The trauma comes from the inherent crack that constitutes one's own determinacy and identity in the first place, the incompleteness that alone makes any coherence possible. Hence one is an "other" to oneself—the indigestible traumatic kernel of X is X itself. Once again we must recall the full playing through of the relation of fire to itself, or any X to itself; its being itself is precisely its not being itself. This non-X is neither correlative to X nor dichotomous with X; it is identical to X. The true disruption of the Xness of X is X itself. Temporally, its appearing is its extinction. In terms of coherence, its being-thus is its not-being-thus. The fire is fire by not being fire, and its fieriness is its nonfieriness.

This brings us to the ethical importance of the question of the "Double," which has already been hinted at in the example given above. Alenka Zupančič has made an interesting distinction among "the similar," "the Same," and "the identical." "The similar" pertains to the register of the imaginary, and necessitates infinite multiplicity. It is what we have spoken of above as the panoramic array of coherences, embraced and made "similar" by an overarching order of being. What is excluded in this array is the Same.

"The Same" is enjoyment (*jouissance*) itself, the excessive something-more which overburdens any and every identity, what is more than any of these assigned roles can bear, what threatens to destroy them and the order they represent. This functions here much like Bataille's "pure continuity," sex/death as what threatens to disrupt the network of social identities necessary for labor and cooperation. It must be excluded in order to unite the multiplicity of the similar, and leads to the loss of identity. For this enjoyment is no respecter of "persons," and has no use for the separate "similar" identities required for the realm of cooperative work. Put naïvely, we all want the Same thing, everything, at the Same time and place, even at the expense of our discontinuous identities. However, for the array to function as an articulated panorama of similars, this Sameness must be excluded. This pertains to the register of the Real.

"Identity" is the realm of the signifier, presupposing the system of differences of the symbolic register. Interestingly, my own "enjoyment" always appear to me as strange, foreign, hostile, but at the same time as the kernel of my own being. Zupančič notes how this tends to represented in literature either as the monstrous—something absolutely alien—*or* as the Double, the twin, the specter of the uncanny Same. In the latter case, "the excluded appears in the image of that from which it had been excluded." The Double is someone "whom we find unbearable precisely because of the absence of any difference. The other does not resemble me, she is exactly the same (as me) and this same, in going beyond resemblance, is also situated somewhere beyond the logic of recognition. My double is absolutely strange to me; I cannot recognize myself in this Same (as myself). The Same (the fact that I am 'absolutely identical' to myself) leads to a loss of identity."[53]

This "loss of identity" which is our sameness with ourselves is precisely what we have called the constitutive impossibility which is the identity of all coherences; and it is not without reason that Zupančič identifies this with "enjoyment," the Lacanian name for the Real which is beyond what any given identity, structure or organism can bear, experienced therefore as unbearable

---

[53] Alenka Zupančič, *The Ethics of the Real* (London: Verso, 2000), 226.

pain or as orgasm. The traumatic kernel which is oneself is one's enjoyment, the pleasure one is and therefore cannot bear to possess. Note that Zupančič insists the Real is lost if made the direct goal of teleological or willed action, that she situates it beyond the passive/active dichotomy, but also sees that this means not that it is a passive waiting, simply because it has no "agent" or subject as such, but rather a matter of *desiring to the end* some other ulterior object which is *not* the enjoyment in question, until it, in our languages, crashes into enjoyment, into the Real as its uncanny by-product.[54] We should also note that enjoyment is not only unattainable, but also inescapable, that the "very act of rejecting or repressing it generates more."[55] We can see here where this is heading, for this is precisely what we have determined above for all coherences without exception; we may perhaps now restate that by asserting that all coherences *are* enjoyment, or are *as* enjoyment.

Desire, for Zupančič, is precisely desire to get rid of this stain of enjoyment—which is for us also precisely the desire to attain it *simpliciter*, both of which are equally impossible, given the fact that "jouissance [enjoyment] does not exist, and that it is found everywhere."[56] Pure desire, on the other hand, is the transitional moment of the crash, the flip-flop on the Möbius strip from desire to what Lacanians call "drive," which seeks and finds satisfaction, but not in the desired *object*, but as a byproduct produced by the consumption of some other object. "We satisfy the drive, whether we want to or not."[57] Pure desire is the limit where desire finds itself confronted with its own support, its own cause, which, in order to sustain desire, must remain invisible, as the frame structuring the array of "similars." If seen, if made a visible object *within* the field, it becomes part of this array of similars, equivalent to others, in competition with them, lending itself to the logic of exchange or substitution. In our language, what should have been seen as the not-seeable, as the Real which formed the invisible center structuring the field by virtue of its absence, as constitutively impossible, incapable of appearing literally (the single term which pervades and conditions the field, but which therefore can never appear in it, like empty space, the Kantian categories, or Davidson's "massive agreement"), suddenly seems to appear literally, and hence to be merely contingently problematic, to be in competition, to be "similar," to be sacrificeable, losable, winnable, part of a panoramic array of beings. This is what happened in your unfortunate escapade with your unfaithful goddess

---

[54] Ibid., 237–38.
[55] Ibid., 241.
[56] Ibid., 242.
[57] Ibid., 243.

cited above. The Real, the Double, the actual object of the desire *of the other* (her desire) appeared explicitly: that other, that clown, who you were, who is your own enjoyment, showed up and ruined everything. (For your desire was fundamentally to be seen as that pervert clown, that dirty old man; but once you really were, it ruined everything. The clown is merely the one true god seen explicitly, moved from the inherently impossible position of the invisible center to the contingently problematic position of the visible object.) The impasse is only overcome when the contingent impossibility is restored to necessary impossibility.

This is done in Zupančič's language by means of "pure desire," the carrying through of desire to the very end, until it flip-flops and reveals that the imagined, visible end was not the real end, that something else came to stand in that place without it being done by anyone—in our language, reversibility as a function of desire as such, which, as Zupančič also notes, is precisely drive itself. As Zupančič puts it, "wanting jouissance [enjoyment] maintains us on the side of desire, whereas realizing desire transposes us to the side of jouissance."[58] Realizing desire means desiring to the very end, desire qua desire, which is to say, desire in its own explicit unsatisfiability, as constitutively insatiable, related to a Real that is constitutively impossible. This alone manifests the Real, as its byproduct. Aiming at the Real as an object, on the other hand, relegates it to the realm of contingent problematicalness. In our example here, this means carrying the desire to be the one true god all the way to the end, until its crash reveals its predevastation, its inherent impossibility, *and* the way this in no way obstructs its appearance, indeed guarantees it everywhere, but only in the form of this impossibility.

The Double then is oneself decentered, moved out of the inherently impossible invisible central position into an uncanny distal position, where one becomes contingently problematic, subject to threat or in need of being established. And all others are one's Double at bottom, among other things. When we perceive our fellow beings as "selves" like us, we are in the same situation. And this underwrites all our relations with other beings, ethical, social and political. To see the importance of this, we should stress again the relation between one's own identity and one's enjoyment, the pleasure that one is but cannot possess, the trauma that exceeds any attempt at an ontological consistency structured according to the dictates of having, or the presence of nonconstitutively impossible entities. As noted above, this innermost kernel of my being, which is "more me than I am myself," is inherently strange and uncanny to me—as strange as the Other whom I confront. As Lacan puts it, "my neighbor possesses all the evil Freud speaks

---

[58] Ibid., 255.

about, but it is no different from the evil I retreat from in myself."[59] The uncanniness and horror of the Other person as prospective Double lies in the fact that he is in fact "the same as" this kernel of impossibility which is more me than me, which is me as non-me, my being, which comes to me as a trauma and an imposition.

This is again why the example of erotic rivalry in the above little tale is important here, for it involves the *involuntary* nature of sexual desire and activity which is nonetheless recognized as precisely what is most intimate to one's self. For to supply a few additional and very telling details about the unfortunate "you" in this story, it is reported that precisely the images and possibilities that caused him to awake literally shaking and sweating every morning were also what aroused him to ecstasy at inopportune moments. This Other, this clown, this pervert—it was his own enjoyment, his own being, but disgustingly relocated to the periphery, as a visible object. It would perhaps not be too much to say that the involuntary physical trembling that came to him in contemplating this case, this gunning of his system with anger and fear, as if threatened in its innermost being, was a kind of interference pattern, an oscillation like the feedback from a microphone placed against a speaker, because he was forced to *be in two places at once*.

And this is the essence of the anxiety and malaise that normally accompany all our relations with Others, and perhaps even with things. We are trying to be in two places at once as self-consistent merely contingently problematic beings, as beings, in a word, which are capable of *simple location* in Whitehead's sense, *instead of everywhere as constitutively impossible*. The Other is our other self, and as long as we think of the self as some sort of potentially or actually simply located being, a being which could *conceivably* simply be in one particular place and disposed in one particular way and no other, this oscillating feedback is inevitable. The necessary impossibility is reclaimed by *being* the enjoyment in question, made impossible here as long as the Other is seen as a discrete other being who is merely potentially simply located, and contingently problematic. For the essence of being any coherence at all is to be precisely enjoyment as such in the sense of something which could not possibly simply be what it is *simpliciter*, is incapable of simple location, and cannot be unequivocally disposed is one particular way rather than any other. To be a coherence is to pervade all times and places precisely as its own impossibility.

To return to the protagonist in our tale, once it was recognized that the shaking of his body in rage, his own fantasmic orgasm, the orgasm of the

---

[59] Jacques Lacan, *Ethics of Psychoanalysis*, trans. Dennis Porter (New York: Norton, 1992), 198.

drooling pervert clown as he enjoyed the beloved woman and even the orgasm of the woman as she enjoyed the clown were *one and the Same inherent impossibility*, that the disgustingly indigestible imagined enjoyment of the Other is precisely the suffering/enjoyment of his own system in its involuntary rage, fear and ecstasy, equally foreign and alien to him and yet equally intimate, what he is rather than what he has, the tension between the two rival centers vanished, and with it his symptom—for now he had become his symptom. This feedback oscillation of split "enjoyment" is exactly what we referred to above as "anxiety" as the fundamental state of ordinary human existence, conceiving itself as a nonimpossible entity that is under constant contingent threat. The essence of ethical relations rests in the same conversion; from seeing the Other as an alternate "similar" being in a panoramic array or system, each of which is "threatened" and contingently embattled, to seeing the strangeness of the Other, the offensiveness of his overflowing presence and enjoyment, as the same impossibility which one is standing on in being oneself. The Other is repulsive and threatening because one imagines he must be some kind of consistent entity, a coherence which is not also its own impossibility. To see him instead as incapable of appearing *simpliciter*, even to himself, and the renunciation of his own coherence in his relation to himself, who is himself only in not being himself, one sees his enjoyment for what it is—not his possession, which would have been unbearable, but as his being, and to see this is just to be the enjoyment that the Other is, for to be is to occupy the position of this constitutive contradiction.

Beauty, Harmony, and the Mystical

Let us return now to the question of beauty, which we raised in a sexual connection above. We can now venture a less restricted definition of beauty, one which will be applicable to natural and artistic examples as well. We define beauty as Unexpected Harmony. (In Bataille's sexual version we have a restricted sense of this: the unexpected harmony between the self-possessed face and speech and social self on the one side, and the throbbing self-abandon of the hairy parts that undermine it.) It will be noted first off that this definition already implies a subjective element, namely "unexpected," which will obviously vary according to what a particular person's expectations are, and will vary for that person at different times and places. We should also hasten to point out that what is meant is not necessarily cases where no harmony at all was expected, but merely that this particular harmony, the one that actually occurred, was unexpected.

Thus we admit most emphatically from the beginning that there is no such thing as objective or absolute beauty; indeed, even the second term of our definition, harmony, implies the presence of at least two terms: no individual thing can be beautiful, nothing can be beautiful in and of itself, since no one term can be harmonious—harmony is a always relation between at least two terms.

What are the terms between which there is a harmony? Most essentially, beauty is a harmony between the subjective element (i.e. the viewer, the experiencer of beauty) and one or many objective elements (that which is perceived as beautiful). The judgment, "It is beautiful," means: "There exists an unexpected type of harmony between it and myself as I am at this moment." It is possible that beauty can be felt merely in an unexpected harmony between a number of the objective elements, which however have no special harmony or resonance with the viewer himself; this would be the case in "formal" art, in literature which one may appreciate without "relating to," in Flaubert's projected novel about nothing whatsoever. In works of this type, the elements of the construction arrange in a new way which is itself perceived as harmonious in an unexpected way, but into which one does not necessarily read one's own heart in any essential sense.

It will be noticed that the two terms of this definition are aspects of Global Incoherence and Local Coherence respectively: we have here in effect an explicit union of the two, the simultaneous occurrence of the two, an explicit union of the two basic aspects of any coherence. For unexpectedness means that we have jumped out of some inferred pattern, have broken the momentum of some system of motion, in other words, a previously accepted coherence has fallen apart or been contravened. But "harmony" is itself another kind of coherence, a joining into a oneness, into a new whole. What we have then is a new and unexpected coherence, an incoherence that simultaneously coheres into some other, unexpected, unpredictable thing that was not a foreseeable part of the previous system or thing. We had assumed a certain fixed pattern that is then broken, the brokenness of which, however, resolves into another unforeseen thing that is equally graspable by us in its moment. In the case of a harmony between ourselves and the objective element, we have revealed to us another sense in which we are not limited and yet at the same time in which we are limited as something else, as a set of habits, as a need for certain conditions; inasmuch as we are living organisms, we need harmonies—between digestible food and our bodies, for example.

Before we proceed any further along this line, we must address the thorny and complicated issue of giving "harmony" a more lucid definition. There is no a priori definition of harmony; harmony will differ to each according to his particular habituations. We have already defined habituation as meaning itself, as the implicit presence of a particular nonnegotiable whole suggested by a part. The part serves as a trigger to call forth a particular expectation for the rest of that whole to be supplied. We may say that harmony is the fitting of something into some category or shape with which we have become familiar through habituation. Habituation itself can perhaps also be described as a snag in reversibility around which some superstructure has been subsequently built. Indeed, we may go on to say that harmony is a union which can be perceived or embraced in a single thought, Zhanran's "single moment of experience," that is, *as* a single "thing," under one definition or act of perception only. This is, of course, wholly dependent on our habituation, including as always the habituation which is built into our anatomical structures, habituated perhaps through the experiences of our ancestors in the course of their evolution. For example, if we see three apples on a table, we can see their "threeness" all at once, as one thing; we need not count the apples, this is a category that is familiar enough to us for us to perceive it instantly, as one. However, most people will not be able to see the "forty-sevenness" of forty-seven apples; they will need to count the group, or see it in smaller groups of three and two perhaps; still these subsets may perhaps arrange themselves in a configuration which accords with some instantly perceivable category in the viewer's mind, spatially rather than mathematically, in which we will still see a harmony in them. A drawing of a circle can be seen all at once, and one need only think one thing, just circle; but if a small scribble is added at some point, or a splotch of ink, one must perhaps think, "Circle and splotch of ink." Perhaps these two can be subsumed into some familiar way of seeing, perhaps not. Some people will see harmony where others see only chaos, for their body of categories and what they feel can be in accord with themselves is broader.

This definition of harmony however is not yet complete, for there would seem to be some empirical difference between mere familiarization and actual harmony. It seems inadequate to define harmony simply as what we are used to, what we can cognize in a single concept. For what shall we do with the sound of traffic, which we have heard a million times? Or with the noise our neighbor makes every night that keeps us awake? Or the argument we have every few days with someone we live with, which come around predictably and which we recognize immediately as "that again" but can never seem to be experienced as "harmonious"? These things are repeatedly felt to be dissonant and annoying; no amount of habituation makes them harmonious in any meaningful sense. This leads us to the perhaps shocking conclusion that the difference between dissonance and harmony is merely quantitative, rather than qualitative. What do we mean by this? Simply that those forms or patterns to which we are deeply or preternaturally habituated, ones that are built into our anatomical structures, our genes, our sense organs, are experienced most immediately as harmonious; they harmonize with our lives, with our bodies—let us say, for example, that they are what have been proven to be in accord with *health* through generations of natural selection. We cannot so quickly assimilate radically new or contrasting patterns to these, patterns that have not yet gone through the sieve of eons of natural selection, and thus we are prone to find them dissonant. Some of these reactions can be modified somewhat with increased exposure and gradual assimilation. But at a very fundamental level, harmony involves the idea of health, that, accord with our most basic life functions, with our whole history of survival experiences going back millions of years. In sum, then, let us define harmony as what is experienced when an organism encounters something that it can integrate into its own equilibrium.

And what is this equilibrium? We may define it as that which allows a system to include two opposite capabilities without conflict. For example, a human being can either sleep or be awake, his ability to sleep does not interfere with his ability to be awake, because he has a way of transcending both sleep and awakeness, a point neutral to them both, to which he can retreat from either one, thus not allowing either to take over his entire economy. If something came along that disturbed this equilibrium, something that made him sleep all the time or be awake all the time, and unable to switch back and forth, this something would not be experienced as harmonious. But this makes it quite obvious that equilibrium is simply another word for what we have been calling Intersubsumption, or the identity between Local Coherence and Global Incoherence, revealed above all as freedom. This type of equilibrium is another word for what is commonly called "health." It applies to all the extremes in our system of capabilities, and keeps us from being snagged in one extreme or the other, leaves us the ability also to be the opposite, preserves our reversibility. That which can be integrated into ourselves, into our system of habits, what we can read ourselves as or read as ourselves without interfering with this equilibrium, that is, without causing us to become fixed as any one thing or another, without obsessing us in any one corner of our possibilities, without reducing the scope of our activities, without further snagging our reversibility, is experienced as harmony.

Thus we can see that harmony is a wholly conventional concept, purely determined by what is familiar to us through habituation, what can be assimilated to our particular set of habits, but that this also includes the structure of our organs as evolved through the habits and experiences of our ancestors. What our mind is able, by these means, to grasp as a totality, or even as a "sameness" (also a conventional concept) is experienced as harmonious. Thus it is clear on the one hand that there is no such thing as eternal objective harmony, inasmuch as it is culturally determined; hence, aesthetics must change with time, since phenomenologically "time" means, among other things, "what was once unfamiliar to me has become familiar." On the other hand, if all human beings have certain things in common (certain habits such as digestion, respiration, cognition, etc.) there may be certain things universally more readily assimilated into a harmony than others.

All this talk of health and equilibrium may well help us understand what harmony is; but harmony is not yet beauty. Beauty is *unexpected* harmony, and as such places us decidedly beyond the realm of health and equilibrium. This can perhaps be appreciated if we turn again to view the realm of sexual beauty, to which the above definition also applies. What happens when a heterosexual man, say, sees a "beautiful" woman out there in the world? We have already examined the explicitly erotic aspect of this beauty, with Bataille: an unexpected harmony is revealed beneath the civilized "person" and the animal crisis of the genital "nonself," between this particular X and its overflowing into its own excluded non-X. Further, we saw already a further unexpected harmony, that is, between the desirer's taboo, what is specifically excluded from the constitution of his identity, and the very constitution of his identity itself; he unexpectedly is his own opposite, his own excluded indigestible taboo turns out to be the kernel of his innermost being, which is more him than he is himself.

We can now take up another aspect of this relationship, and the many-layered experience of beauty that pertains to it. Another unexpected harmony: the unity between her and me, the potential for oneness there, perhaps, to take the old Schopenhauerian line, above all for fertility, that her qualities match mine in such a way as to produce a "harmonious" offspring. Seeing her, I see implicitly the being that could spring from our union, the harmony, the offspring, that could result from our joining. The mere fact that she and I could produce a unified being is itself remarkable enough; and again it is "unexpected" in that before I laid eyes on this particular woman, whose motions and features are not exactly like any others, I could never have formed an idea of the particular child that could result from us. Only upon coming into contact with her do I realize, "ah, yes, this, too, is among my potential offspring, a creature composed of elements from this woman and me is also a possible combination to which I have access, this too could come into being, here is a totality, a harmony which could never have occurred to me before." But it is because the prospect of offspring is itself a severe threat to the equilibrium of my private interests and pleasures, at odds with my personal health, that this harmony is unexpected, and hence beautiful.

But even when looking at the emergence of a community's standards of beauty in the most naturalistic sense, there is more than just health and equilibrium at stake. We might suppose that people who appear ugly to us are those with whom we intuit we would produce "disharmonious" offspring, human beings who do not appear to fit into our categories of "harmony"; and these categories would be determined by the ideal human types propounded by the conventions of our particular society or culture, as filtered through our own habitual idiosyncrasies. On this reading, the standard of what type of humans are desirable would be simply an outgrowth of the will to the continuation of a locally coherent equilibrium, that is, the accumulated habit of surviving, and hence fundamentally concerned with what we have been calling health. The particular conditions of each community's existence, together with whatever other accidental and unique experiences it may undergo, can be seen as creating accumulations of habits, often quite bizarre and oppressive, which have proven profitable or simply habituating, and the perpetuation of these, as well as of particular types of persons which are necessary to a community in its situation, is also implicitly sought in that community's standards of beauty. These standards would have a strong effect on all individuals within the community, who usually cannot stray too far into idiosyncratic personal standards of sexual beauty because their offspring will have to be chosen as mates by members of the next generation; thus they must make children who will be attractive by the standards of the community.

But even if we try to stick to a strict Darwinian perspective, the emergence of beauty in animal species, or of traits that are selected for in mating procedures, seems to follow a more intricate logic. Most instructive here is the example of the peacock's tail, not because it happens to be regarded as beautiful also by humans, but because of the puzzle it poses for evolutionary theory. For this enormous flamboyant tail would seem to be a liability for the survival of the bird to which it is attached. It is large, cumbersome, attracts the attention of predators and makes escape and self-concealment difficult. It can be folded away more or less to avoid these problems to some degree, but this still does not resolve the question of why peahens would find a gargantuan, eye-catching tail so important a criterion when choosing a mate, as the data seem to suggest they do. The currently prevailing explanation for this puzzle is of great important for our discussion. It is said that the visible presence of this enormous liability is read and understood as marking the *unseen* presence of its compensating opposite. That is, only an exceptionally strong male could endure a handicap of such magnitude. That he is alive and also dares to display, nay flaunt, this gaudy, useless, predator-attracting appendage means he *must* have some other invisible strengths which allow him to survive *in spite of it*. As Nietzsche noted, the number of parasites one can endure is a measure of strength. If this is so, we might infer that a community's standards of beauty are derived not from any direct "positive" connection to strength, health, and equilibrium, but involve an essential element of abstraction and misdirection. They are symbolic structures, but symbolic in reverse of their opposites. For health, strength, and equilibrium themselves can never be present *simpliciter*. Whatever appears fully ipso facto loses its value, so value can never fully appear. It must be merely hinted at, suggested, hidden, so that it can retain its role as a true value, commensurate with the moretoitivity and Intersubsumption which are the essence of value; for strength, health, and equilibrium are all modes of overcoming obstruction, stepping over borders—the ability to keep from being snagged in any one determinacy.

But in our current context, this means that all instantiations of beauty must also take the decisive step *beyond* health and goodness. Beauty always has a slight tang of death about it—danger, superfluity, excess, foolishness, weakness, decay. The flaunted presence of all these liabilities is the only way in which the unseen, unseeable perfection, the strength and health to endure them, can manifest itself. It is present as its absence, and only as its absence. Some imperfection, some crack or stain, is necessary for aesthetic perfection, or even sexual attraction, of any kind to become manifest. For the surface is all that is given to the eye, and it is only an imperfection on the surface that provides its putative thickness, makes necessary the supposition of a depth beneath the surface, a moretoitivity to serve as the repository for the totemic representative of Intersubsumption. The latter is the strength or equilibrium that would allow this creature to be able to be not only as it is now, but the opposite way also, without ceasing to be itself, and this as we have seen is the definition of health. Any actually appearing strength would be conditional, subject to threat and damage, able to be placed in contexts and situations in which it would in fact serve not as a strength but as a liability itself; the unseen strength on the other hand takes on the transcendent status of an indestructible, unconditional absolute, which for us means to be a true all-pervasively intersubsumptive center, capable of maintaining itself in the face of any possible recontextualization. Kant's notion of beauty as purposivity without a definite purpose fits illuminatingly into this picture; any concrete, fully present purpose would ipso facto cease to be of value. We may perhaps also see a way clear here to address Nietzsche's counterposition of Kant and Stendhal on the question of beauty. Somewhat oversimplifying Kant through a Schopenhauerian lens, Nietzsche notes the contrast of the Kantian idea of the beautiful as "pleasure without interest" to Stendhal's remark that beauty consists in a "promise of happiness." For the peacock's tail would give a pleasure without interest—in that it is useless, and indeed a liability, to the practical interests of all concerned—and yet also a promise of happiness, in that its uselessness negatively bodies forth the unseen presence of unspecified powers for all sorts of success. The peacock's tail is regarded as beautiful, but the beauty it embodies is the harmony embodied in its unseen opposite (advantageous health and strength), and above all its harmony *with* this unseen opposite. Here is the *unexpected* harmony that moves us from mere harmony into actual beauty. Death and life, weakness and strength, liability and advantage unexpectedly form a harmony; it is here that beauty steps forth.

From this point of view, the creation of new or "avant-garde" art forms could perhaps be read as an indication that certain individuals have already seen through to the formulas inherent in all presently existing art; none of it surprises them anymore, there is no longer anything unexpected in these harmonies to them, hence nothing beautiful. Moreover, they are able to see certain harmonies that none had seen before, that others do not see as harmonious; more fundamentally, they are able to see a greater variety of things as forming a harmony with themselves. Here we begin to verge on the relation of the sense of beauty to the mystical sense. For it follows from our definitions that ultimately all coherences can be viewed as harmonious with ourselves, form a coherence with whatever we might be identifying with at any given time, inasmuch as all local coherences are precisely global incoherencies, and Intersubsumptions of every other coherence. But this Intersubsumption means simply infinite multifacetedness, the potential for being oneself and many other things at once, not being fixed as any one particular definite thing. He who can see the way in which every event is harmonious with something in himself, that he too *is* that event, since neither has any ultimately fixed and definite nature, since both are ever susceptible to transformative self-recontextualization, will perceive a greater range of harmonies than others.

Thus a given piece of music will be heard as utterly dissonant to some. They hear nothing in these tones that corresponds to anything about themselves, to any part of their own experience—"this sound is utterly contrary to all that I am, all that I feel familiar with, all that I can esteem and aspire to or recognize." Another person hearing this same piece of music however, being aware of a greater range of variety in himself, taking himself to be a more multifaceted creature, will perceive that in these sounds that correspond to himself—above all, if nothing else, its lack of ultimate fixity, its indeterminateness.

Perhaps few can bear to know their ultimate indeterminacy, and can recognize the profound level at which they themselves are a chaos, and therefore the sense in which "chaotic" sounds and colors and events are harmonious with their deepest selves. To the extent that they feel this harmony, however, these sounds and colors and events will not be felt as "chaotic" at all, or not merely as chaotic, but rather also as the surest and most familiar order, the order of their own deepest center of experience. Indeed, this order is not separate from or other than this chaos, but is precisely this chaos, is felt exactly by virtue of its being the same chaos as ourselves. Thus we might at least in this local sense judge the broadness of an individual, the breadth of her experience and the depth her perception of herself, by how much she perceives as harmonious (i.e., harmonious with herself), how many different types of experiences and art works she can incorporate into her self, can see as fundamentally in accord with what she herself is; for the more things she herself is, the more things she will feel to accord with herself harmoniously.

Generally, the experience of beauty occurs when seemingly unrelated images are called up, which unexpectedly show some intimate relation or resonance. It always involves a relationship between elements (in the "beauty of simplicity," it is reduced to the smallest number of elements, two: merely one subject and one object). Even in the plastic arts, therefore, the "time" element is essential, inasmuch as unexpectedness implies a before and an after, a moment of initial contact, an adjustment between the former habituations and those after perceiving this new harmony. We see this also in a harmony between the present moment and the past, for example, in literature and music: the work must suddenly assume an unexpectedly coherent shape or arc in time, by which all the seeming randomness that went before suddenly seems an inevitable part of the present resolution. The same can be said for life: it can be perceived as beautiful when the accidental chaos of the past suddenly seems to fall into unexpected alignment or harmony, that is, by virtue of a present "resolution" (harmony). Obviously, then, the sequence and position of the moments is crucial, and all moments are not equal, since in experiencing the past moments of the work we reify, we accumulate habituations that will influence our perceptions of the moments and experiences yet to come.

In plastic art, a collection of images is presented to us all at once; but this juxtaposition itself may be harmonious in a way we previously had not thought of; we had not thought that these particular items and colors and shapes could form any kind of wholeness together in one space, we had not associated them before, we had not perceived any complementariness or resonance or Intersubsumption between them. The artist's task was to indicate that the resonant Intersubsumption between these disparate images existed, that they could be seen as part of some "whole." Moreover, it may evoke images in ourselves, from our own store of experience, which resonate in a way we had not expected. However, this depends very essentially on our accidental state of mind at the moment we happen to encounter the work; our "mood" is never the same, and the images that the same object will evoke at different moments is also never the same. Hence, it may be that many accidental factors of the moment contribute to whether we happen to find a particular thing beautiful; if we had happened to encounter it at another time and place and mood, we may have judged it differently, since it would have resonated differently with the flow of our mind at that moment.

It is also obvious that the second viewing will be a very different experience from the first, since our "expectations" about the work will have been affected by our intial encounter. We will have a memory of it, and now will experience beauty only if our memory has failed to capture something, if what we see is harmonious in a new way, in some way other than what we experienced the first time and had therefore come to expect. The same goes for repeated listenings to a piece of music, or repeated readings of a work of literature. Some works "grow on us," the resonances multiply with each reading, we see a greater number of harmonies that could only come to light with greater familiarity, and hence each new encounter is felt as a new aesthetic experience, a new beauty. Or perhaps what had appeared unharmonious at first gradually and unexpectedly come to be seen as parts of the overall harmony, or as harmonious with aspects of ourselves we were not familiar with before, or had not perceived the connection with before, or which just did not exist before, or were dormant at the particular moment when the first encounter occurred, due to the mood we happened to be in at that moment. As we discover new harmonies in the work, we have new aesthetic experiences, and the work can thus maintain our interest and esteem. What had appeared accidental or superfluous upon first reading or listening or viewing now appears essential and resonates with other parts of the work, parts we had felt a resonance in and with before, or reveals itself, in fact, unexpectedly, to be something very intimately related to us, whereas before we had not seen that it had anything to do with us whatsoever. Thus, no aesthetic experience can occur twice, and no work can ever be experienced in the same way twice. The first encounter can never be repeated, and previous encounters always affect the expectations for subsequent encounters. For indeed, no experience of a work of art (and, by the way, all this applies equally to life and all the experiences therein, which can also be viewed aesthetically, as potential types of beauty) can be "pure," can exist in a vacuum where the pristine work is itself experienced apart from all accidental factors, and judged purely on its own merits, unconnected with anything else. A great deal of other contingent factors also affect our expectations, and hence our experience of the work and whether or not we perceive it as "beautiful." For example, the artist's reputation, what we know about his personality and life, his previous works with which we are familiar, the place and time we first heard of this work and from whom, what they had said about it, what other sorts of reactions it has created in society, when and where it was created, what we had for breakfast that day and so on—all contribute to forming our expectations, which are what must be harmoniously betrayed in order to produce beauty.

Why do we perceive tragedy, the tragic, as beautiful? What is tragic beauty? Aestheticians from Aristotle to Nietzsche have wrestled with this problem, and there is no reason why we should not also get our two cents in. Tragedy is seen when the good and great, those whom we feel should not fail, do in fact fail and are destroyed. Why is this felt as beautiful? Because it reveals the unexpected harmony between greatness and failure, between admirability and destruction; it proves to us that we can also esteem those who are destroyed, that failure and destruction are not at all incompatible with our intuitive conceptions of greatness for humankind. When we see a great man crushed, it does not succeed in making us find him contemptible; on the contrary, we find him all the more admirable for his courage in the face of his ruin. Ordinarily we were not aware that we felt greatness and ruin to be so profoundly compatible, even intersubsumptive. We had assumed that we admired only that which succeeded. But the artist has shown us that in ourselves there is unexpectedly also an appreciation for the harmony of a worthwhile life and character and a ruinous fate—for life is Intersubsumption, and no exclusively fixed results or orders are to be found in it, no success is definitely to go to the virtuous nor downfall to the wicked. This is another aspect of the beauty, a revelation of the full indeterminacy and unpredictableness of the world, its thorough unruliness, the impossibility of getting a firm grasp on it, even by the most sure-handed, its ultimate and indomitable reversibility and Intersubsumption.

The artist's task is thus twofold: to make the familiar unfamiliar (i.e., to de-cohere what has become a coherent single thing in our expectations) and to make the unfamiliar familiar (to make cohere, i.e., harmonize what we had not expected could be harmonized, what does not form part of a familiar grouping to us).

This harmony and resonance can occur in a great number of ways and at a huge number of levels, and the depth of the aesthetic experience may be analyzed in terms of the number of levels simultaneously involved, and the relative "depth" of these levels. At the "deepest," that is, most fundamental and pervasive, level, the harmony of the most disparate things would be perceived in the fact that they are both ultimately Intersubsumption, that is, have no fixed definite nature, they are not *simpliciter* things. Thus, for example, a work or experience which suddenly showed us the harmony of whatever for us represent good and evil, of beauty and ugliness, of life and death, of success and failure, of truth and error, of any set of opposites, would inspire the greatest aesthetic reaction—for all these terms are ultimately not mutually exclusive dichotomous "things," but are rather equally points in various Local Coherences as Global Incoherences, susceptible to transformation into each other, to intersubsumptive reversibility; all are alike in that they share the basic characteristic of incompleteness, indeterminateness, tentativeness, imperfection, dependence, lack of any definite characteristic. Perhaps an even profounder experience would be of the harmony between coherence and incoherence themselves, in other words, Intersubsumption itself, or between harmony and disharmony. (The most radically "unexpected" harmony is that, as we have hinted above, which is found to exist in dissonance itself.) Hence, it would not be going too far to say that "Beauty" is already another name for Intersubsumption itself, which is to say, for Being itself.

But here we enter the realm of the mystical. For the mystic sense is very closely related to the aesthetic sense, and may be perhaps defined as an aesthetic experience of the universe as a whole. In essence, the mystical sense is simply a quantitatively more intense aesthetic experience, in which every component of self and experience come into an unexpected harmony, leaving none out. It differs from the aesthetic experience only quantitatively, not qualitatively. We might go a step further and say the mystical experience is one in which the "mysterious" aspect, in other words, the unknown, indefinable, ultimately unreifiable, intersubsuming aspect of all is itself felt to be harmonious, with this same characteristic (i.e., the lack of any definite characteristics) in all other things and most importantly, in ourselves. In another sense, in perhaps "weaker" mystical experiences, it is perhaps merely that that the deepest types of habituation (i.e., natural law, our physiology, etc.), rather than weaker, more recent ones (our cultural patterns, incidents, or images from our personal histories, idiosyncratic or recently acquired genetic tendencies) are harmonized; in the more complete mystical experience, all these habituations would be involved. For harmonization, harmony itself, is based on snags in reversibility, on habituation, what we are familiar with in various ways and on various levels of consciousness and intuition. We must note here, therefore, that the mystical experience, like the aesthetic experience is dependent on our reification of coherences, our division, our particularization, our limitedness, our finitude, our determinacy—only because of the inherent division of the primordial oneness (noneness/allness) of Intersubsumption can there be reunion or harmony.

One more thing ought to be pointed out here: our definition of beauty extends also to the mystical experience: it must be an *unexpected* harmony. For this reason, the mystical experience cannot persist, unless ever new harmonies, hitherto undreamt of, are perpetually being discovered in the totality of events. This would be a perpetual awakening, not a being awake, a perpetual opening up, not a state of being open; to maintain it would be, to borrow a Buddhist metaphor, like shooting an arrow into the air, and then, an instant later, another that perfectly hit the preceding one and further propelled it, and then, each instant, another arrow perfectly hitting the tail of the last, forever, such that the first arrow never hit the ground, indeed, never stopped ascending. Otherwise, every realization, no matter how profound, will wear off in time.

Thus we might say that the universe as a whole is beautiful in the one paradoxical sense in which it can be considered a single coherent coherence as it were—in that it can be definitively defined as having the characteristic of Intersubsumption, of being incapable of global coherence, of being asynordinate and indefinable.

But let us stop here. It is slightly obscene to define things like "mystical experience" and "beauty" too closely and objectively, with too much clarity and precision, which is to say, with too great a degree of definitiveness. Here more than anywhere else good taste dictates that the fundamental mystery of Intersubumption of all coherences, the face of which hides grinning in everything but shows itself in all its fearsome glory most vividly here, be left as "incoherent" as possible.

Humor

This is a matter directly related to the question of beauty, for in a certain sense, it is humor, not ugliness, that is the true opposite of the beautiful. This intuition would lead us to conclude that the essence of humor is the opposite of that of beauty and that we could, therefore, define it as unexpected discord. This definition has much to recommend it; as in the case of beauty, it would mean that the discord which occurs is other than the discord expected, not necessarily that discord per se was not expected—it could be simply that a different kind of discord was expected. And as with beauty, where expected harmony did not qualify, expected discord here would not qualify as funny; it would be either simply chaos, or some kind of trite joke that we could predict a mile away, that fails to make us laugh. However, despite its symmetry with our concept of beauty as indicated above, this definition does not seem to be the clearest and most effective possible; it could be clarified somewhat by rewording it to emphasize certain elements more distinctly. Therefore, I suggest a more comprehensive and, it seems to me, more accurate phrasing of this definition of humor: *it is the unexpected juxtaposition of disparate habituations*. That is to say, whenever a disparity of habits is suddenly made apparent, it is experienced as humorous. That this is in essence identical to "unexpected discord" in general is evident from the fact that, according to our view, all discord must result from some disparity, and all disparity must by definition be the disparity of habits, since habit, in the broad sense as used and defined in this essay, that is, snags in reversibility, is alone responsible for all manifest diversity, difference, and conflict; disparity and discord are themselves byproducts of habit per se.

But the deep structure of this situation can be described in accordance with our insistence that the setup/punch-line structure, characteristic of humor, is in fact a privileged marker of the structure of reality (Intersubsumption) as such. In beauty, some expectation set up by a meaningful (habituated) marker is subverted, but in such a way that the marker, the original entity, retains its existence as such, revealing that this X, qua X, could also be X as such as a part of some *other* whole besides the one that was expected. An unexpected next step *surprisingly* leaves X's identity in place as X, but as implying another set of completions, so that Xness per se is shown to be more versatile than was first imagined.

Humor is, as it were, more beautiful than beauty, just like beauty only more so, and hence is its true opposite. Humor occurs whenever the completing next step is so radically incongruous that X cannot incorporate it, that X has no way to remain X while forming a new whole with it. It is the limit case that proves the extent to which we are "condemned to meaning": for humor occurs when the perfectly meaningless ensues, when Intersubsumption reveals its being as pure impossibility of Intersubsumption. What happens then is that, necessarily, the initial X must be *reread*. It is no longer X. Two mutually incompatible meanings suddenly appear at once. Meaninglessness simply means that the new token establishes itself as a new center, in terms of which meanings are determined, a new criterion of meaning. When an indigestible other appears, it reads the initial X as part of itself, as some bizarre non-X. But this sudden non-X is precisely what X was, has exactly the same contents as X had. The most extreme incoherence simply reverses the structure, yielding an alternate coherence that re-interprets the initial X.

In beauty, we may say, the Intersubsumption of all of X's possible meanings is manifested, but the continuity of the X whose meanings they all are remains unmolested. In humor, on the contrary, the Intersubsumption of X and some particularly indigestible non-X is revealed directly; each is revealed simultaneously, so that no single synordinate whole is any longer possible which allows both the Xness and the non-Xness to appear at once, except in the single moment of their transformation from one to the other, the breaking of the punch line, where for an instant the two appear as identical and as incompatible at once, releasing the physical tension that had kept each one bound artificially in its nonreversible identity (as a laugh).

This instantaneous single moment should remind us of Zhanran's notion of "totality" and reversibility, cited in the Introduction; for here we have a direct disclosure of Intersubsumption itself, as these two particulars in mutual reversible exchange, each simultaneously the viewer and the viewed, the determiner and the determined. Humor is in effect beauty that has gone too far, beauty that is so beautiful that it ceases to be experienced as beautiful, where the pleasure of beauty is replaced by the violent convulsion of laughter (as similarly, in the violent convulsion of the erotic crisis discussed by Bataille, where the implicit ugliness of the beautiful finally becomes explicit, moves to the center of the relationship and undercuts the last vestiges of the continuity of X's meanings—i.e., the beauty of the face and personality. The trembling interference pattern or feedback oscillation of laughter and orgasm are, as Freud knew, two sides of the same coin, and always imply each other . . .). The equilibrium that was still identifiable as X's own Intersubsumption with non-X in beauty, so that X maintained itself as X in the relationship, has now been undercut—to reveal, as it were, the Intersubsumption of equilibrium and nonequilibrium, or persisting and perishing as X. Humor is the continuity of continuity and discontinuity, the equilibrium between equilibrium and nonequilibrium, the Intersubsumption of Intersubsumption and non-Intersubsumption. It is the ideal case of the total failure of Intersubsumption, which turns out, unexpectedly, to reveal its inevitability at a more profound level; Intersubsumption is as present in its absence as in its presence. What had been center now becomes periphery. What had been a defining criterion in terms of which expectations were set up is now seen to be readable as something else entirely, as determined by the agenda of some new criterion, which appeared as a token in its field of potential markers to be incorporated and interpreted in terms of itself, but for which it was unable to do so. This is the juxtaposition of disparate habits, or what we experience as humor.

Let us explore this definition a little. We may start by noting certain types of situations which seem to recur in comedy: for example, misunderstandings, failures to communicate, absurd teamings, something getting carried away and extending beyond its appropriate or usual measure, the arrival of visitors from distant places or eras whose customs differ greatly from the customs of here and now, and so on. All these situations seem inherently to be experienced as humorous. We see in all these cases that two things are placed together which have become habitually very different, have assumed wildly different shapes, have become more reified, closed off, isolated, separated from one another than we had expected. These very different locally coherent forms have come into being, and they can now interact and contrast without immediately melting into one another or diluting one another, without osmosis occurring, due to their degree of reified local coherence. When we see these two very different shapes—in other words, these two very different habits, for all characteristics are habitual stabilities acquired from previous experience—we laugh; it is the reified local coherence of the overdetermined Intersubsumption, and the great versatility it affords that fundamental Intersubsumption, which creates this pleasure in us. Laughter is in this sense joy in reification of local coherences and the versatility of the universe represented thereby. When the two habits do begin to meld, for example, when the mismatched pair members begin to influence each other so that each becomes more well-rounded, this in itself is not felt to be funny, but rather "touching" or even "beautiful," an unexpected harmony in that these two very different shapes turned out ultimately to be both made of flux, that is, both malleable, both changeable, both influenceable by the other. Very often the habits in question are unstated assumptions, for these are the form that habits take in our daily life; whatever we believe unconsciously and deeply habitually, what no longer comes to our awareness as a proposition but rather has already become a part of our world, a subjective fact as basic to us as the laws of nature, is an assumption. When the assumptions held by two individuals are shown suddenly to differ greatly, or the habitual ways of behaving or dealing with similar situations differ in this way, the result is humor. These very disparate local coherences are both intersubsumptive with the situation they are confronting, allowing that situation to be experienced simultaneously as these two very different things which are nonetheless the same thing, and this is what we experience as funny.

Thus humor, like beauty, has a fundamental philosophic dimension: laughter is essentially an exclamation of joyous surprise that the universe, the intersubsumptive flux where everything is nowhere is everywhere, is capable of assuming such a broad range of differing forms; it is a celebration of the versatility of the universe.

Before proceeding, I should clarify my definition by making clear the different forms in which this "disparity of habits" can appear. As in the case of beauty, two terms are necessary for humor to be experienced; nothing can be funny in and of itself. However, as in the case of aesthetics, the second term might very well be oneself, the viewer's own subjective habit-system, which suddenly comes into conflict or shows its broad disparity with the habit-system implied in whatever is presented and felt to be funny. The greater the disparity between the habit-systems, and the more deeply ingrained the habits are, the funnier the joke. Another very common form of this contrast is in the sudden juxtaposition of two disparate habit-systems which exist simultaneously within the same breast, two habitual ways of acting belonging to the same person but which for some reason are both activated at the same time. For example, a man might have a different way of acting with different groups of people—Jackie Gleason's bus driver character Ralph Kramden boasts of his importance to the bus company when talking to his buddy Ed Norton, but then when he runs into his boss, he must be humble, sycophantic, and obedient. If he is placed simultaneously in a room with Ed and his boss, humor will undoubtedly ensue. Another example of this is the scene of two men at a football game, discussing serious personal matters. They are wrapped up in their discussion and not paying attention to the game, but each time the crowd roars and stands up during the exciting game, they instinctively—habitually—stand up with them, although they have not been watching and do not turn their heads to see what is happening. Here the men possess two different habit systems which are activated at once: their earnest discussion mode and their football game attending mode, each of which demands a different kind of habitual behavior and to each of which a different attitude is appropriate. When both appear at once, the result is humor. Thus we can identify three main types of juxtaposition of disparate habits in humor: between the habits of two different (locally coherent) entities, between the habits of the viewer and those of some entity, and between two different habit-systems of the same entity.

Let us sample a few well-known jokes and look at them in this perspective. *A man is standing on a corner with a dog sitting next to him. Another man comes up and says, "Does your dog bite?" The first man says, "No." The second man, being of a friendly disposition, then proceeds to pet the dog, which promptly bites his hand. "I thought you said your dog didn't bite," he exclaims. The first man looks up and says, "That's not my dog."*

Okay, now what is funny about this old joke? What we are laughing at essentially is the disparity between the habit systems of these two men, and the misunderstanding that therefore ensues. The fact that they have such widely divergent attitudes toward this situation, that the first man has such a different set of assumptions from the second man, and that they can therefore interpret the same situation so differently, is what makes us laugh. More specifically, we are laughing in this case at the very peculiar set of habit-assumptions embodied by the first man, which differ from the expectations and habits of the second man, who represents the average listener's habits. For the first man does not assume, with the rest of us, that the second man's question must be referring to the dog beside him, or that the second man's question already implied the assumption that this was his dog, or if so, that he is in any way obligated to disabuse him of his error. He assumes, whether innocently or out of wanton spite, that he is only obligated to answer the strict literal truth, which is that his dog does not bite. This differs so much from our usual set of habitual assumptions, the assumptions we employ in our daily social interactions, while yet embodying a rationale that we can intuitively understand, that we laugh.

Another common comedic motif that clearly exemplifies this principle is the comedy team, usually a pair of individuals who differ markedly in their basic sets of habits and assumptions about the world. Indeed, it is not uncommon for the two to represent two caricatured opposite attitudes toward the world, or even to be physically disparate, as in the case of the ever popular fat guy and skinny guy motif, which seems to be inherently funny, even when the two individuals in question are real people standing together on the street and not a professional comedy team. In many cases, one of the two, the "straight man," assumes the role of the second man in the dog joke above: he represents the prevailing assumptions and habits of the status quo, of the average viewer, and serves as a foil to further appreciate the disparity of the other member of the team's very different set of habits. The same principle applies to Groucho Marx and Margaret Dumont, or to Bugs Bunny and Daffy Duck, or to a man dressed in drag (for example, one male ballerina in a line of four females; here his masculinity is contrasted with the feminity of the others and of the costume and situation, and the magnitude of our laugh depends on the magnitude of the disparity between the habits displayed by males and females in a given situation). If the straight man is absent, however, we have an implicit straight man, more likely than not ourselves, the implicit habits and thought-patterns of the status quo, with which the comedian displays a disparity. In the case of Groucho, his character is so unique that we see him displaying a disparity with not only Margaret Dumont, but also with Chico, with Harpo, with Zeppo, with the stuffed-shirt, and with ourselves, thus creating at least six different types of laughs.

Another type of humor must be addressed here: black humor. Here we are often made to laugh at the absurd disparity between the common assumptions or habits of cheerful daily life and the consciousness of someone habitually aware of the dark realities lurking behind this optimistic world view. It is important to note that this type of humor, like its counterpart in aesthetics, the tragedy, usually involves the viewer's contemplation of the writer, or some representative consciousness whom the viewer can perceive to be living with this dark view of the world which differs from our common one. In the case of tragedy, we admire the courage of the author in facing this brutal horrible fact, and find beauty not only in the unexpected harmony between the hero's greatness and his downfall, but also in that between the author's composed and even-handed ability to present this horrible tale, and the grim unbearable facts related therein. In the case of black humor, we imagine the dark consciousness of the writer as he presents his innocent or cheerful characters in juxtaposition with the horrible events he keeps creating for them. Or in another variation, a grim-minded character is introduced. For example, we might think of the old SNL routine, "Mr. Mike's Least Loved Bedtime Stories," where the sunglasses-wearing, cigarette-smoking Michael O'Donohue would tell tales of the disembowelment and beheading of cute little bunnies to perky pre-teen schoolgirls. The juxtaposition both of the habitual behavior of the bunnies in such tales with the ending concocted for them here, and the world-view (i.e. habitual assumptions) of Mr. Mike and the young girls reveals a profound disparity, and thus is funny.

Very often the disparity is between the expected development of the story and the actual one, as in the case of the "surprise ending," or even, more generally, the "punch line." Here we have a disparity between our implicit assumptions about the way such a story should go, or how such people should behave, that is to say, between our own total set of habituations, and the behavior actually displayed. The "element of surprise" is employed in a very large percentage of jokes, and yet it is not itself the essence of humor, but rather a special case of the disparity of habits, which is often used in conjunction with other such disparities to achieve the total effect.

Consider Kilgore Trout's tale of the superintelligent visitor from another planet who came to earth to solve the problems of war and hunger. *On this creature's planet, all communication was done by farting and tap dancing. He looked like a vacuum cleaner made of meat. He entered the home of an Iowa family and began to announce to the inhabitants the good news, about the end of war and hunger, farting and tap dancing there in the living room. About thirty seconds later, the head of the house brained him with a golf club.* Now this tale exemplifies a number of the points discussed above. We have two sets of habits: those of the Iowa family and those of the alien, and the vast disparity between them.[60] A failure to communicate, a certain blocking and impenetrability caused by these thick accumulations of different habits, the isolation of the two parties involved and thus the vast difference of their reified coherences, is also an element in the humor. At the same time, we have a surprise ending or punch line, the braining with the golf club, which contrasts with our expectations on how this all should turn out. On another level, we have the black humor dimension; the author's grim consciousness, in coming up with such a story, is contrasted to our regular cheerfulness, or the despised good cheer and optimism of our usual propaganda. Thus this tale causes us to laugh in a number of ways at once, exemplifying as it does several simultaneous habitual disparities.

Another thing that often makes us laugh is the witty insult. Here the humor lies in the hilarious disparity between the object of assault's assumed conception of himself and that displayed by the insulter. It is not funny if the target first disparages himself, and then the wit merely chimes in and agrees with him (unless some other type of disparity is thereby displayed,

---

[60] The same basic idea, but with earthlings travelling to distant points of the past and future of their own history and thus displaying vastly different sets of habits from the people there, was used in Twain's *Connecticut Yankee in King Arthur's Court*, as well as more recently in such movies as Woody Allen's *Sleeper* and the *Back to the Future* series.

for example, between the wit's uncalled-for cruelty and the usual etiquette or compassion expected in such a situation, etc.). If, however, the target seems to think highly of himself, either implicitly or explicitly, the expression of a contrary view by the wit can cause us to laugh. If this low opinion is at the same time expressed in a style which itself embodies some other disparity or surprise, for example, in some pun or literary image, whose use in this capacity we had not expected, the result is a witty put-down. Thus when Groucho says to Margaret Dumont, "I hear they're going to tear you down and put up a building where you're standing," the result is funnier than, "You are fat," because the mental connection between Margaret and a building comes as a surprise to us, contrasts with our own accustomed habits of thinking and associating. At the same time, such a complicated remark is highly gratuitous and uncalled-for in this situation, the bringing in of the image of "tearing down" and "a building" being heretofore completely irrelevant to the conversation and not in accord with our usual habits of conversing. At the same time, we are shown the disparity between Groucho himself, the kind of person who would first have such an intricate and exaggerated image of obesity occur to him and then would proceed to say it aloud, and the habits belonging to both Margaret, with her vanity and desire for self-respect concerning her own appearance which has just been contradicted, and ourselves, who were incapable of connecting these two images, Margaret Dumont's body and an architectural edifice. It should be noted that a put-down is often described as "beautiful"; this is because it does so often involve the use of surprising imagery, and the connection of hitherto unrelated elements. This is, therefore, a form of unexpected harmony and thus, as we indicated above, is experienced as beauty.

The pun in general is another example of our principle. For a pun is the use of a word in two or more senses at once, and it is these "senses" that are juxtaposed, and found to be disparate. The listener had mistakenly assumed that he shared the speaker's assumption about what this word meant in this context; this oneness however is abruptly broken into two when the pun is revealed, and the common symbol, this word, is revealed to have a greater versatility than was expected. By extension, it was revealed that the same symbol can have radically different meaning in different contexts, which is to say, within different habit-systems. The principle involved is essentially that of the "Is that your dog" story above.

I was walking down the street and something caught my eye, and then dragged me along the pavement for about fifteen feet. The idea of someone being ridiculously harmed in this way in itself, as represented by the statement, "I was dragged along the pavement by a hook which had found its way into my eye," would usually not be sufficient to elicit a laugh. The juxtaposition of the two possible ways in which we can "read" the words "caught my eye," the fact that these two radically different habit-systems could both come into use in this particular context, that we have within us this great disparity of ways of reacting, of attitudes, of assumptions, of habits, is the condition of the laughter.

Often a story will go along carefully maintaining ambiguity, seeming to be an ordinary situation that does not reveal itself to be something else, something unusual or absurd usually, until the last moment. For example: *When I was six years old I was playing near the cellar door, and I saw a tiny crack of light in the door. Now my parents told me as long as I could remember: Stay away from the cellar door. But I couldn't resist, I had to find out what was on the other side, and so I went up to it and slowly I opened it up and stepped through; there on the other side, I saw wondrous things, things I had never seen before, things like . . . trees, grass, the sun, the sky. . . .* Here the entire story is ambiguous all the way through, but we only become aware of the other way to read it when the punch line comes around, and then we realize the versatility of our symbol system, the fact that we might be understanding something other than what the speaker means, and that we ourselves have many disparate habit systems within us. All this makes for humor, the celebration of the versatility of the universe in producing so much disparity, so many different forms (i.e., habits), none of which have any fixed nature, all of which are as elusive and changeable and incapable of being definitively pinned down as these signs in our language have thus proved themselves to be.

In the same way, stories of deceit are usually funny. These stories generally involve the way some person cleverly misled someone else. Again what is funny is the disparity between these two people, that they could perceive the situation so differently. A difference in intelligence is invoked, and this is nothing other than a disparity of thinking-habits. This can be seen in Joel Chandler Harris's stories of Br'er Rabbit tricking Br'er Bear and Br'er Fox, for example.

Comparisons of the traits of various ethnic groups are also common comedic material, and for obvious reasons by our scheme. The most common of these is the comparison of Jews and gentiles, or of blacks and whites, especially as performed by a Jewish or black comedian respectively. The gentiles or whites are suddenly treated to a view of themselves from the outside, a view of their own habits from the perspective of a different set of habits; and thus can they see the desired disparity between the two habit-systems. The Jews or blacks, when watching these routines, jubilate in their own characteristics, i.e., the traits that become evident from comparison with the other, dominant, status-quo-defining group, which is to say, their differences from that group and hence the existence of disparity per se, in other words, the possibility of an alternate or deviation from the norm, and therefore of universal versatility. It is for this reason too that the constant feeling of being different, of being a minority, or of being alienated in general from the social norms, usually results in an enhanced sense of humor. There is a social function to ethnic humor of this type too, in that by pointing out differences it also succeeds in creating groupings. We will touch on this point in more detail below.

Sacrilege or irreverence is almost always funny, unless it becomes routine, because it displays such a sharp contrast with the habits of the pious and their attitude toward the objects of their reverence. To them, this is the most important thing of all, the very meaning of life, the crux of the universe, whereas to us it is just so much silliness; here again the contrast is fundamentally between the habits of these two groups of people. For example: *Jesus is on the cross, and his disciple Peter sneaks past the Roman authorities to hear his master's last words. "Peter, Peter," calls Jesus. "I am here, Lord," Peter answers, but Jesus is high up on the cross and delirious from loss of blood, and whatever it is that he says sounds to Peter like, "Ahknchiasoosenear." "Wait, Lord," cries Peter, and sneaks back out to get a ladder. Again the same conversation ensues, and again Peter hear's his master's urgent final message as only "Ahknchiasoosenear." Finally he sneaks back out and gets an even taller ladder, and this time can come all the way up to press his ears to Jesus's mouth to hear the final words of his dying lord. "Peter, Peter," says Jesus, "I can see your house from here."*

This joke works on a number of levels, but for the moment let us just point out the disparity between the habitual attitudes of Peter and Jesus; this contrast, and the different expectations exemplified thereby, are at the heart of the joke, and behind them are the habit systems of the two groups, the pious and the nonpious, respectively. Peter here represents the pious, earnest, and serious about this whole matter, expecting to hear significant words of wisdom about the relation of God and man and so on; Jesus represents us, the joke public, by making a commonplace observation on this occasion. "Golly, I sure am high up here, oh look, over there is Peter's house," was the train of thought going through his mind as he hung on the cross, not anything about humankind's guilt and redemption. There is a certain sympathy for Jesus in this joke as opposed to the pious, for he comes off as a nice regular guy, in implicit contrast with the somewhat ill-tempered and dictatorial know-it-all, who seems to take everything so seriously, who is put before us in the Gospels. But the fundamental contrast is between the two attitudes toward or habitual assumptions about this event, representing the disparity between these two groups, the pious and the nonpious.

Or: *Jesus is on the cross, and calls his followers to gather around him. "Fear not, my flock!" he says. "Soon, very soon, the day of our triumph will come, and I will return on the right hand of power, with the clouds of Heaven, and the end of the world will arrive, where I will judge the quick and the dead, and then you shall get your reward. Verily, I tell you, all this shall happen before some of those standing here shall have tasted death. But in the meantime, while the shape of this world persists, I leave you with one instruction: What you must do at all times is simply this: Play dumb!"* Here we have as it were a combination of the irreverent joke and the insult. We have a contrast between their interpretation of themselves and our alternate insulting interpretation, which amounts to saying, "This is the only explanation for how they can be so stupid." Again, "we" form a coalition, a group, in opposition to "them." I will leave the reader to note all the levels of habit-disparity in this joke for himself.

Such a division naturally also involves a grouping, a consolidation; by being different from you, we become a "we." There is an element of community in humor for just this reason; it contrasts habit systems, and invites all who share a given habit system to feel themselves in communion as opposed to the contrasting group. It is for this reason that humor counts as consummate social skill, and is such a powerful tool, for example, in courtship and flirtation. It is not merely that making someone laugh causes pleasure and dispels boredom, thus making them desire your company just as they would desire any other pleasant experience. The uses of humor go deeper than just as a sign that one person has the power to give another person pleasure (although this is itself would surely be sufficient to make it a useful tool in the courtship process). A deeper function of humor is that it implies that we, two people who can understand the same type of humor, belong to a similar type, have shared habits, form a distinct group as opposed to some other group. This element is always present to some degree in humor, for even to be able to "get" the same joke represents a certain amount of common ground, a common view of where disparity of habits occur, even if we are not on the same side of this disparity. But in some cases this element is much more pronounced, and the "shared experience" aspect becomes almost central. This is the case in most ethnic humor, as indicated above, and in a good deal of "topical" humor or "in jokes." Here the binding, grouping function of humor comes to the fore.

This accounts for a certain common type of humor, which seems at first glance to be the opposite of a celebration of disparity, namely the popular, "Did you ever" type. In this type of joke, a comedian typically describes an experience that he believes his audience has also had, some common trait that we all share but that no one ever mentions. This last point is crucial for an understanding of this kind of humor. For here is where the first layer of disparity comes in: it is a contrast between our public and our private habits, between two sets of habits belonging to the same person but in different situations or times, or between our ideal or public selves and our actual or private selves, or between us, a sub-culture within the culture, and some other group or the culture as a whole. There must be some contrast between some expected experience and this one that actually occurs to us all the time. If the former term did not exist, the latter, a merely shared experience, could not be funny. For example, if the comedian said, "Did you ever go to a restaurant and then order a sandwich, and then when it came, eat it, enjoy it, pay your bill, and go home?" this would probably not incite much laughter. However, if he says, *"Were you ever making out with someone, and one of you had a snot that was whistling,"* we might find it funny. The latter line draws to our attention two disparate sets of habitual attitudes and reactions, and juxtaposes them in a single moment or situation. Our habitual reactions to making out with someone and to a whistling snot are greatly disparate, and seldom manifested in the same moment, but here they are brought out at once, and from this results the humor.

More examples: *Did you ever make a phone call and then forget whom you were calling?* The two selves, the one who dials automatically, by habit, and the one who then must speak, are revealed to be disjunct.

Did you ever look at crowds in old movies, and wonder if they were dead yet? Here, on one level, the disparity between life and death, the fact that a person could be alive and moving around at one moment and later on dead, is itself brought to light, or that in one moment he could be seemingly moving around, in the movie, while at the same time he is actually dead. At the same time, the attitude of the viewer displays a peculiarity, a disparity from the usual habitual attitude one has when viewing people in a film, or when encountering any other person. Great interest in the idea of their being dead at some time, or that a person could be preserved in film even while being dead, is not usually acknowledged, and the disparity with a less astute viewer, to whom this issue did not even occur, is also involved.

Then there is the "bank shot," where disparity is revealed by a misplacement of empathy, or feeling of similarity. This is typically accomplished by means of the "pathetic fallacy." For example, *What do dogs do on their day off? They can't lie around, that's their job.* Here the disparity is between the habits of man and dog. The concerns of the man are erroneously placed into the dog, which reveals that originally the dog's world was something altogether different. To suddenly imagine the dog considering this question, from a typically human perspective, reveals how different his actual perspective and habits are from ours. *What I really can't stand is cruelty to plants. For example, hanging plants. I mean, how do we know they're not scared shitless?* The world of the plant and the world of us, who could be frightened by hanging in the air like that, are here juxtaposed, inductively as it were. To suddenly imagine this foreign set of sentiments, which we had not previously attributed to the dogs or plants, transplanted onto these objects, results in the desired appearance of a disparity of habits in the universe, and the result is humor.

The element of community in humor is also manifest in the fact that a viewer often finds other "types" of people more humorous when he is in the presence of someone belonging to his own "type." When alone, one will sometimes take these things simply as annoyances or even indifferently and as a matter of course. For example, it is not uncommon for adult children to find their parents habitual ways extremely funny, but they are less likely to laugh about them separately than together. A single child in the presence of his parents will not find his parents strangeness particularly funny, but when a sibling is present, who has shared many experiences of these same idiosyncrasies of the parents, with whom they have often been discussed and mimicked and ridiculed, and with whom the disparity with the habits of the children have become a piece of shared knowledge, the remarks and actions of the parents suddenly become hilarious. All this is due to the sense of community that necessarily arrives simultaneously with the appearance of disparity: disparity immediately makes one aware of those whose habits are less disparate that one's own, difference makes us aware of similarity. That is, Local Coherence is Global Incoherence is Intersubsumption. This is another significant level of the pleasure which is inherent in humor, particularly the humor resulting from the disparity between the viewer's habits and those of the observed entity: a joy in one's own sense of community with those whose habits are similar, who implicitly observe this spectacle of different habits with one, and thereby manifest their own sameness with one. However, this somewhat xenophobic and derisive element of clustering, although important, is clearly secondary to the main source of pleasure in humor, the disparity of habits itself, and the versatility of the chaotic locally reifying universe thereby manifested.

Sex and Drugs

One of the most beautifully executed expositions of the vicissitudes of the principle of *asness* in modern times is the Freudian libido theory, to which we should devote some words here, having just explored the realm of humor and the comic, which was one of the fields in which Freud gave the most illuminating examples of his way of thinking. Leaving aside the question of metaphysical duality of Eros and Thanatos for the moment (we shall take it up presently), we see in the many expressions of libido—as art, religion, literature, personality types, and so on—not the effacement or avoidance of sexuality, but rather, in the very attempt to evade it, a display of its irrepressible power, of its all-pervasiveness, of its unevadability. The coherence "sex" is equally present in its absence as in its presence. Indeed, we should say it is more present in its absence, in its repression, where it diversifies into manifold forms and displays its unconquerable power. The direct expression of sex is by this standard a poor, weak expression of sex. It should be noted that considerations of the type elaborated above might lead us toward a Jungian rewrite where the precise "sex-ness" of libido is effaced by virtue of the very fact of its fecundity, of its ability to be so many nonsex things; for Jung libido becomes an indeterminate psychic energy which can assume any form but has no one privileged expression which would allow us to specify its pure content. But while Jung's inference on this matter is accurate, he does not go far enough; he ends up with what a typical metaphysical monistic mistake, where "indeterminacy" itself becomes the privileged coherence which is being expressed in various determinate forms, but which itself is not subject to "asness" at all. This neutral indeterminate tertium quid is what it is, *simpliciter*, pure potentiality.

In Tiantai terms, we have here a variety of the "Exclusive Center," and indeed not the most thoroughgoing sort even of that. Indeed, in an important sense, Freud's naive dualism is more advanced than this sort of monism. Freud's quest for metaphysical duality (first ego vs. libido, then Eros vs. Thanatos) was motivated by a wish to explain the conflict in psychic life, especially the fact of repression. Why did he want to see this conflict as between the instincts themselves, rather than between two contrary manifestations of one instinct (as Jung, Reich, et al. would and did)? After all, it is easy to see that one is the reverse of the other; to want to preserve yourself is to want to destroy others (given limited space and resources), to affirm one thing is to deny another, to love one is to hate another. The simplest answer is, because he wanted to root things in bodily relation; but even more crucial is the fact that he wanted the destructive instinct to be incapable of elimination, not to be just a transformation or distortion of a neutral or positive force. This basic dualism makes the doubleness of forms irreducible to either side. In any combination, there will always be an element of destructiveness—in at least one of its forms: desire to return to the previous state of inanimacy (desire to reduce tension), repetition compulsion, aggressiveness. It can never be eliminated, and even if one is totally satisfied in love, even presumably if one had satisfied his Oedipal desires with his mother and no one had stood in the way, he would still show this trait. It is incurable, it can never be eliminated, it is not adventitious. The only way it can be dealt with is to "fuse" with Eros, and this it does in fact in the phenomenon of life itself. As Brown suggests, this could easily have been seen as a "refusion" (as finding an object is always refinding)—but Freud will not say so. The ego fuses them, as it fuses all, but this is its work and its accomplishment, not something which was the case in the beginning. The point is that no "one" coherence is ever an adequate description of what is appearing; to be appearing *as* love is also to be readable as aggression, and vice versa. In every actual instance, they are outside themselves, they manifest only by being more than what they "are."

In fact, this move is parallel to the classical Tiantai denial that "enlightenment" really existed at the beginning—it is something that is yet to be attained, which only then is seen as having been implicit all along—and enlightenment is in Tiantai also a fusion, an unobstructedness. It is "original" only in a retrospective, inherently paradoxical sense (closer to Freud's notion of *Nachtraglichkeit*); it has "always existed" in just the same sense that any other emergent coherence has "always existed," which is in the sense that all coherences are necessarily intersubsumptive. Tiantai also insists that the evil can never be eliminated; it is built into the constitution of things. In any fresh alloy, even the Buddha, this element must be a discernible component, it is never lacking. But in that particular alloy, it is fused perfectly with its opposite, and their identity can be affirmed from that vantage point. Evil appears then *as* Buddhahood, which for Tiantai also means that Buddhahood can appear *as* evil. Freud could not say this because, first, he could not imagine a principle that was one and yet necessarily also always self-opposed and two, the principle of the Tiantai Three Truths, and second, he was committed to one-way causal descriptions of things which assume the primacy of the term that comes first in time. Whatever comes first is the real thing, what is done with it later is adventitious. So for him the ego's fusion of the death and life instincts cannnot assume any special significance ontologically.[61]

Nonetheless, as suggested, in a certain sense this kind of dualism (or Empedoclean pluralism) is much closer to omnicentrism than any monism would be. For what is being asserted here is simply that in *every* instantiation or

---

[61] But some words should be said also about what is really being asserted in the death instinct. It is claimed that we are aggressive or destructive not only in the senses in which we are so because of frustration or lack of love, or because someone or something has frustrated us and we therefore want to eliminate him or it in order to obtain the libidinal satisfaction that he or it has blocked. Besides all the instances that you can think of of that, there is a fundamental need to destroy things, to return them to quiescence, which is drawn upon by Eros in these cases—and this is how the two are usually "fused." But there is in any case a certain amount of this instinct that has to be used up. This "economic" aspect of the libido theory requires the most thought—perhaps the central error lies there, perhaps the central profundity. In any case, the idea is that we want to be inanimate again—but Eros persuades us to enjoy this return only vicariously, through destroying others, as in Bataille.

manifestation, both (or all) elements must be identifiably present. There are, in other words, no cases of pure love or pure hate, pure aggression or pure libido, as would be possible if they were merely transformations of a neutral tertium quid. If hate were simply distorted love, there could be cases where it was all love or all hate—and then we end up with a real practical dualism, as with the sheep and the goats, some are good and some are evil. Freud's theory is not axiologically dualistic at all. The point is simply that this unity comes in reality, in things, not in the realm of the unseen principles themselves.

However, even in Freud's own terms, a definitive assertion of the separability of the two contrary principles is saying too much. Freud should have been tipped off by the fact that there is no concept of negation in the unconscious, just varying degrees of cathexis of objects. This means that the unconscious cannot distinguish between a desire to touch, be near, love, and a desire to negate, eliminate, destroy. It simply cathects, simply makes that object an object of attention and interest, which will always imply a desire to touch it, break the boundary, interpenetrate with it, make the two part of one system such that their individuality is destroyed but also affirmed, having an impact on other things all the more intimately. From the Tiantai perspective, to posit and to negate are the same thing: to see another as another is already to desire and hate him, to want to incorporate, destroy and preserve him.

A further word may be said here also about the privileging of sex in this context. Contra Jung et al., it is not completely without justification that it is singled out as the master signifier here. Hegel noted, rather amusingly, that the highest expression of the dialectical identity of opposites in animal existence, its caricature as it were in the realm of the functions of the body, was the conjunction of the procreative function and the function of elimination in a single organ, the "highest" and "lowest" functions of animal existence in one place. We may transpose this observation to the register of ordinary consciousness; perhaps the most intense and pervasive form in which Intersubsumption, constitutive impossibility as all-pervasion, appears to natural consciousness is in the experience of sexual desire. (The previously cited example of the Will is generally noted not in ordinary experience but in some form of philosophical reflection.) For where else do we get so tight a tangle of the conditions of possibility and the conditions of impossibility, experienced as a single simple datum? It is impossible not to regard others as both persons and as sexual objects. Each of these contrary coherences pertains to all other beings, each pervades the entire experiential field, and sexual desire may perhaps be described precisely as their clash. As we have seen in our discussion of Bataille, the public persona of control and civilized respectability turning out to be animated by something falling completely outside the realm of any personality at all, a vortex of impersonal drives.[62] To the extent that this is claimed and repossessed by the personality, its quality of satisfactoriness (to the individual personality) is lost. "Good" sex appears in this field as the impossible ideal of a loss of control, but in such a way that control is not lost and the enjoyer is not destroyed. This simultaneous identity and incommensurability is as good a revelation of the fundamental paradox as any; indeed, the emergence of a coherence as an object of sexual desire—say, a breast—out of fatty tissue, a pendulous conglomeration of cells made of the usual elements and chemicals, as harped on in primitive Buddhist meditations on the components of the body—is perhaps the most immediate intrusion of constitutive impossibility that comes into our experience. That beautiful woman over there grew up as someone's little daughter, went to school and goes to a job and eats and reads and watches TV, has a digestive and respiratory and nervous system, and is wearing underwear which was manufactured in a factory and bought in public at a store; this is as profound a paradox as any devised by Zeno.

We may add to this, on the traditionally male side, Žižek's phallic paradox: everything depends on me, and yet for all that there is nothing I can do.[63] And again: Orgasm as both the goal and the destruction of pleasure. Also Freud's "Most Common Form of Degradation in Erotic Life":[64] tenderness and erotic feelings in inverse proportion, but also dependent on one another. The impossible identity between the spontaneous body/genital and the face/mind, which is nonetheless inescapable, is again what is disclosed here.

We may add to this also, on the traditionally female side, the paradoxical ability to elicit a response belonging to another as one's own achievement and enjoyment—doing "being done to," initiating the initiation done by the other. What we have here is a constitutively impossible attempt at possessing "being possessed," enjoying "being enjoyed," and so on. The more I succeed at possessing being possessed, the more I fail; the more I succeed at being the enjoyer of being enjoyed, the more I fail.

The depth of the paradox is compounded by the fact that in reality both the "male" and "female" sides are experienced by each participant, as can be demonstrated, if it is not already perfectly evident, by reference to our consideration of constitutive intersubjectivity. Here we have a prime example,

---

[62] Compare, in this connection, Merleau-Ponty's description of the connection of sexuality to the ambiguity of the body, of being simultaneous subject and object, seer and seen (PhP, 166–69).

[63] Žižek, *Sublime Object*, 223.

[64] Sigmund Freud, "The Most Prevalent Form of Degradation in Erotic Life," in *Sexuality and the Psychology of Love*, trans. Phillip Rieff (New York: Collier, 1970), 58–70.

immediately and insistently experienced, of "identity as constitutive impossibility as all-pervasiveness": the coherence "sex" is such only by being impossible, and thereby is inescapable. For us, this *turns out* to be so not only for the coherence "sex," but also for every coherence whatsoever, for identity per se, as we have already intimated.

A similar phenomenon can be detected in the experience of a smoker trying to quit smoking, or any other kind of addict. For here we have one of the most visceral instantiations of absence as hyper-presence. Once the drug is denied, it is suddenly everywhere, its unavoidability has suddenly become manifest. Every situation puts forth the coherence "cigaretteness" in a way that could never have been as vivid or all-pervasive while actual cigarettes were being smoked. One discovers, as Sartre once remarked in another context, the "capable-of-being-encountered-by-me-smoking-ness" that has been hidden in all situations, in matter itself, in every percept into which one might dream of escaping it. This coherence turns out to have always been playing a foundational role in the construction of the world, which only now, in the absence of smoking, has become fully present. Cigaretteness is built into nature, and what is more, is the meaning of nature, of civilization, of life, of love, of food, of death. It is the first principle and ground of all existence.

It may be complained that I am talking about desire and metaphor here, which is something quite different from the presence of a coherence in experience. This is just the presupposition I wish to overturn. The appearing of a coherence in imagination, as a form of desire, as a metaphorical whimsy, is as much the presence of that coherence as its concrete location, and indeed, as I have said, more so. This requires a rewriting of the notions of being and experience, and this is precisely what is being attempted here. Indeed, what is most crucial here is just what is desired in desire, what sort of presence is acquired with presence, and to what extent the "full presence" of the desired object is identical to its complete absence—and as such can be experienced as either the total fulfillment of the desire or the most excruciating frustration of the desire. Perhaps, as I have suggested in various ways above, what is desired when X is desired is precisely, *per impossible*, to finally *get rid of* X?

Catharsis and/or Addiction: Asness, Art, and the "Repression Hypothesis"

What we said earlier about mindfulness, the power of the word in bringing into focus a peripheral element, making it explicit, and the crashing of a coherence accomplished by full extension of it, which was equated to full awareness of it, can now be applied in addition to another problem, a more broadly cultural issue. The Freudian "repression hypothesis" has become now almost common sense in our culture; to put it crudely, this is some variant of the notion that there is some *quantity* of excitation which is hidden inside, and needs to be released regularly, a kind of displeasure in the form of pressure which demands regular pleasurable discharge, on a vaguely hydraulic model. Hence, evils need to be acknowledged, "brought out in the open," confronted, thereby dispelling their power to pull the strings from the dark, diminishing their force by spending their accumulated pressure. This notion bears a distant relation to the Aristotelian cathartic notion of art—as a harmless channel by which to use up an accumulated negative force. In spite of the intuitive appeal this notion has to us by now, both in ethics and in aesthetics, it is opposed across the boards by the opposite notion, the notion that the bringing into the open of dangerous elements only habituates us to them, creates an addiction, a self-perpetuating momentum. Ethically, this can be seen in vulgar Confucianism and Buddhism, as well as the notion of the power of positive thinking—we must not think bad thoughts, the more we do the more we increase their power. We increase the strength of our good habits by practicing them, and pushing the evils out of our mind—repressing them is good. The corresponding notion of art is perhaps what is operative when we hear pundits complaining about the sex and violence in the media—seeing this sort of thing openly, far from using up and discharging the problematic element, simply reinforces it, creates a habit, and indeed escalates the tendency, so that it now must be had constantly, must even be acted out in more and more extreme forms.

Well, what are we to make of these two opposite views of the moral and artistic function of bringing to full view the most undesirable things? As in most other of these deadlocks between two opposed views, we may again suspect that we have a false dichotomy here, that the problem has been wrongly posed, and this is what I shall try to show, in terms of the concepts so far developed here. We must first redescribe the situation. We have already spoken of the strange presence qua absence experienced as "missing something," which we also described as the most generally applicable human condition. One form of this presence qua absence can be found also when one is "repressing," in other words, when one is haunted by something one does not acknowledge, something one cannot even identify. I do not admit to myself that I hate my best friend; I do not know that this is a fact; I am not aware of it. And yet, I have "tacit knowledge" of it; it is affecting what I do know; in fact, I know *by means of* it, as we have seen. It is an *organ* of my knowing, like my eyes or the nerves in my brain, which I am experiencing *as* the explicit "manifest content." Now in this case, we have an organ of knowing that can be described as distorting or obstructing my present apprehension of what I am aware of; it is interfering with each thing I now encounter, in such a way as to leave its negative imprint on all. By this is meant simply that the reversibility is impeded, that it can appear *as* some explicit term, but not vice versa. The shape of this coherence, if you will, is hyper-present by virtue of its very enforced absence. Its "presence" is experienced by me in that its shape is reflected, as in a photographic negative, by the contour of what is being avoided in each exchange of perspectives, each new moment of experience, whichever the reversible flip-flops of center-periphery relations, and exchanges of "asness" are still unimpeded. The one thing that never appears in all these reversals is the one persistent shape. As we saw, it is indeed a sort of pressure: it is the lack of reversibility, something I can neither "be"—in other words, experience as center/impossible/all-pervasive—nor see as an expression of the coherences I am currently tacitly identifying with. This is, by our definitions, precisely to simultaneously want it and want to eliminate it, which reveals the inner structure of ambivalence characteristic of repression. Given our basic model of what a coherence is to begin with, that is, a figure/ground or setup/punchline relationship, we may picture this presencing qua absence as something like the pattern that might emerge if a magnet were repeatedly applied to a spread of iron filings, changing the configuration of where they were attracted to constantly, so that a vast array of patterns emerges, but in each case having the same configuration of repulsion on the magnet, so that a hole in the shape of, say, a rabbit, forms somewhere in all the different positive figures. Rabbitness appears simply as what is excluded from *every* act of construction (although in each case, many other things are necessarily excluded as well). We may picture this exclusion as a positive presence which refuses to register as such (although it, like the figures formed by the filings, is a presence in the only sense we recognize, namely, a figure against a ground) because one is primed to look for figures in the black rather than the white at the moment, in the groups of filings rather than in their spaces. The figure of the excluded item emerges as it were as the contour of the front line of resistances; it appears in the resistances, in the things that appear instead of it, or, in our language, *as* the things that are there in its place, which are holding it off. It is shaped by the line of sedimentation that describes the point beyond which nothing is allowed to flow.

It is important to note once again the ambiguity of "what does not appear in present awareness"—that is, for us, whatever is appearing *only as* this thing here, but as which this thing may not appear. For this is true first and foremost of the "self"—I am the one thing which never appears in my world, as Wittgenstein notes (in his example of the proposed "world as I found it" book), but also of "the external world" in the sense we defined it above, that is, whatever lies outside of whatever is in my cognitive or volitional control at the moment, whatever overflows the determinations I am able to make on the basis of my self. This apparent paradox should be easily resolvable at this point, and quite fruitfully. It is no accident that the external world and I seem to occupy exactly the same position. The self is the external world; I am outside my self. My self as such is always something yet to be encountered, something that threatens whatever it is I believe myself to be appearing *as* at the moment, a projected fulfillment or undermining of its present expression; all these things can equally be said of "the external world," as noted above. This is simply a fruit of the Three Truths all over again: identity (myself) is a constitutive contradiction, it means the impossibility of its own appearance *simpliciter*, and therefore its omnipresence, it is always necessarily something else, something more, something other than what it is. What lies outside X is more X than X itself. X's external world is the real X. The essence of X is precisely non-X, and vice versa. The self is precisely the external world.

Also involved here however, getting back to the problem of catharsis and addiction, is the transition from contingent to necessary impossibility, upon which we have grounded our ethics, so to speak. For the transition from repressed content which is present only in the form of its absence to confronted and fully aware presence is precisely the transition from contingent to necessary impossibility, from presence as absence to absence as presence, if you like. When a given coherence is repressed—"I hate my best friend," for example—I am excluding it from the circuit of things as which whatever I am presently doing—let us say, "eating dinner"—can be expressed. I cannot be aware of "hating my best friend" as a form of "eating dinner" for the simple reason that I am not aware of the former at all, except as an absence, that is, as eating dinner, as a negative imprint which has appeared as one of the many negativities that constitute "eating dinner" but which has done the same for all previous positive coherences, without being in turn constituted by them, by their absences. I cannot see it as "eating dinner" because I cannot see "eating dinner" as it, and that is because I simply cannot see it. Now this is felt as a kind of interference, as I said, a kind of holding over which prevents the full absorption of all into this present one. A little more Buddhistically, what obstructs "one-pointedness" or a "nondwelling" or doing one thing at a time (cf. again the arresting formulation in the *Udāna*: in the seeing only the seen, you will not be "with that" then you will not be "in this," then you will be nowhere, not here, not there, not in-between . . .) is this retention of an undigested extraneous coherence which tangles with the present moment, which sets up a twoness or array because it has failed to be integrated into the "this"—for in Tiantai terms, the only possible oneness or one-pointedness is that which results from an insight into asness, from focusing on a central coherence interpreted into all other coherences, seen *as* all other coherences, and hence vice versa.

The rest of the story is simple, and once again no more than a Tiantai spin on a pan-Buddhist premise, namely, the Second Noble Truth: desire is the cause of unsatisfactoriness, which means for us, "Avoidance of suffering is the cause of suffering." Eating dinner shrinks from confronting hating my best friend—it thinks it will be damaged by it, will be unable to sustain the affront of this other coherence—that is, my nice dinner will be ruined if I have to deal with this right now. The premise here is that "eating dinner" is some particular "one" which could be ruined, and that "hating my friend" is another coherence that is a particular "one" which could ruin anything; this evades the basic insight that both are already completely bankrupt, that is, all-pervasive, having nothing outside themselves upon which to act or to be acted upon by. Eating dinner is not only contingently threatened by external coherences; it is in its very nature already thoroughly undermined and made impossible by them. Its ruin is necessary. This is true of hating my friend as well. Fully inhabiting either one of them would be enough to demonstrate this. To do this, however, I have to overcome my fear of suffering the loss of them, the loss of something that I do not possess. Eating dinner is a coherence that never appears *simpliciter*; it appears as a bunch of other coherences, a finite set for which can never be determined. "Hating my friend" can be one of these coherences as well, if I just have the hermeneutic chutzpah to include it and read it as dinner-eating. The repressed coherence is absent in the insistent form of a haunting repeated hole, or the contour of the front line of defense, and thus only contingently absent, and capable of promising a genuine but postponed presence *simpliciter*, a presence which would exclude all otherness, precisely because it is not present now, because it has been excluded and thus cannot be disproved as all present things are disproved. It sustains itself by staying out of the process of mutual expression, of involvement in awareness. If it comes into awareness, if I do allow or force myself to "face the repressed," this contingent absence which promises real presence becomes instead another center in its own right, which means a necessary absence, an emptied-out master signifier that appears only as others, and that therefore intersubsumes with dinner-eating and all other coherences. Here we see the difference that still can be seen in the absences we just described of self and of external world. The latter, in its ordinary sense (the one external world) is the absence as contingent, while the self is this same absence experienced as necessary, which by the way equals our modified definition of the external world, that is, the fact that there is always a constitutive outside to every coherence.

But let us return to catharsis and addiction, for we are now in a position to resolve the dilemma. I will put it simply. An instance of, say, sex or violence, whether in personal behavior or as witnessed in the media, will be addictive if it appears simply as itself, and will be cathartic if it appears in the form of something else. That is, if the reversibility of its asness is snagged somewhere, it will repeat endlessly, trying to break through that snag, it will be an addiction. If it is permeated by asness in full reversibility, however, such that it appears also as other things and other things appear as it, it will be cathartic, will flow away in the process of expression. This has nothing to do with graphicness or explicitness of presentation. It is solely a matter of Intersubsumption. Indeed, as we have seen above, in a certain sense, a coherence can only appear as itself only by staying off camera, by staying out of awareness, by not presencing, by existing only in the form of suggestion, allusion, innuendo, and consequence. When violence appears as football, I am forced to realize that violence also expresses itself as strategy, as restraint, as rule-following, as time-allocation, as skill, as teamwork, as hot-dogging, and so on. Even if an act of violence is graphically portrayed in a movie, I am forced to see that violence appears as craftsmanship, as entertainment, as narrative, as symbolic marker, as aesthetic form. Indeed, in both cases I normally say, "It is not real violence." In all these cases, my desire for violence is satisfied by the very absence of literal violence, and it is here that we have the cathartic effect. It will be noted too that this is equivalent to our ethical imperative to embody in a single token the demand for X and the demand for non-X; violence is cathartic when it embodies the constitutive impossibility of violence, the co-extensiveness of violence with nonviolence.

But when then does violence become addictive? Not when it is bare, real violence, stark facticity. Rather, it happens when the violence becomes a symbolic bearer of a dense enough package of non-violence coherences—when it becomes, if you like, a center, but one which I do not quite fully inhabit, so that it remains determinate as violence, as discussed above. That is, violence is a rival center, a "false" center, which unifies all things for me, as which all things appear for me—both desired coherences like strength, freedom, love, intimacy, courage, pleasure, as well as many much more specific and idiosyncratic desiderata, and undesired ones, perhaps death, destruction, failure (I vicariously live my failure through the failure I inflict on the other—and this is a large part of the pleasure), pain. In the case of the desirable coherences, I get them all at once when I get violence; in the case of the undesirable quiddities, I get them as violence, which is to say, as the desirable coherences, thence nullifying whatever was fearsome about them, allowing me to master and accept them. That it remains identifiably "violence" however is due to the fact that I am willing to be the experiencer or perpetrator or witness of violence, but not yet to *be* violence itself; if I were to intensify my commitment to violence just that little bit more, to become it, it would cease to have any particular identity, it would be "self" truly and necessarily impossible and thereby omnipresent. This would not preclude its being identifiably "violence," of course, but it would mean that it was no longer an addiction, violence would come and go like any other expression of this impossible omnipresent self. I would be seeing the contradiction of violence not as contingent but as necessary. So, in a nutshell, if football is your violence, it is cathartic; if violence is your football, it is addictive.

It should be obvious then that for us the repressed can by its nature have no fixed contents—it is not, as on the Freudian hydraulic model, a certain set of repressed coherences which are stored up somewhere; it is simply whatever the present acts of awareness are structured to exclude and resist, the negative image formed by their own resistances. A coherence is just a contour of this contact-boundary; whatever is excluded is the content repressed and present as repressed. There is no end to these, and when one thing is allowed another will be resisted. The only "remedy" for this would be a certain skill, a flexibility in detecting and relaxing resistances and exclusions that are bound to be morphing continually, a kind of flexibility or motility in the clenching and relaxing of the interface between the seen and the unseen. It also means that our descent into the forbidden cannot be restricted merely to the familiar hosts of rape, incest, murder, cannibalism, and so on; the list of the excluded never ends, and is always recreating itself. That is, we have to have the courage to confront and inhabit not only the above atrocities, but also putting spaghetti on our heads, suddenly jumping up and down like a chimpanzee when walking into the bank, rolling around on the floor for no reason and so on, whatever we are not thinking we are thinking of doing. Or, if you like, we must own up not only to "I want to kill my dad," but also, "I want to dress my dad up like a fish," and "I want my dad to be submerged in a sphere of whipped cream orbiting the earth," and so on. Most of these are easy to do—"preconscious," in the language of Freud's first topology—while a few will be recalcitrant pillars of some chronically impacted self—"unconscious" or genuinely "repressed"—but all demand at least their moment in the sun. As Spinoza said,

> The human mind is capable of perceiving a great many things, and this capacity will vary in proportion to the variety of states which its body can assume.... That which so disposes the human body that it can be affected in more ways, or which renders it capable of affecting external bodies in more ways, is advantageous to man, and proportionately more advantageous as the body is thereby rendered more capable of being affected in more ways and of affecting other bodies in more ways. On the other hand, that which renders the body less capable in these respects is harmful.[65]

---

[65] Spinoza, *Ethics*, trans. Samuel Shirley (Indianapolis: Hackett, 1982), 76 and 177 (part II, proposition 14 and part IV, proposition 38).

Only with continual exercises of this absurd, surreal kind does the mind remain supple enough to keep up with its own asness, and the inexhaustible multifariousness of the meanings of things.

The Limits of Sublimation

Another point should be made here, while we're touching on these psychoanalytic issues. For it might be thought that our claim that "each thing is already all other things" would make possible unlimited sublimation; to put it pathetically/naïvely, it might be thought that, since we claim eating Jello is also already having sex, one can completely sublimate having sex into eating Jello with no remainder, and no longer ever literally have to have sex. Or vice versa. But it should be obvious by this point that this will not fly here, for "Intersubsumption" for us also necessarily implies a sense of alternation. We cannot say "since X is already in Y, you can get X just by being Y without ever going to X literally." We have, first of all, indeed wiped away the *literal* distinction between literalness and metaphoricity, taking them as mutually implicative. But more than this, we must say that the readability of X in Y also means that Y must sometimes become X, by whatever standards of literalness happen to be operative in any given (delusive) locally coherent cognitive frame. For whatever Y is there cannot stay, cannot contain itself, cannot coincide with itself or match any conditions of its appearance *simpliciter*. Here we are once again unexpectedly able to agree with Freud; some small grain of direct satisfaction (again, however construed in any given context) is always necessary, since for us the "everything is everything else" and "infinite convertibility between all coherences" does *not* mean you can *exclude* certain things completely, sublimate them, and take them only in other certain forms. This is precisely the thrust of the Tiantai doctrine of inherent entailment of the Three Thousand Coherences, not one of which can ever be eradicated. Since there is no mastery to any coherence (except as this impossibility of *simpliciter* appearance per se), all must fall out their own bottom, and make the rounds again through all other forms; each and every possible coherence haunts every actual, and can never be excluded from actualization once and for all.

Hegel and/or Zen

We spoke of Hegel above, especially in connection with the introduction of the concept of "cunning," the cunning of Reason in this case, and indeed, the case of Hegel deserves closer consideration as we look back over the ground we have covered here. For the explication given by Hegel of a single coherence—in this case, "Reason"—pervading and binding together all other coherences by means of its very impossibility, its very breakdown, is accomplished at a greater level of detail and sophistication than has been demonstrated for any other starting point. The privileging of Reason itself as the starting point for any exposition is, like the privileging of sex, highly justifiable. Since an exposition is by nature a conceptual and linguistic binding together and mutual explication, the explicit raising of the de facto starting point of any thinking—the "divine power of language," Reason—is arguably to be uniquely privileged in any attempt to say anything about anything. And Hegel's sublation of *Verstand* into *Vernunft* is a beautiful playing out of constitutive impossibility as all-pervasion; Reason itself, in its very breakdown, proves to pervade, support, explain, indeed move all that initially appears as nonreason. By means of its breakdown, whereby it becomes no longer recognizably *Verstand*, it succeeds in the attempted project of the *Verstand*, to be that which all other coherences turn out always to have been, or what supplies their definitive explanation. Moreover, we do not have to accept the received reading of Hegel, whereby the standpoint of the Universal, of the Idea, of *Vernunft*, is assumed at the outset and surreptitiously read into the supposedly inherent evolution of the particular, with the outcome assumed in advance. With Žižek, we may see the procedure as arising from the side of the particular; its own impossibility or blockage is what produces the Universal that it thereby always already was. It is not that the Universal simply splits off to produce and subsume the particulars that will provide it with content. The work of dialectics is done by the particular itself, the self-destruction or self-splitting of which is what is called the Universal, or Reason per se. Dialectic itself is the omnicentrism displayed by the particular coherence "Reason."

But Hegel's real shortcoming is still to be sought in his insistence on the *unique* validity of this particular "center," Reason. He is of course aware of the danger of this, and makes a valiant attempt to fend it off in the *Phenomenology*. There, the attempt is to show that any possible standpoint of natural consciousness, anything short of Reason itself, will devolve via its own self-realizations/breakdowns into reason itself "by an immanent dialectic," as the cliché has it. The claim is that the extraneous standard of reason itself need not be brought in to produce these transitions. They are accomplished simply by the self-application of the standard avowed by the standpoint in question, its necessary and inherent attempt to accord with its own Notion. This is what Hegel claims to be doing, but it is highly debatable that this is what is actually happening in the *Phenomenology*—especially in the earliest sections, on sense-certainty and perception. The mere fact that the whole thing is being discussed, that we are already in the realm of language and its "divine power" is one point to be made against this claim. It is arguably only in this sense that "necessary" and "inherent" and "its Notion" can play any part at all in the proceedings. These are retrospective determinations translating into the language of Reason what manifested originally as something else. (In that Tiantai view, this retrospective sense can itself be constitutive, by virtue of the uncloseability, the ineradicable yet-to-be-decidedness, which pertains to the previous moment, as it pertains to any coherence whatsoever.) Another objection would be the mere fact that there remain consciousnesses inhabiting these standpoints that persist in not recognizing the supposedly immanent transitions.

Hegel has ready answers to both of these objections—the necessity of language for self-consciousness, given its provenance in intersubjective encounter, as well as the possible meaninglessness of the idea of "translating into the language of Reason": Hegel will say that there is no other language, language as such necessarily turns out to be the language of reason. The other point can be answered by pointing to the ambiguous position of the Absolute Knower as encompassing these finite standpoints even in their finitude, and therefore by no means calling for their abolition, or for all nature and animal consciousness to become *immediately* absolute knowing—they are *mediately* absolute knowing already, due to their presence as moments in absolute knowing. Both of these counterassertions can be granted if we wish to give Hegel the broadest possible benefit of the doubt. It is clear at least that he has by no means short-shrifted sense-certainty or perception, or anything else he takes up in the body of the text, much less whatever is treated in the *Logic* and thereafter; they are given as thorough and illuminating an exegesis as one could hope to encounter. And yet we end up with an omnicentrism of reason that is pragmatically quite unicentric, with very far-reaching unicentric consequences.

I believe the reason for this can be found before we get into the main body of the text of the *Phenomenology*, in the preface, where we find what is really being excluded and short-shrifted by Hegel's approach. It is not immediate experience, or the particular, or nontotalizable dissemination of some kind that is really left out. It is rather Hegel's constant contempt for "edification," "dreaminess," "laziness," "monotony," and so on that signal what is really being excluded here. For it is these alternate *discursive methods* that Hegel evidently considers completely unable to reveal themselves to be really reason, or rather, which can only do so one-sidedly. Reason can reveal itself in them, can reveal that they were always actually nothing but it, but they cannot reveal reason to be a form of themselves, even after this magical power of reason, and its complete identity to them, has been revealed. That is: these things, like anything else, are only actual to the extent that they turn out to be Reason—expressions of Reason in its self-emptying, or in its own self-blockage or breakdown qua *Verstand*. But "being precisely Reason" in this case does not mean that "it has all the characteristics possessed by the coherence 'Reason'" per se—that is, the characteristic of being that which is expressed in everything by means of its own constitutive impossibility, or that which everything is to the extent that anything is actual. Hegel does attempt to assert this of the standpoints taken up in the main body of the text, in the sense outlined above. But he will not do that for the alternate methods of exegesis—laziness, edification, unseriousness, and so on (for if all are in their actuality nothing but Reason, all are certainly *methods of exegesis*!), which simply cannot be used, even after the advent of Reason, to reveal themselves *as* all other coherences. The complete reversibility of the final position is as it were blocked from the beginning by this work-ethic; in spite of all his precautions, we end up with the impression that, while Reason reveals itself in the very form of its absence in, say, the Unhappy Consciousness, the contrary is not fully true; the Unhappy Consciousness does not reveal itself via its absence in Reason; its all-encompassing-ness is not restored by the final triumph of Reason in Reason's own breakdown. Writing from the final standpoint, Hegel still sees nothing of value in "edification," in "monotonous formalism," in "finding only dreams," in "intuition," in "immediacy," in "laziness."

It may be argued in Hegel's defense that he simply finds no value in these things for undertaking the project at hand, which requires a different approach, or that he is simply opposing a dangerous countertrend of the historical moment in which he wrote. But this is not only belied by his tone here; it cannot stand up to fully omnicentric scrutiny. Hegel's omnicentrism is perfect in every detail of its exposition, with the exception of this inability to recognize itself methodologically in its opposite, in lazy unserious intuitive immediate dreamy monotonous edification. We may perhaps be forgiven for saying that Hegel's dialectic is perfect *in itself*, or in principle, in all its theoretical pronouncements, but not *for itself*, not in its own self-aware execution. Hegel should be able to start again at the beginning and see laziness as what every other form of consciousness is revealing, or better, since "seeing" something "revealed" is arguably precisely the activity of Reason, *live* laziness as the meaning of all other possible coherences. But this sort of possibility is excluded in the first few minutes of the game and never restored. Even Krug's pen is beneath Hegel's notice; so it is no wonder that laziness and irresponsible thinking do not stand a chance.

An almost perfect counterpoint to Hegel here is Zen, construed very broadly, since the Chan/Zen tradition encompasses historically a vast array of approaches and positions. Zen excels in its ability to make omnicentric quilting-points of exactly all those things excluded by Hegel; laziness (no seeking, no practice, various flavors of *Gelassenheit*), edification (half-baked sermons on the pure mind or self, Pure Land recitations), unseriousness and dreaminess of every description. In fact, if we wish to read a doctrinal position into Zen practice, we *can* find here a perfect omnicentrism too, except for its mirror-image defect: its inability to recognize itself in reason, in seriousness, coherence, rigorous thought, conceptualization, theorizing, Hegelizing. The Zen tradition has been magnificently inventive in coming up with devices and approaches to drive home constitutive impossibility as the sole reality of existence,[66] with one glaring exception: extended doctrinal dogmatics. It has not been so pure and naïve an intuitionism as is sometimes suggested by its modern advocates, and has made creative use of language, semantic tangles, doctrinal traces, in its methods. But the particular alienated form of existence known as thinking, piling up concepts and so on, somehow tends to be excluded from what in principle should include all possible entrances. The sound of a pebble striking bamboo, a shout, a blow, a pure ambiguity, a paradox, all these are considered ways to experience the ungraspability of one's functioning identity; but not theorizing, thinking, coming up with theories about what is, arguing, reasoning. The problem then—which would not be a problem at all but rather its own solution if openly acknowledged and as it were dwelt in—is that there remains some doctrinal understanding surreptitiously guiding all the rejection of doctrine—even if it is merely this rejection of doctrine, as it rarely is, this is still a particular position—which then stands stagnant and unchallengeable; no one is allowed to contest it, for it is supposed to be beyond all discussion since it supposedly has no particular conceptual content at all. This is the authoritarian danger into which Zennists almost inevitably succumb, with a few exceptions.

Hegel and Zen both end up as authoritarian unicentrists, in spite of their best efforts, precisely because their omnicentrics fall short of recognizing themselves as, in effect, each other. If Zen could see Hegel as itself, or Hegel could see Zen as itself—to be outrageously sectarian about it—both would already be Tiantai without having to add anything more. However much each may be willing to recognize some coherences as "cunning" versions of others, both fail to recognize the other as a "cunning" deadpan version of itself.

---

[66] I speak here mainly of mature, that is, *Song* dynasty Chan, and a few figures before and after, and of the minority whose work centers on constitutive impossibility as all-pervasion, as opposed to on pure intuition, on pure experience, on the Mind, on pure negation, on constant flux and moving-on, on action, or on simple impossibility, or on simple all-pervasion, or on a simple juxtaposition and copresence of impossibility and all-pervasion; but this requires a more detailed historical analysis, which I will perhaps attempt separately at some point in the future.

The Revolutionary Impulse and Revolutionary Charisma, with Gotama, Jesus, Nichiren, Lennon, Dylan, et al.

As we have seen, to be is to desire, and to desire is by definition to desire change (even if only to change the fact that "things are changing"). This means, at the very least, that in some sense we want to change "the world"—for there is nothing else to change. We usually distinguish two forms of this desire to change the world: the "reformist" and the "revolutionary." The former wants to change some undesirable details of the world as it is, but to leave the overall infrastructure, the rules of the game, intact. The latter, the revolutionary, feels this is hopeless; something more radical is required. Even the rules governing the field of particulars, which create the space in which particular things can be judged to be either relatively desirable or undesirable, is hopelessly skewed in such a way as to make meaningful reform impossible; the game is doomed from the start, given this set of rules. Taking this distinction to heart, we may here make the claim that Neo-Tiantai ethics are the only truly revolutionary ethics. For if the distinguishing marks of the revolutionary as opposed to the reformist are as we have described them, the revolutionary is still not fully revolutionary to the extent that she still wants to change only *part of the world*. If the revolutionary has any *specific* goals at all, she has accepted at least one particular detail from the old world order: the standard of desirability, for example. Otherwise she has no way of justifying her call for revolution. The ordinary revolutionary thus remains merely a more histrionic reformist. If the impulse to revolution is taken seriously, we have something more like Levinas's description of the *metaphysical* impulse: the desire for the *wholly other*. It is the desire for *everything without exception*, including the facts, including oneself, including the rules, including the parameters making the field of experience possible, to be *otherwise*.

But this is exactly the Neo-Tiantai view of every moment of experience. Delusion is any desire which wants only a part to be different, rather than seeing that all things are already *wholly other* to themselves. As long as desire has (1) any specific goal in mind, and (2) any conviction that it, this desire, actually does oneself, or anyone else, or indeed any "one" at all, any "good," it is delusion—for the latter is just another form of the paradoxical desire to preserve one part of the whole while altering other parts, namely some standard of goodness and some one to be there to enjoy it. It should be obvious that, in the Neo-Tiantai perspective, this desire for the wholly other is precisely the same thing as *accepting everything exactly as it is*. For the being thus of all things is precisely their being otherwise, as we have seen. This is what is meant in these pages by "pure desire" which indeed is the desire for everything to be otherwise, the desire which has no specific particular object, the desire for life qua death, the desire that is time itself, the desire for everything to be just as it is, the desire that is in that sense no desire but just the experiencing of Local Coherence as Global Incoherence as Intersubsumption.

Given this groundwork, we may now ask a more specific, socio-historical question. What makes certain persons capable of rewriting the rules governing the field in which they operate, reversing the relation between themselves and the norms of the world they live in so that they become effectively infallible? For if we wish to grasp the "rhyme schemes" that operate in culture and history, as Alan Cole puts it, to understand the way values and world views change, the way groups alter and merge and subdivide and define themselves around their particular symbolic desiderata, we have to understand above all these shifts in desiderata, where they derive their power from. As Nietzsche said, the world revolves silently around the creators of new values. We would emphasize that it revolves primarily around the creators of values, and only secondarily around the values they create. What is this strange "charisma" that accrues to these lawless lawgivers who somehow place themselves in a position where they can, by definition as it were, "do no wrong" no matter how much wrong they do? I have in mind here a type which is perhaps most easily recognizable in the history of religions and popular culture, although I have no doubt that the same dynamic is in play in the more explicitly "political" objects of fascination as well. We can at least note certain similarities between figures like, say, Gotama Buddha, Jesus, Nichiren, and the like, on the one hand, and, to bring this home most directly for lowbrows like myself, popular culture icons of a particular type, for example, pop singers like, say, Bob Dylan and John Lennon. All of them commit outrageous and unjustifiable crimes against fidelity and good taste, indeed against all identifiable existing norms.

Gotama leaves his wife and child, and abandons his father's patrimony, not after fulfilling his Dharmic duties as an old man, but stealthily in the middle of the night. In the Mahāyāna version, in which his charisma is greatly amplified, he then goes on to repudiate all he had previously taught, and even, in the *Lotus*, baldly admits that it was all a pack of lies, and yet that he cannot for that reason be accused of lying.

Jesus breaks the Sabbath, remains a bachelor, cavorts with tax-collectors and prostitutes, disrupts the temple, values himself above the poor, curses the fig tree, makes wildly unjust and self-serving condemnations of his rivals, the Pharisees, and in a final burst of megolamania, damns to eternal torment anyone who so much as questions him, even having the mawkish nerve to define his "friends" as those who "do whatever I command." Nichiren twists the sutras, willfully reverses the Tiantai doctrine, spits poisonous promises of dire consequences for any who doubt him, indulges in wild vainglorious fantasies, curses all other schools, breaks the gentleman's agreement of tolerance that marked Buddhism thitherto, proclaims a panacea with no basis in scripture (the Daimoku) as the whole of Buddhism and attributes to it whatever powers, however contradictory, happen to serve his evangelical purposes.

Dylan fakes his way into Greenwich Village with some bogus hillbilly/carny yarns, masters leftist folkie political outrage, attains success and promptly stabs everyone in the back, laughs off his previous political commitments as mere wordplay, proclaims his identification with Lee Harvey Oswald a week after Kennedy is shot, cynically sells the world surreal word games as poetry, screws everyone, writes angry songs complaining of his mistreatment at the hands of the people he had betrayed, then puts out a country music album to emphasize his new redneck identity, then a deliberately unlistenable couple of works, then becomes a Christian, and so on.

Lennon pisses on nuns, wears a toilet seat around his neck on stage, fatally kicks his best friend in the head, insults everyone, unprofessionally spaces out for several years, then complains that Paul took over the band, then turns up nude on an album cover, leaves his wife (having a flunkey notify her rather than doing it himself) and child and breaks up the band with his new woman, then writes a vitriolic song ("How Do You Sleep") attacking his former partner well beyond what would be called for by either justice or good taste, then leaves the new woman to drink in LA for two years, then becomes a henpecked househusband producing nothing, and so on.

All these people are heroes who *define values*, even *moral* exemplars, who have come to stand, within some subculture, as ungainsayable icons. I myself admire all of them. I would add also a text to this list: the *Lotus Sūtra*. Here, too, we have narcissistic self-advertisement, repeated self-contradiction from chapter to chapter, condemnations of unbelievers, compounded by a notorious absence of any actual doctrinal content, and so on. What is it that distinguishes all of these value-creating icons from mere lunatic sociopaths, on the one hand, or obedient men of virtue, or ideologues, on the other?

The first thing to note about all of them is that their actions are, *by definition*, inexplicable. That is, they each *repeatedly* commit transgressions that admit of no justification by appeal to the context of existing norms. They may scrap together ad hoc explanations from bits and pieces of older standards which are still floating around, and with absolute confidence and persuasiveness, but at the same time the fragmentary nature of these justifications, and the alloys into which these fragments are haphazardly combined, try to suggest secret larger wholes which are putatively profound and consistent; however, what is actually disclosed in these cases is without exception *trans-*

parently inconsistent, vague, incomplete and perfunctory. It is important also that they *repeatedly* transgress, and transgress even the norms that one might have supposed to be implicitly appealed to by their initial transgression; for a single, consistent transgression would make them mere ideologues, proclaiming some *identifiable* new set of values, which is just what they are not doing. Second, they transgress with absolute confidence, even astonishing arrogance and uncompromising narcissism. Third, they are willing to sacrifice everything for their transgression of the moment, even whatever they have gained from their previous transgressions. Fourth, they all offer something that is *strictly meaningless* as a bearer of absolute value.

My thesis is this: the importance of these four points in the creation of absolutely authoritative and literally unquestionable charisma is that they make explicit the principle of *self-recontextualization*. Let us take up these four points in turn.

1. *Inexplicability*. An inexplicable act makes no sense in terms of any existing context. But we are "condemned to meaning," to be is already to plead for sense-making and coherence. Hence these acts bring with them an aura of possible sense-making contexts; they require us to *guess* their meaning, to wonder whether they may not be suggesting the positing of some as yet unimaginable revolutionary frame of meaning when they fail to be explicable in terms of any recognizable contexts. The inexplicable act is *explicitly* self-recontextualizing.

2. *Absolute confidence*. Even if doubts occasionally creep in—they are documented for Jesus, Nichiren, and Lennon, at least—they are never in the form of, "Is this the right thing to do in terms of the norms that are universally recognized?" Rather, they bear a certain self-justificatory, self-dramatizing hysteria, which pushes not toward more familiar values, but toward *even more* ungraspable values, which might be compromised by a particular act that is perhaps too readily recognizable and explicable. Sabbatai Zevi presents an interesting exception here, which shows the flexibility of this category. Zevi was absolutely confident of his transgressions while committing them, in the frenzy of his manic phase, but immediately felt the brunt of the accepted norms the morning after, and accused himself of being a horrible sinner. What is important here is absolute confidence in *whatever phase he is in at the moment*, which can ruthlessly repudiate all former moves as absolute folly.[67] Lennon, Dylan, and the Mahāyāna Buddha are masters of this attitude, and of the ability to make the current project, however inconsistent with everything else they may have stood for in the past, unflinchingly

---

[67] See Gershom Scholem, *Major Trends in Jewish Mysticism* (New York: Schocken Books, 1961), 287–324.

convincing. (Sartre was pretty good at it too, and even notices it in himself in *The Words*). What I am doing right now is, *by definition*, right, even if it means everything else I or anyone else has done is wrong. This coherence, in other words, is not to be justified by reference to any other, to any context. But here again we have the principle of inexplicability, which immediately discloses self-recontextualization. This moment *must* be coherent; this "must" here is translated from an implicit structural necessity to an explicit ethical imperative. If its coherence is not dependent on its cohering in any meaningful way with any previous actions or commitments, then it must be implying some others, vaguely lurking just over the horizon. If enough radical shifts are made, so as to clean out any suspicion of some recognizable specific content, what is left is the pure structure, the "I" itself, as we shall see in point 4 below.

3. *Sacrifice*. This is what most readily distinguishes the charismatic revolutionary from the mere street loony or opportunist backstabber. For to achieve true inexplicability and the limit of incoherence that makes apparent the necessity of coherence, they must also show *practical* indifference to the most basic frameworks of contextual values, such as life, wealth, reputation, pleasure. The quanta of value pertaining to these recognized standards are as it were converted into the new currency of the mysterious new value they are sacrificed for, stand as guarantor for its reality. The value of whatever is sacrificed for the sake of X is immediately transferred, onlookers suspect, to X. It *must be* better than these things, not only different, or he would not have been willing to sacrifice them for it with such confidence. It is this indeterminate "must be" that fills in the missing content of the vague new value. The mere act of sacrificing whatever is "other," negating its value, establishes the value of the "this," and the thoroughgoingness of this sacrifice—one must sacrifice even whatever else one has *hitherto* established, all other moments—denies the basic structure of contextualization, in other words, denies that the "this" can be what it is only by virtue of its reference to a context of "others." But by doing so, the deeper structure of all coherences is disclosed; they are not merely contextualized, not merely recontextualized, not merely constantly recontextualized, but constantly, constitutively, necessarily *self-recontextualized*. The meaninglessness endemic to this relation is here placed front and center. "This," just by virtue of being the current "self" under discussion, is by definition the determiner of its determinants. Anything that this might have been done for the sake of is sacrificed in advance. It becomes autotelic, which, as a relation of means-ends contextualizations, immediately points to self-recontextualization.

4. *Meaninglessness*. This is closely related to inexplicability, taking it one step further, as it were. The two must be distinguished, however. Inexplica-

bility means that an identifiable deed or tenet is put forward, but no context can be found in which to justify it. Meaninglessness indicates that the item put forward in the place of ultimate value is itself devoid of any identifiable content; it plays contradictory roles, it is denied any specifiable determinations, and yet unsurpassable importance is attached to it. The relation between inexplicability and meaninglessness mirrors, if you will, that between contingent and necessary dilemma; meaninglessness is the state that results when the demand for contextualization has reached the point of pervading all possible experiences, and thereby crashes. We may think here of Nirvana, the Kingdom of Heaven, the Daimoku, or the talents and stylistic contributions of the artists on our list, but it is not hard to see why it always quickly devolves into an obsessive personality cult centered around the proclaimer, the person, himself. The contentful message is very quickly eclipsed by the proclaimer of the message as the truly sublime object of fascination. This is because the structure of this meaninglessness is precisely the structure of subjectivity per se. This indispensible, all-conditioning centering item which is nonetheless unspecifiable and ultimately meaningless is a precise disclosure of the structure of subjectivity, the "pure desire," "freedom," "self-being," "necessary impossibility," "Intersubsumption," and so on we have spoken of here. In a word, we have self-recontextualization laid bare here. When this structure is made vividly explicit in the meaninglessness of the message proclaimed, which is allowed to play any and every contradictory role, we have the fascinating charismatic figure.

These four points are meant to explicate only the reasons why such figures exert such a powerful effect on their beholders, not what actually makes them behave the way they do. The efficient causes and motivations of their behavior may be quite prosaic indeed—ambition, greed, confusion, shame, exhibitionism, narcissism, jealousy, superstition—and often it takes only a few glances from a historical eye to discern strings of meaning that tie together the apparently inexplicable, inexplicably over-confident, self-sacrificial and meaningless deeds of such figures in a disappointingly coherent way. We may think here of Schweitzer's account of the historical Jesus, for example, which pulls all the piece together around the idea of an "interim ethic" quite convincingly and tidily; or any textual analysis of the *Lotus*, which quickly discerns adequate justification for its absurd overstatements in the irresponsible enthusiasms of a particular sectarian polemic. Such an explanation, of course, has great power to undermine the charisma in question, for the crucial conditions for authoritative charisma, as we have specified them here, are thereby removed. Indeed, one style of criticism offers such explanations precisely in order to knock the wind out of such overbearing claims of sublimity. This goal may well be praiseworthy, but, from our present perspective, such a method of defusion really cannot be considered thorough; for it merely displaces the fascination from this particular object to some other, some other limit of inexplicability. The structure has remained in place.

Indeed, I offer these considerations not so much as an idle example of the explanatory power of the model we have been developing, much less as a manual for would-be charismatic icons; there is an old-fashioned moral burden to all this. For it is certainly arguable, upon dispassionate consideration, that the harm done by these figures—according to the standards of most local contexts that probably spring most quickly to our minds—at least matches whatever advantages they may bring about. We can leave this matter undecided for the moment, since it is strictly undecidable, or even meaningless; still, many may feel, understandably, that the harmfulness of ungainsayable charisma becomes all the more difficult to deny if we add the obvious examples of charismatic personal authority from the *political* realm to our list—the obvious totalitarian dictators, for example. So for the sake of argument we may well agree that there is much to be gained from a thorough defusion of their fascination. But we suggest another method for doing so.

As we have seen, what fascinates here is precisely the explicit disclosure of the structure of self-recontextualization itself. But we have argued that this is the structure of all coherences without exception. The cup on that table exists as pure self-recontextualization to exactly the same degree as any of our great heroes do. They do so in a way, however, which forces attention to this structure on the participants in some local context, for whom the same structure in "ordinary" objects and experiences has come to be ignored or suppressed. This, indeed, is the "upāyic" *positive* value of this kind of hero worship and fascinating charisma; it does reveal self-recontextualization, and perhaps inspires it in others as well. But the obsessive side effects of this disclosure could perhaps be denuded somewhat if the same structure could *thereby* be revealed also in all coherences without exception. We may find some figure astonishing and nonnegotiably authoritative, and our world of putatively *simpliciter* coherences will thereby be exploded and greatly enriched. But this is potentially disastrous until the same can be said for every other object as well. The harmful side effects of fascination can be thoroughly undercut not by reduction of the charisma to its prosaic synordinate meaning, thereby reducing the presumptuous ranter to another *simpliciter* being, but rather by allowing the same ineluctable self-recontextualization to reveal itself as the rest of the world, opening our eyes, as it were, to the holy insane authoritatively arrogant ranter which is presenting itself at all times, masked as every apparently *simpliciter* Local Coherence—the cup on this table, for instance. When we can come to see its long career to be just as amazing as that of these heroes of history, we will have overcome the dichotomy between *simpliciter* and self-recontextualizing coherences which is the crucial condition undergirding the idolatry and fanatacism in question here. For it is these that truly generate *specific* new values—but as a side effect as if were. Shocking as it may seem, the particular content of these new values is in each case, it would seem, largely arbitrary; if there is any pattern to it, it would seem to reside in whatever loose ends and suppressed shadows already peeking through the threadbare fabric of the formerly recognizable standards of values that could be plucked up by the charismatic revolutionary in his random grasp for justifications, and mistakenly woven by his faithful ideologues into what it must have been he was really secretly going on about, undergirding his inexplicable and self-sacrificial confidence. Cultures are fads—nerdy elaborations of what the cool kids inexplicably did. (Sabbatai Zevi and his sidekick theologian Nathan of Gaza provide perhaps the purest example of this.)

The power to change the field lies in the empty form of pure self-recontextualization provided by the charismatic figure; the content, the specifics about how it is to be changed, is haphazardly filled in later, and indeed, for such a figure to have a *lasting* impact, it must be filled in again and again, as each generation of ideologues is sure that the previous generation got it wrong. This is made possible only by the meaninglessness of the initial message, which provides a blank sheet of paper with a few random words scribbled in at irregular intervals, which may be completed in an infinity of alternate ways. This is really a recapitulation of the old Taoist concept of power, as the empty vagueness that demands filling in. In the Neo-Tiantai universe, however, the dichotomy of the ordinary quotidian fact and the miraculous self-recontextualizing changer of the world is overcome: every moment of experience is inescapably a revolution, setting up a new standard of value with which all the rest of sentient history must forever contend.

Boredom or Truth: A "Critique" of Critique

The above considerations have rewritten all the standard building blocks of common sense, and indeed also of philosophical, religious, and moral sense. It should then be no suprise that they will also have to rewrite the assumptions undermining our most intuitive modes of hermeneutic and critical activity, as has been hinted and touched upon many times already. This will follow from the general epistemological position we have been developing here. This particular application, however, I consider especially timely. For the time has become ripe for an overcoming of the hegemony of the notion of "critique." This has finally come to the notice of the most astute even of the hypercritical French thinkers of recent years (the Lyotard of *Libidinal Economy*[68] (in spite of later recantations) and Latour in *We Have Never Been Modern*[69]), but the instinct to critique—to critique something or other, anything at all rather than nothing—remains the dominant impetus guiding the work of almost all professional intellectuals, perhaps all over the world. It is therefore worth our while, in closing, to say a few words on how the earlier reflections might bear on this topic.

Obviously (as the above named Frenchmen have pointed out, and dealt with in characteristically artful ways) it would be silly to present a critique of critique per se. On our current premises, of course, it is not as impossible as it might seem otherwise. But we, too, will have to admit that in critiquing critique, even if we do engage in such a thing (which from a Tiantai point of view is exactly as legitimate as any other taking of a position, indeed has the virtue of being explicitly what all coherences are implicitly, i.e., a constitutive impossibility) we will also want to affirm the value and legitimacy of all critiques. We can perhaps do so with a simple pragmatic argument to the effect that the aims of critique are better served by precisely the contrary strategy. As an example, we might take one of the by now most familiar forms of critique of any and all propositions, the postmodern poster boy, deconstruction; this will be especially illuminating since we obviously share so many premises with the deconstructive notion of textuality and its consequences. But we can distinguish the Tiantai view from the Derridean in the following terms: although in both cases the constitutive always-truth and always-falseness of any proposition (and even coherence per se) is grasped as a single gesture, as a matter of procedure, when confronted with some claim, some experience, some text, the Tiantai approach will be to elicit its rightness, indeed its hyper-rightness as all-pervasive (and also therefore self-emptying) quilting point. In practice, the Derridean procedure still smells of critique, and one that is, as has often been pointed out, implicitly contrasted to some ultimately substantialist standard of what something would have to be like, *per impossibile*, to be true. Pragmatically, if we may invoke an old trope, in deconstruction, all is wrong and false, while in Tiantai, all is right and true. Tiantai reads all texts, even bubble gum wrappers, as if written by an omniscient genius, rather than by a confused and self-contradicting sneak or panicking presence-invoking ideologue. Indeed, for us these are one and the same thing.

---

[68] Jean-François Lyotard, *Libidinal Economy*, trans. Iain Hamilton Grant (Bloomington: Indiana University Press, 1993).

[69] Bruno Latour, *We Have Never Been Modern*, trans. Catherine Porter (Cambridge: Harvard University Press, 1993).

Why then do we, in pragmatic matters, prefer the former as a hermeneutic approach? Quite simply, for the sake of what might be called epistemological plenitude, which more readily serves to illuminate the intersubsumptive nature of all constitutively impossible dilemmas than the contrary approach (although needless to say, this need not always be the case, so this procedure is not to be unilaterally preferred—we speak only for the present state of the game). Otherwise, we get a monolithic (unspoken) know-it-all lurking at the place of enunciation, who never comes forth but who is implicitly always right and never wrong. The unseen "negater" is always right, the very act of pointing out the problem is itself unproblematic, and, as in old-time Schlegelian irony, everything positive or determinate is always wrong. What we want here, on the contrary, is constitutive rather than contingent problematicalness, and that means for both sides to always be right (all-pervasive asness, interpretable into "truth" or "rightness" *however these may happen to be conceived at a given time*) and also always be wrong (incapable of simply appearing as such), and by the same token, indeed, *as* one another. We read all texts as teaching the truth of identity qua constitutive impossibility qua deadpan all-pervasive asness, but also as any other truth that, by this very token, we might be experiencing that truth *as* at the moment. But pragmatically, this is accomplished by reading everyone as right, rather than by reading everyone as wrong. The only way to deconstruct the hegemony of one view is to produce an overwhelming plurality of equally (not *more*) valid views, not by "criticism." Criticism is just perpetuation. The active role of the interpreter is thus drawn out into a form of learning to find the constitutive contradiction, hence the reversible Intersubsumption, of whatever coherence is currently acting as a block, whatever is getting stuck at the moment. This means training in seeing Intersubsumption itself qua necessary failure. This *skill* more easily applies to itself than the purely negative one (although attempts have been made to work it that way, notably not only in premodern Schlegelian irony and postmodern deconstruction but in many forms of Buddhism as well, for instance, in many anti-predicative interpretations of "the emptiness of emptiness," etc.), that could also conceivably be seen to apply to itself. But even when it succeeds in doing so, this negation of even "the act of negating" fails definitively to leave the circle of one-sided negation, which for us means one-sided positiveness—inviolable rightness—as well. Unless this negation of the negation ends up meaning precisely the proliferation of fully valid new meanings and positions (and this is precisely where Tiantai differs from traditional Mādhyamika), we end up with a nonpervading split, where the act of negating ultimately falls outside its own grasp, cannot succeed in negating itself.

Again we may think of Zen in this connection: Caoshan, asked why, since he is "killing" all he encounters, he does not kill this "killer" also, says, "I can find no place to get a hold of it." Read: Much as I try, I cannot locate this negater itself to be negated in the way all other things *can* be located. This is, as I indicated above, very nearly indistinguishable from the Tiantai position. The difference becomes manifest, however, when we look to see whether new meanings are established, or whether the same operation of negation continues to be universally and "monotonously" (as Hegel, the antipodes here, puts it) applied. If "it cannot be negated" means, "so it continues its work of negation *only*," we have fallen into an Exclusive Center. The Tiantai position is rather, "Whenever I posit anything, this negater is posited as well, and the more I posit the more the negater exists, the more I negate the more the posits are produced." The point is that all coherences, including the negater, are negatable and positable to exactly the same extent, and indeed that the positing and the negating are one and the same deed, that its negation is its positing and vice versa. This is the true "negation of the negation."

Onany, Interpretation, and Love: Truth and the Libidinal Community

This is one form of "critique" to which we have grown accustomed these days. Another is carried out under the auspices of what might be called a certain holistic insight, and thus is also of special interest to us, since omnicentrism too is a form of holism, albeit one which is pushed to the point of a crucial self-overcoming. This is what might be called the "historicist" critique, which, in seeing the necessity for the contextualization of all coherences and further the overlooking of a great number of potentially relevant contexts in the usual treatment of ideas and meanings, attempts to undermine the meaningfulness of posited coherences, in particular world views, by reducing them to ideological smoke screens that are moreover merely reflections of a set of conditions prevailing in the relevant society at the time of production. The question upon which this hinges, in our terms, is as follows: given the seriousness with which we are willing to take the premises of holism, and the expanded sense of "relevance" that goes with it, to the point of asserting that freedom is precisely the fact that everything without exception is relevant to any given thing, does this mean we have to know everything in order to say anything? Are we honor bound to take everything into account before we can "know what something is?" I mean this question to apply at all points in the spectrum of possibilities: to "understand" a thinker, how much do I have to know about his society, his dietary habits, his job, his family background, what time he woke up that day and so on? And to understand myself, how much do I have to know about the economic system of my nation, the political situation, the social conditions prevailing around me and so on?

Where may I legitimately draw these lines? Shall I feel that I am in bad faith somehow if I have no interest in learning about the administrative decisions made by an institution of which I am a nominal member, or if I do not pay attention at budgetary meetings? If I have to know everything to know anything, it is obvious that I will be unable to know anything; and yet here I *seemingly* know a lot of things. On the grounds of traditional truth/opinion contrasts, I have to say that some of these things I really only think I know, and that I have to find out more other stuff, and more about the thing in question, to find out what is really the case about this thing. But when I will really know that I have found out enough other things, and that I have allocated my limited resources of time and attention to the right contexts, are not at all clear, and indeed, as already indicated, very probably impossible to know at all. It seems to me that one of the greatests harvests to be had from the eschewing of the truth/opinion contrast (and its ontological and axiological doubles, the reality/appearance and good/bad contrasts) afforded by Neo-Tiantai omnicentrism is that it allows us to find here a standard of relevance which is both immanent to the material and infallible: in a word, for us *boredom* and *irrelevance* are for any local coherence strictly equivalent terms, indeed are synonymous. Whatever is boring is irrelevant.

We are able to make this claim, first, because of the role that *interest* (desire) plays in our epistemology, that is, in setting the limits of contextualization that afford the appearance of any local coherence, and second, because of our demonstration of the Intersubsumption of all these limited-perspective-dependent coherences. We start in every case with a coherence emerging on the basis of some arbitrary omission of relevant contextual elements—in other words, some always-already operating prejudice, some self-interest, with the "self" here understood in the sense we have delineated above, as an explicitly intersubsumptive and reversible confederacy of coherences. None of these coherences is self-enclosed, or can rest without such interest outward; a coherence is always an embodied demand for more, for more confirmation, more support, more fields of operation; in this sense we can say, with Nietzsche, that to be a coherence is to be Will-to-Power. It persists only through expansion of its contexts, either intensively or extensively, and for us, given the infinite divisibility of each coherence, these two alternatives cannot be strictly distinguished. Which other coherences it will expand toward, or transform into, or resolve into, will be a function of its initial structure, which coherence it is, and where it sees (mistakenly in every case) its self-confirmation to most likely lie. This is the "interest" that inheres in it.

In all cases, even a coherence that is as broad and vague as an overall sense of what the world is like or how it works, we have a certain amount of other relevancies taken into account and a certain amount excluded, a necessary "non-all." However much the expansion or intensive deepening proceeds, as long as this local coherence proceeds, this will continue to be the case. Hence we have no question of realities versus appearances here, or of right or wrong coherences. Each coherence is self-justified to precisely the extent to which it appears as such, as a particular clearly discernible reading of the data, and all do so, for this "apparently-justified" is just what they are. The selective interest a particular appearance of a coherence will bring with it toward other coherences will thus be an immanent part of this project of self-preservation, which as we have seen is really the movement toward its necessary breakdown (self-destruction being on the contrary the avoidance of its necessary breakdown in favor of a contingent one). It need not make a special effort of compensation, to include the neglected portions of all that has been excluded, going against its inclination and interest, so as to ensure its reliability. It is always already involved in the (necessarily doomed) project of seeking its self-confirmation, and however dead-ended it may appear to be, however caught in a repetitive habitual holding pattern, it can never genuinely succeed in limiting its contexts to any finite set—although the attempt to preserve selfhood from its inherent crash is precisely the attempt to do so.

Needless to say, the othernesses that it may feel compelled to regard from its own interest may include specifically, for example, "objectivity per se," or "precisely what I tend to ignore," or "what is of no interest to me, what is boring, and hence more likely to be representative of undistorted truth," as is the case for many professional intellectuals, and this is an admirable way to hasten the breakdown. However, I need hardly point out that this itself constitutes another, more sophisticated form of interest, one that is qualitatively no different from the less self-abnegating forms of interest, or self-interest. The structure here is in essence no different. When the particular form of consciousness that looks systematically outside what it has recognized as subjectively determined (a "scientific" or "scholarly" consciousness) comes to function, it has conceived a new interest, a new type of demand-for-more—for more confirmation and so on—in all cases founded on the initial coherence and its prejudices, which here serve as a kind of exponential springboard to new negations of itself, which for us are simply more and more radical contexts that will transform it, expand its field of meaning, and thereby empty it of its initial meaning. We need not fear that any form of obsession, any starting point no matter how narrow and naïve, will fail to push toward greater and greater Intersubsumption with other coherences. This does not mean all these projects will converge toward a common point, either a unified field of universally accepted knowledge or the pure negativity that results from the breakdown of all of them. This would be a misunderstanding of what is entailed in the crash of a coherence's system.

What we have instead is a plethora of alternate determinings of the entire field of possible other coherences, each of which maintains its difference from the other while at the same time intersubsuming with the others from its own perspective. There is not one world, nor are there many worlds; there are many "one worlds," each being the "sole one" and thus taking account of the whole field of possible coherences. Each one is the all/non-all under the auspices of its particular arbitrary starting point or history of starting points. The foot-fetishist ends up with a universe of foot-fetish relevant knowledge, the whole economy and history of the world, all physics and chemistry, to the extent that they are of interest to his foot fetish, and this changes the meaning of that foot fetish—he can now find foot-fetishistic enjoyment not only in literal feet, but in all the other coherences which turn also to be instantiations of "footness"—while the car aficionado sees the same physics, chemistry, and so on, as car instantiations.[70] These two fields are radically the same and radically different at the same time, as we explained in the initial exposition of omnicentrism in Part One. All that is required is that each intensify his own obsession, that he keep going, that he push it as far as it will go. And that is inevitable, unless he backs out because he regards something as impenetrable to his interpretation, thereby taking the central coherence's failure as contingent rather than necessary. Only if he stops short, telling himself he has crashed into a wall that cannot be read as footness or carness, will the self-emptying and full interpenetration of footness or carness fail to occur. That in itself, directly along the lines of his own most prejudiced and biased interest, accomplishes the Intersubsumption which is identical with the revelation of his starting interest's necessary impossibility, with its crash.

What is called for here, quite obviously, is the thoroughgoing libidinization of hermeneutics. In a nutshell, we follow classical Tiantai, although we may state the case in the idiom of our own age as follows: all interpretation is either a case of onany or a case of love; the final Tiantai position on this will be that these are not two options, but are always already coextensive, or, more strictly, that love is just hyper-onany, and onany is just hyper-love. The classical terms for them, are "habituated desire" (passion, delusion, self-nature-positing, suffering-inducing, etc.) and "compassion" (solidarity). We have already noted that these two are what act as the determinants of any coherence, that is, these are what determine what all coherences will appear "as" in any given situation. Recall also that compassion is always a response to some pre-existing deluded desire, and that the same desired coherence is simply repeated, enframed in the formal gesture of

---

[70] In classical terms, as Zhili puts it, "Whatever brings you joy is what is appropriate to you, and whatever you thereby practice on is what will enlighten you."

universalization, in the compassionate response, which is nothing more than the constitutive self-recontextualization of the initial coherence of delusion. But this is precisely what is at stake in all interpretation.

For heuristic purposes, let us take up the highly simplified example brushed on above. Consider a foot-fetishist, but one whose only genuine interest lay in onanistic gratification based on foot-fetishistic significations. The scholar confronting a text to be interpreted is in just the situation of the foot-fetishist faced with a new piece of pornography. Some material may be easier for him to work with than others; a copy of *Foot Lust* will be easier than *Hot Hats* or *Big Lips* and much easier than *The New Republic*, but if this is indeed his only interest, he will have to find the foot-fetishistic meanings, by whatever metaphorical skills are at his disposal, that will make the texts into pornography which will "work" for him. There is a clear and unmistakable internal criterion for whether a particular interpretation is "successful." He must thread centers together, develop chains of asness, back to his central concern—see hats as a distorted expression, by ironic negative allusion, to shoes, see breasts as obliquely pointing to the stresses or lack of stress their weight would put on the unseen hamstrings, see the floor in the background as walked upon, see the furniture in the background precisely as not-walked-upon, or as sat upon so as to lift the feet off the floor—any aspect of any photograph can be given a foot-connected relevance. But this can go for abstract things as well; perhaps he will have to interpret the political essayist's references to bottom-lines, to gravity, to lowliness and humble conditions of the oppressed, as foot-relevant; obstacles are things to be walked over; desiderata are things to be walked toward; complications make the feet stop in their tracks. I trust this demonstration need not be extended. Why is this ridiculous extension of metaphor, this tenuous string of casuistry, this forced asness necessary? Because only what interests comes to consciousness. Because only what is foot-related will sexually arouse our friend.

Shall we demand instead that he reconstruct for himself, as accurately as possible on the basis of all available evidence, what was going on at the photo shoot itself, or in the office of the editorialist? Shall he lie there picturing to himself the contract signed, the money changing hands, the woman's pained decision, her attempt to look sexy, the thoughts of the photographer, the rent paid on the studio? Indeed, I was once surprised by a friend who told me he imagined just this sort of thing in such situations. "That way it's almost like I'm having a real experience," he added. This was, of course, meant as an ironic comment on his recent lack of good fortune as far as "real experiences" went. One wonders whether interpreters who can see nothing in a text but the imagined scenario of its production—the intention of the author, her historical circumstances, the socio-economic conditions mediating her work—are not undergoing similar bad fortune with regard to "real experiences"—a nasty conclusion I would not hesitate to draw except for the fact that, as we have established, contrary to my friend's self-deprecating remark, these experiences are exactly as "real" as any others.

Nonetheless, this is not the whole story. For, as we have seen, there is no purely nonintersubjective realm, and even the onanist is also really a lover. Indeed, he is necessarily also imputing implied others to his fantasy, he is in interchange with some imagined counterpart, he is talking to someone when he comes. The academy is not only a huge porno palace made up of masturbating loners; it is also a great place for exhibitionists who want to be seen doing it, and voyeurs who want to see others do it, and the mutual desire to incite and participate in the pleasure of others thereby. Shared onany, or an onany that takes into account the fetishes and perversions of an other, is already love of a sort. The academy has its standards, and anyone joining in the fun takes these arbitrary perversions as his or her own, for just the same reason the foot-fetishist puts up with his lover the sadist and vice versa; I will now take my foot-pleasure in the form of (as) pain, for your sake, for the sake of your pleasure. Kick me. But, of course, this malleability of the "as" works only because of what has been established earlier; a skilled thinker is one who can rewrite his own obsessive fetishes "as" whatever is necessary—in other words, whatever accords with his lover's own obsessive fetishistic desires. To state the matter more plainly: we live at the moment with a set of standards—about verifiability, historicity, objective truth, evidence, or about power, oppression, economics, and so on—which bind the modes of expression which can be taken "seriously" in the academy—that is, which will please the pervert we are in love with. *These standards must be observed*; there is no more rigorous taskmaster imaginable. No room for whimsical *laisser-aller* is possible in the face of such forces. No one need fear the deterioration of discourse into lawless subjective fancies, any more than one might fear a breakdown of the norms that govern the foot-fetishist and the sadist when they are together. The enforcers are the love of one and the desire of the other, and vice versa, and no more powerful force exists in the universe. We make do with these rigorous and unbendable standards, and, if our own skill in asness-reversibility is in gear, play the game that way. As Kafka put it, "I take injury to my soul so that you may remain friendly to me." If the relationship is good, we may also make others read their own pleasure *as* versions of our own, out of reciprocated love. Desire and compassion—in the Tiantai universe, these are more than enough to guarantee that the consistency of each "one world" coexists *as* the other. In the academy, too, these hold everything in place.

It may seem that all this rigmarole only gets us to a result which does not really differ from the standard relativist or cultural constructivist story; are we not simply saying, in an infuriatingly roundabout way, that what is true is what a given society says is true, that there is no independent standard beyond what some community agrees on? And will the consequence not therefore also be that, for example, the Pythagorean theorem is not something true about the objective world, or something objectively true, but merely something agreed on in accordance with a certain set of social needs and the standards of inquiry engendered thereby? My answer to this is no, not at all. For it is here that we must recall the difference between the skeptical claim, "Nothing is really true; all we have is what people say is true," and the omnicentric claim, "Every possible proposition is true"—really true, really "out there," recalcitrantly real and not in the control of any "one" (or of the whim or conditioning of any one finite determinable "society"). These do seem to be simply flipsides of one another—in either case, what practically counts as true is determined solely by what someone says or does, whether this is seen as entailing the conjuring up of something where there is nothing or rather the narrowing down and exclusion of a lot of other truths, the choosing of one out of many—but there are crucial differences. This hinges on what I said about "the external world" earlier in this study. For us, the Pythagorean theorem is an "eternal truth." Would it exist if no human minds existed to think it? Yes, exactly as much as it does now. Could we say the same thing about the erotogeneity of feet in the absence of foot-fetishists to be excited by them? Yes, absolutely. What this means is that, unlike what we have in the skeptical or relativist picture, it is not possible that the Pythagorean theorem could simply play no role in the universe, that it could be completely ignored, that it would cease to function if we ceased to think of it; it will always haunt every being, it will be a coherence which wants to break into any enclosed circle that is designed to exclude or ignore it, it is what every other coherence wants to appear *as*, and *will* appear as if it develops itself enough. The Pythagorean theorem does not wait outside other coherences—say, "eating Popsicles" or "the explosion of a supernova"—passively, such that it can either be invited in or not; the more any other X becomes itself, the more it flirts with the revelation that it is the Pythagorean theorem, the closer it gets to seeing itself expressed as that as well.

Needless to say, all this goes for the erotogeneity of feet, or a whimsical passing notion that it would be cool to shave my head, or the proposition, "Dogs are made of cheese and live forever." All of these are eternal truths, they are not at our discretion to exclude from reality; but none of them can possibly exist *simpliciter*, all of them depend on some particular contexts and supports in order to become apparent *as* such. When they are not apparent, they are all always nonetheless functioning, but in the form of something else. When no one is thinking of it, the Pythagorean theorem exists just as much as it does when someone is thinking of it; in the latter case, it is everything else *as* the Pythagorean theorem; in the former, it is the Pythagorean theorem *as* whatever else is going on. In either case it can never cease to function. Whether we like it or not, it will be functioning, and indeed it will have to appear even if something else is what it is appearing as, if that something else persists long enough. Its greater persistence in the role of that *as* which other things appear than, say, my consideration of shaving my head, is due to the onanistic and erotic patterns that persist in particular societies of mutually enjoying perverts; that much we grant to the skeptics and relativists. But its eternal existence, its independence of all human agents, its obligatory status as something that sooner or later forces itself into any consideration that comes near it, its non-negotiable facticity and "out there"-ness in the strict sense, we grant to the realists and objectivists. I realize that this will satisfy neither camp, as it denies each exactly what it really wanted to gain by clinging to its position—i.e., perfect freedom to determine what the truth is and a feeling of exemption from anything claimed as truth, on the one hand, and a firm foundation for science and for standards of judgment on the other—also so that one could feel exempt from any claims held by others which could be shown not to be "true." In either case, one wanted to be free of something, one wanted to transcend something, one wanted a firmer ground to stand on in the face of some others who were clamoring out other viewpoints to be accepted, claiming they were binding on one. But for us, they are indeed binding, every crazy fantasy or whim anyone ever has is binding on everyone, and there is no escape, no transcendence, no support one can have against this constant threat of the "external world"—the truly external world, the world that is necessarily "external" to whatever coherence or set of coherences one has pitched one's identity on. Trying to be any X only makes that X all the more into all those crazy non-X's one was trying to avoid, and fully being X, really making it, only reveals the non-Xness of X itself. So I do not expect anyone committed to either view here to be delighted or to feel vindicated. But this is no objection; quite the contrary.

What is objectionably counterproductive, on the other hand, in the contrary application of the holistic principle, namely the mania for the relevance of all heterogenous coherences, is its current incarnation as a new substantialism built around sociological data (the assumptions that there exists a "tenor of the times" at a certain era, that a particular culture is responsible for the attitudes and behavior of individuals therein, etc.). The problem here is not the premise that all we are is formed entirely by things that were originally outside us—the fact that the world existed before we were born makes this point perfectly obvious, unless we are clogged by bizarre old metaphysics, the soul belief in any form above all. Everything we feel most strongly about, all our most cherished opinions and attitudes and judgments, all these things come from out there, they could all have been otherwise and often become otherwise in the course of a decade or so. Other people, like Allah in the Koran, are closer to us than the vein in our necks. We are them, and when we fight against them it is them fighting against themselves. All this is not only incontrovertible; it is also profoundly important and importantly profound. But what is objectionable in the conclusion drawn from this compulsion to explain everything "socially," is the pathetic clinging to the concept that any behavior is ultimately and definitively explainable and comprehensible at all, that the data is readable and interpretable in some reliable way, that the relevant information is available, that there is some perspective from which these things, concerning other times and places especially, can be objectively known. In fact, our position is that the manner in which any individual binds and constructs these influences is wildly idiosyncratic and unpredictable—not that it derives from some otherworldly inner source that is beyond the pervasive reach of these forces, but simply that the really decisive turnings come from trifling details and untraceable childhood accidents and misapprehensions of the attitudes of others. As Kafka said, trifles decide trifles. The attempt to analyze the institutional factors, the political and economic environment, and so on as a means of understanding any particular act, word, or thought is ultimately both misleading and useless, and would seem to be just a clutching at the final straw of intelligibility and "selfhood" in the cognitive sense, a cowardly act of bad faith in the face of the utter self-exteriority and contingency of everything about us. It assumes that the field of relevant othernesses determining us is limitable, that it can be circumscribed and definitively known, thereby rendering once again, just like in the good old days of foundational metaphysics, a final answer to the question concerning what things are and mean. It would not be unjust to call it the most modern form of superstition.

Proof That All Previous Errors Have Spoken This Truth, and Vice Versa; Or: How to Believe Everything You Read

But shall we then say to the advocate of such a view, or any other view, "You are mistaken! It may appear to you that social conditions—or God, or childhood experiences, or blind matter, or historical necessity—determine in a knowable manner what things are, but this appearance is illusory, you are wrong!" This would be like saying to the person who claims to be in pain, "Oh no you're not! You're at least equally experiencing shoe on foot, and an infinity of other coherences; you have just arbitrarily chosen this one above all others. Just choose another one, and stop your bellyaching!" It is just this sort of conclusion that the omnicentric move allows us to avoid. For to say this would be to privilege a particular coherence as center, that is, the coherence of Intersubsumption, reversibility, freedom to recontextualize, omnicentrism itself, over all others, once and for all, and set it up as a standard by which to condemn all other centerings. Omnicentricism, on the other hand, is precisely a self-emptying "Nonexclusive Center" which, by establishing itself, simultaneously establishes all other centers as equally valid. This includes experiencing this moment as pain. Pain has appeared to this person as a coherence, a mode of organizing the totality of coherences that includes foot in shoe and all others, and this appearing as a coherent figure is all that is required for its validity; there is no other standard. It is the same standard that omnicentrism applies to itself. Simply to appear is to be true, in as strong a sense of true as is possible. The Tiantai position has always been that "existence" and "illusion" are coextensive terms, which of course has very different consequences from calling some subset of all-that-is illusory; the latter move always implies a devaluation in favor of the nonillusory part. But if to be is to be illusion, and to be illusion is to be true, we have quite another situation. Illusion, when predicated of all possible coherences, can only mean ambiguity: whatever appears *as* some coherence is always such as to allow itself to be read *as* some other coherence as well. We may again think of the movie dinosaur: it is illusory because it is not only a dinosaur, not because it does not exist. Illusion in this sense applies to all possible appearances. The plastic props that make up the movie dinosaur are only illusorily "plastic props," because they are also readable as a dinosaur; in this sense, they are illusions as well.

Very well then: the man who says "I am in pain" or "I am a genius" or "This is green" or "This occupies one cubic meter of space" or "This is good" or "All matter is really spirit" of "All spirit is really matter" or "Life is all about courage" or "Life is all about humility" or "Women are superior to men" or "Men are superior to women" or "All history is the history of class struggle" or "Sex is all that matters" or "God is good" or "There is only one substance" or "We can never know the thing-in-itself" or "Truth is discoverable only through careful empirical research" or "I am being pursued by demons" has spoken a truth which can never be gainsaid; we can never tell him to abandon whatever is appearing to him as so. Whatever he says, it has a coherence, hence a truth, in some contexts, the delimitations of context to which he has restricted his awareness so as to allow this particular coherence to appear to him. At the same time, there will be other contexts for all of these claims in which they cease to be coherent or make sense, cease to appear as a figure at all, recede into an incoherent background for something else, for some other coherence. All the claims listed above, as well as all the ones we are making here, are in exactly the same boat. All that is required of them is to appear to someone.

What then can we say? We are not committed to neutrality—that would be the privileging of neutrality. We are committed to our own illusion, the one being described here, Neo-Tiantai omnicentrism. As we have already seen, its own epistemological position should not elicit the usual objections— viz., what is the status of your own statements, when you say all statements are illusions, are you not subject to the same unreliability? The Neo-Tiantai position itself is just one more coherence, one that happens to have the quality of "asserting that all positions are right and wrong and both and neither." Obviously, as already suggested, there should be no objection to it saying the same thing of itself. In that sense, it is right. That it has appeared at all as a coherent picture, even one that falls apart when certain considerations are brought into the frame, as by its own admission it must, is all that is required of it. Its status is somewhat like that of the Lambchop song: "This is the song that never ends / For it goes on and on, my friend / Some people started singing it, not knowing what it was / And they'll continue singing it forever just because / This is the song that never ends / for it goes on and on my friend. . . ." We started singing it not knowing what it was, for purely prejudicial and unjustifiable libidinal reasons; but once this happened, for whatever reason (and the reasons would seem to be the same as those of any other appearance of a coherent coherence, a contingent bunch of mishaps, enmities, avoidances, desperate hungers and hasty conclusions, attachment to conditioning and narrow-mindedness, fear, stupidity, and greed—in a word, as we have seen above ("Why There's Anything"), fearful passionate protection of a putative self manifesting as inattentive habituation, on the one hand, and "compassion" or solidarity on the other), once this seeming got going, it happened to be of a kind that by its nature cannot end; for it establishes itself as visible in all other positions, *as* all other positions, so that it can have no disconfirmation. Whatever other view appears, whatever seeming comes forth, this one will not view it as an other which delimits it, but rather as another example of "asness." In the process, it takes all positions, without having to be changed in the least, as assertions of itself; but this means here that there are an infinity of equally adequate ways of saying just what we are saying here, and none needs to be changed.

On the other hand, they all need to be changed: we are not committed to neutrality, but to the particular partiality which is ours, and which is called omnicentrism, which claims that it, like all partialities, is also a kind of universality. Transformative self-recontextualization is in one sense a change and in another sense no change at all. By seeing all the views listed above as "asnesses," we have transformatively recontextualized them (and they have thereby self-recontextualized themselves). What is the change involved in this nonchanging?

We claim that all the coherences, all the seemings listed above, are equally unobtainable and unevadable. This goes for the coherence being asserted by "I am in pain" or "I am a genius" or "This is green" or "This is good" or "All matter is really spirit" of "All spirit is really matter" or "Life is all about courage" or "Life is all about humility" or "Women are superior to men" or "Men are superior to women" or "All history is the history of class struggle" or "Sex is all that matters" or "God is good" or "There is only one substance" or "We can never know the thing-in-itself" or "Truth is discoverable only through careful empirical research" or "I am being pursued by demons." There is nowhere one can go to be rid of them, and no way to get a hold of them *simpliciter*. To see them through the lens of omnicentrism is to see them as all-pervading in this way. Now we can see the advocates of each of these claims doing some harm to others and some good to others (however locally defined by us or others at the relevant moment), which may inspire us to promote or suppress them accordingly. The man who believes that it is just a plain fact that he is in pain *can* be a great debit to the world; he exacts vengeance, he needs someone to blame, and so on. The Marxist or Freudian or Christian or Kantian or historian or scientist or philosopher of any stripe can also be a great bane and nuisance—again, all that is required to establish this is that anyone might think so, however fleetingly. It is also possible to imagine someone to whom these characters might be beneficial—again, for whatever reason, in whatever context, as long a person *thinks* she is benefiting from them, she is. Now, no one who encounters these persons, or any other claims made by anyone, is simply in no position, starting from no partiality of his own, without some locally coherent program or programs of his own which he is busy pursuing. That is to say, he has his own quiddities, coherences, seemings that he is in the process of coping with, establishing, expanding, combating, and so on. His judgment of these other claims will be determined by the parameters of the horizons of relevance established by his own presently dominant *seeming* coherence. What we say to that person is this: take all these other claims in such a way that they aid your own current project—knowing that there is some way to do so. Twist them as you wish. Expand your own perspectival position to include these, to swallow them, to appropriate them. The violence inherent in all explanation, the swallowing up of the nonself in the self, and "the hegemony of discourse" are heartily endorsed here. We believe they can never be eliminated if there is to be any local coherence at all, and there cannot ever be no local coherence at all. But we combat these at the same time by encouraging them to proceed in all directions at once: omnicentrism, not acentrism, is the only way out of the problem of the violence imposed by centers. The transformation occurs when any of these prejudices is *universalized*, that is, when it became unevadable and unobtainable, such that these two are one and the same in their difference.

So if I am a profligate sybarite, if the thought of omnicentrism happens to come to me, through whatever channels, I will continue being a sybarite, and continue in my view of the world, which sees it as having meaning only to the extent that it provides me with sensual pleasures. When someone comes screaming "Repent!" at me, or "Work for the betterment of society instead of your own selfish pleasure!" or "Yours is a false consciousness; you will never attain satisfaction that way! Renounce, and you will know peace!" or "Work hard at a career and make something of yourself! Become respectable!" what shall I do? Pre-omnicentrically, I can either reject what they say as false while holding to what I say as true, or be convinced by them and possibly change my ways. But omnicentrically, I will instead look to each of these in terms of my own current arbitrary center, which I will thereby try to universalize in the peculiar Tiantai sense. That is, I will start by trying to get selfish pleasure out of being yelled at in this way (if I am simply an opportunist sybarite), or seeing them as expressions of similar desires for selfish pleasure (if I am a hedonist philosopher as well).

Let us take our example along the first path, which is more difficult and less obviously resolved. I want to make being preached to an opportunity for my own sensual pleasure. I want to make being opposed, or else even repenting, working, respectability, forms in which my sybaritic greed are expressed, *as* which it is expressed. Without abandoning my commitment to this greed for pleasure, let me try to recognize it better, so I can better pursue and discover it. In doing so, as we have seen, it starts to splinter into a multitude of nonpleasure and non-pleasure-seeking coherences: wearing shoes, having to prepare my food, looking for a parking space in front of the whorehouse, waiting around for my drug dealer to show up, not finding anything good or at least having the suspicion that something better might be on another channel while channel surfing and wolfing down cheese popcorn, and so on. But to the extent that I am experiencing pleasure at all, or seeking-pleasure, I have succeeded in experiencing all these nonpleasure coherences as *aspects* of my pleasure: I enjoy looking for the parking space in front of the whorehouse, it is part of the whole whoring experience for me; standing on the corner waiting for my dealer, I am glancing around in a kind of reverie of expectation knowing that the narcotic is about to transform everything for me, maliciously to undermine this oppressive objective reality, and so on. These are setups absorbed into my anticipated punch line. If I can do this with these nonpleasure coherences, absorbing them into the coherence of pleasure of which they are a part, I can do the same for repentance, work, respectability, or being scolded. I can see even self-denial as a form of self-indulgence, a maliciously ironic and deadpan version of it which forms, if anything, an even more cynical kind of mockery of the respectable conventions I am now a part of. If I have fully expanded this absorption process, if I can now read everything without exception in this way, as part of my sybariticism, I have attained a kind of free-moving mastery of referentiality within it; I can go anywhere and be as much in my self-indulgence as I was anywhere else. This does not mean I have to stop shooting heroin and whoremongering, but it does mean I will no longer have any reason to choose them in their direct or obvious form over any other form. In fact, in light of our considerations of absence as hyper-presence above, if anything I may be inclined to prefer the latter—a prejudice that perhaps can be the target of a similar "universalization" process at the meta-level. I will retain the ability to shoot heroin or whoremonger, but I will not be compelled to do so; these coherences are not renounced, they are present universally, and I can deploy them in any form I choose, and at will. What will make me choose one form over another? This brings us back to the intersubjective point, "compassion," as we have already discussed.

Of course, the above account is meant to apply equally to all the other obsessive commitments cited earlier; if one is a Marxist, or an objective scientist, or a philosopher, or a Christian, or a historian, or a cynic, or a know-it-all of any stripe, let him be so, but let him be so to the end. We will view his stated foundation as no more or less a foundation than any other, and if we feel in some instances the need to make judgments—and why should we not?—we will do so according to how fully he has realized the arbitrary ridiculous one-sided center he has chosen. Any one, chosen at random, can be the basis of all others. Any one can explain the others, in the process remaining what it always was but at the same time emptying itself of immediate determinate content. This is what it means to universalize in the Tiantai sense. The question will no longer be, "Which is right (or good)?" but, "In what manner right, in what manner wrong, in what contexts right, in what contexts wrong, from the perspective established by my own present arbitrary starting point, in what ways can it be incorporated in the project of my ravenous expansion and universalization of this arbitrary starting point?"

Once more we find that this, the epistemological issue, is really the most central and directly thematized of all topics in the old Tiantai systems, and has remained so for us as well. We regard it as an affront for someone to say to anyone, "You're wrong when you say you're being chased by demons, or that history is of class struggle, or that God is good, or that sex is all that matters, or that you can intuit truth directly"—this is as offensive as if someone were to say, "You're not in pain, although you think you are." On the other hand, we do not need to accept total fragmentalization, an atomization of views that can never communicate or influence each other, coupled with some kind of holy nonjudgmentality. On the contrary, we want total interpenetration and intercommunication; we want to see each and every starting point expressing itself in and through every other, and when we ourselves judge we will do so according to the extent to which this is done in any given case. All we have said is perhaps just a footnote to Blake: The fool who persists in his folly becomes wise. Develop your idiocy to the utmost, and it is wisdom. The only emendation we make is that the folly is not eliminated in this process, but more fully entrenched and developed, and that just this is all that is meant by the "wisdom"—the Intersubsumption of this folly with all possible *other* follies. Such is omnicentrism.

It should be obvious by now also that we are here availing ourselves of Zhiyi's method again; that is, after all our snippy comments in the preceding discussion, dismissal, ridiculing, rejecting various positions and "mistakes," we want now to turn back and say, All that stuff we rejected we now reabsorb, we open the provisional to reveal the ultimate, we engage them in a transformative recontextualization precisely by having so criticized them, and indeed see this equally as *self*-recontextualization. We make the division first, the difference between setup seriousness and punch line humor, only in order to see both qualities on both sides. All the things that we said were wrong above are now right.

We may find it instructive to walk through a few examples of what some other doctrines look like to us now, after being recontextualized and transformed by the Neo-Tiantai considerations, so as to reveal themselves to be expressions of Tiantai, and further, *to reveal Tiantai to be merely peripheral expressions of themselves*. These conditions must be met for all possible doctrines if the Neo-Tiantai claims are to hold; they must be not only subordinate to Tiantai ways of putting the issue, but even, through the intervention of the Tiantai recontextualization, reveal that the Tiantai way of stating the case can equally well be read as a peripheral, partial, inadequate way of putting what they put more exactly, that they are centers as well. This will be most useful if done for those doctrines that, *prima facie*, are most directly at odds with the Tiantai way of viewing the world; I will leave out those with which it has obvious affinities. Let us try a few examples. In each case I will show first why this doctrine is a pale form of Tiantai, obscurely and imperfectly revealing its truths, and secondly why Tiantai is a pale form of it, obscurely and imperfectly revealing its truths. In other words a true meta-level asness between Neo-Tiantai thought itself and any other doctrine, chosen at random, must be suggested if not demonstrated here. Each alternate view must be shown to be both (1) the setup to which Tiantai is the punch line, and (2) the punch line to which Tiantai is the setup. Here we go:

Platonism

(1) I refer here to the vulgar Platonism of the textbook theory of Forms, not the more complex and multifarious thought actually found in Plato's works. I choose the former because it is more obviously offensive to and at odds with everything we have said here. According to this metaphysical doctrine, the Universal Form of any coherence can never be perfectly instantiated in any concrete particular, and the Forms are more real than the empirical world which instantiates them. Although this mistakenly drains the in-itself-ness into the intelligible realm, it does assert that every observable coherence is not quite itself, that every X is an imperfect X, that to be (empirically) is to fail to be (intelligibly, the only way that qualifies for the name of being). For all intents and purposes, then, if it eliminated the intelligible realm, saw that it was merely illegitimately projecting the naïve (pre-Platonic) concept of the empirical world (as a realm of beings which really are themselves) onto the intelligible world, we would see that the work it does to the empirical world is just the work Tiantai does to all coherences. All experience, then, is Tiantai-fied as soon as we choose to ignore the positing of the intelligible realm at the same time. Hence, Tiantai thought is the truth to which the Platonism is obscurely and imperfectly pointing. Tiantai appears as Platonism. Tiantai is fully realized Platonism.

(2) Tiantai shies away from going all the way, from positing "intelligible in-itselfness" per se, such that this determinate in-itself-ness *precisely as in-itself-ness*, that is, as excluding any moretoitivity, would itself prove to be moretoitive as such. It posits no in-itself realm, although by its own premises there should be no objection to doing so, since by the Nonexclusive Center, in-itself-ness *alone* should be enough: to be in-itself as such *is* to be relative. That Platonism does do, for example, in the doctrine of the Form of the Good, which bears the same relation to the other forms that the intelligible realm as a whole bears to the empirical realm as a whole. For what happens here is that the Form of the Good, which is the ground which bestows determinacy on all the other Forms, which themselves serve as the ground which bestows whatever determinacy there may be to empirical things (the shabby, self-contradictory kind that Tiantai likes), is itself indeterminable and self-contradictory. By going full circle, Platonism finally really clears the decks, leaves no stone untouched by truly necessary problematicalness. Tiantai, by a kind of loss of nerve, never even dares to posit an intelligible realm, apparently for fear that this could never reveal itself to be asness, that no punch line could be devised for such a setup. Only Platonism had the muscle to really prove

that any setup, including "lack of set-up-ness per se," was really a setup. Hence, Platonism is the truth to which the Tiantai thought is obscurely and imperfectly pointing. Platonism appears as Tiantai. Platonism is fully realized Tiantai.

Christianity

Here again I will choose the most objectionable, un-Buddhist type of the doctrine in question. (1) I have already invoked in passing a reading of Christian dogma that makes it a beautiful exemplification of Tiantai ideas: Christ takes upon himself all the sins of the world, just as some coherence before us takes on all the problematicalness of the world. He does this as a man of flesh, as this coherence takes on contingency. As flesh he is crucified and resurrected, he is God and a condemned man, the lowest and the highest; as a contingent act on our part, this representative "encountered" coherence is destroyed and made eternal in a single act, or indeed dealt any type of treatment that satisfies two contrary demands. Then Christ is born in us, and is present in the community of believers; the problematicalness now resides everywhere. And so on. This is given an inexplicit and confused symbolic/mythological form, but this symbol can be unpacked to reveal the deep (Tiantai) truths concealed there. Moreover, the doctrine of the trinity gropes toward a representation of the Three Truths. Hence, Tiantai thought is the truth to which the Christian doctrine of the death and resurrection of Christ is obscurely and imperfectly pointing. Tiantai appears as Christianity. Tiantai is fully realized Christianity.

(2) This is a more exact exemplification of Tiantai ethics than anything Tiantai itself has come up with, and indeed most concisely and in the most compressed single token attempts to embody all the contradictions of the world as they exist in temporal, contingent form. Indeed, the doctrine of the trinity (as Hegel realized too) is the assertion that contradiction and impossibility are built right into the absolute, in other words are necessary and constitutive, rather than contingent or even illusory. What is more, for this to really deal with contingency as such as the central problem, as we have outlined it theoretically here, it must deal with a genuinely contingent event—that is, a single, unique, event in history, the realm of contingency per se, and with real flesh, not merely in words and symbols. Hence, the death and resurrection of Christ are the truth to which Tiantai is obscurely and imperfectly pointing. Christianity appears as Tiantai. Christianity is fully realized Tiantai.

Fideism

Here I have in mind the pure faith doctrines like those of Luther and the Pure Land Buddhism of Shinran. (1) Faith and the repudiation of reason are perfectly reasonable expressions of the insight that all propositions which claim to be simply accurate concerning the objective reality are necessarily false. Any claims made are undermined by the moretoitivity of both the referent and the claim. Hence one has faith—and the more "absurd" the faith the better. But this ends up being muddied by the supposedly determinate and non-moretoitive concept of the object of the faith, and even of faith itself, as in the Platonic case. Take these away, leaving only the faith without either the object of faith or self-certainty of faith as faith (i.e., as having no more to it, as, for example, specifically *not* reason), and you have the Tiantai view. Hence, Tiantai is the truth to which faith is obscurely and imperfectly pointing. Tiantai appears as faith. Tiantai is the full realization of faith.

(2) Like any theoretical system, the very position of enunciation of Tiantai thought, as elucidated here, undermines the claims to interpervasion, since it assumes control from beginning to end, and places itself beyond the besmirchment of other-powers, that is, other doctrines. It is one thing to *say* that they can all be it, as in this section, but another to really abandon oneself to the power of another, feeling viscerally that this other is also your own deepest self, that what he does to you will be in fact readable as your ownmost project, and then relinquishment of freedom will turn out to be the realization of freedom. The man of faith does these things, trusts in the other-power and makes no judgment about what the plan of things, and their goodness or badness, might be; he not only knows that he does not know what anything is, that there is necessarily more to what he is and what he is doing than he can fathom, but he lives it. Hence, faith is the truth to which Tiantai is obscurely and imperfectly pointing. Faith appears as Tiantai. Faith is the full realization of Tiantai.

Commonsense Materialism

By this I mean the notion that there are a bunch of things out there, and I perceive them by means of the impressions they leave on my senses, which are clusters of sensitive tissue, and that "I" am this one here rather than any of those over there, and that objective world over there is what it is without any reference to me, whereas I am beholden to it and dependent on it. To this let us add the further belief that being rich, famous, successful, happy, wise, smart, and strong are intrinsically better and more desirable than being poor, unknown, failed, miserable, foolish, stupid, and weak, and that life consists of trying to move this "I" away from the latter set of undesirable conditions toward the former desirable set of conditions. This, after all, is *prima facie* probably the most head-on repugnant view possible from a Tiantai perspective.

(1) In positing a goal of whatever kind, striving to attain it, and identifying oneself with something which is bereft of this attainment, one has made

manifest the primary twoness which is the primal quality of all coherences, namely, their constitutive problematicalness. Of course, here this is conceived mistakenly as contingent problematicalness, and shifted from one object to another as each object is attained. Nonetheless, without this initial experience, revealing what the coherence "problematical" means to begin with, constitutive problematicalness could never be realized or even understood. It must first establish itself in contrast to some putative nonproblematicalness in order to establish what problematicalness means; then and only then can we "open the provisional to reveal the real," that is, the necessarily all-pervasive and constitutive nature of this problematicalness, which was obscurely intuited in the basic structure of ordinary experience, but in a self-contradictory form. Once it expresses itself fully, it is Tiantai. Hence, Tiantai is the truth to which common sense is obscurely and imperfectly pointing. Tiantai appears as common sense. Tiantai is the full realization of common sense.

(2) Tiantai asserts that all coherences are inherently entailed in each coherence, that each coherence can be read as any other coherence, in a condition of mutually reversible, intersubsumptive asness. This also means that all are inherently entailed in what is, that none is eradicable from reality, that all are necessary and justified, and have to them a very strong sense of objective reality indeed. There is nothing I can do about all coherences (in classical terms, the Three Thousand) being just as they are. This is a situation with which any moment of sentient experience is confronted, even if it too is one of these ineradicable coherences. But if this is accepted literally, we might think that full adequation has been achieved between world and self, in such a way that makes adequation no longer problematic. As we saw above, this is only half the story. The adequation between the two sides of this confrontation actually lies in the fact that neither side is even adequate to itself, and hence bleeds toward the inadequation which is the other. It is a mistake to think there is a satisfactory answer to anything, or that anything is finally settled. What Tiantai as a doctrine, which appears on the scene as if it were settling something or helping someone, really comes down to is precisely the unsettled searching which characterizes common sense. The difference is just that Tiantai sees this fact as necessary, common sense as merely contingent. But on the other hand, Tiantai seems to offer a solution, thereby making the problem seem contingent, whereas unreflective common sense sees no escape, indeed cannot even imagine one; the way it defines self and world make inadequation genuinely necessary and inescapable and all-pervasive. Hence, common sense realizes what Tiantai was trying to get at it. Once Tiantai expresses itself fully, it is common sense suffering. Common sense is the truth to which Tiantai was obscurely and imperfectly pointing. Common sense appears as Tiantai. Common sense is the full realization of Tiantai.

I will not belabor this point by continuing this sort of exegesis for each possible alternative view of the universe, nor even for those that are most manifestly un-Tiantai. The reader may wish to connect the dots and extend the lines over to a few of the other obvious candidates—empiricism, intuitionism, rationalism, Marxism, stoicism, scientism, cult of duty, Confucianism, and so on—or perhaps a history of philosophy along these lines might be written by me or someone else sometime in the future. In any case, the point should be clear. Neo-Tiantai thought too is a ladder to be discarded when it has been climbed—with the difference that, like everything else, it can never really be discarded, it continues to haunt every other coherence, to impinge on whatever is landed in when it is transcended. Precisely because it cannot be attained, because it is inherently impossible and appears nowhere *simpliciter*, it can never be left behind, even when relinquished, just like every other coherence.

Invitation to a Recantation

In closing, a final declaration: What we have said above about contrary views held by others applies also to any other view, methodology, or perspective I myself may adopt in the future. I hereby declare my intention to backslide into all sorts of nonomnicentric views—in fact, I confidently expect that I shall do so, for example, when my brain begins to deteriorate, through senility or decomposition after death, and I am capable of taking no position on these matters at all. Such a day, therefore, will undoubtedly come; in the terms we have ourselves delineated, simply losing interest in the view propounded here, or forgetting exactly how it was supposed to work, is tantamount to a full recantation. This much, at least, is plainly unavoidable. Indeed, just the fact that I will be going to sleep and dreaming in a few hours is all that is required to clinch this point. But, of course, that will be no more a contravening of this view than any other "other" view was. It will be an expression of it, from the point of view of this view itself, expressed in this sentence I am writing now. My recantation or dream or nonexistence will be an obscure and imperfect form of the ideas expressed in this book, a confused and one-sided expression of the fully realized Tiantai position. Tiantai is, in that sense, the truly and fully realized version of that recantation. But equally this book will be revealed to have been an obscure and imperfect form of that recantation. My recantation will turn out to have been right now only expressing itself badly, *as* a clumsy avatar, called Neo-Tiantai thought. My recantation will be the truly and fully realized Tiantai. The world has been overturned in these pages, as it is always being overturned—and now these pages must necessarily become just one more book on a shelf, even on my own shelf, and thus be overturned by everything else. A world in a book, and a book in the world: it subsumes the world, and now the world, many worlds, subsumes it. Must we not say again that each of these subsumptions is precisely the others? And? Or? As?

Index

absence, as hyper-presence, 155, 398
the Absolute, as absence/presence, 145
absoluteness, temporality of, 262
addiction, 402–3
   as false center, 403
   object of, 306
adequation, 265–66
affirmation/negation, 34
agreement/disagreement, as intersubsumption, 108
Allen, Woody, 180
alterity, 347
ambiguity and temporality, equation between, 33
Anselm, St., 291
anxiety/boredom, 267–68, 303–4
   and addiction, 306
   alleviating, 305
   and love, 307–8
   and narrative, 305–6
   of "what to do next," 303
appearance, 67–68
   ambiguity of, 68
   moretoitivity of, 68
   as one, 62–63
   as other, 62–63
   tertium quid of, 65–67
   transcendence of, 65–66
   as truth, 429
   as vanishing, 74
appearance/reality structure, 263–64
   as necessary, 199–200, 212
appearing "as," 101–2
a priori intuitions, 115
Aristotle, xx, 44, 378
art, task of, 379
"asness," 36–37, 49, 66, 67, 152, 167, 176
   categories of, 152–53
   as continuity, 321
   as energy, 268
   metaphoricity of, 173
assertion, impossibility of, 35
avant-garde art, 376
aversion, 188
   as invisible center, 276
   overcoming of, 277–78
   snagged reversibility in, 189–91
awareness, 46–47

INDEX

Bataille, Georges, 350–51, 365, 369, 383, 396
  active/passive in, 358
  on beauty, 353, 354
  on continuity/discontinuity, 350, 353–54
  on eroticism, 350–52
  on sacrifice, 351–52
  on violence, 351
  on work, 351
beauty
  and coherence, 370
  and death, 375
  as Intersubsumptive, 380
  time element in, 377
  as unexpected harmony, 369–70, 373, 376, 377
Being/beings, 316
"being" the impossibility, 216–17
being thus/being otherwise, 265
Bergson, Henri, 197
black humor, 386
Blake, William, 434
Bodhisattva path, 14–15, 17, 93–94, 325, 333
Bohm, David, 55, 174
borders, particularity of, 110–11
Brown, Norman O., 394
Buber, Martin, 347
Buddha, 2, 92, 93, 95, 411, 413
  as Bodhisattva, 15
  doctrines of, 14
  as every personality, 288
  and inherent evil, 346
  meaning of the term, 289–93
  as reversible asness, 290–91, 293
  three bodies of, 226
  and tragedy, 346
Buddhism
  on desire, 2–4, 6
  intellectual history of, 1
  liberation, notion of, 7
  on marks of existence, 3
  the Middle Way, 4, 6–7
  nonreferentiality in, 11
  precedents in, for Tiantai, 1–2
  on suffering, 4, 9
  and theism, difference between, 346–47
  theory of momentariness, 7
Bugs Bunny, 386

Caoshan, 419
Carnap, Rudolf, 131
categories/contents, 117–19
catharsis, 399, 402–3
  as Intersubsumption, 403
causality
  critique of, 12
  impossibility of, 204–5
center(s)
  as locus of value, 83–84
  as provisional but necessary, 313
  reversibility of, 192
centrality, as indispensable, 86
Centrality, 31, 55–59, 62
Chan/Zen, 408
Chico, 386
Christianity, and Tiantai, 436
classicism, 254
coexistence of differences, problem of, 25, 26
cognition, 10
  causality of, 10
  as mutual referencing, 10–11
  and repeatability, 10
coherence, 37, 41–45, 143, 318, 362
  as ambiguity, 33
  aggressivity of, 147
  as asness, 157
  atomicity/interpenetration of, 323
  and centering, 54–55, 82–83
  in chaos, 44
  as compassion, 299–300
  constitutive impossibility of, 202–3
  contingent problem of, 210
  crashing of, 156–58, 160, 163

INDEX 443

as delusion, 300
and determinacy/indeterminacy, 49, 51–52, 64
as distanced, 68–70
dual meaning of, 38
as enjoyment, 366
as external, 349
as figure/ground, 64
and Global Incoherence, 146
hostility of, 282
impossibility of, 164, 191, 216
of incoherent notions, 42
as interpervasive, 169
as its own negation, 73
mastery in, 52, 53
as moretoitive, 266, 268
necessary aspects of, 56
as necessary contradiction, 220
necessary failure of, 158–59, 160, 317
necessary impossibility of, 210
as one, 44, 63
and oneness/duality, 51–52
and otherness, 348, 364
part and whole, 49–50, 71–72, 168
persistence of, 317–18, 322
as a possible possible, 43
as presence/absence, 64, 144
and relevance, 63
rhythm of emergence of, 155–56
"seeing as," 22–23
and selfsameness/otherness, 132
as setup and punch line, 141–42, 315
as something, 48
as something other, 48, 51
as tentative, 362
through exclusion, 159
and truth, 43
as two, 63
as unavoidable, 166
as universal, 169
"unseen back" of, 54

coherence/incoherence, question of, 37–38
coherences, relation between, 144
coherence theory of truth, 163
Cole, Alan, 411
commonsense materialism, and Tiantai, 437
compassion, 109, 300, 322, 423
concepts, 72–73
and presence/absence, 72
conceptualization, 45
"condemned to meaning," 320
consciousness, 8, 195
as discerning, 20
expanded meaning of, 20
as interacting with not-self, 240–41
as open system, 240–41
constitutive mutual violence, 349–50
ethical implications, 349–50
content, as contrast, 104
contingency, as necessity, 123, 284
continuity
as discontinuity, 75, 354
as reversibility, 321
control, contradiction of, 164–65, 249
correspondence theory of truth, 163, 209
creation
as transformation, 32
as unchanging, 30
"creation by mind," 22–23
critique, "critique" of, 417–20
the cunning of cunning, 167–68
the cunning of Reason, 167

Daffy Duck, 386
Davidson, Donald, 105–6, 107–9, 349, 366
death
as embarrassment, 309–10
fear of, 308–9
death-drive, 225
deconstruction, 418

demands, fulfilling/subverting of, 219–20
dependent co-arising, doctrine of, 3
Derrida, Jacques, 347
Descartes, René, 291
desire, 2–5, 303
  and affect, 273–75
  aggravation of, 179
  as conditioned, 5–6
  constitutive impossibility of, 206
  of desire, 271–72, 275
  and inattentiveness, 4–5
  as invisible center, 276–77
  mindful of, 6–7
  obsessional, 182, 183–84
  paradox of, 205–6
  and selfhood, 2–5, 184, 186, 273–74, 276–78
  as "shouldness," 215–16
  snagged reversibility in, 184–85, 187
  structure of, 215–16
  subject/object split in, 4–5
  as theist, 192
  to be, explicitly, 187–88
  to have/to be, 183, 186, 187
  two rival centers in, 184–85
  types of, 2
  unsatisfiability of, 181
  as visible center, 183–84
the desired, as contaminated by the undesired, 179–80
determinacy, 44
  as ambiguity, 75–76
  and indeterminacy, overcoming dichotomy of, 242
dhammas, 7
Dharmakaya, 226–27, 229, 232
dharmas, 113–14, 124
  critique of reality of, 12
  as principle, 114–15
Diamond Sutra, 146
dichotomies, overcoming, 242–43
diffusion, randomness in, 125–27

discerning, as feature of consciousness, 20
disclosure, as concealment, 75
doctrine of momentariness, 73–74
the Double, 367
  ethical importance, 365
Dumont, Margaret, 386, 388
Dylan, Bob, 411, 412, 413

Emptiness, 55–57
emptiness, doctrine of, 11–14
enlightenment, 293
entropy, 318, 319
epistemological double bind, of subjectivity/objectivity, xv
epistemology, interest/desire in, 421–23
equilibrium, 372
eroticism
  and the Double, 359
  negations and taboos in, 355–57
  as vicarious self-destruction, 358
ethical meaning, reversibility in, 287
evil, as ineradicable, ethical importance of, 284–85
Exclusive Center, 57, 67, 146
exertion, in overcoming repression, 253
existence/illusion, 429
experience, multiplicity of, 280–81
external world(s)
  as constitutive, 149–50
  as mediated, 150–51

Fahuaxuanyi, 97
false dichotomies, xvi
Fazang, 112
fideism, and Tiantai, 436–37
figure/ground relationship, 48
Five Aggregates doctrine, 7
Flaubert, Gustave, 370
Fliess, Robert, 359
Four Noble Truths, on desire/suffering, 2

freedom, 235–36
  and determination, convergence of, 279–30
  as interchangeability, 220
  and necessity, 236
  and restriction, 243
  as self-recontextualization, 242
Frege, Gottlob, 130-31, 132
Freud, Sigmund, xx, 81, 155, 176, 189, 219, 349, 359, 367, 383, 393, 397, 405
  dualism of, 394–96
  The Ego and the Id, 185
  on fear of death, 308
  on morality, 284

Gendlin, Eugene T., 259
Gleason, Jackie, 384
Global Ambiguity, 127
Global Incoherence, 55–60, 70, 89, 92, 102, 103, 128
  as "natural law," 124
Gödel, Kurt, 41
the Good
  as indeterminacy, 247–48
  as paradox, 250
  as power for self-redefinition, 250
  as reversibility, 250
  as total exertion, 253
Goodman, Nelson, 130
Graham, A. C., xviii

habituated desire, 423
habituation, 371
harmony, 370–71
  and coherence, 370
  and dissonance, difference between, 371–72
  as Intersubsumption, 379–80
Harpo, 386
Harris, Joel Chandler, 389

Hegel, G. W. F., xx, 46, 51, 140, 167–68, 176, 188, 220, 286, 289, 299, 316, 343, 396, 420, 436
  on categories, 116
  on contingency, 221
  dialectic of, 408
  on freedom and determination, 235–36, 238
  on infinity, 255
  Logic, xvii, 44, 235, 241, 407
  on negativity, 239–40
  Phenomenology, 406, 407
  on pure indeterminacy, 241
  on Reason, 405–8
  work-ethic of, 408
  on universals, 221
Heidegger, Martin, 316
Heraclitus, 109
hermeneutics, libidinization of, 423
Hershock, Peter, 63
Hinayana, 14–15, 17
  on liberation, 275
historicist critique, 420
Hofstadter, Douglas, 156
holism, 89
  as centered, 83–85
  and epistemology/knowledge, 420–21
  mania for relevance in, 427–28
  omnicentric, 86–87
  unicentric, 85–86
horizon of relevance, 63
  in coherence, 159, 160–61
Huayan, 343, 344
Hulme, T. E., 254–56
Hume, David, 116
humor
  community in, 391–93
  definition of, 381
  and disparity of habit, 383–93
  and Intersubsumption, 383–84
  as opposite beauty, 381–82
Husserl, Edmund, 195

idealism, specter of, 149
ideals, functions of, 286
identification, selectivity of, 238–39
identity
  as contextual, 89–91
  as difference, 326
  impossibility of, 39
  as necessary contradiction, 220
ignorance, as nonmindfulness, 8
imaginary object, 72–73
  and presence/absence, 72
imagination, 45
incoherence, 37, 43
  and context, 42–43
  real and apparent, 38
  in religion, accommodation of, 38–39
incompleteness, necessity of, 41
incompleteness theorem, 41
incontrovertible proposition, form of, 37–38
indeterminacy
  as determinacy, 247–48
  in self-redefinition, 247–48
infinity
  of alternate meanings, 348
  as self-recontextualization, 255
  as total attention to detail, 255
inherent entailment, 279, 314–15, 325, 327, 334
"innocence of becoming," 278–79
"inside," concept of, 26
inside/outside, relation between, 109–11
institutionalization, Daoist-anarchist principle of, 177
intelligible character, 233–34
interpretation, as either onany or love, 423
intersubjectivity, 209, 280, 293–94
  primacy of, 294
Intersubsumption, 31, 56–62, 64, 68, 69–70, 72, 73, 82, 89, 92, 101, 103, 139–41, 194, 216, 268

  as Central/non-Central, 140
  in pleasure, 222
  as setup/punch line, 202
  three-way, 282
irreducibility, as reducibility, 76
isolation, as unity, 259

Jesus, 411, 415
jia, 68
Jingangpi, 115, 142
joke, structure of, 97, 228
Jung, C. G., 396
  on libido, 394

Kafka, Franz, 425, 428
Kant, Immanuel, xx, 31, 103–4, 106, 109, 318, 337, 341, 343, 375
  on categories, 114–16, 117, 119
  transcendental ego, 119
  transcendental unity of apperception, 31, 103, 106
  unity of apperception, 119
Kennedy, John F., 412
Kierkegaard, Søren, xvii
Kramden, Ralph, 384
Kripke, Saul, 133
Krug, Wilhelm, 221

Lacan, Jacques, xx, 192, 225, 359, 367
language, function of, 257
Laozi, 177, 181, 189
Latour, Bruno
  We Have Never Been Modern, 418
Laycock, Steven, 67
Leibniz, G. W., xx
Lennon, John, 411, 412, 413
Levin, David, 72
Levinas, Emmanuel, 410
  Totality and Infinity, 347–48
li, 33
libido theory, 393

Local Coherence, 55–60, 68, 70, 89, 92, 102, 103
  as Intersubsumption, 157
  three forms of, 139, 143
Lotus Sutra, 1, 11, 14–16, 40, 80, 83, 91, 95, 325, 333–34, 411, 412, 415
  on provisional and ultimate truth, 92–93
  as punch line, 98
  Treasure Tower, 328–29
love, 423
  impossibility of, 206-207
  paradox of, 205-206
Luther, Martin, 436
Lyotard, Jean-François
  Libidinal Economy, 418

Madhyamika, 419
Mahayana, 11, 14, 17, 95, 226
  on dharmas, 115
  on self-knowledge, 28
Marx, Groucho, 386, 388
Marx, Karl, 176
meaning/meaninglessness, 254
meanings
  as changing, 134
  as true and false, 108
Mencius, 215
Merleau-Ponty, xx, 43, 46, 52, 54, 63, 69, 77, 79–81, 233, 310
metaphoricity
  literalness as effect of, 171–72
  as primary, 171–73
the Middle Way, 4, 6
mind/body
  dualistic view, 195
  indeterminacy in, 196
  monistic view, 194–95
  relation between, 194–95
  as setup/punch line, 196–99, 200
mindfulness, 175–76
  implications of, 8–9, 10

mindfulness meditation, 275
mind/matter, 113–14
  indecidability of, 113
  as setup/punch line, 201
mystical experience, as aesthetic, 380

Nagarjuna, 11, 12, 14, 15–16
naïve consciousness, 265
naïve experience, 9, 261, 263
narrative, absorption in, 305–6
Nathan of Gaza, 417
nature
  as nondwelling, 111–13, 114
  as unconditioned/unchangeable, 28–29
"the Nature," 24, 25, 26
"negation of the negation," 420
neither-sameness-nor-difference, 92, 326
"neither thus nor otherwise," 67
neo-theism, 347
Neo-Tiantai, xix, 39
  ethics, 259
  external truth in, 426
  as holistic, 76
  as isolating things, 76–77
  momentary approach of, 77
  as omnicentric, 76
  on perception, 78
  as revolutionary, 410
  on sacred/profane, 100
  standard of relevance in, 421
  on will, 251–52
Nichiren, 411
Nietzsche, Friedrich, xx, 189, 206, 211, 232, 279, 286, 288, 357, 374, 375, 378, 411, 421
  on pleasure and pain, 222–24
Nirmanakaya, 226–27, 229
Nirvana, 95
  as existing reality, 95
Nishitani Keiji, 146
"the nondwelling root," 127

Nonexclusive Center, 57, 66, 90, 92, 143, 146
"nonself" teaching, 3
normativity, constitutive impossibility of, 207
Norton, Ed, 384

objectivity, questioning notion of, xix
O'Donahue, Michael, 386
omnicentrism, 45, 59, 89, 91, 190, 192
   center as empty, 87–88
   and holism, 128
   as meaning of teaching, 91
   as Nonexclusive Center, 429–31
   and relativism, 426
   and skepticism, difference between, 426
   universalizing in, 432–33
onany, 423, 425
"one nature as no nature," 32, 106
oneness, 44
   as impossible but necessary, 44–45
"opening the provisional to reveal the real," 91–93, 97, 141, 197, 315, 325, 326, 434
openness, as primal, 268–69
Oswald, Lee Harvey, 412
the Other, inscrutability of, 295–96

pantheism, 149
peacock's tail, 374
perception, 72–73
   and Gestalt theory, 46
   and moretoitivity, 78
   and presence/absence, 72
   primacy of, 45
   and subject/object relations, 79
personality
   as pregnancy, 288
   as symptom, 288
Planck, Max, 129

Plato, xx, 181, 191, 286, 337, 435
Phaedrus, 39
Platonism, as Tiantai, 435
pleasure
   constitutive impossibility of, 207
   as Intersubsumption, 222–23
   as overcoming of obstacles, 222–23, 225
   and power, 223–24
Polanyi, Michael, xx, 46, 161
   on awareness, 46–48
"polymorphous interpervasion of omnipresences," 220
presence
   as absence, 177–78, 399–400
   as hyper-absence, 155
pre-Socratics, xx
principle of charity, 105–6, 107–8, 132, 349
   reactionary consequence of, 108
private language argument, 132, 137–39
   and sameness/difference, 134–35
private/shared, Intersubsumption of, 139
process philosophy, 198
process thought, 323
   problem of, 335
projects, constitutive impossibility of, 209
proper nouns, 133–34
   as universals, 133
properties, as theft, 54, 294
the provisional, as ultimate truth, 93–94, 96
Provisional Positing, 55–57
puns, 388
Pure Land Buddhism, 436
Putnam, Hilary, 130–31, 133
Pyrrho, 315

quiddity, 41
   as quaddity, 49

radical classicism, 256
radical otherness, 347
radical romanticism, 255
randomness, as lawfulness, 127
the Real, Lacanian, 365–67
realization, as liberation, 105
realness, as obstacle, 261
Reason, function of, 299
reducibility, as correlativity, 348
reference, and selfsameness, 132
reformist, 410
Reich, Wilhelm, 394
repetition, and crashing of coherence, 254
repression, 253, 404
repression hypothesis, 398–400
responsibility, groundlessness of, 284
reversibility, as energy, 268, 270
Reversible Asness, 31, 56
revolutionary, 410
revolutionary charisma, 411
    defusing of, 415–16
    harmful effects of, 416
    sacrifice in, 414
    self-recontextualization in, 413–17
    as transgressive, 412–13
right/wrong standards, 200
romanticism, 254
Rosenzweig, Franz, 347
Roth, Philip
    The Breast, 186
Russell, Bertrand, 223

Sakyamuni, 329–30
Sambhogakaya, 2226, 229, 240
sameness
    and difference, 113
    loss of identity in, 365
samsara, 95
Sartre, Jean-Paul, xx, 72, 73, 78, 79, 115, 167, 179, 195, 233, 251, 304–5, 398
    essence in, 304
    on perception and conceptualization, 45
    The Words, 414
Schopenhauer, Arthur, xx, 5, 198, 230–31, 303
    on the will, 232–33
    will-to-life, 230
Schrödinger, Erwin, 125–27, 129
Schweitzer, Albert, 415
Second Noble Truth, 402
"seeing as," 22, 28–29
self, 182, 193
    anxiety of, 368–69
    as body, 193
    as drive to indeterminacy, 243–46
    incompleteness of, 364
    as negativity, 256
    as Other, 364, 368
    as redefinition of self, 225, 243–44
    as reducible to other, 348
    as setup/punch line, 246
    in two places at once, 368
self-certainty, constitutive impossibility of, 209
self-discipline, and freedom, 248
self-knowledge, 28
self-objectification
    moral implication of, 280
    and other-subjectification, 280
    in reversibility, 279
self/other, 193
    reversibility of, 287
self-worth, constitutive impossibility of, 207–8
sense and reference, 130–31
    and Intersubsumption, 132–33
separation, as connection, 75
setup/punch-line structure, 202
    as structure of reality, 382
Sextus Empiricus, 315
sexual desire, paradox of, 396–97
shi, 33
"shouldness"
    as constitutive of being, 215

as desire, 215
Socrates, 39, 180
Spinoza, xx, 5, 9, 29, 112, 165, 196, 197, 200, 206, 279, 284, 286, 289, 318, 343, 404
Stendhal, 375
subject, as unchangeable identity, 27
subject/object relations, 29–30
   ambiguity in, 225–26
   epistemological double bind of, xv
   impossibility of, 203–4
   as seeing-as, 30
   unified, 121
subject/object split, 8–9
   in desire, 5
   and suffering, 4
subject/predicate, reversibility of, 173–75
sublimation, limits of, 405
suffering, cause of, 10
"the sword cannot cut itself," 28

Thales, 88
Three Thousand Coherence, 18–19, 29, 30
   as categories and contents, 118
   as self-emptying, 32
Three Truths, 15–16, 17, 25, 31, 33, 46, 55, 191, 226, 228, 269, 326
   interpenetration of, 73
   as nondwelling Nature, 111
   and pivotality of presencing, 70–72
   problem of, 26
   as setup and punch line, 141
Tiantai tradition, xviii, xix, 14
   on affirmation/negation, 105
   and agreement/disagreement, 106–8
   on appearances, 264
   Buddhist influence on, 1–2, 11
   on categories, 115–19, 124
   as contents, 117–19
   reducibility of, 335
   on causality, as experienced, 116
   on centrality, 19, 57
   on coherence, 33, 64–65
   on compassion, 300, 322
   "consciousness only," 119
   and deconstruction, difference between, 418
   on enlightenment, 293, 395
   on evil, 395
   on experience, 116–17
   expository technique, 20–21
   on external impingement, 28
   Intersubsumption in, 59
   and Kant, comparison with, 119–20
   on liberation, 275–76
   and *Lotus Sutra*, 14, 15
   and meditation, 25, 106
   on the Nature, 24–26
   new God in, 343
   "principle" in, 122, 124
   and principle of charity, 106–7
   and problem of suffering, 344
   provisional and ultimate in, 97
   reducibility/reversibility in, 19
   teachings of, 17–19
   as theoretical/practical, 31
   on the "two marvels," 94
   unique position of, 92
   on unity/difference, 105
   universalizing in, 433
   value and antivalue in, 97–98, 344–35
time
   as recontextualization, 196–97, 298–99
   structure of, 296–98
   and will, 298
tong, 222, 225
"too much of a good thing," 180
Torah, 40
tragedy, as beautiful, 378–79
transcendental ego, 280, 283
transcendental I, 104
transcendental unity of apperception, 31, 103, 106

transformative recontextualization, 73, 91, 99
transformative self-recontextualization, 263
Trout, Kilgore, 387
true center, as invisible, 182
truth
  as conditioned, 40
  as constitutive impossibility, 209
Twofold Three Thousand, 33
Two Truths, 14, 16
Tynan, Kenneth, 356

Udana, 8, 260
undecidability, 190
unity, through isolation, 259
universal Buddhahood, 347
universalization, as self-emptying, 104

value and antivalue, 94-95
  as aesthetic contrast, 348, 349
Vasubandhu, 19
Vimalakirti Sutra, 33
Visuddimagga, 3

Whitehead, Alfred North, 112, 114, 117, 197–98, 323–26, 334–36, 343, 348
  on eternal objects, 330–31, 336–42, 346
  on God, 331–33
  on Peace, 345
  Science and the Modern World, 336
the will
  and affirmation/denial, 231
  holistic view, 251–52
  as neither same nor different, 231
  and time, 298
  as the world, 230
willing, constitutive contradiction of, 164–65

Will to Power, 321
Wittgenstein, Ludwig, 40, 135–46, 137, 400
word(s)
  constitutive ambiguity of, 136–37
  as focus, 257–58
  justification of, 137
  meaning of, through change, 134
  repetition of, to meaninglessness, 253–54
  as unifying, through isolation, 259

X
  non-X as precondition for, 139–40, 146–48
  as non-X, only more so, 177
Xifying, as deXifying, 146–48

yiniansanqian, 176

Zen, 408–9
  as unicentrist, 409
Zeno, 397
Zeppo, 386
Zevi, Sabbatai, 413, 417
Zhanran, xviii, 1, 79, 103, 104, 106, 115, 142, 371, 382
  affirmation/negation in, 34
  on coherence, 30
  on creation, 21–22, 30, 33
  on field of differences, 31
  on mind and matter, 21–22, 24, 32, 107
  on mindlikeness, 30–31
  on "the Nature"/nature, 24, 29
  subject/object in, 22
Zhili, xviii, xx, 1, 24, 33, 105, 118, 123, 124, 161, 201, 231, 328
  on coherence, 25
  on consciousness, 23
  on creation by mind, 22-23
  on mind and matter, 22, 32, 119

on "same nature," 112–13
Zhiyi, xviii, 1, 18, 20, 21, 93, 94, 95, 97, 346, 434
   Sinianchu, 19
zhong, 68

Zhuangzi, xx, 37
Žižek, Slavoj, 40, 85, 144, 159, 219, 397, 406
Zupančič, Alenka, 365–67

www.ingramcontent.com/pod-product-compliance
Lightning Source LLC
Chambersburg PA
CBHW022006300426
44117CB00005B/56